MY PAPER CHASE

ALSO BY HAROLD EVANS

They Made America:
From the Steam Engine to the Search Engine;
Two Centuries of Innovators
(with Gail Buckland and David Lefer, 2004)

War Stories:
Reporting in the Time of Conflict from the Crimea to Iraq (2003)

The BBC Reports: On America, Its Allies and Enemies,
and the Counterattack on Terrorism
(BBC Corporation and Harold Evans, 2002)

The Index Lecture: View from Ground Zero
(lecture prepared for the Hay-on-Wye Festival, 2002)

The American Century (2000)

Good Times, Bad Times (1984)

Eyewitness (1981)

Suffer the Children: The Story of Thalidomide (with the
Sunday Times Insight Team, 1979)

We Learned to Ski (with Brian Jackman and Mark Ottoway, 1975)

The Freedom of the Press:
The Half-Free Press (with Katharine Graham
and Lord Windlesham, 1974)

Editing and Design (five volumes: *Essential English,*
Newspaper Design, Text Typography, Newspaper Headlines,
and *Pictures on a Page,* with Edwin Taylor, 1973)

The Active Newsroom
(with the International Press Institute, 1961)

MY PAPER CHASE

True Stories of Vanished Times

HAROLD EVANS

Little, Brown and Company

New York   Boston   London

Little, Brown and Company
Hachette Book Group
237 Park Avenue, New York, NY 10017
www.hachettebookgroup.com

First Edition: November 2009

Little, Brown and Company is a division of Hachette Book Group, Inc.
The Little, Brown name and logo are trademarks of Hachette Book Group, Inc.

Credits for endpaper photographs: taking an oath (top left): Dafydd Jones; with
Tina on *Queen Mary 2:* Cunard; Rupert Murdoch (under *Good Times,
Bad Times*): Jane Bown; caricature: Gerard Scarfe; with Tina (under Murdoch):
George Brown; with Henry Kissinger: UPI; ship launch (bottom left):
Colin Theakston; skiing: Bryan Wharton; sketch of St. Ann's (top right): *Manchester
Evening News*, Bert Hackett; with President Clinton on Air Force One: Official
White House Photo; thumbs up on winning Crossman trial, with Mrs. Anne
Crossman and Graham Greene: Press Association; RAF office with German
prisoner Walter Greis (next to *Traveler*): Herbert Gale; editing: Neil Libbert;
St. Mary's Road Central School (bottom right): courtesy of Newton Heath
Historical Society and Peter Charlton.

Copyright acknowledgments appear on page 549.

Library of Congress Cataloging-in-Publication Data

Evans, Harold.
    My paper chase : true stories of vanished times/Harold Evans.—1st ed.
        p. cm.
    Includes bibliographical references and index.
    ISBN 978-0-316-03142-4
    1. Evans, Harold.   2. Newspaper editors—England—Biography.
3. Journalists—England—Biography.   4. Investigative reporting—
England—History—20th century.   5. Journalism—England—History—
20th century.   6. Newspaper publishing—England—History—20th century.
7. Sunday times (London, England : 1931)   8. Guardian (Manchester,
England)   I. Title.
    PN5123.E9 A32009
    070.4092—dc22
    [B]   2009015541

10 9 8 7 6 5 4 3 2

RRD-IN

Printed in the United States of America

Dedicated to my granddaughters,
Emily and Anna

Contents

BOOK ONE   Vanished Times

1	Grains of Truth	3
2	Getting Up Steam	12
3	First, Know Your Enemy	40
4	Hot Metal	72
5	How I Won the War	100
6	*Non Nobis Solum*	112
7	The Sting of Disraeli's Gibe	122
8	Stop Press	138
9	Why Aren't Their Women Wearing Our Frocks?	166
10	Adventures in the Land of Opportunity	192
11	From Delhi to Darlington	235
12	Just Causes	263

BOOK TWO   Scoop, Scandal, and Strife

13	The Rolls-Royce of Fleet Street	301
14	The Third Man	323
15	Children on Our Conscience	353
16	Space Barons	385
17	Death in Cairo	413
18	Divided Loyalties	445
19	Showdowns	479
20	My Newfoundland	504

Acknowledgments	543
Principal Sunday Times *Books*	551
Bibliography	555
Index	563

The Vanished Newspaper Office

If you had x-ray eyes and looked on any newspaper building in most of the years of our vanished century, this is what you'd have seen behind the brick facade: the stacked floors of worker ants and machinery transmuting the typewritten word into newsprint. Starting in the sixties in the United States but delayed until the eighties in Britain, computer terminals replaced the typewriters and editing pencils (1st floor) and the Linotype machines (3rd floor).

Basement
The reel room and the presses. One pressman is objecting to the shape of the plate he is supposed to fit on the rotary press and another is having too good a time to notice a coworker has disappeared.

Ground floor (left)
The foundry casts plates for the presses in between a hand of cards. Right, the newspaper bundles on the way to the world.

1st floor
On the left, the reporters and copy-takers; center, the subs; and right, the wire room collecting agency dispatches and photos. The big man in the subs room collaring a copy boy is the chief sub-editor, who designs the pages and gives orders to galley slaves of sub-editors who sit in front of him with their spikes and glue pots and perplexities of copy-fitting and headline writing. They feed edited copy to the pneumatic tube, sustained all day by infusions of tea.

3rd floor
Linotype operators

Top floor
Proofreaders

I've long treasured the drawing by an art student at Manchester University (who preferred to be known just as "Caesar"). Attracted by his work in the student publications when I was covering the university, I commissioned him to come to the *Manchester Evening News* to sketch the operations for my stint in the fifties as editor of the spoof newspaper the *Manchester Guardian and Evening News,* put out during the university's annual "Rag" week of raising money for charity. "Caesar's drawing" prefigured Martin Handford's "Where's Waldo?" puzzle games — and, yes, I'm in there somewhere, in prominent spectacles.

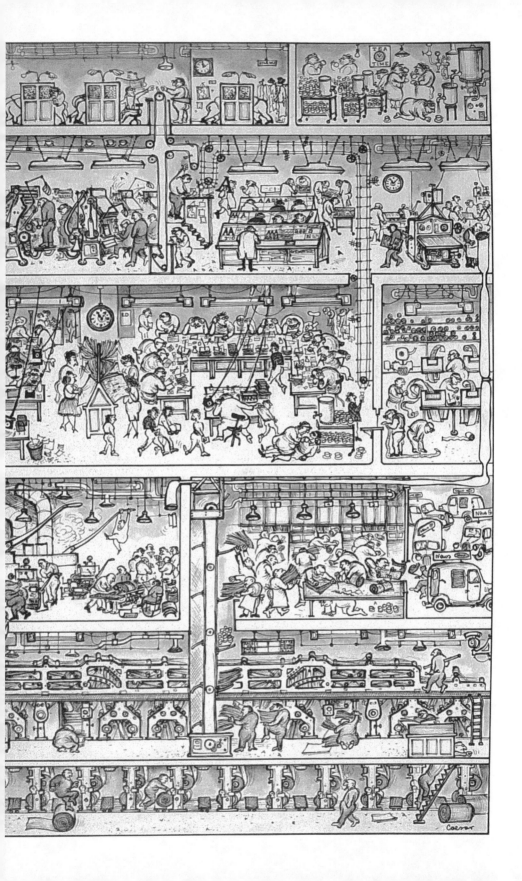

Knowledge will forever govern ignorance and a people
who mean to be their own governors must arm themselves
with the power which knowledge gives.

—James Madison to W. T. Barry,
August 1822

BOOK ONE

Vanished Times

1

Grains of Truth

The most exciting sound in the world for me as a boy was the slow whoosh-whoosh of the big steam engine leaving Manchester Exchange station for Rhyl in North Wales. Every year as summer neared I counted the days to when the whole family—six of us then—would escape the bleakness of northern winters, taking the train for a week at the seaside, buckets and spades in hand.

I was nearly twelve the summer I saw the bodies of the soldiers scattered about the sands.

The soldiers were so still, their clothing so torn, their faces so pale, they looked as if they had died where they fell. And yet they had escaped death, unlike thousands of their comrades left on the battlegrounds of northern France; thousands more were on their way to years in German internment camps. The men I saw were the lucky ones, a few hundred of the 198,229 of the British Expeditionary Force (BEF) who just days before in May–June 1940 had fought their way to Dunkirk. Twenty-four hours before we saw them, they had been on that other beach, being hammered from the air by Stuka dive-bombers, strafed by the machine guns of Messerschmitts, rescue ships ablaze offshore, and every hour the German panzers closing the ring. They were a forlorn group, unshaven, some in remnants of uniforms, some in makeshift outfits of pajamas and sweaters, not a hat between them, lying apart from the rows of deck chairs and the Punch-and-Judy show and the pier and the ice-cream stands. Most of the men who were evacuated had been sent to bases and hospitals in the south of England, but several thousand had been put on trains to seaside resorts in North Wales, where there were army camps and spare beds in the boardinghouses. The bulk of the men sprawled on the Rhyl beach were members of the Royal Corps of Signals attached to artillery regiments; some sixty-four officers and twenty-five hundred other ranks had been sent to the Second Signal Training Center at Prestatyn, which shared six miles of sand with Rhyl.

When we set out for the family holiday, we had no idea that survivors of Dunkirk had just arrived in Rhyl. Nobody in Mrs. McCann's redbrick boardinghouse on the front said anything about the arrivals; they didn't know, and wartime censorship didn't encourage people to talk anyway. Our first day on the beach I bullied my younger brothers — ten, four, and going on two — into helping me build a huge wall of sand to keep out the advancing Irish Sea, while Mum sat in a deck chair knitting and Dad read the newspaper. My father, a steam train driver, had worn himself out taking munitions trains through the blackness of wartime Britain, but he could never sit in a deck chair for long. He would inhale the salt air for ten minutes, then declare we should swim, kick a soccer ball, or join an impromptu beach cricket match. The next bright morning, when I hoped to build a bigger, better sand wall, Dad was restive again. He suggested we should all go for a brisk walk along the sands to work up an appetite for Mrs. McCann's lunch. My mother and brothers preferred to idle by the paddling pool, so with ill grace I fell in beside him. Not only could he not sit still for long, he was compulsively gregarious. Everyone else on the beach was getting on with their seaside relief from factory shifts and holding a family together in the stress of war. To my frustration, when we had gone beyond the pier, Dad saw these sprawling clumps of men, isolated from the holiday crowds, and he walked along to find out who they were. I can see him now squatting among them, offering a cigarette here and there. At thirty-nine, he must have been several years older than most of them, but you would never have known it, so weary and haggard were they. I was always embarrassed by Dad's readiness to strike up conversations with strangers, but Dad moved among the groups of soldiers most of the morning, and I tagged along.

We had been encouraged to celebrate Dunkirk as some kind of victory. A *Daily Mirror* front page I'd seen pinned up in our boardinghouse had the headline "Bloody Marvellous!" How was it, then, Dad found nothing marvelous, only dejection, as he moved among the men?

Only two years later, when my ambitions to be a newspaper reporter flowered, did I understand that Dad was doing what a good reporter would do: asking questions, listening. It never occurred to me to take a note and write it up in my diary, but to this day I remember the sadness of the soldiers who had seen such havoc on that other beach and who knew, too, that they owed their lives to the countless acts of heroism of the rear guard who fought to the last man to keep the escape corridor open.

"They said they had nothing to fight with," Dad told everyone back in the dining room that lunchtime. The men were not triumphant, he explained, as they were said to be—they were bewildered, bitter that the Maginot Line had proved useless because the Germans had bypassed it by coming through

Belgium, bitter with the French Army, bitter with the Royal Air Force (RAF) they felt had left them so exposed to the German Luftwaffe as they lined up on the beach and scrambled for the shallow-draft boats that would take them to the bigger ships. (The histories suggest that the French and the RAF both performed better than it seemed at the time, but misperceptions are the common currency of war.) The newspapers we'd seen had given the impression that the survivors couldn't wait to get back into battle to avenge their defeat. Maybe thousands were, but not those prostrate on the Rhyl beach or the dispirited men who, according to the historian Richard Collier in his 1961 history of Dunkirk, flung their rifles away after landing at Dover.

Dad's account of the mood of the men compared well with the national archives records I checked years later. "We didn't deserve the cheers," said Albert Powell, a truck driver, of their reception after they landed in Ramsgate before entraining for Rhyl. Bert Meakin, a gunner with the Fifty-first Medium Regiment, was critical of the weapons they'd been given to hold back the Germans: "First world war 6-inch howitzers on iron wheels, pretty useless really!" His group fought south of the Somme, then were told it was every man for himself; they abandoned the howitzers in the woods. He arrived in Rhyl with a seven-day leave warrant but without a penny. Powell, a Royal Signals truck driver attached to Third Corps Medium Artillery, got to La Panne on foot. "On the beaches," he recalled, "we huddled together in the sand dunes for protection from the constant bombing and machine gunning from the air. The bombing was ineffectual, just blowing up loads of sand, but the machine gunning was another matter." Once Powell reached a boat, it was swamped by a dive-bomber's near miss, and he was flung into the sea. He swam fifty yards, "arrived at the ship completely knackered and found myself hauled aboard."

Looking back on my boyhood snapshot memory of the difference between what I read and what I saw, I often wondered whether Dad and I were overly impressed with a first-hand experience and hadn't seen the woods for the trees. Dad talked, after all, to a tiny fraction of the evacuated soldiers (and surely, newspaper reporters would have talked to hundreds). So it was interesting to learn later that Winston Churchill got so worried at the presentation of the retreat as a triumph, he felt it necessary to remind everyone that "wars are not won by evacuations." Even more illuminating on the role of the press was Phillip Knightley's authoritative account of war reporting in his book *The First Casualty*, first published in 1975. Of Dunkirk he wrote, "Above all, the stories stressed the high morale of the evacuated troops, itching to get back to France and into the fight again. It was not until the late 1950's and early 1960's—nearly twenty years after the event—that a fuller, truer picture of Dunkirk began to emerge." Alexander Werth, the *Manchester Guardian* correspondent, confessed that after the fall of France he felt guilty at the "soft soap" he had been giving his readers.

The discordance between the waterfront and the front pages was bewildering, the first vague stirring of doubt about my untutored trust in newspapers. As a kid in short pants, I had hardly followed the events of the 1930s with the avidity with which I later read the histories, but I remember how troubled my father was on September 3, 1939, when Prime Minister Neville Chamberlain declared war on Germany. It was so contrary to what we had been insistently told by the *Daily Express*, the newspaper my parents took at home. The paper had reassured its millions of readers that there would be no war with this front-page slogan: "The *Daily Express* declares that Britain will

not be involved in a European War this year, next year either."
Everyone believed it. And why not? The *Express* was a brilliant
broadsheet with a circulation of three million and a huge secondary readership. Most British homes were reached by one
of the bigger newspapers: in 1939 some thirteen million read
the *Express* newspapers, the *Daily Mirror,* the *News of the World,*
or *People,* an audience that by 1948 reached twenty-two million. Newspapers played a crucial role in shaping public perceptions. As the social historian Richard Hoggart noted in his
study of the working class at this time, people often used to say
as evidence of disputed truth, "Oh, but it was in the papers."

But what if you couldn't trust a newspaper to tell the truth
and nothing but the truth? Which institution was more trust-
worthy, the state or the press? Later in adulthood, it was easier
to understand how predictive headlines could turn out to be
wrong than to reconcile what we experienced in Rhyl with the
emphasis in what we read as fact. How did newspapers come
to conclusions? Were they acting at the request of government?
Was there a deliberate and widespread gloss on Dunkirk?
Would that have been justified as a means of sustaining the
nation's morale at a crucial time? Should newspapers take
account of such imperatives or just report things as they saw
them? How did a newspaper decide these things?

Such questions still resonate with me after a lifetime in newspapers. There have been many times when I have found that
what was presented as truth did not square with what I discovered as a reporter or, later as an editor, learned from good
shoe-leather reporters. It was not so much that deliberate lies
were told, though they sometimes were, and not always to
conceal a villainy. "In wartime," Churchill remarked, "truth
is so precious that she should be attended by a bodyguard of

lies." We all understand in an age of terrorism that refraining from exposing a lie may be necessary for the protection of innocents. But "national interest" is an elastic concept that if stretched can snap with a sting. When, in the early 1970s, the *Sunday Times* began reporting the anger building among the Catholic minority in Northern Ireland, a group of Conservative members of Parliament (MPs) invoked the national interest to demand that we stop. They came to tell me, as the paper's editor, that it was "treasonable" to continue. Actually, the real offense was failing to give Northern Ireland full attention in the early 1960s, when the violence was incubated.

A more common issue than outright lying is that people of good faith resent facts that run contrary to their beliefs and assumptions. The nineteenth-century American humorist Josh Billings said it best: "It ain't ignorance that causes all the trouble in this world. It's the things people know that ain't so." No institution has a monopoly of vice in these matters—not governments, trade unions, company heads, lawyers, academia, or the press. In what came to be known as the thalidomide affair in Britain, children were born with deformities—a shortened arm, or no arm at all, or no leg, or completely limbless—because the mothers had taken a prenatal drug prescribed by the National Health Service. They were left to endure their ordeal without help or compensation, a shocking situation that persisted for a decade because the government and the lawyers representing the families assumed that the children had been the victims of an unforeseeable disaster. The lawyers sincerely believed they were making the best of a bad case, but the argument for adequate compensation, properly investigated by the *Sunday Times*, was overwhelming. Revealing it brought furious lawsuits, led by the government of the day, with the attorney general accusing me and the newspaper of contempt of court, punishable by a jail sentence.

Independent reporting has a history of provoking denunciation. Take the legend that "unpatriotic" reporters lost Vietnam. It doesn't stand up to serious examination. Print and TV journalists supportively reported the war in the context of cold war ideology: they wanted the United States to win. What maddened them were the little deceptions of the U.S. government, the hubris of its generals, the corrupt incompetence of the South Vietnamese establishment, and the way the political military bureaucracy deceived itself into telling Washington what it wanted to hear. The corrective correspondents did a real service, and too many of them were killed doing it. Similarly, early in the Iraq War, the George W. Bush administration charged that the reporters on the ground were being lazy, foolish, cowardly, and unpatriotic for reporting that the country was on a vicious downward spiral. It was. The administration deceived itself, and no good came of that. Indeed, a more accurate charge against the press on Iraq would be that it hadn't been patriotic enough before the war began. Faced with a secretive administration bent on war come what may and a popular clamor for post-9/11 revenge, the press forsook its true function. The real national interest required the most searching examination of the reasons for sending thousands of people to their deaths, and it did not get it.

The epiphany on Rhyl beach shook my faith in the printed word, but it did not make me averse to newspapers. On the contrary, as I entered my teens, I grew ever more eager to involve myself in their mysteries. Newspapers were clearly more important and more fascinating than I had imagined, reporting more than a matter of stenography. But how was I to become a reporter and learn the newspaper trade? I was a working-class boy who had already been branded a failure, having failed to qualify for grammar school (the English equivalent, roughly, of American high school). Was I reaching too far? Was I really fit for the work? What were the pitfalls, the ethical dilemmas, and the traps I could barely imagine? How could I equip myself to decode the complex, ever-changing, thrillingly dynamic mosaic of live news and bring it to the public with the raw integrity of truth?

So began my paper chase.

2

Getting Up Steam

When I was three years old, I was expected to die of pneumonia. My first fevered memory of life is staring at the colored counting beads of an abacus at the side of the narrow bed where I was confined in a room with the curtains drawn.

I was born in the summer of 1928 in one of the long rows of two-up, two-down terraced houses off the Liverpool Road, Patricroft, Eccles—part of the sprawl of the cities of Salford and Greater Manchester—and raised in the L. S. Lowry landscape of bent stick figures scurrying past sooty monuments of the industrial revolution. The Renshaw Street houses were so narrow that people shook their heads about how hard it was to get a coffin down the staircases.

Until antibiotics became widely available in England at the end of the 1930s, one in twenty infants died—mostly from pneumonia, meningitis, diphtheria, and tuberculosis. TB was always referred to in a whisper as "the consumption, you know. They'll never rear him." Indeed, it carried off my cousin Freddy around the time I had pneumonia.

During that family crisis my mother was up half the night nursing my brother, who had whooping cough; my father was working nights. I was mostly nursed by a neighbor, Mrs. Amy

Roberts, who lived opposite us, had some nursing experience, and volunteered to sit with me through the nights of fever. In 1978, after I'd become known as a journalist, Amy told the *Eccles Journal* that when she visited my distraught mother, she found that "Harold had been put to bed with whooping cough he had caught from his brother, but was lying on his back, which is dangerous for a sick child." She added, "Harold was a very tiny child with a small peaky face and was too weak to be bothered with anything. He did perk up towards the end of the week but even then he was very shy."

The shyness is at odds with family folklore from when I was two. My mother, on a walk through a local park, stood my baby carriage behind a bench at the duck pond while she chatted with other young mothers. When she turned to go, my carriage was empty. The consensus among the calmest of the young women consoling my mother was that her blue-eyed son had been seized by an international gang of baby smugglers and was even then on his way across the Channel. In fact, the guilty party was happily ensconced in another baby carriage. I had undone my harness and climbed from my own pram into another, where eventually I was found cuddling a baby girl.

My brother Fred, who became the keeper of the family history, told me I was actually nursed through the pneumonia by another good neighbor, Mrs. Matthew (Matt) Newstead, the wife of my father's best friend, which is how my second name came to be Matthew. Perhaps the two women took turns at my bedside. In any event, there are people who feel they both have a lot to answer for.

My grandfather on my father's side, John Evans, was born in 1854 at Llanrhaeadr ym Mochnant in Montgomeryshire, a little village in Mid Wales, where the Bible was first translated into Welsh. He left school when he was nine years old to run errands for plate layers mending railway tracks around Crewe railway junction, the gateway to the north of England. (Compulsory schooling to fourteen was enacted only in 1918.) He later married Sarah Jane Collins, a girl eleven years his junior from Church Minshull, Cheshire, who gave birth to my father on August 1, 1900. She failed to register his birth within the six weeks required, and so fearful of prosecution, she registered Frederick Evans as having been born fifteen days later, on August 21. In this manner, my father acquired a distinction shared with the Queen—two birthdays, and we never knew which to celebrate.

Grandfather John sustained his family in a rented cottage in the village of Coppenhall, Cheshire, in North West England, by repairing shoes and cutting hair at the end of his day's work on the railway. My father told me, "He saved halfpennies so that we'd have Christmas stockings. Mine always had a twopenny mouth organ, an apple, a nut, and a shiny new penny. Nobody had a radio. It hadn't been invented. On Christmas night we blew out the candles and sat around telling ghost stories." Every Christmas in my own childhood, whatever else was in our stockings, there was always an apple, a nut, and a shiny new penny.

My father had little formal education. My grandfather had none—a family secret we didn't learn for fifty years. In 1981, when I was editing the *Times* of London, the paper was delivered to a cottage I had in Shoreham, Kent, where Dad and Mum were taking a break after retirement. "You know, Harold, it's a rum thing," he said, opening the paper. "What would people say if they knew the man editing this newspaper is the grandson of a man who couldn't read a word of it?"

I had six very different aunts and uncles from Dad's

brothers and sisters. One of them, Wild Jack, was a gambler who lost everything betting on horses. The other older brother, Albert, was a railway chief detective superintendent, who slept in freight cars to catch thieves. Dick was a housepainter and Len a very quiet fisherman who didn't seem to have any work. Dad's two sisters were opposites in temperament. Aunt Beattie, the toughest of all my father's family, married a younger widowed farmer in Oswestry near the Welsh border and ruled him and the kids with a rod of iron. Mild Aunt Maggie, the youngest and plumpest in the family, helped in a shop in a backstreet in Crewe, and always fed me sweets when we visited. My first sexual thrill at the age of ten was when her teenage daughter and a giggling friend in another bed in the same room teased me about what might happen to "little Harold" if they came in bed with me. In retrospect, I regret they lost their nerve, but at the time I was terrified. They seemed like fully grown women to me, though they were probably around fourteen.

My mother, Mary Hannah (known to all as Polly), was one of thirteen children, of whom, so far as I could discover, only three survived to adulthood. She was born in Stockport, Cheshire, in 1904, the daughter of Lucy Haselum (née Murray), which gave us a tinge of Irish blood to mix with the Welsh. The Murrays were connected to the Collinses. Grandmother Lucy's father captained ferryboats making the run from Merseyside to Ireland. My mother left school at the age of twelve and helped the family budget by chopping firewood in Eccles. At thirteen she was clattering down the street in clogs on the way to the card room of the local cotton mill. Her older sister, named "Big Eva" to distinguish her from her daughter and my cousin "Little Eva," married a cobbler who had lost a leg in World War I. Her younger brother, Arnold, was a dashing engineer and a Merchant Navy officer in World War II.

15

My mother always had ambitions for a better life. Childhood measles and scarlet fever left her without a sense of smell, and her hearing deteriorated in her thirties, but she never complained. Not only did she manage to bring up four boys with equal affection—five if you include Dad, who was lost without her—but in time she started a business that thrived on their relationship.

My father was the optimist; my mother was the worrier. She had a habit, when sitting in an armchair, of repeatedly running her hand along the fabric, smoothing it out in a rhythmic manner that the British scholar Richard Hoggart perceived (rightly I think) as an effort by working-class women of that generation to smooth out their anxieties. Unlike my gregarious father, she never struck up conversations with strangers and never talked politics. She reserved her energy for figuring out a future for everyone in the family. She hugged us and cared for us—all of us, including Dad—through accidents and sicknesses. Even when I had my tonsils removed at eighteen, she busied herself bringing to the sickbed every day some concoction of egg and brandy with a mystery ingredient I thought might have been brown beef sauce. It seemed to work.

Dad had not much of a better start in life than his father, punished like so many bright boys for being born poor. He was a good all-round student, top of his class in arithmetic and picked for advancement to high school in Crewe, but the family needed him to become a wage earner, so his schooling ended when he was eleven. At thirteen he stoked the furnaces making steel at Crewe Works. "It was a rotten time," he remembered. "We had no electricity in the countryside at Coppenhall; in winter we got up at four thirty to light the fire, thaw the taps. I ran the mile or two to Crewe to get there for six, just in time for a cup of sweet tea and a bun."

In 1916 he volunteered for the Royal Flying Corps, passed some tests, and was downcast when they found out he was sixteen, not the seventeen he claimed, and therefore too young. The war ended before he could be sent to the trenches, but he joined the Territorial Army (Terriers), Britain's volunteer reserve force, the equivalent of the National Guard in the United States. For a time he trained as a boxer, modeling his footwork on a legendary world flyweight champion hardened in a Welsh coal mine — the skinny, five-foot-two Jimmy Wilde. Dad put boxing gloves on all his boys, one at a time encouraging us to take a swing at him and to learn to dodge and weave. "A good little 'un will always beat a big 'un," Dad assured us. It was one of his aphorisms I preferred not to test on the back-streets of Newton Heath, where I collected enough bloody noses simply protecting my marbles from predators.

My father was a bit of a puzzle about martial matters. He was the least belligerent of men, but he loved military ceremonies, like the changing of the guard at Buckingham Palace, and spoke of John Philip Sousa's marching music with almost the same reverence as a run down the wing by his idol on the football (soccer) field, Stanley Matthews, the wizard of dribble. In his spic-and-span time in the Territorial Army, he learned to beat out an impressive tattoo on a kettledrum. He practiced it for years on our bedroom doors when we were slow to get up for school.

My mother was nineteen and my father twenty-three when they met at the "monkey run," as everyone called the Saturday evening dance at a social club on Liverpool Road. The stylish wedding picture of the slim, elegant couple at Patricroft Parish Church in September 1924 belies the bleakness from which

17

they emerged. The newlyweds had to squeeze into a tiny house at 39 Renshaw Street with Granny Haselum and her dying husband, Adam, a laborer in a chemical factory.

My mother and father were lucky in a way: they had jobs when they married. Three million Britons did not. My father had been taken on by the London, Midland and Scottish Railway (LMS) to clean steam engines, and my mother worked in the cotton mill until I was born. They were then wholly dependent on my father not being sacked. The fear that they might have to go down to the labor exchange to register for unemployment money from the government filled them both with horror; they had a prideful revulsion at taking "dole money," which was still vivid in their minds when I was a teenager and they were secure. They radiated a quiet confidence that they were giving us a better start than they had. "I'll see you never wear clogs," Mum said often, and always with uncharacteristic fierceness. They both took it for granted their boys would climb Everest. "The railway's not for you," Dad told each of us.

They saved every penny in Renshaw Street, and with the birth of a second child (my brother Fred in October 1929) they rented an airier, better-built house, one of a row at 14 May Street, Monton. It was just across Liverpool Road, but it was a different world. On Renshaw Street you were in the living room as soon as you crossed the doorstep, so much so that families were judged by how freshly sanded they kept that front doorstep. On May Street, Mum didn't have to kneel every morning at the front door with a bucket of hot water and a pumice stone. Now we had a gate; we had a tiny front garden; we had leaves. In fact, after the abacus my earliest memory is of leaves on privet hedges. To my young eyes, as I was wheeled to a nursery school where we each had a cot for an afternoon nap, the neighborhood of May Street was a corridor of privet hedges—moats around semidetached castles of the English lower orders. Horticulturists value *Ligustrum ovalifolium* for its ability to survive industrial pollution; the self-consciously respectable working class in which I grew up cared more about preserving privacy than combating the then little-appreciated effects of pollution. How sedulously they tended their ligustrum defense against prying eyes! Such was the prevalence of the question "What will the neighbors think?" that I got the idea God had planted busybodies as prolifically as privets.

My father was a genius with numbers. If you named a date five, twenty, thirty-seven years ahead, in a flash he'd tell you what day of the week it would be. Or tell him the date of your birth, and he'd name the day you were born. I never knew him to get it wrong, and I never knew how he did it.

At work on the railway, he became a legend among his workmates—"a ruddy marvel"—for being able to calculate in his head what any one of them was due in his pay packet at the end of a string of complexly different wage rates and irregular hours. The first railwayman who took him at his word got a brusque reception at the "gaffer's" office until they discovered they had indeed shortchanged him. This happened so often that when a worker took the pay slip back to the cashier and said, "Freddie Evans says it is five pennies out," they'd pay it without argument. Ken Law, a Manchester steam fireman, recalls encountering my father at the Newton Heath rail depot's large glass casement that displayed all the assignments of some thirty or more "links" (groups of drivers, firemen, and cleaners); each link was assigned twelve weeks of work. "If you stopped for a word, he would suddenly amaze you by saying that number three link had four hours more night rate in twelve weeks' work than number five link, or that number two link had more Sundays than number seven link and so on.

19

It was no effort. Freddie could work out these statistics just in his head while he waited to be given his engine number. Few could do it today even with the aid of a pocket calculator. Of course nobody had those then. We had Freddie Evans."

In his middle years Dad experimented with the laws of chance. "Gambling is a mug's game" was his mantra, derived from the experiences of his crazy older brother Jack. Among workingmen, all sorts of foolproof betting "systems" enjoyed brief vogues, all ending in disaster, so Mum was fearful when Dad said he had devised a mathematical system for betting on greyhounds. Off he went to the track in Salford with four pounds (about one hundred dollars at the time). He lost it all.

He was depressed, but he knew why his scheme had failed. "I'm sorry, Polly, I got greedy," he told my mother. Henceforth it was his iron rule that once he had won a pound, he would walk off the track. His railway hours did not allow him to go as often as he would have liked, but month after month, year after year, he won his pound and came home, eventually accumulating enough to pay for every family summer holiday.

He didn't impose any kind of regimentation on his boys, so I didn't associate him with discipline. But he was disciplined with himself, apart from being unable to control an appetite for conversation. In his mid-forties he suddenly decided to give up smoking because the price went up. "That's my last cigarette," he said one day, and it was. I'd tried a few cigarettes with our street band of boys. We collected discarded ends called "dimps" and rolled the tobacco into handmade cigarettes for secret group smokes. A few puffs made me cough, and I never touched cigarettes again.

My father's phenomenal numeracy was of no interest to the railway company then, nor in the 1950s and 1960s to nationalized British Railways, which swallowed the LMS. However conscientiously a cleaner, fireman, or driver performed, however well he did on tests, whatever ideas on efficiency he put forward, however long he served with distinction, however much he was esteemed by his peers, he could never hope to achieve advancement into the officer class of supervisors and above. That was ordained by the hierarchies of class.

The question I asked myself often about my parents was what they might have done if they'd had a real chance. Like millions of others, they'd been held back from birth by the belief among the ruling elites that education could do nothing for the working class—nor should it. The Liberal Party in power after World War I set about introducing universal secondary education to the age of sixteen, reducing classroom size below sixty students, and opening a door to university, but the Tories dominant after 1922—the hard-liners, not all of them—abruptly reversed the progress. Growing up, I got bored when Dad went on and on about "the Geddes axe," not realizing then how frontal an assault it had been on any hope of equality of opportunity.

Sir Eric Geddes (Lord Inchcape), a Tory grandee and Minister of the Crown and a former manager of the North Eastern Railway Company, had a predictable contempt for the working class. It expressed itself most nakedly in his advice to Parliament not to waste money giving poor children a secondary education—"children whose mental capabilities do not justify it" was the way he put it in the report of his committee examining public expenditure. This was unappealing as rhetoric; it was appalling as policy. It was exactly the wrong prescription when Britain was suffering from chronic overreliance on unskilled labor in declining industries. Naturally it was greeted with applause in the press, just as was chancellor of the exchequer Winston Churchill's disastrous return to the gold standard in 1925, which priced British exports out of world markets. The conviction of the conventional wisdom in the press and politics was that if it hurt, it must be good for you. Those who were most hurt, of course, were not the advocates of salvation by masochism. They were the coal miners, factory hands, and shipbuilders who endured wage cuts, longer hours, and lockouts.

Recollection of my father's dim view of Churchill pains me, since like millions of others I came to see Churchill as a hero for his wartime leadership. From the perspective of the 1920s, however, my father's attitude was justified. It was hard to forgive the consequences of Churchill's gold standard blunder, his ill-fated assault on Gallipoli while first lord of admiralty during World War I, or his virulence in the General Strike of 1926, a failed attempt to stop a reduction in coal miners' wages. He edited the government newspaper, the *British Gazette,* attacking the miners and persistently printing foolish fabrications — for instance, assuring Londoners that buses and trains were running near to normal when, having to walk to work, they knew they weren't. When later in my career I took a look at the record, I was shocked at the distortions coated in hysteria and shoved down the throats of the public (the fledgling BBC also was hardly a beacon, suppressing anything that might help the strikers, including a conciliatory appeal from the archbishop of Canterbury). Even Prime Minister Stanley Baldwin and the government's commissioner in charge of information, Mr. L. C. Davidson, were alarmed at Churchill's reckless conduct. Davidson wrote later that Churchill and his ally Lord Birkenhead were "absolutely mad.... [Winston] had it firmly in his mind that everyone who was out of work was a Bolshevik; he was most extraordinary and never have I listened to such poppycock and rot." Churchill simply allowed political passion to swamp journalistic principle.

The distrust carried over into the darkening 1930s, when Churchill was so valiant in his efforts to awaken Britain to the menace of Nazi Germany. Dad called him a "warmonger," a common perception among his mates. They were quietly patriotic but disillusioned by World War I—the heady parades through the streets; the senseless slaughter that hit every family; the slow realization, as the histories filtered down, that the men marching off so proudly had been sacrificed by stupidity and that the war itself had been just a terrible accident. Daily at work Dad passed a memorial to the twenty-seven local railwaymen who had not come back from Gallipoli and the Somme:

Forget us O Land for which we fell
May it go well for England, still go well?
Keep her proud banner without blot or stain
Lest we may dream that we have died in vain

The wretched years of appeasement have to be understood in that context. Men like my father had no faith in "that talking matchstick" Neville Chamberlain, but nor did they have any enthusiasm for a rerun of 1914–1918. Dad was by no means a pacifist, though the Labour Party lessons in history and geography he had taken had made him otherwise a disciple of Jimmy Maxton, a militant Scottish socialist and pacifist who was elected to Parliament in 1922 (an admiration later shared by Maxton's biographer, Prime Minister Gordon Brown). What really inspired my father was faith in the brotherhood of man, a characteristic he shared with the giant who walked the full length of "the world's longest platform" at Manchester Exchange station to shake hands with the footplate crew who had brought him safely to his destination. The giant was Paul Robeson, who was finally free to tour outside America after eight years of being denied a renewal of his passport. In the cold war hysteria of the 1950s, it had been judged treasonable for Robeson to have said, "Our will to fight for peace is strong. We shall not make war on anyone. We shall not make war on the Soviet Union." The egalitarianism of Robeson's handshake appealed to my father; certainly it was something no British political leader of the era would have dreamt of doing.

Robeson, like my father, had a romantic view of the Soviet Union. Dad believed that it exemplified Karl Marx's slogan "From each according to his abilities, to each according to his needs," an illusion fostered by Sidney and Beatrice Webb's 1935 book *Soviet Communism: A New Civilisation?* read by my father in Labour Party and trade union courses. Dad was as unaware as millions of others of Joseph Stalin's mass murders, nor was he of a revolutionary disposition. When I got him to talk about his part in the General Strike of 1926, I said he must have felt bitter when it was broken. "No," he said, "I didn't feel bitter. I just felt sorry for the way the miners were let down."

The job my father had when I was born, engine cleaner, was a bigger deal than it sounds. It was the first rung on a very long but very coveted ladder to becoming a locomotive driver.

Train drivers were an aristocracy among the working class. They had a job for life, the social esteem that came with security, and better-than-average pay. The downside was that the job was brutally hard in its physical and mental demands. The hours of work were horrible, beginning variously at 2:00 a.m., 3:00 p.m., or 5:00 a.m. It was a matter of pride to my father that he never needed the knocker-up to rap on the window with his long pole (an essential profession before alarm clocks were common). But the shifts meant that week to week we were asleep when he was up and he was asleep when we were up.

The railway historian Frank McKenna observed that "the eyes of a footplateman appear to be a decade younger than the rest of his physique." Dad's were striking, deep in his sockets. Perfect eyesight and physical fitness were demanded of an engine cleaner as of a driver. A slight falloff in the eyesight test, a hint of color blindness or any physical limitation, and a driver would be demoted to sweeping the sheds, shunting wagons in a freight yard, or cleaning lavatories — or even dismissed altogether. Dad was so sensitive about his fine vision that he would not hear of it when as a teenager I thought I was becoming nearsighted. I was, but he was in a state of denial I didn't understand at the time. Now I see that the eye-rolling exercises I picked up from a book by an Indian doctor would have alarmed anyone.

Every schoolboy then might have wanted to be an engine driver, but there was no glamour in the first step. On his night shift, among other dirty jobs, Dad had to go under the engine and climb into the dark belly of the beast to oil the big ends of the pistons, fearfully trusting that nobody would move the engine (as occasionally some lunatic did). He had several years of this before he was tested for work on the footplate (that is, in the open cab), first qualifying as a "Passed Cleaner," which carried the prospect of some turns as a fireman. What back-breaking work! I have a mental picture of my father coming home, exhausted from an all-night firing job on a goods train, keeping a foothold on the rocking engine while hour after hour shoveling coal from the tender, maybe six tons of it, and hurling it through the small fire hole into the right places in the firebox to raise the necessary steam pressure. "Where's my steam?" was the yell no fireman wanted to hear from the driver.

In time, a Passed Cleaner could hope to become a Red Ink Fireman, on the footplate for a few months; then, all being well, a Black Ink Fireman, on the rosters for regular firing; and finally a Passed Fireman, tested to drive any train in his depot.

As a Red Ink Driver he would be on the roster for driving in holiday periods, and then eventually, as a Black Ink Driver, he would be at the top of the ladder. No other craft or profession exacted such a lengthy "apprenticeship." Dad carefully annotated the details of every driving turn he acquired after becoming a Red Ink Fireman. It typically took at least twenty years to get to the top. "Dead man's shoes," said Dad.

A driver could not take a train on a route until he knew the route's every particularity—the sighting of every signal, the sounds and shadows that might guide him in fog or a snowstorm when visibility was near zero, the shape of every curve in the track, the length and darkness of every tunnel, the trickiness of every ascent where extra steam and sand might be needed, the occurrence of every set of points where the train might be switched to a different line. They called this familiarization "learning the road," and Dad learned many roads, rattling most happily along the North Wales coast, where many years later, at Bluebell Wood cemetery at Coed Bell in Prestatyn, he was to find his final resting place.

Drivers and firemen were subject to strict military discipline, and it was easy to see why. A railwayman who did not read, memorize, and follow the hundreds of regulations in the precious rule book risked his own life, as well as the lives of his workmates and his several hundred passengers. Dad knew the rule book back to front. In the kitchen, testing himself, he'd ask questions rhetorically: What do you do with a runaway train on a hill or a train slipping back? How in an emergency do you signal to the guard at the back of the train? If you pass through facing points onto a curve, what is the safe speed? What if you have to run backward? What's the right thing to do if there's an obstruction on the line, an uprooted tie, a snowdrift? If you run out of steam, what lights do you lay down on the track and where? The work ethic was puritanical—clean overalls, no drink, no swearing, no smoking on duty, and no tolerance for misdemeanors. If he was ten minutes late at the sheds, he risked being sent home with the warning that next time he'd be fired. I remember a railway inspector coming to our house to see if Dad had taken home one of the high-quality hand rags issued to footplate crews for oiling work. He hadn't. He knew better.

We worried about my father's daily risks. Usually he came home chuckling over some incident. It was ominous when he didn't:

"What's the matter, Dad?"
"Something terrible."
"But what?"
"Bad accident."
"What kind of accident?"
"Finish your tea."

We'd eventually discover that a plate layer had lost a leg, a shunter had been crushed between wagons, a fireman had been scalded, or a driver had been killed walking across a track to check a frozen signal. His own most common affliction was grit in the eye from looking out of his open cab at high speeds. There was no protective eye shield for footplate men.

He tried to educate his union, the Associated Society of Locomotive Engineers and Firemen, not always to campaign for wage increases but also to aim for medical benefits and for decent pensions, pointing out that an extra shilling or two now would be better invested for retirement. But he could never persuade them, so when he did retire, his pension after fifty years was seven shillings a week (about eight dollars at today's values).

*　　*　　*

In the early 1930s the composition of the manpower at the LMS Newton Heath sheds, way across the other side of Manchester, offered a better prospect of graduating from Passed Cleaner to Red Ink Fireman. Newton Heath was a very big depot with more than two hundred locomotives. Also of some relevance was Dad's passion for soccer: he never saw a ball he didn't want to dribble around an imaginary fullback and, scorning players who could not shoot with both feet, drilled us hard on that. Naturally he liked the idea that the Newton Heath sheds were the birthplace of a soccer team—not any old team, but the Heathens, a bunch of railwaymen who managed to get into the Football League, nearly went bankrupt, and then did rather better after 1902, when they changed their name to Manchester United.

Dad at once applied for a transfer to Newton Heath. He and my mother took the plunge of putting down all their savings as a deposit on a £300 house a few miles from the railway sheds, their first time out of rented accommodations. It was a barely finished, semidetached place at 54 Ashworth Street, a new estate close to Manchester City's wooded Brookdale Park, famed for its birds, grasslands, and Victorian bandstand. (Many were the times irate park keepers chased Fred and me for getting into the park by climbing the iron railings instead of walking ten minutes to the park entrance.) Our new house was right on the edge of open countryside and farms. In the early days before the war, a farmer in pony and trap came round before breakfast time selling milk he ladled out of a big churn strapped to the trap; in the summer everyone joined in haymaking.

This was the place where, for more than twenty years, my three brothers and I, sleeping two to a bed, grew up. All our fun was very much homemade—marbles, yo-yos, hopscotch, tag, whipping a spinning top along the street. Fred and I would go out to the big paved space at the three-way junction where our house stood to stage a cricket match with a rival street, using a tennis ball and a lamppost for a wicket. In winter we made long ice slides, and when it snowed Dad hammered together crude sleds, lining the runners with metal from discarded tins of Heinz beans. I collected scrap lead, boiled it on the kitchen stove, and used clay impressions of tin soldiers to create armies for battles with cannons firing matchsticks. From a smelly works along the Rochdale Canal we "lifted" bits of ebonite tubing for peashooter contests. We were manic competitors in everything with all the kids in the street, but most of all in completing cigarette card series of soccer teams, cricketers, kings, aircraft, cars, wars, and film stars.

Very occasionally we'd test our parents' good temper by venturing into enemy territory to engage in running stone-throwing battles with kids from other streets in Newton Heath, everyone scattering at the sight of the angry red face of the potbellied Police Constable Robinson. He had a truncheon and lived opposite our school, Brookdale Park Elementary.

Communal goodwill broke through, though, every November 5, when Guy Fawkes brought our neighborhood together. After three hundred years there wasn't any lingering resentment of Captain Fawkes for trying to blow up Parliament in 1605 — quite a few in 1936 thought it was a great idea — but the passage of time hardly lessened the appetite for a bonfire feast of baked potatoes, boiled ham and cheese, treacle tart, toffee apples, and Yorkshire's gingerbread, known as "Parkin pie," accompanied by fireworks and singsong. Fred and I enthroned a stuffed, bearded effigy of the conspirator in a cart made from old carriage wheels and begged around for "a penny for the Guy" to be spent on fireworks. Every household made a contribution to the bonfire, which lasted past midnight, fueled by logs from the fields, broken-down settees and chairs, and our "Guy

Fawkes" on top, exploding with firecrackers. I can still smell the cordite.

Mum and Dad gave their four sons warm encouragement at every stage. They were devoted to each other, too, but they didn't let it show. None of my brothers can recall any cross words between them — nor any show of open affection. I don't think I ever saw them embrace or kiss. But if Dad was there to help Mum with the dishes after supper, sometimes we'd hear him attempt the lilting lyric of a music hall song: "If you were the only girl in the world, and I were the only boy."

He was moved by music from America. My nostalgic ear catches now the innocence of the refrain of "Home on the Range," which Dad puff-cheeked out of his mouth organ. He wished he had been born in Wyoming, not Crewe, so he would sit at our kitchen fireplace imagining that he was playing the song by a prairie campfire under the stars before rolling up in his horse blanket, with his saddle for a pillow. Sometimes he sang it to us: "Oh, give me a home where the buffalo roam/ Where the deer and the antelope play;/Where seldom is heard a discouraging word,/And the skies are not cloudy all day."

He wanted us to appreciate the harmony of Nelson Eddy and Jeanette MacDonald singing "Rose-Marie" in the film about the Canadian Mounties, the majesty of Paul Robeson's "Ol' Man River," and the romance of Stephen Foster's "Camptown Races." When we were toddlers, he would hold us on his knee and give an unsteady version of Al Jolson from the movie *The Singing Fool*, which came out the year I was born: "Climb upon my knee, Sonny Boy/ ... You've no way of knowing, there's no way of showing / What you mean to me, Sonny Boy." He took the words to heart. I grew up when boys were regularly beaten by their fathers. There was only one occasion when Dad took a strap to my backside — for playing with matches.

My parents were affectionate, but they were reticent—no, downright obscure—about anything to do with sex. My worldlier younger brother Fred claimed superior knowledge, but until I was about ten, I sincerely believed that babies were delivered in the little black Gladstone bags that doctors carried. That doesn't say much for my powers of observation, since my mother had by then carried another brother to term.

The only hint that my parents were aware of the hormonal turmoil of teenage life was a book—from the Boy Scouts, I think—on the awful consequences of masturbation, which just happened to be left lying around and of course caused immediate and unmentionable panic among us boys. We subsequently struggled between the Boy Scout reign of terror and a *Naturist* magazine featuring sepia nudes that was slipped to me in an exercise book at school.

Nowadays my father would be considered a prude. Mother's brother Arnold, who looked like Clark Gable and rode a fast motorcycle, once began to tell Dad a risqué joke and then had the sense to stop when Dad's face dropped. He liked the kind of riddles stuffed in Christmas crackers, music hall impersonations, and idiomatic radio sketches of northerners coping with the frustrations of their lives. Ken Law told me, "If you met your dad in the very early hours of a cold, damp, frosty morning or in the middle of a rain-lashed railway shed yard, he'd always come up with something funny." Never would it require the prop of profanity. He'd "damn" and "blast it," but I can't recall him saying "bloody," and indeed the "effing" and "blinding" that is the vernacular today was not then a feature of respectable working-class speech in the north.

Most of all, my father liked telling daft stories about himself, and the family loved to have him act them out. One night, he told us, he went to a rough workingmen's club to collect a small debt. He climbed to the top of the stairs. "When I got to the top, there was no light, and I could just make out the shadowy figure standing there. I said, 'Hello, I've come to see a friend of mine.' He didn't reply, so I told him again. And he stood there saying nothing, so I took another step forward and so did he! I thought, *He's coming for me."*

And at this point Dad, who was no more than five feet six but muscled from all that coal shoveling, would hunch into a boxing stance.

"I was such a fool!" he explained. "There was a big mirror at the top of the stairs. I was talking to myself! I'd been misled because I'd done something I don't normally do—wear a hat!"

He was indeed a creature of habit. We knew the ending, but we hooted with laughter every time he told the story in exactly the same way. We were part of the performance, and his performance, like good theater, always seemed fresh, as if he were discovering it himself for the first time.

Rituals were a big part of our happy family life. Mum tossed pancakes on Shrove Tuesday, baked treacle toffee for the campfires on Guy Fawkes Night, hid eggs at Easter, and made sure that the first person to enter the house after midnight on December 31 carried a piece of coal for good luck.

Most of all, on occasional Saturday nights Mum and Dad enjoyed opening the house to relatives and neighbors for cold meat and pie suppers and games, pitting teams of adults and kids in musical chairs, charades, bobbing for toffee apples, blindman's bluff, scavenger hunts, memory games, and on and on through a repertoire filled with excitement and laughter.

My father was enthusiastic about his quaint ceremonial rituals at club nights in the workingmen's fraternal association the Royal Antediluvian Order of Buffaloes, or "Buffs." (Dad would have joined the Freemasons if anyone had asked him.) In my adolescence I dreaded when we moved into the company of strangers. He would always open a conversation, while

I curled up in embarrassment and affected not to be with him. For me, Dad on holiday at breakfast in the dining room of a seaside boardinghouse was a recipe for importing anxiety by the bucketful. He would make the opening sally to the family at the next table, and vistas opened on an infinity of world controversies while we fretted to get out to the beach before it rained. Without Mum giving him a kick under the table, we'd have been stuck for the day.

Writing about my parents and their role, I realize how easy it is, just as it was in her lifetime, to allow Mum's more contained personality to become overshadowed by memories of Dad's ebullience. But it was Mum's down-to-earth practicality and native intelligence that were key to a rise in the family's fortunes. The girl who had started out working in a mill and wearing clogs developed an entrepreneurial streak.

Our house at 54 Ashworth Street was on the edge of open fields and farmland stretching for miles in the direction of Daisy Nook, a sweet valley of woods and water, and toward hills dominated by Hartshead Pike, where the druids, we were told, had made sacrifices and the Romans had lit beacons to warn local garrisons of heathens on the prowl. At Easter more pacific modern hordes made the trek to Daisy Nook for a big annual fair, but on every weekend there was a steady flow of ramblers passing our door for picnics there or boating on the adjacent Crime Lake. Often they'd knock on our door and ask if we could give them a glass of water. My mother always obliged. There were so many knocks at the door that she came up with the idea of making lemonade and selling it for a half-penny a glass. She sold it all, and her ambitions soared.

My parents walked the two miles to Rothwell Street and asked to see Antonio and Fred Sivori, who owned a little ice-cream factory. The Sivori brothers had their own horse-drawn "ice-cream parlor" traveling the streets of Newton Heath, but Dad persuaded them to deliver to Ashworth Street, on Sunday morning, a big tub of ice cream at wholesale price, packed around with ice (we had no refrigerator), along with a scoop for making cornets (ice-cream cones) and a wafer maker for ice-cream sandwiches. That first Sunday as nascent capitalists, my parents were apprehensive. Dad painted ICE CREAM HERE on a big piece of cardboard, and they stood by the garden gate. If it rained, they'd lose the investment.

By late afternoon they'd sold out, and Dad went cheerfully off to the night shift. They tried it again the following Sunday: another sellout. The third week, the ice cream was all gone by lunchtime. It was a long way to Rothwell Street for a refill, and the container was so heavy they carried it between them along the streets. They were almost at the Sivoris' when one of them—neither would ever take the credit—realized that the weight was mainly melted ice that could be poured away. The Sivori brothers ferried the refilled tub back to Ashworth Street, and it was empty by teatime.

Soon there was a growing parade of Sunday and then Saturday customers at No. 54. They'd ask if Mum had sweets, or pop, or cigarettes, or a bun, and her answer was always the same: "Sorry, no, but we'll have it next week." She got Dad to take down the garden gate and build shelves in the hallway. The litany of promises led to stock spilling out from the hall into our front room, so she removed all the furniture, installed a big counter, started stocking groceries and haberdasheries for neighbors, and in time installed a plate-glass window and a refrigerator—wonders in the Ashworth Street neighborhood. Within a year, a full-scale corner shop flowered in our old parlor—managed, staffed, and maintained by Mum. Under her canny eye it became wildly successful. While she could not match the virtuoso calculations of my father, in the blink of an eye she could add up a long column of pounds, shillings, pence, and halfpence—twelve pence to a shilling, twenty shillings to a pound—and get it right the first time. Out of one pound of the takings, she'd make two shillings, a nice 10 percent profit that she stored in an old Oxo tin.

Sometimes she allowed Fred or me to help in serving. This was a great treat. I put on a white apron, scrubbed my hands, and slicked back my hair with a helping of butter. Boys and girls I played with in the street outside incredulously pressed their noses against the plate-glass window and the array of sweets displayed. My stock rose. I served customers simple items: cigarettes, bread, milk, tinned food. Bacon came in a big roll that had to be sliced. I was not allowed anywhere near the horrendous slicing machine; seeing Mum with her hand feeding the bacon so close to the sharp, swift-circling blade gave me nightmares. The most glamorous job was filing the colorful dust jackets (and rejacketing the returns) of the books Mum lent in the library she started. Fred and I came to blows over this privilege, wrestling furiously in the back room until one of us got the other in a headlock and won a concession.

When his shifts worked out, Dad liked nothing better than to come home, discard his overalls, and put on a clean white apron to serve in the shop—such a contrast from what he had been doing all day. This was sometimes to my mother's exasperation when the shop filled with people. Dad listened to every tale from every customer, whereas Mum knew who was a gasbag to be deftly cut off at second breath. Dad's style was altogether free and easy; asked for half a pound of boiled ham, he'd sacrifice his passion for precision in numbers and let the Avery scale ride over the eight-ounce mark. He redeemed this liberality, though, on one occasion when a woman came in and asked for a back stud for her husband's shirt collar.

Dad rifled in the haberdashery drawer and presented it to her. "That's one penny," he said. The woman responded sharply, "No, I want a *good* one; it's for a wedding." Dad took the back stud from her, rummaged around in the drawer, and pulled out the same stud. "Twopence," he said. She beamed and went off happy that she had a good-quality stud.

I still marvel at how my mother managed to give birth to two more boys—Peter was born in January 1936 and John in December 1938—look after Fred and me and Dad, run the shop six days a week (which meant ordering supplies, pricing them for retail, and dealing with customers), and never lose her temper. When she closed the shop, her working day wasn't over. She'd sit at her Singer sewing machine doggedly making clothes for us, including a billowing nightshirt for Dad (the cause of much hilarity) and white satin blouses for us to wear in the All Saints' Whitsun procession. (The family didn't go to church, but we were regulars at Sunday school.) Mum darned socks, knitted pullovers, ironed shirts, washed our laundry by hand, and saw Dad off to work with his can of loose tea, sugar, and milk to be brewed up on the engine; sandwiches; and playing cards in an old tobacco tin. If something bothered her, she retreated into silence, her lips tightening.

And then came bad news.

As more of the fields filled with housing, two neighbors copied Mum by turning their parlors into groceries, and the Co-operative Society chain announced that it would open one of its big stores and butcher shops in Miriam Street, a few hundred yards down Ashworth Street. The Co-op had the appealing message of being owned by its customers. Buying in bulk for many branches allowed the Co-op to cut prices, and thrift-minded customers became "members" who could accumulate a cash dividend on purchases. George Orwell, in *The Road to Wigan Pier* in 1937, observed that the arrival of a Co-op was a disaster for independent shopkeepers. Local authorities that built housing estates (large blocks of flats) rigidly limited the number of shops in the area and gave preference to the Co-op. "Many a small shopkeeper is utterly ruined... their whole clientele taken away from them at a single swoop," Orwell wrote.

Mum and Dad debated whether they should keep going. While they worried, an inspector came around from our controlling local authority, Failsworth Council. "I have the power to shut you down forthwith," he told all three front-parlor entrepreneurs. "Not one of you has a license, and you don't stand a chance of getting one if I'm not satisfied with the way you store food." Having inspected ours first, he then went off to look at the others. When he came back in the afternoon, he told Mum, "I must speak to the man of the house." In the 1930s women were not presumed to have any competence at business of any kind; very few ran anything. The inspector waited around until my father came home and took him aside.

"Mr. Evans, I take it that Mrs. Evans is in charge?" Dad said yes, she was. "In that case," said the inspector, "I have to tell you, Mr. Evans, you are a lucky man. I have never seen a better-run grocery in all my years as an inspector. I am giving you a license. I am closing down the others."

The day after the Co-op opened its doors, Mum went in to check its prices. The employees didn't know who she was, so they indulged the slightly deaf lady who asked for prices on a lot of items. Only a few of the Co-op prices were cheaper, and Mum immediately marked down hers. She lost a few customers in the first week, but most drifted back, probably because my mother identified with her customers in a way the Co-op staff, conscious of their elevated position, could not match. As the semidetacheds expanded farther into the countryside, we stopped worrying. It was plain there was room for both ventures, and indeed Mum's shop was still flourishing under Korean management in 2007.

The Evanses were moving up! By the time I was nine, my parents were doing well enough to buy a secondhand red Hillman Minx, an unheard-of acquisition in our area. A car outside a house had always meant bad news: only doctors had cars. I heard years later from my schoolmate at Brookdale Park Elementary Alf Morris that I was known behind my back as "Posh" Evans on account of the purchase. In truth, I did not enjoy the car. The smell of leather inside made me sick, so when the family went on Sunday drives into Cheshire, I stayed at home, moping around and looking at the terrifying representations of hell in an illustrated Bible—where the Boy Scouts' helpful literature on the perils of masturbation assured me I was undoubtedly headed.

Much more exciting to me than any car was the day Dad became a king of the iron road.

Dad had washed and had his supper before he told us he had at last been promoted to Black Ink Driver. It must have been an effort for such a talkative man to say nothing, but he waited until Mum had closed the shop. There were handshakes at the sheds but no ceremony. He would still be doing the same work, rising at all hours, taking out trains in all kinds of weather, but as a full driver he had acquired a certain majesty, meriting respect and deference all along the line as a reflection of the responsibility he bore.

He had taken his licks as a fireman working with cantankerous drivers, and as a part-time driver he'd had to tolerate a few lazy or careless firemen. Now he was indisputably in charge. Nobody could tell him to take out a fireman he thought incompetent or an engine he considered defective. He could insist on a replacement. Railway management rarely authorized any visits to the footplate, not least when it was moving, but nobody could mount his footplate without his permission, and while he was in charge of the big engine, he was answerable to no one.

I longed to see my father at work, but the hours were unhelpful. As a driver, he often set off in his new glossy peaked cap and serge jacket just as I was spreading out my homework on the living room table. I had to wait for the privilege, and it came by chance when I was sixteen. One summer evening when I arrived by train at Manchester Victoria station, Dad was on the opposite platform about to drive a few hundred passengers home to Oldham. "Hop on quick," he said. I seized the moment.

Sitting in the comfort of a railway carriage, as I had been on the way in, gave passengers no idea of the ferocious goings-on up there in front on the open footplate as the train gathered speed out of the station and up the line—of the heat and noise that made speech impossible; the roar and flames of the firebox; the sweat of the fireman with his long-handled shovel feeding the red-hot maw; the noise of iron meeting iron on the swaying footplate; the intensity of Dad's concentration looking up the line for pinprick signals of red and green, checking the boiler pressure, and opening and closing the steam regulator arm according to gradient and track. And then at the end, at the station platform, the carriage doors slamming as the passengers got off the train, their voices drifting into the night, oblivious of what we had been through, I was astounded and bursting with pride.

3

First, Know Your Enemy

I was eleven when Prime Minister Neville Chamberlain told forty-seven million Britons, "This country is at war with Germany." That Sunday morning at 11:00 a.m., on September 3, 1939, I listened to his broadcast with the rest of the family, all of us huddled round the vibrating fabric of our brown-enamel wireless set.

Dad was unusually silent, but Mum commented, saying of Chamberlain, "He seems to be more sorry for himself than the rest of us." Reading the speech today, I can see what she meant: "You can imagine what a bitter blow it is to me that all my long struggle to win peace has failed. Yet I cannot believe that there is anything more or anything different I could have done and that would have been more successful."

Mum was right. It was all about him.

No sooner had Chamberlain finished speaking than the air raid sirens howled. Fred and I rushed into the street. It was a crazy thing to do, but it was a false alarm. We were disappointed not to see Stuka dive-bombers tangling with the big, fat blue barrage balloons in the blue sky. We were even more upset when, the same day, the government shut down all the cinemas. What would we do for the rest of our lives?

The sound of Chamberlain's plaintive voice has stayed with

me all these years. At the time I could not get out of my head the posh way he talked about our "embessador" in Berlin and the "plens" we would all have to make. The plummy announcers on the BBC had made me acutely conscious of accents as an indicator of class, of ineluctable superiority. Just turning on the radio made me ashamed. Nobody in my universe spoke like that; therefore, we must be outcasts, belonging to some inarticulate barbarian tribe. These were the years when the announcers and newsreaders all spoke so-called Standard English, meaning the soft tones of the alien south: harmonious Oxbridge voices of long vowels, distinct *p*'s and *t*'s, and effortless aspirates. The BBC tolerated J. B. Priestley's Yorkshire accent for a few months from June to October 1940 in his series of morale-boosting talks, but not his political opinions: seen by the Tories as too socialist, the program was axed. In 1941 it was front-page news when Wilfred Pickles brought a Yorkshire accent to BBC news reading—one would have thought a cathedral or two had been sacked—but he too was soon removed from the national airwaves, and Standard English prevailed for the next thirty years.

Our teacher at Brookdale Park Elementary interposed her good soul between civilization and us aural barbarians, struggling against centuries of cultural history to get us to "speak nicely," which meant mimicking the BBC. Chastised early in reading class for referring to an "'ospital," I approached every "aitch" as a pole-vaulter running at a high bar. (Of course educated youths now use a slovenly "mockney," which is more affected than ever we BBC imitators were in the Brookdale English lessons.)

Chamberlain's announcement created hardly a ripple in our neighborhood compared to the excitement of the night before he spoke. Every Saturday a half hour between 5:00 and 6:00 p.m. was sacrosanct. We could count on being undisturbed by the shop bell because every household was poised by the radio for the BBC's pip-pip-pip prelude to the day's football scores. Seeing match results on television or the Web today doesn't begin to compare to the effect of hearing one calm, authoritative voice announce the end of the world: "Manchester United 1, Charlton Athletic 7."

The scores were of paramount importance because predicting the results could take you from the hard grind and dreary backstreets to a fantasy life of ease and luxury. The football pools were not quite a lottery; there was a certain skill in assessing the clubs and their key players. Fortunes were made overnight; getting all but a few matches right might win hundreds of thousands of pounds, zillions more than anyone could earn in a lifetime. Before mailing in the coupon with his sixpenny bets, Dad spent hours studying the form, then used his little stubby pencil to mark the match lists with a 1 for a team's home win, an x for a draw, or a 2 for a win away from home. If he'd bet that the star team of Blackpool, playing at home, would beat Leeds, the radio announcer's pause after "Blackpool 1" was excruciating. The disembodied voice of fate seemed to extend every letter in "L-e-e-d-s" before ruining everything by declaring that Leeds had scored 2. Crueler still was "Middlesbrough 4," Dad's prediction for a home win, followed by "Everton...4." The house rule against breathing a word couldn't stand such freak results.

Fearing that British stoicism could not bear the strain of the Saturday pools and at the same time win a war, the Football League suspended its matches "for the duration." It was a phrase we came to hate, along with "Don't you know there's a war on?" Knowing now of the years of convulsions that were to follow Chamberlain's declaration of war, it is weird how calm and confident the people were, sitting down to roast lamb and mint sauce after his speech.

Perhaps that was partly because we were under the illusion that we were ready. We had already collected our identity cards and gas masks. Fred and I paraded around in the masks parodying "Heil Hitler" salutes, but the smell of the rubber made us gag, and after that we wore ours only for the drill at school, when on the command we assumed fetal positions under our desks.

We helped Mum and Dad stick tape all over our windows to hold the fragments in a bomb blast, put up blackout blinds and double curtains, and hated it when a bossy air raid warden knocked on the door to say a chink of light was showing: he was just a neighbor in a tin hat. Riding the electric tramcar along Oldham Road, we could see sandbags heaped around Failsworth's ceremonial flagpole. And at supposedly key points in the straggling communities of small terraced houses served by clusters of fish-and-chip shops, haberdashers, pubs, hairdressers, newsagents, bookies, savings banks, pawnbrokers, butchers, and the occasional cinema and church, iron railings round the churches and graveyards and everywhere else had already been taken away—to make tanks we were told. The flowers in Manchester's Piccadilly Gardens had been dug up for trenches and air raid shelters. The more active householders had dug deep holes in their gardens and roofed them with six sheets of curved corrugated iron supplied by the local council. The finished bunker was called an Anderson shelter after its progenitor.

Dad thought the Anderson useless. Many in our street filled with water. Some people did not bother to prepare at all. Everybody knew the war would be over by Christmas. The mass of people had no idea of just how ill prepared our military was. They were betrayed by the newspapers, led by the *Times, Daily Express,* and *Daily Mail,* and even by the BBC, which had shamefully soft-pedaled and suppressed the years of alarms from a small band of Chamberlain's critics in his own party (including future prime ministers Churchill and Harold Macmillan, but not a vain and timid Sir Anthony Eden). "Germany's tanks are made of cardboard," a know-all boomingly reassured a shop full of our customers. "Joe, that can't be right," said my father, who was helping out that day. Then he delivered a numbing recital of figures of German steel production, recalled from his well-thumbed *World Almanac and Book of Facts*. (This didn't go down at all well. My mother had to remind him that never mind his blessed almanac, the customer was always right.)

Dad's irregular shifts at the railway meant we often didn't see him for two or three weeks. He drove trains carrying thousands of children out of Manchester, their schools closed and relocated miles away from industrial areas, considered prime targets for bombing. Schoolmates from Brookdale and Briscoe Lane Junior, with their name tags and mandatory gas masks, were put on a train to Ramsbottom, a village on the West Pennine Moors, where the local families could pick and choose whom to welcome into their homes for the duration. By all accounts most of the evacuees, even the scruffiest, were kindly received in foster homes more comfortable than the dwellings they'd left behind, in the process happily finding out about the mysterious "countryside." Schoolmate Alf Morris, who in the fullness of time became a Labour minister and later Lord Morris, was one of the unlucky ones. Separated from his brother and sister, who were taken in by a well-to-do family, Alf was billeted with a mean old couple who sent him out hawking firewood they chopped for a living and half-starved him on suppers from the fish-and-chip shop. Alf was back home in a month or two.

As the city emptied, my parents kept us in Ashworth Street. They wrote to my father's mother, Sarah Jane, to ask if Fred and I could stay with her on the Welsh border. She was now Granny Jones, having married a gravedigger called Jack. Anything remotely to do with death upset me, but I was not wild about the prospect of going to Ramsbottom either. I'd heard too many comics on Rhyl pier mouthing "Ramsbottom" as if the name was a joke in itself. My inclination to stay away was clinched when a postcard came back from a Brookdale classmate saying that it was once known as Tupp's Arse (Tupp being old dialect for "sheep").

Once or twice a week a Brookdale teacher came to the house and gave us homework, but Mum and Dad worried that we were falling behind. While we waited for Granny Jones to write back, a neighbor told Mum about another possible sanctuary. It excited me most of all: Somerford Hall, which was an old manor house in the countryside near Congleton in Cheshire where the Manchester Education Committee had set up a boarding school.

To appreciate the attraction of Somerford Hall, you have to know about the *Magnet*. Of all the comic books we bought at the newsagent's every week — *Beano, Wizard, Dandy, Hotspur* — the *Magnet* most insinuated itself into my imagination. This is where Frank Richards (aka Charles Hamilton) recorded the adventures of the fifth form at Greyfriars, the ancient ivy-covered public school secure in its gentlemanly traditions. The setting represented some of the lyrical features of English life evoked by Rupert Brookes's Grantchester poem: "Stands the Church clock at ten to three? / And is there honey still for tea?" The class overtones should have grated on me, I suppose, but they didn't. After the asphalt playgrounds of Newton Heath, I liked the idea of surviving the war with toffs on the lawns of Greyfriars, and I relished the *Magnet* stories where beastly cads got their comeuppance and good eggs and goodness triumphed. Here were Harry Wharton, Bob Cherry, Frank Nugent, Johnny Bull, the Indian cricketer Huree Jamset Ram Singh, the Form Master Mr. Quelch (too ready with the cane), and the crafty Billy Bunter, "the Fat Owl of the Remove," plotting to steal someone else's tuck. I identified most with Harry Wharton, captain of the remove and editor of the *Greyfriars Herald*. I saw myself seeing out the war at Somerford Hall, toasting crumpets for tea with Bob Cherry after hitting one of Ram Singh's googlies for six to acclaim from the whole of Greyfriars.

One glorious morning we heard that Fred and I had been accepted at Somerford Hall. Arriving a week later, we found no gracious hall and no ivy. The school was a collection of six or seven wooden sheds in soggy fields, an encampment on the grounds of the shut-up old country house. None of the city evacuees had time to acknowledge my resemblance to Harry Wharton; they were too busy jostling for sheets and blankets and fighting for jelly sandwiches from the makeshift kitchen. At bedtime I was assigned the upper berth of an iron bunk in a bare board hut with about thirty others. The first night, as the wind howled, I sobbed my heart out, homesick and disillusioned. "Shut up, crybaby!" yelled everyone. The protesters hurled shoes at my bunk; even Fred told me to put a sock in it. Cripes! I was Billy Bunter, the object of execration. The next day we had lessons. In English class we were told to write home and present our letters to the teacher, who would check the grammar before putting them in the post. I wrote two pages about my disappointments and handed them in. I was called to the teacher's high desk up front. "This just won't do," he snarled, screwing up my effort into a small ball that he lobbed into the wastepaper basket to giggles behind me. "Go back to your desk and write something cheerful."

That night, with a thumping heart, I sneaked out of the back of Somerford Hall after lights-out and found a postbox to send a letter to Ashworth Street pleading to be rescued. I had no stamp for it, but at the weekend both my parents arrived at the camp and took me home. The hut was glad to see the back of me. Fred, less infected by the Greyfriars fantasy, elected to stay and had a great time for six months. Down the years he developed a number of different theories concerning my lack of moral fiber, none of which bears scrutiny.

Brookdale was still closed when I came home. Within days I was bound for the Welsh hills, more precisely for the hamlet of Hengoed in the county of Shropshire, but a slingshot east of Offa's Dyke, the ancient earthen rampart separating the wild Celtic tribes from the English. Dad had no petrol ration for his car, so we took two trains to Gobowen, the railhead for Oswestry, then walked four miles in the fading sunshine along winding, densely hedged lanes, through tunnels of over-hanging trees, trying to find the Old Vicarage before dark. To baffle German parachutists all the signposts had been taken down, but eventually we were directed to St. Barnabas Church, where Grandfather Jones plied his trade. Down the hill from the church we opened a door in a high wall of mellow stone to find Granny Jones scattering grain among scores of chickens.

She was a pale wraith of a woman in her mid-seventies, inherently graceful and affectionate and very attentive to the needs of her new husband, who must have been fifteen years younger. She scurried around in her flowered pinafore to take off Gravedigger Jack's boots when he clumped into the stone-floored kitchen and dropped into a high-backed wooden chair by the fireplace: his chair, his hearth, his house. He was a red-faced man in corduroy trousers hoisted by a fat leather belt he said he would apply to my backside if I didn't behave. I convinced myself he had a twinkle in his eye. It was good to hear he had spent the day cutting hedges and clearing ditches in the next hamlet, there being a shortage at St. Barnabas of candidates for the next world.

Gravedigger Jack rarely spoke, and he had an iron routine. If supper was not on the table sharp at six, he wouldn't eat it. For hours after eating, he'd sit silently smoking his pipe while I read *The Count of Monte Cristo* by the light of an oil lamp and Granny filled the kitchen with the warm smell of homemade bread. Her secluded old house, set in meadows with an apple orchard and a brook at the back, had no electricity, no gas, no radio, and we drew water from a pump in the yard. On Sundays we sang in the Hengoed church's little choir, smug in our white surplices. Not a whisper of the war percolated. It was paradise.

Finding shortcuts across fields to the village school in Gobowen was a daily adventure: seeing the flash of a fox in a copse, leaping brooks, slashing a path through banks of nettles and brambles with a "sword" fashioned from a stripped elderberry branch. It was 1066, and I was on Senlac Hill with my namesake king, driving the bastard Normans back into the sea. I was romantic and reckless. When a route skirted a wasps' nest, I set fire to it and was stung in the eye for my folly; so much for acting King Harold. Still, the hazard that gave regular pause to my impetuosity was the cow pasture, where there might be a possessive bull. Every boy at school had a fanciful story of racing death against thudding hooves and sharp horns. I had been the fastest runner at Brookdale and fancied myself to beat any bull. After I saw one on the loose, I decided against putting my speed to the test. I checked every beast for balls and every pasture I crossed for an exit.

At school there were some sixty boys and girls from ages eight to about fourteen, scrunched up at little desks, all learning the same things. I could not concentrate much on what was going on because I soon fell madly in love with a poised thirteen-year-old evacuee from London called Gwyneth: a southern beauty! I wooed her with horse chestnuts. The big prickly fruits, which dropped in the autumn or could be brought down by hurling a stick, have a white pith encasing the chestnut seed — a big nut called a "conker." For our most popular game in Gobowen we drilled a hole through the nut, threaded twelve inches of string through, and knotted it. You dangled your conker as a target to receive the blow of your pal's stringed conker; if he broke yours, his became a oner. If you had already broken four other conkers, then he could claim all your precedent victories, and his conker became a fiver. I sacrificed a niner to Gwyneth — just think of it. I forbore to tell her that to make it harder I had peed on it. This was no perversion. It was common practice to urinate on the conker, soak it in vinegar, and expose it to heat. Big juicy conkers often succumbed to a blow from a hard little conker. Blissfully unaware, she appreciated the gift.

My next gambit, proof of manhood, was to announce that while Gwyneth ate her sandwiches in the midday break, I was going to climb to the top of a spectacular tree in the playground. I did. The effect of my bravado was rather ruined because I couldn't get down before the bell went for classes. I never saw her again. Lovesick, I hung around the cottage where she stayed for days until someone told me she'd been called back to London, where her school had reopened.

Eventually I was summoned home, too. I'd had four happy months with Granny Jones, followed by a Spartan two months under the thumb of Aunt Beattie on Uncle Ted's little farm at Old Stone House. He had six fields, twelve cows, a couple of horses, and countless pigs, to which he fed swill from the Oswestry army camp. To Aunt Beattie, stomping through the mud in big rubber boots with a cigarette hanging from her lips, I was a city sissy: I failed miserably at milking a cow.

In the absence of German warplanes, classes had resumed at Brookdale, but my return was required anyway because I had reached the age to take part in the all-important national "eleven-plus" examinations—tests administered to eleven- and twelve-year-olds, the results of which would determine whether a child would stay in elementary school or ascend to secondary school. Sitting in a drafty classroom for four hours with forty others, I didn't appreciate that the curious questions, some of which seemed easy and some of which were incomprehensible to me, would decide my future. The aim of the examinations was to identify a handful of really bright boys and girls who would be offered a superior "grammar-school" education to the age of sixteen, and with that the opportunity to win a Joint Matriculation Board certificate, the passport to a good job. There were places at grammar schools for no more than 10 percent of the eleven-year-olds. The other 90 percent were destined to remain at elementary school and leave for work at the age of fourteen—trade apprenticeships if they were lucky, menial work if not. Put another way, the results of the eleven-plus would decide the course of the rest of my life as surely as a switch in the railway points would decide whether Dad's train went east or west.

My fate was contained in a buff envelope Mum brought up the stairs to the bathroom one morning when I was washing my face. I opened it with soapy fingers. "Harold Evans has been selected for St Mary's Road Central School."

I was at once bothered and bewildered. I had not been selected for a cherished grammar-school place, but neither had it been decreed I should stay in the elementary school. St. Mary's Road Central School, I discovered, was one step up from elementary school, an intermediary school where you could stay until you were fifteen, and a few pupils might have a chance to take the crucial Joint Matriculation Board examinations along with the grammar-school boys. I fretted that I had been held back by evacuation and country school, yet when Fred came home later from the Congleton camp, he sailed into a grammar school. Alf Morris, too, was selected for grammar school, but his family could not afford the uniform, and he stayed at Brookdale until he was fourteen.

I was excited all the same. It was not so much the education—there was a rumor that St. Mary's expected its pupils to learn French—as the blue cap, school tie with lion rampant, and crested blazer I would be entitled to wear and the leather satchel for my exercise books.

Fearful that sporting this lot risked jeers and jostles from the lads who were staying on at Brookdale, as I passed my old playground I sprinted up Albert Street to the No. 7 bus stop at the entrance to Brookdale Park. Fifteen minutes later I was looking up at the gaunt Victorian redbrick edifice of St. Mary's, across the street from the coal heaps and rusting ironmongery of the Newton Heath rail yard and the great sheds that housed the steam locomotives Dad drove. Not a single blade of grass was in sight; the playground was tarmac running into brick walls.

Looking down from the schoolrooms, we could see a rail line leading from the locomotive sheds to a turntable at the foot of our red cliff. I always hoped I would catch a glimpse of my father in command of a steam locomotive, but I never did. Gazing out of the high windows, we ran the risk of being discovered doing nothing by the school's dominating person, the headmaster, Mr. W. L. Marsland. He appeared to us a sinister figure. He glided through the school without apparently moving his legs and held his head well back so that he appeared to be looking down on you. I was in a high state of nervous tension. I'd just discovered Dickens, and the cruel schoolmaster Wackford Squeers was fresh in my mind. For a few weeks

I avoided stepping on cracks in the pavement and obsessively touched every third lamppost just to be sure the gods were on my side. Going up the road from school to the bus stop for home, we always ran past a spooky derelict building that was once an inn called the Duke of York. The body of a young woman killed crossing the railway line in the nineteenth century had been brought there, and we believed it when we were told her footsteps could still be heard around the shattered old bar.

But if the exterior of St. Mary's was workhouse grim, its environs bleak, and the headmaster forbidding, I soon discovered that the school was infused with an appealing spirit—a nurturing combination of respect for traditional values and zestful competition created by Marsland. We were all attached to one of four houses honoring British heroes. I was in Scott; others were in Livingstone, Gordon, and Stephenson. I'm sad to think I'd better add a word about these icons of the British Empire. Robert Falcon Scott (1868–1912) was the explorer of the Antarctic who died with three companions on returning from the South Pole. David Livingstone (1813–1873) was the African explorer, medical missionary, and antislavery crusader whom the American journalist Mr. H. M. Stanley was eager to meet. General Charles George Gordon (1833–1885) led military campaigns in China and the Sudan and died defending Khartoum, beheaded by the Mahdi. And George Stephenson (1781–1848) built the Stockton and Darlington Railway, the world's first permanent public railway line powered by a steam locomotive. Various privileges, whose nature I've forgotten, were awarded to members of the house that had accumulated the most "good house points" in class and our infrequent visits to a sports field where we wore our house colors (I regretted Scott was yellow).

Marsland's disconcerting way of looking at us, I discovered, was not an expression of contempt. It was physiological:

his eyelids were stuck because he'd been gassed in World War I. I never heard him talk about his experiences, but he wanted us to remember the price of freedom: St. Mary's "adopted" Czechoslovakia, sacrificed by Chamberlain at Munich in 1938, and each day in assembly, while a flower was placed on the school war memorial plaque, a boy or girl read out the lines of Laurence Binyon's memorial poem: "They shall grow not old, as we that are left grow old;/Age shall not weary them, nor the years condemn./At the going down of the sun and in the morning/We will remember them."

Marsland had pride in his school. He expected us to behave like grammar-school boys, and we—all grammar-school rejects—strove to justify his faith and ourselves.

Sixty years later I can still see all the teachers and recall their names and mannerisms. For the first few lessons with the science teacher Eddie Whipp (a precise representation of his name), we focused only on the *dees* and *doze* of his nasal speech, but he was a masterly choreographer of chemicals. Every time I passed the somber Philips gasworks at the end of Briscoe Lane, I thought of Mr. Whipp's magically enriching hydrocarbons dancing within. There was the (still tangible) first-time thrill of seeing litmus paper turn red, proving the substance in the beaker was an acid, and the excitement of summoning up hills and valleys after the angular, testy John Bateman had shown how the contour lines on maps could be converted into shapes. I was enthused enough by the suave Joe Abbott describing the day Oliver Cromwell had King Charles I beheaded to spend hours at home memorizing the dates and events leading up to that dreadful sequel.

Early on I picked up the journalist's habit of never throwing anything away, and I still have the school reports of those years. It is nothing less than saintly of me to acknowledge that in the first year I scored a disgraceful 2 percent on the music exam set by the ample Miss Polly Wardle, whom I couldn't help but think of as "Miss Warble." This "terrible result," as she described it, puzzled the good Miss Polly because she certified I had indeed "worked in class." But this may have been a reference to my countertenor rendering of Handel's "Where'er You Walk," a promising diversion from reading scores until I fell out of favor when my voice broke mid-song.

Meanwhile, in geometry and algebra I was damned as "often careless," "erratic," and "disappointing," and my efforts in physical education were dismissed as "tries hard but has no sense of rhythm."

I had such a dim start for all my efforts that I thought the eleven-plus examiners had me right. As the terms went by, however, I began doing well ("promising"), then very well ("excellent worker"). I was always top of the class in history exams; scored high in French and English composition, language, and literature; and battled a brainy brunette called Betty Ogden for top place in science and geography. Even the demon physical training instructor in the third year was moved to dub me "nimble, a very good performer." My surviving little blue English composition exercise books reflect my romantic addiction to the adventurous historical novels of Jeffrey Farnol (*The Amateur Gentleman*), Henry Rider Haggard (*King Solomon's Mines*), Arthur Conan Doyle (*The White Company*), P. C. Wren (*Beau Geste*), and Walter Scott (*Guy Mannering*)—all borrowed from my beloved Failsworth Public Library. But a degenerate streak soon showed itself. I had the idea I would grow up to write enthralling fiction. I had no talent for it. No subject was safe from the pestilential prose I inflicted on S. J. Pawley, a gentle English teacher with a withered arm. He set us a composition innocuously entitled "Village Shop." I submitted one beginning "I looked up from the bare uncarpeted floor. There she stood, no longer young, but a huge mass of fat. Wiping her bare red arms on her dirty apron she waddles towards me."

In the fourth year I was elected school captain by some combination of staff nominations and school votes. A blue shield was ceremoniously pinned on the lapel of my blazer, and I kept it on at home. My brother Fred, who was rebelling at Chadderton Grammar, said I was a goody-goody, and while the badge was supposed to confer authority over all my schoolmates, Fred made it clear my writ did not run at home. My main school duties were to organize the prefects to watch out for bullies and troublemakers on the playground and when the bell went for classes to resume, keep order in the long lines on the stairs and in the corridors. There were many bigger, stronger boys in the school. I'd been terrified of one brute who liked to grip smaller boys in a rib-cracking bear hug. The blue shield was like invisible armor: I was no longer singled out for his embraces. I fretted a lot in these adolescent years about being skinny and flat chested. There weren't nearly as many musclemen on the beach as there are these days, but I felt I was exactly the pale seven-stone weakling featured in a comic-strip advertisement for the bodybuilding system of Charles Atlas. The ads we saw featured a sand-kicking bully on a beach humiliating a scrawny boy walking with his girlfriend. Weeks later, rebuilt by Charles Atlas, the weakling sees off the bully and wins the admiration of the girl. It was my first experience of the power of advertising. Brother Fred was stronger than I was, but the ads got to him, too, so we persuaded Dad that he should invest in our taking the correspondence course. With all that heavy work on the footplate, Dad didn't need the course, but when he was home, he joined us in our bare-chested nightly efforts to look like the glistening Mr. Atlas. Mum tolerated the sight of the three tensed-up men in her life straining to pit muscle against muscle in their own bodies in the system called "dynamic tension" so long as our efforts did not delay our arrival at the supper table.

As school captain I was supposed to set an example to the whole school. This was complicated by the fact that I had fallen in with bad company. Howard Davies, a youth who lived nearby, was so slick he had a toothbrush mustache at seventeen, Brylcreemed his hair, and claimed to have had carnal knowledge of several members of the Women's Royal Naval Service (Wrens), promising that he would initiate me, too. He was the Stromboli to my Pinocchio.

Among other things, Howard taught me magic tricks. Of course I hated him at first, not just for his sexual prowess but also because in my Christmas stocking I received a velvet bag that could make an egg disappear, and he was better at the trick than I was. He became a good enough conjurer to be engaged by Uncle Mac's amateur concert party and later by the semiofficial body for entertaining the troops. Uncle Mac, though, was on a lower plane than many of the stars he toured with. His main gig was putting on shows at night for the servicemen and servicewomen in the North West bored out of their minds when they weren't operating the searchlights and ack-ack batteries. He also organized summer shows in the parks for the Stay-at-Home Holiday campaign (which encouraged people not to travel on their holidays), for which I was drafted as the rear half of a donkey.

Mum and Dad didn't like Howard, but I quickly became stagestruck. The world of Leichner makeup, footlights, and frenzied changes backstage between acts was even more exciting than banging the school gong, but one night offered an experience that was unnerving for an adolescent. A pretty young actress in a sketch had just rushed offstage while I awaited my cue. I looked back and through a gap in one of the changing room curtains my eyes lingered on her beautiful white bottom wriggling out of a pair of tights. I had no psychological mechanism for the shock when moments later the curtains parted to reveal that the favored backside belonged to a boy.

I was haunted by the ambiguity and regarded as condign punishment the subsequent drama of the red ball. After the Peeping Tom trauma I rededicated my spare time to practicing Howard's sleight-of-hand card tricks. He taught me how to acquire dexterity by rolling a little red ball from finger to finger, and I did it furtively at all times of the day in school. Classes would stop when I lost the grip and the ball rolled to the front. I would retrieve it with a "Sorry, sir." One day I was practicing in the washroom next to the teachers' recreation room, and the ball fell down the drain. I did not see it again until a week later. Mr. Marsland held it up before the whole school in assembly. "Who is the boy who owns this little red ball? Who is the boy who has blocked the washrooms with it? Who is the boy who flooded the teachers' staff room? Let him have the decency to own up and see me in my room after assembly."

I was punished with three strikes of a leather strap on my open hand. Hand-strapping was commonplace in the classrooms, but the pain here was in letting Mr. Marsland down.

Marsland was something of a mystery, for though he wasn't a university graduate, he was a more cultivated man than the Manchester Council required or expected. St. Mary's had no playing field, so he taught us the refinements of cricket on expeditions to a city park.

In the final year, five of us were thought to have a chance of passing the Joint Matriculation Board examinations normally reserved for the grammar schools. Marsland organized after-hours coaching. When everyone else went home at four o'clock, we five, three girls and two boys, stayed behind in his study. The school's emptiness echoed around us as he read passages from *As You Like It* and *A Midsummer Night's Dream* in a lovely lilt. At first we were hard put not to giggle when he acted out Pyramus on tiptoes talking to Thisbe through the wall's chink, but we soon hung on every syllable. He brought the same intuition to directing us gorily in the school performance of *Sweeney Todd: The Demon Barber of Fleet Street*. It has always been a sadness to me to think how little we were able to respond to his graciousness and learning, and his courage in trying to raise the academic and athletic standards of his school. He died some years later from the effects of his World War I service, and St. Mary's Road Central School was demolished by an education committee that could have known nothing of the magical forest summoned up behind our redbrick walls as the shades of night fell over the railway yards.

In 1940, when Hitler smashed Norway in April and then the Low Countries and France in May, I was more concerned that the end of the phony war marked the demise of the *Magnet* comic book, closed by paper rationing. The fictional Greyfriars vanished along with the universal illusion that the war would soon be won. My days of careless youth ebbed away, too, after the morning on the beach at Rhyl with the Dunkirk survivors. I resented the time Dad spent with them instead of with me, but I came to see the encounter as cathartic. And while I didn't suddenly grow up, I read more and more about the war. I was already intoxicated by the *Express* and by newspapers altogether as a manifestation of a more potent magic than Howard Davies's. The "Daily Surprise," as I came to think of the newspaper, simply amazed me. How did they do it not once but differently every day? How was all this information gathered? How was everything fitted on a page with nothing over? How did the photograph get taken on the battlefield, and how was it reproduced? Who were these dazzling figures with note-books sitting at the feet of Churchill and Roosevelt? How were the newspaper's strong opinions determined? Little opinion seeped out of the radio. On political questions the august governors of the BBC would rather be caught naked in Whitehall than be seen trying to influence people.

Oh, yes, and who was the mysterious anonymous columnist in the *Daily Express* who signed himself "Beachcomber" and wrote a few hundred words headed "By the Way"? Those words convulsed me with insane laughter I could never explain to Fred or anyone else. "Sixty Horses Wedged in Chimney" was a typical Beachcomber headline, followed by "The story to fit this sensational headline has not turned up yet." Beach-comber was nonsense on stilts but comically perfect in his parodies of newspaper style: "Erratum. In my article on the Price of Milk, 'Horses' should have read 'Cows' throughout." As a toddler, I'd been hooked on a comic strip in the *Express,* the adventures of Rupert the Bear; the incentive to finish my por-ridge in the morning was to see his antic figure painted on the bottom of the bowl. But Beachcomber was a lifetime's addiction even after I soured on his host newspaper for its vendettas and political distortions. For thirty-very-odd years I was to follow his surreal daily reports from an asylum populated by Dr. Stra-bismus of Utrecht Whom God Preserve (inventor of Bracerot juice designed to make Hitler's trousers fall down); Mr. Jus-tice Cocklecarrot at the Court of Uncommon Pleas (adjudicat-ing the right of Mrs. Renton continually to ring the doorbell of Mrs. Tasker for the purpose of depositing twelve red-bearded dwarves); Great White Carstairs (the overpatriotic ambassa-dor who could not talk on the telephone to the Foreign Office without saluting); and Narkover School's cunningly villainous headmaster, the light-fingered Dr. Smart-Allick, all of them in a funny-mirrors gallery of grotesques similar to the daily procession of frauds and fools who, happily for us, provoked Beachcomber, aka John Cameron Andrieu Bingham Michael Morton, to put on his countryman's boots and scale mountains of absurdity. No word or phrase was safe from his mischief. A clue, he wrote, "is what the police find when they fail to arrest a criminal." And again: "One disadvantage of being a hog is that any minute some blundering fool will try to make a silk purse out of your wife's ear." Morton's ink flowed into the veins of Spike Milligan, Peter Sellers, and Harry Secombe (the BBC *Goon Show*); John Cleese, Michael Palin, and Eric Idle (*Monty Python*); and Richard Ingrams (*Private Eye*). He had a place in my pantheon with Evelyn Waugh, P. G. Wodehouse, Stephen Leacock, J. K. Jerome, and S. J. Perelman.

Hollywood reinforced my infatuation with newspapers. Our local cinemas—the Magnet, the Pavilion, the Picture Palace, the Ceylon, and the Grand—reopened in the autumn of 1939. Every Saturday at the Magnet matinee, Fred and I jostled others kids lining up to get in and then scrambling for the sweets the manager threw into the mob. The run of movies in those years still seems remarkable: *Gone With the Wind, Citizen Kane, Ace in the Hole, The Gold Rush, Stagecoach, Casablanca, Foreign Correspondent, 49th Parallel, Beau Geste, The Front Page, Gunga Din, In Which We Serve,* and Bob Hope and Bing Crosby on the road some-mad-where with Dorothy Lamour. Heroes— and hilarity—aplenty. I loved them all, but it was the movies about newspapers I tried to see over and over again. I identified with the small-town editor standing up to the crooks, the tough reporter winning the story and the girl, and the foreign correspondent outwitting enemy agents. That was the easy part—cops and robbers in different costumes—but some of the newspaper movies stayed in my mind when the adrenaline rush had gone. How could *Ace in the Hole* reporter Kirk

Douglas be so greedy for a scoop on a man trapped in a mine that he delayed the rescue just to keep the story alive for the media circus he created? Charles Foster Kane begins as a tribune of the people, the immigrants and the unions, against the "octopus" of the Southern Pacific Railroad, the bosses of Tammany Hall, and the banks and Wall Street, and he ends up manipulating the news as a crypto-fascist crusader for capitalism. Was that a true portrait of William Randolph Hearst? I learned in due course that it was a distortion of Hearst, but I relished the moment when Citizen Kane's managing editor, Mr. Bernstein, pulled out the proofs of two front pages made up in advance, one announcing that Kane had won New York's gubernatorial election and the other announcing that he had lost, one banner-headlined KANE ELECTED and the other FRAUD AT POLLS! What fun!

The war became intensely personal when bombing of the Manchester area began in August 1940. It was only sporadic at first, but Dad was much at risk out there in the blackness in some godforsaken tangle of railway lines. Schoolgirl Enid Parker, who was to enter my life ten years later, saw an exploding ammunition train light up the sky near her home on Queens Drive, Liverpool. Much more was to come. The full-scale blitzes began on September 7, with heavy bombers pounding London for fifty-seven nights in succession. People in Manchester kept saying jocularly, "Well, we're bound to get it next."

We did. The awesome two-day Christmas blitz of Manchester began at dusk on Sunday, December 22. After the bombing of Liverpool, Mum made up camp beds in the brick shelter that the Failsworth Council had built to replace the waterlogged Anderson shelter dug into the back garden. As soon as the sirens sounded on the Sunday, she shut the shop and hustled baby John, four-year-old Peter, and me out of the house and into the shelter with a big basket of sandwiches, hot water bottles, thermos flasks, and a flashlight. Two of the family were missing. On Saturday, December 21, Dad, on a day off work, had taken my ten-year-old brother, Fred, with him to Gobowen, the village near Oswestry, to see if Granny Jones had a turkey she could spare for Christmas. Without a telephone, we had not expected to hear anything from them, but sitting in the brick shelter in the cold candlelight without the perennially cheerful head of the family, we were lonely and very afraid, our shelter isolated in a vast cavern of echoing noise — the drone of more than a hundred bombers overhead, the crump-crump of our ack-ack guns, the blast of the bombs.

We'd no idea we were smack in the bombers' sights, our very street clearly to be seen on the high-level aerial reconnaissance photographs of targets made by German planes on October 5, 1940. I came across the dated and marked photographs only when I started to write this memoir and visited Peter Charlton, a school friend from Brookdale Park and St. Mary's Road. He had become the historian of Newton Heath and in German archives had unearthed one headed:

Manchester–Newton Heath
Flugzeugzellenfabrik A. V. Roe & Co Ltd.

Superimposed on the image were black rectangles of areas to be bombed. The perimeter of the principal target, the aircraft factory A. V. Roe, was just down the road from us. The aeronautical genius Alliott Verdon Roe, born, as I was, in Patricroft, designed the RAF's most successful bomber, the Lancaster, which flew 156,000 operations from 1942 to 1945. Lancasters delivered the bouncing bombs that broke the dams of the Ruhr Valley in 1943 and the thirty-one Tallboy bombs that finally sank the mighty German battleship *Tirpitz* in November 1946. Three other targets in our neighborhood are marked on the Luftwaffe map: Gaswerk am Philips Park (which featured in my science lessons), the Mather and Platt gun factory, and the Crossley Brothers diesel works.

Apart from starting a fire in one building of Crossley Motors, the 270 bombers missed all the targets so meticulously pinpointed. Instead, their 272 tons of high explosives and 1,032 canisters of incendiaries fell three miles to the southwest of the factories, blowing up and burning the area from Manchester's city center of Piccadilly Gardens to Victoria station, the cathedral, and into Salford and Stretford. Had the bombers erred in the opposite direction, missing A. V. Roe as much to the northeast as they did to the southwest, they'd have obliterated the Brookdale area and 54 Ashworth Street, and all of us with it. As it was, around the devastated city center seven hundred people were dead.

We could smell the smoke, and fires were still raging when we came out of the shelter the next morning. My uncle Arnold and his wife, Gertie, emerged from their garden shelter near Trafford Park to find their home was gone, burned to the ground. By lunchtime Dad and Fred had still not reappeared. We worried all day. Mum refused to go down to the Newton Heath police station to ask if they had heard anything about bombs falling on Welsh border villages. "We can't bother them," she said. "They have enough on their hands, and Dad can look after himself." She reopened the shop, and I helped to look after John and Peter, while popping out from time to time to stand watch on the street corner.

At dusk, when nobody was about, I saw figures coming up Farm Street, but moving very slowly. I ran down the street, and it was Dad and Fred, laden with a turkey and other good country things. (Throughout the war, rationing restricted everyone to tiny quantities of everything—bacon, butter, meat, tea, sugar, jam, cereals, eggs, milk, sweets, clothing, biscuits, canned fruit—but the countryside fared better for eggs.) They'd caught a morning train from Gobowen to Crewe and another to Manchester, but a bomb had torn up the track from Eccles, so they had to walk, jumping on any bus that was still running in the hope it was heading in the right direction: all of the destination markers were blanked out. They arrived just in time for the second full night of bombing. It was just as bad as the first night, but with them back with us the fear evaporated.

The only consolation for all the bad news on the evening radio in the early years of the war was that the steadiness of the ice-clear baritone voice of the BBC announcer Alvar Lidell suggested there would always be an England. In these radio years, voices were so important to us, the anchors of our hopes as much by tone and inflection as by the words. Churchill had no better news for us than Chamberlain, but his voice evoked the spirit of St. Crispin's Day; Chamberlain's would not have scared a sparrow hawk. We suffered a sense of isolation until the marvelous moment in December 1941 when Mr. Lidell at last had something good to relate. America had entered the war. Fighting spirits rose hearing Churchill growl his epic phrases; FDR's voice soothed. Having just learned about the Gulf Stream from Mr. Bateman, I thought of FDR's words as a powerful warm current crossing the ocean to keep us calm and cheerful. His words were uplifting—"We will gain the inevitable triumph—so help us God"—but the almost languid calm of his rolling articulation was essential to the reassurance.

The words became gloriously manifest when in Manchester's

bomb-gutted Piccadilly I first saw a lanky, leather-jacketed American airman on a weekend pass from the Flying Fortresses at Burtonwood, Warrington. Soon after I saw my very first black man. The British Empire had dominion over millions of black and brown people, but before the war we were still a homogeneous race of pale whites living insular lives, never hearing a foreign accent in the provinces or venturing across our narrow moat into Europe. When Dad, in 1938, took us all on a day ferry from Ramsgate for a few hours in Boulogne, it was the talk of our neighborhood for weeks.

What color and dash the smiling Americans brought to our bleak gray world! We saw them all as rich film stars, so sleek and well tailored in their smooth uniforms. Any one of the big-boned American servicemen sighted in the city drew a flock of kids asking, "Any gum, chum?" and they always got something. Women, we heard, were given gifts of nylon stockings and cigarettes, arousing some resentments. My widowed cousin Little Eva was the happy recipient of this generosity from one of the black servicemen she brought home to tea in Eccles, to some spiteful gossip according to my mother; later she had a lovely baby daughter by another airman. The odd sourpuss in our shop might recycle the crack by the comedian Tommy Trinder that the Yanks were "overpaid, oversexed, and over here," but as far as I could see, the Americans were warmly welcomed. Most English people just were too inhibited to express much emotion beyond an occasional thumbs-up gesture.

The war dragged on. It was a strain for Mum the shopkeeper. The histories I've read about the home front highlight how hard rationing was on the public; nobody bothers much with what it was like for the shopkeeper, the hub of the system. The administration of it was complex. Some foods were rationed by weight, some by quantity, some by groups so a customer could opt for jam rather than marmalade or swap the jam for extra sugar. Early in the war holders of ration books were also given sixteen points they could spend on unrationed foods, such as a tin of Fray Bentos corned beef, a packet of Kellogg's corn flakes, a box of Peek Freans assorted biscuits, or a tin of Tate & Lyle golden syrup—on the label a defunct lion plagued by bees—which made such a difference to the morning porridge. But supplies of such luxuries were erratic. Mum was so scrupulously honest that when there was a lucky break—one month the arrival of six unrationed tins of salmon—she agonized about whose need was greatest among the several hundred registered customers, and she had to distribute the tins by stealth to avoid jealous fights.

The unseen burden was counting the coupons from the ration books. The number of coupons in various categories returned to the Ministry of Food offices in Failsworth determined what supplies the shop would get the following week. No coupons, no food. It was an awful chore counting and recounting those fiddly bits of paper; the coupons for sweets and chocolate were tiny and easily lost. Some shops had to close. Everyone in the family had to help out at the end of the week, all of us kneeling on the carpet for four or five hours on a Sunday night. It was the burden of rationing, which continued after the war, that induced Mum to sell the business.

I'd no ambitions to be a shopkeeper. By the time I was thirteen, I had grand ideas of myself as a journalist-historian of the war. In my fourth year at St. Mary's there was an election to choose an editor for a new school magazine. The English teachers nominated a handful of candidates, and I was utterly shameless in campaigning to win the editorship.

The magazine I produced was a limp little thing. My incipient journalistic juices must have gone into my pet project at home. I scoured the *Daily Express, Daily Dispatch, Manchester*

Evening News, and any magazines I could get my hands on for maps, drawings, and pictures. I pasted them in Manchester Education Committee exercise books from night bookkeeping classes I took later, so that the tumult of the war overlay neat balance sheets of assets and liabilities of fictional companies. I still have these war books with my copperplate captions and their headlines:

> "First, know your enemy: silhouettes of new Luftwaffe warplanes"
>
> "Achtung! Britain's perfect bomber-buster comes off the secret list"
>
> "German tanks burn on a Tunisia battlefield—British six pounders hold the position"
>
> "Iron Crosses for seven but look at their boots"
>
> "Over mountains, through steaming jungle, to smash the Jap toe-hold at Buna"
>
> "These Italians are happy to be out of the struggle"
>
> "Gurkha rescued under fire at Mareth"
>
> "RAF aimed well—factory is hit; the homes are spared"

The pictures that most excited me were panoramas of our invincible armies on the march in the Western Desert, cutaway drawings of our deadly fighter planes and flying boats dominating the skies, and gallant destroyers on heaving seas sinking U-boats. British nationalism was intense, but the Free French cavalry in the desert was allowed to gallop into the pages in sepia. I also gave a page to bearded Cossack guerrillas in the snow, and one to a portrait of Lenin. Any number of my classmates were superior in identifying aircraft silhouettes; I was in for the drama.

The impression the pages give is of a "Boy's Own" jingo paper: we were winning gloriously. Of course all of us of that generation had grown up with an exaggerated idea of Britain's prowess. The schoolroom maps of our world were mostly colored red for the two-fifths of the globe that was the British Empire and its dominions; half the traffic through the Suez Canal was British. How lustily we belted out "Rule, Britannia! Britannia, rule the waves:/Britons never, never shall be slaves." In the end it was assumed without question that the nation of Wellington and Nelson would triumph. My selections were loaded with optimism, because they were, again, a reflection of what was in the newspapers, though leafing through the two crammed books today, I rather scent the mephitic vapors of the time: a dread recalled that the next day's news might be bad. The magazine was a comfort, something to hold on to in a depressing yearning for certainty. Just look at that Mosquito, the world's fastest reconnaissance bomber, on its way to attack Gestapo headquarters in Oslo!

I kept my little war books to myself. I didn't show them to Dad. I glowed with his constant encouragement, but about the war I feared his skepticism. He still had reservations about Churchill. He admired Franklin Roosevelt, but as the war ground on, he talked most about the Russians. "That Marshal Zhukov!" he'd say with a chuckle, gripping me in an imitation of a grizzly bear's squeeze. "He'll get them in a pincers movement. Just watch." Only years later, writing history myself, did I think that Dad may have been doing more than indulging his romantic view of Russia; he may have divined from the numbers what most people did not at the time: the bulk of the fighting against Germany was being done by the Russians, so the European war would be won or lost on the eastern front.

I don't think any of us St. Mary's graduates thought at all about the distant future that summer of 1943 as we stood in the last assembly belting out "Forty years on and forty years after, / parted are those who are singing today." The war was too much in the way. There was no future; there were only black lines and arrows on newspaper maps marking the clash of armies and navies in the infinities of Russia and the Pacific Ocean.

I had done well in the examinations for the central school certificate (distinctions in literature, French, science, geography, and history), but what really counted were the results of the Joint Matriculation Board examinations the select five of us had taken.

I was on edge that summer. Most of the boys in my class had, within days of graduation, signed on as apprentice merchants of death, the cleverest working on blueprints, others in the Avro factory riveting the fuselages of Lancaster four-engine bombers destined to do to the Germans what they had done to Manchester in the Blitz. I'd see these boys on the streets in blue overalls, schoolkids who had been kicking a tennis ball round the playground a few weeks earlier, joining the droves of men and women headed for the factories around the time the milkman was leaving bottles on our doorsteps. Other classmates vanished behind the long camouflaged walls of Mather and Platt as trainee draftsmen, making drawings for parts of big guns. These factories were just round the corner on Briscoe Lane in Newton Heath. A few others trekked across Manchester's suburbs to Metro-Vickers in the great sprawling Trafford Park, the misnomer for the world's first industrial estate, a prime target for the Heinkels. When I bumped into former classmates, they'd pull out a pay slip. "Take a look at that! Two quid! Two quid! I got to keep ten bob" (a quid being a pound, and ten bob being a lovely red note worth half a pound).

My own pocket money was a fraction of that, two shillings and sixpence, the satisfyingly heavy silver coin we called "half a crown." I was not envious but glad the war effort depended on their skills, not mine. These were the boys who had made perfect dovetail joints in the dark basement at St. Mary's where we were taught woodworking. The carpentry teacher, the bristling, red-faced Joe Hall, had been so disgusted by my efforts, he threw the finished joint the length of the room, yelling, "You one-eyed kaffir!" The joint's disintegration in flight proved his point: I was not good with my hands. I could not get an apprenticeship even if I wanted one.

Partly as an insurance against academic failure, my parents had been saving pennies and shillings in those little tins around the house. In that summer of 1943, they told me they'd accumulated £70 (about £6,000 at today's values) and starting right away they were ready to pay for me to acquire the tools of the reporter's trade by taking full-time classes at Loreburn Business College in the city—shorthand, touch typing, and a little German to add to my so-so French. I was as much impressed by their foresight as by their sacrifice. I'd talked about shorthand and typing but hadn't worked out how I would get the skills. Now I had the opportunity.

The Loreburn classes were all girls learning to be secretaries, giggling about having two sissy boys do what they were doing. Dick Walton, the other boy—as thin, pale, and nervy as I was—aspired to be a writer, too. I found Pitman shorthand as exciting as a spy code and took to it, as did Dick, so that we beat the girls for speed and transcription. We reached 180 words per minute (and examination diplomas for 120 wpm). But not all was triumph: thumping our Underwood machines hard as we might, the keyboard covered by a shield, we never outmatched the nimblest of the girls in touch typing.

With some vague idea that if I ever became a reporter, I'd have to unmask embezzlers and fraudsters, I enrolled in classes at Brookdale Night School for double-entry bookkeeping.

I wouldn't say I shone. I was distracted a lot by a table tennis table in the hall and became so obsessed with the game, I played every night—and then off and on for the rest of my life. I teamed up as a doubles partner with a neighborhood friend, a much better player, Ron Allcock. We entered all the tournaments, and he played for England in international matches.

I was still high from a winning match at the Manchester YMCA when I returned home to find a buff envelope reminiscent of the one from the Manchester Education Committee telling me I'd failed the eleven-plus. This one was marked Joint Matriculation Board. I wasn't eager to open it. I took it into the back room to read it alone before Dad came home. Mum was in the shop serving a crotchety customer, but I broke into the transactions exclaiming, "I've passed! I've passed!" I'd done more: I'd passed in all six subjects, with credits in five of them.

I was forgiven the interruption. It was a huge moment, bigger even than I realized at the time.

I had a chance in life.

4

Hot Metal

In 1944, when I was sixteen, I applied for my first job in newspapers. I raided my mother's box of Basildon Bond notepaper, calculating that the fine blue sheets would make an impression of refinement. I had to clean up after family supper before I could sit down at the kitchen table with a steel pen and a bottle of ink. I succeeded in ruining several drafts with blots, so it was dark when I went out with my stamped letter to the little red postbox at the end of the street. By then the wartime blackout had been relaxed a little. People were allowed to use a flashlight provided the glass was covered in cardboard with a tiny hole in the middle.

At Failsworth Public Library, my home away from home, I had found the addresses of eight or nine daily newspapers in the city where I was born, Manchester. I wrote a letter a night for a week. With each letter I enclosed a stamped, self-addressed envelope "for courtesy of a reply." I didn't get many and wondered if some miscreant had steamed off my precious stamps. The replies that did come more or less said get lost.

In three weeks or so, I was stuck, like the British Army at Caen following the D-Day landings in Normandy that month. So I abandoned the big-city newspapers and scouted more obscure titles in the urban wastes of Lancashire and then the posher towns of Cheshire, trying to outpace the rejections and silences with bolder advertisements for myself. Captain of the school! Editor of the school magazine! School certificate! Shorthand and typing! I had also included a testimonial from the headmaster of my school. What more could they want?

In fact I hadn't expected much of a testimonial from Headmaster Marsland. His end-of-school testimonial, at first reading, didn't suggest I had been a disappointment, so I had a copy typed to send with each application. I still have it after all these years.

Harold Evans, who has been a conscientious and successful School Captain, is a boy with very lively intelligence, possessing powers of original thought along with a very retentive memory. He is perhaps too impetuous at present, but will outgrow that. He has won his success, both as a Captain and in the classroom, because he never spares himself, and seldom flags in his interest. His success in the athletic life of the school is largely due to his determined energy. We shall miss his integrity and willing service, and we wish him all the success he deserves.

When none of my letters had any effect, I had the dark thought that the testimonial was not foolproof, in fact might be a hostage to fortune. Wouldn't an editor contemplating a risky hiring be quite put off by "too impetuous"? Not just impetuous — that was bad enough — but *too* impetuous. Clearly this was an alert that the applicant was foaming at the mouth. "Seldom flags in his interest"? Could that be read as a hint that he flaked out when the going got tough? And that reference to energy in athletics suggested brute force rather than exquisite skill. As for being wished "all the success he deserves," it could be a backhander; perhaps this youth deserved only a tiny bit of success—or none at all! For one mad moment I impetuously drafted a letter asking Mr. Marsland to withdraw this reference to impetuosity and conclude with something like "we wish him the glittering success he so thoroughly deserves." Fortunately, the paranoid parsing was preempted. One of my scattershot applications produced a returned envelope with a peremptory command beneath the magnificent blue Gothic title *"Ashton-under-Lyne Weekly Reporter* Series": "Come to Ashton at 10 a.m. the following Wednesday and ask for me. (Signed) John W. Middlehurst, News Editor."

I knew nothing of Ashton except that it was one of a cluster of cotton and coal towns east of Manchester with odd names like Stalybridge and Dukinfield. It proved to be an initiative test in itself just finding a way there. Manchester was criss-crossed with rail and bus lines, but every bus and train anywhere accessible from our house in Failsworth shied away from Ashton-under-Lyne.

It was a miserable wet day that Wednesday. My father had been on the footplate all night but insisted on giving my shoes "a special railwayman's shine" before he went to bed, and Mum ironed a fresh white shirt between serving customers in our corner shop. It took three bus rides before I was deposited outside the sooty town hall of Ashton-under-Lyne. Across the cobbled market square, asserting equality in its authority, rose the Victorian redbrick headquarters of the *Ashton-under-Lyne Reporter.* It was market day. Vendors in the square huddled from the drizzle beneath their canvases, and there was hardly anybody about. I took shelter by a stall selling teapots until two minutes to the hour, then ran across the street through the revolving front door of the *Reporter.* In the front office I asked to see Mr. Middlehurst, speaking in my best BBC voice to disguise my flat, north country accent. A sniffy clerk told me I'd have to use the back entrance. Where was that? "Just round the corner. Use your eyes!"

He didn't say which corner. I found an unmarked side door that opened onto a narrow flight of worn stone steps. I ran up them to the second floor and discovered another world: the floor was filled with long lines of iron monsters, each seven feet high, five feet wide, decked out with an incomprehensible array of moving parts—gears, pulleys, camshafts, levers, and bars. A man crouched in communion at the foot of each contraption. This was my first sight of the Linotype machine, at whose ninety-character keyboard a deft operator could automatically render words into metal slugs at the rate of five column lines a minute. There was an exciting smell to which I would become addicted. It was hot news. Lead, antimony, and tin bubbled in each Linotype's melting pot, kept at three hundred degrees centigrade by a gasoline burner. Digital typesetting at a computer has consigned the Linotype to the museum, but the speeding electron has none of the aromatic urgency of hot metal marinated with printer's ink.

I interrupted one of the Linotype operators at his devotions. "I'm here to see Mr. Middlehurst."

"Jack or Dennis? They're both in there!"

Behind a flimsy wooden partition at the side of the big room were six or seven desks piled high with papers, telephone directories, pots of glue, spikes, and a full-size glass kiosk with a chair and a candlestick telephone inside. One ginger-haired middle-aged reporter with a pipe clenched in his teeth sat bolt upright at a typewriter in the corner, and another wizened walnut of a man was hunched over a desk writing with a pen in front of a window overlooking the market square. Neither acknowledged that the savior of British journalism had arrived.

At the end of the room stood a big disheveled man with thick glasses, running his hands through thinning hair and steaming at a stolid man in a printer's apron, who had his hands on his hips in what looked like a posture of defiance. The big man broke off in midstream. This was clearly my quarry, Mr. Middlehurst.

"Evans?" Without any more ado, without even looking at me, he scooped up bunches of paper from the turmoil of his desk and thrust them into my hand.

"Asparagus," he mumbled in a rapid monotone. "Asparagus—four copies, an' quick about 'em, laddie!"

He went back to his confrontation with the printer. Asparagus? It was a delicacy unknown to Lancashire dinner tables; I'd barely heard of it. The little old man at the window desk gave me a wad of coarse newsprint copy paper, about six inches wide by three inches deep, and gestured to an empty chair by an Underwood typewriter.

I skimmed the papers Middlehurst had given me, mostly handwritten scrawl on letters, postcards, and sheets torn from an exercise book. There were names of winners of a women's whist drive in Audenshaw; a note about a gift day at a Rotary club; a typed sheet from an undertaker naming a list of mourners; a rambling report on "Christianity in action" at the Welbeck Street Baptist Church; a letter about a clergyman back from China "after thrilling adventures," maddeningly unspecified; and a handwritten page about a burst pipe at a Methodist church that doused the choir in steam and drenched the conductor. The correspondent testified that "Mr. Joseph Thornrey carried on unperturbed."

I was at a loss. No mention of asparagus in any of these disconnected vignettes of local life, not even a flower show. The hunched figure at the window radiated *You're on your own*. The ramrod ginger-haired typist was on automatic pilot, pounding away without pause. The sight of Mr. Middlehurst frothing at his desk behind a big spike impaled with paper and a gallery of column proofs deterred me from going back to inquire what I was supposed to be doing.

I typed *asparagus 1* at the top of the copy sheet and prayed for inspiration, whereupon there appeared at my elbow a fairy godmother in the shape of a handsome, slight youth my age with dark wavy hair. As he spoke, he kept washing his hands together Uriah Heep style. "You're new. I'm Laurence Taylor. Let me show you the ropes. Yes, yes," he chuckled, "just write up these submissions separately as paragraphs."

"Asparagraphs." As paragraphs!

He had decoded the sibilant Middlehurst mumble and saved my life. I rendered each of the submissions neatly into six-line typed paragraphs, removed the messy carbon paper required to make four copies, and took the lot to Mr. Middlehurst, his head down as he fertilized another heap of "asparagus." He ran a stubby black pencil over my first efforts in professional journalism, slashed out some words, and put the top sheets in an "out" tray. Glory, could it really be that my first words were bound for print? That they were is evident in the files I consulted in the Stalybridge Public Library years later.

Middlehurst spoke again, raising his bushy eyebrows several times. "Spitman, eh?" He wanted to test my ability to take down a note in Pitman shorthand. My Pitman was easily up to the pace of his brief dictation about some council committee or other. It was the way he spoke that made it hard, first decoding the mumble into intelligible words; then coding the words into the Pitman phonetic code of loops, hooks, and dots; and then decoding the squiggles back at the Underwood.

The transcription passed muster. I was rewarded with a wedding: four folded sheets of blue paper bearing the pre-printed blanks for names of bride and groom, their addresses and occupations, what they wore, what the bride's mother wore, who played the organ, who performed the ceremony and where, who arranged the flowers, the names of the bridesmaids and the best man and their relationships to the happy couple, where the reception was held, who spoke, and what the bride wore as she headed off on honeymoon. Only at that point did the *Reporter* restrain its curiosity. Laurence took me over to the bound files of previous editions so that I could learn how to render the bullets of information into imperishable prose that would support the headline "Stalybridge Man Marries Ashton Woman" or "Ashton Woman Marries Stalybridge Man" or, with any luck, something more graphic like "War Workers Marry." Even then flights of fancy were clearly not in mode. I could type up "the marriage was solemnized of..." or "Ada Briscoe and John Tomlinson were married" or "the wedding took place on Friday of..."

My effort was rewarded by another rapid elevation of Middlehurst's eyebrows. I was to learn that if they were elevated three times in rapid succession, it was a sign of benevolence.

He offered me a three-month trial. "Pound a week. Righty, laddie?"

A pound a week was about half what my classmates were now earning in factories. I didn't care. I might have to be on trial, but I had my first job in newspapers.

The offices of the *Ashton-under-Lyne Reporter* were too difficult to get to by bus from our home in Newton Heath, so I cycled fourteen miles to get there each morning.

The *Reporter* had thirteen editions serving eighty thousand readers living in the dreary backstreets and industrial sprawl of Gorton and Openshaw, as well as the beautiful vales and villages of Derbyshire's High Peak district. Correspondents who walked the hills around Mossley, Saddleworth, and New Mills put their copy into envelopes stamped NEWS URGENT and gave them to bus drivers. One of my first tasks as a junior reporter was to hang around at the bus stop in Ashton waiting to identify the right bus to collect those stories and feed them into the Middlehurst mowing machine. To miss the bus was a capital crime; not only the flow of news was imperiled but vital advertising revenue as well. Every weekly newspaper in the *Reporter* group gave up its front page to classified ads, as they had since 1855, and the inside pages were packed with news with no bylines. The only personal credit allowed was initials for a reviewer's critique, thereby bowing to the arts. Much of the news was collected by what was termed "parring," or "paragraphing"—forays to gather the news on foot. None of us had desk telephones; they were regarded as an extravagance. Very few homes, including mine, had the luxury of a telephone.

The kindly Laurence Taylor, whose hand-washing turned out to be exercises for his advanced piano lessons, initiated me into the labor of "parring." He paid the bus fare to Droylsden, then we walked the streets for hours making house calls, scavenging for names of the recently dead and the lucky.

I was very self-conscious. I hated going in to see the undertakers. They were unforgivably cheery when they had a lot to report. I was glad Laurence was with me, though he too was of a morbid temperament. We roused grumpy caretakers in innumerable workingmen's clubs rancid with stale beer and sawdust, drank tea in vicarage and rectory, dropped in on union secretaries and Catholic priests, youth centers and political party offices. We wrote down the names of winners of whist drives, cribbage contests, and darts championships, of speakers and candidates for office, of cake makers and soup servers in the Meals on Wheels service for those confined to their homes. Names, names, names! In search of scoops, we asked everyone if they had any news and usually drew a blank. In time, I learned that people didn't recognize "news" the way journalists defined it; you just had to get them talking freely and then fish out the bits and pieces that might add up to something significant. The police stations, promising drama, invariably delivered nothing at all, and we meekly accepted a duty sergeant's brush-off. No doubt we were thought not grown-up enough to be exposed to crime stories. The county coroner's office was more forthcoming. We were invited to view a body ready for an inquest, someone who in the blackout had fallen into a canal. I couldn't face it.

We schoolboy reporters were filling in for men who were fighting the war. The senior newspapermen at work, like my teachers at school, were among the walking wounded. The robot at the typewriter I encountered on my first day had a wheezing chest complaint. He was Dennis Middlehurst, the taciturn son of the news editor, Mr. Middlehurst. The other man, a reporter by the name of Billy Mee who lived to be ninety-eight, looked as if he was beyond recruiting age for the Boer War. When I first encountered the third senior reporter, he was lying inert and silent on the newsroom floor with his hat on. He was a plump man with a clubfoot. His nose was bleeding. "Just step over him," said Middlehurst junior, without looking up from his typing. "Raphie has these attacks from time to time."

When not prone, Raphie (Ralph Alder) was the most considerate of men, who encouraged us juniors. We were all very circumspect, never referring to his disability—a sensitivity not respected by the chief photographer, a ball of energy in his late thirties, Charlie Sutcliffe, who would burst into the newsroom and say with a big grin, "Come on, Raphie, don't drag your bloody feet."

Charlie had his own problem. His right hand had been severed at the wrist during factory war work. His leather glove concealed a prosthetic hand, but he nonetheless wielded the blinding flashlight of his big Speed Graphic camera like a tomahawk. He was our very own Weegee in a rakish trilby hat, and a cynic. "You're Boy Scouts," he'd needle us. "We're all in it for the money, right?" But he was very professional about getting his exposures right. (His bullied young assistant, a thin youth with a squeaky voice, got his revenge by winning £250,000 on the football pools and quit newspapers.)

We novice reporters were nervous about Charlie's vulgar energy, but we all loved going on assignment with him. He had gasoline coupons for essential war work, so we got to ride in his car, Charlie laughing his way past any resistance. "Give the lad the bloody story!" he'd yell at some stick-in-the-mud official or difficult cop. None of us dared hang back from persisting when Charlie was present.

The tumult of the war was represented in the newsroom by Charlie's polar opposite, a scholarly young reporter with a prolonged brainy forehead, rimless glasses, and the elaborately courteous manners of a diplomat at the court of Louis XIV. He sported a brown beret and a shoulder patch that proclaimed him a member of the Royal Army Pay Corps. This was Private John David Michael Hides, doing a little journalism as an arts reviewer. His initials, JDMH, at the end of his music and theater reviews were regarded as a royal seal.

Michael was destined to be chief subeditor (copy editor) of the *Manchester Guardian*, a key man in its perilous 1961 transition to London printing, and then the editor of Sheffield's *Morning Telegraph*, who against all odds got his paper out during a strike. I learned later that even when I first met him, he had assumed a high responsibility: seeing that money got through to Popski's Private Army, Popski being a Belgian of Russian parentage who worked behind enemy lines in North Africa and Italy blowing up fuel dumps and aircraft on the ground.

Of these adventures, JDMH said nothing. He was more concerned to tell us that we should catch Gustav Mahler. I'd never heard of Gustav Mahler. "I'll alert the Droylsden police on my calls," I told him. He seemed pleased.

The most striking figure among the younger reporters resembled Franz Kafka on the back of my Penguin copy of *The Castle*. This was Frank Keeble, who had a habit of clenching his jaw and promising to thump people who put obstacles in the path of truth and justice. I was in awe of him; he radiated glory. His friends included famous reporters such as Tommie Thomson and Walter Terry, both of whom had graduated from the *Ashton Reporter* into the big time of political reporting with bylines in the *Daily Mail*. Frank wasn't a man to be intimidated by anyone—even the august directors of the Stalybridge and Hyde Transport Board. They thought it was unconscionable that he should have reported a complaint about a bus driver who got stuck on a hill in the snow. According to the intrepid Keeble, the driver had ordered all the passengers off the bus with the command, "If tha' wants to get home tonight, tha'll have to get out and push."

Such an order, protested the directors of the transport board, would have been contrary to the best traditions of the bus company. Keeble stuck to his story, and Middlehurst stood by his man. To us juniors, all this was stirring stuff.

At the end of my first week as a reporter, I was beside myself. Bundles of newspapers came up from the printing presses in the basement. Incandescent on a number of pages were those paragraphs I'd written on the first day and others, and a couple of wedding reports of mine to the tune of about two full columns of paragraphs. Nobody acknowledged the glow these contributions shed over the whole paper. The room had become crowded with strangers—pipe smokers in tweedy jackets from the hill country talking among themselves—and my new pals, the junior reporters who were busy rushing about with brooms and shovels. They swept the floor of the week's wadded-up balls of discarded copy paper, cleared the desks of incriminating cups, straightened up the newspaper files, and emptied the ashtrays and extinguished cigarettes. Soon the place looked like a bank.

All this labor was performed for one singular man: "Mr. Will," namely William Hobson Andrew, justice of the peace, captain of the Third Volunteer Brigade of the Manchester Regiment, and governing director of the entire *Reporter* series—i.e., our employer. Each Friday he appeared in the newsroom carrying a quart-size metal canister of milk, which he deposited on Mr. Middlehurst's desk, specially cleared of papers for the occasion. We were a pale, fidgety bunch in off-the-rack suits. Mr. Will was from another planet—silver-haired, slim in his hand-tailored suit, and suntanned from daily hours on the golf course. He stood erectly among us, bracing his shoulders and gleaming with purpose.

"Good paper this week," he said, exposing several gold teeth.

He made a few more comments, then after an awkward silence Mr. Middlehurst indicated I was the new boy. "He cycled all the way from Failsworth," he added.

"Very good," said Mr. Will. "Now, Evans, how many spokes are there in a bicycle wheel?"

"I don't know, sir."

"Find out! Curiosity is the thing in journalism. Curiosity. Ask questions, Evans."

Then he nodded to us all and was gone, taking his milk can with him.

A clerk in the front office often met Mr. Will at the entrance to the building and carried the milk can for him. He told me he was rewarded for this task with an apple fished from Mr. Will's pocket and polished on his very own sleeve. (The clerk, Derek Rigby, became a reporter with a world scoop to his credit: he was the first to report the discovery on Saddleworth Moor of the bodies of two child victims of the so-called Monsters of the Moors, Myra Hindley and Ian Brady.)

That Friday after Mr. Will had gone to his office, Mr. Middlehurst wasn't finished with me. He beckoned me over, his head down, avoiding eye contact.

"You're expensive," he said.

I felt tempted to retort that a pound a week wasn't a lot for the long hours I worked, but I'd misheard him again.

"Your expenses! Your expenses! Where's your expense report, laddie?"

"I haven't spent anything," I explained.

"You must have. You must have taken bus rides."

"No, sir, I walked."

He glowered. "Downstairs will think you're not working." Then he scribbled on a slip of paper. "Take that to the cashier." I read it on the way down the stone steps to the front office: "Harold Evans, Bus fares, Droylsden calls, 3 pence. Approved, J. W. Middlehurst, News Editor."

I took every penny.

Everyone was a little scared of Mr. Will, including Mr. Middlehurst, who wore his jacket for these Friday encounters with him. The irreverent Keeble was the only one of us who dared to risk the wrath of the owner by entering the office at the main entrance like management. This meant surviving the glaring disapproval of the clerks and junior managers as he ascended the stairs and passed Mr. Will's office. One day Mr. Will sprang out at him. "Well, young man!" he said indignantly. "Well!"

But Frank had an inspired response. He duly explained

that he'd come to thank the governing director for his leadership and guidance—and was it not time he was rewarded for his own dedication? A week later he found an additional shilling in his pay packet.

Mr. Will was represented every week in the paper by six asterisks at the foot of his own column, called "Golf Causerie." He wrote anecdotes about personalities and course records and ordered that not a syllable of his copy should ever be changed. Thus it was that one of his columns informed us, "There is no greater thrill than to drop your balls on a damp green."

Perhaps "Golf Causerie" was Mr. Will's arcane indulgence, but I see now it was a nice, chatty little enrichment even for those who didn't know the difference between a birdie and a bogey. Mr. Will was a shrewd owner-manager. He had worked in every department of the business since taking over twenty-six years before; he'd helped to push the transition from hand-setting to Linotypes and had set up branch offices; and he'd committed the *Reporter* to solid nonpartisan community news reporting at a time when even weeklies tended to be conspicuously Conservative or Liberal (never Labour). We juniors had little appreciation of these matters; we were more concerned with the vast areas of human activity about which he required information. One week his parting shot to one of us was "Do bones make good soup?" He left another junior slack-jawed with the parting question "How long, young man, does it take a banana to ripen?"

A junior named Bob Sands, who later became deputy northern editor of the *Daily Mirror,* had labored hard on a detailed report of a Stalybridge Council meeting, and Mr. Will, who lived in that town, challenged him: "Well, Sands, how many steps on Stalybridge Town Hall?"

"A lot," said Bob.

"Count them, count them! Look about you. Good day to you all."

We juniors were lucky to be on a weekly newspaper during the war. Chronicling darts winners and blushing brides might have palled after a while but for the adrenaline of being by proxy on the battlefronts.

War Office service bulletins about local men in action came into the office regularly, and Middlehurst doled them out selectively like lollipops. Sometimes we arrived on the doorstep with information the family did not have. A woman whose husband was killed in Holland had no idea why the army had sent her a ribbon in an envelope, but we had details of the action. We were allowed into the front office when readers came in with letters from the war fronts, and when we heard someone was on leave, we could go round and see if he had a story: a sailor rescued after an hour in icy waters following the torpedoing of his cargo ship; an airman who had disposed of a live bomb just before it exploded; a navy telegraphist on how he had managed to keep in touch with all the ships in a convoy to Murmansk beset by seven days of blizzards and U-boat packs; a prisoner of war in a German camp with a surprisingly cheerful take on life in the stalag.

I arrived one morning to find I had been taken prisoner myself. Mr. Middlehurst fluttered his hand like a priest sprinkling water and waved me over to a young man in a double-breasted suit tightly buttoned over an incongruous sweater. I had not seen him around. He had a lordly air, but he looked like a bouncer: he was squarely built and had a boxer's nose and a strangely hooded left eye. The bad news was that he would "keep watch" on me for the remainder of my three-month trial as a reporter. This sinister figure, named Eric

Marsden, was not enthusiastic about his new charge. I learned years later that the ancient warrior Billy Mee had taken him aside and said, "That boy Evans will never make the grade."

Marsden plucked from my desk a piece of copy I'd written and barely glanced at it. "I don't know what I'm supposed to do with you," he said disdainfully, then added, "We may as well make a start with film reviews." This was promising.

"Gary Cooper's on round the corner at the Pavilion in *Casanova Brown*," explained Marsden. "David Niven's at the Roxy in *The Way Ahead*, and Tyrone Power is in *Old Chicago* at the Palace. See what you make of them. Make it snappy."

I leapt up.

"Where are you going?"

"I see the matinee starts at two at the Pavilion. I can just make it."

"Control yourself. All you need, Harold, is here in the files. And no more than thirty words a film." With a wave of his hand he left me a few dog-eared publications published by the cinema trades, whose cryptic phrases — "bodice-ripper," "good thick ear," "great smoocher" — I had to translate along with their breathless plot summaries.

Marsden was smart: he'd been a star scholarship student at grammar school and won a prize for an essay on Thomas Hardy's *Mayor of Casterbridge* — and dammit, he'd seen war action. As a junior fireman in the Auxiliary Fire Service, he'd manned a stirrup pump to extinguish incendiaries dropped on Manchester roofs in German night raids, and at seventeen he was an officer cadet, training to be a pilot in the Fleet Air Arm. I felt inadequate. I didn't have a double-breasted suit and wouldn't have filled it so impressively. I'd not doused a single incendiary in the Blitz, and I was the only one of the juniors who had failed the eleven-plus to get into grammar school.

At the end of the week, though, I was invited to join

Marsden, Taylor, and Keeble for the lunch they had regularly at the Co-op café. I was flattered. They were all grammar-school boys, though my shorthand and typing were better than theirs. The routine was for the ace reporters to swagger into the upstairs café with a copy of the paper to give to a pretty waitress. After baked beans on toast, Marsden pulled out a pocket chess set, soon checkmated Taylor, and challenged me to a game. He beat me with ease. That night I took a chess book out of the Failsworth Public Library and spent the weekend memorizing openings for the next Friday encounter.

I was convinced that Marsden was a complication to my hopes of being taken on the staff. As it was, I already lived in constant apprehension that I might mishear the mumbling Mr. Middlehurst and be fired. He was all detonator and no fuse. He blew up when I blundered in completing the worst task in the office—transcribing the eye-straining, interminable, and complex results from marked-up dog show catalogs. It took but a second to mix up the results of the Border Collie with those of the Border Terrier class. In these days of "recovered memory," I could have blamed the error on the black mongrel that sank its teeth into my leg when, at the age of ten, I was innocently cycling in the street. Truth was I couldn't tell one dog from another. As punishment I was assigned to be Middlehurst's runner for Mossley United's Saturday football match in the Cheshire League. I sat with him in the stands while he wrote up the game in longhand, and every fifteen minutes I was sent off to a telephone booth to read it to the *Sunday Empire News*, which paid him by the line.

Another form of torture was to be sent into the readers' department adjacent to the newsroom. It was like a cave with little pools of light from desk lamps, and in the shadows two or three murmuring men curled like commas over galley proofs. I was assigned as the copyholder to a reader, a retired headmaster of vinous complexion by the name of J. R. Hall, who practiced his pedagogy in the margins of text in type as I slowly and quietly gave voice to the reporter's original words. But I did at least learn to be on the alert for the curious interloper in newspapers known as "Etaoin Shrdlu." He sounded half-Irish, half-Indian. I'd seen him make random appearances in the pages of all kinds of newspapers, sometimes in the byline position but most often and bafflingly in the middle of a story, so it read like this:

Several demonstrators had
minor injuries and one of
tawk Etaoin Shrdlu
the leaders was taken to
hospital. Thirty-two were

The start of the incomprehensible third line represented the operator's mistake in trying to key "the leaders" of the correct fourth line. Operators who erred in casting a line of type (called a slug) quickly strummed down the first vertical keys in the letter section of the board. These were *e-t-a-o-i-n s-h-r-d-l-u* and represented an alert to copyreaders and compositors to discard that line. (In these digital days, Shrdlu no longer haunts newspaper pages.) Hall explained that Etaoin was a saboteur and it was our duty to apprehend him before he made print anywhere in the *Reporter* series of newspapers. Never on his watch had the fellow slipped through as he did in newspapers conducted more carelessly than ours. Mr. Hall let me know every time he made an arrest and scrawled a large "must delete" mark in the margin of the galley.

The experience in the readers' room also yielded an insight into how Mr. Middlehurst wrung water out of copy. His speaking manner might be woolly, but he brought a very sharp mind to the editing of text. He had no time to instruct juniors directly, still less for small talk, since he edited every line in the entire series of newspapers, wrote the headlines, made all the assignments, wrote the (anodyne) editorial comment, and also contrived to contribute a chatty column of notes called "Round and About" under the byline "Pilgrim." ("One wonders how much time is spent by those who take a delight in obliterating the red labels on the windows of non-smoking railway compartments.") Mr. Middlehurst never made a comment on copy; he talked through his black pencil. He had been on the job since 1930 and would die at his desk with his pencil in his hand.

Soon after his triumph on the chessboard, Eric Marsden picked up a review I'd written of a Droylsden comedy and held it like he held a pawn, between thumb and forefinger. "Nice intro," he said, and seemed to mean it. To my surprise he now wanted me to review theater. It was a break: We could use adjectives; we could make judgments. We could imagine being the James Agate (the legendary *Sunday Times* theater critic) of our generation. I kept a note of Agate's critical shafts ("Theatre director: a person engaged by the management to conceal the fact that the players cannot act") with the hope of somehow matching him when taking on local community theater productions.

When I was used to being a drama critic, I had the cheek to review a new church company, the Clayton Players, whose performers included Marsden. My review of their debut in *Doctor's Orders*, a two-act farce, was proudly signed with my initials, HME. I wrote: "Eric Marsden as Banks gave a good impersonation of the legendary butler, Jeeves. His chief fault, like that of most of the cast, was a tendency to lower his voice in his longer speeches." The amazing thing is that Marsden

90

did not raise a voice of protest the next day in the office when he saw my copy. I decided he was a man of discernment.

I was right, for the wrong reason. In fact, I had misread him altogether. Marsden looked twenty-five, but was only nineteen. Fixating on the menacing eye, I'd missed his tolerant humor. And the prosperity suggested by his new double-breasted did not exist: the suit was a farewell gift from the navy. Gradually I learned that his imperious air masked privation. His family was really poor, living in a mean terraced house amid factories. His father was a drunk who had abandoned his sick wife, so Eric had been forced to leave grammar school to be the breadwinner, working as a clerk in the Manchester textile company of Tootal Broadhurst Lee. This meant giving up the near certainty of a university scholarship. Only a handful of working-class boys had any hope of college then, however brilliant they were. He'd volunteered for the Fleet Air Arm at age seventeen, but his billet in Skegness, Yorkshire, while he waited to leave for flying training in Canada, was a thin plywood shack cursed with a coke stove leaking toxic fumes. Endless winter rain coursed down the inside walls and onto his bed, and he shivered the nights away. The pleurisy he developed, which ended his flying career, would dog him all his life.

It was a cruel outcome for such a brave spirit. I discovered he was a sturdy romantic who did his own thinking. His gods were Beethoven and Shakespeare, and he made them mine. At sixteen I had not heard a note of classical music. Eric, while clerking at Tootal's, had got into the habit of relieving the drudgery by walking over to Manchester Central Library for its lunchtime recitals by pianists and violinists, then he'd saved up to go to the classical concerts by Manchester's famous Hallé orchestra. He studied the composers by playing secondhand records on a wind-up gramophone.

That was the way he introduced me to an enduring joy of my life. He lent me a tiny 48 rpm record of "Dance of the Hours," the ballet music by Amilcare Ponchielli. To the family's amusement, then irritation, I played it dementedly on a portable wind-up in Ashworth Street. It's a trifling sugary piece, lampooned in Walt Disney's *Fantasia* as a dance for hippos.

Eric taught me the etiquette of concertgoing and how it had changed since the nineteenth century, when people talked and sometimes played cards and clapped at anything they liked. I was not to talk, not to cough, not to sniff, not to tap a foot, not to rustle a paper, not to breathe, in fact, unless absolutely necessary—and for Pete's sake not to clap when they stopped playing but wait till I was absolutely sure from the program notes that they really had finished what they were about. The first time I heard Beethoven's Third Symphony, the *Eroica*, I was exalted. I read all I could on Beethoven in the Failsworth Public Library, learning the most from J. W. N. Sullivan's Pelican paperback *Beethoven: His Spiritual Development*. Who could not be moved by the drama of the composer's struggle against deafness and depression: "I will take fate by the throat; it shall not overcome me!" I found myself reflecting, albeit immaturely, on the dissonance between physical appearance and character. Ludwig—and Eric—were both ill-favored, so clearly the face was not a window on the soul.

Thereafter I begged to write stories about the Hallé; I couldn't afford to pay for a regular ticket.

It was no reward for Eric's beneficence that on the following Friday at the Co-op café I tried out one of the chess openings I'd learned, the queen's pawn gambit, and about which I had breathed not a word. It enabled me to control the center of the board against both Laurence and Eric. "Once more unto the breach, dear friends," cried Eric, but I was merciless. Thereafter every Friday for two years, when all the other customers had fled, we tussled from lunchtime to teatime in the empty café as I matched my book learning against his originality. Eric probably still had the edge but became careless in his crusading style, his mating mind divided between the tiny chessboard and the vivacious Co-op waitress with the frilly lace apron. She had a curious accent — flat Lancastrian with some extra zing in it that made her seem snooty. This was a contradiction. Ever acute to the nuances of class, I couldn't work out how someone with a working-class accent could manage to be as haughty as the upper class.

It transpired that she was a Belgian aristocrat, Jacqueline Henriette Alphonsine Marie Dirix de Kessel, who had risked her life in the Belgian resistance. She'd been interrogated by the Gestapo and let go. In 1945 she'd married a handsome British soldier who'd brought her home to Ashton. It must have been a terrible shock — a disillusion suffered by thousands — to come from war dramas to the rainy vicissitudes of a cotton town and find that the dashing liberator was a bully who regarded a wife as a chattel. She divorced him, and now everyone lusted after her.

We knew "Ereek," as she called Marsden, had no chance. The unstoppable Charlie Sutcliffe was in hot pursuit. It was obvious that, unversed in the nuances of the English class and educational system, Jackie would see the dashing photographer as the war-wounded Cavalier and the much cleverer Eric as the plodding Roundhead. Charlie had a car, and a Fleet Street career beckoned. He would sweep her off her feet, and she would be glamorously at his side in a Hemingway-style life of adventure in the world's capitals. My asthmatic hero would be left to grow old on the *Ashton Reporter,* like the wrinkled walnut Billy Mee I'd encountered on my first day.

You can't script someone else's life, let alone your own. Jackie and Eric were married in 1947. And while Charlie stayed rooted to the same spot for the rest of his life, it was Eric who became a brave and accomplished foreign correspondent. When night work subbing in the Manchester office of the *Daily Telegraph* became too much of a strain on his health, he moved to Kenya in 1957 to work for twelve years for Nairobi's *East African Standard*. He reported on war and civil strife in Africa and the Middle East; he risked exposing abuses that governments preferred to cover up. In 1969, invited to cover an Arab League conference, he was nonetheless marched at bayonet point through Cairo as a suspected spy. The league apologized. Later the same year, now deputy editor of the *East African Standard*, he was deported from Kenya for displeasing President Jomo Kenyatta by publishing reports of machete attacks but was then invited back after protests by the African journalists. When he and Jackie started receiving death threats in Kenya, I invited him to join the *Sunday Times*, where I was the editor, as our correspondent in Israel and later South Africa.

Whatever doubts there may have been about my fitness to join the staff, they were put to the test by the Red Wharf Bay murder, in which the victim was a local army sergeant's wife. Mr. Middlehurst dispatched his son, Dennis, to report the sergeant's trial in Anglesey. But there was a problem. The court hearing opened on a Thursday, and the paper went to press that night. The only way Dennis could get his long report back in time was to phone it through to the office, and the only person with sufficient touch-typing speed to take his dictation was me.

At 4:00 p.m. I was locked in the newsroom telephone booth. The Underwood was lifted onto the little ledge inside. I was given dodgy earphones, and Dennis dictated his story at top speed. Everyone crowded round outside the booth looking in on me, the typing fish in the aquarium. It was hot inside — so hot that the windows misted up. I could see Mr. Middlehurst pacing urgently outside. Every time I finished a page his paw came into the booth and took it out to the Linotype operators. I was three hours in the aquarium, we made the edition, and Mr. Middlehurst never said another word about my being on trial at the paper. The following Friday I had an extra shilling in my pay packet.

I soon got better assignments. A gaunt, suave senior named Jameson, just medically discharged out of combat missions for the RAF, initiated me into the art of reporting the dispensation of justice. He had once worked on a Manchester daily, and policemen nodded to him as we crossed the icy cobbled square and climbed the many steps into the Ashton Town Hall, where the magistrates decided local cases.

This was March 1945, when the Allied armies had crossed the Rhine and we were winning the war in Europe. None of this made any difference to our life in Ashton. It was twenty degrees below freezing, and coal, already rationed by the bag, was not to be had. (Coal fires were the only form of heating in drafty buildings, where the wind rattled the windows. Nobody could afford electric heat, and nobody had heard of central heating, except in the American wonderland.) Hot and cold water pipes froze all over town, as did my fingers trying to write shorthand in the arctic courtroom to which I was now assigned.

Disconcertingly one morning, Mr. Will, bristling with good purpose, appeared high up on the bench as one of the presiding magistrates (mental resolve: count the town hall steps on the way out), but even he, for all his milk vitamins, was not immune to the cold. The court adjourned after fining one publican for embezzling the brewer and dismissing the case of another man accused of being "absent from essential war work without reasonable excuse." Ten minutes later the magistrates came back in overcoats and scarves, four men and a woman, banging their feet and rubbing their hands, not in the proper mood to deal with a wretch accused of stealing coal. Jameson, languid on the wooden bench, left these cases to me. He perked up when a police sergeant took the witness box and solemnly described what he'd seen when he'd entered a house of ill repute. Mr. Will looked flushed. Jameson whispered that it was too big a case for town magistrates and I should take down the depositions verbatim. Back at the office he edited my notes into a short report, sanitized for our Methodist readers, then carefully put the longest version in an envelope addressed to the *News of the World*, the seamiest of the Sunday papers. "We'll make a pretty penny out of this," he confided, and so we did. The splash on Sunday in the *News of the World* was GIRL OF FOURTEEN WANTED TO BE TAKEN FOR SIXTEEN. I received three shillings as my share of those wages of sin.

These many years later, I had forgotten what a slog it was on the *Reporter* until I looked at the pocket diaries I'd saved and deciphered the shorthand, a ridiculous subterfuge for a blameless life. The night work, when I thought it advisable to abandon the bike and go by bus, was onerous:

6 Feb 45: Manchester after work in freezing fog for NUJ
   lectures at Young Journalists' Club on interviewing.
   John Beavan of Manchester Evening News talked on
   importance of college education for journalists

7 Feb: Hard day. Court in morning, then two inquests
   back to back and stuffy old Englishe night at
   Rotarian dinner. Home about 11.

9 Feb: Worked like hell. Long Ashton Council meeting.
   Missed 10 pm bus.

Some weeks I filled ten columns of the paper. My fingers ached from all the typing on the heavy keyboard, but the personal demands were the hardest. I was given the name of a parachutist who had died in action in Italy. "Make sure," I was told, "you bring back a good photograph and a few lines on his life." I was to call on his parents; he was their only son. I walked toward the door of the terraced house, spiral-bound notebook in my raincoat pocket, then walked away.

I felt a terrible intruder, a teenager not long out of short pants sent on a man's mission. I imagined a reporter calling on my own mother announcing my death. I canvassed my conscience with the idea of going back to the office to say sorry, nobody was in. I had to keep telling myself this was it — this was the real test — and picturing what it would be like returning to the office empty-handed with a lame excuse.

When I finally knocked on the door, praying nobody would come after all, I was quite drained. "Sit down, lad, and have a cup of tea," said the mother, while the father extracted a photograph from its frame. They were sorrowful but proud, ready to talk about their son for hours to someone from the *Reporter*.

I found time and again we of the *Reporter* were regarded not as nosy intruders but as friends of the family. That was not because of any magic we had as individuals. It was a reflection of respect for the paper; it bothered with the little things in people's lives, the whist drives and flower shows, so it was trusted to be part of the big things. A Royal Signals sergeant, in a letter describing their months' long advance down the Railway Corridor in the Burmese jungle, wrote, "In spite of the rain, mud, sticky heat, insects, we are quite a happy crowd. I must give thanks to the American Air Force for the splendid way they supplied us with the necessary things of life, including little luxuries such as canteen supplies, etc. and most of all that great morale booster, mail from home—along with a few welcome *Reporter*s."

For all the respect the *Reporter* enjoyed, encounters of this kind never came easy to me. I eventually perfected a little mental trick to play on myself in rough waters, imagining the shame I'd feel if I surrendered to embarrassment or shyness: if I failed to knock, shirked a tough question, accepted an obvious lie, retreated from the glare of a VIP.

What I most of all took away from these years going into so many homes was identification with the people of the backstreets and appreciation of their fortitude, too often in the face of a vast official carelessness. I got worked up about the way they were used and tossed aside. And while the *Reporter* style was deadpan, without a hint of comment in the news, I couldn't contain myself after I knocked on a door in Abbey Hey, Gorton, and was welcomed in by Mr. William Henry Adams and his widowed father.

William, a skeleton of thirty-seven, had volunteered for the army within days of the outbreak of the war. Even though he had been ill for two months with double pneumonia and was still somewhat groggy, he enlisted and was rushed to the front in France. Conditions at Cherbourg with the Royal Engineers were grim. Bivouacked in heavy rain, he was diagnosed with tuberculosis in both lungs. He was discharged, unfit for active duty, unable ever to work again, and yet denied any form of war service pension. He had been appealing for four years when I met him and had just been rescued by the local MP, Alderman Will Oldfield, who had taken up his case. Rescued? The pension was all of two pounds and five shillings a week. I wrote, "This is the story of a man who sacrificed his health to serve his country and was all but forgotten when he was no longer needed. He is grateful for the pension but those years of waiting are no credit to England."

Mr. Middlehurst let it through and even gave me a personal reference, inserting "writes a *Reporter* representative."

In the bitterly cold February of 1945, just after the Allied armies had finally blocked Hitler's panzers thrusting from their Ardennes lair to the English Channel, Mr. Middlehurst murmured that I was to go and see General Carpenter, who was in town for a night. He gave me a scrap of copy paper with the name Major Bagworth, who would introduce me to the general, and the address where they were to be found. It was a hall packed with uniformed men and women. I could not find the major. It was hard to ask questions because the uniformed ones were banging tambourines, clapping hands, and singing a hymn to a brass band. The headgear of the women revealed that they were Salvation Army bonnets, and General Carpenter was their general—in fact, the leading general of the Salvation Army. The Salvationists kindly made room for me to squeeze into the front row when I mentioned the *Reporter* and took out my notebook, ready to report his speech.

The general had other priorities. Instead of mounting the platform, he walked into the body of the hall and asked every individual to stand so that one by one he could commend their souls to the Lord's care. He started on my row, at the far right, speaking to every individual. I remained seated as he advanced toward me.

"Won't you stand for Jesus, son?" the general asked.

"I'm press."

He looked at me and smiled. "You can still be saved!"

5

How I Won the War

The record of my war years need not detain us long, particularly as the war was over.

I answered the nation's call on Monday, August 12, 1946. His Majesty's Royal Air Force needed me and would brook no delay. It didn't seem to have remembered its urgent need when I reported for duty at the RAF station at Padgate, near Warrington. I was one of hundreds of pale young men sitting on the floor of a big hut, waiting for something to happen. For days we were in a no-man's-land between civilian and service life.

Among us somewhere, though I didn't know it at the time, was another numberless man whose words would shake governments, Aircraftsman William Rees-Mogg, later the distinguished editor of the *Times*. He was going through his own culture shock, mystified by the frequency of the *f* word, applied to almost every noun: "I had not previously come across an effing knife and an effing fork on my effing plate. Nor oddly did I often come across it much later in the RAF." Someone in the Air Ministry must have had a premonition that this numberless one would become an august member of the establishment because, on emergence from limbo, he was compensated with one of the cushiest of billets as a sergeant in the Education Corps.

When I was given a number, 2318611, I clung to the seven digits of my new identity as a baby to a mother. I'd have been no good under interrogation by an enemy. Just the word "number" would have triggered a reflex response.

The transmutation from reporter to recruit was complete when I went through one door in a sports jacket and came out the other in a uniform and an improbable forage cap with the even more implausible motto *Per ardua ad astra* (Through adversity to the stars). We were all given effing haircuts and effing kit bags, huge sausages designed to dislocate shoulders and impose hours of ironing time for everything stuffed inside. Then as numbered freight we were dispatched in groups to Compton Bassett, Wiltshire, for six weeks of square bashing to make men of us. Opinion is divided to this day as to whether they succeeded.

I found it a relief to be turned into a robot for six weeks; no need to plan, worry, or think for oneself, just do what the man said when he shouted a number. It gave me a glimpse of how a fighting unit that didn't happen to have me in it could perform acts of incredible bravery. The challenge set for me on passing out of the drill squad as an AC2 (aircraftsman second class) was how to escape from the clerical Colditz to which I was immediately dispatched, the dreaded Ministry of Aviation Records Office at Innsworth. There grown men recently trained in warfare went on paper chases into the endless rows of filing cabinets and were never seen again. Redundant aircrews flew metal desks.

I was pretty miserable myself; collecting the names of whist drive winners was thrilling by comparison with my duties at Records. I was in a division responsible for compiling and filing movement orders that sent airmen to their new stations. I tried hard to get the RAF to realize it had a wasting asset. I filled in lots of forms for reassignment. I volunteered for aptitude tests whose results suggested I had no aptitude for anything. I never heard another word.

When, resigned, I'd all but forgotten these escape attempts, I received one of the movement orders we sent to others. With effect immediately, 2318611 was posted to Hullavington, Wiltshire, home of the Empire Flying School (EFS) and headquarters of No. 23 Group in the Flying Training Command. There was no hint what 2318611 would be doing there. I didn't care; it was such a relief to exchange the claustrophobia of Innsworth for the vicarious excitements of an active airfield. Flying school! It was as if I had stepped through the pages of my wartime scrapbooks.

Hullavington was in the countryside not far from the charming old town of Chippenham, but the fumes of the war lingered. Bombers and fighter planes lined the runways; fitters and armorers sweated in the hangars; the aroma of combat was as strong at the base canteen as the tea was weak.

The military police at the guardroom directed me away from the airfield, but I found myself in the stratosphere entering the offices of an air commodore on his way to being an air vice marshal, Claude McClean Vincent. He was air commandant, in charge of the whole station, home of the crack pilots in the All-Weather Squadron, which specialized in flying on instruments into electric storms just to see what the hell happened. He'd asked the station adjutant to get him a shorthand typist. If he was expecting a comely Women's Royal Air Force officer to brighten the all-male station of eight hundred officers and enlisted men, he kept a stiff upper lip, as you'd expect of a pilot with a Distinguished Flying Cross who'd flown in World War I and most recently commanded a group of Spitfires in the Middle East.

"Dog's dinner, I'm afraid," he said, asking me to type a manuscript of crabbed handwriting and convoluted revisions. It didn't take much imagination to see why he reminded me that I was bound by the Official Secrets Act. The terse reports I sent to the Air Ministry could have been turned into news leads: BRAVE TEST PILOT'S ORDEAL IN STORM: EXCLUSIVE FULL DETAILS by our air correspondent somewhere in Wiltshire. Unfortunately, I also saw the effects of the flying errors I recorded, being several times ordered to lead a guard crew when one of our planes crashed.

I had a lot of dog's dinners from the air commandant and from his successors over the next two and a half years. They were all apologetic, as if asking me to undertake some dangerous mission. In addition to being the secretary to the air commandant I had paperwork to do for all five RAF stations in No. 23 Group, but here, too, my boss, Squadron Leader Papworth, was so courteous I forgot I was the lowest of the low in RAF ranks. He was intrigued that I had been a newspaper reporter and took me home for tea with his wife in his cottage in lovely Bourton-on-the-Water, a village in west-central England nicknamed the Venice of the Cotswolds.

Nothing remarkable about that, you may say, but the RAF was my first realization that my mental map of class boundaries was a stereotype. I'd not before been in close contact with the officer class. I was disarmed by the lack of pretense among the majority on the station, who'd been through the war. Being shot up over Düsseldorf and seeing your mates die night after night didn't leave any taste for affectation. Commissioned and noncommissioned officers shared the same risks on bombing missions.

Visiting the airfield and the hangars, I noticed the ease of exchanges between officer pilots and other ranks working as airframe fitters, armorers, and maintenance technicians. A sergeant bomb aimer I got to know playing table tennis introduced me to a flight lieutenant whose north country accent was so much more marked than mine that I got called "educated Evans." This officer took a Lancaster bomber on "training flights" and one weekend invited me to go along for a flight that ended very conveniently at Ringway Airport near Manchester, his hometown and mine. It just happened that his bride lived there, and a few mechanics who came along also happened to be from Manchester. In this way, qualified by geography and accent, I had my first-ever flight in any aircraft—and subsequently as many as I could contrive in all sorts of RAF planes. Getting from Wiltshire to Manchester by the worn-out and indirect train service used up most of a forty-eight-hour pass and always risked running afoul of some officious military policeman at the station intent on finding my brass buttons and badge not bright enough to blind passersby. When I traveled by air, my weekends at home were blissfully extended.

This is how, when I am describing how I won the war, I can discourse on what it was like freezing at twenty thousand feet in the rear gun turret of a Lancaster. If I have the right captive audience, I can also describe my first German prisoner of war, Oberschütze Walter Greis, a tall, good-looking, blond Aryan of Hitler's fevered dreams. Actually, he was an eighteen-year-old bank clerk who'd surrendered to the U.S. Army at the end of the war and been sent to Hullavington to work. He was not an enemy but an ally of mine against the endless "bumph"—RAF slang for useless paper—flowing into my office.

Nobody had any idea why we had to fill in and dispatch so many forms, so after a year of this I invented a form of my own. I circulated an official note to all stations saying that in accordance with the No. 23 Group medical officer's determination to limit flyborne infections, commanding officers were henceforth required to ensure there was a weekly examination of the sticky flypaper hung up in various locations and a record submitted of the number of flies caught. "Group expects," I wrote, "that the numbers of intruders brought down should increase if careful study is made of the optimum placement of the traps."

The compliance was gratifying, though I never got round to visiting the stations to check the accuracy of the reports. No doubt they are still being submitted.

I was desperate to get on while my career in journalism was stalled. I applied for every promotion, every examination. One examination to do with RAF regulations that I passed with a 100 percent score was so obscure that nobody on the station had ever taken it before and so important that I cannot remember a single thing about it.

Within a year I had moved up from AC2 to AC1, then to leading aircraftsman (entitled to a propeller on my sleeve), then to corporal. All that the corporal's two chevrons did was put me in charge of my barrack room, theoretically responsible for the good conduct of forty airmen and their performance on the hated kit and rifle inspections. Let us say that my writ was lightly applied and more lightly accepted. The biggest call on my authority was who should next have the room's ironing board and iron to get a razor-edge crease in his trousers. I considered drawing up a waiting list, then thought better of it. Was I an ace reporter, or was I Corporal Jeeves?

Papworth encouraged me to apply for a commission. I could tell you the idea appealed for the extra money, the greater freedom, the uniform smoother than my blue serge, the snob appeal to women in town, the equality of status, the privilege of easier weekend passes, and the pleasure it would give my parents. It was all those things, but it was also a question of grub. The food in what was called the other ranks' mess (as if we were an afterthought) was notoriously inferior to the officers' and sergeants' messes. Every night, though, an officer moved along our crowded mess tables, asking us to approve of what we had just consumed — that is, to lie. The duty officer was preceded by a sergeant calling out, "Orderly officer, any complaints? Any complaints?" We might have gagged on the greasy lamb, but nobody ever said a word. The officer might be amiable enough, but the menacing demeanor of the sergeant, a stiff-backed soldier from the RAF Regiment, made it clear that there would be a penalty. On one historic occasion, much celebrated thereafter, I heard that a leading aircraftsman from Air Traffic Control had broken ranks. When the sergeant bellowed his "any complaints" question, Traffic stood up:

"Yes, sir, it's shit!"

Everyone froze. Officer and Sergeant stopped dead in their tracks.

"What did you say, airman?"

"It's shit, sir," said Traffic in the silence. "But it's beautifully cooked."

I had a better idea than trying to become an officer, which meant signing on for three years anyway. In the summer of 1947, a full year into service, I finally realized what I should be doing. There were eight hundred men, plus some favored ones with families in married quarters. What they needed was what I needed—a station newspaper. I got permission, provided I did the work in my spare time. Officers and sergeants volunteered to be reporters and printers. There was a wartime can-do spirit about the whole enterprise.

A local printing company said they'd let us have several sacks of old type they didn't need but warned that the sizes and letters were all mixed up. In a mountain of metal deposited in the hut, we had to pick up each thin sliver of type by our fingertips, guess the size, read the single character on the surface, and dispose of it in the correct little box in a composing tray so that we could pick out *t-h-e* to form "the" in a composing stick. There were ninety boxes, the size varying according to how often the letter was likely to be needed.

We all chipped in at night after the day's duties were done. It was eye-straining work under a single lightbulb. It was cold, too, with just one fire. I tried Tom Sawyer's trick of telling friends what a fascinating time we were having exploring the mysteries of print. Then another difficulty pressed. In my mad whirl to stay occupied before the newspaper was approved, I'd been cast in a station production of a play, *Men in Shadow*, about the French resistance. I was to play Polly, a downed flier hiding out in the roof of a barn. The nights I had reserved for editing copy and writing headlines were the nights I was supposed to be dropping out of a trapdoor to link up with the lead character, Kenny, none other than our own printer, Sergeant Mott.

Since we lacked the gift of being in two places at the same time, our days through November consisted of morning parade, a full day's work followed by rehearsal or performance, and then print shop duties until midnight. This was so fraught an enterprise that I took in my stride the first blemish in the editorial content I'd ordered up: a review of *Men in Shadow* concluded, "It would have been better if Corporal Evans as Polly had been more consistent with the Lancashire accent and left the Shakespearean gestures to John Gielgud."

A clerk called Jock McPhee joined with a few others to sort type as we neared Christmas. The night before the camp was due to close for Christmas we still had to finish setting the final page to run off on our flatbed press. We worked through the night. By 9.00 a.m. we were all drooping around the setting table and still had not set enough type. Out of time and material, we slapped the words STOP PRESS on four inches of blank space at the foot of the page, as if we were a regular newspaper expecting late news at any minute.

As the pages came off the press, the ink still wet, Jock ran out of the shop to the camp gate with the first hundred copies of the *Empire Flying School Review* to sell at threepence a copy. Following with the second batch, I met him on his way back to the print shop—he was empty-handed. We sold all we could print.

After Christmas the station welfare committee voted to float the cost of professional printing if we would commit to repaying the grant from advertising income and sales. This mighty enterprise would cost twenty-five pounds. If we sold six hundred copies at sixpence—double our initial rate—we'd have fifteen pounds and could make up the rest from advertising.

Sixpence? To justify that price, we'd have to concoct a magazine whose price and quality of paper might draw more advertisers. This meant devising a cover each month, an art that was not part of the Middlehurst curriculum. I had the idea of having small silhouettes of six of the station's most celebrated planes fitted into the spaces of the letters *E-F-S* (for Empire Flying School). The concept was a disaster. Our customers recoiled from being reminded of work. "We've enough of kites [planes] all day. Give us a break!" Sales were off target on two issues. This much of a failure with a third issue would kill us.

What to do?

Our first newspaper had included a photograph of Veronica Lake's thighs, and I had flash recall of it pinned up in a barrack room. Would I pander to these baser instincts?

Ask me another. The third glossy cover design featured the lovely redheaded actress Hazel Court. Sales shot up. One of the civilian workers suggested we feature a blond bombshell of a girl from his hometown of Swindon. It sounded unpromising. Diana Fluck, as he knew her, was a little-known film actress, but I liked the sound of how she had responded to a studio's request to change her name: "I suppose they were afraid that if my real name was in lights and one of the lights blew..." She changed it to Diana Dors and eventually became known as Britain's answer to Marilyn Monroe. I think we were the first magazine to make her a cover girl. Soon after we featured her in her bare skin sitting on a snowy stile with a strategically placed fur muff, she was cast in *Oliver Twist* and made into a star by Pinewood Studios.

Just when the August 1948 date neared for my demobilization, Joseph Stalin intervened. He stopped all road, rail, and water traffic crossing the Soviet zone in occupied Germany at the end of June, threatening 2.5 million people in the western sector of Berlin with starvation. The RAF and the U.S. Air Force immediately joined in the great Berlin airlift, carrying coal and food round the clock. It was good news for the Berliners—among them the repatriated Walter Greis—but it was bad news for me. The airlift required selectively postponing the release of thousands of airmen, and I was one of them.

I was kept back eight more months, but the time flew. The day's paperwork assumed an air of relevance and urgency, the *Empire Flying School Review* had its deadlines, and in every spare minute, now that I had been snared by the big world outside camp, I tried to understand what was behind some of the more worrisome headlines in the newspapers: DOLLAR DRAIN! PAYMENTS CRISIS! AUSTERITY BUDGET! BANK OF ENGLAND ROW! In my barrack room were two airmen, junior to me in rank but way ahead in being able to follow the ups and downs of the economic trials of the new Labour government. They'd been called up during their first year at university—one at Oxford, one at Cambridge—and had made a nodding acquaintance with people I'd never heard of, such as John Maynard Keynes and Alfred Marshall. With the encouragement of my clever new friends I wrote away to Wolsey Hall in Oxford, which was offering to teach economics by correspondence course. Wolsey Hall was not an Oxford college (as I'd imagined) but a commercial enterprise. Still, it was a first step into what they called "the dismal science." "Why is a pound of diamonds valued more than a pound of bread?" Wolsey Hall asked. I couldn't for the life of me see how to apply the lessons to Mum's grocery, which is just as well, but I conscientiously wrote up the short answers in the station library and waited anxiously for the red ink marks from Oxford.

In the library one day, a typed note crammed among many on the bulletin board announced that Manchester University was offering servicemen a two-week residential course of lectures and discussions titled "The Rights of Man."

I raced down to the education department to apply. Happily nobody else did, and a few weeks later, with the permission of the air commodore, I was installed in civvies in the university's Holly Royde House in Didsbury, Manchester, cerebrating with men and women of all ranks from all the armed forces. Here I met Thomas Paine and Edmund Burke, John Locke and Thomas Jefferson, Jean-Jacques Rousseau and Thomas Hobbes. I made no more than a nodding acquaintance with these strangers, but I got the idea that somewhere in their writings they might, in the urgent clamor of postwar politics, furnish a better compass than the newspapers.

I reentered civilian life in March 1949 in a shiny demob suit, returning to Ashton-under-Lyne and weekly newspaper reporting. I'd been promoted and was now chief reporter of the edition called the *Gorton and Openshaw Reporter*, but I carried around the cold streets a fever incubated at the Empire Flying School. I burned to learn more about politics and economics.

I just had to find a way to get to university. My new ambition marked me out as some kind of freak. When I was unwise enough to express it in the Ashton head office, the general refrain was "You've lost three years in the RAF, now another three for university? You can say goodbye to Fleet Street!" Even my old colleague the erudite Michael Hides was skeptical. He wrote me a long letter explaining why academic studies would not only be a diversion from acquiring the skills for journalism but actually distort them. He'd been taken on by the *Manchester Guardian* and was deep into the mysteries of his new craft as a subeditor, the first of our batch of Ashton juniors to make the big time. But the flicker of envy I felt was expunged by the prospect of exploring mysteries of my own.

6

Non Nobis Solum

It must seem an unexceptional ambition today, but in the 1940s for a working-class boy to say he was going to university was like announcing he was about to marry Betty Grable. Our only idea of a university was through movies like *A Yank at Oxford,* which was less about book learning than rowing boats, robbing someone of his trousers (debagging), and heavy breathing over Vivien Leigh. College just never occurred to the brightest of my schoolmates, nor to any of the newspaper people I met. I knew of nobody in Newton Heath who had gone to a cap-and-gown university, as distinct from a few wizards who had attended a technical college.

There were very few places open in the handful of universities, and only a tiny fraction of those qualified could hope for admittance. I continued to post short essays to Wolsey Hall but tried to keep up with my education in journalism. Every Thursday night, after handing in the last Gorton story, I'd take the bus into Manchester for a series of talks by leading daily newspapermen organized by the National Union of Journalists. I learned some tricks of the trade, but the major impression was made by the writer-editor John Beavan (later Lord Ardwick) descending from the clouds, which is how I then regarded the *Manchester Guardian*. Beavan informed us in his silky way that we were all ignoramuses.

How could we explain what was really going on, Beavan scolded, if we had not read Macaulay and Tawney? His barbs were resented by the group. The bitterness of postwar politics made imperative some understanding of economics and political history, however I acquired it.

In training for the attempt to enter a university, I abandoned cycling to the office through Daisy Nook in favor of three bus rides because they gave me a chance to catch up with a few centuries of political philosophy. I have an aptitude for losing things, so it is quite astonishing to me that I still have the tiny blue hardback book I carried everywhere in my jacket pocket: *The History of the Peloponnesian War*, written by Thucydides and edited in translation by R. W. Livingstone.

Sitting with Thucydides on the top deck of the Oldham to Ashton bus, rain spattering the windows, I was not carried back to fifth century BC in Athens but rather into the middle of the twentieth century and beyond, since the Athenians' arguments about democracy and equality, power and patriotism, war and imperialism, so lucidly reported, will be with us for some time. Of course the Athenian democracy had no role for women and was dependent on slave labor, but I was moved — then and now — by Pericles' evocation of the spirit of the idealists striving for a liberal democracy: a society which honors excellence and beauty but gives equal chances to all its citizens; where individuals give the state due service of their own free will and without compulsion; where they are free within the law to lead their private lives their own way without black looks and angry words. "Wealth to us is not mere material for vainglory but an opportunity for achievement; and poverty we think it no disgrace to acknowledge but a real degradation to make no effort to overcome. Our citizens attend both to public and private duties, and do not allow absorption in their own various affairs to interfere with their knowledge of the city's. We differ from other states in regarding the man who holds aloof from public life not as 'quiet' but as useless."

The useless man is with us still. He does not vote; he dodges taxes; he volunteers for nothing; he does not speak up for any cause; he turns a blind eye to the propagation of hatred; he "minds his own business." For any social ill he deals in the coinage of cowardice: "They should do something about it."

I marked another passage where the historian of the fifth century BC spoke directly to the reporter of AD 1949: "With reference to the narrative of events, far from permitting myself to derive it from the first source that came to hand, I did not even trust my own first impressions, but it rests partly on what I saw myself, partly on what others saw for me, the accuracy of the report being always tried by the most severe and detailed tests possible."

That Thucydides had never attended a secondary school, let alone a university, did not deflect my determination to secure a grander degree. I wrote to every one of the fourteen English universities, offering to study there for a bachelor of arts degree. None of them was impressed. Although I had those precious five school certificate credits, not one of them was in Latin, and Latin, I now learned, was required to read for an arts degree. I wondered if I could take a crash course but was told that adequate preparation to take the examination would entail three years of evening classes, not very feasible with so many night reporting jobs. There was also even more daunting arithmetic: I could not conjure up anything like enough money to pay for college accommodations and teaching, nor could Mum and Dad. They had four sons to prepare for the big world. There was no organized system comparable to the American one of working one's way through college.

I can't remember who told me that the wartime coalition government had passed further education and training legislation, within the Butler Education Act, whereby the Ministry of Education was empowered to give grants to men and women who had served in the war. Well, I had almost done that, hadn't I? Wasn't the Berlin airlift a key conflict in the cold war? The act was much more circumscribed than the GI Bill in the United States, but I wrote to the ministry. The answer was swift. Sorry, mate, you must have a place in a college before we can even begin to consider whether you qualify for an ex-serviceman's grant. No Latin, no college. No college, no money. Catch-22.

I'd been through all the brochures for degrees in politics and economics, but I started again, this time spending summer nights after work looking at everything universities had to offer. Time was running out for applications for admittance in September–October. Amid some small print, I discovered there was a three-year course called Social Studies leading to a bachelor of arts degree. I'd skipped past it, but now I noticed Latin was not mentioned in its entry requirements, only "matriculation." Was it an oversight? And what was Social Studies? There was a brief reference to political theory, industrial history, economics, and psychology. What was the catch? Would I emerge adept in the social skill of settling disputes in a soup kitchen when the underpaid chef ran amok with a cleaver? Or divining at close quarters the emotional impulses of depraved juveniles? Further research was needed.

I wrote to Durham, the university offering this degree, and specifically asked if they really would admit someone without Latin. Durham promptly wrote back, saying yes. I could apply to enroll for Social Studies unconjugated by Latin—but I could not be admitted to the degree course unless I had also been admitted to one of the five men's residential colleges in Durham City or to St. Cuthbert's Society, whose members lived at home or lodged in town. They kindly attached the fees. Any residential college would want first to be assured that I was acceptable to the Durham colleges' academic authorities. Catch-22 redux.

Nevertheless, in the leaflet from University College, Durham, one of the residential colleges, there was a tiny picture of an undergraduate's room in Durham Castle complete with a fireplace and mantelpiece, and I could not resist imagining myself there. I wrote to University College and was told I could put in an appearance for an interview on September 13, provided I had satisfied the registrar that I had matriculated. Clutching my five credits, I took a train—and the chance they would not spring a Latin trap on me.

I had imagined the city to be one vast coal heap with Social Studies graduates toiling somewhere in the dust. Instead, an incomparable vista opened up when the train steamed through the last obscuring hedges and over the spectacular viaduct. The magnificent Romanesque cathedral the Normans had built on the rocky wooded peninsula high over a loop of the river Wear was the most inspiring single scene of my life, then and ever after. If men could build that prayer in granite in the service of God, what could they not do? Across from the cathedral, where lay the bones of Saints Cuthbert and Bede, stood the redoubtable Norman castle: "Half church of God, half castle 'gainst the Scot" proclaimed Sir Walter Scott's ode to Durham, those words cut in the stonework of the graceful Prebends Bridge (1777), where J. M. W. Turner planted his easel to paint the peninsula.

After Oxford and Cambridge, Durham was England's third-oldest university. I found the registrar in a dainty pastel-washed little house in a cobbled side street by the cathedral. I presented my school certificate parchment. In the blink of an eye a "W. W. Angus" signed a valuable document: "I certify that Harold Matthew Evans is qualified without further examination to matriculate in the University of Durham, to read for the degree of BA in Social Studies." It meant I was admissible to the university, provided a college... Yes, yes, I knew the refrain by heart. Now to gain a college place I first had to scale the ramparts of the castle, the headquarters of University College.

Founded soon after the Norman conquest, the castle had for eight centuries been the palace of the immensely rich prince bishops of Durham. It is the oldest inhabited university building in the world and surely the most grandly housed college in the universe.

The moat had been cobbled over, but the castle still had defenses against pretentious interlopers. First of these was the dragon lady who popped out from a crevice in the wall to bar my way when I dared open a little door in the great iron-studded castle gate beneath the embattlements of the crenellated keep.

"Castle is closed," she was pleased to inform me.

"I'm here to see the Master of the College."

It made no difference.

"No visitors."

I protested: "But I have an appointment!"

"Are you a university student?"

"No, but I will be."

She paused to consider the impertinence, then vanished back into the crevice. I was left to contemplate the University College arms, a shield of four lions rampant and two bishops' miters with a scrolled inscription. It was Latin: *"Non nobis solum."*

What did it mean? I thought better of asking the dragon lady when at length she reappeared to admit me into the courtyard. But what would I say when the Master asked me to discuss the inscription's relevance to college life? It was humbling enough just to be in the presence of the Master of University College, Lieutenant Colonel Angus Alexander MacFarlane Grieve, MC, MA. I stood in the doorway to his room. He looked at me without saying anything. I calculated that through his Coke-bottle glasses I must be much diminished in size. I was not much to start with—five feet seven inches according to the RAF— but I shrank with every passing second. I was probably about twelve inches high when I advanced, braced to babble about Thucydides if he broached the importance of a classical education. He offered a gentle smile.

"Do you row, Evans?"

I'd been in a paddleboat in Rhyl amusement park, but I didn't go into that. I said there had not been much chance of rowing in the RAF, but what a strenuous and exciting sport it was, relying on what I'd seen of oarsmen sweating it out along the Isis in *A Yank at Oxford*. It was as well not to claim knowledge. The Master had been captain of boats when he was at University College as an undergraduate, and he was the author of a history of rowing in Durham. As he discoursed on how well the university's oarsmen had been doing in races on the river Wear, I noticed he wore no socks. I found the incongruity of the formal demeanor and this manifestation of individuality strangely relaxing for all of the five minutes before he ended the meeting. He sent me to see the senior tutor, a physicist and doctor of philosophy: "You will find him on the Norman Gallery. Good morning, Evans. And close the door on your way out."

To reach the Norman Gallery I had to confront the dragon lady again and ask her to point the way. There was a door off the courtyard, then beyond that an obscure crack in an ancient wall leading to a sharp spiral of a very narrow stone staircase. As I climbed, I came upon a tiny paneled doorway in the rock. I knocked. No answer. I waited, knocked again, and waited. I eased the door open, coughed politely, and fell on my knees. It was not a prayerful posture. There were several steps immediately behind the door, catapulting one forward—no doubt some crude Norman's idea of a practical joke. Beyond the steps there was no head tutor. I had stumbled into a toilet.

I returned to the ascent, and the staircase finally opened out on a beautiful gallery of fretted Norman arches and pillars, its windows looking out over the courtyard and gatehouse to the cathedral. I found the head tutor secreted off the gallery behind a big black door with black iron bolts. He was running his hands through his hair, a work of supererogation, since he had none that I could discern in the dim filtered light. He sat reeking cleverness in a wood-paneled room. There was the deliciously musty smell of books and of the dust of centuries of crumbling stone. The cathedral bells tolled the hour and the crucial interview began.

Why did I want to be in Castle (as University College was known)? Why not in St. Cuthbert's Society? What about King's College, Newcastle (then part of Durham University)? I extrapolated about residential college life from those weeks at Holly Royde. Why spend three years away from the headlines? Did I realize how long three years was? What did I think I would get out of Social Studies? Why not an honors course? "Mmm, no Latin, no Latin, eh, well, never mind. You'd learn something, I suppose." What had I learned in the RAF? What books had impressed me? What was I reading now? What did I think of the literary quality of English newspapers? What did a reporter do? What did I consider good writing? I emerged about an hour later and flew over the cathedral: I had been offered a place in Castle for the Michaelmas term just a month away.

Now all I had to do was find the money. I told the ministry the good news. They were equal to the challenge. To qualify for a grant, they now informed me, as well as winning a college place I would have to satisfy them that I was "ex-service" enough, and they asked me to confirm that my RAF service had disrupted an original intention to go to university. They couldn't have hordes of ex–national servicemen suddenly deciding they wanted three years at a university, could they?

It was going to be hard for me to prove my intentions of 1943, especially since I didn't have any then. In a rush, I entreated supporting letters from St. Mary's headmaster Marsland, the head of Brookdale Night School, Loreburn Business College, and the lordly Beavan. The best they could do for me was to testify that I had always wanted to be a journalist, that the RAF had stopped my rise, and that they believed a university education would make me a better man. It was not quite what the ministry had demanded, but I posted these letters and spent hours in Manchester's landmark Central Library collecting any book references on leading editors who had been to college and how Western civilization would collapse if insufficient numbers of newspapermen had a college education.

There were not many, but I sent these, too, and waited.

And waited.

I did my rounds in Gorton. Mum optimistically began knitting a pullover in Castle's colors of maroon and white. I adopted her attitude. I gave notice at the paper. I found a translation of *Non nobis solum:* "Not for ourselves alone." I sent another letter to the ministry.

Ten days before I was to be at the freshman's dinner at Castle on October 10, the day before formal registration, I reminded the Ministry of Oblivion that Durham was expecting me and my trunk was on its way by British Rail. Again, silence. On the day before I was due to leave home, I sent the ministry a telegram in desperation. The next morning Mum finished the pullover. The household was depressed. Nobody knew what to say. The train to Durham was leaving Manchester just after noon. Two suitcases stood in the hall. We fretted on the doorstep. A Post Office boy cycled up the street and stopped at our door asking me to sign for a telegram. It was from the ministry and had the oracular tone of a communiqué from Dumbledore to Harry Potter:

PROCEED TO DURHAM

7

The Sting of Disraeli's Gibe

I proceeded to Durham and my higher education Hogwarts with three pounds in my pocket—and Dumbledore's telegram. It said nothing about a ministry grant for university and college fees, but I presumed the college bursar wouldn't be so ill-mannered as to ask for cash on the nail as soon as I climbed the hill to Castle that night for the first college dinner in Great Hall.

I mingled with the other freshmen, all of us wearing black academic gowns as we stood on the steps of Great Hall, looking out on the courtyard, clock tower, and splendid Norman Gallery. I was convinced that half of them must be baronets. I heard a few ask the defining question of the English class system, "What was your school?" meaning one of the all-male public schools.

At the gong we trooped in to stand by long tables, awaiting the arrival of the top table of dignitaries and dons. I noticed the Master among them; I was to learn he might look forbidding, but he was shy, less happy mingling with the dons than with his Dumfriesshire sheep. It was exalting just standing there, looking up at the fraying battle flags left by the Duke of Wellington when he dined in the college after the Battle of Waterloo. By this stage I would have been disappointed if the grace, read that night by the college chaplain after a bow to the Master, had been in anything other than Latin. Until I knew it off by heart, I learned to listen for the ending, "per Christum Dominum nostrum," and say amen. More challenging was the array of knives, forks, spoons, and glasses at my place. I worked out the etiquette by sly observation of my fellow diners.

Gradually we all thawed out into recognizable human beings, shedding diffidence and self-consciousness. There was not a baronet at our table, and it turned out that a goodly proportion were ex-servicemen. We were an eclectic mix of ambitious undergraduates hoping to become business managers, explorers, schoolteachers, composers, research scientists, industrial chemists, translators of French literature, and, in my case, a newspaper editor. A few were on the way to being vicars, though most of the future parsons were on their knees in St. John's and St. Chad's colleges, located in the shadow of the cathedral. Perhaps the best thing about us was how biologist talked to geographer, music scholar to mathematician, geologist to theologian, chemist to historian. By the time the carafe of port—vintage port!—was passed along the table, we felt we had become Castlemen. The college, and indeed Durham itself, was small and concentrated enough—no more than two thousand students—for the sense of community to be real.

After such a heady first evening I sweated my two suitcases down the cobbled streets all the way through town, past the arches of that spectacular Victorian railway viaduct, and up steep Western Hill to a terrace house where I had been allocated lodgings with six other Castlemen. There were no rooms for freshmen in college that first year. My trunk occupied most of the tiny room I was to share with a music scholar and his cello. Here, too, we brave six had our first encounter with a landlady who liked to catch one of us on the stairs and pin us to the wall with her outsize bosom.

My first lectures on Palace Green took place in old alms-houses under the shadow of the cathedral. The alms location seemed more appropriate the more days passed and I heard nothing about my grant. It was some ten days into college life, when I was down to my last pound, that I found in my mailbox at the Castle Gatehouse a buff envelope marked ON HIS MAJ-ESTY'S SERVICE. My imagination worked overtime as I opened it amid the Castlemen jostling to unload books and shed their gowns for lunch in Hall. Conceivably the letter might say, "Unproceed from Durham; you have been unmasked."

I read it twice before the wonderful news sank in: ex-corporal Evans had been awarded an ex-serviceman's grant of 315 pounds a year for three years—on condition he survived the first-year examinations. With the ministry paying university teaching fees directly, it was enough for living, as well as travel to and from home, though not for all the books on the extensive reading list. Those gaps could be filled in the rambling library on Palace Green.

I took happily to the routine of college life—the lectures, the one-on-one tutorials, the intercollegiate sporting rivalries, the parliamentary debates in the oak-beamed Union Hall, the ritual and ceremony, the black academic gowns billowing in the breeze as we rushed about, the ponderous hum of the still incomprehensible grace in Latin, the solemn processions of dignitaries into the cathedral and castle. The agreeably disputatious political radicals on campus, anticipating the 1960s rebels by a decade, saw college rituals as symbols of reaction and wanted to abolish all ceremony. In the show-off arguments at coffee breaks they explained that if we all turned up for lectures without gowns or refused to stand for grace or boycotted the Union Society debates in favor of political agitation, it would be a blow for the depressed proletariat. And where was I at this historic moment in British history?

I'd thought of myself as a radical eager for reform. To my surprise I recoiled from their brave new world where everything "unnecessary" was to be swept away in favor of a rational new order without ornament or ritual. The best I could muster against the rationalists were naive incantations about how much families enjoyed Easter eggs and Guy Fawkes Night. Why, I argued defensively, "you'll be saying get rid of Christmas next." They hooted with derision: "Commercial exploitation of religious myth!"

I aspired to be a journalist partly because I thought good journalism could identify the consequences of the use of power or the failure to use it for the common good. In 1950, having just read E. S. Turner's polemic *Roads to Ruin: The Shocking History of Social Reform*, I steamed about how "tradition" had been repeatedly invoked to defend the indefensible as it had been in slavery, denying votes to women, sending children into the coal mines, and so on. ("Don't talk to me about naval tradition," Winston Churchill said. "It's nothing but rum, sodomy and the lash.") But what was to distinguish between the customs and traditions I thought benign and those I thought repressive? Had I taken Edmund Burke to heart as well as E. S. Turner, I'd have been better equipped to argue that we should espouse those uses of power that reaffirmed traditional values and resist those that eroded our heritage of a liberal, humanistic society. I'd have cited Burke's remark that the individual is foolish but the species wise, that our common law, the majority's tolerance of minorities, our respect for private property, and even my tolerance in listening to the rebels spout nonsense had all come to us as customs in the trial-and-error evolution of civilization. But I'd yet to hear any lectures on Burke, so such ammunition was not at my disposal.

The vehemence of my sparring partners made me wary of the warriors of cold reason. Years later, I think the Durham encounters gave me a framework of sorts for deciding when we were defending a precious custom and when legal theory was being used to sanctify injustice. The sardonic remark of a French diplomat in a negotiation has stayed with me: "Yes, we agree it will work well in practice, but how will it work in theory?"

My grant dependent on getting through the first-year examinations, I immured myself in the past. In the silent solitude of the library I absorbed the notion of the sanctity of property from John Locke, of free opinion from John Stuart Mill, of free will and the immorality of treating others as a means to one's selfish ends from Immanuel Kant. I recoiled from the mob-rule totalitarianism, as I saw it, of Jean-Jacques Rousseau and found myself at one with Burke again in loathing the mob in the French Terror—my favorite Dickens was *A Tale of Two Cities*—while sympathizing with the revolutionaries in America. It was thrilling to read how the abstractions of Enlightenment philosophies became muscle in the American Declaration of Independence. I got so carried away by that dangerous thing, a little learning, that I offered to give a paper to the pipe-sucking intellectuals in University College's "Read and Weed Club" on the modern relevance of absolutism and determinism in Thomas Hobbes's *Leviathan*. It served me right that my effort reached print in the colleges' newspaper as "Harold Evans talked on hobbies today."

Later, practical experience in journalism made me question and qualify the philosophies I had absorbed like a sponge. I could have questioned them when I sat in my tutorials with the professors of politics and economics. There was Frances Hood, the gaunt head of the department of politics, who was so nearsighted that his nose literally swept along the undulating contours of the handwriting in the essay he was judging;

his utterances in a deep bass voice with a refined Scottish burr fell like mortar shells among my assumptions. There was the diminutive bow-tied Edgar Allen, who created arches with his fingertips while analyzing elaborate economic models, always prefaced with the Latin *ceteris paribus* (meaning he was assuming that other things remained static). There was the darkly handsome Viennese psychologist Dr. Wolfgang von Leyden, the heartthrob of the women undergraduates, who schooled us in the ambiguities of perception. Dr. Peter Bromhead, the owlish authority on political constitutions, challenged me to stay awake long enough to track all the legislative processes of Labour's parliamentary bill nationalizing the gas industry. He returned my report and its labored tabulation with a lot of J's penciled in the margins: "J equals journalese. You can take this as a compliment or not, as you prefer."

Whatever it was that did the trick after I took the first-year examinations, the professors promoted me to the second year of the honors course in politics and economics, though *ceteris paribus* was my only working Latin. The ministry renewed its grant. I'd taken the precaution of working during all the vacations, at Christmas ensuring that the Royal Mail got through hail, sleet, and snow, and at other times writing shorthand instructions to relay to the engineers at Mather and Platt and to drivers at British Road Services. I saved to buy a second-hand Triumph motorcycle — Dad taught me how to handle the beast. It was as well I had wheels, since in the second year the college authorities decreed I was to be rescued from Western Hill and afforded sanctuary in the fourteenth-century fortress of Lumley Castle, Chester-le-Street, fifteen miles from Durham City. Others given rooms at Lumley, after spending the day in lectures at Palace Green, had to suffer a long bus ride, while I raced up the A1 highway into Lumley's thickly wooded parklands in time for tea.

I threw myself into college life that second year. I joined the boat club as a gesture to the Master; I participated in Union Society debates; I ran the half mile for Castle, played squash, and started a Durham University table tennis club. Some of the heavies from the rugby and boat clubs derided "ping-pong" as about the level of tiddlywinks, a weakling's sport not worthy of the sporting honor of the colors we coveted. It made no impression on them at all when I bragged that I'd played in the 1948 English Open championships, the Wimbledon of the sport. I didn't stress that I'd been knocked out in the first round, nor offer my lame excuse that the ball was a bit of a blur because I was nearsighted and too vain to wear spectacles. (My myopia was a weakness cruelly exploited in the men's singles by the French national champion, Maurice Bordrez, who went all the way to the semifinals.) But the issue of whether "ping-pong" qualified as athletic was satisfactorily resolved in Durham by inviting the loudest objectors to play a game where a mix of angled long and short shots had them running round the table until they dropped.

Not surprisingly, in that hectic second year I succumbed to the imperatives of journalism. There was competition among the colleges for one of their own to have the distinction of editing the university's biweekly *Palatinate*, though nobody was rushing to do any of the slog of collecting enough news and putting it in the newspaper. At one point there had been a Union Society debate on the proposition "The journalist is a man who has sold his soul." It had been carried overwhelmingly. From the masthead only three people seemed to be engaged in this activity. I volunteered and was sucked in. It was so time-consuming going round to all the colleges, I gave up coxing a Castle racing four, which was a relief to the crew. During one training session, fiddling for glasses in my pocket as we headed back to the boathouse, I saw my driving license fall in the river and retrieved it only by frantic commands as we drifted into the weir.

I was rewarded for my *Palatinate* industry with the masthead title of assistant editor. This was an inflation of my role, sitting in a cold room in the Union proffering the glue pot to the editor, pasting up his columns into pages, and reading proofs. Nobody could hope to edit the *Palatinate* for long given all the lectures, tutorials, and examinations, but when the editor resigned, I let my name go forward to the owners of the paper, the Student Representative Council (SRC), an elected group of the most active undergraduates and graduates. I was summoned to a meeting to learn that I'd been elected, then was promptly sandbagged: I inherited a newspaper practically bankrupt by the cost of paper and zinc (used to reproduce photographs). What, asked the president of the SRC, did the wizard of Ashton-under-Lyne propose to do about it? Was I going to ask for a bigger subsidy? Hand on heart, I recklessly declared that every journalist worth his salt would never take a penny in any subsidy from anyone because it would compromise his independence. Rhetoric wouldn't pay our bills, so I proposed that we be allowed to increase the price and maybe the advertising rates. Some jibbed at this, urging that it was preferable to reduce the number of pages from ten to eight. "You'll have a job filling them anyway."

It was a proposition I was to hear many times in my newspaper life. Believing then, as I do now, that the way to kill a newspaper is to ask more for less, I pleaded that we should be allowed to charge 33 percent more but go up two pages to twelve. This was rash. I didn't know a thing about newspaper management, but I boasted of my RAF experience in doubling the price of the *Empire Flying School Review*.

The SRC was persuaded to give us a trial, which meant that the three of us committed to the paper had to think very fast to justify the extra pages and the higher price. We concerted our plan of attack: more sports and news, of course, but we'd also introduce features, which meant recruiting more help. We wooed widely among second-year students, varying the pitch a little according to our judgment of the tastes of the quarry. "Look what a spell on the *Palatinate* can do for you," we'd say. "Do you realize who's the chief subeditor of the *Times*?" If that glazed the eyes, we'd try, "And do you know who edits Britain's largest-selling daily newspaper, the *Daily Mirror*? Both Durham men!" We weren't sure that either Reginald Easthope at the *Times* or Silvester Bolam at the *Mirror* had actually worked on the *Palatinate*, but why cloud the issue that Durham men were stars in journalism? There seemed no point either in mentioning that Bolam, a fervent defender of the virtue of tabloid journalism, was currently in prison for documenting the crimes of a vampire murderer before the courts had decided the killer's guilt.

Among our recruits was an undergraduate who displayed an encyclopedic knowledge of the books by Evelyn Waugh in a letter he wrote to the famous author and thereby secured an interview with the writer himself on Waugh's Gloucestershire estate. After alighting at Stinchcombe station he paused to ask directions and by way of thanks explained to the stationmaster the influence of T. S. Eliot on John Betjeman's railway poems. When he arrived at the Georgian mansion, Piers Court, an upstairs sash window opened, and Waugh's angry red face appeared. "You are five minutes late. I will not tolerate rudeness! Good day to you, sir!"

Without our literary scoop, we fell back on a loquacious member of Hatfield College, an irreverent gadfly poet who proposed that he should visit all the Durham pubs within staggering distance of Palace Green to report on how far the natives were friendly and whether their beer was drinkable.

To support this enterprise he required expenses. In justification he wrote, "Around the peninsula lies a permanent challenge to wit and conversation and beneath in its black earth, lies the constant reminder of laughter, bright cups and tinkling glass." We were moved. We gave him a pound of SRC money. Our undercover pub reporter wasn't seen on Palace Green for two whole weeks, but bang on deadline he came into our office bursting with intelligence: Did we know there was a pub over Framwellgate Bridge where you could debate capitalism with Marxist miners? Did we know the one where a leading lecturer suitably primed could be guaranteed to lose all sense of discretion in a vivid dissection of his fellow dons? He confided this intelligence with a flourish: "Amid the smoke-filled air, to the strange sound of one of the most fascinating English dialects and the monotonous clink of the dominoes, the student can indeed say in after years that this is where memory both begins and ends."

I was less moved by the prospect of dominoes than his identification of a hideaway upriver ideally placed for cool refreshment after a long summer punt beneath the willow trees. I made a note of it for a personal campaign. I'd lately been taken with the grace and vivacity of Enid Parker, a biology undergraduate in St. Aidan's Society. I liked the way an apparently gentle question from her punctured hot-air balloons in the gabfests of Union Society coffee breaks. Though she had been seen on campus with a college tennis star, I got in early with a fast service. The moment I learned the date of the elegant garden party Castle staged in the Fellows' Garden in the spring, I passed her a note in the Union. She accepted. Fifteen love to me. I next discovered we had a bond in both being from the north, albeit she was from Liverpool, Manchester's rival. Thirty love. And she liked the ride on the Triumph I gave her. (In those days it was hugely impressive for anyone to have wheels.) Forty love. The punting expedition recommended by our intrepid pub reporter might in due course be game, set, and match. She erred only once in her impeccable judgment that I know of, which was a year later in agreeing to be my wife.

Here are a few extracts from my college diary of these momentous days:

Monday, January 29, 1951: Lots of *Palatinate* copy to edit and an essay to do for tomorrow. Couldn't get out of table tennis match with miners, took bus, still editing copy, then came back to late night at Lumley and finished the essay such as it is.

Tuesday, January 30: Ethics tutorial in Harrison's cat-infested room. He pads about in slippers and flannel bags talking in an Oxford voice about the concept of good. Took notes at evening emergency meeting SRC. Late back Lumley. Copied economics notes before bed.

Wednesday, January 31: Windy bike ride in from Lumley, very tricky. Dashed to Hood tutorial on Hobbes. Did headlines. Noisy college meeting made me captain of athletics. I'm taking on too much! Girl in Union is Enid, Edgar Jones says she goes with Danny F, so forget it.

Thursday, February 1: Missed lecture in the morning, but it was only by the odious man from Cambridge so I didn't miss anything. A little late, too, for tutorial. Page makeup in the afternoon and evening. Hectic. At one point we seemed a page down. Went for a drink. Late at night John Nettleton helped me decide we did have enough for 12 pages. Doors locked, so went down a fire escape with a torch and ran to the printers with page proofs.

The final acquisition for the new *Palatinate* was to find someone to write a gossip column under the pen name Argus. We
knew we had found the right man when he sent in a little note
about one of the prominent Communists on campus, a tough
former shop steward called Michael McVeigh of St. Cuthbert's
Society who was constantly recruiting comrades:

> Mr. McVeigh I understand has changed his lodging due
> to a disagreement with his landlady about the propor-
> tion of water in the milks supplied with his porridge
> each morning. Obviously no Scotsman could be fooled
> on a matter connected with porridge, and for her pains
> the good lady is now no doubt blacklisted by the Com-
> inform. However, even a clash on so fundamental an
> issue hardly explains why he left so quietly as he did,
> and at midnight.

My first issue was published on Friday, February 2, 1951. "*Palatinate* came into the Union coffee bar earlier than I thought it
would. I was in a funk," I learn from my diary. "Had to find
somewhere to hide. I bolted to obscure corner of the library,
had lunch in Lyons in town instead of Castle and read the
paper. Such sensitivity!"

When I summoned up the nerve to venture back on Palace Green, I found we were fast selling out. The new features
were popular, especially "Palace Green Notes" by Argus, and
on page one we had a hot news break. University campuses in
the 1950s were riven by discord about just how serious a menace was international communism. Mao's Communists had
taken over China, Stalin had tried to starve out West Berlin,
Communist North Korea had invaded the South, but even so
our Union Society in 1951 seriously debated the motion "The

United States is as much a menace to world peace as the Soviet Union," and another time voted 2:1 in favor of "We could not conscientiously take part in any future war." America was seen as provocative and dumb for backing Chiang Kai-shek's corrupt Kuomintang regime; Senator Joseph McCarthy and the House Un-American Activities Committee were derided and despised for their witch hunts for "Reds" in Washington and Hollywood. Alger Hiss, we now know, was indeed a Soviet spy, but at Durham then *he* was the campus hero, not the courageous Whittaker Chambers who exposed his betrayal.

It was in this fevered period that Durham's ice hockey team accepted an invitation to take part in the ninth World University Games. The warden of the Durham colleges, Sir James Fitzgerald Duff, and the Academic Council of professors banned the team from going. The official explanation was that the four-day interruption of studies in term time was too much. This was regarded as whitewash. Everyone believed that the real reason was the anti-Communist hysteria of the time. The games were in Poiana, Romania, behind the Iron Curtain. Memory tells me I accompanied our report with a brave and stinging editorial rebuking the Academic Council for its paranoid worry that Durham men could be suborned or bullied into pro-Communist "peace statements": I had tried out for the ice hockey team and had the bruises to testify that they were not deeply interested in peace with anyone. But finding the editorial again now, I see that the roar I imagined was all weasel. "Whatever views may be taken of the attitude of the authorities on this subject," I wrote, "all will welcome a better indication of the extent of undergraduate liberty during term, for we cannot but notice certain inconsistencies in this matter."

In fact, read today almost all my editorials for *Palatinate* were lamentable. They were affected, studded with quotations I'd looked up. A reasonable critique of an SRC vote concluded,

"Perhaps this sounds too much like a homily on democracy or 'that fatal drollery called a representative government....' Can we, though, make ours work a little better and escape the sting of Disraeli's gibe?"

I cringe.

The only editorial I wrote that was any good came out of my baptism of fire in political journalism. The members of the Durham Colleges' Conservative and Unionist Association were always complaining that they did not get enough space in the paper. They were wrong, but the assaults made me acutely aware that an editor had to be, like Caesar's wife, above suspicion. I'd variously been invited to join the Conservative, Liberal, Labour, and Socialist societies. A sixth sense held me back from allegiance to any political party. Two years after graduating I was invited by the Liberal Party in Altrincham, Cheshire, to be its parliamentary candidate in the next general election against the sitting Conservative MP. I felt flattered—and ran a mile in the opposite direction. After my Durham experience, I knew that pinning a party badge on my lapel would make it harder to be seen as unbiased, which by this time I was. (I have to say, though, that I've known many leading journalists who've been party men in both Britain and the United States without it in any way making their work suspect or hindering their rise.)

These were somewhat discomfiting years in terms of class consciousness. When our table tennis team traveled to play against clubs in the mining villages in South Durham, we were disconcertingly regarded as toffs. In town the shopkeepers were deferential to "gentlemen of college," which made me feel fraudulent. And in my third year, living in Durham

Castle itself, I had the privilege of a college servant known as a "scout." I was gloriously accommodated in two rooms on the Norman Gallery, where I'd taken the crucial entrance interview. My rooms looked over the town and down on the terrace, where I could admire the sockless Master doing calisthenics at the crack of dawn. Returning from lectures, I was happy to find my scattered books and papers neatly stacked on my desk, my coal fire ready, and a tray laid for tea with jam and crumpets for toasting. I remained uneasy that the scout was a woman of my mother's age.

I had a precious privacy. From my quarters the door opened not directly on the gallery but on a second door, this one being an inviolate "oak" that could never be opened by anyone, so that the scholar within would not be disturbed while reading. Closing the outer of the two doors was called "sporting the oak," a ritual signaling private study—or a woman visitor arriving for tea. Visitors to our rooms were all clocked in and out by the vigilant dragon lady who had met me at the lodge when I first arrived.

I'd resigned my editorship in good time for the third-year purgatory of finals. I frequently retake those examinations— mad recurring dreams of me staring at the blank paper, wondering who on earth is this David Ricardo to demand rent and what did he have to do with the categorical imperative and question time in the House of Commons and marginal utility and anyway how can it serve the greatest good of the greatest number of people if someone has taken the lovingly long-preserved head of Jeremy Bentham out of his cabinet at University College London? I got through, though. Mum and Dad came early for the graduation, looking long and proudly at the degree notice board on Palace Green to see I headed the "Honors Politics and Economics" list. Their pride was tempered by calculation. My brother Peter recently came across a picture postcard of the cathedral that Mum sent home with just these words: "Harold has had a lot of expense. See if there are any pounds or such like in my club moneybox. Bring it along and the pound out of the brass box in the living room."

I had already started looking for work, writing applications this time on the Castle's red-crested letter paper. At the end of that idyllic summer of 1952, I left Durham with a telegram in my pocket as peremptory as the one from the Ministry of Education that had sent me there three years before:

REPORT MONDAY
Manchester Evening News

8

Stop Press

There had been no individual signatory on the telegram summoning me to the *Manchester Evening News*. I landed in the office of T. E. Henry, the editor in chief, an imposing, beefy presence with forbidding spectacles, a military mustache, and slicked-back hair. He barked into an intercom and passed me like a hot coal to his assistant editor next door, a soft-spoken man who smiled and immediately got on his intercom to summon a tiny man bristling with urgency, who grimaced and hurried me out of the inner sanctum and into the hands of a dapper, bow-tied No. 4.

The pass-the-new-boy game came to a halt in a big room, starkly lit by fluorescent tubes. One end of the room was hectic with reporters lassoed by telephone wires hanging from the ceiling, hotfooting messengers, and banks of copy takers— girls wearing headsets and clacking away on sit-up-and-beg Underwood typewriters. The noise of the newsroom then! Today's tippity-tap at computers, like mice dancing on a keyboard, can never set pulses racing in the same way. At the other end of the floor there was silence. Cigarette smoke drifted from a score of men in shirtsleeves, curled up in prayerful postures before the dominant feature of the room: a schoolhouse clock with big Roman numerals.

These were the paper's subeditors (subs), called copy editors in the United States. I had applied for a job, outlining my reporting experience. The net result of the morning's lightning transactions was that I was to be given a trial—not as a reporter, but as a sub. Everyone knows what reporters do—collect information and write it up in "a story," whereupon it becomes "copy." But nothing reporters write gets into a newspaper without passing through the hands of the subs, the hidden impresarios of news. Subs take pride in translating the complex into the comprehensible, in making sense of conflicting information from divergent sources, in making sure the story fits the space allotted to it, and in writing read-this-or-die headlines. In the first stage of the process, text goes to a sub designated to assess the worth of every story from everywhere—from staff reporters, freelance reporters, and above all the news agencies, notably the Associated Press in the United States and the Press Association in Britain. I'd bet that only a handful of the millions then and now who get their news from newspapers know how much they depend on the sub as the human filter of the torrent of words and pictures from reporters and the wire services. The thirty-two-page *Evening News* got enough information every day to fill five hundred pages. (Today with the Internet, it would be many thousands of pages.)

In British parlance the sub who filters the copy is called the "copy taster," for he must have a palate sensitive enough to differentiate instantly between the fresh and the stale. He will skim maybe 100,000 words in an hour to make the preliminary selection of the best stories. In those days, he impaled the discards on a basic tool of his trade: a sharp metal spike. Nowadays the term "spiked" means that a story has gone into electronic trash.

The copy taster passes his selected stories to the chief subeditor, a Chinese tailor of page design. He fashions page layouts to express a range of priorities and distributes the copy to his gang of subeditors with instructions as to story length and headline size and style.

Subs never know one minute to the next whether the packet of copy coming their way will be a shout or a murmur: a short story requiring a small headline ("Small Earthquake in Chile; Not Many Dead") or a story calling for a front-page thunderbolt: EVEREST CONQUERED or AT LAST THE FOUR-MINUTE MILE. The packet may contain only a few paragraphs, dispatched in a few minutes, or two thousand words to be carefully trimmed to five hundred. The good sub is an artist in economy. The news feed that unedited would make a full column of space is often enough rendered in half that space without losing a single relevant fact or sacrificing good writing. These skills have been but poorly developed in the United States and Canada, where copy editors have been accustomed to grazing on acres of newsprint; in Britain the effect of wartime newsprint rationing put a premium on conciseness. To be described as a "tight sub" in Britain is a high compliment. (The practice I've wearily observed on too many American news desks of simply lopping off the end of an overlong story is an abomination. It assumes that the reporter has assembled the essence of the story in the first paragraphs and that the portion on the spike is impossible to condense.)

Saving space is a necessity in itself, given the cost of newsprint and the prodigious flow of information; but clarity, as much as economy, is at stake. Meaning is fogged when sentences are freighted with unnecessary words—whether in print, in broadcasting, or on the Internet. A good sub would no more hesitate to remove unnecessary words than an engineer would to remove unnecessary parts of a machine. Excess words and abstractions impose on the receiver's time and attention. This morning as I took a walk along the beach at my house in Quogue on Long Island, I checked the weather report on my cell phone. By the time I heard "Abnormal weather conditions resulting in bursts of heavy precipitation are a likely eventuality for the Northeast," it was already raining.

Not surprisingly, reporters everywhere have a lexicon of rude words for the sub. The color and detail on which the reporter labored have to be reconciled with the imperatives of time and space, and subs have to be merciless. They struggle to retain all the details relevant to the central idea of a story, changing the woolly into the concrete: "Provision for increased retail opportunities" becomes "more shops." In addition to all this, the sub also does a score of checks—for grammatical barbarisms, for inner consistency and coherence, for apparent errors of fact, for fairness, for double meanings, for propaganda, for libel, for nonsense: "The truck driver said he was going north when he saw the deceased walk into the road."

All this editing and checking has to be done with an eye on the clock. Kipling biographer and essayist Edward Shanks put it well: "Sub-editors, when I meet them, seem to have only two eyes just like other people; where they keep the other two I cannot say, but I know they must have them." These unlikely supermen may not be very good writers; they may have been undistinguished as reporters. The skills are just different. When I arrived at the *Manchester Evening News*, they were still talking about a young man before me who'd flopped as a reporter. He was too shy to go out into the city and ask questions of people he had never met before. I knew the feeling. He pleaded that instead of being fired, he should be given a chance in the subs room, and from there his rise was meteoric: copy taster; chief subeditor; editor in chief; joint managing director of the whole company; wartime editor in chief of the BBC; director general; and finally Sir William Haley, the much-feared editor of the *Times*, who thundered about moral issues and replaced the classic first page of classified advertising with front-page news.

While plodding round for paragraphs in Droylsden, I'd gorged on the 1944 edition of F. J. Mansfield's *Complete Journalist* and the anecdotage in Fleet Street's *Inky Way* annuals. I loved the photographs of hunched men in cardigans reducing cataclysms to column inches. I knew what daily newspaper subs were supposed to do, but my only practical knowledge of a sub's role had come from seeing scissor-hands Middlehurst at work in Ashton. I did not know then how much British subs are a breed apart, their work more intense and more highly specialized than their apparent counterparts on American newspapers, the copy editors, who are expected to do so much less and rise to the challenge. It remained a question of whether Harold Evans, BA (Honors Politics and Economics), could do it well enough as a greenhorn to survive with the gunslingers on the biggest, fastest, slickest, most profitable, and humdingiest popular regional daily, with its million-plus readers.

The subs' end of the room seemed tranquil compared with the reporters' end. It wasn't. The turmoil was psychic. All the subs, in tight balls of concentration, were too preoccupied to raise so much as an eyelid as Mr. Bow Tie, who turned out to be the day's copy taster, indicated an empty chair at the long table and equipped me with the tools of the trade: spike, glue pot, two pencils, scissors, a galley listing deadline times for every page of the day's editions, a pad of copy paper, and an office book of typefaces. I had no time to open it. The tiny man I'd met in the final sequence of my arrival turned out to be the chief subeditor, Norman F. Thornton, known as "Nifty"—except to the man himself, who froze the room on any suggestion of familiarity. We were all "Mister." Having lost all of ninety seconds in meeting me, he was now emitting steam.

"Boy!" he called. "Boy! Boy!"

The summons was addressed not to me but to one of six teenage copyboys, usually a dead-end job then.

"Mr. Evans, and sharp about it."

I received four folios of teleprinter copy about a mother of five who had won £50,000 on the football pools on her first attempt. Nifty's headline instructions were written on top: "24 xi xi, p.4 Home."

The sub next to me uncoiled long enough to whisper, "Two lines twenty-four-point round here is three pars, no more." From reading the paper I knew its paragraphs were short, two or three sentences at most. From Mansfield I remembered the vital little rules devised for fast newspaper production. Head printers shared the typesetting among scores of Linotype operators; a sub who failed to number and mark every folio would create chaos. I identified my little story with the catch line "Mother," then I numbered every folio — Mother 1 for the headline; Mother 2, 3, and 4 for the text. I marked every folio "xi" for single-column setting, double-ticked the capital letters, circled the periods, indented for new paragraphs, defined the destination and edition on every folio, wrote "mf" (for "more follows") at the end of each folio, and made a double-gated pound sign at the end, so that the printers assembling the story would know not to wait for more. Routine clerical stuff really, but as important as a bank teller being able to count.

More time-consuming was that the story I had been given to edit ran ten paragraphs and had to be contained in three. Clearly, if I couldn't do that by now, I should seek another line of work. But according to the time sheet I had only twelve minutes for text and headlines. I had almost no experience writing headlines. The type book, each line measured off against column widths, told me that at the size of 24-point Century Bold — the standard headline face of the paper — no more than twelve characters, including word spaces, would fit in a single column. Having squeezed the text, I turned to the headline. I tried:

> Mother of five
> has big pools win

No good. "Mother of five" counted out at fourteen characters, and *M* was a wide letter and the second line bust. I fiddled and fiddled. Five minutes left:

> Mother hits
> jackpot

It fit, but it was rather vague.

> Five lucky
> children...

Even vaguer.

With three minutes to go, I had a brain wave. I wrote:

> Mum wins big
> first time

and self-consciously shouted, "Boy!" He scooped up the folios and dumped them in the chief sub's wire basket.

Other subs sent their text straight up to the composing room, but mine had to be scrutinized. It was a relief to hear the "plop!" as Nifty made it vanish up a vacuum tube, but he held back the single folio with my headline written on it. "'Mum' isn't style," he rapped. "Mum! We're not the *Daily Mirror*."

He might as well have told the room I had syphilis. How

the hell was I to know what the office style was? They hadn't given me the house stylebook. In a blink, Nifty scribbled his own headline. When the galley proofs came down, I saw what he had written:

Mother's big
pools win

By now I was deep into copy bundles piling up in front of me for the next edition. Help! It was only fifty minutes away. My desk was right under the schoolhouse clock. Out of the corner of my eye, I caught the blur of a mustache in motion. It adorned the upper lip of the editor in chief—Mr. T. E. Henry, Mr. Tom Henry, "Big Tom." As razored mustaches go, it was not exceptional, but it was spotlighted by two patches of high color in his complexion, the whole ensemble lending urgency and authority to the words issuing forth as he strode without pause through the subs room, his slipstream buffeting a retinue of assistant editors and copyboys, and often the excitable photo editor trying to get him to glance at a print. A herd of wild elephants could not have caused more commotion. A few minutes later the intercom buzzed. Nifty sprang to it. Everyone sat up. "Who the hell," asked the harsh voice reverberating through the squawk box, "who the hell subbed this twenty-four-point that's as long as Cross Street?" It was Big Tom speaking from the stone—the composing room where all the type was assembled in iron frames (chases) laid out on flat stone tables. It wasn't my 24-point; it was someone else's, whose text had run to five paragraphs and would not therefore fit the three-paragraph space Nifty had allocated for it on his neat page plan. The excess paragraphs were a double waste of time—for the Linotype operator and the editor overseeing the page to press. Simply discarding those lines in hot metal might also discard a key point, even the basis for the headline, yet there might not be time to have the galley reset. Nifty choked on his anger.

The erring sub shriveled in his chair. You could feel the room stiffen every morning when Big Tom swept through on his way to the stone for the first edition, catapulting commands and lobbing questions, answers to which were shouted back as if they were grenades about to explode. We all dreaded the sound of "Darth Vader" on the squawk box. His wrath fell on anyone who wrote a politically slanted headline, a commonplace on other dailies, left and right. He was insistent on the unbiased presentation of news — so long as it did not concern the Manchester United football club, which occupied a different universe of gods and supermen. (When they lost 5–1 one Saturday, Big Tom was inspired to write: "United in Six-Goal Thriller.")

The tendency in the newsroom, cowed by the intercom blasts, was to regard Big Tom as a vulgarian. He'd risen through subbing sports, for Pete's sake. He chomped on a cigar. He wore red braces and spotted bow ties. His voice was hoarse. The two editors before him, ice-cold Haley and the glossy John Beavan, were accomplished writers with the air of university dons. "Had an excellent weekend, thank you," Haley would say. "Read eight books and reviewed three of them." Tom gave himself no intellectual airs, but he was an organizer of genius. For the big scheduled events like the presentation of the national budget, six or seven foolscap sheets from his office would tell forty individual subs and reporters precisely what they were to do at 3:10 p.m., 3:15 p.m., and 3:50 p.m. Subs assigned to the stone with him hated to admit it, but they were in awe of his speed and skill, his relentless drive to get the paper out on time. He had no equal. Printers loved his decisiveness and expertise. Gothic heads emerged from the Ludlow machine seconds after he had scrawled a banner that fit perfectly. Like all good stone men, he would read the story in mirror image, cut it, change a dumb headline, and issue boil-in-oil curses on its writer.

At the end of that first week I was shaking, not at all sure I would make the grade. On Monday morning I got in bright and early. Bow Tie was already at his desk, spruce in a white shirt, sleeves rolled up, two shiny spikes ready for the day's torrent of copy. "It's hard for you as a novice from a weekly," he reflected between satisfying puffs of Churchman's in his pipe. "Not to worry. A lot of subs from the dailies who come just can't take the pressure here, no sir, just can't hack it."

Nifty, he kindly informed me, kept a book of the comings and goings, which showed that in four years ninety-four subs had joined and left the paper, some sacked on the spot, most running for the exit. That was close to one departure every two weeks, which meant that by the law of averages another head was due to roll. Mine, I feared.

Nothing before, and nothing I have experienced since, working for newspapers, radio, television, and Web sites in London and New York and Washington, matches the speed demanded of everyone on the *Evening News*. Newspapers were the way millions got their first inkling that we had been invaded by men from Mars; there were no cheap transistor radios, cell phones, or Internet sites then.

Reporters and subs had to operate like a souped-up Internet news service, producing eight editions in six hours—more if big news broke—and without the crutch of desktop computers. We had trains to catch and vans to race into the suburbs. In the words commonly (but mistakenly) attributed to the Confederate lieutenant general Nathan Bedford Forrest in the American Civil War, we were desperate to be "fustest with the mostest." The crowds on the city streets had to carry home the *Evening News* rather than the hated *Manchester Evening Chronicle*, our direct challenger. Both papers wrote "contents bills"—news placards designed like the bikini to titillate but not satisfy: SEX TRIAL SHOCKS.

As the two evening newspapers slugged it out, hundreds of other reporters, critics, feature writers, subs, and photographers were competing like mad to beat us and everyone else. Manchester was Newspaper City. Six million people in the north of England got their news through Manchester. Daily and Sunday, no fewer than twenty-six newspapers were written, edited, and published within a couple of square miles of the four central railroad stations.

The twenty-four-hour inner city simply throbbed with news day and night in the newsrooms and all the smoky watering holes where journalists and compositors loved to gossip, keep an ear out for any clue to what their rivals were up to, and uniformly agree that the gritty northern editions of their newspapers were much superior to those put out by their effete bosses in Fleet Street.

Every day on the way to work I had to walk by the embattlements of the enemy in Withy Grove, a rabbit warren a few yards from Victoria station where three thousand people in Europe's biggest printing plant produced twelve papers, including the *Evening Chronicle*, the *Daily Telegraph*, the *Daily Mirror*, the *Daily Dispatch*, the *Sporting Chronicle*, and three Sunday papers; from Deansgate, out rushed the delivery vans of the *Daily Mail* and *People*; the trade unions' *Daily Herald* was tucked away on the other side of the railway tracks in Chester Street; and to the west rose the glass black Lubyanka, where the slickest of the slick produced the *Daily Express* and *Sunday Express* for Lord Beaverbrook (William M. Aitken), the press baron for whom the phrase "whim of iron" was invented.

The *Guardian*—then proudly named the *Manchester Guardian*—and the *Evening News* were both owned by the Scott Trust. We had offices on different floors and separate composing rooms, but we shared the presses and the cafeteria. (With a nod to liberal principles, company chairman Laurence and his brother Charles shared the same meat-and-potatoes menu.) At the lunch table where the *Guardian* editorial people tended to assemble, you'd find the gentle Bill Weatherby; Bob Ackerman, an American intern from Brown University who decided he would rather dissect the brains of chimpanzees as a neurologist in Boston; and a pale, emaciated new reporter with a lupine smile, who amazed us by saying how entertaining that morning's proceedings of the North West Gas Board had been. The gas moguls were not amused by his report in the *Guardian,* but the experience was great training for becoming Michael Frayn, playwright and novelist. I was entranced to hear that Frayn, another Cambridge alum, had learned Russian so as better to appreciate its literature, a linguistic accomplishment that catapulted him into journalism. He was approached to become a spy and made up his mind on a newspaper career instead when Control—or whoever, maybe Alec Guinness as Smiley—laid a venturesome hand on his thigh. The North West Gas Board paid for the indiscretion.

At the *Manchester Evening News,* we always liked to show Newspaper City how we could turn on a dime. Of course, delivering news by casting it in hot metal took an age compared with transmitting it electronically, but it was the rush of the raw editing time that was so taxing. It was not uncommon for our subs to be physically sick from the tension. In the second week I felt so queasy that I made lunch a boring glass of milk, forsaking the corned beef sandwiches Mum had put in my raincoat pocket. Nifty gave each of us only twenty minutes for lunch anyway; if during the day we got up to go to the toilet, more copy would be piled up for our return as punishment for indulging human weakness.

The survivors around me were all used to the sound of gunfire. The artist who drew our maps had been a lieutenant in the Royal Naval Volunteer Reserve. His Japanese captors had made him kneel for a beheading, then changed their minds and chopped off an arm instead. Bob Gibbons, the soft-spoken sub who had rescued me from letting that first story run too long, had been a tank commander, decorated with a Military Cross for battlefield bravery (a fact discovered only when a buff envelope crested ON HIS MAJESTY'S SERVICE was left on his desk on his day off). A sub who came and went every day without saying a word to anyone had been a bomber pilot, badly shot up over Düsseldorf. A vehement blond man with a black eye patch had lost his eye in the army but was still a quicksilver sub. The amiable Bow Tie, who looked like such a dandy—he came to work every day in yellow gloves and for the 1956 Suez invasion turned up in a pith helmet—had for four years been Quartermaster Duncan Measor on the destroyer *Hotspur,* dropping depth charges on U-boats in the Atlantic. Nifty himself had been a regimental sergeant major. He expected everything to be done on the double and without complaint. In that spirit, on the occasion when he rammed discarded copy on his spike and the spike went right through his palm, he uttered no cry of pain. He simply took out the spike and picked up more sheafs of copy from Bow Tie, who was a kindly man but knew Sergeant Major Thornton too well to express sympathy.

Nifty was the fastest and best sub and layout man in the room, and I daresay on the planet; his instructions on copy, written at speed, could be read by a man on a galloping horse. He was also a tight-lipped disciplinarian. No banter, no jokes, gentlemen; keep your heads down; get the copy out. He had a watertight memory. When a story ran through two or three news cycles, he knew precisely which elements were fresh. A sub might be rebuked, "Wake up! That headline was the page-four lead in the *Express* this morning." The subs took these chastisements quietly; Nifty was always right.

We might as well have been on a spaceship, receiving signals from all over the world but stuck in our chairs, hermetically sealed off from the daily life of a vibrant city. In the mornings, having memorized all the headlines I could from half a dozen dailies on the train from Failsworth, I walked with the city crowds, inhaling the aromas of French cheese and Latin American coffee seeping out of the cellars of the wholesale houses along the damp streets near the cathedral. It was the nearest I'd get to foreign parts for some time. At the blackened Victorian building in Cross Street near the corner of bustling Market Street where the tramcars stopped, there'd always be a gaggle of people pausing to look at our news pictures in the display windows of the front office, a matter of pride when I'd edited the captions. I'd pause to savor a little romance. Here was where the legendary *Manchester Guardian* editor C. P. Scott ("facts are sacred, comment is free") jumped off his bicycle every day, having ridden the three miles from his home at The Firs, Fallowfield, and back again at night, a practice he continued until he was past eighty. Here, in January 1932, the crowds stood ten deep for his funeral cortege. Here, too, is where Neville Cardus, a bastard son of a prostitute from a Rusholme slum, came to gaze up at the *Guardian*'s lighted windows, dreaming he might one day write for the paper. And eventually he did, gloriously, as the doyen of cricket and music critics.

In the first weeks I was happy to take home a paper to show off the stories I had edited. But they weren't much, little single-column efforts. The family was nice about it but clearly baffled by my sense of achievement. No, I hadn't written anything really, I'd say, not like for the *Ashton-under-Lyne Reporter*. But you see this story and this one, well I edited them, and they all caught the page in time, and you should have seen what they were like before I did the editing.

Two months into the work I was being trusted with inside-page leads and was officially taken on the staff. But I became jealous of the aristocracy at the subs table, the three or four "top-table" subs who were given the really big stories and made it seem effortless. One of them, the unflappable Bill Lloyd, edited while he lay back in his chair like a nonchalant Battle of Britain pilot awaiting the siren, his pencil, with a life of its own, gliding over the copy and oozing headlines. If only I could take home a front-page splash I had edited! When there was a loud bang on the shutter between the subs and the wire room, indicating the arrival of a "rush," some kind of sensation, I'd sit up like a puppy dog, tongue out for a juicy bone. Nifty would look round and invariably award the prize—"Rush this, please, ninety-four-point Gothic caps"—to Mr. Lloyd, Mr. Finnegan, Mr. Futrell, Mr. Batchelor. He might as well have announced, "To anyone but Mr. Evans."

He was correct in that judgment. I was in the right place as a down-table sub. I still made mistakes in the endless rush, sending up two folios numbered four, writing a headline that didn't fit, one day taking three minutes too long to squeeze the best juice out of a complicated court case. Big Tom had to rewrite one of my Saturday sports headlines when the Port Vale soccer team beat Chester. My headline was a succinct summary of the play, but the comps fell about with laughter when they set it in metal before Big Tom: "Port Vale Thrusts Bottle Up Chester." Nifty's punishment for infractions was a rain of "K's"—the three-line fillers at the ends of columns which required a headline in small bold caps, meaning there were too few letters to do more than grunt. It was Chinese water torture all day: drip, drip, drip. Someone recognized that my soul was in torment. Every week two or three of the editorial staff were handed books for review. The others got histories and novels. Not me. The first one on my desk was

Eclipse of God by Martin Buber. ("All journeys have secret destinations of which the traveler is unaware.") The following weekend I had to devote myself to studying Paul Tillich's *Systematic Theology,* and the third was consumed by two sledgehammer volumes on the philosophies of the East and West. I was a marked man.

When the big day came, it was more than I'd bargained for. At 8:25 a.m. the wire room shutter banged, signaling a rush story. Nifty shouted, "Boy! Mr. Evans!" I was sharpening a pencil. A single Press Association folio landed on my desk.

RUSH 1
Train
TRAIN CRASH 8.19 XXXXX IN FOG XXX PASSENGER
TRAIN IN STATION XXX

Oh, no, please not Dad! But I'd no time to fret. "Rejigging page one," Nifty called to the room, giving instructions for new displays. And to me: "Crash for lead replate at nine."

A boy gave me Nifty's folio of instructions for head and text setting.

8:38: Another folio:

RUSH: TWO TRAINS LONDON MIDLAND REGION COLLIDE HARROW WEALDSTONESTONE STATION. COACHES PILED UP. WRECKAGE BLOCKS LINE. FOG. AMBULANCES. FIRE BRIGADES POLICE RUSH TO SITE.

Not Dad's region. More folios followed, in summary:

8.40: Express from Perth with four sleeping cars ran into back of local on fast line. Est sixty miles an hour.

8.41: *Local Tring-Euston train nine coaches stopped at Harrow-Wealdstone station for minute-plus, running seven minutes late in fog....Rear coaches telescoped by impact of Perth express. People still on platform scythed down. Unknown numbers trapped inside wreck....*

8.46: RUSH RUSH
One minute after primary crash, wreckage hurled across adjacent tracks derails two engines pulling Euston-Manchester-Liverpool express approaching at 60 mph. No word of casualties....

So now we had three trains in a wreck—two express trains and one local in which an unknown number were trapped in smashed coaches.

8:54: Four minutes to deadline. I'd translated the cryptic rushes into sentences and sent the story to the printer. The banner was easy: THREE TRAINS IN HIGH SPEED COLLISION. Second deck: "Many feared trapped in coaches."

8:58: I'd made the edition, but now an important nugget came two minutes to deadline: *Police: Casualties bound to be heavy on Tring train. Twenty bodies on stretchers.*

"Boy!" I yelled at the same instant I marked the folio for a bold flash intro and wrote a new substitute head that Nifty accepted: TWENTY DEAD IN EXPRESS PILE-UP.

I was feeling pleased that I was keeping up with the pace of the inflow but suffered remorse the instant the page had gone to press. I'd presumed "bodies" meant people who were no longer alive, but...

9:02: *Twenty bodies unconfirmed dead. Repeat unconfirmed dead.*

Nifty brushed aside my concern. He was already calling instructions for the next edition in fifty-eight minutes.

"Streamer cross eight twice ninety-four point. Second deck thirty-six point cross four. Close ten o'clock. Let it run."

9:05: I killed all the type from the first edition and started to compose a new story from all the fragments.

> 9.06: *The station foreman assXXXX assigned igned to count passengers for rail census says, "I counted 332 passengers coming down the stair from the footbridge. God knows what's happened. I heard terrific noise and screams."*

9.06: RUSHFULL
Twenty now confirmed dead. Police say total likely higher. Names withheld pending notification of next of kin.

> 9.07: *Rescuers trying to reach Driver of Perth express R. S. Jones and Fireman C. Turnock of Crewe North Sheds. Buried somewhere under mountain of twisted iron Rescue crane due 9.40*

> 9.09: *Loudspeakers command quiet so rescuers can listen for cries from the trapped passengers under the mountains of twisted iron.*

The separate folios, a sentence on each, were falling like snowflakes in a blizzard, mixing the urgently important, the relevant, the repetitive, and the disposable:

> 9.09: *Harrow-Wealdstone 11 miles from Euston. Six tracks for 17 miles....*

> 9.12: *Witness: "We came up on the local line, then crossed to the express line. Our train was packed. We hadn't shut door of our coach. There was one hell of a crash. Our train leaped off the ground. We were hurled against one side of the*

compartment. Then another engine flashed by in the opposite direction. It was a nightmare."

9.16: *Guard J. Kent in rear Perth Express survived. Linked up with Perth express Driver Jones at Crewe. Jones told him had difficulty backing new engine onto train in fog. Express running 32 minutes late, would do best to make up times.*

9.17: *Minister of Transport heading to scene.*

9.17: *Driver Perkins Manchester-Liverpool Express killed in derailment.*

9.18: *Worst train crash 22 May 1915. Troop train collided with passenger train at Gretna Green, Scotland. 227 killed.*

9.20: RUSH: *Electric train from Watford headed into wreckage scattered across electric line but stopped by alert signalman switching off current. British Rail keeping him secluded. Said to be shaken.*

9.21: *Tring train passenger in ambulance: "The most terrible thing is the screams coming out of the middle of the great heap of the wreckage from the poor devils trapped inside."*

9.25: *Injured Perth express survivor in hospital: driver must have run through signals. Must have been drunk.*

9:30–9:40: Half an hour to deadline. I edited the first half-dozen folios into a sequence, trying to make the story flow and writing cross headings every four or five paragraphs, taking note of my numbered folios, holding back the intro for the hardest and latest news. I set aside the allegation about the driver. Not because of family ties. How did the survivor know? The driver was still in the wreckage.

9.40: *Lucky escape Guard W. H. Merritt of Tring train along train to his van at rear said heard express approaching at speed and dived under coping of platform, then ran to signal box to sound alarm to close all lines.*

9.43: *Express sleeping car attendant says brakes went on hard seconds before crash. None of sleeping car passengers hurt.*

9.44: *All the station clocks stopped at 8.19*

9.45: *Firemen climbing 40 ft into piled-high twisted debris. Score of stretchers laid across tracks. Coach and wreckage jammed under station footbridge.*

9:50: "Five minutes to close," called Nifty. "Banner, please."

I'd now written a lead paragraph on twenty confirmed dead in a three-train collision. No sooner had it left my hand than a new flash landed:

9:51: *Total thirty-one bodies pulled out of Tring train wreckage.*

I wrote a new intro, marked it as substitute for the intro just sent ("substitute" meant the earlier one had to be thrown away), and warned the stone.

9:59: A minute before deadline I gave Nifty the banner: THIRTY-ONE DEAD IN EXPRESS CRASH.

Nifty had replanned the page for noon. A crude diagram showed the paths of the three trains on two lines. There were picture captions to write, new headlines for a jump to the back page to report names of the dead—including a Manchester Queen's Counsel—miracle rescues, interviews with the hundred-plus in hospitals, the arrival of bigger cranes, and now, if I wanted, I could use a new Press Association lead reconstructing the crash with descriptive writing: Hundreds, six deep, chatting and reading newspapers as they waited for the tube across from the doomed Tring platform, "suddenly heard the roaring and vibration of an approaching express, the shriek of a whistle, the hiss of steam. Before horror could shape itself upon the faces of the crowd, they saw the express from Perth smash into the rear of the waiting train and in that eerie frozen moment of horror there came from the direction of Manchester the thunderous pounding of the express from Manchester gathering speed into the wreckage."

I subbed the best of the new material into yet another version of the story for the noon edition. So it went all day: edit this, spike that, change this, number that, check the number, insert a paragraph here, delete a paragraph overtaken, shout for a proof, mark it and send it back…and watch the clock. I was oblivious to all the activity in the subs room, utterly immersed in a story changing every minute, writing and rewriting the narrative, waiting for the last seconds for the final headline, heart pounding, praying that what I was rushing into metal read well. By the final edition the news was much bigger than it had begun. At 4:00 p.m. I wrote the Late Night Final edition banner:

75 KNOWN, 110 FEARED DEAD IN RAIL DISASTER
Full platform "scythed": Children trapped hours

The Harrow-Wealdstone disaster, my baptism of fire, was the worst crash since 1915: 122 people died. The official inquiry concluded that express driver Jones had died on impact, and so had his fireman. The signalmen were exonerated, so the explanation offered was that Jones, a healthy experienced driver of forty-three who knew the road, had almost certainly not reduced speed when taking the train past a distant signal showing yellow for caution. He passed two "not very conspicuous" semaphore signals at danger, running through "a deceptive patch of denser fog."

Even with a computer today, that kind of fast-changing, multisourced news report is tricky to handle; with hot metal it was the supreme test of a news sub. My anxiety was whether I had passed. The next morning I opened an envelope on my desk. It was from Big Tom. "To mark your excellent work yesterday I am putting you down for one pound [about $116 today] special work bonus." My euphoria was such that I have kept the note all these years.

Thereafter I got a fair share as a top-table retailer of disaster: floods, a ship drifting packed with explosives, a plane crash, a building collapse. I told myself that four months into the job, I was almost up there with the aristos. Then I was pitchforked into page design and thought again. Late every afternoon, when everyone else was putting on his coat to head for home or pub, one sub stayed late as editor of the "Star" edition. This was the first edition the next day. The Star editor had to lay out and sub five or six inside news pages for the early shift of printers. The first edition, with a newsy front page and runners at various horse tracks, could then be on the street before noon. "Here you are then, Mr. Editor," said Bow Tie, depositing a bundle of timeless agency copy, photographs, and layout sheets. "Make the pages sing! Good night."

The reporters' room was empty. The tea trolley was cold. Within an hour the cleaners had coped with the day's debris, and I was alone with a lubricious library girl. She swayed over for a chat but quickly decided that filing old clippings was more exciting than my impromptu exegesis on the challenges of page design. I laid out pyramids of headlines on top of one large photograph and one small, with a boxed panel and text stretching over three columns, descending into two columns one inch deep and then into a single column. It was an arresting new look for the *Evening News*. It was also utterly unworkable, a jigsaw that would not fit together unless the relevant words in text and headlines once cast in hot metal matched exactly the number of lines the layouts required. I also discovered how little I really knew about scaling a photograph for the engravers so that it would occupy exactly the space I'd allotted in the layout. As for a fancy enlargement of the second photograph, I hadn't a clue how to work out the scale for that. (It seems very unfair that today the calculation is done by the computer before you can say George Eastman.) I was in the middle of exasperated fiddling with the photograph, hunched over a light box, when a lovely soft voice said, "Still here? Like to come to the Opera House when you're done?" Ah! The library girl, a second chance! No, it was a perfect entry, stage left, by Denys Futrell, a sunny plump sub obsessed with the theater and Yorkshire cricket, who had come back on his day off to pick up tickets from the news editor's desk. In his evenings away from Nifty's lash, he directed amateur theatricals and wrote innumerable reviews. I showed him my comic opera of a page. "Trying too hard, old lad, trying too hard," he said with a sigh. "Till you get the hang of it, just copy some layouts from other days. Nobody in Ancoats is going to complain that they've seen that layout before." He showed me how to measure the enlargement, then headed off to the more satisfying drama of Ibsen's *A Doll's House*. "You should be through in an hour. I'll leave your ticket at the box office," he said.

Denys needed plenty of time to get there, handicapped as he was by a clubfoot resulting from a childhood accident, after which his leg had been badly reset, but I had no chance of catching up with him. I did as he suggested, subordinating originality to sanity, but I still had to sub all the copy, write all the headlines and captions, and do it all over again for four more pages. They were just about ringing down the curtain at the Opera House when I crawled up to the composing room with the copy and layouts for the Star edition. Next day nobody complained that the layouts had been seen before.

Eventually I became a fast page designer. A few months

later when I was again the Star editor, my diary affirms I was home at 7:30 p.m., in time for Radio 3's broadcast of Mozart's "Coronation Mass," and a week later "a furious attack" on the Star pages had me out of the office at 6:00 p.m., impelled to catch a 6:30 train to Leeds with a big backpack loaded with tent, blankets, ground sheet, and Primus stove. I had inveigled Enid Parker, then teaching at a Quaker progressive school in the Yorkshire village of Wennington, to realize that her biology teaching would be much enhanced if she camped with me in the Yorkshire dales. (We married a year later.) Beyond that attraction, I also took any chance I could to get out of the city, walking the vales of Derbyshire and climbing the moorlands to Kinder Scout with other subs gasping for clean air.

The first year of subbing on the *Manchester Evening News* was a companionable roller-coaster ride. In the second, I was restive. I more and more lived for the big days. In the summer of 1953 we were all keyed up for the coronation of Queen Elizabeth II. Everybody was. The *Guardian* got in trouble for publishing a cartoon by David Low which mildly questioned the millions of pounds to be spent on the proceedings, while its historian David Ayerst noted the "quasi-religious fervor" sweeping the country. Certainly the community spirit was infectious. Across the city and into the suburbs, streets were outdoing each other in profusions of Union Jacks and red-white-and-blue bunting; mothers and grandmothers in pinafores with buckets and soap were on their knees scrubbing even the pavements so they'd glisten for the street parties on Tuesday, June 2. Everybody in these streets knew each other: "Flo is good for sausage rolls. Jill will ice the cake."

The excitement at the *Evening News* was in preparing to outdo the *Manchester Evening Chronicle* and the dailies with a souvenir issue. (The excitement would have been even more intense if we had known the British conquest of Everest would become known the same day.) Nifty took me aside the weekend before the Tuesday. He confided, "You have been handpicked for our special edition." He said no more about my anointment, but I knew at once I was going to be asked to comment on the significance of the crowning. At home that weekend, I read Walter Bagehot's essay on monarchy and made notes on the role of religion and the history behind each ceremonial act in the crowning. Big Tom's multipage battle plan, circulated on the Monday, described other intents. Photo captions: H. Evans.

I was deflated. It was actually an important job on a coronation edition filled with pictures, but I had already begun to wonder whether Michael Hides had been right in our Ashton-under-Lyne days that reading Hobbes and Keynes was all very well but irrelevant to getting on in newspapers. There was a common feeling, too, that the painstaking act of subbing to save words ruined the fluency for writing. "Show me a good sub, and I will show you a dead writer" was the newsroom's jaunty challenge, not so much directed at me as at all the subs who kept threatening to write novels. On the day there was a surprise cut in the Bank Rate, everybody had an opinion about what it meant for the average man in Manchester. I sulked that nobody asked me. When I finally volunteered a paragraph I'd written, it was brushed aside as too late and too complex. Doubtless it was both those things. Another day I fretted at the London political correspondent's analysis of the annual economic survey. I thought we could do better and said so. A diary entry records the fallout: "It was a mistake to speak of Bank Rate, etc. to colleagues. They will only think of me now as a know-all." When I was given the splash that the new Tory government was going to break the BBC monopoly by permitting commercial television, Bill Lloyd ribbed my pretensions, calling out, "What's Aristotle got to do with it?"

The frustrations came to a head when my newspaper—

which is how I thought of it—joined the chorus endorsing the death sentence for an illiterate youth for a murder he had not committed. Sydney Silverman, the tiny, silver-haired Labour member of Parliament, a passionate abolitionist, was leading the protests. "Silverman is only doing this for personal publicity," declared Big Tom out loud on his quick way through the subs room. He was not inviting a discussion; he was venting. The sub opposite me protested by repeatedly jabbing his cigarette stub in the ashtray. I shared his feeling.

Derek Bentley, the condemned youth in the cell, was a weak-willed nineteen-year-old who had suffered a head injury from V-1 rocket debris and was judged to have a mental age of eleven. His pal Christopher Craig was sixteen, but he was brighter—and he'd carried a gun the night the pair had tried to burgle a warehouse. Four policemen cornered them on the roof. One policeman caught Bentley. He made no attempt to escape, even though the policeman had been shot in the shoulder by Craig, who, still free, kept firing and shot Police Constable Miles dead. Craig was undoubtedly guilty of murder, but he was spared the death sentence on account of his age. Lord Chief Justice Goddard—"the hanging judge" to his critics— ignored the jury's recommendation of mercy for Bentley. Parliament was not allowed to debate whether Bentley deserved to hang until he had been. Silverman called for the home secretary, Sir David Maxwell Fyfe, to make a recommendation of mercy to the Queen. Silverman had the support of two hundred MPs, but the home secretary turned them down.

Though Mum and Dad were not opposed to capital punishment, as I was, they could not understand why Bentley should be the one to die. I was empowered to go to the public phone booth at the end of the street and dictate a family telegram to the home secretary. I followed up with a letter in the *Guardian*, which did not meet with universal approval around the subs table. "Why do you think you know better than the people in authority?" asked Jimmy Entwistle, one of the most capable and charming men on the newspaper. Bentley went to the gallows on January 28, 1953. Forty-five years later, three Court of Appeal judges quashed the conviction on the grounds of misdirections to the jury by the "intemperate" and "blatantly prejudiced" Goddard. Lord Chief Justice Thomas Bingham said that Bentley had been denied "that fair trial that is the birthright of every British citizen." Craig, age sixty-two and long out of jail, having served ten years, said, "I am truly sorry that my actions on 2 November 1952 caused so much pain and misery for the family of P.C. Miles, who died that night doing his duty. A day does not go by when I don't think about Derek and now his innocence has been proved with this judgment."

Six months after my family telegram of protest, my diary tells me I abandoned my scruples about the death penalty. "John Reginald Halliday Christie," I wrote, "forfeited the right to be treated as a human being. Seven murders and an innocent man executed!" The innocent man was Timothy Evans (no relation), who a decade later was to haunt my first editorship.

Fortunately, for everyone's peace of mind on the paper, I found an outlet for the didactic impulses I never knew I had: I volunteered to be an evening tutor on politics and economics for the Workers' Educational Association, founded in 1903 to help adults who had missed out on education. Twice a week that October, after the day's subbing, I took a bus ride into Tyldesley, near Bolton in Greater Manchester, crossing a darkened playground to a schoolhouse where a gallant group sat at children's desks: retired coal miners, clerks, a watchman, a sprinkling of housewives, and a couple of shopkeepers. There were never more than sixteen of them. I had an idea that the room would soon be packed when word got around that I was lighting the sky; it didn't happen. Two dropped out in the second week and another in the third week. If this went on, I'd have no class.

The survivors were embarrassed by the defections. They were so nice, trying to put me at my ease, but I'd missed a trick. I'd not engaged them. They'd lived much of the interwar political and economic history I proposed to teach. They'd seen the thuggish behavior of the Blackshirts of Oswald Mosley, the incitements in the Jewish area of Cheetham Hill. Mosley was a Manchester man; one of the main thoroughfares was Mosley Street. He'd had his second wedding in Joseph Goebbels's house in Berlin, and Hitler had been the best man. So I made the evenings more of a discussion than a lecture. It took more preparation, not less, to plot a kind of sub-Socratic question-and-answer dialogue that led somewhere, but the classes got livelier. Short-changed by the education system, just like my father, the group was touchingly eager to explore—but not uncritical. One of the housewives and a storekeeper, in alliance, were not convinced (nor was Mrs. Thatcher years later) that in the Great Depression they'd lived through, the government should have increased spending instead of sticking to balanced budgets: they had to stay in the black in their household accounts, why shouldn't government? They attended the twice-weekly classes in all kinds of weather—one dropout even came back—and they all signed up (with newcomers, too) for a second year. At the end of the course, they took up a collection to buy me a going-away present of an *Oxford English Dictionary*, which I still cherish fifty years later.

In truth I was in their debt. Face-to-face, I'd been made to appreciate what schoolteachers learn painfully but journalists behind a shield of print rarely do: transmitting information is easier than creating understanding. For me it was a step toward grasping the art of popular explanatory journalism.

I was not able to teach a third year. Big Tom had a better idea.

9

Why Aren't Their Women Wearing Our Frocks?

Late on Friday, December 18, 1953, just as I was putting the lid on the messy glue pot to head home, the editor's secretary dropped an envelope on my desk. I'd seen Big Tom stride out of the office in his cashmere overcoat, cigar between his teeth, and a copyboy trailing behind with an armful of books. I sliced open the envelope. The letter was headed PRIVATE AND CONFIDENTIAL, underscored in red.

It was good news. "My dear Evans," the three-page letter began, "I feel quite sure in my own mind that you are qualified to have a shot at the job of Evening News Editorial Writer, and I want you to take up duties for a trial period of three months. In the first place your salary will be increased to 14.10.0 pounds per week plus Cost of Living bonus."

My old paranoid instincts fastened on the phrase "in my own mind." Did it imply everyone else thought he was off his head? But he went on: "I will now develop one or two matters arising from this appointment."

I'll say.

He acknowledged that there would be "a great deal of political and economic reading"—no more novels on the weekend, only the *Economist, Hansard Parliamentary Debates,* and Chatham House reports. I was also to get out of the office and interview Labour, Conservative, and Liberal organizers; MPs in their constituency clinics; councilors; and anyone who might lead me to a story. "Do not forget the political leaders outside Manchester, say in Altrincham, Knutsford, and other divisions. Never let up on them. Follow and probe indefatigably; keep stories flowing and watch for good tips for Mr. Manchester's Diary. I think this could be very rewarding and I am keen to have it done thoroughly. The test is how many stories and how many tips you can produce. Let me see them all."

He hadn't finished: "Afternoons at 2:30 pm (except Friday), I want you to go into the subs' room and lead the parliamentary subbing team." What this meant was that I could select who would stand with me to protect the sanity of Mancunians from the tsunami of verbiage from the Commons. I selected Bow Tie. He was fast and genial, and not someone who would blow cigarette smoke in my face. I was even authorized to become a Nifty in training, giving work to other subs if we could not cope.

To be acknowledged as a top-table sub would have been promotion enough, but writing the editorials (commonly called "leaders") was the big deal. They had struck me as sensible and lucid for the most part, and the phlegmatic man who had been writing them, Sidney Cursley, certainly fit the role. He would emerge from his inner sanctum next to the editor and stand stock-still sucking on his briar pipe, incubating great thoughts as he looked on our bowed heads. Happily for me, he was sailing to New York to head the British government Information Service explaining our eccentric ways.

I was thrilled to accept the trial, but with the Bentley hanging still in my mind I fretted about what I would do when asked to write against my conscience. This was a preposterous exercise in self-regard. The editorial column was not my prerogative. I was there to express the viewpoint of the paper for which the editor was responsible, and if faced with an impossible demand, I could take my conscience with me back to the subs room.

There were, moreover, new perplexities to humble my pretensions. Britain was in transition from a Labour government headed by Clement Attlee to a Conservative government headed by Winston Churchill. Attlee's ministry had nationalized major industries, established the welfare state—of which the jewel was Aneurin Bevan's National Health Service—and emphasized the planned collectivist economy. "Collectivism" and "planning" were incendiary words to Churchill. He announced that "at the head of our mainmast we, like the United States, fly the flag of 'free enterprise.' " How should the two philosophies be reconciled? And while Attlee's government had begun shedding the empire that Churchill loved, giving India independence in 1947 over his vehement objections, it had not pulled up the drawbridge. It had vigorously fought an insurgency in Malaya (where Britain had rubber and tin interests). It had committed itself to the North Atlantic Treaty Organization (NATO) and the development of an independent nuclear deterrent. Churchill, an unashamed imperialist, was even more determined to maintain Britain as a big power. But could Britain afford the military means to protect its overseas interests, especially in the Middle East, maintain the welfare state, and meet the rising expectations of the trade unions? World War II had cost Britain a quarter of its wealth. Fully 10 percent of the gross national product was spent on defense during the Korean War, just ended. The pound sterling was vulnerable.

How could they expect a boy from Failsworth to solve all this, even with his precious degree?

On the Monday, wearing a bow tie as Big Tom did, I walked through the subs room into the office of the assistant editor

I'd met briefly on turning up in Cross Street, Bill Pepper, the meditative consigliere to Tom's brusque Corleone. I was given a small desk there, looking out on the newsprint trucks.

At 8:30 a.m. I was alone at the typewriter Cursley had abandoned for Manhattan. At 8:31 a.m. Big Tom's frame filled the doorway. "First leader, the Queen of Tonga, second the Canberra jet bomber." Then he was gone. Over the weekend I'd read myself ragged on all the economic and political news. In these preparations Queen Salote, the South Sea Islands, and indeed the whole Southern Hemisphere had not figured at all. I was abandoned on a coral reef without a clue as to how to get off.

I sent for the clips and then remembered the caption I'd written on our coronation special in June, when Queen Salote had enchanted the crowds by sitting in the rain in her open carriage. Now the young Queen Elizabeth and the Duke of Edinburgh were her guests in Tonga, and luckily it was raining in paradise, too. I was able to say how pleasing it was that the queen of the world's largest kingdom and the queen of the smallest shared an umbrella—and that they shared certain ideals et cetera. (My first editorial was not the place to recycle Noel Coward's wicked response when asked who was the little man sitting with Queen Salote in the London celebration. He replied, "Her lunch.")

The new Canberra jet bomber was easy. Flying London to Cape Town in record time, it had beaten every major long-distance world record, but the chief engineer of British European Airways, a Mr. Shenstone, had chosen that moment to condemn the quality of the work on British aircraft, and vaguely at that. We took him to task for a damaging generalization. (Note the editorial "we." And as a former RAF corporal hiding behind the royal "we," I'm relieved all these years later that "our" vigorous defense of the Canberra was vindicated by its versatile life of fifty-five years. Not until July 31, 2006, did it go out of service.)

I could never guess what bee buzzing in Big Tom's head would fly out to sting. Every morning at the paper was a lottery. The space was usually half a column, but he would sometimes ask for double the normal length for a major foreign affairs subject—our role in Europe, say, or what we had to do in the Middle East to make friends with Arab nationalists without sacrificing Israel. It served me right that having felt frustrated in expressing the occasional opinion on something I knew about, I should now be called upon to express an opinion on *everything*. There was no Google or Ask.com, no Aladdin's lamp I could rub to bring me facts from the vasty deep of cyberspace. I was reliant instead on the snip-snip of the library girls' press clippings and the prayer that whatever reading I had been able to do was pertinent to the editor's impulses. Should we arm Germany? Should the Church of England conduct marriage ceremonies for divorced people? How much of a menace was Egypt's Colonel Neguib? Was the government right to impose a fourteen-day ban on television discussing anything down for debate in Parliament? What should be in the chancellor's upcoming budget? Did women over thirty-two become unattractive, querulous, and antisocial, as an American airline maintained in rejecting them as "air hostesses"? Guerrilla strikes! Income taxes! Delays in court! The Common Market! Nationalization! Cricket manners! Algeria! Cotton exports! The slums! Neighborliness! Joseph McCarthy! Food prices! Immigration! I became a rag and bone man of the opinion trade.

Big Tom himself edited the copy on all these efforts. He did not fiddle with the wording, apart from a startling "For why?" he wrote into sentences that he thought needed more pep. I'd spend the first fifteen minutes of the precious writing

time throwing scrunched-up balls of paper into the wastebasket. If the editorial was a tiny bit long for the space, most often
because of an advertisement, he'd invariably just lop off my
precious first paragraph. He didn't say anything, but I got the
message: no throat clearing.

Working closely with Tom, I gradually came to know a
more sensitive and prudent man than the fairground barker
I'd seen from the subs table. At the end of a day scuffling with
news, he would go home to his violin and wrestle with Bach.
In circumstances he never explained, he had played with the
Berlin Philharmonic after World War II. The evening he was
due to collect an award at a city banquet, having been named
Mancunian of the Year, he came into the office with a heavy
suitcase. "All the family silver," he said, index finger tapping
nose. With a touch of pride he explained, "Burglars read our
paper, too, you know." He had an uncanny instinct for news.
In 1945, by elaborate preparation and shrewd interpretation of
a stray message from Rheims, this same Tom Henry secured a
world scoop and had his prepared WAR IS OVER edition on the
streets well ahead of the official announcement, every other
newspaper, and the BBC.

Big Tom's attachment to Manchester, its needs, and its
achievements no doubt came with the job like his black Jag-
uar Mark VII, but it was heartfelt and justified. "What Manchester thinks today," he was fond of intoning, "the world
thinks tomorrow." He was the reason for the soaring success
of the paper, reaching peaks of circulation and influence no
provincial evening newspaper is likely ever again to reach.
The profits generated under his leadership kept the *Manchester
Guardian* alive when it edged into loss in 1961 and plunged ever
deeper thereafter to the brink of shutting down for good in
1966. Some of my friends on the *Evening News* in the 1950s felt
that the *Guardian* staff patronized them as being from a lower

universe. I didn't sense that, but stories of *Guardian* eccentrics had a ready currency. "One of their leader writers came up in the elevator with me carrying six umbrellas—on a dry day. Can you believe it?" said Bow Tie. It was later alleged that the *Guardian*'s editor, lacking an editorial from the leader writer, had sent a messenger along to retrieve it and found he had passed out, his head resting on the typewriter on which the only written word was "notwithstanding."

Big Tom bristled with certainties, but the secret of his success was the way he identified with his diverse Manchester readers, though he was born in the East Midlands and had an Irish background. The sacred hour in his day was when his secretary carried in the "Postbag" (letters to the editor). He fell on them, licking his lips, read every one, and then gave over huge amounts of space in the next day's paper to these missives. He enabled citizen journalism long before the blogging era. Later one of my jobs was to edit the letters for publication. On many papers this was regarded as the ultimate ignominy for a sub. Not on the *Manchester Evening News*. Indeed, the editors whom I later heard boast that they didn't ever bother to look at readers' letters invariably ran second-rate papers.

Big Tom was on the board of directors of the *Manchester Guardian* but rather relished his different point of view on Manchester, most notably on the city's plan to build new towns in the greenbelt of the Cheshire plain, which the *Guardian* supported and we didn't. The *Guardian*'s housing specialist was outraged by Tom's conviction that the city was chasing moonbeams in applying for compulsory purchase orders to build two little Manchesters in Mobberley and Lymm. It took eight years for the government to say no. In the meantime Manchester had 20,000 homeless and 68,000 houses unfit for habitation. We argued that given the land famine—sites available for only a tenth of the housing needed — the city should immediately build upward, not outward. We envisaged six-story housing in attractive landscaping, emphasizing that they must not be designed as soulless barrack blocks. I had my doubts whether the city had the imagination to achieve that, but it was a better bet than waiting for unfit homes to collapse. They were already falling down at the rate of two a day.

The slums were a legacy of Manchester's leadership of the industrial revolution. Benjamin Disraeli, prime minister and novelist, said in 1844, in his novel *Coningsby*, "What Art was to the ancient world, Science is to the modern.... Rightly understood, Manchester is as great a human exploit as Athens." It was true. The invention of the world's textile industry in and around "Cottonopolis" (as Manchester was called) was only part of it. Whitworth, Fairbairn, Nasmyth, A. V. Roe, and Royce developed revolutionary discoveries in engineering; Ferranti in electronics; John Dalton in chemistry. The first pilots to fly the Atlantic Ocean nonstop were two former Manchester Central High School students, J. W. Alcock and A. W. Brown. It was at Manchester University that Ernest Rutherford knowingly split the nucleus of the atom, Hans Geiger invented his Geiger counter, and William Jevons devised his Logic Piano, the proto-computer that was the first machine that enabled a problem to be solved faster with the machine than without it.

Manchester paid a price for industrial pioneering. Too often we lived the opening page of *Bleak House:* fog everywhere. No, it was worse. This was not gray fog rolling down the river, misty clouds creeping in from marshes. This was black fog hanging over us day after day, still and suffocating. We went to bed breathing fog and we got up breathing fog and we worked breathing fog. People coughed themselves to death: the black spots spoiling the washing hanging to dry in backyards was the stuff being breathed into lungs.

We called it smog—fog enveloped by coal smoke from a million chimney pots like ours at home, from thousands of factories and coal-fired steam trains. On clear days, just from our house in Hale Lane, Failsworth, adjacent to the rail line, we could count scores of belchers, tall redbrick cotton mill chimneys. It was a double nightmare for Dad; hundreds of passengers' lives were dependent on him seeing the signals. The smog was so dense that in January you could not see them; in fact you could not see a yard ahead. It was not unknown for men walking home from work to fall into canals and drown. The only warning you were about to collide with some other struggler was the cough, mysteriously disembodied.

The London newspapers had chosen to call the terrible December 1952 fogs "Pea Soupers." In the subs room we had favored "Darkness at Noon" banners until Nifty said, "Enough literary allusion; stick to the facts." (We had our own smog makers. While I was at the paper, I was about the only nonsmoker.) Everyone seemed to accept the smog as an act of God. I'd recognized the fatalism of the working-class communities. "Where there's muck, there's money, Harold," wheezed a bronchitic neighbor. But it was the same among my more or less middle-class colleagues: "Price of progress." Perhaps I'd been reading too much Dickens. I didn't just want to record the smog; I wanted to get rid of it. It pained me to hear Dad coughing all night in the next bedroom on the occasions he came down with bronchitis. One morning, before Big Tom could issue his command, I ventured to suggest that I press for control of both industrial and domestic smoke. "Go to it," he said.

The Manchester City Council had some years before decreed that in the heart of the city nobody could burn coal, only specially treated smokeless briquettes. This had created one of the first smokeless zones in the country, and we had applauded it. But the order was still confined to the limited area around the town hall, leaving most of the city as smoky as ever. National measures lagged, as they had for decades, until some four hundred people died in London. Why did it take deaths in the capital city to spur action when people in the north had been suffering for years? Three years after London's smog, a national clean air bill was making its way through Parliament, ostensibly banning the burning of coal in domestic chimneys. But it had lots of loopholes, exemptions, and long delays before enforcement. It had too few teeth, and Tom let me say so, time and again.

For this campaigning, we got bitten on the ankle by the *Economist*—until that moment, more or less my bible. We did not understand what we were talking about, they pronounced. Mustn't rush things, you know; think of industry. I got steamed up imagining them in their ventilated London offices. Of course London had had its smog, but day in and day out the workers of the industrial north breathed the most polluted air in the world. They were five times more liable to die of bronchitis than people in country areas. Since the founding doctrine of the *Economist* in 1843, laissez-faire economics and free trade, had been borrowed in the early nineteenth century from our own liberal-minded "Manchester School," I felt entitled to correct their interpretation. You couldn't go to a concert at the splendid Free Trade Hall without thinking of how, from a temporary wooden hut here in Peter Street, just more than a hundred years ago, Richard Cobden and John Bright had stirred the whole country to win the repeal of the Corn Laws, taxes on food imports which fattened the farmers at the expense of the mill workers. Cobden and Bright had fought for cheap food for workers, not for poisoning them.

Looking back, it is shocking that the clean air advocates had to face so much resistance. In the end we got significant improvements in the Clean Air Act passed in 1956. An empirical investigation into the effects of the act published in 1994 concluded that it markedly improved air quality: average urban concentrations of smoke down by 80 percent and sulfates down by 70 percent since 1960. We won that battle, but the war goes on into the age of global warming, when new interests put up a familiar resistance.

Even before we pursued the clean air campaign, I already shared a primitively biased north vs. south complex: we all thought southerners, apart from Cockneys, were "stuck-up" folk who wore stiff white collars and never got their hands dirty with real work. They were "them," not "us." They were "the beastly bourgeois" of D. H. Lawrence's savage little poem. It was a silly prejudice, but the condescension of the *Economist* and the torpor of the responsible Tory ministers stirred embers of resentment left by incendiary histories of social reform.

St. Peter's Square, in the center of Manchester, where I frequented the grand circular library, stirred my overactive imagination. Back in the nineteenth century, all the industrial cities—Manchester, Birmingham, Liverpool, Leeds—were denied representation in Parliament. On the hot summer day of August 16, 1819, middle-class families and workers in their Sunday best assembled in St. Peter's Fields to hear speeches calling for universal suffrage (for men). The people were peaceful, and the speakers did not incite violence, but the crowd was so big—fifty thousand crammed the fields—that the magistrates panicked and ordered the arrest of the platform. Several hundred ill-trained amateur cavalrymen of the volunteer Yeomanry force rode into the crowd, wielding their sabers. Eleven citizens were killed, 8 died later, and more than 650 were wounded, a quarter of them women. When Richard Carlile published a firsthand account in his newspaper, *Sherwin's Political Register,* his complete stock of newspapers and pamphlets was seized, and he was thrown into jail. So was James Wroe, who documented the attack in his *Manchester Observer* and gave it the name "the Peterloo Massacre." Years later, in editing, I took inspiration from the greatest editor of the *Times,* Thomas Barnes, who defied the authorities and published an account of the massacre by his reporter John Tyas, who'd been arrested and jailed just for being there taking notes.

For all its heroic history in political and industrial innovation, for all the renown of its Hallé orchestra and its Gaiety Theatre (where British repertory was born), its great university, its art galleries, and its standing as Newspaper City, Manchester was neglectful of its heritage. After my years in proud Durham City, I was dismayed that the brass chamber in which Rutherford first split the nucleus of the atom ended up in the Cavendish Laboratory in Cambridge; that William Jevons's logic machine, made in Manchester at Ferranti, went to Oxford. I'd grown up in the city, I'd seen it come through the Blitz, and I felt it should make more of itself. Perversely, the German bombing had given us a chance to create something special, but typically the great center of Piccadilly Gardens remained nothing but a big, ugly traffic rotary.

One day, dodging cars in St. Ann's Square, which was quite near the office, I had an idea. What a jewel it would be if the geographical heart of the city wasn't so lacerated by traffic, so noisy, so defaced by ugly street clutter. My thought was to return the spacious square to its Georgian tranquility—a pedestrian area like St. Mark's in Venice. There was a splendid focal point at the King Street end in the towered neoclassical St. Ann's Church in pink sandstone, probably built by a pupil of Christopher Wren in 1712. There was J. E. Gregan's graceful corner palazzo with its arches and Venetian windows, and the

well-mannered and genially grouped terraces of the Edwardian and Victorian buildings. There were fashionable shops
and a bronze statue of Richard Cobden. But one could almost
see Cobden shrinking from the racket of heavy trucks, buses,
and cars, holding his nose from the exhaust fumes. The Boer
War soldiers featured in another statue seemed on the point of
surrender.

Back at the office, I sought out Bert Hackett, a pale young
man in the art department who had difficulty swallowing, the
residue of some accident. He was confined to drawing maps
and little sketches, but I was to discover that he had an unex-
ploited imagination for larger tasks. Presented with my vague
idea, he swiftly completed a fine sketch of how St. Ann's Square
would look without traffic, with silver birch trees, fountains
and an ornamental pool, and sidewalk cafés where Mancunians could pause to admire the view and gossip. I presented it
to Big Tom. I told him that there was a rear service road where
shops could be supplied and, hand on heart, that there would
be as many days in Manchester when people could sit outside
as there were in northern France.

Tom was so enthusiastic for Manchester that he'd long ago
decided it *never* rained, just as Manchester United never lost a
match. He embraced the new St. Ann's Square as an *Evening
News* campaign, giving it a page in the paper headlined "This
Could Be Manchester. Picture a Peaceful Plaza in the Sun."

I called on the Civic Trust in London, an independent
national philanthropy formed to help regenerate decaying
urban areas. The deputy director, a town planner, came north
and enthused. Laurence Scott, the chairman of the *Guardian*,
and Bill Mather, head of the great engineering firm Mather and
Platt, rallied round, and so did St. Ann's canon, Eric Saxon. We
called a public meeting of city officials, property owners, and
businessmen. The buzz was good. I had high hopes when the

chairman of the city's planning committee reported that the city surveyor found it "an attractive scheme." Then he added, "But the surveyor thinks it should wait until the ring road is finished" (which might be many years). Bill Mather argued that the world's biggest industrial area should have such a showpiece without delay. The objections were fewer than I expected; most of the traders said they would happily cope, but a Mr. R. R. Stoker argued that to deprive people of a place to park their cars threatened life, liberty, and the pursuit of happiness. Instead of a plaza, he advocated "flower baskets, trees with colored lights, and taxis painted pink and green."

St. Ann's is now a pedestrian square. My idea was not exactly an overnight success; it took twenty years. But more came out of the initiative. With Scott and Mather doing the heavy financial lifting, we formed the Civic Trust for the North West to work for a cleaner, more agreeable city. I went around with a photographer identifying areas of remediable squalor. My old stamping ground of Ashton-under-Lyne reversed the slogan "What Manchester does today, the rest of the world does tomorrow." Two months after the St. Ann's meeting, Ashton adopted an attractive design for its market square, where I had sheltered from the rain opposite the *Reporter* office. With guidance from the national Civic Trust, the borough adopted a plan to turn the area into a traffic-free shopping and social center—and to do it that year.

Long before anyone heard the phrase "green revolution," the initiatives of the Civic Trust caught on. Within a few years, citizens in no fewer than three hundred places were giving their time and money to conserve what was beautiful and pitch out what was not. The cause united Rottingdean with Wigan; craggy folk with snow on their boots in Inveresk with villagers on the Downs; burghers of Bristol with potters in Burslem; men and women in Godalming with those in Glasgow. In Stepney a group turned blitzed sites into gardens. In Lincolnshire and Stafford-shire volunteers cleared away from the countryside the debris of pillboxes, Nissen huts, and concrete left over ten years by the big-gest litter louts of all—the Air Ministry and War Office.

I was proud to have played a part in all this. Enid and I later moved from our rented apartment in Altrincham to a house on the edge of the wildly beautiful High Peak national park. We formed a society to lead volunteers in the weekend clear-ing of woods and fields and ghastly water holes filled with three-piece suites, mattresses, broken television sets, prams, and other throwaways of civilization.

I was on the opinion treadmill for nearly three years, then after an interlude I will describe, Big Tom promoted me to feature writing. One day he lingered in my office for a record three minutes. "Where did you get the shirt you're wearing?" he asked to my surprise.

"Lewis's. My mother…"

"Why don't the Swedes wear shirts like that?"

"No taste?"

"And why aren't their women wearing our frocks from Manchester?

"Look what's happening, my boy," Big Tom went on with indignation mounting. "Lancashire cotton exports way down, mills closed. I want you to go to the continent and find out why. Leave right away."

"Of course," I replied, praying my passport was in order. Those were the days when going to "the continent," as we called Europe, was a vast mystery. Beyond a day trip by ferry from Ramsgate to Boulogne as a schoolboy, I'd been out of the country only once.

Tom hadn't finished. "And what about the Norwegians, eh?

Whose pajamas do *they* wear? They could be wearing German pajamas! Think of it, the Germans!"

He seemed ready to fight World War III over pajamas, but exploring the bedroom attire of the Vikings struck me as chancy. "You want me to go to Norway as well as Sweden?" I ventured.

"Yes, yes, Oslo. And while you're about it, swing down through Denmark and come back through Germany and Holland."

By night trains and planes, I was soon deposited in snow-etched Oslo. I called on various offices, starting with the Han-delskammer, the city's chamber of commerce. Everyone seemed to speak English, which was fortunate since the phrase books didn't have anything like "I am an Englishman from Manchester. Kindly help us understand why you don't wear our shirts."

The officials I spoke with were very helpful in explaining import and export rules and custom duties, but they had no more idea than I had myself why Lancashire cottons were no longer as popular as they used to be. On my bewildered first night, I nursed a beer at a table looking out on the Volkswa-gens scudding round the city square. Where on earth was I to begin the next day? This was my first big overseas assignment. All I had now were the names of a few import agents, none in Oslo. A talkative old Norwegian materialized, putting his beer down next to mine. "See, we buy from our enemies and not from Britain, our old friend," he mused. He became uneasy and moved away when I asked him if he would mind turning back the collar of his shirt to see where it was made.

The waitress was more obliging. I asked her where she bought her clothes, tablecloths, and curtains. Next morn-ing I trudged through the snow to the department store she mentioned. It was advertising a clearance sale. I found a rack of poplin raincoats at the bargain price of two pounds, two shillings (around twenty-five pounds today). I checked the label—a Manchester manufacturer. I tried it on. "Anything wrong with this?" I asked a salesman.

"Nothing wrong. It's good quality, and it looks good on you," he said. Flattered, I bought the coat but asked why they were selling our poplin raincoats for so little. "The English style never changes," he explained. "It's out-of-date."

I went to another store and watched various women choose curtain material. It was all German, French, Swiss, Italian, Norwegian—except for two languishing pieces from Lancashire with designs as cheerful as cold porridge: on one a network of the old familiar pallid rosebuds, on another what looked like a sickly green bird in an ocean of turquoise. An import wholesaler explained the popularity of German pajamas: "Your people offer me five colors, the Germans fifty. And on piece goods you fob us off with gaudy leftovers from the colonial trade. You're stuck in the Victorian era."

The refrain became depressingly familiar from agents and store buyers throughout Norway, Sweden, and Denmark; design and service were more important than price. The decor in the homes I was invited to was so different from the oak sideboards, floral curtains, and stuffed sofas of the pre-Conran English homes. My hosts' style of richer woods, ornamental glassware, trailing plants, and angled spotlights demanded fabrics as striking. At twenty-seven, I was feeling out-of-date myself.

When I stopped off in Malmö, Sweden, I finally solved the mystery of the Cottonopolis shirts that had sent me on the journey in the first place. A kindly and effusively pro-British director of two leading men's stores told me how for years he'd asked a quality British shirt company to package its merchandise more attractively. He'd been told it wasn't necessary. "Just recently," he told me, "the Swiss have come in with shirts in an attractive transparent wrapping, folded with a broad front. Just look at

Cartoonist Mark Boxer ("Marc") takes a rise out of my skiing obsession in the mid-seventies. Luckily, I left the extravagant Astrakhan overcoat in a cloakroom somewhere. *(Mark "Marc" Boxer)*

Wedding day photograph of Frederick Evans and Mary Haselum, 1924.
The next day Dad was back in the steamy grime servicing locomotives
at Patricroft railway yard and Mum was in the cotton mill.

Vanished times....The sooty grittiness of my dad's daily life for nearly fifty years as a steam-train driver is epitomized for me by Stephen Dowle's photograph of a Newton Heath loco heading into the winter darkness. *(Stephen Dowle)*

Rhyl seaside front, 1938. Dad and three of his four sons (left, Harold; back, Fred; and Peter). Yet to arrive: John—and World War II.

Dad didn't share the romantic feelings about steam—"too dirty"—and was glad to graduate to driving diesel passenger trains. "It's a toff's job."

Dad's expression is truer: the North Sea was choppy and chilly.

Mum and Corporal Evan

Diana Dors to the rescue.

My room!

Non nobis solum. University College, grandly housed in two castles, one at Lumley and the other (above) in Durham City. In my third year as a "Castleman" in Durham I had a room on the Norman gallery (marked), well placed to administer boiling oil to invaders. *(Durham University)* I rode to Lumley Castle on my fairly trusty BSA bike (below).

It had rained, and nobody was about for the promenade photographer at Llandudno, North Wales, except a couple of newlyweds. One year after graduation from Durham University, Enid was teaching and I was trying to survive on the subs' table at the *Manchester Evening News*.

The battlefield: time and space were our enemies on the subs' desk at the *Manchester Evening News*; our weapons—black pencil, spike, glue and scissors, and caffeinated concentration, always fearful of the call from Big Tom. (*Manchester Evening News*)

Big Tom: Tom Henry, the editor in chief of the *Manchester Evening News*, pushing the last page to the foundry—a rare honor from the comps on the occasion of his last edition. (*Manchester Evening News*)

The *Northern Echo* sub-editors' room during the BBC filming. The news editor, Michael Morrissey, leans over deputy editor Maurice Wedgewood. I'm on the right, in black-rimmed spectacles, pointing at something. In the foreground the sub in rimless glasses is Don Berry, who went on to become a managing editor of the *Sunday Times* and, later, a power at the *Daily Telegraph* and *London Evening Standard*. *(Ian Wright)*

Campaigning: We circulated thousands of pamphlets on the wrongful hanging of Timothy Evans (in the photograph with wife and baby he was falsely convicted of murdering). The front of this four-page effort carries a strong call for a judicial inquiry from Sir Frank Soskice. He made it when he was in opposition, then forgot about it when he became home secretary. *(Northern Echo)*

Enid and I had three children under three. They've grown a little in this photo with me and Enid at Elton House in Darlington in 1964: Michael (in my arms), Ruth, and Kate. The house had lovely grounds (the site of Mike's experiments in eating daffodils). The *Northern Echo* offices were but five minutes down the road.

them." Had I seen them side by side, I had to admit, I would have bought the Swiss, even though it was a little more expensive. "See," said my new friend, "that's why I have two hundred English shirts I can't sell. Take one, take two. Help yourself."

In Düsseldorf, soon rebuilt after the RAF devastations, I scoured one huge department store after another and discovered something extraordinary: not a stitch of Lancashire cloth anywhere. And I noticed something just as odd: the same German fabrics I'd seen in Copenhagen were more costly here in the home market—and that despite the Danish tariff. The plump export manager of a large German textile company invited me to dinner because his wife, a dazzling beauty, was grateful for being treated kindly by British troops at the end of the war. He sketched a confusing system of high German tariffs and tax relief that basically enabled German manufacturers to charge high prices in their protected market while sending below-cost fabrics abroad. "Dumping" I called it in the third article I wrote.

By this time two of the three "Cotton in Crisis" articles had been published under the rubric "How Not to Sell Cotton." Big Tom was pleased; the cotton kings were not. But a few months later the president of the Board of Trade intervened. He announced that his department and the Cotton Board would send a special commission in my footsteps to investigate all I had reported about design, selling and after-sales service, price, and dumping, to be followed by a "hell for leather drive to take Lancashire cotton out of the doldrums." Big Tom made it a page-one splash: COTTON AWAKES!

Big Tom's next idea was to send me back to Germany to ask how lads from the Greater Manchester district in the Guards Division of the British Army of the Rhine liked life over there. It looked like a boring assignment—until I stumbled on real news, rather as my father had done that morning we came across the Dunkirk survivors on Rhyl beach. I just happened to arrive at the barracks when the officers and grenadiers were boiling over about their obsolete weaponry. They were stuck with old-fashioned bolt-action Lee-Enfield Mark IV rifles (while other NATO armies had the automatic self-loading FN); far too heavy Vickers medium machine guns from World Wars I and II; radios that did not work; and the Sten, the emergency submachine gun that had been introduced to me in my RAF training as having killed as many of our soldiers as the enemy because of a defective safety catch. A tank commander said his radio equipment for keeping track of his squadron was nothing near as good as the Germans' in World War II; the enemy had been able to keep in speaking contact at night over a distance of fifteen miles. "On one recent night maneuver I had to sit on top of a haystack to speak to artillery one hundred yards away," he said. "Amazing we won the war, you know. God knows how we'd cope with the Red Army."

The stir created in Lancashire by the cotton articles was nothing compared to the outcry about the army report. It was cited in a full-scale debate in the Commons and the Lords, and the responsible minister promised swift action—as he put it, "a concentrated phase of renovation and re-equipment such as has never been seen before."

Subsequently, Tom piled on the assignments. Go into the baleful and bleak Communist zone of East Berlin (I did; when I pointed my camera at a Red Army soldier, he summoned me over because he wanted to pose properly); examine the case for equal pay for women; go check on whether the new West German Army was something to be scared of; see what was cooking at our major science research institution, the National Physical Laboratory (the birthplace of radar and much else was starved for resources); examine technical education; explain atomic energy and look at solar power. I was split three ways:

foreign correspondent, science correspondent, northern political correspondent. They were all rewarding assignments. In West Berlin it was a joy to call on my liberated prisoner, Walter Greis, back at work in a bank and happy with his wife, Alice, in their new apartment. I had only one question: could they please explain the strange customs in their bathhouses? On the first night, exhausted by the difficult journey, I had gone into a public facility for a massage, wearing a swimsuit and over it a fur and leather astrakhan coat I'd invested in for my Scandinavian travels, intending to use it as a blanket for a little sleep afterward. Inside the bathhouse, the Berliners stared and laughed at me. I was the only one dressed; they were all naked, men and women. I reentered fearlessly, bravely unclad: even the RAF unarmed combat course hadn't prepared me for this. The massage was so good, I went back the next night for a swim, disrobed, and walked in. Cries rang out on every side. Everyone was wearing a bathing suit or dressing gown. Walter explained that my German would have to cope with tricky little notices the bathhouses changed every night. The first night I'd missed a sign that said *Entkleiden Sie sich bitte vor Eingehen* (Please undress before entering) and the second night *Badeanzuge erforderlich vor dem Zugang heute abend* (Bathing suits required before entry tonight).

The job of northern political correspondent gave me a front seat at the seaside spectaculars at Blackpool, where the Labour Party—political leaders, humble constituency workers, and trade union rank and file—wrestled for the party's soul in the annual party conference. The Labour government had just been turfed out by the Conservative Party, and the vociferous Marxist left claimed this was because voters had been so bamboozled by the press, they'd failed to understand the issues.

185

This was akin, said Labour leader Hugh Gaitskell, quoting Oscar Wilde, to saying that the play was a success but the audience was a failure. I admired the way Gaitskell stood up to the catcalls of abuse he got for defending the wisdom of the voters and the virtues of the Atlantic alliance and a mixed economy. I thought he represented Labour's best hope (though it took four decades for Tony Blair to convince the party that nationalization was no panacea), but for me the revelation at Blackpool was from Gaitskell's leading critic within the party, Aneurin Bevan.

I saw for the first time how conviction can be suborned by a particular kind of eloquence. The resonant generalities and voices of, say, Winston Churchill and Barack Obama inspire, but that is different from the gifted debater's ability to take an opponent's case apart piece by piece and substitute a glittering alternative. I'd known Bevan could do this from reading his dazzling attacks on the Suez intervention: "Sir Anthony Eden has been pretending that he is now invading Egypt in order to strengthen the United Nations. Every burglar of course could say the same thing, he could argue that he was entering the house in order to train the police." But to see and hear Bevan in full flow was a singular experience. Nobody in the party or press ever risked missing a minute of him. He'd take the expectant crowd through the labyrinths of a policy argument with wit and passion, his index finger quivering in admonition; his silver forelock flopping; his lilting Welsh cadences beautifully calculated between mocking vituperation, intellectual analysis, and beseechment; his face flushed (I learned he soaked in a very hot bath before he spoke).

Big Tom was relentless. Now he suggested that I combine political and parliamentary reporting with organizing our book reviews and cover activities at Manchester University.

As an afterthought, he dropped me a note: "I am told you are keen on table tennis. I'd like you to cover the sport for us."

Will that be all, sir? No, now you ask, said Big Tom, "I want you to write a column. Every Thursday. Make it snappy. It will pay a guinea." (The guinea always sounded grander than the one pound, one shilling it represented.) He told the features department that this new assignment should be presented as "The Column of a Manchester Man Who Speaks His Mind" and headed with my name in bold type. In the guise of modesty, I told him I preferred to write under the pen name Mark Antony (ambition is made of sterner stuff). He agreed but told the features editor to have a sketch of me at the top of the column. Artist Bert Hackett drew a tight-lipped, jaw-jutting profile of someone with the kind of steel-rimmed glasses that went out of favor with Heinrich Himmler. But about the column itself, I was given not a clue. It surely had to be personal, but being personal cut across the grain of my training. I'd been schooled in the anonymity of neutral reporting, to eschew any personal note except in theater and book reviews or features. "Never," said J. W. Middlehurst, "let me see the word 'I' in anything you write for the *Ashton-under-Lyne Reporter*."

I found the new cloak hard to wear. My first column was passable, with three or four shorter items, but it was not personal, and it could have been written by anyone. I was rescued by the antic behavior of the nationalized Electricity Board responsible for serving the whole of the North West. During lunch hour, I walked into its showroom in Manchester to buy an electric cooker displayed in the window. It was an older model at a knockdown price. I was so newly married with furniture bought on credit, we couldn't afford a new model. I paid and gave the salesman the address for delivery at our apartment in Altrincham, a suburb of Manchester. He revoked the sale. In no circumstances would he deliver to Altrincham, he explained. It was in the rules. Not giving up, I went to the Altrincham showroom of the same board. They didn't have a cheap model. Would they kindly order it from their colleagues in Manchester? "Oh, dear me, no. We're not on speaking terms with Manchester." I went back to the Manchester showroom. I said I'd buy the cooker and arrange my own pickup and delivery. "We're a state enterprise," said the salesman triumphantly. "We can't deal with a private trucker." He didn't thank me for apologizing for thinking that I was in Manchester, not Moscow.

Recalling the farce, I found a voice—and my grand alias Mark Antony found an audience. It led to a newlywed couple inviting Mark Antony to their brand-new home, where they handed over a bag filled with tiny brown pellets. Crushed between thumb and finger, the pellets formed a small, sandy deposit on my desk. They were the remnants of defective mortar supposed to be holding together the bricks of their house, which was already shifting on its foundations. It turned out to be just one example of a wave of jerry-building. Newspapers and the BBC followed up. Mark Antony would survive. Indeed, he was even invited to speak.

I was admittedly only one of a hundred eager Manchester newspaper writers auditioned for the role of broadcaster. After furious debates, the Conservative government had deemed that the BBC monopoly of television, paid for by the license fees of viewers, should be challenged by a handful of independent companies that would finance their programs on the "dreadful" American model of carrying paid-for advertising. In the north, only just recently reached by the BBC's flickering blue signal, the commercial franchise was won by the irrepressible

Sidney Bernstein, a silver-haired smooth talker of creative vitality, who looked like a cross between a Roman emperor and a beaten-up boxer. On his father's beginnings in cinema, Bernstein had built a huge chain of splendid cinemas inspired by what he'd seen in America in the 1920s. He'd sought the northern franchise in preference to London, he said, because he preferred to get away from the London metropolitan atmosphere and move to a more distinctive close-knit culture. With his brother Cecil he set out to make his Granada Television synonymous with the north: he called it Granadaland. His soap *Coronation Street* introduced northern life to the south and became the longest-running drama on British television—still running some fifty years after its launch.

Granada didn't have a news operation, so it made a deal with the *Manchester Evening News* to cut and paste our stories and present them as its own Granada news bulletin. None of us knew anything about television, including the Granada executives, who'd come from print, marketing, and the Bernstein brothers' interests. I presumed their inexperience explained why when I'd said all of twenty words to the camera, they invited me to undertake some of their first outside broadcast interviews—a few hours I might take off from the *Manchester Evening News*. Later, the producer, Barrie Heads (also fresh from newspapers), explained to me that I'd just been lucky. Sidney Bernstein had a list of characteristics of performers he loathed—anyone who was bald or bearded or had a foreign accent or wore a metal watch strap, suede shoes, or a bow tie. In a hurry that morning, I'd not bothered tying the bow tie I often wore, hence I escaped the automatic rejection inflicted on others. Barrie told me it was the ambition of several frustrated producers, hoping to end their careers on a high note, to find a middle-aged, bow-tied, and bearded Bulgarian in sandals they could put under a lengthy cast-iron contract.

The laconic Barrie Heads was the supervising producer of my first interview with L. S. Lowry, the reclusive eccentric whose paintings capture the fortitude of the Manchester working class in the toils of the north's urban decay. Lowry was in his seventies when I went to see him in his remote moorland stone house at Mottram-in-Longdendale. His modest home—which had no telephone—was his studio, too, with paintings piled up. I was in awe of him; not so Barrie. As if directing a scene in a TV studio, he had the nerve to tell the great man that a finished painting of moorland hills and valleys lacked something—the familiar Lowry skeletons in drab suits perhaps. A few days later Lowry told Barrie he was quite right: "It needed some folk in it. I've put in a picnic party."

The show itself went surprisingly well for a first effort, mainly because the unassuming Lowry made it easy to ask questions. I did a couple more shows, with Big Tom's agreement, then someone had the bright idea that Granada would do a public service if it introduced traveling gypsies to a wider audience. A gypsy encampment was selected in a siding just below the busy East Lancashire Road linking Manchester and Liverpool. As a program idea, it was hardly earth-shattering, but viewers then were known to switch on just to watch the signal for an idle hour.

The extrovert director assigned for the gypsy show, H. K. Lewenhak, was said to have come from making movies in Hollywood. For a couple of hours of television in the afternoon, he directed me to wander among the caravans with a microphone, earnestly asking various gypsies about their lives. There was no script. We made it up as we went along. I was on camera, but basically rehearsing set positions for the shorter main evening show. One grouping around a caravan's steps, seen by Lewenhak as the climax, was aesthetically unpleasing to him in the run-through. He didn't like the way I'd had to lean over with the microphone to catch what the gypsy chief was saying. "Harold, on the show," Lewenhak advised, "give him the mike with your left hand, then when he gives it back, turn full face to camera two, wrap up with a four-minute summary, smile, count three, then smile and say, 'Good night, viewers, from all of us at Granada.' "

This was Hollywood talking! I'd be ready for my close-up. The gypsy chief had stars in his eyes, too. Under the blaze of the spotlights, he answered the question. I proffered my hand for the mike. He kept it and segued expertly into a litany of grievances. He named one town for its intolerance, then another and another—a gazette of local councils and cruelty the width and breadth of the land. Starting in the south in Surrey, he was working his way north to the Outer Hebrides. Lewenhak's alarmed floor manager was holding up two fingers. I had two minutes to close. I leaned over to retrieve the mike from the chief; he leaned back. I moved forward; he moved farther back. He was clinging to the mike. We struggled for possession. He was still talking as I managed to get a hand on it. These politically correct days, I would be denounced for oppressing a minority. I didn't see it that way; it was *my* mike. But the chief wouldn't stop talking. Police sirens were now blaring. Trucks and cars, drawn like moths to the spotlights, had stopped to see what was going on. One car ran into the back of another. It was chaos. Lewenhak rolled the credits over the unstoppable talking gypsy and doused the lights. I had no close-up.

It was time to get back to print.

10

Adventures in the Land of Opportunity

I am addicted to print. That is different from being addicted to reading. An addiction to print means that you get your fix by looking at the shapes of letters in type even when the words don't make any sense. I savor the design of letters—the ascenders piercing the skyline, the fugues created by the descenders. On those assignments in Europe for the *Evening News*, I felt compelled every day to scour the Norwegian, Swedish, and Danish newspapers without understanding a word. It was a guilty pleasure to be relieved of the burden of comprehension. I scan newspaper pages of classified advertisements even when I'm not looking for anything. Today I waste emotional energy nursing grievances about the migraine-inducing type on medicine bottles and the ridiculously emaciated compressed capital letters of credits on DVD boxes. What are they trying to hide?

Early in 1956, in the midst of my quick scan of the first pages of the *Economist*, I found myself mesmerized by five lines of small type. The longer I looked, the larger they got, expanding into a new world: *the* new world. British and Commonwealth graduates, the advertisement announced, were offered the opportunity to travel and study in the United States at the expense of a body called the Commonwealth Fund.

So many millions now visit America every year, it's hard to appreciate how magical those few lines were in 1956. Even crossing the Atlantic was an adventure then; nonstop flights and mass air travel were years away. The everyday material pleasures of Americans — their hamburgers and hot dogs, their jeans and gadgets for everything — are now a commonplace in every community in the world, but they were curiosities then. America was at once a vast mystery and an inspiration.

Its universal luster was dimmed in the years of the George W. Bush presidency, but as a schoolboy who'd shivered in an air raid shelter during the Blitz, when England seemed unlikely to survive, I can never forget the America that came to the rescue. Franklin Roosevelt was as large in our imaginations as Winston Churchill. Then, when the war had been won in the West and in the East, I'd seen this same America sustain Western civilization by acts of courage, generosity, and vision. The Americans didn't occupy the freed lands as Stalin did; they created a new liberal world order.

What kind of people were they? In 1933 during the Great Depression, they sang, "We're in the money," when all they had to live on was hope. In America, it seemed, it was permissible to dream. How had they survived so many crises, achieved so much abundance, fostered so many innovations, transformed so many immigrants arriving at Ellis Island with their pathetic bundles into American citizens making a mark in the world? See, there in the line on Ellis Island, Albert Einstein, Bob Hope, Fred Astaire, and Alexander Graham Bell. And there's Irving Berlin, Frank Capra, Enrico Fermi, and Yogi Berra. There's a more nuanced image of America today than mine in 1956, formed by movies and novels. But who with an atom of romance in his soul could not feel the pull of the mythic

America? To walk into a small-town diner in a Norman Rockwell painting; to follow Raymond Chandler in a roadster up Sunset Boulevard; to steam down Huck Finn and Jim's Mississippi; to see Faulkner's Yoknapatawpha County, Gatsby's Great Egg, Zane Grey's Wild West, and Damon Runyon's Broadway. Yes, there was heartache in the history and in the literature, in the Okies of Steinbeck's *Grapes of Wrath* fleeing the Dust Bowl and finding California not such a promised land, and most of all in Gunnar Myrdal's *An American Dilemma* on discrimination against black people. But how were things now, in the 1950s? Were these Americans as open, as breezily uninhibited, and as welcoming as their GIs? And were their newspapers anywhere near as exciting as they were in the movies?

I responded to the advertisement in the *Economist* as soon as I got into my office at the *Evening News*. It transpired that the Commonwealth Fund had nothing to do with our far-flung British Commonwealth. It was an American foundation established in 1918 by Anna Harkness with $10 million of the fortune left to her by her husband, Stephen Harkness, who'd discovered a more profitable business than making harnesses in Cleveland, Ohio: he got together with John D. Rockefeller to cofound Standard Oil. Anna had made her Anglophile son Edward president of her foundation, and he saw the Commonwealth Fund Fellowships (later called the Harkness Fellowships) as reciprocating the Rhodes scholarships. The idea was that returning home after seeing the other country firsthand would promote "mutual amity and understanding between Great Britain and the United States."

The Commonwealth Fund seemed mostly to have been seeking genius scientists who would further their research on the cosmos, but three Harkness Fellowships were open to "graduate opinion-forming journalists" who would be required to commit to a research project and promise that when finished they'd not linger in Hollywood.

My heart sank when the Harkness Fellowship application forms arrived. The British selection committee included none other than Sir James Fitzgerald Duff, the fierce warden of the Durham colleges whom I had criticized in the student newspaper *Palatinate* for banning Durham's ice hockey team from playing in matches behind the Iron Curtain. Could he have taken offense? Could he even have read it, heaven forbid, as an indication that I was soft on communism? I wasn't—after all, it was the Soviet attempt to snuff out West Berlin that had prolonged my time in the RAF—but any suggestion of deviant socialist tendencies was a sure disqualifier for entering the United States.

The fund stipulated that an application had to be accompanied by a substantive proposal for study in the United States, identifying the university and a program of travel. It would be a lot of work. Given the presence of Sir James, I doubted it would be worth the effort. I put the forms aside. Yet as the deadline approached, every story I read about the United States revived my initial excitement. If I succeeded, I'd be in America for the 1956 presidential election!

I dug out the *Palatinate* editorial; it was much less forthright than I'd thought. Nevertheless, I'd have to overcome any residual hostility on the part of Sir James by presenting the selection committee with a proposal so reeking of responsibility, so central to the future of mankind, that my previous acts of rebellion would be forgiven.

The study idea I hoped would take me across the Atlantic came in a circuitous way from Big Tom. When he vanished for two weeks in my first year on the *Evening News*, everyone assumed he was following Manchester United in Europe. In fact, he was more cerebrally engaged at a conference in Delhi called by the International Press Institute (IPI), an association of daily newspaper editors from around the world that was to play a critical role in my career. Formed in the early postwar years with support from the Ford and Rockefeller foundations, the IPI had become concerned at distortions in the flow of news that complicated relations between nations and sometimes led to conflict. The institute had commissioned twenty-two foreign correspondents in ten countries to assess the way their native countries were portrayed. I sent off to the IPI headquarters in Zurich for the two resulting reports, "The Flow of News" (1953) and "As Others See Us" (1954). The stereotypes were startling. The IPI had supplied Alex H. Faulkner, U.S. correspondent for the *Daily Telegraph,* with a four-month collection of reports on Britain from 105 American newspapers. Americans, he found, were being presented with a Britain that was "an inefficient, old-world, rundown country at the end of her tether, a 20th century anachronism with no part to play in the world of atom bombs and jet planes...a chronic panhandler always trying to touch Uncle Sam for an extra dollar."

It didn't sound like home, but that was the point. We had no idea how we looked to others. Surely, I wrote to the Harkness selectors, we ought to analyze how those impressions were formed and fixed, how justified they were, and what influence they might have in the making of foreign policy. I trusted the selectors would see valor in my intention to choose Chicago as my headquarters. The *Chicago Tribune* under Colonel Robert "Bertie" McCormick was the citadel of midwest isolationism, rivaled only in the pungency of its expression by the city's three-time Anglophobic mayor, William Hale "Big Bill" Thompson, a pal of Al Capone's. He, too, had claimed to be speaking for the Midwest when he said, in the 1930s, that if ever the King of England came to Chicago, he'd punch him in the nose.

I wasn't just being quixotic in choosing Chicago. Its university, founded by Stephen Harkness's workmate, had an entire department concerned with the influence of reading and media, and its chancellor Robert Hutchins had raised the sights of journalism, I thought, when he had chaired a commission on the responsibilities of a free press.

It was a nice surprise to be summoned to an interview at Harkness House in London, but the selection committee presented a terrifying spectacle. The florid Sir James Duff, bushy eyebrows twitching, sat with a convocation of university vice chancellors; Oxbridge college heads; a professor of physics; Geoffrey Crowther, the managing director of the *Economist;* and a man justly described as one of the founders of the postwar world, Oliver Franks, former ambassador to the United States and then chairman of Lloyds Bank. I got the impression they did not go to bed at night worrying about stereotypes of Britain formed in other countries. Sir James asked me hardly anything; if that *Palatinate* editorial had made any mark on his consciousness, he didn't show it. Years later, when I met him at a function in Durham, he told me what happened. "You were up against some very formidable competitors—there were long odds against you. I need hardly say I myself had almost to lean over backwards against any semblance of favoring a candidate from my own university."

Apparently a key question in my interview had nothing to do with foreign reporting. It was whether I had met any American professors. I could recall only one visitor from Chicago, who'd talked on society and crime, and I told the selectors, "I think he called himself a criminologist." The idea that crime should merit a whole "ology" to itself and be practiced by a professor from Al Capone's city tickled the selectors, according to Sir James, as if I had deftly epitomized the eccentricities of American academia. So the British committee recommended me for a fellowship on the strength of a witticism I didn't know I'd made.

It is intriguing the way unreflective, transitory moments like this can change the trajectory of a life. It changed mine for good, as a similar one changed the life of the Blackpool boy Alistair Cooke, who'd applied for a Harkness before me. At his interview, straight out of Cambridge in 1932, he happened to look Lord Halifax in the eye. Halifax took this as a sign of self-confidence and on this recommended him to the other selectors, explaining, "What's more he's from the North Country and they're always the best types." I wasn't going to cavil at advertisements for northerners, but I did object when the sponsors in New York sent a document I had to sign as a condition of their accepting the British committee's nomination. The "Conditions of Tenure" were explicit: if I were to become a Harkness Fellow, I would have to be celibate. "Fellowships are vacated by marriage," the rules announced.

Wasn't it, I suggested, carrying New England Puritanism too far? The New York office stood fast. Wives diverted a fellow from the pursuit of knowledge. Also, they had no budget for them. The other two "opinion formers" who got through the eye of the needle that year were Brian Beedham of the *Economist* and Alastair Burnet of the *Glasgow Herald,* later editor of the *Economist* from 1965 to 1974, editor of the *Daily Express* from 1974 to 1976, and the anchor for Independent Television News for many years. Both bachelors, they had no Harkness dilemmas. (When Burnet married nine months into his two-year tenure, he vacated his fellowship.)

At the *Manchester Evening News,* newsroom mates thought I should forfeit the Harkness. They were aghast not so much that I should cavalierly abandon a new wife for the ivory tower, but more that I could even think of losing my grip on the greasy pole of newspapers. I didn't intend to do that; I thought I might learn a thing or two from American journalism. But they had a point. Two years was a long time to be absent from an industry where reputations were made or lost in minutes. Indeed, there were moments when I flirted with the idea that a Harkness Fellowship was an open door to a change of career. I was tempted by beguiling images of myself as a history don delving into dusty diaries in a university library, relieved of the clamor of scoops and deadlines. I must have been deranged. In any event I was not prepared to leave Enid teaching biology in a rough Liverpool school while I swanned around the cloisters pretending to be a monk.

The Harkness man in London, Gorley Putt, encouraged me to attempt a transatlantic negotiation. The deadlock was resolved when New York finally said if I would go to America as a bachelor for the first six months, they would waive celibacy as a condition of tenure for the rest of the fellowship. This was on the understanding that I would be responsible for my wife's upkeep when she arrived. Enid accepted the six months of purdah with customary good grace and on September 8, 1956, joined Mum, Dad, and my youngest brother, John, in waving me off with a simulation of cheerfulness as Cunard's RMS *Franconia* steamed out of Liverpool harbor.

On board I shared a tiny cabin with a white-haired Welshman going back to California for the sun after trying to retire in the rain-sodden hills of his birth and a young Merseysider leaving his seaside town to be a mate on a dredger. We learned to avoid the bearded artist next door, returning to Philadelphia from a scholarship, who was keen to explain the sexual maladjustments leading him to contemplate divorce. We were nine days at sea, most of which, one gale excepting, I spent crouched on deck over a chessboard, combating Carl, a German soldier who had become a naturalized Englishman. It was a rerun of the ebb and flow of World War II until the liner picked up a pilot for the tricky navigation of entry into New York harbor, and we all rushed to the foredeck. We couldn't see a thing for the fog.

This, though, is the only way to arrive in America, as the first Virginians and Pilgrims did. The millions who now come by air every year to JFK or Newark miss the euphoria of landfall as the sea mists dissolve into Lady Liberty and syncopating skyscrapers, and soon enough you are tasting the cosmopolitan street life of the city. P. G. Wodehouse said that arriving in New York was like going to heaven without the bother and expense of dying. I woke the next morning floating on a cumulonimbus cloud, my soul borne up by the glorious sound of Bach's "St. Matthew Passion."

The prosaic explanation for this was that I was in a high-rise apartment on West Twenty-third Street, the guest of a friend of a friend who'd installed loudspeakers under the beds, each wired to the perpetual loop of a tape recorder. Herb Ertheim could not live without round-the-clock music, therapy for his days spent manufacturing metal coat hangers for the Seventh Avenue garment trade.

When I wandered round Herb's apartment, I had a measure of how we'd fallen behind America. Herb's high-tech kitchen had a dishwasher, four-slice toaster, deepfreeze, washing machine, and spin dryer. Everyone I knew back home was still washing clothes by hand in the sink and making toast with a fork held over the fire. I'd seen nothing like the giant supermarket on Herb's block, a single warehouse serving everything you could possibly think of to more than twelve hundred families. Back home we shopped for the family at four or five corner shops like my mum's. Years of doing without everything had dulled my appetite for acquisition. Britain's food rationing had only just ended, nine years after the war, with the liberation of the banana. Here I felt like a Visigoth in imperial Rome. Thirty varieties of ice cream! Tectonic layers of steaks! Gallons of orange juice!

All of this, of course, had to be sustained by salesmanship. Away from the supermarket one had to appease news vendors, diner counter cooks, waiters, department store salesmen, and hotel staff. Every purchase I made provoked the same challenge: "What else?" There was no escaping the hard sell. A newlywed friend of Herb's took an apartment high above the Hudson River, cozily safe, he thought, from the hustle of the marketplace. No way. Sign writers for a church got to work on a facing wall across from the apartment, and every night the couple found themselves staring at a spotlit warning: "The wages of sin are death."

It would take more than doomsayers to shake America's satisfaction with itself in the mid-1950s. I'd arrived in the middle of the presidential election campaign in which the eloquent Adlai Stevenson was again challenging Dwight Eisenhower, running for a second term. America was at peace. The Suez crisis had not yet erupted; the cloud of McCarthy's anti-Communist hysteria was lifting; there seemed to be a thaw in the cold war with the new Soviet leader, Nikita Khrushchev, denouncing Stalin's crimes; and Eisenhower himself had ended the Korean War with a veiled nuclear threat.

I could see why the mass of people liked Ike; he was a reassuring figure. Stevenson exuded erudition, Ike goodwill. I saw the effect at a small airport I went to with some friends of Herb's, all wearing ALL THE WAY WITH ADLAI pins. When Ike stepped out of a light plane and waved to us, he was so presidential but so friendly—the most powerful man in the world waving to us, his supposed critics—that we all cheered him.

They were no doubt mindful of the good times. Americans

were enjoying a level of prosperity never before seen in the history of the world, splurging their three- and fourfold increases in purchasing power on new homes with kitchens like Herb's and longer and longer automobiles with ever more extravagant tail fins. The majority of people in Britain did not have cars or telephones. In America between 1951 and 1956 the number of *two-car* families doubled. Most homes had a television set, not yet in color, but they had more programs than in Britain, including *The $64,000 Question, Gunsmoke, Wagon Train, I Love Lucy,* and *The Honeymooners* (Alice and Ralph Kramden in Bensonhurst).

I found that the brighter western light buoyed the spirits, and the pace of New York was exhilarating to someone from a gray Britain that had yet to boom. The sense of impermanence in Gotham was pervasive—in the helter-skelter erection of new skyscrapers taking the place of the ones built in the previous generation; the number of going-out-of-business sales (all bogus, I learned); the Brooklyn Dodgers deserting Brooklyn for Los Angeles. Something new was invented every minute. It was the decade for the debut of novelties that are still with us—Kentucky Fried Chicken and McDonald's—and others that are not. I miss the carhop—the waitress in roller skates ferrying hamburgers to your car—and the iconic images of Monroe and Brando framed against the night sky as I passed drive-in movie theaters. I miss the diners where the jukeboxes offered Elvis singing "Hound Dog" and the Five Satins doo-wopping "In the Still of the Night."

Of course there was a darker side. I had the familiar angst in New York of trying to reconcile the plenty with the beggars and vagrants; there were ten thousand of them sleeping in the parks, in the screeching subways, in the flophouses, gutters, and sheltered doorways. Alarmed by the gap between those who had and those who had not, Herb's friends met weekly to discuss questions such as what an intellectual should do for a cause he believed in, such as relieving poverty. They were all anxious for me to know that New York wasn't the real America. Wherever I went in the next two years, all over the country, I would be told the real America was somewhere else.

I loved it all the same, but I could not linger scrounging off friends. The agreeable folk at the Commonwealth Fund's splendid headquarters at Seventy-fifth Street and Fifth Avenue put a new $100 bill in my hand and wished me Godspeed to the University of Chicago. Once in Chicago, the quickest way to the university area was the elevated railway. I bought a ticket and said, in the English manner, "Thank you very much." The man behind the grille snarled at me, "Did ya say sumfin, wise guy?"

Was this the real America? No, I was assured by Professor Douglas Waples, my academic adviser at the University of Chicago. The real America was in Gary, Indiana.

The University of Chicago was a study in dissonance: the pseudo-Gothic architecture copied from Oxbridge; the students in sandals and T-shirts sipping Cokes together through sweetheart straws; one of the wealthiest institutions in the country set down in the middle of a slum called Hyde Park. The whole area was in flux, every day receiving hundreds of blacks escaping from the South.

It was from Chicago's South Side that fourteen-year-old Emmett "Bobo" Till set out in August 1955 for a summer visit with family in the Mississippi Delta, and it was to this Chicago that he came home in a pine box, a disfigured corpse, his face battered to a pulp. His mother, Mamie Bradley, insisted that he be returned to Chicago so that she could display "what they did to my boy." The thousands who walked past the open coffin would talk for a long time about the shock of seeing Emmett, whose only offense, if it existed at all, had been to chat up a white female storekeeper (northern version) or to "put his hand on her and make a lewd remark" (Mississippi version). His two killers had only recently been acquitted, on the 166th anniversary of the signing of the Bill of Rights. Clearly, I told myself, I must find out more about the perverted values of the American South.

I found it hard to decelerate from newspaper life. To a mind still subliminally on an edition time sheet, the cleverness in the academic studies on media seemed for the most part to consist of making the obvious obscure. Where was the headline point? Courtesy of the university, I had a room in International House, living with people of fifty different nationalities. I had to save if I was going to keep my Oliver Twist pledge not to ask for more support when my wife arrived. Like Rockefeller, I counted the dimes. In the cafeteria I was charged 35 cents for breakfast—20 cents for cereal with milk and 15 cents for a banana—but I found a grubby supermarket where I could buy ten tiny packets of Kellogg's cereals for 33 cents, enough milk for 10 cents, and a whole bunch of bananas for 15 cents. This meant breakfast for ten days on 58 cents instead of $3.50.

The theory of International House was that by living together as individuals we would be able to help the nations of the world live together more easily. I wondered about this when my neighbor, the engagingly rambunctious thirtyish Swedish novelist and broadcaster Par Radstrom, in Chicago to study "contemporary American culture," made a habit of banging drunkenly on my door at 3:00 a.m. to discuss the ethics of his involvement with American women. Like me, he was a "Harkness bachelor," his journalist wife remaining in

Sweden. He had no enthusiasm for my suggestion that a diet of cereal and bananas would solve his hormonal problems.

Par made up for his nocturnal intrusions by giving me a copy of one of his novels, in Swedish, embossed with a vamp's pouting red lips, and introducing me to a jazz hangout he'd found, Club de Lisa. It was open 24/7, boasting, like the Windmill Theatre in London, "We never close." There was nothing fancy about it, no cover charge, just cheap tables jammed together in the darkness and a solitary spot on a small stage for a cabaret. The first night I went there, the place was packed with black people, many of them fresh from the South. Nobody seemed to mind that the only white people in the crowded hall were Par, myself, and the saucy young French novelist Babette Rollins, whom Par also had brought along. Suddenly a dozen Negro matrons appeared on stage in their best dresses and flowered hats, and the room went respectfully quiet as they presented a check to a local charity. I'd thought I'd been living dangerously, but I might have been in an English church. It seems that Club de Lisa doubled as a community center catering to black migrants. It made me more determined to spend time in the South they'd fled.

A sterner test of the principles of international amity by contiguity came on October 29, only days before Americans would decide between Eisenhower and Stevenson. In the months before sailing to America, I'd written editorials in the *Evening News* on the cascade of events in Egypt: Colonel Gamal Abdel Nasser's military coup in 1952; his arms deals with the Soviet bloc; U.S. secretary of state John Foster Dulles's abrupt withdrawal of funds for Egypt's damming of the Nile at Aswan; Nasser's seizure of the Suez Canal, owned by British and French stockholders, earlier in 1956, throwing down the gauntlet to Churchill's just-elected successor as prime minister, Sir Anthony Eden; the abortive efforts, never entirely sincere, to fashion a diplomatic solution. The *Evening News* did not trust Nasser having a grip on "our lifeline," and we condemned Egypt's refusal to let Israeli ships through the canal, but we were critical, too, of the "whirling dervish" volatility of Dulles.

The news that Israel had invaded Egypt to destroy commando bases—and that Britain and France were intervening militarily, without consulting Eisenhower—plunged International House into a frenzy of excitement, bewilderment, and dismay. A crowd of us at the dining tables—Israelis, Egyptians, Iranians, Australians, Nigerians, Japanese, Brits, and French—raced downstairs to the television. We yelled abuse at the set when the network abruptly abandoned the United Nations Security Council arguments in full flow, switching unconcerned to the regular programming.

That first night after the invasion I barely slept, with International House becoming a mini-UN. Two scientists from Tel Aviv asked whether Israel was supposed to do nothing when more than a thousand Israelis had been shot or kidnapped by Egyptian raiders since 1950. "And you've killed a lot of Arabs," a couple of Egyptians retorted, albeit calmly enough. An American professor (in an argument prefiguring those over the Anglo-American invasion of Iraq in 2003) suggested that military action would inflame the Arab world without achieving its objectives. The professor asked me to "speak for Britain" in response to an Arab student's charge that the British had secretly put Israel up to the whole thing so that we could regain control of the canal. Were we capable of this perfidy? I hardly thought so.

In the cafeteria the next day, I couldn't get to a table with my tray, accosted by people rushing up with the news that the Royal Air Force had begun bombing Egyptian airfields. Memory has long encouraged me to think I heroically defended the British-French intervention, but a letter Enid found recently expresses a depth of revulsion that memory had muted: "I am on fire with the Suez Crisis. I hope by the time you receive this someone has put Eden in a lunatic asylum. I thoroughly despise Eden, the gentleman turned bully. And he's wrecking the Anglo-American alliance."

International House, already smoldering, was incandescent when the Soviets used the cover of the Suez crisis to crush the Hungarian Revolution. Someone hissed at me, "See—you've sacrificed the Hungarian patriots!" Then Khrushchev threatened to rain rockets on "imperialist" Britain. It was horrible being four thousand miles from home and imagining the worst.

With study impossible, I escaped the hothouse. Alastair Hetherington, a former Harkness Fellow now only a few days into the editor's chair at the *Manchester Guardian*, telegrammed asking me to assess opinion in the Midwest. I was flattered. As a *Guardian* correspondent, I was untried. Hetherington was only thirty-six. Did he know what he was doing?

Since Professor Waples had said that the real America was in Gary, Indiana, I went there first. Mammoth cauldrons exhaled flames, lighting the dreary industrial wastes of the world's biggest steel plant. Most of the brawny and highly paid workers were Polish. They were not very welcoming to an English reporter. They'd just seen Władysław Gomułka win their country a measure of freedom from the Soviets, after the summer suppression of an insurrection in Poznan. Now they blamed Britain's Suez adventure for giving the Soviets a cover to do to Poland what they had done to Hungary. A local Polish newspaper suggested that there should be new Nuremberg trials with Eden and Khrushchev in the dock. I was too close to their furnaces for debate on the subject. I made my notes and left.

Purely in the interests of research, I spent time in Chicago's city center bars. My timing was not great. Britain had just had to ask the United States to waive interest on its 1948 loan. In one darkened bar where the patrons were watching the election results on television, my accent caught the attention of a belligerent barstooler: "Look, son, America paid for the drinks in the first two world wars, and this time you've gotta pay for your own."

The *Chicago Tribune,* renowned for fostering this friendly attitude, was having a field day. There was no escaping where duty lay. I had to venture into Tribune Tower, the *Tribune*'s imposing neo-Gothic redoubt on Chicago's "Magnificent Mile" (Michigan Avenue), to ask if they would discuss Suez with a representative of perfidious Albion. It was snowing. In the forecourt I genuflected to the American patriot Nathan Hale, unflinching on his pedestal. The Revolutionary War hero had been hanged by the British for spying, declaring, "I only regret that I have but one life to lose for my country." My lesser regret was that I wouldn't get to meet the former owner of the "world's greatest newspaper," Colonel Robert McCormick, six feet four inches of megalomania.

He had been barely a year in his grave, but I hoped to find that his spirit still flourished. McCormick had been more than a bombastic libertarian of the far right. It's inevitable that we pin epithets on public figures; newspapers do it all the time in marshaling the stage armies of the good and the bad, and the most egregious characteristic tends to stick. It may not be untrue, but it obscures complexity. McCormick undoubtedly fulminated against the British Empire, against Woodrow Wilson and the League of Nations, Franklin Roosevelt and the United Nations, the World Court and the Nuremberg trials. He was convinced that all Rhodes scholars came back to the United States to spy for Britain, and he campaigned to have them fingerprinted. His worst excess, in his anxiety to keep America out of war, was to behave like Geoffrey Dawson of the *Times,* in the thirties suppressing his own correspondent's accurate reports of Hitler's evil ways.

Yet it required more than polemics for the *Tribune* to become the most widely read full-size morning newspaper in the United States. At its zenith it had a million readers daily and a third more on Sundays, and its influence was not confined to the Chicago area. McCormick was a bold and innovative newspaperman, versed in all its skills. He could take a printing press apart and put it together again. He saw the future of color very early and the possibilities of facsimile transmission, and he backed the *Daily News* in New York, the first successful American tabloid. He campaigned and investigated with a vigor that makes so many corporate American dailies today taste like cold custard. The diversity of his life, rich in paradox, defies caricature. He was an inventor, explorer, engineer, municipal reformer, civic booster, artilleryman, and athlete. He was an apostle of free enterprise who despised Wall Street. He was ruthless in crushing newspaper rivals but won epic battles for freedom of the press. It was the cranky Colonel who beat the villainous Mayor "Big Bill" Thompson in a libel defense that established the principle that every citizen had a right to criticize the government without fear of prosecution; it was the cranky Colonel who valiantly bankrolled a Minnesota scandal sheet to win the famous Supreme Court case *Near v. Minnesota,* which gave the American press the vital freedom from prior restraint we did not enjoy in Britain. He was, as Fred Friendly wrote in his study of the case, "the Daddy Warbucks of the First Amendment." The Colonel had standards; duty came before profit. He loved private gossip but would not run a gossip column—keyhole peepers, he called them. He deplored Eleanor Roosevelt but would not print a story about an old affair of hers with another woman, nor a story about a homosexual advance said to have been made to a black railway porter by Undersecretary of State Sumner Welles.

The editorial writers I met in Tribune Tower did not disappoint. They were glad to talk about the Colonel and what it was like to be summoned to his twenty-fourth-floor aerie, where armed guards and German shepherd dogs protected him: "Hizzoner" Big Bill Thompson had once sent goons to rough him up. The Colonel's men were pleased to be able to practice their swordplay on a real live Englishman who would bleed. "Let's face it, Britain is finished," said the chief editorial writer by way of opening pleasantries. I retorted that Britain had just opened the world's first atomic power station; it was one of my last science features for the *Evening News.* "That's nothing. You're desperate for economic power. We don't need it. You've got corrupt unions, lazy bosses; soon you'll be kicked out of your last colonies." In rebuking Britain, Ike had invoked the United Nations and the rule of international law, so I wondered whether they would have second thoughts about condemning the UN. "Nah," the chief came back. "We like Ike, but Ike's like Woodrow Wilson at Versailles: he's the preacher trapped in a bawdy house calling for a glass of lemonade." McCormick would have liked that.

I could have filed for the *Guardian* on the strength of the anti-British sentiments I'd heard in Gary and Tribune Tower alone, but I didn't. I called up congressmen, editors, churchmen, academics, local Democrats and Republicans; no one I bumped into was safe from interrogation. It was intoxicating to say "I am a correspondent for the *Manchester Guardian*" and find doors opened, phone calls to powerful people returned within the hour, even invitations to drop in for a coffee. It was my first taste of the different attitude toward the press. And though I didn't find anyone in the Midwest who was uncritical of the British-French intervention, the alligator of isolationism seemed largely confined to the banks of the Chicago River.

It was gratifying to see my report—airmailed in those days—appear as a page lead in the *Guardian,* bylined "from a special correspondent," and even more satisfying to hear that the special correspondent was denounced by the director of the British Information Services in New York as getting it "entirely wrong." He'd been telling London that Eden had the support of the whole country, including the Midwest, while I had reported the opposite.

Having broken the ice with the *Tribune,* I insinuated myself into the rival afternoon paper, the *Daily News,* which had just sent a public official to jail by proving he'd milked public funds of $1.5 million. Running the *Daily News* was a legendary newsman by the appealing name of "Stuffy" Walters (after a famous second baseman). Working for Walters, newsmen said, was like being pecked to death by a duck. He was shaped like a beer barrel and spoke in rat-a-tat machine-gun sentences. "Tell it," he told reporters. "Don't write it. Tell it. Period." Jabbing the air with a fat cigar, he gave me a staccato account of how they'd caught the official with his hand in the till. Stuffy was rolling up his sleeves for intensified news warfare with the *Tribune,* which had bought another afternoon daily, the *Chicago American,* so he swiftly took me to the newsroom, where the crackle of the police radio was counterpoint to the usual hubbub. "Tell Evans about the funerals!" he instructed a cardboard cutout of what a city editor should look like—crew-cut, bow-tied, under thirty but gray-haired. A reporter had noticed, I learned, that a certain mortician seemed to get all the business when people died intestate. The reporter had spent weeks on the case and concluded that the official entrusted with intestate funds had been authorizing $4,000 funerals, although the ones the reporter had seen carried out were cheap $100 affairs. The pair of grave robbers had been splitting the profits.

The city editor was constantly in the hot seat, but he said it was not as bad as working for United Press International (UPI). In the competitive agency business where every second counted, a UPI man he knew in Raleigh, North Carolina, had been so short-staffed that he'd been forced to have one operator frenziedly punching copy on two teletypes at the same time. His boss at the receiving station in Atlanta telexed, "Hurry. Why so slow?" Raleigh replied, "He only has two hands." Atlanta shot back, "Fire the crippled bastard."

Even the vigorous Chicago papers had their work cut out for them monitoring the Ike vs. Adlai 1956 presidential election. On voting day I went with a reporter to various polling stations in the tough, largely black area to the north of the university. At one station, normally a barbershop, we were not welcomed by the Democratic precinct captain, a nasty piece of work. We caught him bullying a middle-aged woman. "See here," he shouted, "I know your crowd's goin' and blastin' about what Jack Wilcox did and did not do last time. I've changed my name—legally!—because of your mudslinging, see!" The woman was one of three election judges charged, among much else, with watching the voting. It was not unknown for someone to slip into a voting booth and set the machine the way his party wanted it so the next person voted Democrat or Republican, like it or lump it. Apparently the captain, a master of such arts, was lambasting the woman for her insistence that one of the booths be moved into the line of sight.

The voting machines were too complicated for many. One perplexed woman was ten minutes in the booth. A judge went in and voted for her. The next day at the *Daily News*, Stuffy vented. The rival paper had a better story—a page of pictures showing a Democratic captain in the act of passing dollars to voters. Stories of fraud and intimidation by Democratic operatives ran for several days. (One can hardly say fifty years have purified the electoral system.)

The smell of printer's ink had been seductive. After two months of thrashing around on my project, I was depressed. In Theodore Roosevelt's phrase, I found relating the abstractions of mass media theory to my concern with stereotypes like trying to nail jelly to a wall. Fortunately, my truancy pointed a way out of the morass. Suez! It had been so obvious I hadn't seen it. Here was a concrete, finite event in foreign relations that I could put under the microscope. Britain and America were at the center of it, so any stereotype, any bias one way or another, would surely become clear. And from this empirical study maybe I could construct a model for assessing press performance generally.

The truth about Suez, I recognized, might take decades to emerge. But we could expect the press at least to record the contemporary raw material of the crisis. I'd heard numerous disputes about who did what to whom and when. Did the press report the public statements fairly, fully, and accurately? Did it publish rebuttals as well as allegations? Did it publish speculation as fact? Did a newspaper's opinion page color its reporting? Just how much of an understanding did a reader get of what was going on?

Getting to work, I collected three weeks' worth of eleven publications covering the crisis—eight newspapers (independent and chain) representing different environments and three newsmagazines.

I drew up a checklist of verifiable and freely available facts.

I also noted wherever unsourced, pejorative, nonfactual color was introduced ("he arrogantly refused"). It was a considerable task, and awkward in my cramped room at International House.

I did not, in fact, finish the thesis elaborating a test for bias until I had steamed back across the Atlantic—which was perhaps just as well in view of the critical nature of the findings. Surprisingly few facts made it into print, but performance varied in unpredictable ways. The *Chicago Tribune* would have been expected to score poorly in the factual reporting of the British-French arguments. Not so. It performed better than any other newspaper or magazine in the study. It did have a lot of color words and unsourced material, but the *Tribune's* animosity toward Britain did not affect its news coverage; it gave readers enough facts to make their own judgments. In the British press, however, patriotism made it a risk even to raise a question about the Suez venture. Alastair Hetherington's *Guardian* and David Astor's *Observer* suffered heavy losses in readers and advertising for opposing "Eden's war."

All American newspaper coverage, though inadequate, was fuller and straighter than that in the newsmagazines—*Time, Newsweek,* and to a lesser extent *U.S. News & World Report.* All three magazines offered a confusing mixture of fact, supposition, distortion of chronology, and angled writing. Fact and opinion were so mixed that the casual reader would have no idea which was which. *Time* was easily the most adulterated— twice the amount of nonfactual material compared to *Newsweek* (344 entries to 154). Here is *Time,* for instance, on Eden's speech in the Commons: "When he had finished the House was chill with silence." But *Newsweek* reported, "His fellow Conservatives, including an enthusiastic Sir Winston Churchill, responded with a three minute ovation, probably the loudest of Eden's career." *Newsweek* was accurate. For a reader who hadn't the time or inclination to read the newspapers during the crisis,

U.S. News & World Report was the erratic best for gaining some unbiased appreciation of the crisis.

Whatever misgivings my younger self had about American journalism as manifest in the reporting of the Suez crisis and Joseph McCarthy's witch hunts, a seminal influence on me was the way American newspapers consistently engaged in time-consuming investigations of a kind virtually unheard of then in Britain. In this time before satellite transmissions, the United States was too vast for the distribution of remotely printed national newspapers, so the regionals and locals had a chance to star. While I was traveling in the West, I was mightily impressed by the dogged courage of two reporters in their thirties at Portland's *Oregonian*, Wallace Turner and William Lambert, who busted a conspiracy to control a vice empire in the city. Behind it were officials of the International Brotherhood of Teamsters and a compliant district attorney. The two reporters had seventy hours of incriminating tape recordings of gangsters, obtained from an ex-con who broke with the mob and subsequently was threatened. The suspect nature of the source meant that Lambert and Turner had to double-check everything on the tapes—three months of risky work once Portland's underworld got wind of what they were doing. They stayed in hotel rooms, moving often; switched rental cars almost every day; and stored the tapes in a bank vault. The management of the *Oregonian* showed courage, too. The Teamsters were sure the paper wouldn't expose the racket because their union had threatened to disrupt production (a tactic I was later to become all too familiar with).

The work of a number of other investigative reporters ended up central to the U.S. Senate's McClellan Committee investigation of corruption led by chief counsel Robert Kennedy.

Among those reporters were Clark Mollenhoff at the *Des Moines Register and Tribune* on the trail of Jimmy Hoffa; Harold Breslin at the *Scrantonian* in Pennsylvania; and John Seigenthaler at the *Nashville Tennessean*. It's painful to recall now how I watched the two fated Kennedy brothers, Bobby and Jack, brimful of eager life as they sat side by side in confronting day after day the dregs of American society.

We liked to think that British public life was less stained by corruption, and by and large that was true, but the big national newspapers at home were profoundly uninterested in grassroots journalism. The quality newspapers preferred the rarefied air of Whitehall and Westminster (where so many "scoops" were partisan leaks); the popular press was more or less confined to reporting sex scandals. It wasn't just that the British laws on libel, contempt, and official information were more onerous. It was, I came to see, the difference between two cultures: a British population conditioned to limited access; the Americans demanding openness.

Pretty well everywhere in the United States the status of editors was high in their communities. No doubt this was partly because the role of the press is honored in the First Amendment to the Constitution; partly because local ownership tends to boosterism, much appreciated by all being boosted; and certainly because the better newspapers were vigilant in exposing abuse (except in nearly all of the South, another story altogether). Of course, in visiting forty states I passed through many a Gopher Prairie ill served by a slovenly monopoly sheet, met many Babbitts as editors, and discovered that much of the work on the average Main Street paper would drive anyone to drink. I had modified raptures, too, about the use of freedom of the press when people were accused of crimes. In San Francisco, where I lived for a few carefree months, I was shocked when both the *Chronicle* and

Examiner effectively convicted an innocent man of serial sex killings before his trial. Day after day they branded this poor fellow, name of Rexinger, announcing with glee, for example, that they'd come across love poems he'd written. Love poems! Must be guilty! But the police and the papers had the wrong man. It was a shameful episode. In Britain editors faced jail for reporting on crimes that prejudiced a fair trial. The Rexinger case was no better than a southern lynching.

Along with the high regard I developed for newspapers' dedication to good firsthand reporting on local and domestic issues, I questioned foreign coverage even before finishing the Suez study. The trauma of Senator Joseph McCarthy's attacks on the press earlier in the 1950s seemed to have made editors nervous on anything to do with the cold war. The coverage of McCarthy by most newspapers, wire services, and radio stations had been inept and timid. I was bothered that throughout the 1956 election, the press was in lockstep in letting Eisenhower and Nixon brush aside Stevenson's unanswerable case for stopping the poisoning of the air due to the continued testing of atomic bombs in the atmosphere. "Catastrophic," Nixon called it, falsely suggesting that ending the tests would leave America defenseless. Eisenhower, too, was allowed by the press to distort Stevenson's proposal. We learned later that he actually favored the idea, and he decreed a test ban only the following year.

The Suez turmoil had died down by the time I said goodbye to International House and freezing Chicago in February 1957 and began the travels expected of a Harkness Fellow. I headed first for the warmer climes of Raleigh, North Carolina, where Enid joined me. All my scrimping had enabled me to save for a car and camping gear. I would have to bear the humiliation of not driving one of Detroit's latest models, but my 1953 cream and chocolate Plymouth (without a prehensile fin) was special, a gift of history. I had taken it to a dingy space below the elevated railway where a shaky man in his seventies, with four cats, a couple of dogs, and a barefoot wife, had gone to work on it. In the 1920s he had owned a big factory doing specialized bodywork until the Great Depression had put him out of business. He'd survived all these years by fixing baby carriages and bicycles, but he could still summon his old bodywork skills. With hinges and bolts and upholstery, he made it possible and easy for me to join the front and back seats to form a double bed (cost: $62). "What else?" I paid another $7 for two copper gauge screens to keep out mosquitoes on sleepovers in national parks. It was the best investment of the entire expedition.

Eisenhower's interstate superhighways were as yet unbuilt, and with Enid as navigator we stayed off the main arteries, such as they were ("Get your kicks on Route 66"), and explored the quiet blue highways. I won't forget the thrill—absurd as it sounds today—of my first motel stay one night when we couldn't find anywhere to camp. To a Brit reared in the war, the motel was the pinnacle of romantic luxury: a television, a telephone, free bedside tissues the colors of the rainbow, and a toilet seat sanctified by a strip of paper like a Good Housekeeping seal of approval. What more could puritan American civilization offer?

I was keen to see something of the West, the America of legend. We joined cowboys on a roundup of cattle on a Montana ranch. We shared an improbable tea in Fort Sill, Oklahoma, with Mr. and Mrs. Jason Betzinez—improbable because Jason was the last surviving member of Geronimo's Apache band, and his wife was a former missionary teacher. He was ninety-three. As a prisoner of war and later an army scout, he had been taught the blacksmith's trade, but on his release from army service he was too proud to accept the government's gift of a forge and the tools of his trade.

In the eastern highlands of the Sierra Nevada, we trekked through blinding dust storms to the wild gold-mining camp of Bodie, California, now a ghost town of tumbledown saloons, storefronts, and a church, long empty of human life. We stayed among the Cherokee Indians in the Great Smokies of North Carolina, where mothers carried babies in cradleboards, the Hopis in their cliff-top dwellings in New Mexico, and the Navajos in their hogans at Bluff, Arizona.

Aware of why so many blacks in Chicago had left the South, I was keen to see how this other minority was faring. The Navajos, herding their sheep and goats and gambling and trading, seemed happy enough, but they were undernourished, with a high incidence of tuberculosis and illiteracy (only three in one hundred could read or write). Uranium and vanadium had just been found on their reservation, however, portending big royalties for the Tribal Council, and an active Catholic mission ran two schools and a clinic. The Southern Cheyennes we visited in Hammon, Oklahoma, had nothing so promising on their horizons. The ten bands of the Cheyenne nation were once among the fiercest tribes of the Great Plains, but all the families we saw depended on government handouts of food. They were living in leaky wooden sheds with piles of rags on the roof to keep out the rain, no electricity, no gas, and no running water. The women did their cooking over open fires on the ground. A Cheyenne proverb had a prophetic ring: "A nation is not conquered until the hearts of its women are on the ground. Then it is finished, no matter how brave its warriors or how strong its weapons." A chiefly looking man of eighty-three sat on an upturned bucket, staring into space, oblivious of the drops of rain falling on his head.

Big Tom, always looking for feature articles, read somewhere that you could put all the people of the world in the Grand Canyon and roof it over. It wasn't clear what he had in mind, but when we saw the huge hole a mile deep and four to eighteen miles wide, the idea seemed feasible. It was a fine day in June when we set out to walk from the North Rim to Phantom Ranch at the bottom. We were practiced hill walkers in England, even having backpacked the entire two-hundred-mile Pennine Way from the Cheviot Hills to the Yorkshire dales.

Fourteen miles downhill was a small thing to attempt for one of the world's most spectacular sights, each mile of the descent revealing the chasm's geological history through the millennia. Eight miles down, in the cactus desert, we found Bright Angel Creek roaring across the trail, its footbridge a wreck of broken planks and wire. We were stuck. Eight miles was a long climb back up. It was hot. Swimming was out of the question: Enid had never learned how. The swollen creek was about twenty feet wide. We tried a running jump to get as far across as possible. The rushing water knocked us both down and wet the backpacks, but we got up on the other side and triumphantly resumed the trail to the ranch.

We didn't know there were five more crossings, all destroyed by the melting of exceptionally high snows on the North Rim, and not even a hint of a bridge left on any of them. At the next crossing, the creek raced even faster between rock faces. Looking round for a wider, slower course, I interrupted the sunbathing of a rattlesnake. It hissed. I ran and stumbled on a long strand of telephone wire, which gave me an idea. My plan was to tie the wire to a tree, take both backpacks, and somehow get across the creek, trailing the wire so that Enid could hold on to it for her crossing. I jumped from a ledge jutting out over the creek. Once I hit the water, I was swept along but was able to scramble onto a rock, still holding the lifesaving wire. I dumped the backpacks and yelled for Enid to come over. Waist-deep in water and holding the wire, she made the first few yards all right. Then the current swept her up so she was stretched horizontally downstream, and I was straining every sinew to hold her by the wire. I had made a mistake: I should have tied the cable to a tree on my side. Enid might have inched along if the wire had been taut. I could not keep my grip. She vanished.

I went after Enid in the same instant, reached her, and got her head out of the water, more by panic strength than skill. We ended up far downstream, very wet and frightened—and on the wrong side of the torrent, with our backpacks of food, matches, maps, and flashlight on the other side of the creek.

We couldn't go forward; we couldn't go back. So we went sideways up and along the tops of the cliffs. In two hours we had gone upstream a few hundred yards, but we'd had to climb hundreds of feet, and the enterprise looked more and more foolhardy. Gaps opened along the cliffs. The rock face crumbled. We negotiated a retreat to return to the creek and try again to ford. Without a wire, we were both tossed about like twigs, once more dumped on the wrong side. The spires and buttes of the canyon passed into shadows. Night fell too soon. We made a shelter of logs and leaves, aware of every stirring in the undergrowth.

At dawn, not having been devoured by mountain lions, we spent eight hours inching along the canyon walls, then came to a full stop where the cliff wall rose a sheer, sharp, vertical one thousand feet from the torrents. I'd have to reach the ranch alone and get help. I found a high spot with an overhang and took a running jump. I went under in the torrent. I surfaced and got tossed around trying to swim. I wasn't in charge, but

I'd got far enough across to make it to the other side, albeit with a cracked shinbone. I had four miles to go in the heat and four more crossings to make.

The last two crossings were wider but easier, and in late afternoon I reached Phantom Ranch. Within a few minutes ex–bronco buster Jay and kitchen hand Ray, just out of the U.S. Marines, were off up the canyon. They took two sturdy mules. The mules lurched and lunged in the rapids, but Jay — who'd made a living riding outlaw horses and Brahma bulls in rodeos — drove the mules across. At dusk Enid returned in the saddle of one of them.

We recovered quickly enough at Phantom Ranch, but to go back up to the North Rim and retrieve our backpacks on the way was considered impossible. We had to climb to the South Rim (much easier) and hitch a ride for the two-hundred-mile drive to the North Rim and our Plymouth.

The adventure in the Grand Canyon was scary, but what followed was the darkest experience of my time in America. I approached the states of the Deep South with foreboding. There were ghettos in the North, as I'd seen in Chicago, and there was discrimination for sure. The white northerner, if he had an opinion, could be indignant about the way black sharecroppers in the South were still treated almost like slaves, but he hardly thought about the black man with a PhD who could get a job only as a waiter and was excluded from buying a home in certain residential districts in the North. Even so, racism was of a different order in the South. Since the end of World War II, scores of Americans had been murdered simply because they were black; hundreds more had been maimed, thousands abused, and millions deprived of basic rights.

The America that elected Barack Obama in 2008 is a very

different place from the America of the 1950s and 1960s, but only those who lived through those years can fully appreciate how dramatic the transformation has been. The full fury of what African Americans endured has faded in the popular imagination, and with it an appreciation of how extraordinary it was that the rights they achieved were largely of their own making. They had no new revolutionary doctrines, only the old ones enshrined in the Constitution and the Bible and a dedication to peaceful change. Most of the people I met on my travels expected that reform would have to be instigated and enacted by the white community. Almost no one anticipated that blacks would take the lead themselves.

Zigzagging my way south, I spent a few days in Kentucky at Barry Bingham's *Louisville Courier-Journal,* which by cool, positive reporting and quiet editorials had coached the city so well on school desegregation that all fifty-four public schools opened to black children without incident only two years after *Brown v. Board of Education,* the 1954 Supreme Court ruling ending segregated (and inferior) schooling. It was an inspiring example of what a newspaper could do with reporting and advocacy. It was cold water in my face to stop off farther south in the sullen town of Clinton, in the Cumberland Mountains of eastern Tennessee, where the influence of a decent enough paper, the weekly *Clinton Courier,* had not prevailed against baser passions. An outside agitator had gone about showing a picture of a black man kissing a white woman, and a riot had ensued. The National Guard had restored order, but I didn't like the looks of the knots of young toughs hanging about in leather jackets and jeans or the thin-faced mountain people who sat unsmiling in a pinball diner; they stared hard at me when I stopped for a coffee.

I was relieved to leave the ferment in Clinton (where the high school was blown up a year after my visit). I found an antidote to the poisons in the resolute manner in which the professors at Tuskegee Institute (now University) in Alabama faced the indignities inflicted on them. "It's not conducive to confidence in the system," said a doctor with the irony of the long-patient, "when I come back here from my home in Atlanta, there's not a single place where I am allowed to stop or eat or go to the restroom. That's one hundred fifty miles of willed restraint." Whenever I could, I talked to black people of all kinds about their experiences. They were usually uneasy talking to me in a public place: I might be compromising them if I instinctively put out my hand for a handshake. Why should they trust a stranger? And how could I, a privileged white foreigner, possibly understand what it was like to be an ordinary black man relegated to the most menial work and degraded services not just in schools but also in restrooms, parks, waiting rooms, elevators, bowling alleys, bars, cinemas, restaurants, beauty parlors, hospitals, professional organizations, trains, buses, and hotels? When I mentioned this to a white reporter in Mississippi, his response was "How'd you like to be one of eight thousand whites in Holmes County among twenty-four thousand blacks?"

At Morehouse College in Atlanta, I talked about newspaper responsibilities with the mentor of the newly emergent Martin Luther King Jr. — the scholar and humanitarian Benjamin Mays. Editors, he told me, had an inescapable duty to be sensitive to the wrongs and injustices perpetrated against blacks and to strive by faith and reason to close the gap between America's ideals and its practice. Only a handful of newspaper editors anywhere were doing that. The watchwords of liberalism were "moderation" and "patience," as if the denial of the fundamental right to vote could wait another century or two. In the North the interest was sporadic even among liberal organs such as the *New York Times, Newsweek, Time,* and the *Washington Post*. A sensational crime like the Till case or, earlier, the brutal blinding of World War II veteran Isaac Woodard Jr. in South Carolina would make its way into the headlines with strong editorials. Then the case would be allowed to fade; the reporting (not controlled by the editorial page editor) would diminish or vanish, as would the editorial pressure on local leaders, business, and Washington's lawmakers and bureaucrats.

Mays's words were the origin of a conviction I was to carry with me into my editorship: it may not be enough to print the truth once. Amnesia is a characteristic of all newspapers; it is natural. They have to move on to the next day's story and the next. It's an effort to keep connecting the dots and worthwhile only when the dots look like they're adding up to a significant picture.

In the South editors such as Ralph McGill at the big *Atlanta Constitution*, Hodding Carter II at the *Delta Democrat Times* in Greenville, Mississippi, and Harry Ashmore at the *Arkansas Gazette* were pinpricks of light in a dark scene, if not rallying points for reformers. But I was disappointed at the gradualist caution that considered it brave to give a black man the prefix "Mister." At the time I was there, McGill was regarded in the North as the conscience of the South, but he felt that *Brown* must be obeyed not so much because it was social justice but because nine men had said it was now the law. In that view there was no passion to right a historical wrong. Those newspapers making a moderate, reasoned case for accepting the Supreme Court ruling were speaking out not against Jim Crow laws that relegated blacks to second-class status, but rather against the brutality that went into their enforcement.

That ritual hypocrisy was made clear when I spent time working on the liberal-minded *News & Observer* in Raleigh, North Carolina. The newspaper was edited by the doughty

Jonathan Daniels, a New Dealer and for a short time press secretary to President Harry Truman. Not to be confused with
the civil rights activist of the same name who was murdered in
1965, Daniels was a fine writer and open-minded, as were his
staff. Tagging along with the paper's columnist Charlie Craven, who could see the funny side of anything, I half-forgot the
predicaments of blacks. Then one hot day I stopped to drink at
a town water fountain, one marked "White," situated next to
one marked "Colored," and looking up I saw that the adjacent
statue was dedicated to "Liberty and Equality."

In due course, Ralph McGill came around to despising
the "chloroforming myths" of white supremacy, but he was
exceptional in his society. Even before he took this stance,
most southern editors and their readers regarded him and
anyone else who advocated obeying the *Brown* decision as a
radical.

I traveled extensively through the plantation belt of the Deep
South, sweltering in the humid one-hundred-degree heat, as
big flying beetles hit the porches while I sagged listening to
the same expositions on how well the races had been getting
on before outsiders started to interfere. The insistent theme
was this: "Leave the South alone. We'll solve our 'problem'
in our own good time. We understand our 'nigras,' and you
don't. The North can't talk about segregation; look at the race
riots in Chicago." At lovely dinners given by gracious hosts, I
knew it was my job to listen, but I got to the point where I had
difficulty restraining myself from protesting as I heard again
how kindly "good Negroes" in their towns were treated, how
much happier they were here than in the ghettos of the North,
or how any attempt to "rush things" would only stir up the
"ignorant mob" terrified of miscegenation.

Accustomed to the homogeneous conformities of home, I was psychologically unprepared for the succession of shocks in the divided South—the way the respectable white leadership looked the other way when violence was done to blacks, the fact that all too often the crimes were committed with the acquiescence of law enforcement. Most of all, perhaps, I was tormented by the contradiction that the white middle-class people I met were ostensibly kindly folk of generous impulses. We British thought of ourselves as a generous nation, but compared to American philanthropy, ours was meager. In every town on my American travels, I was aware of middle-class groups organized for benevolence. In the mid-1800s, Alexis de Tocqueville wrote of this American gift for association, and it was just as true a hundred years later. Alas, in the Deep South in the 1950s, I saw the dark side of the gift in community after community: clergymen, shopkeepers, politicians, bankers, auto dealers, lawyers, doctors, and dentists organized for repression through the White Citizens Councils, a movement inspired by a Yale-educated Mississippi circuit judge. The councils declared that they forswore violence and would resist school desegregation by legal means. It sounded like democracy in action, but it wasn't. They were determined to keep blacks down in every respect and especially to stop blacks from voting.

The councils' weapons were not billy clubs but denial of work, credit, supplies, and housing, as well as a boycott of any white newspaper advocating compliance with the Supreme Court on any issue of segregation. By 1957 only 5 percent of Mississippi blacks had been allowed to register to vote. The immediate past president of the American Chamber of Commerce took me around black schools in Jackson to show me how happy the students were, and I asked him about this denial of the vote. "Only isolated cases," he said. The attorney

227

general of the state was more blunt. "Yes, we don't encourage them," he told me in a disquisition on African Americans' inferiority. "Maybe a wrong was done to the babbling natives of Africa brought here, but I am not willing to accept that the race of Negroes can get to the same position in two hundred or three hundred years that yours and mine attained in several thousand years. Would you know, I saw a Negro boy urinating in the street today?"

There were many acts of individual decency among news-paper editors in the South. Eugene Patterson, who succeeded McGill as editor of the *Atlanta Constitution*, rejected an FBI offer to let the paper catch Martin Luther King Jr. in a com-promising position with a woman. That was not surprising for a progressive like Patterson, but even the most rabid segre-gationist editor in the state refused to touch the story. Rarely, though, was any white brave or imprudent enough to express an outrage proportionate to the outrages committed against blacks. I spent time with such a man in the small town of Petal, Mississippi, across the river from Hattiesburg. His name was P. D. East, and his house had just been firebombed when I visited. East was thirty-three years old, six feet two, and heavy: a rawboned product of the lumber camps, a million miles from the colonnaded pretensions of plantation homes set among their azaleas and Spanish moss. In the army and in civilian life heaving sacks in a store and working on the railroad, he had never thought twice about blacks and segregation before the Supreme Court ruling in *Brown*. He did not think about them much then either. The year before, he had talked himself into starting a weekly newspaper, the *Petal Paper*, having learned the ropes on a union paper. He worked eighteen hours a day to build a six-page newspaper with two thousand readers and was making money. He never entertained any thoughts of coming out against the mores of the society in which he had been born and raised. And then he found that he could not live with himself.

The way he put it to me was that he just got sick of the daily hypocrisies: a cunning law to stop blacks from voting; the humiliation of black leaders who turned up at a meeting called by whites to discuss the town's schools, then were told they couldn't stay because according to Mississippi law, whites and blacks could not be in the same room together. "One Sunday morning last month," he said, "I was in my office, and I felt that if I didn't say something about what was stuck in my craw, I'd explode." Who can imagine what a nightmare of the soul it was for a man like East to pull himself out of the swamp of a deep-seated prejudice that seemed a natural way of life, and do it in such a way as to hazard his livelihood and even his life? His epiphany took the form of a satirical column comparing the progress in his native state to that of a crawfish. The progressive Hodding Carter II wrote to him from Greenville: "I hope you leave a forwarding address." He stayed, in pursuit, as he put it, of his hobby of self-destruction. Week after week he poked fun at the beasts in the "Magnolia Jungle," reckoning it was a complete waste of time to deliver sermons. He offered membership in the "Better Bigots Bureau," the privileges of which included "freedom to interpret the constitution of the United States to your own personal advantage!...Freedom to yell 'nigger' as much as you please without your conscience bothering you!" A typical send-up announced, "Don't suffer the summer heat by using your regular uniform of muslin bed sheet. Be modern! Inquire about our complete stock of cotton eyelet embroidery; Klanettes may enlarge the holes for the arms but your heads will fit nicely through the eyelets as they are."

His telephone calls would tell him he was a nigger-loving, Jew-loving, Communist son of a bitch. He met everything with humor. While he was stopped at a light in Hattiesburg, a man on the curb said, "Aren't you P. D. East? If you'll get out of the car, I'll mop up the street with you." East replied, "I am sorry, that's not sufficient inducement." The *Petal Paper* was outrageous—silly, if you like—and effective in killing his business in Mississippi. But to me it was the gold standard.

I'd had a taste of the feudal pathologies at work in the Deep South from reading the novels of William Faulkner (a quiet admirer of the *Petal Paper*) and the 1941 classic *The Mind of the South* by Wilbur Cash. But by the end of my months there, I found myself simply unable to take it any longer.

One day I argued with the belligerent Robert Patterson, the organizing genius of the White Citizens Council movement, who'd been signing up thousands of members all over the South at Kiwanis, Rotary, and Farm Bureau lunches. Sitting in his office in Jackson, I told him that I'd shaken hands with a Negro, and yes, I'd have a Negro to dinner, and no, we didn't discriminate in England (I was too sanguine on that score). He was a big, hulking man; I was intemperate, and he took offense.

It was probably just bad luck, but when Enid and I left Jackson, we had a nasty experience on a lonely mountain road heading into Arkansas. I saw cars coming up fast behind me. The lead car had me in a dazzling spot. I pulled over to let the cars pass, but they pulled over, too, and several men in rough farm clothes got out and approached. "Didya notice that little bitty of a stoplight at the crossing back there?" one asked. Well, I said, I'd seen a blinking amber light, and I'd paused several seconds to make sure both roads were clear. "Yeah, well, round here we say that an amber is a stoplight. Come with us."

We were taken back to a little town and escorted into a dimly lit, bare room, while the gang kicked stones outside. My imagination had been inflamed by all the stories of police brutality I'd been hearing. Were these men even police? "Ya been in Mississippi, right?" said a man who claimed to be the sheriff. "Not from these parts?" I said we were from England. It seemed an age before he absorbed this information, then he asked me for $20, which I gave him. It was a lot of money in 1956—$140 at today's values—but worth it when we were allowed to go. I had a shameful feeling: I was glad I was white.

Which was the real America? The schizophrenic towns of the Deep South, the dour enlightened German city of Milwaukee, the Li'l Abner country in the wooded hillsides of Kentucky, or hedonistic San Francisco? At the end of thousands of miles of travel through forty states, defeated by the immensity of space and the infinite complexities of the people, I decided there was no real America. When pressed on my return home to give an answer, I settled for a small town in the corn-and-hog belt of the Midwest.

Smalltown USA: what is left of it? In one decade exposed as a small-minded hell by Sinclair Lewis's *Main Street*, in another pickled in nostalgia by Norman Rockwell's *Saturday Evening Post* covers, more recently satirized in the movies *American Beauty* and *The Truman Show* and then claimed as the heartland of Karl Rove's "red state" empire. But in 1956, Smalltown USA was epitomized for me by Paris, Illinois, a township of thirteen thousand people with fifteen churches of fifteen different denominations, all the races thoroughly integrated as Americans. They lived in white clapboard houses overhung with maple and elm trees and fronted by unfenced lawns and pole-perched mailboxes. While at the University of Chicago, before Enid arrived, I drove through the little town square with its sandstone courthouse and tower, and past the Farm Bureau, where men in earmuffs stamped their feet in the cold. Five miles of gravel roads brought me in sight of a corncrib and the sturdy redbrick farmhouse where Ed Gumm and his family had offered to put me up.

It was what I came to see as an act of generosity typical of Smalltown USA, where strangers were welcome. The Gumms had no idea who I was; they had just extended an invitation to any foreign student to spend Thanksgiving with them. The family consisted of Ed, age forty-one, a short sturdy man with sharp blue eyes, of German, Scots-Irish, and Swiss ancestry; his schoolteacher wife, Isabel; and their six-year-old daughter. His grandmother had crossed the Atlantic alone at age twelve. His grandfather had built the twelve-room farmhouse and planted the screen of trees. The Gumms were Christian Scientists. They told me that when Ed broke his collarbone in a fall from a corncrib, he let the fracture heal itself while he read from his Bible.

The temperature was fourteen degrees below freezing. Icicles hung from the long, white front porch. It was snug inside, warm with the smell of beef stew. I looked out on the desolate prairie. A heavy silence pressed down from the sky. Ed predicted snow. It was not hard to imagine the icy, howling wilderness this had been a little more than one hundred years before, when the pioneers had come with their oxen and covered wagons and crude rafts. Then, there were seven-foot-high prairie grasses; swamps and mosquitoes; wolves, panthers, and bears; and marauding Sac Indians, led by the pro-British Black Hawk, finally defeated by the settlers' militia in 1832 in a battle an arrow's flight away from the Gumms' farm. An old tomahawk turned up in the soil while I was there.

I was up at 5:00 a.m. with Ed and his one hired hand, making the rounds of his 480 acres of corn and soybeans. The federal government offered subsidies to farmers like Ed, but he told me, "They can keep their dollars. All those government dollars come out of the pockets of poorer townsfolk paying taxes. And I don't like government officials on my land." That meant turning down $2,000 a year (around $20,000 today). Money like that would quiet the conscience of most men, but Ed, when I pressed him, insisted in his slow, cheerful voice, "A man's substance is what he believes in."

In Paris, Illinois, I felt I was very close to the old Midwest and the men and women who had turned the wilderness into America's larder. When I mingled with people like the Gumms, they seemed to me to have inherited not just the land but also the pioneer virtues that had been lost in the big cities. In the cities the primitive vigor remained, titanic and miraculous, but unaccompanied, I thought, by those other original qualities, such as devoutness, simplicity, patience, deep independence of thought, and neighborliness. If Smalltown USA seems in retrospect like a product of my imagination, individuals like Ed Gumm, Benjamin Mays, Jason Betzinez, and P. D. East were real enough. And people like that were the real America.

I was going back to England conflicted by all I had experienced: exhilarated—outside the Deep South—by the restless optimism; warmed by the breezy, unpretentious friendliness of a society that was more open than my own, with similar values but more vigor; moved by a common unabashed search for redemption in doing good; inspired by what a truly free independent press might achieve; and for the same reason inflamed by its passivity in securing equal protections for the most vulnerable. I admired how editors and reporters had achieved a fruitful status by demonstrating a commitment to their communities, as much as to their corporations, as well as the way they had done it through public-spirited investigation, professional pride, and a sense of decency. Yes, their newspapers were duller than ours, and profligate, too. I envied the big-city editors who had imaginative separate sections for books, science, business, and society, yet the news pages everywhere were slackly edited and designed with rivulets of news on pages leased to supermarkets.

I now longed for a chance to marry the best of American and British journalism. Whether I would get to do so after such a long absence from the battlefront was another matter.

11

From Delhi to Darlington

One of the most versatile, courageous, and creative editors in the history of newspapers perished on the *Titanic* on April 15, 1912. William Thomas Stead (1849–1912) was on his way to lecture in America. Men desperate to get into one of the last sixteen lifeboats were held back at gunpoint while Stead, a solitary bearded man in his sixties, sat in the first-class smoking salon, apparently oblivious to the dramas around him or his own mortal peril. One survivor saw him reading his Bible as the ocean flooded in below. Another said that Stead gave his life jacket to someone escaping in the last lifeboat.

At the *Pall Mall Gazette* Stead had investigated and exposed the evils of child prostitution, sanctioned by Victorian high society, and gone to jail for it. He'd made his name long before that in his very first editorship when he wrote passionate editorials that roused the whole of Europe against Ottoman Empire atrocities in Bulgaria—the holocaust of the nineteenth century. Only in his twenties, he did this from the relative obscurity of the market town of Darlington, in the northeast of England, where for nine years he edited the regional daily newspaper the *Northern Echo*.

As I steamed safely back across the Atlantic at the end of

the Harkness Fellowship, I could never have imagined that I would soon assume my own first editorship in Darlington, sitting in Stead's worn leather editorial chair.

Curiously the route to Darlington was to be through Delhi. On my return, I became an assistant editor of the *Manchester Evening News*. Eleven months into my duties, which included editing the paper on Saturdays (but only Saturdays), Big Tom suggested that I might like to step off the treadmill and spend a few weeks in India. He may have indulged me because, as I learned many years later, he had secretly vetoed the intention of Alastair Hetherington to invite me on my return from the Harkness trip to be his assistant editor at the *Manchester Guardian*. "You can take time off to help out Mr. Nehru" was the grandiloquent way Tom released me.

Ten years after independence, Prime Minister Jawaharlal Nehru was exasperated that the Indian press was still stuck in the Victorian mode bequeathed by British imperialism, in touch with officialdom but out of touch with the newly literate masses. The country had 40 million literates in a population of 465 million, but the total circulation of all the newspapers, vernacular and English, was less than 3 million. "I can't reach the people through the newspapers," Nehru told Jim Rose, the visionary first director of the International Press Institute (IPI). One of the founders of the IPI, Rose was passionately concerned with human dignity and freedom. As a high British intelligence officer in the war, he'd protested directly to Winston Churchill that bombing Dresden would be a crime. After the war he became literary editor of the *Observer*. He was a sensitive, graceful man, gifted with the ability to listen with such evident appreciation that the speaker of the most mundane truisms felt elevated in his presence. He followed up on

Nehru's remark at once by getting the Rockefeller Foundation to fund a program of technical training at the shirtsleeves level of newsroom, printing shop, and accounting office.

Big Tom, a keen member of the IPI, had suggested that I teach newspaper editing and design for two or three weeks. As soon as Big Tom's recommendation was accepted in Zurich, bundles of newspapers rained down on me from the subcontinent: a score of titles in English and another score in the scripts of Hindi, Punjabi, Tamil, Urdu, Malayalam, Marathi, Bengali, Kannada, Gujarati, Konkani, Oriya, and Assamese. I could see what was wrong with the disorganized layouts and unimaginative photographs, and even wonder at the apparent rambling prolixity of multideck headlines I could only scan. The English-language papers that I could understand had news columns written in treacle and topped by don't-read-this headlines ("Fissiparous Tendencies Remarked in State Government Report").

At the first workshop I conducted with thirty or so Indian editors in Delhi, I urged that news headlines should focus on people and be written in short, simple words with a verb in the active voice. On the blackboard I chalked as a basic example of a good headline the old definition of news: "Man Bites Dog," shorter and superior, I suggested, to "Canine Bitten by Human," whereupon I was denounced from the front row by a silver-haired man in a dhoti. What I had proposed, he flared, would corrupt the Hindi language. It was cheap, nasty sensationalism to have verbs in the active voice and present tense. Furthermore, he knew of no case in India where a man had bitten a dog.

Jim Rose gravely explained that Mr. Evans was attempting to make a point by parody, but then there was another eruption of protest—not at my insensitivity, but at the obduracy of the older man. "We must change!" cried one of the younger editors. "He resists it because he belongs to the old India of the Raj. Yes, 'Man Bites Dog.' Yes! Yes!" From round the room came a rapid-fire declension of "Man Bites Dog" in Gujarati, Bengali, Urdu, Punjabi, and Malayalam. The discussions about the state of Indian journalism, afire with enthusiasm, spilled over from the hot seminar room into the hotel, and they were still going on when I went to bed very anxious. I learned later I worried too much about all the head shaking I'd encountered: for an Indian a head shake is a sign of agreement, not dissent.

It's fair to say that the IPI workshops, of which this was only the first of many over the years, encouraged a revolution in Indian newspapers, broadening their appeal and reinforcing their viability and their capacity to monitor government and business. But by no means was this renaissance inspired only by British and American missionaries, and it was certainly not carried out by them, but by editors such as K. M. Mathew of the *Malayala Manorama* in Kerala, who put everything he learned into practice and doubled his circulation. His newspaper became the foundation of a media empire of twenty-five publications and various television stations.

Lightning struck the subcontinent most effectively in the form of a chubby-cheeked ebony Asian, Varindra Tarzie Vittachi. He appeared to be as urbane as "the brown sahibs" of the postcolonial era he satirized in his book by that title, but it was merely a convenient mask for passion. Editor of the *Ceylon Observer* at age thirty-two, he'd fled the country after exposing the role of the government in the incitement of race riots. Jim Rose had persuaded him to be director of the IPI Asian program, in charge of training missions in Southeast Asia, and Tarzie and Jim had made prodigious journeys throughout the region, identifying the new generation's leaders in newspapers and the opportunities open to them for reaching a vast untapped readership at moderate expense. They found, for instance, that

10 percent of the costly newsprint was wasted by bad press-room practices: there was no concept of copy flow. Only six of India's five hundred dailies used a makeup sheet to instruct the printer on the placement of headlines, stories, and pictures, so the printer just threw the paper together with much confusion and delay. Tarzie demonstrated the utility of the sketched page plan, from which editor and printer could work. For decades afterward, until the arrival of computers, the layout sheet was referred to throughout the subcontinent as a Vittachi.

Tarzie burst into our Delhi discussions with the fire of a revivalist preacher—he was a member of the spiritual brotherhood of Subud—but he was also Rabelaisian, vastly entertained by life, and a champion deflator of pomp. He visited practical, informed vehemence on any journalist unable or unwilling to relate the columns of his newspaper to the hard daily life of the people: children dying from dehydration during the yearly "diarrhea season," families caught in the toils of debt to loan sharks, street traders persecuted by petty officials. For twenty-five years he mocked the paraphernalia of bureaucracy by traveling everywhere with the documents of the fictitious "Republic of Amnesia," bearing, for the health regulators, a stamp of approval by "Dr. Portly Rumbel of the Quarantine Department."

Working with a variety of British, Asian, and American advisers, I sweated design and editing for several years on other periodic ventures into newsrooms in Malaysia, Korea, Japan, and the Philippines. In Manila we wrote headlines about an earthquake even as it arrived to shake our desks. In Davao I joined in designing a discretionary code for reporting racial and religious tensions. Thousands had died in India because newspapers and broadcasters had carelessly publicized rumors, but community tensions had exploded in Northern Ireland and the United States, too.

I learned much from what I saw and from the others in the traveling circus. Amitabha Chowdhury, from the Bengali paper *Jugantar,* inspired us all in leading what was almost certainly the first-ever professional discussion in India of the ethics and purposes of investigative journalism. He described how he'd got into it when two shy middle-aged clerks in the office of the director of statistics of the West Bengali government came to see him because they were uneasy about the way their boss manipulated statistical reports to serve a political group. Small beer, you might think, but the fake figures that were used to justify a fare increase on the tramways provoked a week's bloodbath in the streets of Calcutta. Chowdhury spent months tracking nepotism and corruption in the department and had no hesitation in fixing blame. "For positive journalism," he said, "there is no role for the neutralist, no scope for timidity in the name of so-called objectivity." Chowdhury made waves.

I remember most the young Serajuddin Hussein, news editor of the Bengali-language daily *Ittefaq* in Dacca, then East Pakistan. Serajuddin took to heart Chowdhury's mantra that if you stayed with a story, your paper would become a magnet for people with information. A missing child was not a story in Dacca. Serajuddin made it one. Every time he heard of a child vanishing in the busy streets and bazaars, he noted it on his front page and reminded everyone that this was the second, third, fourth, fifth, sixth child that month and none of them had returned home. His persistence revealed that not a handful of children were missing, but scores. He asked the authorities to investigate the possibility that a kidnapping gang was at work. They laughed at him.

A month or so later he went to the authorities with a tip from an informant. Police raided a remote village eighty miles from Dacca and found most of the children, deliberately maimed—some of them blinded—so that they would make pitiable beggars on the city streets. The gang leaders were hanged. Within six months the *Ittefaq* nearly doubled its circulation. Serajuddin was so proud that he wrote to me and others about his plans for investigating other abuses. When East Pakistan rebelled in 1971, he was among the "intellectuals" sought out and murdered by the Pakistani Army.

When I landed in London after a very long flight from Kuala Lumpur, I almost missed a small item in the *Guardian* telling its readers that Mr. Harford Thomas, editor of the *Oxford Mail*, was joining Alastair Hetherington as deputy editor. No successor was named. Could it mean that an editor's chair was going begging in Oxford? But who would I have to beg? Nobody in Oxford. The *Mail* was the property of the Westminster Press group, owner of a number of provincial newspapers and the *Financial Times*. All the editorships, I discovered, were in the gift of the editorial director in London, one Charles Fenby, whose work I had admired without knowing it was his. *Picture Post* and *Leader* were two of the wartime and early-postwar magazines, both dazzling in their different ways (*Leader* was more literary). Fenby had been assistant editor of *Picture Post* from 1940 to 1944 and editor of *Leader* from 1944 to 1948. He had also helped found the *Oxford Mail* (he was an Oxford graduate), and with his best friend at Oxford, the future poet laureate Cecil Day-Lewis, he'd compiled *Anatomy of Oxford* in 1938. He'd been editor in chief of the *Birmingham Gazette* before becoming editorial director of Westminster Press.

A thin, dry voice I could hardly hear came on the line when I telephoned Fenby. "Ah, yes, the *Oxford Mail*. Applications have been falling on my desk like confetti. What makes you think you could edit the *Oxford Mail*?" I told him. Silence. My pitch had been too long. Clearly while I'd waffled, he'd gone off to read *War and Peace*. I bit my tongue. A small movement of air I interpreted as a sigh eventually struggled along the cable from London to Manchester, followed by words. "I suppose you'd better come down for a little chat if you don't mind what might be a wasted day. Good morning." Click.

Arriving at Newspaper House, Great New Street, a few days later, I found Fenby to be a pale, dome-headed man in his early forties who punctuated his glacial speech with light, mocking laughs. He'd warmed up since I'd phoned. It transpired that my IPI connections had come into play. Jim Rose's beautiful actress wife, Pamela, was the sister of Pat Gibson, who was vice chairman of Westminster Press. Jim had mentioned our adventures in India to Pam, she'd mentioned them to Pat, who'd mentioned them to Charles, who also just happened to be chairman of the British committee of the IPI.

"The *Oxford Mail* is not for you," said Fenby at once to my disappointment. But he went on, "I've heard about the work you did in India. Rather surprised you didn't tell me about *that*. You'll know our *Northern Echo* in Darlington from your Durham days, read by the coal miners' families, edited by the great W. T. Stead. You know Stead, I trust?" He then drifted into a rumination as if I weren't there. "Now Mark Barrington-Ward is the editor of the *Echo,* Balliol man, not too happy in county Durham. Perfect I'd think for Oxford." Pause. "As indeed Evans may be for Darlington. Let me think about it."

So it was that in June 1961, Westminster chess master Fenby designated me as the bishop to move diagonally north from Manchester to edit the *Northern Echo* and Barrington-Ward as the castle to move directly south to Oxford. "It comes as no surprise," said Big Tom in a generous note about my nine years with him.

It did to me. Finally given the challenge of editorship, I stood astonished at my own pretension. I'd been inordinately ambitious to succeed in all the stages of newspaper life. I was assiduous in learning the crafts. An editorship had always seemed the logical goal, so I had applied, but now that it was about to be realized for something more substantial than the *Empire Flying School Review,* I had a sudden loss of confidence.

I knew I could do all the nuts and bolts of newspapering, but there was more to editing than a sequence of crafts. It was all very well to carry out the instructions of Big Tom in reporting and editing or to find fault with papers in Asia and America. I didn't really risk much beyond the shame of getting it wrong. As a critic I was not hazarding a whole newspaper. Here I was about to have care of a venerable title, but one beset by competition, its circulation ebbing, headquartered in a small town, staffed by people whose skill I could not guess, whose attitude toward a stranger might be unfriendly, and whose management I didn't know in the way I knew Big Tom and Laurence Scott. I was thirty-two. This was it.

I arrived in Darlington, a pleasant market town, in August 1961, with Enid and our one-year-old daughter, Ruth, who'd been born in Manchester. I touched for good luck a large granite boulder outside the redbrick offices of the *Northern Echo* in Priestgate. Stead used to tether his pony to the ring on the boulder at his home in Grainey Hill, a village two miles out. I saw the boulder, which had been moved to Darlington in the 1950s, every day when I walked to work, its bronze inscription identifying the granite as a fitting symbol of Stead's indomitable courage and strength of character and proclaiming "His Spirit Still Lives."

Charles Fenby had something approaching reverence for Stead's professionalism—Stead had invented the big-time newspaper interview and the cross heading to break up slabs of text—but he admired Stead most for his crusading journalism. Fenby had seen to it that I read "The Maiden Tribute of Modern Babylon," Stead's exposé of white slave traffic in London. To shock Victorian society into acknowledging what it furtively condoned, in 1885 Stead bought a girl of thirteen for five pounds to expose how the trade and hypocrisy were locked in embrace. The sensation of what he called his "infernal narrative" in the *Pall Mall Gazette* succeeded in shaming the House of Commons into raising the age of consent for sexual intercourse from thirteen to sixteen, an overdue reform that had been blocked in the Commons after its passage in the Lords. His enemies saw to it that Stead was prosecuted for spoiling the fun. He was jailed for three months for abduction on the trumped-up technicality that although he had the permission of the mother for his symbolic transaction, he hadn't secured that of the absent drunken father.

Enid and I renewed Barrington-Ward's rental agreement for a spacious ground-floor apartment in a solid Victorian house by a park. I was so puffed up at finally being an editor, and one in line of descent from a legend, that the first morning I was due to start work, I marched naked from bedroom to bathroom declaiming, "Here comes the editor!" forgetting that along with the apartment, we'd retained the services of Barrington-Ward's spinster housekeeper, Miss Edith Mullis, who wished me "Good morning, sir," and got on with folding towels. All her life she had been "in service," as she put it, meaning that she had been one of the aproned downstairs ladies facilitating the upstairs life of the landed gentry in the heyday, long gone, of North Yorkshire's fashionable country-house parties.

The *Northern Echo*, in its antiquated appearance with a fake Gothic title piece, small type, and rambling headline style, resembled one of those faded Edwardian establishments. It had a history and character, but its carriageway was unweeded, and its plumbing gurgled all night.

Reginald Gray, editor for the fourteen years before Barrington-Ward, was a Darlington grammar-school boy who'd been at the paper all his life—chief sub for twenty-two years before reaching the chair. He was a big man, saddened by disappointment; he'd lost a leg in the fighting at Arras in France in 1917 and didn't for a decade return to his field of dreams, the cricket pitch. His left-arm spinners still eviscerated the opposition, but he was reclusive. He mixed little with the staff and was very strict with those he did encounter. He did not encourage visitors to his office, where he read a great deal and wrote book reviews. Reporters dare not show up in Fair Isle pullovers or corduroy pants. "Few of you need to be told, I expect," he told a training conference, "one does not wear a white tie with a dinner jacket or a black tie with tails."

The female secretaries and copy takers invited censure if they wore makeup or earrings. He imposed a lot of unbreakable rules on the newspaper, too. One was that no regional news could appear on the front page. Another was that on the inside pages a place name had to feature in every headline. He was an excellent judge of subeditors and was content to hand over the paper to the chief sub when he left the office in the early evening.

The *Northern Echo* of his day, and Barrington-Ward's, too, was assiduous in covering an impressive range of local news, but it had not even the whisper of a voice. The editorials were written in London, exclusively on national and foreign affairs; so were the main editorial features (including a canned half page for women). Only London writers were allowed bylines. When statistics were released or someone made a speech, the paper duly reported the adversities facing the basic industries of coal, chemicals, steel, heavy engineering, and shipbuilding, but it took them as a given, an act of nature.

Fenby told me the London editorials and features were not imposed. They were on offer as a service to all the newspapers in the Westminster Press group. I took him at his word; I intended relying less on London. How could I not, sitting every night in Stead's very own chair, confronted by a letter in his copperplate handwriting framed on the opposite wall: "What a glorious opportunity of attacking the devil, isn't it?"

Stead had written the letter to a clergyman friend on being appointed editor in 1871, to ask whether a God-fearing man could edit the Monday morning edition when it meant being in the office later than 7:00 p.m. on Sunday. His contract stipulated that he did not have to work after 9:00 p.m., but evil being no respecter of the clock, he was often still at his desk later than that every night, including Sunday, doing the Lord's work. In those days he conceived that as attacking Benjamin Disraeli and the Tory Party, Stead was a committed member of Gladstone's Liberal Party. I liked the definition by Sir Linton Andrews, editor of the *Yorkshire Post*, that an editor of a great newspaper was the temporary custodian of a tradition, but much as I admired Stead, I couldn't follow him undeviatingly down this anti-Tory road. I was tired of partisan journalism; it wasn't the opinions I minded, but how they corrupted the news pages.

Of course I knew too well how prewar Tory administrations had neglected the industrial regions, the North West and North East, but five years of Labour government hadn't made an appreciable impact, and in 1961 we had in Harold Macmillan the best Tory prime minister we could have had. "Supermac," as he was called for picking up the broken bits after the Suez crisis, had in 1929 been the MP for Stockton-on-Tees, a key town in my area, when every third man was out of a job.

The old Etonian and classics scholar at Balliol affected to be a tweedy Edwardian patrician, but he'd seen the hardships firsthand and understood what it meant for a man to be out of work for years and without the dignity of owning a home. In the 1930s he'd broken ranks to press for social reform, just as he had to defy the policy of Chamberlain and the Tory machine, which he saw as asking Hitler what he wanted and gift wrapping it for him. During my editorship, the conviction born of his Stockton experiences led Macmillan to give jobs and expansion a higher priority than preserving the exchange rate for the pound sterling, the cause of the walkout of his entire treasury team of monetarists. He neatly dismissed the exodus as "a little local difficulty."

So I regarded Supermac as a good bet. If we reported and argued effectively, the region might win a better share of public-sector investment to tackle its twentieth-century devils: a male unemployment rate twice the national average; little new industry; thousands of slum homes without a bath; air and water pollution; schools falling down; landscapes scarred by derelict spoil heaps from exhausted coal mines. My view was that the industrial areas had contributed so much to the nation's wealth—indeed, sacrificed so much—that reparations were due them.

Of course, for all his virtues, Macmillan couldn't by himself regenerate the region. It was psychologically depressed by daily life amid the debris of the industrial revolution and the careless 1930s. It had to be roused from stoicism to strenuous endeavor; it had to inspire more civic service; it had to nurture its own culture: two cathedral cities, two universities, the Northern Sinfonia orchestra, and the creative talents that had somehow flowered in the privations of the pit villages, most notably in the paintings by Norman Cornish, thirty-three years underground, and the novels by Sid Chaplin. I envisioned the

Northern Echo as forging the agenda here, yet the paper itself hardly relieved the gloom with a design in typography and layout ideal for Dickensian times. The single-column editorial was sometimes flanked by a black tombstone, an advertisement placed by a local undertaker. Nor could I expect to find eagerness for change among a staff long drilled in working to formulas.

Entering the *Manchester Evening News* office in 1952 had been like being tossed into the rapids of Bright Angel Creek. Nine years later, entering the *Northern Echo* office the day Barrington-Ward was to hand it over to me was rather different. For a start, I saw no human life on the editorial floor until I reached the editor's sanctum down a long, dark-green corridor. Inside, Mark bore the cares of the world on his shoulders (a genetic disposition: his father, Robert M. Barrington-Ward, DSO, MC, and Balliol, too, had been editor of the *Times* from 1941 to 1949). Tall, waistcoated (with a pocket watch on a chain), droll when he wasn't melancholy, charmingly shy for a man of intellect (he took a first at Balliol), Mark was very generous in describing all the problems he'd encountered in his eighteen months in the chair, getting sadder and sadder as he gave me his note to self, listing changes he thought imperative that he'd not yet been able to carry out.

I began to get one idea why after he strode off to catch the train to Oxford and I sat alone in his book-lined office. Editors work by command; there was nobody to command. The first day was emblematic. Nobody came into my office except the secretary I'd inherited, a young Darlington woman called Joan Thomas. (She was to prove a treasure; I knew she recognized my difficulties when she came in one day wearing a Salvation Army bonnet.) She asked brightly if I'd like to dictate. I would have liked to rattle off something on the lines of "Editor's Note to Staff: Where the hell are you all?" Nothing else was on my mind, but never having had the privilege before of dictating to anyone, I wrote a redundant note to Fenby saying I had arrived and seen the granite boulder. I noticed that Miss Thomas's outlines were very good and said so. As a former teacher of Pitman shorthand, I was referring to the clarity of her penciled loops and dashes. These days I would no doubt have been reported and drummed out of office by a sexual harassment tribunal, but Joan Thomas had a sturdy common sense, coupled with knowing where the bodies were buried; she was to save me from many a misstep.

Of course I'd not expected that a daily morning newspaper, going to press around 11:00 p.m., would be anywhere near as busy during the day as an afternoon newspaper like the *Manchester Evening News,* but my isolation was uncanny; no, it was unnerving. I'd failed to realize quite what it meant to have the main reporting energies stationed outside the office. Darlington was the only town in the country producing a paper with a daily sale (then 100,000) bigger than its population (60,000). Its area of circulation was the largest of any provincial newspaper in England: 120 miles long and up to 60 miles wide, stretching from Berwick-upon-Tweed on the border of England and Scotland in the north to York in the south, and from the east coast to Penrith. This meant the paper was serving readers spread over 5,000 square miles of cities, towns, villages, and hamlets, and nearly 50 reporters were not in Darlington but scattered in 14 branch offices, supplemented by 130 correspondents, 20 of them professionals and the rest part-time amateurs—clergymen, teachers, clerks, owners of newspaper shops, retired policemen.

Even so, I was disconcerted by the absence of any executives. The *Northern Echo* did not have a news editor. It had a chief reporter, the rather suave, dark-visaged Dick Tarelli, but only half of him: we shared him with the *Despatch,* the small-circulation Darlington evening newspaper published from the same building by the North of England Newspaper Company, the Westminster Press subsidiary that owned the *Echo* and two thriving weeklies (the *Durham Advertiser* and the *Darlington and Stockton Times*). The evanescent Tarelli was preoccupied with pleasing the *Despatch*'s editor, the immaculately tailored Frank Staniforth, a senior figure of uncertain temper in the North of England Newspaper Company whose responsibilities as group managing editor then included administration of the weeklies, the *Despatch,* and the *Echo.* Tarelli, like the chief photographer and the editor, was accustomed to going home at 6:00 p.m.

The lassitude enveloping the floor was also partly a product of head-office geography. There were separate quarters for reporters, subeditors and photographers, and wire room. In all the daily newspapers I'd known, in Europe and even in India, there'd been a news hub, a big central arena where people could be seen at work to the same clock and you could feel news rippling across the floor, a place for newspaper shoptalk and gossip, a place where directions could be defined, instructions shouted, enthusiasm raised, arguments concentrated, layouts examined, and disputes resolved by crossing a few feet to another desk. If Darlington was the cortex of the *Echo,* it appeared to be without synapses.

Not until near dusk did some semblance of activity occur. A frail, stooped figure in a cardigan knocked and very timidly advanced into the room. "Would you like to look at hear all sides?" I got it. This was the letters feature "Hear All Sides," destined for that night's editorial page, for which Dick Yeomans was responsible. He wished he'd never asked. He was unlucky that it was my first chance to edit anything.

My pent-up energy fastened obsessively on a letter from a Shildon man who wrote that "like all women," his wife loved a nice cup of tea but had been asked to pay ninepence in a small Lake District café (as near as I can work out, that would be like paying four dollars now). Our outraged correspondent had calculated all the costs of making seventy cups from a quarter-pound packet; added the cost of sugar, milk, and overhead; and concluded that the 100 percent profit was capitalism at its most rapacious. I asked Yeomans if we should check it out with a tea-brewing experiment of our own. Could you really get seventy good cups from the leaves of a quarter pound of tea, or would it taste like dishwater? Should we challenge our readers to do it? Was a small café's overhead as high as the correspondent suggested? Yeomans, with good reason, got paler and paler. Was I joking? Miss Thomas came in to say the subeditors had started to arrive. I settled for a headline, "How Much Profit on a Cup of Tea?" enthusing to Yeomans that his page would ignite a national controversy we could run for weeks. He gently suggested it wouldn't start unless we got that page to press on time. I released him.

While I was fooling around with tea brewing, the world had moved to the boiling point. Khrushchev, working through his East German stooge Walter Ulbricht, was threatening to close the East–West Berlin border, isolating West Berlin. President John F. Kennedy, facing his first test since the ignominy of the Bay of Pigs cock-up, was dispatching Vice President Lyndon Johnson to Berlin; Britain was sending more fighter aircraft to West Germany. All this was chattering out of our four news agency wires as I went down the corridor to the subs' shabby quarters opposite the composing room.

There were about eleven men and one middle-aged woman, their heads down over piles of dimly lit copy. In the absence of the deputy editor—on a perfectly timed holiday—a roly-poly, balding man called Stanley Senior was in charge. He was the chief subeditor, occupied in riffling through bundles of copy from the far-flung reporters phoning in or sending packets by train. It was early in the evening, but already the printing room overseer was pressing a maddening buzzer to indicate he had men at the Linotype machines and no work to give them.

I was disinclined to breathe down the amiable Senior's neck when I hadn't yet met the deputy editor who ran the room. I wanted to see how the pulleys and levers worked before I tried to pull one, but a few days later, on a somnolent Sunday, I had to change my mind. At 5:00 p.m. the chief reporter in the Middlesbrough office phoned in to say his copy would be a little late because of the riots. What riots? Hadn't we heard? On Saturday several thousand people had taken to the streets. Colored people had been attacked. A Pakistani café had been set on fire. There hadn't been anything like it before. Oh, yes, I felt like saying, thanks a lot, and while you were on the phone I forgot to mention that World War III broke out this morning.

One of the characteristics in which I'm deficient as an authority figure is that I don't scare people. To say I'm even-tempered is not a boast but an admission. I should have thrown a fit in the subs' room that night. Tantrums are useful for making people sit up; they tiptoe around the volcano. Big Tom's incipient growl kept everyone on their toes. Rupert Murdoch has only to pick up the phone, and men a continent away genuflect before he utters a word. Some geniuses have had very short tempers—Ben Jonson and Isaac Newton seem to have exploded with ease—and some well-regarded political leaders have had horrible tempers: Truman for one, Eisenhower for another. Senior decently made excuses for the reporter, a taciturn older man, he told me, who did things by the book. We would catch up somehow. Besides, the riots had happened too late on a Saturday for the Sunday newspapers, so we still had the first bite at the story.

The lapse was actually quite useful. I told Senior I'd help out by handling the editing and layout of the story, and please to tell his good friend not simply to file the facts of the night but write five hundred words on the history of relations with colored people in Middlesbrough. I was sensitive on race, having smugly told the segregationists in the Deep South that British people were immune from any kind of racial prejudice.

On that Sunday night, immersed in subbing the story, I woke up with a start. I'd done nothing about Dick Yeomans, and there he was on his way to the composing room to send his page to press. The editorial was another London offering on West Berlin. I told him we'd surely want to replace it with a local comment on the riot and please to hold off for the moment. He came back into the subs' room paler than he had exited: "It's too late." The composing room overseer had refused to accept the request. "I told him it was the editor's wish," said Yeomans wanly.

I went into the composing room. The overseer had already sent the page to the foundry for platemaking. I cut him off at the pass by intervening with the stereo (platemaking) department. I told the bearded young stereo department chief (who belonged to a different union from the overseer) not to make the plate of the page he'd just received because a page with a new editorial was coming. He didn't know what to do. He was trapped. Who was the boss — the new editor or the established composing room overseer? The standoff between overseer and editor got rather tense. I decided to proceed as if all we had was a little local difficulty and rushed back to write a Middlesbrough editorial.

It was as imperative for the *Echo* to find a voice on issues like this as it was to excel in the reporting. The trouble with my impulse was that I was too busy to write the editorial myself, and the only writer around was a young man so shy he had difficulty getting to the end of a sentence. I had only just met

David Spark and had no idea that his prematurely bald head contained a keen analytical intelligence, a rapid-fire writing ability when required, and a profound knowledge of everything about the North East. I should have been reassured by the reaction of Yeomans. He regained his color; he knew that Spark would deliver insightful comment in double-quick time, and so he did. The overseer set the new editorial; the pages were a little bunched going to press on the first edition, but we were not late. The very nimble, thirtyish stone (composing room) hand, one Bill Treslove, made a lightning change on the editorial page, shuffling type slugs like a cardsharp. I designed a simplified front page, half of it given over to the riot.

The facts from the reporters at the scene made it clear the violence in Middlesbrough was only superficially a repeat of the 1958 riot in London's Notting Hill (in which seventy-six whites, mostly youths, were charged with offenses, as were thirty-six "colored" people). Notting Hill was undoubtedly a "race riot" in that both whites and blacks were charged with assaults. Middlesbrough's was more like hooliganism. Drunken youths coming out of the public houses had exploited a Friday night street fracas between an Arab and a white youth to attack anyone of color: West Indians, Pakistanis, Africans, Chinese. The minorities, only three thousand to four thousand in the whole town, had not retaliated; they had run away. So I wrote the simple banner MOBS OUT IN MIDDLESBRO' (instead of RACE RIOT IN MIDDLESBRO'). The editorial endorsed the point, and so later did the police chief and the magistrates.

No sooner had we sent the edition to press than the public houses closed and the drunken mobs came out again. The chastened chief reporter was on the telephone within minutes of a baton charge by the police. We rushed to press again. The simplified layout made it easy to change, and the next day we had a double gratification: all the nationals with earlier dead-lines missed the baton charge, and they did not get around to an analysis of race relations in Middlesbrough until a day later. We stayed way ahead of the competition and, I thought, put the riot in the right perspective.

Or did we? A local teacher wrote to differ. He agreed that the riots were the work of louts, but he believed there existed a deep-seated color prejudice—about jobs, about lifestyles, about sex. It smoldered, and it would burst into flames unless we could deal with it. I published his views prominently on the editorial page on the Wednesday—but with another feature on two big North East soap firms fighting it out for a monopoly of dishwashing liquids. Here was the glimmering of the kind of editorial page the *Echo* should have. For the first time I felt I was editing the paper instead of going through the motions. Charles Fenby sent congratulations. The staff, once roused, had done all I could have asked.

Still, news and photo editing didn't exist, sharing reporters in Darlington didn't serve either the evening or the morning paper very well, the feature pages had no sparkle, and the editorial page had no authority. You would have had to try very hard to diminish an editorial in the way the *Echo* routinely did, with small type in a single column mixed in with the cinema and theater ads and random display advertising. But if we were to get anywhere, we'd have to redesign not simply the editorial page but the entire paper, as well as rethink the way it was created. We needed a news editor of our own, reporters specifically allocated to the *Echo*, and a night production editor.

I was eager to discuss all these matters with the deputy editor when he returned from his break. Maurice Wedgewood was a small, dapper man in his forties, with big glasses, a wispy mustache, a words-per-minute rate of utterance almost beyond comprehension, and a conviction that the world was going to hell and that it would happen on his watch; no, it would happen that very night, in fact it would happen right now while he was wasting time giving the new editor a rundown on the night's news. (There was no written news schedule. It was all in Wedgewood's head.)

The structure of his utterances was marvelously complex, with subordinate clause upon subordinate clause; and then having erected the structure, he would take it apart bit by bit with qualifiers, so that what began as an imposing edifice ended up as dust in your ear. To render it into prose is to do violence to a work of art, but here goes:

Considering all the circumstances, and in the light of the fact that the story was in the *Despatch* last week and picked up also by the *Darlington and Stockton Times*, I've put the outbreak of foot-and-mouth disease on the front page because I think this thing is going to blow up. Though one never knows. One never knows since the last time we had an outbreak on a pig farm at Barnard Castle, it turned out not to be what it was feared to be. You weren't here at the time of course and can't be expected to remember what happened in Reg Gray's day. He was very keen on this kind of story, said the farmers were the heart of the region and — Goddammit! — we ended up looking very silly. In fact some of the farmers in the area said we had caused needless perturbation because the pig in question only had a cold and Gray got upset though he had no reason to be since he was the one who had told us to watch out for this kind of story. So perhaps you may not think page one a good idea after all and we might be better off running a short paragraph on the front and cross-referring to a page inside, which I think would be prominent enough in the circumstances, don't you?

All by himself, Wedgewood made up in kinetic energy for the inertia that marked the days. He had four editions to see to press every night except Saturday and immersed himself in editing the front page with frenzied concentration. When it neared time for the page to go to press, he got up a head of steam. If the phone rang, he didn't just replace it on its cradle—he slammed it with a force that rattled the tea mugs. Then the sound of the composing room buzzer provoked him to flush, roar, break his pencil in half, and fling it at the door. Nobody ever took any notice. It relieved the tension. One time a damp inside-page proof held for his inspection was a mess in its layout because the stone sub had not followed the plan. Wedgewood raised himself to smash his fist through the page. Senior barely blinked at such outbursts. A day or two later, when Wedgewood was working pell-mell to close the edition, the messenger put proofs on the wrong nail. Senior, sensing Wedgewood's exasperation, wordlessly handed him a pencil so he could break it in triumph.

I was alarmed. Clearly, to get a moment for reflective discussion I'd have to wrestle Wedgewood to the ground. (It was doable; he was smaller.) A few days observing what he did to agency and staff copy won him a reprieve. He was a text editor and judge of news values in the class of Norman (Nifty) Thornton. His assistant, Frank Peters, was, so to speak, just a whisker behind his boss in editing and theatrics, with dramatic Dundreary whiskers, a tartan waistcoat, a thesaurus of oaths from his service days on a Royal Navy cruiser, and a long cigarette holder tilted at the angle made famous by Franklin Roosevelt.

He began the night with a quiver of sharpened pencils, all reduced to stubs by the end.

I came to regard the Wedgewood-Peters histrionics as a small price to pay for the way these two hirsute Horatios stood on the bridge every night to intercept the verbiage that got through into so many newspapers. We regularly had fewer pages than our competitors and had to make every inch count. When they were hard-pressed, I gave them a hand. I had an early wager with them both that for every unnecessary word I could save on any story they'd subbed, they would owe me a penny, and I would owe them a shilling for every challenge. I'd have made a fortune on American or Indian newspapers, but very little money changed hands in Darlington.

As I geared up to change almost everything in the time-honored conduct of the paper, starting with the tortuously fussy design, I still didn't quite know how to deal with Wedgewood. It must have been cruel to have been passed over first for Barrington-Ward and then for me. I wanted my deputy to be a partner in the adventure, but in my first months he seemed to regard himself as the custodian of the archaic. I mentioned that I thought place names deadened the headlines and robbed them of universal appeal ("Missing West Hartlepool Boy Found" instead of "Gang of Kidnappers on the Run"). Wedgewood repeated at length all the reasons that place names had been the style for "donkey's years." I came to see he wasn't being obstructive. He could only guess whether I knew what I was doing or just making change for change's sake. And over my shoulder he could see the shadow of his former boss Reg Gray. Wedgewood had a very quick mind, but like any batsman in cricket facing a spin bowler, he could see all the horrible possibilities of any batting stroke. He felt obliged to do justice to the cons as well as the pros of every alteration in the *Echo*'s normal practice. This took time.

In the end I simply promulgated my first edict as editor: place names are to be dropped from headlines! The editor's memo explained that the main effect of place names was to deter the circle of readers who didn't live there—that is, the vast majority. Place names were henceforth to be included in new small-type bylines that had the virtue of advertising our on-the-spot presence. I waited for the ceiling to fall in. Senior plucked up the courage to whisper that the change would be much welcomed by the subs who had struggled for years to fit the seventeen characters of "Chester-le-Street" into a headline of twelve characters per line. Wedgewood, without a word, faithfully executed the first Evans rule, and not a single reader complained.

If I was developing some hope for the night operation, I had none for the day. There was no morning conference to discuss news and photo assignments and establish priorities. I tried starting one with Tarelli and Charles Westberg, the chief photographer. I had developed a toothache looking at the pictures in the paper. There were innumerable small "grip and grin" photographs of retirement ceremonies, flower shows, well-equipped bulls, empty buildings, and councilors on rostrums. These were fine for the group's weekly papers. They were the kind of pictures for which I'd written a lifetime of captions in my first year at Ashton-under-Lyne. I couldn't believe they represented the changing dramas and personalities of life in a region as vast and diverse as ours. Westberg's five photographers were run off their feet trying to cover all these repetitive functions, to the exclusion of more irregular happenings. I laid it down that we had to be more selective, shunning routine images, seeking out scenes of promise, and always ready to cover breaking news. Westberg got the point, but Tarelli had half his mind on the *Despatch,* and the news lists from the districts were thin and predictable. The conferences were a flop.

I was flying blind. We were assailed round the clock by competition. We had a few hours' grace over the national dailies printed in Manchester, but to the north, in Newcastle, we had the big morning daily the *Journal;* to the south the *Yorkshire Post*, regarded as the leading provincial morning paper; and evening newspapers in Newcastle, Middlesbrough, West Hartlepool, and our own Darlington. In Darlington, moreover, I shared reporters with the *Despatch*. Day after day we'd nothing distinctive planned. In desperation I suggested a sally in consumer journalism. Enid, who knew about these things, had found fruits and vegetables in Darlington expensive by comparison with similar provisions in Manchester. Perhaps the newsroom might check the prices and quality in the region's major towns? "Can't do that," said Tarelli sweetly. "Too busy with the Darlington Show for the *Despatch*."

I was downcast when I walked home through the busy town at midday. I wasn't getting anywhere with the news operation. I vented my frustration on the cavalcade of truck drivers thundering through the center, their exhausts belching black fumes. The Great North Road ran right alongside the elegant esplanade shops on High Row. I felt so impotent in the office that I there and then in the street began a little campaign, pointing at the filthiest high-pipe exhausts and shouting at the drivers to look at how much they were poisoning us. They roared on. It was ridiculous and a wonder I was not arrested as an eccentric, menacing the flow of British commerce. Well, Stead had gone to prison, hadn't he? So what if I got in trouble. Yes, but Stead had used his paper, and that's what I should have been doing. The daily scenes of havoc created by the heavy trucks running through towns and villages reminded me of the campaign for St. Ann's Square, how hard it had been to civilize it, and how very far I was from making the *Echo* anything like as effective an instrument as Big Tom's *Evening News* or, for that matter, Barry Bingham's *Louisville Courier-Journal.*

At home for lunch I banged on a bit about what I called "the lorry menace" to my waiting guest, the newspaper's industrial correspondent, Don Evans, as if he were to blame. I knew he was a very sensible fellow when he agreed it was worth looking into why a long-planned bypass of Darlington hadn't come about and why railways weren't carrying the bulk loads for which they were most suited. After all, Darlington was the birthplace of the first railway in the world to run freight and passenger trains: George Stephenson's *Locomotion* did it from Darlington to Stockton in 1825. *Locomotion* now graced Darlington's Bank Top station, and I saluted it every time I rushed into the station for Westminster Press conferences in London.

I'd asked Don if he could introduce me to his friend Sid Chaplin, and my clouds lifted when the novelist arrived. He was so warm, so unpretentious, so full of zest for what the *Echo* might do. I felt a kinship with him. Chaplin had gone underground as a miner but got an education from the Workers' Educational Association (WEA) through Durham University. His portrait of coal-mining life, *The Day of the Sardine,* spoke to me of my life as a working-class boy, and he was intrigued by my own WEA experiences. Over a jolly lunch we identified the causes and the people who could make things happen. "There's an ache for leadership," said Chaplin. He thought the *Echo* was better placed to do it than the flashier *Newcastle Journal.* Lunch was exhilarating. By the time it was over, I felt we had already retrained miners displaced by pit closures, grassed over the scores of hideous slag heaps, diverted the heavy lorries, cleaned up the beaches and rivers, purified the air, and capped it all off with a spectacular celebration concert in Durham Cathedral.

I felt emboldened to ask management to end the practice of shared staffing so that we could have reporters of our own and a news editor and night editor reporting to me. I'd be sunk if our sales continued the slide that had begun the year before. (They'd fallen by ten thousand after a price increase.) One of the hardest things for a newspaper to do is to halt a slide.

I began to see Stead's letter facing my desk as a nightly rebuke from the grave.

12

Just Causes

The BBC's television crews, setting up their paraphernalia of cameras and cables and lights at the *Northern
Echo*'s Priestgate office, created a stir in Darlington. Somebody
famous must be coming.

Not so. The TV crews were there because I'd somehow
convinced the Newcastle studios that they had the chance of
a lifetime to create a documentary on the remaking of a newspaper. I cringe when I see the film today. There's nothing
wrong with the production. What makes me cringe is the sight
of the owlish, clench-jawed editor trying to give the impression he's in the middle of one of the greatest news stories of
all time when all he has on his desk is a report of a Women's
Institute dance.

The BBC broadcast helped the *Echo* in the North East—it
certainly irritated our regional competitors—but we were
still obscure nationally. We were not quoted in roundups of
national opinion, and I was made to feel we didn't count. We
had no money for promotion. How could we break out? Darlington was regarded as a dead end, and I was having difficulty even finding a news editor. We couldn't compete in
salaries with the big nationals in Manchester, or for that matter
with the pay scales of the *Newcastle Journal* to the north or the

Yorkshire Post to the south. When I went to Newcastle and York, I made a point of stopping in newsagents as an ordinary customer, asking for a copy of the *Northern Echo,* and expressing amazement when they didn't have any. I seemed to be the only one surprised.

In my search for a news editor I went south — far south. The editor of a weekly paper called the *Independent* in Ibadan, Nigeria, had read about my appointment as editor and inquired whether I'd have an opening for him sometime in 1962, when his contract ended. The name was familiar — Mike Morrissey. I remembered a terse, slim industrial correspondent on the *Manchester Evening News* moving mercurially through the newsroom before he took a chance and left for Ibadan to start a Catholic newspaper there.

I tried him in Darlington for two weeks as a sub. He didn't shine. I sent him to cities and towns all over the circulation area to find stories. He dazzled. By insistent sleuthing, he discovered that unthinking magistrates were mistakenly sending children in need of care to detention homes. His story put a stop to that.

It was investigations and campaigning journalism that would put us on the map. I didn't have a deliberate plan to do that; it was circumstantial, arising from frustrations and disquiet as we encountered instances of a vast carelessness in public life. I recoiled from the partisan political filters of the dailies and resolved never to start a campaign of any kind until we had first investigated thoroughly and had an achievable target. And if we began a campaign, which meant intensified reporting and opinion writing, we had always to give space to dissenters — and not give up after a few days. All this was as yet an untested theory of mine.

I appointed Morrissey the *Northern Echo*'s first news editor. He made an astounding difference with no more full-time reporters than we'd had before. He wasn't everyone's favorite. He irritated the branch offices by his insistence on follow-ups; when they complained, I told them he was right. After the street riots in Middlesbrough, for instance, it was important for us to keep on eye on relations between the colored and white populations. Six months after miners were thrown out of work by a pit closure, we had to find out what happened to them. We had to check where in the bureaucracy the bypass around Darlington was stuck or when the ground would be broken for the factories promised for the new town of Newton Aycliffe.

Such efficient news editing was essential, but we'd not get very far with follow-ups and recycling all the events the dailies and weeklies were covering. We had to be different, but with an eye clearly on the community's needs. We had to monitor speeches and reports from councils and courts, but I'd grown impatient with the notion, common then, that covering these scheduled events was about all a newspaper needs to do.

Fortunately, Morrissey ran on one of those batteries that never wear out. This became quite clear when I gave him an early endurance test in an investigation that led to a significant improvement in the well-being of hundreds of thousands of people.

It was a perfect spring day in the village of Hurworth-on-Tees, four miles south of Darlington. We'd moved to a house there, the family having grown with the arrival of our second daughter, Kate. It was refreshing to escape town and go home for an hour or so at lunchtime before returning for night work that tended to get later and later. Hundreds of daffodils bloomed on the village green; we thought it would be nice for Kate and Ruth to see the celebrated display. On the walk home, a mist swirled in, blotting out the bright sky. It was not a mist of mellow fruitfulness. It stank of rotten fish, and it didn't go away. It made me gag, and it followed us into the house. I mentioned it in the subs' room that night. "Oh, yes," said the chief subeditor, Stan Senior, "that's the Teesside Smell. Everybody hates it, but not to worry; it comes and goes."

I couldn't leave it at that. No doubt being a father again made me overanxious about the Hurworth haze. I fretted that it might be not only noxious but also a health hazard for infants. I sent to the library for clippings but drew a blank. I asked around and got the same response from everyone: The smell wasn't news; it was a fact of life. Get used to it.

Had I raised the question in my first year of editing, I'd have had little hope of getting anywhere; I'd have felt like apologizing for the distraction from the routine news gathering. By the middle of 1962, however, my morning news conferences had begun as I'd hoped. When I put the Teesside Smell on the daily agenda, I volunteered to carry a test tube into the thick of the next noxious mist. We'd have it analyzed and then send a sample for Prime Minister Macmillan to sniff. As the former MP for nearby Stockton-on-Tees, he'd surely come to the rescue if he got a whiff of it.

I've had better ideas. Carrying a test tube in the hope of ambushing the smell was tedious; I broke a couple. Nor did the odor soon come back. Morrissey applied himself doggedly and duly reported that nobody in local industry would acknowledge responsibility for *any* smell. He asked the Darlington Rural Council, in the person of a Mr. J. D. Collins, if he'd investigate. He ran a mile. "No comment. Least said the better, I think," he replied. A few regional patriots assailed Morrissey for asking around, contending that it was bad publicity for the region to admit it smelt of anything other than roses and new-mown hay. Some maintained that it was all in the editor's imagination: wasn't he from some effete metropolis to the south?

During a long spell of clear air, I began to doubt the authenticity of my olfactory senses; I almost longed for the nuisance to return to reassure the staff that I was not an obsessive hypochondriac. Then one morning a haze thickened, and with it came the Teesside Smell. Our Stockton office reported coffee bars suddenly crowded with refugees. All who caught the merest whiff wanted to know the source and what "they" were doing to suppress it. Clearly "they" were doing nothing, and we'd not been very effective ourselves either, until David Spark, visiting Westminster Press in London, had the bright idea that we should check with industrial chemists whether there were pollutants that gave off a distinctively fishy smell. The answer was methylamine, used in the production of pesticides, dyes, and solvents. But where did it come from? And why did it linger?

Our chief suspect became the Imperial Chemical Industries (ICI) plant at Billingham. They made amines there, did they not? A public relations manager we asked wanted to know why we were picking on ICI. They'd had no complaints locally, said the manager. Surely it was obvious that when there was a temperature inversion, low stratus clouds coming off the cold North Sea, known locally as the fret, would carry a whole cocktail of pollutants over a large area of Teesside, not just downwind of Billingham. In short fog wasn't a local issue; it was an inescapable regional phenomenon—God's work.

At the end of the next morning conference, I suggested to my team that when the smell returned, we should be ready to photograph the track of the persistent noxious vapor. A giggle ran through the building: "Guess what now, he's asked Charlie to photograph a bloody smell!"

Not long afterward, Ossie Stamford, one of Charlie Westberg's photographers, was driving through Houghton village in Teesside on a lovely day. No mist, no smell. But when he reached Stockton-on-Tees downwind of Billingham, there it was: a pall enveloping the High Street. He photographed it, then rushed back ten miles inland to Houghton's clear skies. The images came out wonderfully—the first photograph of a smell ever published! I splashed the two pictures across a whole news page. They proved that the Teesside Smell was localized. Nor did the haze disperse quickly, as did the sea fret blowing inland. The haze, with its pollutant, lingered. So we had two mysteries: the source of the smell and the persistence of the haze that carried it.

We called ICI again and received a long letter from the process investigation manager at Billingham. He strongly protested "bias in *The Northern Echo*'s implication that pollutants and smells come only from the ICI factory at Billingham, ignoring the other numerous sources of pollutants and smells among the busy industries of Teesside." Furthermore, he maintained, "the smells observed and described at various distances from the factory cannot be related by 'nose' with any smells inside the factory." But he followed that blanket denial with an admission: "With one or two exceptions such as the amines or 'fish smell.'"

One or two exceptions? The game was up!

I was invited to lunch at Billingham with the division chairman, Rowland Wright (who became chairman of ICI), and the factory's top managers. I brought the incriminating photographs. ICI came clean. Yes, they'd been plagued by leaks of amines and were working hard to stop them. It wasn't easy because the stuff was so potent that a thimbleful would smell across a county. As their process investigation manager put it, "The quantities involved are very small indeed, and obtaining large enough samples and their subsequent analysis calls for methods of very great precision." So my test tube idea wouldn't have worked, but persistence did.

ICI now conceded that the mists carrying the fish smell weren't just naturally occurring sea frets. Instead they were principally created by leaks from their own ammonia plant which rapidly combined with the amines to form malodorous mists. ICI committed urgently to plug the leaks, install more gas scrubbers in the ammonia plant, and replace worn-out equipment at considerable cost. It refined its detection techniques for leaks. It installed electrical precipitators to reduce emissions from the sulfuric acid plant. It sent out a mobile laboratory sucking in air and making analyses.

We'd done well following our nose. Only years later did I think we'd missed a trick: early in our inquiries, we should have called the relevant union officials. They knew all about the Teesside Smell, though perhaps they would have been too embarrassed to brief us. The men working in the amines tank wore protective clothing and breathing gear and then changed and showered, but they still complained that the smell accompanied them home and put their wives off sex.

ICI had performed a perverse service. Their reaction to the attention we gave the noxious lingering problem dramatized how feebly other firms controlled gases from other chemical factories and the grit and fumes from the steelworks, power stations, and brickworks. Black smoke also poured out of the thousands of household chimneys in the area. We applauded the housewife who took her laundry to a council meeting to show them the sheets she'd washed white and hung out to dry that morning, only to have them ruined by black smoke.

Despite all this, Darlington and Stockton authorities still did not insist that fuels should be smokeless (as Manchester had done years before). Individuals smoldered with resentment but hadn't formed into a well-organized pressure group. We had to speak for them.

*   *   *

Some of our critics saw our reporting as hostile to industry. On the contrary, as industrial editor Don Evans confirmed, the entrepreneurs invited to establish highly necessary new businesses in the region were not infrequently deterred by pollution. Perhaps it was as well we didn't stumble on the difficulties ICI had created for the sex lives of chemical workers; we'd have had to report it, and the region would never have appealed to anyone.

Out of the desire to attract new jobs we conceived a series of features highlighting the experiences of companies who'd chosen the North East as the location for new plants. The results justified the title: "They Came North to Success." But there were too few of these new companies. Government policy for the so-called depressed areas was to induce manufacturers to locate wherever unemployment was highest. It was good politics but lousy economics. Most of these areas lacked the communications, skilled labor, and infrastructure to support fledgling enterprises. What the *Echo* was able to add to the relevant academic analysis were insights derived from grassroots reporting. David Spark had written two hundred profiles and a series on the centers of Stockton, Darlington, Durham, Ripon, and Newcastle. Don Evans had slogged round shipyards and steel mills and heard the grouses of management and union leaders. I asked Don and David to join me in defining the paper's policy. Trained as reporters, they were uneasy about opining. Soon enough, though, the three of us were sharing the writing of a double column of argument on a new editorial page uncluttered by advertising from mortuaries.

With each passing week, the news got grimmer. The last shipbuilding yard on the river Tees closed; so did Darlington's railway workshops. We hammered away at the piecemeal, short-term, and incoherent government policies for the region. We emphasized the crucial interaction between the economy and the environment. You couldn't walk in the shadow of the giant pit heaps without wondering why everyone had not fled long ago; skilled labor migrated south all the time. The vile winter of 1962–1963, the worst in living memory, exposed the inadequacy of the road system. Giant snowdrifts cut off thousands of people for days. The effect on the local economy was devastating: nearly ninety thousand were unemployed.

Amid the never-ending storms that winter, a tornado touched earth at Middleton St. George Airport (now Durham Tees Valley Airport) one chill February morning in the person of a bleary-eyed man with flyaway hair, tie askew, boots untidily laced, and a cloth cap pulled down over his pugnacious face. This was Quintin McGarel Hogg, Queen's Counsel (QC, or counsel to the Crown, an honorific title), then the second Viscount Hailsham, Tory leader in the House of Lords. An anti-appeasement supporter of Churchill, a platoon commander in the North Africa campaign, a barrister of charismatic brilliance, and our very own Merlin, Hailsham had been charged by Prime Minister Macmillan with conjuring up a long-term brief for the regeneration of the North East. The press cynics scoffed at his cloth cap as a gimmick to identify with a mythic regional figure, Andy Capp, the earthy *Daily Mirror* and *Sunday Mirror* comic-strip character supposedly located in Hartlepool, who was into pigeon racing, snooker, football, getting drunk, and abusing his wife. No, Hailsham witheringly explained, as if talking to an idiot, he wore the cap to keep his head warm.

Hailsham was perhaps easy to underestimate. He'd been regarded as something of a clown for his stunts for the television cameras—rushing into the sea in baggy pants to celebrate an election victory, closing a Tory conference by ringing a big hand bell to symbolize Labour's death knell. But Tom Little, our veteran chief reporter in Newcastle, had seen officials come and go and testified that not since Winston Churchill visited the region during the war had a Minister of the Crown seemed so seriously possessed by the urgency of his mission. Hailsham defined it as "lifting the quality of life at all levels." He was shocked by the dereliction. He drove through South Durham and thought much of it should be pulled down. Lights blazed into the night in his Newcastle headquarters as he worked himself and his team from 8:00 a.m. into the small hours.

He didn't finish the Hailsham Plan until the autumn, but we were thrilled to read it when an embargoed copy arrived in the office in November. Our managing director even agreed to increase the size of the paper so that we could publish four full pages. Her Majesty's Stationery Office heard what we planned. They told us it was too much: "It's our copyright." Yes, I replied, but it's our lives. You'd think they would want the widest dissemination of such a key report, but they lacked the imagination Hailsham possessed. We went ahead, hoping they wouldn't sue (and they didn't).

The Hailsham Plan—"as long as a washing list"—projected a bright new future for the region. The conurbations of Tyneside, Teesside, and the Darlington-Aycliffe area would become "growth zones" for investment, with new airports, motorways, and revived seaports. A regional council would make decisions on the spot so that everything didn't have to await the nod from London. Hailsham envisaged making towns and villages more pleasant by providing decent housing, schools, and hospitals and by removing the industrial scars, tackling pollution, and fostering the arts.

I couldn't contain my glee, hopping about the editorial floor like a kid with candy. In my exultation I felt emboldened to contact the region's leading industrialists—Swan Hunter, ICI,

Vaux Breweries, Head Wrightson—as well as the heads of Durham and Newcastle universities and others, and urged the formation and funding of an organization to sponsor schemes of improvement. They seized the moment with vigor and generosity, setting up an office for the Civic Trust for the North East in 1965. The paper meanwhile attacked the Coal Board for dumping waste on a once lovely beach and highlighted shoddy development in villages of real architectural merit. But I wanted us to be creative as well as critical.

Geoffrey Broadbent, an architect friend from Manchester, toured the region for us with Bert Hackett, who'd drawn St. Ann's Square for the *Manchester Evening News*. We couldn't pay this pair enough; they just liked the challenge. Their illustrated series, "The Big Clean Up," showed how wretched and squalid landscapes could be made inviting.

Our own fake Gothic title piece and Dickensian editorial offices were now glaringly at odds with what we were preaching for the region. The management agreed to refurbish the gloomy subs' room with good lighting and new furniture designed to assist copy flow and page layout; we even got a light box for measuring photographs.

I knew that changing the title piece was about the riskiest thing a newspaper could do, putting its identity in pawn as it were, nor was management filled with joy at abandoning a tradition. On the other hand, Bill Treslove in the composing room agitated for modernity, so we experimented with this and that typeface, all woebegone failures. Finally I turned again to Bert Hackett. He designed a new *Northern Echo* title piece based on the English slab-serif face Clarendon, in bold upper- and lowercase. The sturdiness of style spoke well for the identity of the *Echo* and its region. Our Conservative MP Anthony Bourne-Arton protested, but the mobs stayed indoors.

*   *   *

There are no small stories (though some are bigger than others), and so to the Battle of the Broccoli. It was the fate of a clever bluestocking by the name of Valerie Knox to be assigned the investigation originally inspired by my wife, that of local produce. I'd abandoned the story in the face of the lassitude prevailing in the old shared newsroom, but Valerie was new blood, one of Fenby's graduate trainees. Doubtless wondering why she'd worked so hard for her Oxford degree, she took her shopping basket around Darlington, Newcastle, Middlesbrough, West Hartlepool, and Manchester, buying fruits and vegetables. She found that the prices were indeed higher in the North East than in Manchester, and highest of all in Darlington.

On the morning of publication, a posse of angry Darlington greengrocers arrived in the office of our managing director, demanding that the editor come down and eat his words — and their broccoli. Nervous that I could easily have been tripped up by an inability to distinguish between a mangel-wurzel and a yam, I offered up our investigative reporter Valerie instead and asked the beatific David Spark to go along as a pacifier. (I also calculated that his presence would calm management, still not sure whether London had imposed a madman on them.) As I fretted in my office three floors above the battleground, a telex arrived from Fenby. He liked the story; in fact his wife had also noticed how highly priced vegetables were in Darlington. I felt the telex should be put in a cleft stick and rushed by runner to the managing director.

Spark reported back that the confrontation with the greengrocers had been heated but essentially came down to an argument about the comparative quality of broccoli and King Edward potatoes. I offered to repeat the exercise with an independent shopper and a Darlington greengrocer riding shotgun. The result was pretty much the same. We "won," but it was another lesson in how sensitive local communities could be when "their" paper seemed disloyal.

I read fifteen newspapers daily and ten on Sundays. One Sunday morning, scanning the heavyweight *Sunday Times,* I came across a three-line "filler" paragraph at the foot of a column. It said that Vancouver, British Columbia, was expanding a program to save women from dying of cancer. That was all. A hundred questions buzzed in my head, propelled by one of the most consistent emotions of my life since the days I'd seen people in Lancashire coughing up blood from soot-blackened lungs: If preventable, why not prevented? Why did it take so very long for medical knowledge to percolate and have effect?

Ken Hooper was a six-foot-two history graduate and cricketer from Wadham College, Oxford: rather enigmatic, certainly not prone to my emotionalism, and likely, I thought, to wrestle every fact to the ground. He was by now fairly experienced, having joined the paper in January 1961 and survived the subs' room and reporting for both the *Echo* and the *Despatch.* I could ill afford to lose him from the reporting staff, but I gave him the clipping on the Monday morning and asked him to go to Vancouver straightaway. I knew I'd have to worry about the impact on the budget, but I was eager to get started before the *Sunday Times* or someone else followed up. Nobody did.

Hooper saved me the expense. He started his research in Britain (much tougher to do before the Internet) and never went to Canada. He spent endless hours in libraries, hospitals, and ministries, heaping his findings in a shopping bag to the amusement, if not derision, of some of the big shots he visited. He was gone about seven weeks, but four well-informed articles landed on my desk. They were disturbing. Thousands of women who were dying from cervical cancer might have been saved, thousands of others had died already, and thousands more were certain to die because of chronic inertia in the National Health Service.

The technique that could save lives was called exfoliative cytology, the study of the characteristics of cells shed from body surfaces. The possibilities had been known to science on both sides of the Atlantic since the 1920s, thanks to George Papanicolaou at New York Hospital and Cornell Medical School and Professor L. S. Dudgeon and his colleagues at St. Thomas' Hospital in London. It was another twenty years before their work was put to practical lifesaving use by Dr. Joe V. Meigs, a Boston gynecologist, assisted by a biologist, Ruth Graham. Graham took vaginal smears of three of Meigs's patients. The patients appeared perfectly healthy, but the smears, read under a microscope, showed very early cancer cells. Given the state of medical knowledge then, it was risky/courageous of Meigs to remove the uteruses of the three women, certain he would see tumors not detectable in a routine examination. He didn't. He was horrified. He was roundly condemned — then vindicated. Three days after the visual inspection, the sections of each uterus examined under a microscope showed it contained early curable cancer that would have been fatal if undetected.

What all this meant was that a simple smear test, requiring only a few minutes of a patient's time, could detect a threatened cancer in women. The danger could then be obviated by a simple cone biopsy or removal of the uterus, depending on the condition. It was another five years (1949) before the potential was realized by two doctors in Vancouver and one on the other side of the world, Mr. Stanley Way. (As a surgeon he was entitled to "Mr." The honorific "Dr." was one notch down in British medical parlance.)

Hooper reported that all his findings kept bringing him

back home not with the finished articles, but to see Way, who was just up the road from us in Gateshead. Beginning in 1949, Way's gynecological research unit at Queen Elizabeth Hospital had screened upwards of 150,000 women and found 601 of them harboring very early cancer. None of the women treated had died; of those having the minor operation, 46 of them had gone on to deliver 57 children.

Way's sample was smaller than the one in Vancouver. By 1963 researchers there had screened 214,900 women over age thirty and compared the records of another 248,400 who hadn't been screened. The death rate was seven times greater in the unscreened group.

When Hooper called on Way, he heard how Way had tried for years to have screening adopted as a routine national test. There was interest in a few centers (London, Birmingham, Derby, Edinburgh), but none in the Ministry of Health. So every year something like twenty-five hundred women died needlessly, about double the number dying in road accidents. It was so different in the United States. Early in the century more women died from cervical cancer than any other form, but the death rate began to fall remarkably after the American Cancer Society started to campaign for Pap smears in 1957.

I took up the Hooper articles with passionate urgency, running all four in June 1963, with editorials asking the Ministry of Health to start a national program to save women. I sent everything the *Northern Echo* published to news organizations and wrote personal letters to a group of MPs. They sprang to it, all of them submitting parliamentary questions for the minister of health, Enoch Powell. They ran into a brick wall. "I am advised," Powell intoned, "it would be premature to aim at a general application."

How many more women had to die, we asked in the paper, before the minister acted on the evidence, already years old?

He acknowledged that there had been 2,504 deaths in 1961, but every time the MPs went back to him — as they did month after month — the answer was always some variation of no: "I cannot estimate how many deaths would have been prevented.... I cannot suggest an average cost per smear.... I would refer the hon. Member to my previous answer(s)."

So it went on through the whole sickening year as we pounded away and the minister stonewalled. Regional hospitals, Powell said, would consider any proposals, but they'd have to find the money. We learned that the city of Stoke-on-Trent had done so but had had to wait three years for ministry permission to establish a clinic. One of the MPs I'd recruited, Jeremy Bray, did not let it rest. At the end of the year, on December 2, he asked what further consideration the minister had given to setting up a comprehensive early diagnosis and treatment service for cervical cancer.

The gratifying answer was "I have asked regional hospital boards to expand cytology services. Before screening can be offered to all women in the age groups at risk, more trained staff are needed and I have asked five hospital boards to set up special training centres." It didn't represent a miraculous conversion. Powell had been replaced by Anthony Barber.

It was a victory, the road to a comprehensive national program, but I couldn't help doing the arithmetic. A national program could have been started ten years earlier (Stanley Way had been screening women for fourteen years). Since 2,504 women had died in 1961, I calculated the unnecessary loss of life over the past decade at ten times that number, or 25,040.

Besides our campaigns for public health and revamped economic policies, we were now getting some recognition for our news reporting. We proved at least as good as the nationals in responding to the assassination of President John F. Kennedy on November 22, 1963.

I heard of the Dallas shooting on the radio when I was in a dinner jacket driving to the Teesside press ball and turned back to the office. Wedgewood was busy editing the diverse flow of copy—from the agencies and from the London office—with just over three hours to deadline. I added to the tension by saying we would publish a four-page special on Kennedy's life and discuss how often the U.S. presidency had been ended by murder. We sent for photographs from the library. None could be found. The day manager of the picture library, Shirley Freeman (known as "Shirley Fileroom"), had gone home, and the night manager, Bill Webster, had the night off. The indispensable Joan Thomas suggested we call Shirley's parents. "Oh, she's out with her boyfriend." Where? "I think they went to the cinema."

The Odeon was the most popular cinema. Joan got the Odeon manager on the telephone for me. He hadn't heard of the Kennedy shooting. He was aghast when I asked him to stop the film and find our staffer. Then I had a better idea, with the result that Shirley and her boyfriend, canoodling in the back row, saw a flash on the screen—a handwritten message on a Perspex slide: "Miss Shirley Freeman call the *Echo* urgently." Her date was ruined; the paper was saved.

By 1963 circulation had risen by 10 percent, on the way to a rise of 14 percent, and year on year our profit had tripled. Winston Churchill had been a big help. I came across an old copy of his *My Early Life* (1930). I'd read his war histories but not this, and I suspected few of my generation had. I was so enchanted by it that I wrote to him and asked permission to serialize it. He sent a warm note back saying go ahead. It proved popular.

Nineteen sixty-three was a significant year, as the poet Philip Larkin made clear:

Sexual intercourse began
In nineteen sixty-three
(which was rather late for me)
Between the end of the Chatterley *ban*
And the Beatles' first LP.

As a happily married man with now three children (Michael had arrived that year), I too missed the sexual revolution — but I kept pace with the music. I could hardly miss the Beatles' first record, "Love Me Do." My wife was a Liverpudlian; our Granada TV broadcast the Beatles' first studio appearance in October 1962; we bought their first album, *Please Please Me;* and I could hardly forget how my sharp producer friend Barrie Heads had told me he'd thrown another new group out of the Granada studio because they weren't as presentable as the Beatles. "Mick Jagger and his group were so scruffy."

The break into music for the *Northern Echo* came out of a snowstorm. George Carr, Westberg's deputy, took a sixteen-year-old printing assistant, Ian Wright, on a long slog to reach people trapped in a blizzard along the route that went over the Pennine hills. Carr and Wright had a broken-down Ford Popular car (Britain's lowest-priced car) with no snow chains, no snow tires, and no heater. They loaded the trunk with four bags of coal to weight down the back axle, along with a shovel and hessian coal sacks for when they got stuck. In this way, with thermos flask and sandwiches, they got through the traffic jams and jackknifed trucks when all others — including the police, rescue services, and ambulances — had failed. Between taking photographs and conducting interviews, they helped people get their cars out of snowdrifts.

As it happened, the best photograph was taken by Wright, who was normally an unseen elf, filing the negatives, mixing the chemicals, and cleaning up. I put his dramatic picture on the front page. Soon after the first edition had arrived, there was a knock on my door, and there was Wright, asking very nervously if there was some reason why he'd not been given the credit. It was an oversight. I put his name under the photograph in the next edition, and so began Wright's career as a photographer. He was the only photographer with any interest in pop groups. Westberg despised those long-haired rockers. It was a hard day's night getting him to concede that if Wright took the pictures on his own time, Charlie wouldn't impede him.

Week after week Wright was out with the Beatles, the Rolling Stones, the Searchers, Lulu, the Dave Clark Five, Manfred Mann, Dusty Springfield, Cilla Black, Roy Orbison, Billy J. Kramer, and Gene Pitney. I assigned junior reporters to write the stories. They knew more than I did about who was worth covering, though I was keen enough to drive them to and from Newcastle for the first North East tour of the Beatles in March 1963.

Our youngsters struck up a rapport with the new pop stars and with managers such as Brian Epstein and Neil Aspinall. Wright and Guy Simpson were the only pressmen who showed up when the Beatles gave a concert at the Globe Theatre in Stockton, and they had no problem getting backstage. "John Lennon," Wright remembers, "was always asking for complimentary prints. 'Wrighty, don't forget to send those photos; the family love 'em.'" I was so impressed by the initiatives of these juniors that I started the paper's first weekly supplement, the *Teenage Special*, which attracted some thirty thousand sales on Mondays — almost a 30 percent increase. With Tyne Tees Television, the *Northern Echo* organized very loud talent shows in Newcastle — the *American Idol* of Tyneside.

The music juniors all went on to make names for themselves. Philip Norman won a *Sunday Times* magazine essay contest, then became a best-selling author with *The Stones, Shout!, Rave On*, and biographies of Elton John and John Lennon. David Sinclair wrote biographies of Lord Snowdon and the Queen Mother. David Watts became the Southeast Asia correspondent for the *Times,* John Cathcart editor of the *National Enquirer,* and Guy Simpson picture editor of the *Independent* newspaper in London. They must have taken their cue from Tyneside's own Eric Burdon and the Animals, whose great hit was "We Gotta Get Out of This Place."

Granada Television came calling on me at the *Echo*. Since returning from America I'd written a couple of documentaries for them and a pamphlet on their fight to televise a parliamentary election. It's an indication of how suspicious the authorities were of this dangerous new medium that Granada had to mount a full-scale legal and public relations assault before it managed to bring TV cameras to the Rochdale by-election.

The call was from whiz kid Jeremy Isaacs. He would become renowned for producing a series on World War II and the cold war and later become the founding chief executive of Channel 4 and Sir Jeremy, director general of the Royal Opera House. But in 1961–1962 he was winning his spurs commissioning a rotating group of commentators for a program critically examining the week's newspapers, *What the Papers Say*. (One of the world's longest-running television programs, this show is still on the air today, now on the BBC.) Would I care to audition for the program?

Had he not heard of Lewenhak and the talkative gypsies? Five years had gone by, which for television people must have meant it was lost in the mists of time. I didn't bother to brief him on that history. I wrote a script for the audition and did a dummy run in Manchester with Michael Frayn of the *Guardian*, Colin Welch of the *Daily Telegraph*, and Tom Lambert of the *New York Herald Tribune*. The outcome was a letter from Isaacs: "I hope I can persuade the boys here to let you have a bash on behalf of the provincials."

The boys apparently weren't in any hurry to risk a hick from Darlington, and it was a few months before Isaacs was back. He was, he explained, bringing cameras for the parliamentary by-election in Harold Macmillan's old constituency, Stockton-on-Tees. He asked me to provide commentary on the press treatment of the election. In a howling wind I stood in the town square, orating into the gale and feeling foolish, as I squinted at the teleprompter, watched by a group of giggling urchins.

Soon afterward Isaacs was succeeded by Barrie Heads, who'd produced my interview with the painter L. S. Lowry. He invited me to join what was now a regular panel. This was hard. Brian Inglis, the anchor for the series, was dry, ironic, and authoritative; Michael Frayn and Peter Eckersley were very witty. Barrie's main problem with me was my north country pronunciation. The Queen's English was still the standard on television. Any regional accent was judged déclassé, except in a slice-of-life show like Granada's own *Coronation Street*. In one run-through of my script, Barrie rushed out of the control room shouting, "Butcher, butcher!" He meant that my Lancashire accent was overly stressing the *u:* "Don't say 'boo-ocher'! Say 'butcher'! Try it again." I did. It satisfied him. But on the show I was so concerned about pronouncing it right that it came out "betcher." Thereafter, I continually rehearsed to myself, reciting "butcher, baker, candlestick maker," but the flat *a*'s and deep *u*'s kept coming back all the same.

For the next two years I was on about once a month. It was

a slog in Darlington scouring scores of newspapers scattered amid the children's toys, as well as writing and rewriting, counting and recounting the words to fit the allotted fifteen minutes — all in between hours at the office, followed on the Wednesday night by a long drive over the Pennines for a recording session in the Manchester studio the next day. The newspaper extracts were read by actors, and the tone of their voices, pace, and timing had to be rehearsed.

How I sweated over the early scripts! I had not merely to read all the papers but also to compare them for news getting, accuracy, and fairness. I'd known from childhood, for instance, that the *Daily Express* (circulation four million) believed in putting an optimistic gloss on all news (unless it was about the Labour Party). Its most famous editor, Arthur Christiansen, laid it down that the *Express* "should make everyone feel it is a sunny day." Nice sentiment, but it was remarkable how far the paper was prepared to go to make everyone believe all was for the best in the best of all possible worlds. Milk in Britain was being contaminated by radioactive iodine from a fifty-seven-megaton Soviet bomb test in the atmosphere, reported the Agricultural Research Council; the government made a statement in Parliament that it was keeping a day-to-day watch in case the contamination got to a danger point. These two items were in every paper except the *Express*. Instead it wrote, "There is little danger milk will become contaminated." When all the other papers reported that Britain could expect additional strontium 90 to arrive the next spring, the *Express* reported that "many experts" believed the Soviets could produce "clean" bombs with little fallout. But they hadn't produced them; theirs was a singularly dirty bomb. "All this talk" about fallout, said the *Express,* was "unpatriotic, because it made the Russians think they could scare us." Next,

I said in my on-air commentary, we'd be told by the *Express* that strontium 90 was good for us.

Though that sort of absurdist journalism was meat and drink to *What the Papers Say*, I also tried to highlight any great reporting I'd read in the national papers. I contrasted the *People*'s robust pursuit of the crooks running football pools for bogus charities with the malicious invasions of privacy by the *Daily Sketch* gossip writers simply to make someone miserable. I praised the *Sunday Times*' exposé of the slum landlord Peter Rachman, I chastised the *Daily Mirror* for rejecting a Conservative advertisement without saying why, and I teased the *Sunday Express* for not disclosing that the lively letters it ran were all written by staffers posing as readers.

Some took this better than others. The editor of the *Sunday Express*, John Junor, invited me to lunch. The editor of the *Daily Mirror* slammed me, thundering prominently in the paper, "Evans dedicates his spare time to denigrating the rest of the press. Loftily he lectures the national newspapers as if Darlington exudes a special degree of insight and wisdom denied to newspapers in London and Manchester." I did the most detective work tracking how the newspapers had failed to find out what lay behind the resignation of Lord Mancroft from the Norwich Union Insurance Society. It transpired that the Jewish Mancroft had been forced out by Arab business interests that had dealings with the society, but the *Financial Times*, which had first reported the resignation, was slow to find out why and even slower to comment.

My commentary did not win friends on Fleet Street. I heard that Lord Drogheda, the fastidious chairman of the *Financial Times*, was upset with me; and I was well aware that Pearson Industries, which owned the *Financial Times*, also, through Westminster Press, owned the *Northern Echo*. Drogheda was far from alone. Big Tom wrote a friendly warning letter from the *Manchester Evening News:* "It so happens that at a large gathering in London last night I saw a number of our top boys, one of whom went into a long diatribe that your Granada program was intended to try and kill newspapers and that you were determined to single out *The Sun* for often quite unjustified criticism which, if persisted in, could put the newspaper and 2,000 employees out of business."

I'd actually commented very little on the struggling *Sun* (then owned by the Mirror Group, which got tired of trying to make it succeed and sold it to Rupert Murdoch, who made it a building block of his empire). Tom wrote, "I tried to reason with one editor but the conviction appeared to be that instead of one of their own kind trying to help newspapers at a critical time, 'a newspaperman is selling us down the river to the commercial television companies who are delighted at the spectacle.'" He concluded, "I can also tell you that one of the top boys let it drop that they're watching your paper like hawks every day and they even quoted headings and certain things to me. Keep your powder dry!"

I told Big Tom I had the curious notion that if helping newspapers survive was the criterion, surely improving their performance would help. And no Granada producer ever once tried to influence me one way or another in the commentaries. Big Tom understood; I thought the storm clouds had lifted. So I was stunned when Charles Fenby told me I had to stop appearing on *What the Papers Say.* The icicle I'd first encountered had become a warm and perceptive booster, but now he noted that my contract required me to seek the permission of the Westminster Press board for doing anything other than edit the newspaper, and he was not giving it.

I could not lightly accept the ban, I told Fenby, because the publicity had drawn attention to the *Echo.* It was now being noted and quoted much more often. Fenby was adamant, so I requested permission to appeal to the Westminster Press board. It so happened it was meeting on the Thursday I was due to do the show, which Fenby insisted should be my last.

As soon as I'd finished the recording that afternoon in Manchester, I drove straight back to Darlington. Fenby and the board had just finished viewing the actual program going out at 10:30 p.m. I entered the boardroom in trepidation. They all applauded. It was a tremendous relief, a ruling in character with the open way Westminster Press ran their newspapers. Fenby took his defeat with grace, and I continued the program until the end of my editorship of the *Echo*.

When I'd met Sid Chaplin at the start of my editorship, the region had been sunk in gloom, and we'd wondered whether we could persuade someone to stage a spectacular celebration of its heritage—its art, architecture, and scenic beauty. In 1964 Tom Little, the *Echo*'s chief reporter (and music critic) in Newcastle, watched a son et lumière concert in the radiant white basilica at Vézelay, France, and in his review for the paper he wondered why we could not do the same in the much grander and more glorious setting of Durham Cathedral. Well, why not? I called in David Spark. "We're going to have a son et lumière concert in Durham," I told him, "and you're going to organize it."

Of course it meant borrowing the cathedral, and having the city of Durham amenable, and finding a writer and composer, and raising money for script and music, and finding a brilliant lighting engineer, and selling tickets, and praying that people would come. We started by seeking the blessing of Durham's dean, the Very Reverend John Wild. He and his wife gave us lunch in the cathedral close, which David remembers was trout with a delicious sauce. I can never remember anything

I eat, and on this occasion I was concentrating on not talking like an irreverent show business impresario. But the dean warmed to the proposal, the mayor of Durham City came in with enthusiasm, we persuaded Flora Robson to narrate, and we dragooned the cathedral choir and bell ringers, the Horden Colliery Band, and the Cornforth Men's Choir.

The son et lumière we staged was the single most exciting and uplifting experience of my time in Darlington, a magical marriage of North East enterprise and artistry to reflect the splendors of human faith and endeavor. You could hear the intake of breath among the crowds as the lighting revealed the hidden beauties of the interior of the cathedral and the pageant of nine hundred years unfolded: the translation of the remains of St. Cuthbert from Holy Island, the start of building on the rock, the battle at Neville's Cross, Charles I praying alone on his way to London, a murderer seeking sanctuary hammering on the great doors, the entry of miners' bands to dramatize the role of the common folk as well as that of the ambitious princes and clerics.

When it was over, we were able to give the cathedral the profit of around £70,000 at today's values. It was agreed that most of the money should go to pay for the installation of permanent floodlighting. In the years since, I've never been able to look on that glorious heritage of the cathedral shining in the night without a rush of exultation and gratitude.

I'd edited the *Northern Echo* for four years when I received a letter that would provoke the biggest of the paper's campaigns. It was March 1965, and I was on an express train from Darlington rattling down to London for a Westminster Press conference. I'd caught the train with seconds to spare, which was normal in those madcap days. I made it to my reserved seat only because Joan Thomas had pushed me out of the office and—as always—had phoned ahead to the station staff, so that when I ran onto the platform with the train about to leave, they had the right carriage door open. She never told me this at the time. I just knew there were sixty-one minutes in an hour and assumed everyone else did as well.

In my haste I grabbed sheaves of articles and correspondence reproachfully piling up in my "pending" tray. Among them was an article submitted for publication by a Darlington man I didn't know. Herbert Wolfe had escaped the Nazi persecution of the Jews in 1933. He'd brought with him to England one shilling—from which he'd built a thriving chemical business—and a passion for justice. The story he told in his letter and article accelerated my racing heart, carrying me back to a cold night fifteen years before, in March 1950, when a young man called Timothy Evans sat in the condemned cell in Pentonville Prison waiting to be hanged. He was twenty-five, a bakery van driver and not very bright. He'd had no normal schooling and couldn't read. He whiled away the time playing Chinese Patience and chatting about football and boxing. His companions said later he didn't seem to realize his position.

"The one thing that sticks in my mind," Evans would say to the warders in the cell with him, "is that I'm in for something I haven't done." He'd been found guilty at the Old Bailey of the murder of his baby daughter, Geraldine. He was charged with, but not tried for, the murder of his wife, Beryl, whose strangled body was found with the baby's, bundled up and hidden in the washhouse at 10 Rillington Place, a small, squalid house in a seedy area of Notting Hill, London, where the Evanses had a poky apartment. The trial excited little attention. The chief prosecution witness was a bespectacled clerk called John Reginald Halliday Christie, who lived in the ground-floor apartment at 10 Rillington Place.

All that Evans could say in his defense was that "Christie done it." He couldn't suggest a motive. The jury was out only forty minutes; the appeal was dismissed. Our neighbor in Failsworth, one Albert Pierrepoint, the official executioner, was summoned from the pub he ran, called Help the Poor Struggler. It was just another of the several hundred hangings he'd carried out with great efficiency at fifteen pounds per. There was no crowd at Pentonville at 9:00 a.m. on March 9, 1950, when the uncomprehending Evans was executed for a murder he did not commit.

The cold facts that Wolfe summarized gave me an urgent feeling that I should pull the emergency cord that would stop the swaying high-speed train so I could shout to the world that here was a monstrous injustice we must lose no time in correcting. It pained me that I'd put off reading through the "pending" tray, for the sequel to Evans's execution was as horrifying in its way as the terrible crime.

What the judge and jury didn't know, what counsel didn't know, what Evans didn't know, was that the star witness for the Crown was already a psychopathic strangler. Even as Mr. Justice Lewis donned the black cap and pronounced sentence on Evans, the bodies of two of John Christie's victims, Ruth Fuerst and Muriel Eady, were lying buried, undetected, in the little back garden in Rillington Place.

Three years after the execution of Evans, there was a new tenant in Christie's old ground-floor flat. He started to put up a wall bracket, pulled off a piece of wallpaper to reveal a papered-over cupboard, and found himself looking at the bare back of a human body. There were two more corpses in the cupboard, another under the floor in the front room (Mrs. Christie), plus the two female skeletons in the garden—six in all. Three years after the trial of Timothy Evans, Christie stood in the same dock at the Old Bailey and confessed that he was a necrophiliac and that it was he, not Evans, who had strangled Beryl Evans for sexual gratification at the moment of death.

The Christie confession confronted the public and legal system with an appalling probability: British justice had hanged an innocent man—and had done so on the evidence of the man who'd framed him, a man of such sangfroid that when his garden fence had slipped, he'd propped it up with a human femur.

How could it have happened? It wasn't surprising that judge and jury at the time chose to believe Christie. He was fluent, he was ingratiating, he'd been in France in World War I and been gassed in his country's service, and from 1939 to 1943 he'd been a War Reserve policeman with two special commendations. What a nerve this illiterate wretch Evans had, trying to blame an upstanding ex-policeman! And hadn't he admitted the crime? But it was a bogus confession. Christie had offered to perform an abortion on Beryl Evans—one of his tricks to indulge his vice—and Evans felt guilty when Christie told him it "didn't work" and Beryl had died in the procedure.

We can still get a very good idea of the diabolical nature of Christie from the movie *10 Rillington Place,* where the wily, whispering serial killer (played by Richard Attenborough) is the cobra and the pathetic Timothy Evans (John Hurt) the mouse. "Playing Christie," Attenborough told me at the film's world premiere, "was the most disturbing, distressing role I've ever played."

In Parliament and the press, following Christie's conviction and confession in 1953, there was an insistent demand to reexamine the case. The minister in charge of internal affairs, Home Secretary Sir David Maxwell Fyfe, announced that he'd asked for an inquiry by a QC. The QC he chose was Scott Henderson, a selection that proved to be a landmark in hypocrisy. The home secretary gave Henderson only nine days to review the complexities, on the grounds that Christie's execution shouldn't be delayed. It was an absurd request, and Henderson complied by rushing out an absurd report in only seven days. He did not merely say Timothy Evans was guilty after all. "There is," he concluded, *no ground for thinking* that there may have been a miscarriage of justice." Nobody else got a chance to interrogate Christie. On July 15 he was hanged on the same gallows where the man he'd framed had died.

The home secretary, a devout believer in the infallibility of trials for murder, declared it a "fantasy" to think there could have been a miscarriage of justice, but there were a number of people in Parliament and the press who remained disturbed, for good reason. Michael Eddowes, a London solicitor, published an investigation revealing that pressure had been brought to suppress the testimony of witnesses to Christie's lying and violent nature. Christie, "this perfectly innocent man," in the words of Mr. Christmas Humphreys, the QC prosecuting Evans, had in fact six entries on his police record, including six months in jail for maliciously wounding a woman he nearly killed. The authorities ignored Eddowes. The *Daily Mirror*'s Peter Baker interviewed the Roman Catholic chaplain at Pentonville and concluded that Evans didn't confess to either murder before he died saying the rosary. The authorities were unmoved.

In her work for the great book series Notable British Trials, Ms. Tennyson Jesse, a crime reporter and editor (and a grand-niece of the poet Alfred, Lord Tennyson), again underlined the fallacies in the prosecution's case. The authorities dug in. Ludovic Kennedy, the celebrated writer, TV performer, and Liberal candidate for Parliament, was moved to spend five years writing a masterly demolition of the case. It produced a parliamentary debate in June 1961 in which the Conservative home secretary, Rab Butler, conceded that no jury of the day would convict Evans, but he made no attempt to explain the crime committed in the public's name or to exonerate the victim. There was nothing he could do, he murmured; it was all too long ago.

Among a number of speeches from the Labour opposition was one by Sir Frank Soskice, QC, which passionately demanded a new inquiry, a free pardon, and the handing over of Evans's body to his Catholic family (a mother and two sisters) for burial in consecrated ground. "I believe," he said, "that if ever there was a debt due to justice, and to the reputation of our own judicial system and to the public conscience of many millions of people in this country, that debt is one the Home Secretary should pay now." Three and a half years after that, Sir Frank himself became home secretary. He then had the power to do what he'd urged the government to do in 1961. He didn't, proclaiming, "I really do not think that an inquiry would serve any useful purpose."

Sir Frank was the fourth home secretary in eleven years to reject a reopening of the case, and MPs and editors had other things on their mind. Given the caliber of the people who'd already protested, the fate of Timothy Evans was a lost cause.

To Herbert Wolfe this was intolerable. The integrity of British justice was precious, and it had been polluted. He convinced the Liberal Party to pass a resolution demanding an inquiry; it made no impact. He wrote letters to the press; they were discarded. He chose the fifteenth anniversary of Timothy's death, March 9, 1965, to send me that short article. As soon as I returned to Darlington, I read all I could on the case and was overwhelmed by the magnitude of what we'd been led to believe.

If Timothy Evans and John Christie were both killers, we were being asked to accept that there were two stranglers of women in the same two-up, two-down house, operating independently and in ignorance of one another. Both men used the same method of strangulation, and both made confessions to the police using the same language. Both confessed to "using a piece of rope," and not just any piece of rope but one "off a chair." Both disposed of the strangling ligature; both concealed their victims' bodies; both temporarily used the same place of concealment; both wrapped their victims' bodies in blankets; both left them without shoes; both left them without underclothing.

Not only were these men independently strangling in the same way at the same time in the same house, but it was pure chance that Evans accused Christie, who, unknown to him, shared his own supposed murdering characteristics. Evidence to overwhelm this series of coincidences would need to be formidable. The likelihood of finding two people with the same fingerprints is four billion to one (twice the number of people in the world then). The Evans-Christie "coincidence" was like finding two people with the same fingerprints in the same house.

I published Wolfe's article on the editorial page, along with a full editorial setting out the reasons justifying a new inquiry. I knew it would take much more than this to break officialdom's wall of certitude. What could a provincial newspaper and one of its readers possibly accomplish after all these years when all the distinguished testimony had been to no avail?

Soon after my trauma on the train—and it was that insistent—I was back in London, sitting on a cold stone seat in the lobby of the House of Commons. The man I'd come to see had written the fatal words "Let the law take its course" on the death warrant for Timothy Evans. This was Lord Chuter Ede, Labour's home secretary at the time. He was the man with the least to gain from reopening the case, yet he had the humility and courage to say that he now believed he'd sent an innocent man to the gallows and society should make amends. I asked him if he'd visit the current home secretary with a group of MPs, and he agreed. This would be a unique event; no former home secretary had ever appealed to a successor for a pardon for a convicted person.

I put that news on the front page with a little white-on-black box (a logotype) I intended to use to flag every story about Timothy Evans: "Man on Our Conscience." I wrote personal letters to all our regional MPs. In an editorial the *Echo* asked: Why has Sir Frank changed his mind? If he's discovered some new element in the case, he should tell us. If not, how could he explain his volte-face? But Sir Frank would not be provoked. Chuter Ede had warned me how hard it would be to make any impact: "We are up against the full weight of official Whitehall."

I sent Wolfe's article and my editorials to every regional and national editor and broadcaster. Nobody picked up on either the case or the Soskice contradiction. The silence was broken only by the chief whip of the Liberal Party, Eric Lubbock. He put down a House of Commons motion for a new inquiry and invited signatures from members of all parties. A month later he had only nine signatories.

An editor asked me, "Why are you flogging a dead horse? Why give a dead man any space?" I sent him a quotation from Michael Stewart, MP (later foreign secretary): "The moment we say we cannot be bothered, we have other important things to do, we turn from our progress and start walking along the road that leads to Belsen." A radio interview I secured after a few weeks brought a stinging rebuke from Douglas Nicholson, the chairman of the Vaux Brewery in Sunderland. He wasn't clear, he said, whether my call for an inquiry was "a newspaper stunt," but it did seem to him and others he had spoken to that an inquiry would "waste the time of important people."

It was a strange period for me. I don't have a thick skin; emotional, rather than phlegmatic, is the adjective that follows me around. But as the discouragements multiplied, I grew preternaturally calmer. It was a weird out-of-body experience, like the time in New York when I was mugged and regarded the mugger with a gun to my head with ridiculous detachment. I just went on publishing everything I could. Every time an MP signed Lubbock's motion, I put it on the front page with the Man on Our Conscience logo. Every day I selected one question after another about the conviction and put it under the logo. This got to be a bit much for Maurice Wedgewood and Frank Peters, who saw their precious front-page space taken up by Man on Our Conscience paragraphs. Peters asked, "Isn't it time to call it a day?"

I fell back on the famous editor Horace Greeley, who'd observed that the point when a newspaper begins to tire of a campaign is the point when readers are just beginning to notice it. But how to keep up the momentum and not bore everyone to tears? I assigned a bright reporter, Jim Walker, to examine how the authorities had reacted when confronted with other miscarriages of justice. Sir Arthur Conan Doyle, the creator of Sherlock Holmes, exposed the wrongful conviction of Oscar Slater, who nonetheless had to spend nineteen years in jail before the Home Office admitted the error. Then Doyle, after a Sherlockian investigation, campaigned for a pardon for the former solicitor George Edalji, erroneously convicted of mutilating animals. The authorities held out against a pardon but had to concede the establishment of the Court of Criminal Appeal.

Letters began to trickle in to the paper. Ludovic Kennedy came back from abroad, and we formed a Timothy Evans committee of all those who over the years had campaigned on Evans's behalf. On May 19 I collated all the editorials, news reports, features, and letters in a four-page *Northern Echo* pamphlet and mailed it to BBC radio and every MP, every editor, every television station. Gradually Lubbock gathered allies, and by four months into the campaign, 108 MPs had joined the call for an inquiry. I was now regularly interviewed about the case on radio and television. Supportive comments began to appear left and right—in the *Catholic Herald* and in the left-wing *Tribune* and from the scorching columnist Bernard Levin in the *Daily Mail,* though nowhere else in the national press. The going was made easier by the provincial newspapers. I urged all the editors to collaborate on a joint letter to the prime minister. They took up the *Northern Echo*'s campaign without a trace of jealousy.

On July 22 Lubbock's motion had 113 signatures. With Chuter Ede, he led an all-party group to see Sir Frank Soskice, who agreed to think again. A month later he gave in. He overruled the advice of his civil service officials and returned to his original position, appointing Mr. Justice Brabin to conduct an inquiry in public in the Royal Courts of Justice.

I was there in the Queen's Bench Court No. 6 in the Strand Law Courts on Tuesday, November 23, 1965, with Herbert Wolfe and Ludo Kennedy when Brabin opened the inquiry. The court was packed with QCs, treasury officials, press, witnesses, police, and Evans's relatives. Day by day the inquiry revealed the missteps in the dreadful labyrinth to the execution; we reported them all, and Wolfe wrote a commentary for the *Echo.*

The judge took a million words or so of evidence and examined seventy-nine witnesses, and then on October 12, 1966, he presented the oddest judgment of all: Timothy Evans had probably not murdered his baby, for which he was hanged, but he probably had murdered his wife, for which he was not even tried. "This was certainly an arresting theory," remarked Ludo, "especially as there is virtually no evidence to support it."

I wrote an examination of the flaws in the Brabin maneuver based on all the evidence that had been taken over a year, and the Timothy Evans committee joined in urging the new home secretary, Roy Jenkins, at last to do the decent thing. The testimonies at the inquiry, the judge's findings on the murder of the baby, and the years of advocacy were enough for Jenkins, a man who made all the Whitehall stonewallers look like straw men. Wolfe and I were in the House of Commons on October 18 when Jenkins rose to make a unique announcement. On his recommendation, the Queen had granted Timothy John Evans a free pardon, and the state returned his remains to his family for burial in consecrated ground.

Many people had worked for years to end the death penalty on religious and ethical grounds. The execution of Evans and the long refusal to face the shame of that brought the cause to a climax. Two weeks after the Brabin inquiry was announced, our ally and the stalwart abolition campaigner Sydney Silverman, MP, won a parliamentary motion for the suspension of the death penalty which that century had sent 799 men and 16 women to the gallows. On November 9, 1965, the House of Commons voted to suspend executions for five years. Four years later, on December 18, 1969, on a vote free of party dictates, the death penalty was abolished altogether.

BOOK TWO

Scoop, Scandal, and Strife

13

The Rolls-Royce of Fleet Street

Twenty-five years almost to the day since my father sat on the sands at Rhyl with the burned-out soldiers rescued from Dunkirk, I encountered a survivor who was to change my life.

Denis Hamilton was one of the most powerful people in British journalism. In 1940 this debonair, soft-spoken man had been a twenty-two-year-old junior officer shoulder-deep in the English Channel desperately trying to save the remnants of his battalion. He got to Dunkirk with only 160 men, the survivors of his Eleventh Battalion of the Durham Light Infantry. Now he was not only the prodigiously successful editor of the *Sunday Times*, the flagship of Thomson Newspapers, but editorial director of five Sunday, five morning, and eleven evening newspapers. He'd ended the war as the British Army's youngest brigadier, decorated with a Distinguished Service Order for holding back a German thrust near Arnhem. He was close to Field Marshal Bernard Montgomery, Prime Minister Harold Macmillan, and South African prime minister Jan Smuts. He was photographed with members of the royal family, the shah of Iran, President Kennedy, and President Nasser. He was friends of the Grahams at the *Washington Post* and the Sulzbergers at the *New York Times*.

The three-hour-plus train ride from Darlington deposited me in King's Cross station, a good long walk from the copper-faced Thomson House at 200 Grays Inn Road. Passing through the imposing double glass doors at the entrance embossed with the coat of arms of the owner, Lord Thomson of Fleet — motto: *Nemo me impune lacessit* (No one provokes me with impunity) — I was intercepted by a very martial commissionaire in a white peaked cap, his uniform ablaze with battle ribbons. I had the impression he checked the shine on my shoes as he telephoned someone to confirm the authenticity of my letter of introduction to Hamilton. Once confirmation arrived, he showed me into the elevator to the fifth floor, where I was escorted to an outer office and then the inner sanctum, which the secretary breathlessly told me had been designed by Lord Snowdon, then the husband of Princess Margaret. It was more like an elegant drawing room, with sofas and silk cushions. Hamilton seated me in a stylish Eames chair while he took a corner of a sofa beneath a Matisse print. There was no sign of a typewriter anywhere.

He was unhurried with me (the former corporal) and not at all intimidating. We established a bridgehead in our shared attachment to the North East — he'd been born in South Shields and worked in Newcastle — then he veered away to Asia and the training assignments I'd carried out for the International Press Institute. "I heard what you did for all those newspapers in India," he said. "Very important." He said nothing more for what seemed like an eternity, his mind, I imagined, roaming the subcontinent during the absences that I later learned were unnervingly characteristic of him. I didn't interrupt his reverie. Then his soft voice resumed. "The Timothy Evans affair in the *Northern Echo* and the campaigns on pollution and for a big cleanup of pit heaps...well done. A really good provincial newspaper can make a difference to a community."

I presumed he must be sounding me out on switching sides to join his Thomson regional newspaper group; at the *Northern Echo* I was competing against three of them every day. After the geography discussion, however, it seemed it was the *Sunday Times* that was at the top of his agenda. The *Sunday Times*! I hadn't allowed that possibility to enter my mind when he'd asked me down to London. I'd guessed it was either about the regional papers or the role of the provincial editors on the National Council for the Training of Journalists, where I'd joined discussions in which Hamilton occasionally took part. I tried to look calm. It was harder when I caught up with his ruminations. "I'm looking for a practiced newsman who might be groomed to be managing editor here."

Managing editor? Now that was a heady thought. The job was impressive enough in itself, and a managing editor was also clearly in the line of succession to the editor's chair. But "might be groomed" was tentative; the list of potential assignments—features, news, campaigns, sports, long-term planning for the color magazine—was long without it being clear whether I would run all these departments; and how many jostling managing editors were there at the *Sunday Times* already? Then Hamilton murmured something about looking for a successor to Pat Murphy, a seasoned professional who reported to Hamilton on the performance of Thomson's twenty regional editors. Murphy's current job held no interest for me, nor did I think I'd be much good at it. Twenty editors! I'd found it distracting enough to be looking over the shoulders of just three editors of an evening newspaper and two weeklies after I was promoted to editor in chief of the North of England Newspaper Company group while still editing the *Northern Echo.*

The opportunity of the *Sunday Times*, though, did make my head spin. How could it not? This was the biggest of what we called the quality Sundays. It broke news more often than the others, and its staff was legendary. Not every newspaper could boast Ian Fleming, the creator of James Bond, as the manager of its foreign correspondents, and where else in an elevator could you meet critics such as Cyril Connolly, George Steiner, and Raymond Mortimer and ask if they'd read any good books lately? The newspaper's critics and foreign correspondents trailed clouds of glory. The magnetic Fleming, coming out of the war as assistant to the director of naval intelligence, had recruited eighty-one gifted men and seven women for Lord Kemsley's Mercury foreign service, their locations indicated by colored lights on a world map behind his desk in Grays Inn Road. He liked to say, with a wave of his long ebonite cigarette holder, that their average age was thirty-eight and they spoke 3.1 languages apiece. Godfrey Smith, then the young personal assistant to Lord Kemsley—known as "K"—endeared himself to the irreverent Fleming by letting him have the key to K's very private loo. He remembers Fleming instructing the awed young men in his circle never to use a subordinate clause and to call only God and the King "sir." Fleming's "Atticus" column, like the man himself, was sophisticated entertainment.

Admittedly, the paper's political history was less impressive. In the 1930s owner and editor in chief Kemsley was an errand boy for Chamberlain in appeasing Hitler, and in 1956 he'd been a cheerleader for the invasion of Suez (and gained circulation at the expense of rival owner-editor David Astor's anti-Suez stand in the *Observer*). Under the ownership of the Canadian-born Roy Thomson and Hamilton's editorship since 1961, however, the *Sunday Times* had become less of a mouthpiece for the Conservative Party's Central Office. It was a far richer, more influential newspaper than my provincial daily, with fifty-six pages then to our sixteen, and at 1.3 million it had more than ten times our circulation, nationally and internationally.

I was flattered, but I didn't dive in, as I sometimes did without checking whether there was any water in the pool. Editing the *Northern Echo*, I was "with child." The paper was thriving as part of the community. My family had moved to a graceful period house in town, where we gave strawberry tea parties on the lawn while my two-year-old son, Michael, ate the daffodils. I'd identified so much with the North East and Darlington that a year before I'd written to the *Sunday Times* to protest a book reviewer's slighting reference to the town, typical of the south's snotty disdain, I felt, for anything north of the London suburbs. Hamilton himself had telephoned to apologize; the values he prized most were civility and loyalty.

London itself—the alien Metropolis—was a splendid mystery. On my fleeting visits I remembered the bewildered excitement of the pair of Newton Heath cubs just before the war when Dad had used a free railway pass to take Fred and me, in our best suits, to London by night train from Manchester. We arrived at Euston as the streets were being cleaned early in the morning, and then he proudly showed us Big Ben, the Houses of Parliament, Madame Tussauds waxworks, the Regent's Park zoo, and the Tube. We had tea at the Lyons Corner House, where the nippies, as the waitresses were called, wore white aprons and white lace caps. And then the magical day ended, and we were on the night train back to Manchester.

I was thirty-six. I'd watched all my young friends and colleagues in the provinces head for Fleet Street as soon as they could. I'd had the occasional envious pang seeing their bylines from foreign capitals or hearing of this or that ascent in the hierarchy, but I hadn't looked to London as my future, and looked still less after I became editor of the *Northern Echo*. One of Lord Beaverbrook's top editors at the *Sunday Express*,

John Junor, had pressed me to go for lunch, but I had never got round to it. In any case, there were just too many big guns firmly in editors' chairs of the papers that interested me.

Of course Fleet Street had its magic then. It's become a dull London thoroughfare since the electronic diaspora to south of the river, powerfully assisted by Rupert Murdoch's gratifying defeat of the Luddite print unions. But it wasn't like that in 1965. Nearly all the national newspapers had their headquarters in the street or nearby, with their presses roaring in the basements, the barons barking in the penthouses, news vans and reporters racing out, and enough watering holes for a thirsty newsman, gossip diarist, or cameraman to run from one to another in a rainstorm without getting wet. In the satirical magazine *Private Eye*, Fleet Street was the "Street of Shame," but how could anyone with ink in his veins not be entranced by the tales of daring scoops and backstairs scandals, much improved in the telling by the bibulous hacks in El Vino or the Printers Devil, Cheshire Cheese, White Swan, Punch Tavern, Old Bell, or Stab in the Back? Or by the sight of Megalopolitan House in its sheath of black glass, where Evelyn Waugh's bewildered antihero in *Scoop*, country diarist William Boot, arrived for his unforgettable interview with the foreign editor of the *Daily Beast* and its owner, the autocratic Lord Copper, doppelgänger for Lord Beaverbrook.

The *Sunday Times* was regarded as the most exciting paper in Fleet Street, albeit located in Grays Inn Road, where its solitary watering hole was the Blue Lion. But I'd heard quite a few stories of newcomers to national papers being squeezed out of a role. At least at the *Echo* I could get some things done, ungroomed.

Sensitive to my reservations about moving south, Hamilton suggested that I have coffee with his deputy, William Rees-Mogg, the donnish epigrammist (who in 1981 became the celebrated editor of the *Times*). I did so two weeks later, an encounter eased by the discovery that although Rees-Mogg was a country squire from Charterhouse and Balliol, we were both graduates of RAF Padgate. The columns of his I'd read in the *Sunday Times* resounded with such authority, it was a relief to find a shy bibliophile with an appealing little sibilance in his speech. His solemn ecclesiastical manner, hands fingertip to fingertip as if in prayer, dissolved into a self-effacing giggle when he confessed a cheerful unfamiliarity with questions of typography and production. "Joining the paper would be like joining a freeway," he explained, equably ensconced in his Georgian home near Smith Square, in the political heartland of Westminster, within division-bell distance of the Houses of Parliament. "If you come, I'm sure you'll soon gather speed and get in the right lane." With the caution I came to see as characteristic of Rees-Mogg, he added, "Of course we can't see round corners."

Rees-Mogg asked if I was inclined to accept "Denis's" invitation, then persuasively sketched why I'd enjoy the weekly operations and the personalities I'd be working with if I joined. "Perhaps you'll care to write some editorials, too," he said expansively, as he saw me out into the sunshine of Lord North Street looking toward the baroque church of St. John's. I visited the church before catching the train back to Darlington and happened on a lunchtime concert of Beethoven sonatas. It seemed a happy augury.

Back in Darlington I did some homework on my prospective new boss, Charles Denis Hamilton — known to his associates as C.D. — as well as on the über-boss, Lord Thomson of Fleet. Who were these controllers of the destiny of the *Sunday Times*? Would I be able to pursue the journalism that had most

engaged me at the *Northern Echo* as freely as I had with Westminster Press? Would Hamilton's position as an establishment figure be in any way inhibiting? If an investigation had
to be defended legally, would Thomson balk at the costs? The
self-made tycoon had amassed most of his fortune after he was
sixty. He was flagrantly frugal. The gossip diarists were agog
in 1964 to find the newly ennobled Baron Thomson of Fleet
standing in line at Burberry for a cashmere coat reduced from
seventy pounds to forty.

I soon discovered that Hamilton was not the upper-class
officer I'd assumed. He'd been brought up in a terraced house
in Middlesbrough, his father an engineer who'd been forced
by lung cancer to retire early from the heavily polluted iron
and steel works at Acklam, with a miserable pension of only
ten shillings a week. Hamilton's scholarship to Middlesbrough
High School put him among the handful of youths from the
industrial slums, separate from the paying sons of professional
people. He'd started in journalism as a junior reporter, as I had,
but he had never sought to go to university.

So how had he risen in the ranks so quickly to become
an army officer? He'd learned leadership in the Boy Scouts,
achieving the highest level of King's Scout (similar to Eagle
Scout in the United States). After Munich he'd volunteered for
the Territorial Army (think National Guard) when the Durham
Light Infantry needed thirty officers by the end of the month.
He wasn't qualified by the standards of the time (meaning he
wasn't a public-school boy, he hadn't played rugby for Durham, and his father didn't know the colonel's family), but he
did have an acute eye for the relevant social signals. Mixing
with officer candidates who'd been solicitors, bank managers,
accountants, and men from minor public schools, Hamilton
assumed an upper-middle-class disguise like a second skin.

His establishment aura — his commission, his decoration,

his accent, his Savile Row clothes, his whole demeanor—enabled him to advance toward the redoubts of privilege. Absent the illusion that he was an honorary member of the ruling class, his very real native abilities might well not have carried him into a position of power with the deeply snobbish Lord (and Lady) Kemsley, even though he was a war hero. Control of the so-called quality or serious national broadsheet newspapers in Britain, circulating among the more educated, tended to be the preserve of the traditional elites, with the graduates of public schools and Oxbridge predominant. In 1965, when Hamilton was talking about my joining the *Sunday Times*, the top four positions below him were all held by Oxbridge men. Hunter Davies, who'd followed me as a Castleman at Durham and editor of *Palatinate*, was the only provincial university man to have come, via reporting in Manchester, to an envied position as the successor to Fleming writing the entertaining Atticus column. It was similar elsewhere. The *Guardian* was edited by an Oxford man, and the *Telegraph* and *Observer* were owned and edited by Oxford men. But the Canadian Roy Thomson, the son of a barber from a more open, nondeferential society, who'd appointed Hamilton on buying out Kemsley, didn't care where a man came from so long as he knew where he was going. And William Haley, who edited the *Times,* had educated himself by omnivorous reading, so perhaps there was hope for me.

The press was just one strand of British life touched by the social changes accelerated by the war. In his 1941 essay "The Lion and the Unicorn," George Orwell predicted, "This war, unless we are defeated, will wipe out most of the existing class privileges." The victory of the Labour Party five years later seemed to fulfill his dream that England would assume its "real shape" through a conscious open revolt by ordinary people "against the notion that a half-witted public-schoolboy is better fitted for command than an intelligent mechanic." The two most powerful and able members of Clement Attlee's 1945 cabinet, Ernest Bevin and Herbert Morrison, were uneducated working-class lads. The Butler Education Act of 1944 opened the door for secondary education for all, as I described earlier, but by the 1960s higher education was still very much a privilege. In 1959, seven years after I graduated from Durham, only 4.2 percent of the eighteen-to-twenty-one age group had become full-time university students, hardly a lightning advance on the 3.2 percent admitted in 1954 and nothing compared with the United States. Orwell had been right to protest that the working class ought not to be "branded on the tongue"—a phrase borrowed from Wyndham Lewis—their status determined more by accent than ability. He could not have foreseen how liberation from that perception would be more powerfully assisted by satire than by polemics or politics. The surreal mockeries of class in the phenomenally popular *Goon Show*, on BBC radio, inspired the satirists of *Beyond the Fringe*, leading to *Monty Python* and *Fawlty Towers*. My generation did not feel any need to affect the standard English accent of the BBC newsreaders and the dukes posing as hotel concierges. It was not that we were brave; it would just have exposed us to ridicule.

I was a beneficiary of the late-breaking waves of political, cultural, and social changes that gathered force in the mid-1960s. By 1965 the Conservative Party had fallen apart in the aftermath of the Profumo call girl scandal. The prime minister no longer was Harold Macmillan, who appointed thirty-seven Etonians to office, seven in the cabinet, and played to perfection the role of the grand English gentleman. Now it was Harold Wilson, a scholarship boy at grammar school and university, with a nondescript accent who liked to be photographed in his ordinary Gannex raincoat, taking every opportunity to be seen as a middle-class, middlebrow, nonconformist Little Englander.

Labour's "New Vision," epitomized by Wilson's bending the nation's ear about the white-hot technological revolution, narrowly won the 1964 general election over a Conservative Party now seen as too much under the influence of the "fuddy duddy right." It was led by Sir Alec Douglas-Home, who'd had to demote himself from being the fourteenth Earl of Home so as to be eligible to sit in the Commons as Sir Alec and succeed Macmillan. He'd been cruelly caricatured as the prime minister who did his sums with matchsticks and had been given only tepid election support in the *Sunday Times*.

The stars were thus not badly aligned for me, a young working-class non-Oxbridge graduate with a northern accent, whose political genes were suspect. Lord Thomson said of Hamilton, "He's a fellow that doesn't display himself." He was indeed very private about his origins and his war, but I believe I was lucky that Hamilton's own rise from obscurity, his well-hidden resentment of the way his father had been treated, and his command of men in battle from all walks of life combined to make him exceptionally open-minded for his time and his position.

My sense of Denis Hamilton's civic virtue, as much as his achievements with the *Sunday Times*, was a powerful attraction. His boss was more of a puzzle. Roy Thomson was plainly tightfisted, but he'd risked millions launching the first color magazine in British newspapers in 1962 and installing the machinery for bigger newspapers. Visiting Thomson House I got no sense of hair-shirt austerities. But what of his attitude toward editorial? I'd watched a number of television interviews of Thomson on his purchase of the *Sunday Times* in 1959. He was a tubby, cheerfully Pickwickian figure who blinked at the questioner from behind Coke-bottle glasses, occasionally twitching his neck as if his collar was too tight, as I had seen Dad do. The impression I had, reinforced later, was that he was psychologically incapable of lying or dissembling. He just blurted things out. (I'd heard that Thomson, in Egypt for negotiations to buy a failing Cairo newspaper from President Nasser, had told Nasser, "You certainly are a cunning old Jew.")

His political philosophy amounted to a few homespun pioneer principles about honesty, humility, and thrift, drawn from the life of a self-made man. He'd left school at fourteen but absorbed into his bloodstream the romances of Horatio Alger, poor boy made good. He had the conventional political opinions of the business class. The death penalty was good, socialism a sickness, government regulation bad. But enfiladed from right and left by tough interlocutors such as Randolph Churchill and Keith Waterhouse, he wouldn't be shaken from insisting that he would never impose editorial policy.

Thomson didn't disguise that he was a cultural philistine indifferent to all the arts, or that his views were not those of the chattering classes, but he didn't expect anyone to take any notice, least of all copy him. After all, he once remarked, "part of the social mission of every great newspaper is to provide a home for a large number of salaried eccentrics."

His attachment to editorial independence had deep roots, practical rather than philosophical. Failing early on — in trying to grow wheat, sell motor supplies, sell radios, sell anything — he'd learned the hard way how much expertise he needed to realize his ideas. He had his policy printed on a card he carried around for twenty-five years like an oath:

> I can state with the utmost emphasis that no person or group can buy or influence editorial support from any newspaper in the Thomson group. Each paper may

perceive this interest in its own way, and will do this without advice, counsel or guidance from the Thomson Organisation. I do not believe that a newspaper can be run properly unless its editorial columns are run freely and independently by a highly skilled and dedicated professional journalist. This is and will continue to be my policy.

He'd fish it out of his pocket when accosted by critic, favor seeker, advertiser, or politician wanting him to pressure an editor. "You wouldn't expect me to go back on my word, would ya?" he'd say, showing the person his card.

The word of Thomson and Hamilton was good enough for me. In June 1965 I accepted an invitation to become chief assistant to C. D. Hamilton, and in January 1966 I passed through the crested glass doors to start work. Hamilton's formal letter of invitation spelled out a clearer prospect of being "indisputably the key managing editor within a reasonable time," while still floating the idea of my succeeding Pat Murphy as the regional newspapers' editorial director if that didn't work out.

I left Enid and our three children — Ruth, Kate, and Mike — in Darlington while I tested the ice, traveling home on weekends aboard the midnight sleeper, with an inky third edition of the *Sunday Times* for company.

Longtime foreign manager Ian Fleming bequeathed his successors a warning of the hazards of being deceived by the editor's Tuesday conferences of department heads: "Beneath the surface friendliness, lurk all the deadly sins with the exception of gluttony and lust. Each one of us has pride in our department of the paper; many of us are covetous of the editorial chair; most are envious of the bright ideas put forward by others; anger comes to the surface at what we regard as unmerited criticism, and sloth, certainly in my case, lurks in the wings." The "sloth" was the giveaway, an obvious exaggeration for effect, since this was the time—between 1945 and 1959—he was turning out a succession of his James Bond best sellers (*Casino Royale, Live and Let Die, Moonraker, Diamonds Are Forever, From Russia with Love, Dr. No,* and *Goldfinger*). Well, so I told myself, hoping the rivalries were not so intense as he described. It seemed to me on arrival that Hamilton and Rees-Mogg set an agreeable, gentlemanly tone for the weekly proceedings, more reminiscent of an academic seminar than the frantic ways of Fleet Street dailies. There were no women in the conference and hardly any on the newspaper. Still the men who assembled in Hamilton's office each week were an impressive bunch, and it would have been surprising if there wasn't hot competition among them for the managing editorship, or even the editorial chair in the unlikely event of Hamilton leaving it. I'd only been in the office a day or two when my friend from Manchester and Durham, Hunter Davies, the only person I knew on the paper, took me aside: "What are you doing here? You'll get eaten alive. You haven't even got a proper job [as he had as Atticus]. You've been a big fish in Darlington, but you'll just get carved up by these *Sunday Times* slickers."

The leading players were exceedingly clever Oxbridge men who'd vaulted over the traditional route to Fleet Street from the provinces. Presidents of the Oxford Union were in two of the top four positions: Rees-Mogg, the political editor and columnist, and Godfrey Smith, the irrepressibly creative editor of the color magazine. The foreign editor who controlled Fleming's old domain was Frank Giles, whom Hamilton had filched from the *Times,* where he'd been chief correspondent successively in Rome and Paris. The fourth Oxonian, editing the business news, was Anthony Vice, who'd started out at the

Financial Times, like Rees-Mogg, and was for five years city editor of the *Daily Telegraph.*

Among the older stalwarts were Leonard Russell, who'd been literary editor for thirty years and was married to Dilys Powell, doyenne of film critics. Russell was now in charge of the Review Front, the most cherished spot in the paper for features, most often ones he'd culled from well-written books, though he indulged in adventure stories. ("Three men in a boat on a boiling ocean" was his apologetic characterization.)

In contention for managing editor, I could see, were a number of young Turks: investigative editor Ron Hall, news editor Michael Cudlipp, star writer Nicholas Tomalin, and Mark Boxer, the wild card.

The scintillating founding editor of the color magazine, Boxer had first made headlines at Cambridge where, editing *Granta,* he'd published sacrilegious doggerel, including the lines "You drunken, gluttonous seedy God / You son of a bitch, you snotty old sod." He left Cambridge without a degree but subsequently proved the sharpness of his eye as art director of *Queen* magazine. He was known, too, for a facility for making enemies via the sharpness of his tongue as well as the wit of his pen-and-ink caricatures. Boxer had resigned the editorship of the color magazine, and when I arrived he was features editor without controlling any space, so he wandered round in a vaguely insurrectionary role. In conference he was often deftly offensive, which gave an edge of excitement to the proceedings. People resented his disdainful manner and Byronic good looks as much as the substance of his remarks, since he was usually right about what was "dreadfully dull."

Hamilton's style in the editorial board—a grand name for his Tuesday morning conference—was like none I'd seen before. There were no news schedules, no clipboards, no set agenda, no inquest on things that had gone wrong the week before. It was more of a conversation about what people had seen or read or were puzzled or entertained by. Hamilton let it drift. Having no agenda meant that people just talked about what interested them, and this often led to material for the paper. A remark about the prevalence of short skirts on the streets elicited the information that a revered Parisian film critic had referred to the phenomenon as the "English Revolution," and then someone else said that the revolution was in the moral standards the English young were developing, so different from their boring parents.

Hamilton took hold of that balloon. Who might understand what was happening, someone with authority but wit? Names were batted around. He didn't reject any, so a kind of cultural bidding war developed, everyone trying to come up with a still more appropriate, still more distinguished, still more surprising name.

I tried to keep up. Memos to myself survive in a tiny diary of 1966 and reflect the eclectic collisions as I struggled to come up with ideas and writers for all sections of the paper. I'd caught the tail end of a dismissive remark: "He's just a newsman." Was it about me? Not wanting to be typecast, I tried to cover all the bases:

- Rebecca West on Feminism
- Court magistrate who thinks 70 miles an hour speed too slow. Eccentric magistrates? Justice as comedy? Tomalin.
- Who Lord Goodman? Lewis Chester to write.
- Jean Shrimpton's knees
- Find husband/wife writing team, perceptions each other.
- Hector Berlioz letters. Other composer letters?
- Malcolm Muggeridge and Jesus. Fix lunch.

With Leonard Russell's approval, I got to know the London publishers and agents, in the hope we might have early warning of literary coups. I was not used to long, lavish lunches where pound notes were discreetly palmed for the wine waiter. I took bags of books to skim in my cheap room in the loft of the National Liberal Club that I shared with the pigeons and the cleaning ladies outside my door rattling their buckets. I made good use of the ideas and contacts gained as the host of a new weekly BBC radio discussion program, *A Word in Edgeways.*

I can no longer remember why I thought we might bring fresh light to the question of Jean Shrimpton's knees. But I do remember that a breakfast with my old friend Tarzie Vittachi of the International Press Institute led to him writing a stunning two-part Review Front for us revealing what had gone on in Sukarno's Indonesia during a news blackout. First the Communists murdered generals in an attempt at a coup, then Sukarno's generals murdered the Communists, and then fanatical Muslims started killing "infidels," so that 300,000 died before Indonesia returned to normality.

In the third month I was with the paper, Prime Minister Wilson called an election, giving me an opportunity to observe how far the paper's Conservative sympathies affected news coverage. I was in charge of the election pages, writing up the polls and monitoring the press. The *Sunday Times* reporters, I found, were wholly free to report what they saw, hardly commonplace in the fiercely partisan press.

These were difficult months for me, because in about the third week Hamilton told the conference I'd be revamping the sports pages. Boxer whispered, "That's the kiss of death." Apparently none of the executives cared to tangle with Ken Compston, the highly professional but belligerently independent sports editor of seventeen years. He blew smoke in my face, making it clear he didn't want any bloody fancy new ideas mucking up his pages. Yet he came round in the end. I signed Michael Parkinson as a sports columnist (Parky was not yet a TV celebrity) and cut a deal with the renowned yachtsman Francis Chichester. He'd announced he was going to attempt sailing single-handed the twenty-eight thousand miles to Australia and back, following the romantic and dangerous path of the famous clippers. We gave him a marvelous send-off on the Review Front with a profile written by Philip Norman, last seen earlier in these pages reporting pop concerts for the *Northern Echo*. He'd become a staff writer on the magazine, having won a writing contest set by Godfrey Smith. The Chichester signing turned out to provide an exciting yearlong series with regular dispatches (exclusive to the *Sunday Times* of course), and the whole world was absorbed when he set out from Australia to brave the perils of Cape Horn. It was the start of the *Sunday Times* in adventure journalism.

I was tense at Hamilton's first Tuesday conference after the launch of the new sports pages. There was bound to be criticism. I just hoped it was specific so I could try to grapple with it. Leonard Russell knocked his pipe on an ash stand and spoke before anyone else: "Damned good sports pages this week." Whatever anyone was about to say, Russell's endorsement was enough; a quiet murmur of assent, and we were off on other topics. All that was required was for England to win the World Cup, which it did in July against Germany. The following week Hamilton announced I was to be managing editor.

A few weeks later Hamilton made a dramatic announcement. The separate companies of Lord Thomson's profitable *Sunday Times* and Lord Astor's loss-making daily *Times* had agreed to merge into the new Times Newspapers company, 85 percent of whose stock would be owned by the Thomson Organization.

"The main obstacle to the merger," said Lord Thomson, "had undoubtedly been me. I don't think Lord Astor could stomach the idea of giving control of his paper to a roughneck Canadian." Thomson volunteered to give up the chairmanship, though he remained the principal risk taker. He said he calculated that the ample profits of the *Sunday Times* would cover losses by the *Times*—£285,000 that year—but if the company moved into loss, he and his son pledged their private fortune. And he reiterated his promise that neither the organization nor any individual Thomson would ever interfere with editorial policy.

The merger was approved by the government's Monopolies Commission in December 1966. Both William Haley at the *Times* and Denis Hamilton at the *Sunday Times* relinquished their editorships, Haley to become the first-year chairman of Times Newspapers, Hamilton to become editor in chief of both papers. Both promised the commission they would not attempt to impose identical policies on the new editors of the *Times* and *Sunday Times*.

Rees-Mogg was clearly destined for the *Times*. I had no great expectations I would be high on the list to succeed Hamilton at the *Sunday Times*, and I was surprised when Mark Boxer remarked casually, "You'd have been a candidate for editor, you know, but you're considered too left-wing." I'd originated several big features, led an Insight investigation of a crooked car insurance company, revamped sports, and overseen news, but I'd been on the paper for only a year, managing editor for only three months, and there were several senior contenders. The clear favorite was the foreign editor Frank Giles, an unruffled administrator who was also an accomplished linguist and writer. He'd been labor leader Ernest Bevin's private secretary at the Foreign Office and knew many world leaders.

After Giles it turned out the rivals for the *Sunday Times*

chair were fewer than I'd expected. Godfrey Smith made it clear he had no ambitions to edit the paper. Michael Cudlipp and Anthony Vice were privately earmarked for the *Times;* Ron Hall, Mark Boxer, and Nicholas Tomalin were, it seems, judged not to have sufficient experience setting political and economic policy. This left two older formidable front-runners inside the building—Giles and Pat Murphy, the Thomson group's editorial director—and one powerful outsider, Charles Wintour. The volcanic Randolph Churchill was hoarse in his incessant and often drunken private lobbying of Hamilton and Thomson for the appointment of Wintour, the acerbically clever editor of the excellent *Evening Standard* (and the father of American *Vogue's* future editor Anna Wintour).

In the week the decisions were made, Hamilton took Giles to dinner at Prime Minister Harold Wilson's official weekend residence, Chequers, along with Lord Thomson, William Rees-Mogg, and the paper's political correspondent, James Margach. They didn't get to bed until 3:00 a.m. because Wilson reminisced for hours. Only later, when it was announced that Rees-Mogg had been appointed editor of the *Times,* did it occur to Giles that he and Rees-Mogg had both been eyed as top prospects and that, for some reason, Hamilton changed his mind about giving him the editorship of the *Sunday Times.* Or it could have been that Frank's eye drooped mid-Wilson. Roy Thomson had told Hamilton that he preferred my "north country cheek" to Frank's more polished style (an assessment I was to learn about only years later).

All I knew was that on a Friday, Hamilton summoned me to his office and asked for a brief, to be delivered on Monday, on how I would develop the paper. I was so nervous typing it at home, I filled a whole wastebasket with crumpled false starts. (In those days every second thought meant retyping the whole thing.) Hamilton said nothing about the report I gave him on Monday, but the following day he sent me over to the *Times* offices to see Sir William Haley. Though we both had got serious ink on our hands at the *Manchester Evening News,* this was my first meeting with the editor who his subordinates at Reuters and the BBC had said was the only man in London with two glass eyes. Haley was warm enough, but not in the mood to reminisce about his days in Manchester. His rectitude during the interview was focused on how, if I were made editor, I would resist any pressures or temptations in the conduct of the paper to promote Thomson's commercial interests in magazines, holiday travel, book companies, and directories.

Two days later I was wheeled into the grand boardroom of the *Times* at Printing House Square for scrutiny by the full board of the new Times Newspapers. I sat isolated in a chair facing twelve solemn directors around a long walnut table, with intimidating oil portraits on the walls. In addition to the chairman, editor in chief, and general manager, the board included three Thomson nominees (one of them Kenneth Thomson, Roy's son), two Astor nominees, and four independent "national directors."

"How independent will you be as editor?"

"I'm certain that the judgment of the Monopolies Commission was correct. I shall be completely independent. Unless I was certain of this, I would not be prepared to accept the job."

"What is your attitude to the Thomson commercial interests?"

"The same as my attitude to any other commercial interests."

"Even if it is news adverse to the Thomson interests, say in travel?"

"If there is any news in it, we will print it."

The directors spent a full hour examining my halo as someone who would embrace and defend the freedoms defined in the Monopolies Commission report—not to sell out to

Mammon or twist the news for a political agenda. Looking back at the commitments they demanded, I can't help but wonder at how much journalism has changed.

I was confirmed as Hamilton's successor.

Frank Giles, for his part, accepted the deputy editorship. He was forty-eight; I was ten years younger. Often, talking to colleagues when I was out of earshot, he got into the habit of referring to me as "the young master." I didn't mind. It was good-humored; he was incapable of malice, and for the next fourteen years he was an engaging and steadfast deputy.

On the last Saturday of his editorship in January 1967, Hamilton, in his immaculately tailored suit, looked down from the steps leading to the composing room floor where shirtsleeves subs scurried about with galley proofs and page plans. "I'm handing you a Rolls-Royce," he said. It was true. His *Sunday Times* purred. I was determined to match his dedication to quality, though constitutionally incapable of achieving it in his inimitable style. He was a master delegator; I was a meddler. He was reticent; I wasn't. But we shared the same high hopes of what journalism might achieve. At my back in the years to come, I could always hear the Boy Scout in Denis Hamilton asking, as he'd frequently done when I was managing editor, "Have you done your good deed for today, Harold?"

14

The Third Man

A gale is blowing in from the Atlantic. It rattles the windows of the cottage behind a beach dune in Quogue, Long Island, where I'm writing this. If I take my eyes off the pines bending in the gusts and glance to the right of the windows, there's a framed photograph on the wall that carries me back to the heart of a great newspaper that had more than its share of storms—and created a few of its own.

The black-and-white photograph is of a news conference at the *Sunday Times* in London. It's unremarkable in itself—a dozen people sitting on sofas below a spotlighted world map. It would mean little or nothing to anyone else, yet for me it has the exalted resonance of a "Nocturne" painting. I'd admired James McNeill Whistler's work in the Tate gallery on the Embankment near my last home in Pimlico, but John Ruskin hadn't. The celebrated critic had said that Whistler's *Nocturne in Black and Gold* was nothing more than a pot of paint flung in the face of the public. Whistler sued him. Asked in cross-examination by Ruskin's attorney how long it had taken him to paint it, Whistler famously replied, "All my life."

That's what the photograph on my wall represents, the culmination of my life in journalism, thirty-five years in newspapers, from weekly reporting in Lancashire; to subbing and editorial writing for the *Manchester Evening News;* to foreign reporting in Europe, Southeast Asia, and the United States for the *Evening News* and the *Manchester Guardian;* to five years of daily newspaper editing in Darlington; and finally to fourteen years editing the *Sunday Times* of London.

I'd started this national editorship in January 1967, feeling very much an imposter as I was driven by a chauffeur to Grays Inn Road and the grand office where Hamilton in the spring of 1965 had first broached my joining him. I'd barely got used to being managing editor of the paper. Now I'd taken his place at the helm, and he'd moved across a bridge to the *Times* offices. In the perpetual remodeling of the editorial floor ordained by management, I ended up in the photograph's large white and chrome office planned by Terence Conran—benefactions a million miles from all my previous newspaper habitats— after moving from a smaller one decorated in rather startling red and black tones decreed by Lord Snowdon. Snowdon had explained that it was to match my character (I'm still working that out). He'd designed it very practically for transactions with galleys and page proofs, but he was always darting in to remove any object that offended his taste—one day an ashtray, another a cushion, another a clipboard, another a small potted plant. My secretary predicted, "You'll be next."

One day two Scotland Yard detectives did come in looking for me. They wanted a civil service report we'd published which revealed that Ministry of Transport officials were privately pressing to shut down one-third of the nation's railway system. The report proposed leaving large areas of Scotland, Cumberland, Lincolnshire, East Anglia, and central and west England without any trains at all. I truthfully told my visitors they wouldn't find the incriminating document in my office; I'd taken home the background paperwork after seeing the story to press on Saturday night.

I don't think their hearts were in the investigation, but I was duly cautioned that by publishing the information I could be charged with a criminal offense under section 2 of the Official Secrets Act, or OSA (section 1, dating back to 1911, being concerned with espionage). In the outcry after our report, the minister rejected the scheme, and the detectives didn't come back.

Other stories we ran or wanted to run, however, provoked so many subpoenas and writs summoning me to the Law Courts in the Strand that I could have found my way there blindfolded. I didn't seek confrontations with the law. They arose only because government, corporations, and individuals sought to suppress information of public concern discovered by diligent, painstaking efforts by the *Sunday Times* staff and its contributors.

Collectively the conflicts provoked by our attempts to answer numerous questions dramatized a chronic but unsuspected malaise in the functioning of British democracy. The resulting confrontations with authority also proved the severest of tests for the *Sunday Times* itself. Closer to home, would the solemn promises of editorial independence made by Denis Hamilton and Lord Thomson be maintained under unprecedented pressures and at grave financial risk?

I would soon find out.

In my audition memorandum for Hamilton, I'd suggested the paper needed a full-time investigative unit. I wanted to reflect W. T. Stead's governing functions of the press — "its argus-eyed power of inspection." My appetite had been whetted by the *Northern Echo*'s unifocal investigative ventures (cervical cancer and Teesside pollution); by the big car insurance fraud I'd worked on as managing editor; and by the earlier three exposés by the *Sunday Times:* the investigation of the crooked landlord Peter Rachman; the piquant case of the Chippendale commode, by which the newspaper was able to prove the existence of an antiques dealers' ring swindling sellers; and the "bogus Burgundy" story, in which we found a bottling factory sticking prestigious but false labels on cheap blended wine. These three stories had been published under the rubric "Insight," but the title was otherwise used to identify a weekly page of short, undifferentiated background features contributed by several writers. I devolved the feature writing to three staffers with a more focused mission, charging them to keep watch on all the scientific "ologies" on a page we would call Spectrum. Then I created a new investigative Insight team of four reporters and a researcher. Their exposures of unsuspected scandals of significance and compelling narrative reconstructions of major events (the Yom Kippur War, for instance) soon powerfully reinforced the identity of the *Sunday Times.*

Team journalism is difficult to manage, but I'd no doubt then and none since that it facilitates the best investigative journalism. No single reporter then or instant blogger today could be expected in a timely fashion to follow a multiplicity of trails, false and real, and grapple along the way with unpredictable technicalities in civil engineering, company law, accounting, aeronautics, physics, molecular biology, or whatever the relevant area of expertise. At various times over the next few years when I visited the cramped Insight offices, I'd see engineering blueprints of a DC-10 airliner tacked to the wall, along with a scale model of its defective cargo door, which sent 346 people to their deaths near Paris; another time there'd be diagrams of the chemical structure of thalidomide, which had robbed children of arms or legs or left them limbless trunks; and later annotated maps of the maze of streets in Derry plotting the moves of civil rights demonstrators and the British Army paratroopers who shot thirteen of them dead on Bloody Sunday.

But it is no easy matter to create and monitor a team. The chemistry and direction of the group are crucial. This is a subtle business, and there were periods when I got the mix wrong. You don't want four clones on the team; you want distinct but complementary skills. Each member has to like and respect the others' professionalism; all must be prepared to subordinate their egos and thirst for a byline and to accept direction from a team leader. Then they have to be willing to yield control of the final writing to someone they trust to respect their words and judgments—without being pushovers when the writer doesn't. The most persuasive criticism of team journalism touches on this point. As an anonymous Conservative Party critic of Insight's reporting on Northern Ireland wrote, "While the subjectivity of one writer can clearly be seen in a newspaper under his byline, that of a team is blurred and made more difficult to spot by the common, but unfounded, assumption that anything written by a team must be more dispassionate than that of a single writer."

In the early years the pace and style of the Insight team was set by Ron Hall and his deputy, Bruce Page. Hall and Page were both in their late twenties or early thirties and shared a taste for exuberant hairstyles—Hall a curly black mop, Page long angry sideburns. They had very different temperaments, however. Hall was a scholar in skepticism, honed by his study of statistics at Pembroke College, Cambridge. It was Hall who made the breakthrough in investigative journalism for the *Sunday Times* with a three-part series on the slumlord Peter Rachman, giving birth to tighter regulations and a new word for tenant exploitation: Rachmanism. But Hall didn't regard himself as a dragon slayer. In fact he distrusted crusaders in journalism.

He felt they'd make the facts fit the thesis. He affected boredom, yawning ostentatiously when someone pitched a story that seemed freighted with virtue. For me as editor it was comforting to see Hall, a pipe clamped in his mouth, slowly taking a reporter through the backup for his assertions and analysis. He was a lucid writer and a rigorous editor of text. He'd had a flair for headlines and display introductions beaten into him during his apprenticeship at the *Daily Mirror*. The worst thing Hall could tell you was that he was "combing a dog," which meant the story scheduled for the feature page he controlled had come in with a full consignment of fleas.

Page was not at all interested in the art of presentation but as scrupulous as Hall in deciding what was fit to print. He was a member of his local Labour Party, but never once in all the years I worked with him did a hint of partisanship infiltrate his work. A certain creative tension developed between the two men. In contrast to Hall's more measured approach, Page was zealous to set the world right. Whereas Hall, a dogged Yorkshireman, concealed his analytical sharpness in lethargy, Page, a dropout from Melbourne University, displayed his in breathtaking pole vaults over the collected works of Hume, Burke, Popper, Coleridge, Marx, and Keynes. His long, autodidactic digressions were relieved by an ironical style, and his energy was contagious.

Page and Hall developed strong opposing views on team journalism. Page believed that everyone involved, from the reporters to the designated collating writer, had to trust the judgment of competent colleagues or team journalism could not flourish. He was very careful, though, about who qualified as technically and morally honest enough for membership on the team. Hall thought Page's concept imposed too great a sacrifice of individual integrity. He was not prepared to have an article articulate a view until he was personally intellectually satisfied to the last comma. His statistical training inclined him to calculate the odds against a story having the level of accuracy he required—i.e., 100 percent. He was the kind of editor who would not publish a chess annotation until he'd played the game through himself. As Insight developed, Hall became the chief "space baron" for the whole first section of the paper, selecting and editing the pages he controlled; no second-rate work would survive his scowling scrutiny.

Page had particular gifts for investigation, along with an eclectic mind. He was an ingenious originator of theories to connect apparently unrelated dots, but he had the remorseless intellectual integrity to discard them when the dots didn't connect, as well as the imagination to construct another working hypothesis. Some people found him hard to take. He could be summarily dismissive of individuals he suspected of deviating from his standards, he could be tempted into fascinating but unnecessary digressions in his writing, and his search for the definitive put deadlines in peril. But he was also able to inspire a group with a common animating curiosity.

Much of the renown Insight would win was due to Ron Hall and Bruce Page and the path they set for the varied editors who followed: Lewis Chester, Godfrey Hodgson, John Barry, Simon Jenkins, and Paul Eddy.

Insight had a baptism of fire.

"Does the Flap of a Butterfly's Wings in Brazil Set Off a Tornado in Texas?" Edward Lorenz didn't present his chaos theory paper until 1972, but I've often thought of the principle in relation to a major investigation we began in 1967 in my second month on the job. The dynamics of the saga were such that small changes produced unpredictably large effects. For my own part I had no idea that an idle remark I picked up at lunch would nearly a year later lead to my being denounced by Foreign Secretary George Brown.

The lunch was with Jeremy Isaacs, my Granada producer on the first *What the Papers Say*. Isaacs had become head of current affairs at rival Thames Television. He remarked in passing that the *Observer* had bought the serial rights to a memoir by Eleanor Philby—"You know, the wife of that other man Philby in the affair of the missing diplomats." Sixteen years before, in 1951, two British diplomats, Guy Burgess based in Washington and Donald Maclean based in London, had disappeared together and resurfaced in Moscow in 1956. They were presumed to have been Soviet spies. Kim Philby—"that other man"—had been in Washington with Burgess. In 1963 he'd vanished from Beirut and six months later showed up in Moscow, too.

Back at the office I remarked to Page how interesting it was that all three defectors had been undergraduates at Cambridge in the 1930s. Maybe we could identify the subversive don who'd recruited them to the Communist cause. It didn't prove difficult to identify the don (Cambridge economics professor Maurice Dobb), but the unpredictable trajectory of Project X led us to a far bigger story about Harold Adrian Russell "Kim" Philby.

The Philby investigation was the most taxing one we ever undertook—a frustratingly tedious process of assembling and assessing tiny scraps of information from hundreds of interviews with denizens of a closed world whose stock-in-trade is deceit. Central casting couldn't have selected a more suitably varied bunch of independent minds for penetrating Philby's secret world. Australian Phillip Knightley's quiet, unassuming manner exuded an empathy that attracted confidences despite his distinct resemblance to Lenin—bald dome, black goatee. He'd knocked about the globe as a seaman, vacuum cleaner salesman, South Sea Islands trader, and reporter. David Leitch, like Guy Burgess, had been a golden boy at Cambridge, though twenty years later. Both were good-looking, charming, bohemian romantics—and brilliant. Leitch was already showing the writing gifts that would win him acclaim for describing his days among U.S. Marines at the siege of Khe Sanh in Vietnam. John Barry, a dropout from Balliol, was a contrarian with a quicksilver mind. The austere, cerebral Hugo Young was not on the regular Insight team—he was chief editorial writer and an impeccable political reporter—but he contributed because he knew the ways of Whitehall and Washington as both a Harkness Fellow and a Congressional Fellow.

Most of the ink over the years had been spent on Burgess and Maclean and the mysteries of their last-minute getaway, rushing together onto the ferry from Southampton to St.-Malo at 11:45 p.m. on Friday, May 25, 1951, one of them drunkenly shouting "Back on Monday!" to a sailor concerned about the big white Austin they abandoned on the quayside.

There had been articles about Philby, but nobody had even begun to peel the onion. Nothing had been said on what he'd done, when he'd started spying for the Soviets, how he'd escaped detection, and, importantly, what damage he'd caused, if any. He was assumed to have been a low- to mid-level agent in Britain, and in Moscow he'd become the invisible man. His address was a secret; his telephone was ex-directory; there was nothing about him in the Soviet press; and in the city if he was glimpsed one minute, he was gone the next. For our part we knew next to nothing about him. Leitch had tried to use an interview with Khrushchev in Moscow in 1964 as an avenue to the mysterious exile, but nothing had come of it. Right at the start of our inquiry, we tried again, writing to Kim Philby, Moscow. (It seemed necessary to do that, but in retrospect I'm glad he maintained his silence. If he had talked to us, we would have been accused of being his mouthpiece.)

In the biographical sketch with which we started, Philby surfaced only as a series of snapshots: the blazered head boy at the elite Aldro prep school; the handsome youth who's won a king's scholarship at Westminster posing with his proud, bearded father—Arabist explorer, scholar, and convert to Islam St. John Philby, who had to struggle financially to send him there; pipe-puffing Kim in flannel bags and tweeds at Trinity College, Cambridge, working hard to get a good degree in economics and history; and Kim at twenty-five, an adventurous journalist reporting the Spanish Civil War for the *Times*, his head bandaged from a shell burst. He appeared to be the quintessential upper-middle-class Englishman, a member of the Athenaeum, the premier gentlemen's club in London; decorated as a commander of the Order of the British Empire (CBE); addicted to the *Times* crossword, cricket, and premier cru claret; and repelled by displays of emotion. Even when he was under stress in 1955, when he'd just been accused by a Labour MP of tipping off Burgess and Maclean to flee in 1951, we see him unruffled by the uproar, debonair in a gray pin-striped suit as he smiles into the press cameras admitted to the living room of his mother's home in Drayton Gardens, London. In the tape we watched, he was calm and assured, speaking with amused condescension, controlling his charming little stutter; he had a get-out-of-jail-free card in his pocket, a statement to Parliament by Foreign Secretary Harold Macmillan: "I have no reason to conclude that Mr. Philby has at any time betrayed the interests of this country or to identify him with the so-called 'third man,' if indeed there was one."

The press, too, exonerated Philby. Poor fellow, they concluded; he'd lost his job as a diplomat just because he'd been unwise enough to let the wild, drunken Burgess, an old friend, have a basement flat in his large house in Washington. This was the period when there was revulsion in Britain for the witch hunts of Senator Joseph McCarthy. The MP who'd made the charge against Philby had to withdraw, shouted down by his fellow Labour MPs.

After his official clearance we next see Philby in shirtsleeves at a picnic in the hills outside Beirut, squatting on the ground all smiles and sunglasses, the Middle East correspondent of the *Observer* and the *Economist* at work on a bottle of wine.

And then we don't see him at all.

On January 23, 1963, he got out of a taxi in Beirut "to send a cable" on the way to a party with Eleanor and never showed up at the party. Six months later Edward Heath, the Lord Privy Seal, told a questioner in Parliament that Philby had confessed to having "warned Maclean through Burgess," but this was all that emerged. The government had maintained total silence since. It had never even officially acknowledged that Philby had been a spy working for Britain's Secret Intelligence Service. (The SIS is authorized to operate abroad and is popularly known as MI6, for Military Intelligence section 6, as distinct from MI5, the domestic counterespionage agency.)

We made some progress putting together the jigsaw of Philby's life. Leitch snooped round Cambridge, his old university, looking for leads. Burgess and Maclean were members of a Communist cell started by Maurice Dobb. Philby did not join but did become a Marxist, spending his fourteen-pound prize money at Trinity on the complete works of Marx. He was moved by the sight of hunger marchers who'd walked all the way from the North East and organized meals for them. At Dobbs's suggestion he visited the Paris Comintern, and on graduation in 1933 he rode his motorcycle to the bloody ideological battleground of Vienna. Page called Eric Gedye, the *Daily Telegraph* correspondent who'd been in Vienna then. The news from him was that Philby had married a vivacious Communist—we tracked down her first husband in

Israel—and worked with the underground to smuggle Communists out of Austria to safety.

How could such a dedicated Marxist win entry to the Foreign Service a few years later at a time when the fear of "Bolshevism" was acute? The answer is that by then it was not the same Philby. The Philby smuggling clothes to Communists hiding in the sewers of Vienna was next lending his energies to the hated fascists. Back in London, he was named editor of the Anglo-German Friendship Society magazine. "Look," said Page, coming excitedly into my office with a framed photograph and a shrewd deduction, "here's Philby building a new identity." The picture was a swastika-bedecked black-tie dinner given by the Anglo-German Friendship Society in July 1936, and there clearly was young Philby. Maclean and Burgess also had both conspicuously and abruptly retreated from their Marxism.

When the Spanish Civil War broke out in 1936, Philby took himself off to the battlefront as a freelance reporter—not, like most of his generation, allied with the uneasy coalition of the left on the Republican side supported by the Soviet Union, but on the side of General Francisco Franco's coalition, which included monarchists, fascists, and the Roman Catholic Church. In 1937, when he was only twenty-five, he became the special correspondent of the *Times* with Franco. We looked at his dispatches in the *Times* library. They were slanted in favor of Franco's Nationalists, even after the bombing of Guernica by the German Condor Legion, the first mass air attack on civilians. One thing stuck in the minds of journalists we spoke to who'd observed him in Spain. He wanted to know the details of Nationalist troop movements—numbers, directions, and regiments—way beyond what readers of the *Times* needed.

"Maybe," said Page, "he'd already been engaged by Soviet intelligence."

It was a prophetic insight. He had. But he had also been talent-spotted by MI6, the reason we deduced for his abrupt departure from the *Times* in July 1940. What did he do in the service? We went through all the reference books to find the names of the staff in our embassies where Philby had worked. There were some clues about which ones had been intelligence officers: for example, an entry in the biographical reference book *Who's Who* identifying someone as a member of the diplomatic service but whose name did not appear in the Foreign Office list. Few of the people we approached at first in MI6 would divulge anything. "Sorry, Official Secrets." Click.

Things improved when we knew enough to appear knowledgeable—the conversation might then inch us forward—but I got used to the expression of apology that my depressed reporters brought back from a fruitless day. Knightley had a typically tantalizing talk with a retired MI5 officer who told him, "Of course it was the defector in 1945 who put us onto Kim. After that you had only to look in the files to see it all." And what did you learn? "Better leave it at that, old boy. Don't want to get into trouble with the OSA."

I had known it would be a difficult assignment. We were asking questions about a nonperson, a disgraced member of a secret intelligence service that did not officially exist, whose head man was a letter of the alphabet ("C"), and whose headquarters address was a state secret. I could not keep Insight knocking on closed doors if there was nothing behind them. Perhaps I had given them a bum steer and there wasn't much more to Philby.

What happened next was like a fluke in a crowded pool hall, where as you make a shot, someone jogs your elbow and the cue ball caroms wildly round the table and ends up potting the black. Two high officials, striving to be unhelpful, jogged our elbow at the right moment.

The first was the former head of MI6, who'd retired to Wiltshire and was no longer the anonymous "C" but the aristocratic Major General Sir Stewart Menzies. He'd been in charge of the agency during the war and through the defections — a decent, canny man, much sounder than the upper-class clown portrayed as the head of the service in *Our Man in Havana* by Graham Greene (who served under Menzies in the war). We wrote to him for an interview. No, he said politely by mail, he wouldn't talk to us. He was known in the service as the man with sealed lips, who wouldn't agree it was a nice day for fear of giving something away. But he could not resist adding a sentence in his letter: "What a blackguard Philby was." Oh, really? A man of such notorious discretion as Menzies must have been driven by deep feelings to resort to the vocabulary of Victorian melodrama.

The second elbow jogger was Lord Chalfont, a new minister at the Foreign Office. Leitch, who'd previously been on the staff of the *Times*, had known Chalfont before his elevation on joining government, when he was Alun Gwynne Jones, the newspaper's defense correspondent. When Leitch and Page met Chalfont at the Foreign Office and mentioned Philby, the minister began by saying that Philby was a man of no importance, not worth a reporter's time and effort: *Let me save you the trouble. Anyway you couldn't possibly uncover anything about Philby. And if you did, you'd not be able to publish it.* Then, like Menzies, he felt compelled to say more: "You must stop your inquiries. There is the most monstrous danger here. You'll be helping the enemy." He was more charmingly restrained with me when I had a drink with him at the Garrick Club. Would the Foreign Office at least answer some questions I had? "Afraid not, but we'll not stand in your way."

I told Denis Hamilton that we were going to find out what Philby had done that caused so much alarm. He was troubled.

"How can you be sure you won't help the Russians?" he asked.

"Well, we can't tell them more than Philby must have already told them. Denis, we're the ones in the dark."

"And what about the Official Secrets Act?"

"Can't we judge the risks of that when we know more?"

"Let me think about it."

He didn't tell me the results of his deep think until a few days later. I was surprised. He called me to his office to say that "in great secrecy" he'd been to see Prime Minister Harold Wilson and the current "C." "The Foreign Office is alarmed. I told them you're not a man who would want to damage his country. But I've seen too much slaughter in my life, Harold. Will you let them see a draft to make sure you don't put anyone at risk? All I've said is that you will consider representations."

I said I would. None of us wanted to risk the life of an agent by some unwitting reference. The trouble is, we had nothing about which anyone could make representations. The trail was not just cold by 1967; it was frozen. I took up Hamilton's suggestion that I see Sir Denis Greenhill, deputy undersecretary at the Foreign Office. I discovered later he was the main link between the Foreign Office and MI6. Our first mutually wary meeting was in his Travellers Club in Pall Mall. Later we met in a Bloomsbury hotel; once in his unpretentious house in West London, where his vivacious wife, Angela, served tea and biscuits; and once in the Foreign Office. He was then fifty-four, silver-haired but well-muscled, dressed in a double-breasted chalk-striped suit, curt and brisk in manner. The son of a top manager in the Westminster Bank, he'd reached Christ Church, Oxford, by way of the lesser public school Bishop's Stortford and then got a job as a traffic apprentice on the London and North Eastern Railway, the ladder by which young middle-class men became the bosses of railwaymen like my father. He'd been a staff colonel in the Royal Engineers in World War II before entering the foreign service in 1946. He was not a typical Foreign Office man, but he exhibited the same hostility to our probing Philby as had Lord Chalfont.

About Burgess he was droll in his detestation. Burgess had been foisted on Greenhill when he ran our Washington embassy's Middle East department during the time Burgess and Philby were there. He recalled Burgess as an idle, shambling drunk who dropped cigarette ashes on other people's papers, drank other people's whiskey, paraded his homosexual promiscuity, and told entertaining tales to discredit the famous. "I've never met a name-dropper in the same class," Greenhill said. Burgess had a gift for caricature and once drew a Christmas card for Greenhill's small son with Stalin as Father Christmas. "I should have paid more attention to it at the time," Sir Denis noted, somewhat wistfully. But Greenhill's agreeable facility for recall eluded him over Philby. Not a word would he say about the man who'd fooled them all.

"You'll do more damage with the Americans if you write about Philby. Who's this fellow Page? What's *his* game?"

Why did this minor figure, Philby, continue to excite such anxiety? Any number of people we'd reached were willing to reminisce about Philby as a Special Operations executive trainer of men and women dropped into occupied France. We were regaled with the prowess of Philby as 007—a master of unarmed combat, night sabotage, pistol shooting, and seduction of women. He shone, too, we learned, as an executive within MI6, which he entered in the summer of 1941, though his style was not to everyone's taste. Sir Robert Menzies, a Foreign Office security officer, was dazzled by Philby's "sense of dedicated idealism" and his mastery of the English language in his reports, submitted in neat, tiny handwriting. Miss Kennard Davis, from the vantage point of the typing pool, told Insight that Philby was harsh in his rebukes for mistakes. "I used to shrivel up like a worm. He used it on the men, too, just as effectively. I can remember walking into Graham Greene's office, and his eyes were glinting with anger. I asked him what was the matter, and he said, 'I've just had a caning from the headmaster.' "

All this was very helpful for sketching the outlines of Philby's personality, but none of it told us where the "most monstrous danger" lay.

Around this time I had call from Michael Frayn. I'd seen him socially from time to time in the years since we'd shared a canteen table while I was at the *Manchester Evening News* and *Guardian*. (That was long before he was acclaimed for his farce *Noises Off*, the intellectually brilliant dramas *Copenhagen* and *Democracy*, and the rollicking Fleet Street novel *Towards the End of the Morning*.) He'd told me then how out of a passion for reading the original Tolstoy and Chekhov, he'd learned Russian at an army course after leaving Cambridge—Cambridge again— and then had an invitation to join MI6, which he declined. He called me to say he had a bright acquaintance of his who wanted to start a new career in journalism. I'd have seen him on Michael's recommendation, but I did so with alacrity when he added, "By the way, he's in the Foreign Office at the moment."

John Sackur was a mystery. A pale, earnest man in his late thirties, he presented himself as a crusader for black Africans. He was upset that Britain had not quashed the coup in 1965 by which Ian Smith imposed white minority rule on what was then British Rhodesia (now the benighted Zimbabwe). But was that really his motive in seeing me? I'd expected to draw the usual blank when I mentioned our interest in Philby.

Sackur appeared incredulous.

"Philby? You'll never be able to print it."

"Why not?"

"It'll get stopped—D [Defense] Notices, the Queen. It goes

to the highest in the land." And then he bit out with real emotion, "Philby was a copper-bottomed bastard."

It emerged that he had written a report on the damage Philby had done, but he would not say any more. He'd already met Frank Giles, my deputy and foreign editor, who'd asked him if he was "a friend," the Foreign Office term for someone in MI6. He said he was. When later I accused Michael Frayn of foisting a spy on me—he recalls I was "very angry"—he said that he had no idea Sackur was in MI6, and I believe him. "John was a natural deceiver," Michael said. "He deceived me on several occasions at Cambridge."

I introduced Sackur to Bruce Page, who took him off to Manzi's seafood restaurant in Soho. The one clue Page pried out of him was that if we ever got to the bottom of Philby's betrayal, we'd realize that it mattered less what Philby had done in the cold war than in World War II. Eventually we discovered this was a reference to Philby's role in blocking evidence in 1944, before the German officers' plot to kill Hitler, that the German Army was putting out feelers for a separate peace with the United States and Britain. He may also have had a hand in the fate of a number of Catholic activists in Germany who'd been identified as possible leaders in an anti-Communist government after the war. They did not survive.

Knightley, who has become a specialist in writing on espionage, believes today that Sackur tipped us off because he represented a small group of young rebels in MI6 who suspected the service had not had enough of a purge after Philby. It is also just possible that MI6 encouraged Sackur to seek a foreign correspondent's job with us as a cover for working for the agency in the Middle East, just as they infiltrated the *Observer* and the *Economist* with Philby. Sackur's hints about Philby (and Blunt; see below), on this supposition, might not have been indiscretions but cunning bait to suggest he was disaffected enough to be a genuine defector whose integrity could be trusted. Recalling the intensity of expression on his chalk white face as he expounded on foreign policy at our first meeting, a lunch at the Ivy restaurant, I am inclined to conclude that he was not a plant but a young man whose conscience would give him no rest. I intended to talk to Sackur again when I conceived of writing this memoir, but he died before we could meet.

Only later did I realize the significance of Sackur's glancing reference to the Queen. Leitch had given Page the names of a number of leftist undergraduates in the *Trinity Review*. One was Anthony Blunt. At the time, in 1967, he was surveyor of the Queen's pictures, a part-time job in which he oversaw the care of the Queen's publicly owned collection. He was a pale, chilly, fastidiously mannered aesthete; a compulsively promiscuous homosexual; a favorite of a small group of the more arty courtiers—he dined often at Marlborough House with the Queen Mother and her set; and an enigma even to his friends. Twelve years later, in November 1979, Margaret Thatcher named him as a Soviet spy after Andrew Boyle, the founding editor of the BBC Radio 4 program *The World at One*, had featured Blunt in his book about the Philby scandal, *The Climate of Treason*. Boyle had disguised Blunt as "Maurice," the figure in E. M. Forster's story of homosexual love. Blunt became an object of universal execration and was stripped of his knighthood. But Sackur must have been disturbed, as I was among many, at the immunity Blunt had been given in 1964 and the retention of his job at Buckingham Palace in return for a confession. (By contrast, three years earlier the less well-connected gang in the Portland spy ring had been sent to prison for fifteen to twenty-five years for stealing naval secrets.)

Page wrote to Blunt in 1967 asking for an interview. Knightley took the request round to Blunt's grace-and-favor apartment at the Courtauld Institute of Art. Blunt read it and slammed the door in Knightley's face. The next morning Page got a letter from Blunt's solicitor warning that he would sue for harassment if we ever tried to contact him again. We would not have been deterred by that if we'd had anything on Blunt, but we didn't. He'd been investigated by MI5 fifteen times and proved to be small-fry by comparison with Philby, but we didn't know that at the time. Not pursuing Blunt was a mistake I regret, but we were by then excitedly preoccupied with leads developing on Philby.

Our collection of espionage books had netted one titled *British Agent,* written the year before by someone named John Whitwell. Knightley winkled out his real name, A. L. (Leslie) Nicholson, who'd been an MI6 man in Prague and later in Riga. Knightley found him to be a drunken burnout living on a miserable pension over a seedy café in East London. It was hard to believe he had ever been an MI6 officer. *Another wasted expense,* thought Knightley as he treated Nicholson to a good Italian lunch and several brandies. But as Knightley gently pressed questions, inevitably revealing that we knew Philby was important and by implication that we didn't quite know why, Nicholson's enjoyment increased. He was aware of the seriousness of his illness (he died two years later from cancer), and over coffee and another brandy he told Knightley what Philby had really done.

"The reason for the flap, old man," he said, "is that Kim was head of our anti-Soviet section."

As Knightley put it, "I can remember trying to clear my head of brandy fumes." He pressed Nicholson. "Let me get this straight. The man running our secret operations against the Russians after 1944 was a Russian agent himself?"

"Precisely."

This meant not only that any intelligence operations against the Soviets were doomed from the start but that the days of all

The Tuesday conference in the editor's office at the *Sunday Times*. The "Uganda Sensation" on the contents bill is the detailed revelation of the atrocities of Uganda's dictator, Idi Amin, by a fugitive hiding in my cottage in Essex. Prince Charles (left) happened to come to the conference that week. *(Peter Dunne)*

Roy Thomson: the beloved Canadian who bought the *Scotsman*, the *Sunday Times,* and the *Times* was a frugal owner but generous in according his editors freedom. He was ennobled as Lord Thomson of Fleet. *(David Low)*

Twelve years into my editorship of the *Sunday Times* and William Rees-Mogg's of the *Times,* we were asked to pose with the "indispensable, elegant" Denis Hamilton (seated), as Cyril Connolly called the chairman of *Times* Newspapers. William is left, I am on the right, looking rather smug. The photographer was one who had to be obeyed, Arnold Newman, in Britain preparing a show for the National Portrait Gallery and the *Sunday Times* magazine. *(Arnold Newman)*

The Insight trio who led the Philby investigation: David Leitch, Bruce Page, and the Lenin look-alike Philip Knightley. The intrepid photographer Bryan Wharton managed to get them to stand still for a minute. *(Bryan Wharton)*

David Blundy interviews Israeli leader Ariel Sharon on the Golan Heights during the Yom Kippur war of 1973. He survived his hazardous years as an irrepressible reporter only to be killed by a random bullet on a street corner while covering El Salvador's civil war on November 17, 1989. *(Sally Soames)*

Frank Hermann at the anti-Gaullist riots in Paris in 1968, snapped by his colleague Bryan Wharton. Both were soon overcome by CS gas. *(Bryan Wharton)*

A day in the life of an editor at the *Sunday Times,* first with reporters on a tricky story about abortion.... *(Ian Berry)*

(Sunday Times)

...then the lawyer takes a look at the story on the page... *(Ian Berry)*

finally the hot metal page, attended by the news editor, editor, comp, and chief sub, is ready—on time, it seems. *(Ian Berry)*

Tatler magazine in London was about to expire when Tina assumed the editorship. I didn't notice at the time that the window display behind spells FUTURE. She'd only recently returned from New York, where she made friends with an author I'd signed for the *Sunday Times:* Sid Perelman, the celebrated *New Yorker* humorist and scriptwriter for some Marx Brothers films and Mike Todd's *Around the World in Eighty Days. (Ken Sharp)*

At the age of seventy-four, Perelman declared he was going to drive his 1949 MG YT tourer in a rerun of the epic Paris-to-Peking motor race (9,317 miles). He told me he had a blonde from Pine Bluff, Arkansas, as traveling companion: "She knows zilch about engines, but she's six foot two inches of dimpled beauty." Perelman and I are explaining all this to the London meter maid when Sid parked the MG for a farewell lunch. *(Bryan Wharton)*

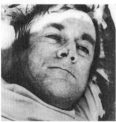

(Sunday Times)

Our debonair foreign correspondent was found in Cairo with an assassin's bullet through his heart. *(Cal McCrystal)*

The Communist union leader in the fur hat is having fun parading a mock coffin of the *Sunday Times*. One and a half million readers didn't get the paper for a full year. *(Sally Soames)*

Who wouldn't look glum standing in the deadness of the strike-bound composing room, normally the hectic scene where the word became metal? *(Sally Soames)*

Saying good-bye on the composing room floor, on my last day as editor of the *Sunday Times* after fourteen years. *(Mark Ellidge)*

As a former corporal, I was outranked by General Colin Powell (left), the retiring chairman of the joint chiefs, and his associates, but we all got the joke about "the one that got away." *(Random House)*

Truth in Travel hits the road. We celebrated the first issue of *Condé Nast Traveler* with a smiling chairman, Si Newhouse; his publisher, Ron Galotti; and a cake iced to represent the first cover photo, from an adventurous voyage up the Amazon recorded by Christopher Buckley. *(Condé Nast Traveler)*

I stood in line with hundreds of others waiting to take the oath of citizenship at a courthouse in New York. It was a moving moment. *(Dafydd Jones)*

Our refuge, the 1928 cottage by the sea in Quogue, Long Island. The view from the top of the ocean dune. *(Mike Evans)*

And then there were four...with George casting a wary eye on the camera. The birth of Isabel Harriet in October 1990, recorded by photographic royalty Annie Leibovitz. *(Annie Leibovitz)*

In the courtyard of Buckingham Palace in 2004, having bent the knee to be dubbed a Knight Bachelor of the British Empire. They've been awarding KBE's since the reign of King Henry III (October 1, 1207–November 16, 1272), so I was a Johnny-come-lately.

the MI6 agents already in place in the Soviet Union and Eastern Europe were numbered.

In the *Sunday Times* office we puzzled over why Philby's crimes had remained undetected for so long. Two luminaries who talked to us about their wartime experiences with MI6—the Oxford historian Hugh Trevor-Roper and the journalistic provocateur Malcolm Muggeridge—spoke freely of their contempt for the quality of MI6's staff, apart from the clever code breakers. Trevor-Roper said that the permanent officers were drawn from two classes of men—"ex-Indian policemen and metropolitan young gentlemen whose education had been expensive rather than profound and who were recruited at the exclusive bars of White's and Boodles." But even if Philby's colleagues were as dim as alleged by these critics, both of whom took a poor view of the human race anyway, wouldn't one of any number of KGB defectors from the Soviet Union surely have given the game away?

The sheriff of Shropshire gave us an answer. He was then Mr. John Reed, living in a great house in a forest, but before retiring to Shropshire he'd been first secretary in our embassy in Turkey in the last year of the war. He was worried how our series might portray his role in a great blunder.

I sent Knightley to see him. He would talk only anonymously for the moment, concerned that the Foreign Office would not approve. Thus masked, he told a fascinating tale. On a hot August day in 1945, the area head of the Russian secret service (the NKVD, later the KGB), one Konstantin Volkov, had walked into the consulate in Istanbul seeking asylum. For a safe passage to Cyprus and living money, he would identify Soviet spy networks. "In return he told me he would offer the real names of three Soviet agents working in Britain, two of them in the Foreign Office, one the head of a counterespionage organization in London," Reed said.

The ambassador, Sir Maurice Peterson, wanted nothing to do with the nasty business of spies. He told Reed to let London handle it. Reed sent the information to London in a secure diplomatic bag and waited for a response. It took two weeks for an agent to arrive to debrief Volkov. That agent was none other than the head of the anti-Soviet section, Kim Philby.

Volkov was never seen again. Philby, who must have had a fright that he was so nearly outed, had taken time with his Soviet masters to organize a safe passage for Volkov—but not to Cyprus. A Soviet military aircraft made an irregular landing at Istanbul airport and within minutes took off again after a heavily bandaged figure on a stretcher was carried to the plane. "The incident convinced me," said Reed, "that Philby was either a Soviet agent or unbelievably incompetent. I took what seemed to me at the time the appropriate action." Nothing happened.

Knightley reported, "The memory of the betrayal made Reed's voice shake."

If Philby was that important in 1945, what was he doing in Washington from 1949 under the cover of being first secretary in the embassy? All the public attention had been on his possible role in tipping off Burgess and Maclean. There'd been nothing about what he did day to day. Nobody had asked, and nobody had talked. In view of the runaround we were getting in London, Knightley was entranced to be in Washington. He called the CIA and was directed to several retired officers who'd known Philby.

Lyman B. Kirkpatrick had been with the CIA since it was set up in 1947. This was a few years before Ian Fleming created the Bond fantasies—which Kirkpatrick regretted for misleading the public about the painstaking nature of intelligence work—but the Americans had been in awe of MI6 for its legendary history and the dazzling code-breaking achievements that had won the Battle of the Atlantic. The doors were wide-open for Philby, whose experience was so much richer than anyone's in the fledgling CIA.

When Knightley found Kirkpatrick, he had just retired as executive director of the agency. He had contracted polio in Asia on CIA business and was teaching politics from a wheelchair at Brown University. He combined secret knowledge with an intellectual zest for freedom. He wouldn't go into detail, but on the main point he didn't equivocate: "Philby was your liaison officer with the CIA and FBI." This was as astounding as Nicholson's revelation. It meant that for three years of the cold war, Philby had been at the heart of Western intelligence operations. Put another way, having penetrated the SIS, he was then able to penetrate the CIA. The director, General Walter Bedell Smith, gave him clearance at all levels, which meant that in a secret service's typically compartmentalized operations, Philby would have known as much as anyone except the director himself and perhaps one or two assistant directors, like Kirkpatrick. Kirkpatrick would not say much more than "have a look at Albania," but that chimed with vague hints we'd already picked up. Tom Driberg, MP, had told us that the Foreign Office had expunged from his book on Guy Burgess a scornful reference by Burgess to Western meddling in Albania, and a former MI6 man in Rome had told Leitch, "Philby lost us a lot of lives in Eastern Europe."

Back in London, Page asked a researcher, Alex Mitchell, to see if among the émigré groups in London there might be some Albanians who could give us a clue as to what lay behind Kirkpatrick's cryptic remark. When Mitchell found a bunch of them working as lumbermen for the Forestry Commission, he was directed to one of the few survivors of an ill-fated joint

MI6-CIA operation. The two agencies had armed, trained, and funded a small army of guerrillas and put them into Albania by boat and parachute in the spring of 1950. The Communist rebels in Greece were faltering, Yugoslavia's Tito had broken with Stalin, and it was hoped that a Communist collapse in Albania would ripple throughout the Balkans. Hundreds of Albanian exiles, including the exiled King Zog's royal guard, were trained in a fort in Malta. They were doomed from the start. One of the few who escaped alive told us, "They always knew we were coming." At least three hundred died.

The disaster, reminiscent of President Kennedy's Bay of Pigs blunder infiltrating anti-Castro guerrillas in 1961, was put down to leaks from the infiltrators and the extraordinary efficiency of the Albanian frontier guards and police. Super-clever those Albanian cops, you know; they must have worked out the radio code by which the first infiltrators would signal back that it was safe to send in more men—then sent that signal when it wasn't safe at all

The operation was jointly commanded by a CIA man and the British liaison officer Kim Philby.

Hugo Young, meanwhile, was making good use of his inside knowledge of Washington. He found that the significance of Maclean, too, had been missed by everyone. The urbanely supercilious diplomat didn't go home after the Washington cocktail parties. Several times a week, unbeknownst to Admiral Lewis Strauss, chairman of the Atomic Energy Commission (AEC), Maclean was wandering unescorted in Strauss's headquarters.

It was a crucial time in the transition from hot to cold war. The Russians were already making good use of the Allied bomb-making secrets given to them by the German-born physicist Klaus Fuchs and company, but they were desperate to find out all they could about the Allied policy for the atomic bomb. Britain, Canada, and the United States had all cooperated on the Manhattan Project, but in 1947, through the McMahon Act, the United States had abruptly ended the exchange of information on atomic weapons. An Anglophile manager, feeling it was unfair to exclude their British allies, had given Maclean a pass without checking with his superiors at the AEC. Young found that Maclean had access so rare that it had been denied even to General Leslie Groves, who'd supervised the building of the bomb, and J. Edgar Hoover, head of the FBI. Between August 6, 1947, and June 11, 1948, Maclean had been in the AEC headquarters twenty times, sometimes at night.

One of the strengths of the leaders of Insight was a readiness to admit a weakness and a resolve to remedy it by identifying people in the know. We didn't have the expertise to determine the significance of the information Maclean had likely gathered, so we asked the atomic energy historian Margaret Gowing to assess how important it might have been to Maclean's Moscow masters. Her answer: very. Especially useful were the quantities of uranium the United States was buying, from which Stalin's scientists could calculate the projected size of the U.S. nuclear arsenal. In the geopolitical poker game, this was a valuable face card.

We'd compiled many hundreds of thousands of words in notes and drafts, with multiple cross-references. Page, ringed in cheroot smoke, was at his typewriter early in the morning and late at night, collating and sifting through what we knew and what needed more checking into a longer and longer "state of knowledge memorandum." If he was not doing that, he was testing hypotheses on the inner circle; we kept Project X as tight as we could. I wanted to publish before the *Observer* began its serialization of Eleanor Philby's memoir, scheduled for October.

By the first week in September Ron Hall had the text ready for the first of a four-part series. Greenhill was still protesting: "Drop Philby; he's a bore."

On September 1 I received a letter from the Services, Press and Broadcasting D Notice Committee. The key injunction (my italics) read: "You are requested not to publish anything about identities, whereabouts, and tasks of persons of whatever status or rank who are *or have been* employed by either Service [MI5 or MI6]."

This was a direct attempt to wipe out our entire investigation.

The D Notice (now called a DA, or Defense Advisory, Notice) was a request approved by a joint committee of government and media representatives. The system was set up to warn the press against inadvertently publishing or broadcasting information that would "compromise UK military and intelligence operations and methods, or put at risk the safety of those involved." The D Notice did not have the force of law, but it could be cited against us if the attorney general chose to bring an Official Secrets case. Our lawyers were anxious. I told Denis Hamilton I was ignoring it. He didn't argue.

The team wanted another two weeks, and I agreed to hold off publication for two reasons: we were following a lead about "another defector" (who turned out to be Volkov), and we had our own Philby in Moscow — not Kim, but John, his son by his second wife, Aileen. Leitch had had the inspiration to check the London telephone directory and rang "Philby, J." He was living in a basement apartment in Hampstead with two Alsatians and an ambition to be a war photographer. Leitch, who had an engagingly jolly manner, casually asked him if he'd like an assignment to photograph his father in Moscow. He would.

The secretive Kim Philby broke his cover to greet his son and came out to stand in Red Square in an open-necked shirt, looking into the distance, his left hand nonchalantly in the pocket of his jacket. "My father told me," said John, "the Russians had given him the task of penetrating British intelligence in 1933 and that it did not matter how long it took."

We'd already worked that out. What we hadn't calculated was that John would have dinner on his return with the journalist Patrick Seale, who was at the rival *Observer* and directly responsible for the Eleanor Philby serialization. The first installment had been scheduled to begin in late October, but the *Observer* rushed it into print. A copy of the newspaper dated October 1, 1967, landed on my desk at 6:00 p.m. on Saturday, September 30. Not so fast! By 6:30 our "Spy Who Betrayed a Generation" was on the presses, with the scoop picture of Philby on the front page and the lead headline "Philby: I Spied for Russia from 1933."

As photojournalism, it was dramatic, but a short-term tactical error on my part. The combination of photograph and quote could give the impression that our investigative series had sprung from Philby or from the Soviet ministry of disinformation. We had enough disinformation coming from our own side. When Philby let us know he had written a memoir, we all recoiled. I couldn't stomach the monstrous egotism — what else? — that had allowed him to stay loyal to his masters after the Nazi-Soviet Nonaggression Pact in 1939 and the years of Stalinist terror. (He offered to suppress his manuscript in return for a deal in which the Soviets would release a British prisoner, Gerald Brooke, and Britain would release the Krogers of the Portland spy ring. His sardonic memoir eventually appeared in the *Sunday Express*.)

Disturbing as our findings of Philby's betrayals were, to me the most sobering revelation was how long Philby had been able to exploit the class-conscious and social attitudes of the club and old school echelons of MI6. Here was a Soviet agent within a breath of the final triumph, his appointment as head of MI6, yet his friends in the service still continued to resent the vulgarly suspicious security men of MI5. Even after he was dismissed from the service, "cleared" by Harold Macmillan on the understanding that MI6 would reorganize and institute a "general clean up," MI6 continued to employ him as a field agent in the Middle East and assured the *Observer* and *Economist*, both of which hired him, that he was no longer active. It was simply impossible for these gentlemen to accept that one of their own could have been a traitor to his class, let alone his country.

When we published our revelations in September–October 1967, I naively expected a demand for reform. Instead there was outrage, directed not at Philby or those who protected him, but at us. Sir Stewart Menzies, the former head of MI6, who at the outset had revealed his anger about the "blackguard" Philby, now somersaulted to vouchsafe that Philby had never been important in the MI6. In the eyes of Donald McLachlan, a former intelligence executive and editor of the *Sunday Telegraph*, we had even undermined the concept of the English gentleman. Several newspapers ran stories—not discouraged by official sources—that our life story of Philby was a Soviet plant. The accusations that we were handmaidens of the KGB seemed to me the product of minds incapable of confronting a real spy story without constructing an ersatz conspiracy around its origins. Only a political paranoid could have imagined, as the Foreign Office put about, that the iconoclastic Bruce Page was a Communist. I reassured them that he was safely locked up in a slave labor camp in Grays Inn Road.

Next the rumbustious foreign secretary and Deputy Leader George Brown got into the act. The first I knew of it was a late-night phone call to my home from a very upset Denis Hamilton. "The foreign secretary has just denounced you as a traitor at a business dinner and in front of Roy [Thomson]. You'd better be in the House of Commons tomorrow, when the foreign secretary will speak." I opened the next morning's *Times* with some trepidation. "Ebullient Mr. Brown Hits Out" was the euphemistic headline, "ebullient" being a press parlance adjective to get round the libel risk of saying he was drunk.

The next afternoon I sat in the House of Commons gallery waiting to be dragged out by the sergeant at arms. The victim turned out to be the foreign secretary himself, carpeted that morning by the prime minister for once again showing undue ebullience in a public place. The *Daily Mirror*'s front page the next day was headlined "The Bowed Head" and featured a penitent foreign secretary in a morning coat facing a stern Wilson on the platform at Waterloo station as they awaited the arrival of a dignitary.

When Roy Thomson was asked about the protests over our Philby series, he had an economical answer: "Bunk!"

My experiences as a provincial editor had given me some inkling of the barricades behind which the bureaucracies conducted the nation's business then. The Philby story was my first prolonged experience as a national editor dealing with central government and what, for want of a better name, I have to call the political establishment: those overlapping "charmed circles" of influence and power whose strands of DNA were the elite public schools, Oxbridge, the aristocracy, the City and the blue-chip boardrooms, the civil service, the legal profession, and the conservative press. British society had become more solvent, more meritocratic, and less deferential than it had been in the 1930s, when the Soviets saw very well how it was run by their recruitment of Burgess, Philby, Maclean, and Blunt. I don't for a minute believe that there was in the sixties or is now a homogeneous conspiratorial establishment—a "tightly knit group of politically motivated men," to misappropriate Prime Minister Harold Wilson's phrase against striking seamen. Obviously, people in the establishment and the various professions differ on issues today: the privately educated Labour men contend with the privately educated Tories. But a penchant for secrecy, social privilege, and the nurturing of an educational elite remained pervasive in the culture and strikes me as not having been entirely expunged in the twenty-first century.

A secret service is a secret service; I accept that. But the well-tried administrative precept that efficiency improves with accountability is not irrelevant even to the secret service. It was shocking to me that Blunt, having condescended to betray his country, was still in place at Buckingham Palace, a socially sought-after figure. It was a revelation that the closing of the ranks that had allowed Philby to survive was manifest again in the rebukes we earned for exposing him and the cover-up.

The consolation at the end of the Philby affair was in the awareness of my good fortune: Thomson and Hamilton had been steadfast in their support, and the staff of the paper, if I could manage it well enough, was a resource of extraordinary intelligence, vitality, and independence of mind. We could tackle anything!

15

Children on Our Conscience

I never heard the word "teratogen" until 1963. After that I would never forget it. Between 1958 and 1962 pregnant women who reported morning sickness, anxiety, and lack of sleep to their doctors were prescribed a "wonder drug"—a pill with supposedly none of the side effects of barbiturates. It was thalidomide, a teratogen, meaning it interfered with the normal development of an embryo. Taken between the fourth and twelfth weeks of pregnancy, it caused babies to be born with foreshortened limbs or no limbs at all. More than four hundred children were affected in Britain, and worldwide it is estimated that between fifteen thousand and twenty thousand babies were affected in some way. Dr. Martin Johnson, who has made an extensive study of thalidomide, writes that apart from war and genocide, thalidomide was the cause of the largest man-made disaster in European history.

I first became aware of the thalidomide children, as they came to be called, in 1962. In 1963 we published some early pictures in the *Northern Echo* of thalidomide infants at Chailey Heritage in Sussex, a hospital, home, and school for disabled children. I expected an outpouring of sympathy. I was wrong. Most of the readers who wrote did so to protest that it was not right for "a family newspaper" to do this: "We don't want to know."

I should have known better than to expect anything else. I had already experienced the awkward emotions in encountering people who are severely disabled. One of the patrons of St. Cuthbert's, a Catholic hospice in the trees by the river in Hurworth village where I lived, had promised a few of the patients there that she would find someone who "knew about print." She nominated me, so I called at the hospice one morning and met John Tinsley. He could not control his limbs. His head bobbed and his mouth twisted when he spoke. His vowels were prolonged and his consonants lost so that what came out was part howl, part speech. It took me some minutes to work out what he was saying—a plea not to laugh at his idea. He wanted to print a magazine created by patients like him at St. Cuthbert's.

John had been born with athetoid cerebral palsy; he was highly intelligent and could get around in a cycle chair (an electric cycle of sorts). Peter Jackson, the sports editor of the magazine he conceived, was a severely spastic young man who had to be strapped into his wheelchair—"thaaaat's J-J-Jaaaco," John said, jerking an elbow into him. And the magazine's cartoonist was a boy with spina bifida.

I said I'd be glad to help, but to be honest my heart had sunk at the thought of spending time with John and Peter and their group. Of course I felt sorry for them, but what was it Graham Greene said about "pity" being a way of distancing ourselves from the other? It's a form of reassurance, an acknowledgment of our own wholeness. That was an uncomfortable thought.

It took me a couple of visits to St. Cuthbert's to stop regarding the patients as victims and treat them as people, real personalities with their own individual identities rather than a "case" of spina bifida, a "case" of muscular dystrophy, a "case" of spastic diplegia. When I said what I really thought about an article, a poem, or a cartoon, we all started to have a good time.

John would then tell me with a huge convulsive laugh why I was wrong.

The thalidomide scandal was the most emotionally draining of all the stories I became involved with at the *Sunday Times.* I came to think of the letters to the *Northern Echo* as a metaphor for how the British legal and political institutions had responded over and over again to the tragedy. They'd made the thalidomide children invisible.

The children who had been affected by thalidomide were between the ages of four and eight when I became editor of the *Sunday Times.* Having published those early pictures in the *Northern Echo,* I wanted to find out what had happened to them. In 1967 I learned that not one of them had received a penny in compensation.

This was a consequence of a heartless decision taken by my old political adversary in the *Northern Echo*'s cervical cancer campaign Enoch Powell, who was the minister of health between 1960 and 1963 and thereby responsible for the National Health Service. In all the attention paid to the thalidomide story, his crucial role in the long nightmare has been neglected.

Powell was a baffling figure. There was no doubting his academic brilliance: he was a double-starred first at Trinity, Cambridge, and a professor of Greek at the University of Sydney when he was only twenty-five. Nor was there any question about his bravery: he was the only man in the war to rise from private to brigadier. He had high velocity, too, as a political thinker. He ricocheted from the impeccably lucid to the paranoid crazy: it was one thing in the 1940s to accuse the United States of wishing to see an end to the British Empire, and something else again to blame the CIA for the bomb that blew up Lord Mountbatten in Ireland in 1979, a crime clearly committed by the Irish Republican Army (IRA).

Millions paid attention when, in a carefully prepared speech in Birmingham in 1968, he said the threat posed by West Indian and Asian immigrants to Britain was comparable to the threat posed by Hitler in the 1930s. Britain, he said, was madly building its own funeral pyre by allowing in fifty thousand immigrants a year, and the antidiscrimination bills before Parliament would be match to gunpowder: "Like the Roman, I seem to see the River Tiber foaming with much blood." As policy, Powell's speech was defensible. But the tone and language were something else—an incitement. The speech blamed immigrants for all the social problems of the cities, indicting every person of color on the basis of a number of unverifiable ugly anecdotes and using such emotive language as "wide-grinning pickaninnies." Then he refused to disavow the personal and mob violence that followed.

William Rees-Mogg in the *Times* called the speech evil, but it was the *Sunday Times* criticism that roused Powell to sue for libel. Shortly afterward, when I bumped into him at a reception in the House of Commons, he turned his pale, mustached face toward me and said, "I will bury you." In fact, when ordered by the courts to produce letters he'd quoted to justify his extravagant rhetoric, he refused to obey and then did not proceed with the libel action.

Like many people, I was puzzled by the loose screw that turned Powell's brilliance corrosively inward. That he refused to help the dispirited and powerless thalidomide families is hard to understand or forgive. He received a delegation of affected parents in January 1963 and rejected their every request: No to a public inquiry on the origins of the disaster. No to immediately setting up a "drug-testing centre"—"anyone who takes an aspirin puts himself at risk." No to a public warning against using any of the pills that might still be in medicine cabinets—"a scare-monger publicity stunt." No to giving a statement afterward—"no need to bring the press into this." And no to his setting eyes on a thalidomide child: no to Frederick Astbury without legs, arms, and right hip; Louise Mason, no legs; David Bickers, no legs, no arms, and just three fingers from his shoulder; Gary Skyner, a short left arm and no thumbs; and Eddie Freeman, no legs and foreshortened arms.

It was an extraordinary lapse of public duty to deny society the knowledge essential to understanding the origins of the tragedy and preventing anything similar from happening again. Powell's intransigence left the families with only one remedy: to sue the manufacturers for negligence. It was bad enough thus to condemn the parents and their children to live in Bleak House legal torment. The courts, in any case, could not be relied on to find the facts. The primary objective of the judicial system is to settle conflicts; it is not to find the truth come what may. A civil action for damages is an indirect, laborious, very slow, and costly way of unraveling the facts. The families were not well-endowed for that exhausting exercise.

They were up against a formidable defendant. The thalidomide pill was marketed by Distillers Biochemicals, a subsidiary of Distillers, the giant liquor and spirits company retailing famous brands of whisky, such as Johnnie Walker. It had assets then worth more than £400 million—£4 billion at today's values—and pretax profits of more than £500 million at today's values. Its chairman, Sir Alexander McDonald, was a Glasgow University graduate of accountancy and law who'd been with the company since 1946. He'd gathered a reputation as a man of granite, which suited the Distillers image, and he'd engaged the rapier mind of John Wilmers, QC, much feared for his capacity to eviscerate witnesses.

While the families' counsel changed four times, Wilmers

stayed on the case throughout. The families had to rely on public funding through the Law Society, the body representing solicitors which administered government funds for people who could not afford going to court. It begrudged spending on what it regarded as a weak case. Three and a half years passed before it authorized paying expert witnesses.

Distillers wasn't a long-established pharmaceutical company. It had no research scientists and didn't hire a pharmacologist until it decided to manufacture thalidomide under license from a German company called Chemie Grünenthal, which was also relatively new to the business. By one of those mocking twists of history, the *Sunday Times* had a part in the company's decision. Aldous Huxley, the author of the prophetic 1932 novel *Brave New World,* contributed an article to the paper in June 1956 in which he speculated that modern science might be able to produce a happiness drug (called Soma 6 in his novel). "Will the pharmacologists be able to do better than the brewers and distillers?" he asked. Provoked by the question, a Distillers director read Huxley. Might a pill be found that would eventually become an alternative to whisky? This new "nontoxic" sedative from Chemie Grünenthal seemed to fit the bill. Distillers sold it as a safe sleeping pill and tranquilizer called Distaval beginning in April 1958. Another company, Richardson-Merrell, sold it as Kevadon in the United States. Millions of American mothers escaped the catastrophe because Dr. Frances Kelsey, at the Food and Drug Administration, while not predicting the phocomelia deformities, became suspicious of Richardson-Merrell's sloppy procedures. Even so, some ten to sixteen American mothers were known to be affected by the premature release of the pill. What a savage irony that a "happiness" drug was to cause so much human misery.

So upset were hospital midwives and doctors at the births of the first thalidomide babies that they often concealed the children from the mothers—making excuses until it came time for their discharge. The mothers, isolated from one another but struggling with the same emotional and physical difficulties, did not know where to turn. They had paroxysms of guilt; something must be deeply wrong with them or their families or their husbands' families. Some believed that God had punished them for a lapse in their lives. Some felt ashamed that they'd complained of the symptoms that had prompted their doctors to prescribe the dangerous pill. Scores didn't know for several years that they were victims of thalidomide. They didn't connect the news stories about the drug to their own predicaments. The psychological traumas were intense. Mothers hid at home rather than encounter people who recoiled from the sight of an afflicted child. Marriages were wrecked. "If you bring that monster home," said one husband, "I'll leave." And so he did.

The impulse to put the tragedy swiftly out of mind was understandable. It was too painful. Somebody, surely, would look after those unfortunate children and their families so that we could get on with our lives. Somebody didn't and wouldn't.

Here again Health Minister Powell was no help. He'd left the families no choice but to seek redress through the courts, then put the whole weight of the ministry behind discountenancing the very grounds of negligence they'd have to prove to win damages. Thalidomide, he said in Parliament and in a television interview, had been properly tested by Distillers according to the standards of the time, when nobody thought a drug could reach the fetus. And unanimity prevailed on this key question. The *Economist, Times, Manchester Guardian,* and *Sunday Telegraph* all said the same thing. As we were to discover, none of those statements was true.

*   *   *

In fact reproductive studies had been routinely done by pharmaceutical companies a decade before Distillers made thalidomide. The tranquilizers in direct competition with thalidomide
were tested for teratogenic effects, and the results were published by the manufacturers, including Hoffman–La Roche;
Lederle; Pfizer; and Smith, Kline & French in America and
Burroughs Wellcome and ICI, under Dr. Edward Paget, in Britain. If reproductive tests had been done with thalidomide, they
would not necessarily have produced the precise deformities,
but they would have shown that it might endanger unborn
children.

How could it be that everyone got it wrong? We learned later
that all the assertions, which is all they were, had originated
with Distillers. The senior civil servant signing the letters to
parents and advising Powell had taken his cue from a Distillers
medical executive who'd been with the ministry and had called
to brief him. The newspapers also found the company most
helpful. Like some primitive medicine man's incantation, the
unceasing repetition — the standards of the time, the standards
of the time — hypnotized everyone who heard it.

When I first arrived at the *Sunday Times*, I longed to take up the
cause of the thalidomide children. Some sixty-two of the abandoned families had begun civil actions in August 1962, while I
was still with the *Northern Echo,* and the British law of contempt
of court meant that their writs sealed the whole affair in a legal
cocoon. Once the writs had been issued, it became illegal to
bring out facts or comment on a pending trial, whether civil or
criminal, on pain of a heavy fine or even jail. With thalidomide

this meant that nothing could be published that might influence a judge until every case—every single case—had been settled by the courts. This is plainly a denial of free speech, but the common law had long held that this right of free speech had to be balanced by the right to a fair trial uncontaminated by outside pressure on any party or information or comment that might sway a judge or jury.

I'd had a narrow squeak in my first months at the *Sunday Times* when, thanks to a slip by a writer, compounded by a duty lawyer's misjudgment, we'd accidentally published the previous convictions of a man about to stand trial. I was personally exonerated, but the newspaper was fined £5,000. The thalidomide actions were in civil court, to be tried by a judge alone, but the law was no different. It didn't matter to the court that there had been no movement on the cases between 1962 and 1967. (Indeed, in 1973 a law lord referred to the eleven-year-old pending thalidomide cases as being "in the early stages of litigation.")

The families had been told by their lawyers on no account to talk to "mass media," but what we most wanted to know at this stage was how the disaster had occurred. Nobody at Distillers or Chemie Grünenthal would help, but we suddenly got the chance to look into the files of both companies. Reporter John Fielding brought a Dr. Montagu Phillips to see me. Phillips had been engaged by the families' solicitors, Kimber Bull, as a consulting pharmacologist and chemical engineer. He was a small, rumpled man who fidgeted a lot—not, I thought, likely to be impressive in the witness box under Wilmers's brand of interrogation—but he possessed ten thousand Distillers internal memoranda and reports that he said documented the scandal. They'd been made available through the legal process known as "disclosure," by which both sides are obliged to supply all relevant files. In short he was a whistle-blower, or what we called a FINK—fair insider with necessary knowledge. But was he "fair"? He had a grievance. His wife had taken thalidomide as a sleeping pill, which he believed was the cause of her irreversible nerve damage, known as polyneuritis. How much was that influencing his judgment? Moreover, he was breaking a legal honor code and was asking me to risk a breach of journalistic ethics: he wanted £8,000 to help care for his wife.

Was this the checkbook journalism I'd inveighed against on the television program *What the Papers Say* and in speeches criticizing newspapers that paid for the memoirs of criminals? I'd never done that. In the office and at home, I debated the ethics of paying him. It was a consideration that he offered us his technical advice and, more important, promised to keep us informed on what went on behind the closed doors of the legal negotiations. Every last doubt fell before my intense curiosity about what the documents revealed on the origins of the disaster. Was I to put my precious journalistic conscience before gaining access to crucial information that might never see the light of day if, as seemed likely, an out-of-court settlement was reached? No. We collected the documents, and I assigned the unflappable Phillip Knightley to evaluate them and prepare a narrative for publication sometime when we were free of legal restraint.

More urgent was a second set of documents from Chemie Grünenthal. Henning Sjostrom, a Stockholm lawyer representing 105 Swedish victims, was concerned that since it had taken the Germans seven years to mount a criminal trial of nine company executives, it might take another seven years of court testimony to resolve the case: the prosecution alone said it had 352 witnesses. Other than wanting his expenses paid, Sjostrom was looking for international publicity to shame the company that had caused so much havoc. The German newspapers dared not publish anything for fear of punishment under their own contempt laws.

Collected in three suitcases, the German papers, when translated and indexed, were to reveal a get-rich-quick mentality at Chemie Grünenthal. The mother's safety during pregnancy while taking Contergan (as they called the drug) was a main selling point, but the company had not tested Contergan to see if it could pass through the placenta to affect the unborn child. Chemie Grünenthal sales leaflets for doctors stressed the drug's safety, quoting a March 1960 article in the *American Journal of Obstetrics and Gynecology* by Dr. Ray O. Nulsen, practicing in Cincinnati, Ohio, the hometown of Richardson-Merrell. In his deposition for the German trial, however, Nulsen admitted that he had not tested the drug on pregnant women at all and was not even the author of the article. It had been written for him by an employee of Richardson-Merrell—who'd relied for information on Chemie Grünenthal!

In light of what I knew was in the German documents and was emerging in the Distillers documents, I was very surprised when Mr. Desmond Ackner, QC (later Lord Ackner), appeared in court for the families in February 1968 to say they were withdrawing charges of negligence. Distillers had agreed to pay 40 percent of what it might have had to pay if the legal actions had been wholly successful. Both parties still had to agree on what sum of money would represent an award of 100 percent, but the 40 percent, said Ackner, would amount to "very substantial" damages. If the actions had continued, he added, "the plaintiffs could have failed to recover a penny apiece."

Judge Sir Raymond Hinchcliffe endorsed Ackner: "I have given anxious consideration to the issues and to the prospects of success in law and fact, having regard to what the reasonably careful manufacturer would have done before marketing the drug in the then state of knowledge. In my judgment the plaintiffs are well advised to accept."

This sounded absurd to us. By this time Godfrey Hodgson, the new editor of Insight, had constructed a shocking four-page narrative of the history of the German company's invention and marketing of thalidomide. James Evans, the elegant and indispensable full-time staff lawyer at the *Sunday Times,* advised me that the law of contempt almost certainly made it too dangerous to publish. Not only would revelation of Chemie Grünenthal's reckless conduct cast Distillers in a bad light, but the announcement of Ackner's interim settlement had stimulated more families to sue Distillers, so the gag order on discussion of the cases extended into the unknowable future.

Evans had to be heeded. He was not one of the legal fraternity schooled in the scholarship of suppression; he was a facilitator. If publication was in the public interest, he regarded it as his duty to justify it in law. Now, unusually unsure, he suggested we seek yet another opinion by consulting a specialist in one of London's grand Inns of Court, a new experience for me.

We'd hardly taken a chair in the Brick Court rooms of David Hirst, QC, before he pronounced, "Contempt! Flagrant contempt!" I tried suggesting that on this logic, when the German trial started every British newspaper reporting it would be in contempt. Mr. Hirst (later Judge Hirst) was disturbed by my belligerence (so was I). All these years later I see his eyes, unblinking behind his glasses, evoking the sensation of being in *The Great Gatsby* looking up at the gigantic blue irises of the oculist Dr. T. J. Eckleburg brooding on his billboard over the valley of ashes. There is no escape! Flagrant contempt!

Sulking on the way back to the office, I pressed James Evans, who went back to Hirst and got the same answer in writing. His own doubts, as much as my persistence, led him to seek yet another opinion. Mr. Peter Bristow, another QC on the way to the bench, spelled out the risks, too, but ended on a somewhat less alarming note than the steely Hirst.

I decided to ignore them all and publish. This was not only my heart speaking but also my head. I realized that in the long run, without any challenge, the oppressive British press laws were not just a threat to the thalidomide victims and their families but a real threat to democracy itself. These laws were a teratogen in themselves, stunting and deforming our freedom and liberty. I was so appalled by the way Chemie Grünenthal had disregarded early warnings, I emotively juxtaposed photographs in the Review Front of a deformed German child and one of the architects of his misfortune, a white-coated head of research at Chemie Grünenthal.

I waited in a defensive crouch for action by the law officers of the Crown or Distillers, but they stayed in their battlements. Distillers had clearly blundered in relying on Chemie Grünenthal. Its own documents revealed how little independent testing the company had done and how similar were the unjustified marketing and the inexcusable delays in withdrawing the drug from the market. The Australian obstetrician William McBride had notified at least two, and possibly six, Distillers Sydney employees of his suspicions of problems by the first week of July 1961, but the company had continued to promote thalidomide as safe for another four months (during which time about a quarter of the British children known to be affected were damaged in the womb).

Our publication of the German story would, I assumed, stiffen the sinews of the families' lawyers about what constituted "substantial" in the damages Ackner had said were in train. But we had to wait a whole year to find out what that meant. Unable to agree on what 100 percent of damages would be, the parties came back in July 1969 to ask Judge Hinchcliffe to resolve the deadlock by making monetary awards in two test cases. One was in the top bracket—David Jones, then nearly nine, who had neither legs nor arms and would need help for the rest of his life, never being able to toilet himself or dress and undress. The other, Richard Satherly, was in the middle bracket. He had legs, but only a single digit protruded from his shoulder; he brushed his teeth by holding the toothbrush in his toes.

The press hailed Judge Hinchcliffe's resultant awards with the usual "fortune" headlines associated with lottery winners. We didn't. I made space on the editorial page for a critical article by Nicholas Harman, who had joined us from the *Economist*. He noted the judge's conclusion that his award to Richard of £32,000 "would be sufficient to keep him free from financial worry and would go some way to ameliorating the discomfort and deprivations that he is bound to suffer." All very well, said Harman, but if £32,000 was "sufficient" to these ends, then the 40 percent he would actually receive, £12,800, would be 60 percent insufficient.

It was a temperate article, but I wrote the aggressive headline "What Price a Pound of Flesh?" and soon had one of James Evans's duty lawyers in my office. "Afraid this is risky.... Not happy about your headline.... Contempt." He pointed out that since even more families were now suing, the contempt restrictions continued. "You could be accused of interfering with the course of justice."

I let the article and headline run.

Partly as a result of these stories, families kept coming forward to press their claims. By 1971 some 266 had secured waivers from the three-year statute of limitations, and another 123 victims had identified themselves, making 389 not provided for by the first settlement. The contempt rules, having kept the tragedy in the shadows for nine years, now extended until the unknowable future date when every last one of these cases would be settled.

In the meantime outrage followed outrage. The lawyers representing the 266 new claimants as a group went back to Distillers, but ice had formed on the Scottish granite. The company declared that it would set up a trust fund worth only £3.25 million—about £7,500 for each victim—half the 1969 settlement. Moreover, the offer was conditional on every single family accepting the offer.

The lawyers commended the offer to the group of families. Six families objected, led by David Mason, a sophisticated Mayfair art dealer who was the father of Louise Mason, who had no legs. The six dissenters regarded the offer as miserable charity, whereupon their own legal advisers—yes, the parents' legal team!—took them to court on behalf of those ready to settle. Judge Hinchcliffe removed parental rights from the dissident six. Henceforth a treasury solicitor would decide what was best for their children—that is, accept the Distillers offer.

Mason had a friend who knew David English, the editor of the *Daily Mail,* so he took his personal story there. English published three articles under the title "My Fight for Justice by the Father of Heartbreak Girl Louise." When the attorney general warned the *Daily Mail* that these articles constituted contempt of court, English backed off. The Court of Appeal resoundingly restored Mason's rights, but the *Mail* published no more articles, BBC television's *Twenty Four Hours* canceled a related program, and Mason stopped giving interviews that never appeared. Once again the cloak of invisibility enveloped the thalidomide children.

As we entered 1972, I had plenty of other issues to deal

with, but I just couldn't get the thalidomide negotiations out of my mind. I was convinced: something was badly wrong. If the Knightley article presented, as a judge later said, "a powerful case of negligence," why had the lawyers been eager to accept only 40 percent of the less than adequate 100 percent? And why were they now ready to settle for something like half of that? What made me even more determined was a new perspective in a long memorandum from Bruce Page. His successes as head of Insight had led me to create the Special Projects unit around him, with Elaine Potter to assist. Elaine was a South African whose tenacity matched her scholarship. She'd not had a great deal of experience in journalism, but she'd acquired an Oxford PhD and, as important, squatter's rights to a freelancer's chair in the features department. Some of our most successful recruits were squatters; they were tested by the exigencies of sudden demands for labor, and the best, like Elaine, survived with the complicity of editors until I could find a place for them on staff.

I'd asked Page to revisit the whole thalidomide project with Elaine. His first initiative was to compare the money awards with a more precise assessment of the children's needs; his second was to send Elaine to pharmaceutical laboratories in the United States and Britain to check the defensive refrain that Distillers had done all the tests that were standard at the time—exposing the myth I mentioned earlier. Page's memorandum on the compensation money was startling. In the *Modern Law Review* of May 1972, he read a two-part article on the absence of any coherent method by which judges assessed personal injury damages. It was written by John Prevett, a fellow of the Institute of Actuaries with the London firm of Bacon & Woodrow. Prevett, it turned out, had given expert evidence to Judge Hinchcliffe in 1969 that the lead test case in the thalidomide trial, that of David Jones, required £135,000. The judge had awarded half that amount, with that half in turn subject to the 60 percent reduction agreed upon by the lawyers. This meant that David's actual cash for the rest of his life was only £20,800.

When recently I spoke to John Prevett, now in his retirement, he remembered wondering whether he was making any impression at all on the judge: "He seemed to be asleep during the long time I was cross-examined on the numbers by the Distillers lawyer [John Wilmers]." The judge said he had to be fair to Distillers as well as the children, but he must have been hypnotized by the mesmerizing Wilmers to swallow the QC's contention that inflation should be disregarded because the government had promised to control inflation. Ah, yes, said the learned judge, all "speculation" and "hearsay."

As for the inflation that the judge and Distillers' counsel regarded with such amused disdain, the value of the 1969 award was by 1972 worth 20 percent less, and in 1975 alone the inflation rate was 24 percent. Prevett told me, "Altogether the awards were sixteen percent of what I reckoned was justified. I worked out that the money the judge awarded David would run out by the time he was twenty-nine."

Why did nobody, including the *Sunday Times*, fully report on Prevett when he was in court in 1969? It was hardly rocket science. And here's a terrible thought: if the *Modern Law Review* had not, three years later, asked Prevett to write on actuarial advice, and if he had not chosen thalidomide as his example, and if Page had not read the journal, it's possible we might have underestimated just how rotten the personal injury system had become.

The priority now had to be making the case for decent compensation and to do it before more families were sold down the river. It was hard to find out what was going on in the negotiations. The Distillers solicitors refused our every request for information with heavy breathing about contempt, and our contact, their adviser Dr. Phillips, was not privy to the secret negotiations. But Knightley had formed such good relations with the families that a number of them confided in him, including the fearless Mason. The shock of the Page-Prevett assessment was searingly with me when Knightley strode into my office, his phlegmatic personality unusually agitated. "Can't we do something? They're being told they'll lose their legal aid certificates if they don't sign. Most of the parents are ready to give up, and yet they'll still get only half of what the 1969 families got. Half 1969!"

The new pressure on the families was the last straw for me. The much-feared law of contempt was going to sanctify a gross injustice. It was urgent to shout that it must not be allowed to happen. Was I emotional about the thalidomide families? Yes, I was, but my decision that Tuesday to launch a campaign in the next issue of the paper, five days hence, was not a sudden impulse. My experience of campaign journalism at the *Northern Echo* had convinced me that certain conditions had to be fulfilled before a newspaper undertook a campaign. The paper had to have investigated the subject thoroughly enough to be sure that there was a genuine grievance, it had to have defined a practical remedy, it had to be ready to commit the resources for a sustained effort, and it had to open its columns to counterarguments and corrections of fact. No campaign should be ended until it had succeeded—or was proved wrong.

I called James Evans: "I'm going to campaign on thalidomide starting this Sunday come what may, contempt or not." He preserved his celebrated equanimity. "I have the picture perfectly," he responded. "Alpine tourist asks guide to take him to the top of the Eiger by the safe route. Let me think about it, hmm?" I told Denis Hamilton we were going to denounce the proposed settlements and was phoned by the advertising manager, Donald Barrett. "You know, Harry, Distillers is our biggest client, sixty thousand a year." Then he added, "I know that won't stop you, and it shouldn't."

Page came in from vacation to convert his Prevett memorandum into a three-page analytical narrative for the upcoming issue of September 24, 1972. It was a bitingly cool piece, but the display by Ron Hall and our new design chief, Edwin Taylor, incorporated an editorial across the top of the page with a picture of a pretty young girl who had no arms. James Evans drafted the editorial. We would, he proposed, acknowledge Distillers' duty to its shareholders and its denial of negligence but also demand that the company fulfill its moral obligation: "The law is not always the same as justice."

I did very little to James's draft. I headlined it "Children on Our Conscience" and devised the emotional slogan for the coverage I hoped we could continue: "Our Thalidomide Children, a Cause for National Shame." At the end of the three pages demolishing the levels of compensation, I intended to announce our upcoming article on Distillers' documents. "May I say that it would be wise," murmured James, "to give yourself and the courts a little more time to sort that out?" Wise indeed. I simply wrote that "in a future article" we'd trace how the tragedy had occurred.

It proved to be the matador's cape.

We were engaged in a high-risk enterprise, but after all the delays, all the anxieties, all the legal frustrations, this was an exhilarating time. We all felt as if we'd been let out of prison.

I invited David Mason and his wife, Vicki, to watch the presses start up. Over the din he yelled, "Until now I never believed it would happen!" It was quite a contrast with the media silence that followed, but that first Sunday morning a most important telephone call came to my home from a man who lived in permanent silence. Jack Ashley, the Labour MP for the Midlands potteries town of Stoke-on-Trent, was stone deaf. I was amazed to conduct a telephone conversation with him: his wife, Pauline, listening in, enunciated my words to Jack; he read her lips and responded.

Ashley was one of my heroes. He'd left school at fourteen, then became a laborer and crane driver in Widnes, a sprawling industrial area, and a shop steward for the Chemical Workers Union. Later he won scholarships to Ruskin College, Oxford, and Caius College, Cambridge; produced radio and TV documentaries for the BBC; and got elected to Parliament the same year, 1966, that I joined the *Sunday Times*. He wasn't deaf then — just one ear was less good than the other — and since he was in line for a ministerial appointment, he decided to have an operation to equip him for the rapid exchanges in the Commons. It went wrong. His first instinct was to give up his seat, but there was an uprush of support for him so spontaneous and moving that it encouraged him to stay — and to do what he could in Parliament for all handicapped people.

Ashley came to the office with Pauline to meet Page and Knightley, asked questions, and said, "Well, that's decided it. I'll give up writing my autobiography until we've won." It's a little commentary on the postwar social changes that Ashley was swiftly joined as an ally in Parliament by another northern working-class boy who'd left school at fourteen and gone to Oxford on an adult scholarship — my old schoolmate Alf Morris (who later became the first minister for the disabled). So we had a partnership of Widnes and Brookdale Park elementary schools, embellished by Oxford and Durham. The cause soon became bipartisan when two Tory physician

MPs—Gerard Vaughan, a pediatrician at Guy's Hospital, and Thomas Stuttaford—joined with Ashley and Morris.

Yet we might as well have been publishing on the moon for all the attention we got. One BBC radio program gave us a few minutes of airtime—with a jumpy BBC lawyer hovering in the control room—and that was it. To the media we were Typhoid Mary. Twenty-three days went by without another mention on radio or a single story in print or on television. Even David English, the enterprising editor of the *Daily Mail*, was unwilling to follow up his newspaper's original Mason series. Not until the eighth week of our campaign did the *Mail* comment. "Saving our space to cover your trial" was the joking response I got to the calls I made to the media.

There was silence in Parliament, too. The efforts of the four Labour and Tory MPs to get the issue raised were squashed. A letter from Ashley to Prime Minister Edward Heath brought only a rebuke: "Legal matters are not for this or for a Labour government." This was a fair statement of the long tradition that Parliament never intervened in any subject being decided by a court of law, but it meant that Ashley couldn't get a resolution before the House of Commons or even raise a question. I went to see the melancholy minister of health, Sir Keith Joseph, in his gloomy office at the Elephant and Castle south of the river. I came back empty-handed, as depressed as Joseph— another very clever man who, like Powell, was averse to getting involved. The law must take its course etc.

The first intimation that we might have legal trouble came three days after our September 24 blast. I was handed a letter in an embossed envelope. It was from the solicitor general warning that our editorial and article could be considered contempt of court. The attorney general was in Strasbourg and would deal with me upon his return. Meanwhile, said the letter, "you will no doubt wish to consider your position." I replied that we were canvassing moral obligations, not legal, and were not to be deterred from continuing. James Evans then applied his emollient forensic skills in several phone conversations with the attorney general's office.

In the third week of the campaign, we got another embossed envelope: "The Attorney General instructs me to say he has now considered the material in *The Sunday Times* of 24th September and 1st October and does not propose to take any action over the matter already published." By not accusing us of contempt of court for the first article, he legitimized the moral campaign. I put in an immediate call to Ashley to give him the news but didn't get through all morning. I had to leave the office for a lunch appointment, not knowing that Ashley had that very afternoon arranged to see the Speaker of the House of Commons, the nonpartisan figure who controls the conduct of business, to make one last plea for Parliament to discuss thalidomide.

I'd just arrived at the Ivy restaurant when a call came through to me on the cloakroom attendant's phone in the vestibule. It was Ashley speaking, with Pauline listening on an extension so as to enunciate my words for Jack to lip-read. What I heard from Jack above the bustle of the lunchtime crowd being greeted by the maître d' was that he could not speak for long because he was due any minute in the Speaker's room on a last-ditch effort to have the parliamentary restrictions removed. I had a rush of blood to the head. In my excitement to tell him that the attorney general was not taking us to court over the first article, and hence was recognizing the distinction between moral and legal justice, I forgot that everything I said had to be mouthed by Pauline so that Jack could read her lips and respond. Jack's patient voice came on the line. "Sorry, Harry, didn't get that. Say again slowly, please." When I'd calmed down, I was able to say that if the attorney general accepted the distinction between moral and legal justice, surely the Speaker would have to follow suit.

It was not that easy. It meant the Speaker would have to overrule the prime minister and shake, if not sever, the precedents of barring any parliamentary discussion when an issue was before a court of law.

Jack argued his case that afternoon, and the Speaker said he would rule the next day. It was then Jack's turn to rush a call to me. The Speaker had just authorized Jack to put down an Early Day Motion (a procedure for collecting signatures, rather like a petition) and they'd agreed on the language Jack might use. This was a vital breakthrough that opened the way for parliamentary activity. Within days 265 MPs had signed in support of the Early Day Motion.

Two days later I got another letter from the attorney general. He was going to court to ban publication of our promised future article on the manufacture of thalidomide.

The campaign I began on September 24 was to run more than three months, into January 1973, and the reverberations continued for years after that. Just as in the Timothy Evans case, there were misgivings from within the newspaper regarding my obsession: we'd offend some readers, bore others. Elaine Potter still remembers the theatrical yawns she encountered from some staffers as she produced "yet another thalidomide story." I understood the concern. There was clearly the risk, too, that I'd get distracted, that I'd not organize enough talent, time, and space for other stories. The world was not standing still. On September 5, Palestinian terrorists murdered Israeli athletes at the Olympic Games, and in October three of the killers were released in Germany following a hijacking. In November Nixon was reelected president of the United States, but there was now a shadow called Watergate; Stephen Aris in New York was agitating to investigate; and Secretary of State Henry Kissinger said "peace was at hand" in Vietnam. Ulster was reeling from the killings of civil rights protesters on Bloody Sunday; Prime Minister Edward Heath was campaigning for Britain to embrace the European Union more fully while the Labour Party wrangled with itself about whether to stay in Europe or pull out; and Idi Amin was terrorizing Uganda.

I was in the thick of all these events as an editor but determined to keep faith with the thalidomide children by campaigning week after week, month after month. The challenge was to keep readers interested.

The editorial template was human interest stories, argument on personal injury law, news of the Ashley-Morris activities, and powerful photography that would engage readers' compassion and dare them to look away. I wouldn't have done this without my experience in Darlington with the program to save women from cervical cancer and vindicating Timothy Evans. I was as eager as the next editor to find something new and exciting, but living close to the readers as I did then, I'd noted how we in the trade, absorbed by every story, became bored before the readers did. Our challenge was to keep dramatizing the pain. We achieved this with photographs, such as one by Michael Ward of an adolescent figure, hung up on a steel stand, wearing laced black shoes and white ankle socks. The shoes and socks were attached to the artificial legs on a body harness for a limbless person. The artificial arms attached to the harness were equipped with metal talons. I remember thinking that there was no way the person in the harness could put on the socks or tie the shoelaces. He'd have to be hoisted into the frame like a medieval knight lifted into his armor.

I identified everything we published with the "Our Thalidomide Children" logo. Readers reacted quite differently than they had ten years earlier in Darlington. Now they didn't turn away, perhaps habituated to the shock. Instead I received hundreds of letters and telephone calls of support, asking what they could do. Many of the letters came with checks; scores came from thalidomide families. In the legal profession and the press, however, we had severe critics. The *Law Society Gazette* (representing solicitors) denounced the campaign as having "all the subtlety and legal justification of Robin Hood's activities in Sherwood Forest." The columnist Peregrine Worsthorne in the *Sunday Telegraph* condemned it as nauseating, saying that the company had only done what the country had willed. The Oxford historian A. J. P. Taylor described it as "a witch hunt, an exploitation of popular feeling such as Dr. Goebbels would have rejoiced in."

That the *Sunday Times* had been attempting to print the truth was a nicety Taylor and others chose to ignore. But I was buoyed by the letters from ordinary readers, especially those from thalidomide families. David Jones's father, a nurse, had taken on the full-time task of looking after his legless son while David's mother, a teacher, went out to work. "When the compensation awards made headlines," he told us, "people withdrew their sympathy. They treated us as if we'd had a lucky win on the pools. After the years of struggle it took time to register what a piffling sum we had. Had I fully appreciated the problems we are facing now—David is growing too heavy for me to lift—I'd have stood up in that courtroom and shouted."

I said we'd run a family story every week until we succeeded. "And what will you do when you've run out of all four hundred fifty families?" someone asked. "Start again," I said on the spur of the moment. "They'll all be older!" To do that we recruited Marjorie Wallace, who was directing television programs for the BBC. She had a gentle nature and a degree in psychology, and she managed to depict the struggles without being mawkish. It was she who found nine-year-old Terry Wiles, a highly intelligent two-foot-tall limbless trunk with one eye, abandoned by his mother and adopted by an inventive sixty-year-old van driver, Leonard, and his young wife, Hazel, living in a dilapidated cottage near Huntingdon. The National Health Service equipment had been of no use to him. From scrap metal and old army surplus, Leonard had invented a "supercar" chair for Terry on the principle of a forklift, so the boy could press a button with a shoulder and raise himself to talk to people. These tragedies could not be ignored, but the authorities were about to try again to switch off the light.

We lost 3–0 in the High Court on November 17. We were forbidden to publish the Knightley article based on the Distillers documents revealing the company's unjustified reliance on Chemie Grunenthal science and Distillers' own questionable marketing activities. The ban probably earned as much ink as the article would have if we'd been allowed to publish it.

Sir Alexander at Distillers counterattacked. When shareholder Tony Lynes, who'd inherited sixty Distillers shares, took up the cause in a letter to the company, he got a stiff lecture from Sir Alexander on the chairman's legal responsibilities. It was easy for a single shareholder to take a moral stand, Sir Alexander declared, "even easier for a newspaper editor," but the chairman could be sued by any of the 250,000 shareholders holding 300 million shares if he gave money away without their unanimous approval. Legally, he said, the parents were probably entitled to nothing. And if the *Sunday Times* campaign led to the breakdown of negotiations with them, well, that's what they'd get, nothing. The company would go to trial—a danger to the families because their lawyers had already unwisely conceded that they had no case on negligence.

It sounded like blackmail. "For three hundred and seventy children," said Ashley, "the sword of Damocles has been replaced by the jagged edge of a broken whisky bottle." Alf Morris, too, had been working in the background. He invited me to come to the Commons to meet the leader of the opposition and soon-to-be prime minister, Harold Wilson, and Sir Elwyn Jones, a former attorney general who was to become lord chancellor. Morris was the front bench spokesman for social policy, and in the meeting, with me cast in the role of Greek chorus, he begged Wilson and Jones to give up precious opposition time for a debate.

The Labour opposition had only four days in the whole year they could claim as their time, but they agreed, and on November 29 Morris and Ashley spoke to a packed House, calling on Distillers to recognize its moral debt and on the government to set up a trust fund for the children.

On the way to see the Labour leaders, I'd been stopped in the lobby of the Commons by Prime Minister Heath's parliamentary private secretary, Timothy Kitson, asking whether we'd end the campaign upon hearing the information they'd just received: Distillers was willing to increase its offer of a trust fund from £3.25 million to £5 million. I said no; I'd been advised that any realistic assessment of need had to be closer to £20 million.

Distillers' £5 million proposition, announced by the government, was brushed aside in a debate in which massive emotional indignation and vivid personal testimony swept both sides of the House. "How can an eleven-year-old girl look forward to laughing and loving," said Ashley, "when she has no hand to hold or legs to dance on?"

Heath relented with the announcement of a £3 million fund

for the congenitally disabled, with a further £3 million for the thalidomide children. Moreover, he set up a royal commission to examine the whole question of personal injury damages.

Two months into the *Sunday Times* series, the campaign was self-sustaining. It gathered momentum from an unexpected quarter—Distillers shareholders. Tony Lynes joined with Sarah and Roger Broad to take up Sir Alexander's challenge. They circulated a letter to thousands of shareholders. Sir Alexander had blithely assumed that the shareholders were interested only in maximizing their dividends, but that proved a misjudgment. Ron Peet, chief executive of the Legal and General Assurance Society, the second-largest life insurance company in Britain, which had 3.5 million Distillers shares, concluded not only that corporations had moral as well as legal responsibilities, but also that the obduracy of Distillers was provoking such consumer hostility that it would damage its own commercial interests. A trade union pension fund chairman declared, "Distillers is blundering around like a Glaswegian drunk."

Peet's snowball started an avalanche. More big companies, insurance brokers, merchant bankers, and local authorities joined in. Stores and customers boycotted whisky made by Distillers. The duty-free stores in London and at European airports reported customers saying, "Anything not from Distillers." In the United States Ralph Nader planned an international boycott, briefed by the indefatigable David Mason (who lobbied passengers on his transatlantic flight). Over nine days Distillers shares lost £35 million in value. This was arithmetic Edinburgh understood.

On January 23 the company gave in with an immediate commitment of £20 million, about ten times the original offer. Jack Ashley rang me on the Saturday to say that he'd discovered the treasury intended to tax the money. I wrote an editorial for the next day. With intervention by Ashley and Morris, the prime minister, now Harold Wilson, made the trust good with £5 million from government funds. The families and the campaigners were overjoyed by the victory and a settlement by which Distillers, in the end, accepted a liability of £28.4 million, embracing all the actions started in 1969.

I was delighted but strangely numb. I'd never doubted we'd win more money for the victims once we were able to let people know what was happening; my faith in free journalism and in the common decency of ordinary citizens had been reinvigorated. But I'd lived with the story for so many years that I kept imagining the victims' daily lives—getting into that harness, opening a bottle with one's teeth, holding a toothbrush between one's toes, wondering if ever they'd know the joys of marriage and family life.

And the fact remained that we had not yet laid bare how the whole appalling mess had been created. I kept Page and Potter on the investigation, and a few months after the monetary settlement—not years—they were able to conclude that there had been an excellent case waiting to be developed, but the parents' legal advisers had failed to assemble it. Because the contempt rule still applied, it was not until June 27, 1976, that we were able to publish the Page-Potter findings documenting the powerful and scientifically sound case that the parents might have had all along. Solicitors and counsel had not secured decisive testimony available in Britain and the United States. No doubt the legal aid system had restricted them, but we spent relatively little energy establishing the falsity of the position taken by Powell and the "quality" press that Distillers was blameless. In this regard, Dr. Phillips turned out to be a poor choice of expert adviser. The documents he gave us were significant, but his advice on why the tragedy had been foreseeable was not. Insofar as we mentioned him, our draft article would have been seriously flawed.

The occasion for publication was our triumph—no other word for it—in a declaration by the European Court of Human Rights. By a vote of twenty-four international judges, the court ruled 13–11 that by banning our report on the origins of the tragedy, Britain's law of contempt had breached the free speech article of the European Convention for the Protection of Human Rights. This meant that the British government had to enact a statutory reform so that the years of silence on thalidomide could never be repeated. Report and comment could henceforth be allowed in civil litigation until a case was actually set down for trial.

In the end it was all worthwhile. We exposed the real reasons for the disaster and achieved reasonable compensation for the families, a royal commission on personal injuries, and somewhat more freedom of the half-free British press.

An extraordinary coincidence provides a coda to this chapter. As I was writing this account, a stranger telephoned me from Yorkshire. It was Guy Tweedy, a property investor in Harrogate, wanting to come and talk about a campaign. Not the *Sunday Times* campaign of the 1970s, which he knew very well, but one he'd started with Nick Dobrik, who ran a jewelry business. Both are relatively able-bodied thalidomide victims who've joined with other more typically damaged thalidomiders to advocate for victims' rights. They've already, with the help of Jonathan Stone, a former law partner of Lord Goodman, succeeded in getting Prime Minister Gordon Brown to rescind his decision as chancellor to tax benefits payable through the

Thalidomide Trust. (Does the treasury have a tin heart?) Furthermore, they've briefed the successor company to Distillers, the Guinness group (now part of Diageo, the world's largest beer and spirits company), to such effect that it is repairing the damages of that "hearsay" inflation with another £160 million over thirty years.

Still, the payments from the trust, very fairly distributed, cannot meet the needs of the most affected of the 457 surviving thalidomiders. Money that seemed adequate three decades ago is no longer able to ensure a decent life for someone like Lorraine Mercer or Vivien Barrett. Lorraine has no legs or arms and only one hand emanating from her shoulder; she longs for the independence of being able to get about in a car with wheelchair access, now possible thanks to advances in technology, but such a car would cost £50,000. Vivien Barrett, no arms, legs, or feet and only one hand, teaches music theory part-time but fears how advancing age may affect her. Those thalidomiders who were able to work are finding they cannot continue.

The indomitable Jack Ashley has been moved to action again, calling for the state to recognize its responsibility for the disaster. Unfortunately, the then Labour minister of health, Alan Johnson, was in the Powell mode. He said he was "not persuaded" there was a case for financial aid.

The thalidomiders feel a bond with their "brothers and sisters" in other countries. In Italy, Spain, and Austria, the victims have had no financial compensation at all. In Germany, where there are more than five times as many thalidomiders as in Britain, the maximum annual payment is meager. And Chemie Grünenthal insisted in the stingy private settlement made in 1969 that none of the victims there could ever complain or campaign.

I called the *Sunday Times* editor, John Witherow, who immediately took up their cause.

I find it inspiring that the thalidomider activists, whose early years were such an ordeal, are now extending a helping hand to others, and then I realize with stab of pain that many of them have no hands at all.

16

Space Barons

Did I mention how invigorating it was to have a big-time national newspaper with the best staff in town? I still get a high from the fumes of those Saturdays when a vague idea from the beginning of the week—or an investigation started months back—crystallized into a thriller package of story, headline, photograph, and graphic. Or the glorious moments when we got our hands on the first copies of the newspaper, expunging all the raw, urgent untidiness of the passion and fine-tuning in the making of it. How authoritative everything looked! How delicious the smell of the still warm newsprint! How envious the rivals would be! Truth requires the admission that the rivals, the *Observer* and the *Sunday Telegraph,* sometimes arrived with a story that had eclipsed ours or had escaped us altogether. Once we'd reduced the shock by declaring to each other "nothing new in that," we scrambled like mad to catch up.

The week began at the editor's conference on Tuesday. Early on I had felt it necessary to issue my first edict. The head printer knocked up a sign I pinned to my office door: "Smokers are welcome but not their cigarettes." My peace offering to ease the pain was a souvenir I'd brought back from a Moscow trip, a samovar that was supposed to keep a flow of hot tea going.

Most of the talking was done by "collectors," heads of departments who said what they hoped to bring in from reporters and columnists, photographers, graphic artists, critics, and reviewers. These executives were responsible for people, not space on the pages. As the week accelerated, they bid their best efforts to the space barons, the handful who decided what should go in the premium spots in the paper.

I found it impossible to stay away from the "backbench" where managing editor and chief subeditor assessed stories, chose photographs, and planned pages. The Saturday news pages were designed by Robert Harling, who'd worked with his chum Ian Fleming on black propaganda operations run by the navy's Unit 17Z. Ingenious ways had to be devised to keep me from making observations that might impede the haste to go to press. I heard later that Harling had been instructed to distract me in the last minutes of closing page one. "Tell me, Harry," I can hear the saboteur say even now, "which do you prefer, sex or skiing?"

I had my own source of relief from the week's tensions: squash. It required careful calculation and downright furtiveness to get away with it. At some stage during an afternoon, at a time decided at the very last minute, I went down Lord Thomson's private elevator, jumped into a waiting car, and sped off to the Royal Automobile Club (RAC) in Pall Mall for a match. "Sped off" is the wrong description of the times I got snarled in Trafalgar Square traffic and had to run the last 220 yards to make my game. I think it was then I decided to renew my motorcycling. Every minute counted. I could not be out of the office for more than an hour (and since there were no cell phones then, I had elaborate arrangements with my secretary, Joan Thomas, for how to get word through if the Russians landed).

I varied squash partners week to week, almost always people from the paper. The urgency of chasing news carried over into the precious half hour we had rushing like maniacs about the court. Sometimes the small black ball metamorphosed into the wily barrister who had convinced the judge that there was no possible public interest defense for our newspaper's desire to report on, say, the bribing of a British MP by a foreign government. Sometimes it was the lupine grin of the Communist union leader in the pressroom who had once again sabotaged our production. (Calls to him from Moscow came collect, which was a bit much.) In any event, just hammering the ball, even though it was too often returned with nonchalance, was therapy lasting several days.

I came to share the half hour with different discreet staff players at the paper, not one of them, curiously, willing to give the editor the benefit of any doubt about questionable line calls. I will say in our defense that we often continued *Sunday Times* business in the locker room, although I didn't join the regulars who repaired to the Blue Lion pub opposite the office to discuss what had happened that week to "their" paper (everyone regarded it as their paper).

Over the years various allegations have been made about my treatment of staff and guests: that I sent a ninety-eight-pound woman reporter into a field with a bull to illustrate a story on the risks hikers face; that I had to be cornered in the men's room to sign "pink slips" for cash advances for indigent reporters; and most commonly that I'd invite visitors arriving for lunch at the paper to decamp for a brisk cheese salad at the RAC, then keep them waiting poolside while I swam my customary twenty laps. These stories and worse are all, regretfully, true. Very few

appreciated the offer to jump in the pool with me. One inter-
viewee, in something of a hurry, obliged me to conduct our
discourse standing at the shallow end between laps.

The *Sunday Times* staff was small by American standards,
never more than 160 men and women on the newspaper and
its color magazine, about a tenth of the size of the editorial
staff of the *New York Times*. But one of the strengths of the
Sunday Times, as it grew to sixty-four and then seventy-two
pages, was that it was informed by a pool of unconventional
talents. Today, when journalists tend to come into newspapers
and television by the same conventional route—college, journalism course—the staff of the *Sunday Times* in retrospect
seems eclectic to the point of parody, but they knew how the
real world worked. Time and again the richness of their back-
grounds enhanced the paper. Among those who'd come to
newspapers in mid-career were a molecular biologist, a professional pilot, a clinical psychologist, a civil servant, a university
lecturer, an antiques dealer, a television producer, a research
chemist, a bond salesman, and an accountant going straight—
very helpful when we were looking into the financial records
of some crook or other.

Most of the staff were university graduates, but a number
had not completed high school. Insight's Paul Eddy, a relentless investigator who is now a best-selling thriller author, left
school at fifteen. The newsroom's pertinacious Anne Robinson
had been expelled from school and worked as a chicken gut-
ter and saleslady before trying journalism; later she became
a transatlantic television celebrity as taskmistress for *The
Weakest Link* quiz show. By contrast, Oxford classics graduate
Anthony Holden, who was only twenty-five when he joined
the *Sunday Times*, had already written two books on Greek

poetry and another on Graham Young, the Neasden teenager who'd tried out poisons on his family and continued his mad murdering ways when prematurely released from Broadmoor. While reporting for a local evening newspaper, Holden had come top in the examination held by the national training scheme. These days he maintains his humiliating versatility by writing literary biographies, competing in the world poker championships, and running a poker website.

A number of staffers had reached the *Sunday Times* via the cauldron of the Fleet Street populars; a few had experience on American newspapers; many had pounded pavements in the provinces. We had regular infusions of renegade "colonials" from Australia, Canada, and South Africa, never inclined to take anyone's "no" for a final answer. And we fostered active relationships with a corps of freelancers, paying the ones we'd learned to trust for their efforts even when the story turned out not to satisfy our standards: next time it might.

Our coverage of wars was powerfully assisted by people with experience of both front lines and deadlines. Among those who'd seen military service of some kind, we had a company of infantry, an instructor in desert tank warfare, a tail gunner, a trio of army colonels and naval commanders, a sprinkling of wartime intelligence officers, and at least one corporal I know of. When Tom Stoppard became intrigued about pressmen coping with concepts of freedom in the context of reporting the murderous idiosyncrasies of an African dictator, the theme of his play *Night & Day,* he explored the experiences of our roving foreign correspondent Jon Swain and photographer Bryan Wharton, who'd dodged a lot of bullets. In fact paratroopers regarded Jon as a talisman.

The staff photographers like Wharton struck me as rather like Battle of Britain pilots, lounging around with their cameras round their necks, ready to take off on hazardous missions at a moment's notice. Wharton, in fact, looked the part, down to the handlebar mustache and fur-collared leather jacket, sauntering into the newsroom with a pretty girl on his arm. The entire news photographic team were on the battle-fields almost as soon as a shooting war started. Photographers with their equipment were more conspicuous in danger zones, and they'd all absorbed the great photographer Robert Capa's injunction, "If your pictures aren't good enough, you're not close enough."

It's no exaggeration to say that our cameramen had more experience with combat than many of the young soldiers. Don McCullin always went with the frontline troops. He advanced with U.S. Marines foxhole by foxhole in the battle for the citadel at Hue and carried a sniper victim to first aid; in Cambodia he was wounded in a Khmer Rouge ambush; in Uganda he was held in the mad Idi Amin's Makyinde jail with prisoners led out to execution; when the Israelis fought yard by yard for the old city of Jerusalem in the Six-Day War, he (and our Colin Simpson) was with them. McCullin's reputation for coming through gun and mortar fire alive preceded him wherever he went. Israeli soldiers were seen to touch his jacket for good luck.

I had loved selecting and editing photographs at the *Northern Echo,* enchanted by the way the photographers, bored with flower shows and factory openings, took advantage of their freedom. But none of that had the acrid taste of danger that came with the prints the *Sunday Times* men brought back from conflicts and disasters.

During students' anti-Gaullist street battles in Paris in 1968, for instance, Wharton and Frank Herrmann were in the thick of it ducking tear gas, then found themselves overwhelmed by military-strength CS gas wildly unleashed by the backup riot police, the CRS (Compagnies Républicaines de Sécurité). The difference from tear gas was devastating. Wharton got more of it, since he was with the students. It dropped him to his knees and blinded him for about twenty minutes. Yet he went back into the gas twelve times to photograph the CRS beating everyone in sight with their rifle butts. In a note to me he wrote, "I saw them corner a sixteen-year-old girl, pummeling her in the face with rifles, dragging out defenseless old men and women from cafés and beating them without mercy. I slipped on the blood on the floor when they charged and went down with camera straps entwined round my neck."

Team journalism was vindicated by the way it worked in Paris, with Herrmann and Wharton feeding their experiences to the group of reporters coming in from the tumult to write in the old Gestapo haunt, the Hotel Meurice. The reporters telephoned copy to us in fragments, and John Barry in London, working through Friday night, pulled the strands together into a single arresting narrative we ran over eight pages. Wharton, after a mad drive from a blockaded and blazing Paris, had to catch the ferry from Ostend, in Belgium, to bring back his and Herrmann's film in time. I say "bring back" because in those predigital days, getting images to London required ingenuity — and stamina. One Friday afternoon, with little more than twenty-four hours to Saturday's deadline, we dispatched Wharton to an earthquake in Osoppo, Italy. The local airport was fogbound. He drove 350 miles through the night to arrive at dawn, took his pictures, drove 350 miles back, flew home from Milan, and raced into the London darkroom just in time for the first edition.

Photojournalism had center stage in the color magazine, although the magazine irritated fastidious media critics by the dexterity with which it could move from serious reportage to glamour and celebrity chic. The *Sunday Times* was particularly responsive to the vibrant popular culture and fast-moving social currents of the 1960s: the Beatles and Stones; the Pill; liberal new laws on hanging and homosexuality; race and abortion; theater censorship formally abolished; the satire boom sparked by Peter Cook and Dudley Moore, *Private Eye* and *That Was the Week That Was*; London's eclipse of Paris as the fashion capital.

We weren't aware of it at the time, but the magazine was itself a tiny chip in the mosaic of the swinging 1960s, its long-serving editor Godfrey Smith and art director Michael Rand matching the counterculture with innovations of their own. They employed gifted young artists such as David Hockney and Peter Blake to go abroad and paint the story for us, and they deployed such big-name photographers as Robert Freson, Arnold Newman, Norman Parkinson, and Bruce Davidson. Those artists and photographers were happy to work for the magazine at a fraction of the pay they could get from advertising because it gave them worldwide prestige (and they kept their copyrights). Lord Snowdon was on the staff, liberating himself from the confines of fashion and theater by pursuing serious photojournalism of the highest order. The flow of photographers was classless, with the East End boys Terry Donovan, Brian Duffy, David Bailey, and Patrick (Lord) Lichfield trooping in. Even more pleasing to all the males, drawn like moths to the light box, was when Julie Christie dropped by to see our new pictures of her.

We felt affinity, too, with a group of young men in the advertising industry. Until the very early 1960s, advertising was stuck in the time warp of social class and condescension: don't even think of being an adman if you're bereft of a military background, a public school–Oxbridge education, or a southern counties accent, preferably all of the above. Then John Pearce, padding the corridors of the small, bright new ad agency Collett Dickenson Pearce (CDP) in his stocking feet, attracted an electric group of talents in their early twenties—David Puttnam, Alan Parker, Ridley Scott, Frank Lowe, and Charles Saatchi. We borrowed Puttnam for six months to help with the nerve-racking launch of the color magazine.

These CDP youngsters transformed advertising much as the color magazine transformed Sunday newspapers. The ad industry in the 1960s was like the TV series *Mad Men:* lose an account, and you're fired. But when Ford Motors rejected a daring piece of creativity from CDP, the agency turned the tables: it fired the client. Creativity, the agency wanted to suggest, was king. Puttnam, Parker, and Scott became celebrated filmmakers; Saatchi joined with his brother Maurice to create what would become the world's largest ad agency, Saatchi & Saatchi.

I can claim a small part in the brothers' launch in 1970. Having seen how uncontrolled display advertising played havoc with good design in American newspaper, I'd laid down the maximum size of a display in the *Sunday Times.* The advertising director asked me if I would see the young ad executive Maurice Saatchi to hear his pitch for our making a single exception. Saatchi was preceded into the room by the largest pair of horn-rimmed glasses I'd ever seen, a fitting ad in itself for the twenty-four-year-old with a first-class honors degree from the London School of Economics. He made a cunning appeal to my vanity, patriotism, and compassion. As an innovative editor, he wheedled, I should support an innovative business; as a citizen, I should support a new business for Britain's sake so that the advertising trade would not be dominated by American companies; and as a compassionate person, I should bear in mind that without the prestige launch in the wonderful *Sunday Times,* the Saatchis would never make it.

I relented, just this once, and their launch in our paper put their new agency on the map. I've not been forgiven for this by some of my friends, since the Saatchi agency went on to devise devastating attacks on the Labour government, which sadly were entirely justified. (A billboard of a long trail of men lining up for unemployment money was headlined "Labour Isn't Working.") Their agency was a powerful promoter of Margaret Thatcher's ascension to prime minister, and Maurice eventually became Lord Saatchi, chairman of the Conservative Party.

I must admit I inflicted on the staff every half-cocked rumor and vague hint I picked up. I cannot recall anyone blinking; whatever they might have said out of earshot, they invariably delivered. I came to expect them to make gold out of flax. I got a taste of my own medicine from Lord Thomson himself. He called me up on a Saturday night to ask whether I'd like to sit down with Howard Hughes. If so—"entirely up to you, Harold"—I was to meet Ray at the London airport the next morning. Thomson knew Mormons in the entourage of the famously reclusive Hughes, and they'd told him that Hughes was ready to discuss how we might interview him for a book and newspaper serial.

We flew to Miami and met with Chester Davis, Hughes's lawyer, and Hughes's Mormon aides, who were shuttling back and forth between our waterfront room and wherever they were keeping their nutty boss. Hughes remained elusive, but it was satisfying in its own way to see how Roy negotiated money matters. He sat on his bed in his underpants and calculated the sum he intended to offer.

For me there were two tricky moments with Thomson on this abortive mission to see Hughes. The first morning, when I arrived in the dining room for a very early breakfast with Roy, I was carrying both the *Miami Herald* and the *Wall Street*

Journal. "Why'd ya buy two newspapers?" he growled. At the end of the trip, when we went to the front desk to pay our departure bills, he had another spasm. He reckoned that since we were leaving at noon, he hadn't incurred a charge for a full day, and he began myopically going through the charges item by item. The duty manager was summoned, and an unseemly argument loomed between frugal peer and frosty manager. I suggested to Thomson that he leave me to sort it out while he accompanied the porter to his room. I volunteered for this because when I ran my own eyes down his charges, I was horrified to find that the hotel had charged him for some of my expenses—a massage, a suit pressing, and two calls to home in London. I suggested to the manager in the privacy of his office that merely transferring the charges to the right room was not sufficient recompense for inflicting a peer of the realm with all this embarrassment. Roy's satisfaction, when I told him that the hotel had made an error and his bill was being reduced, made him beam for the whole trip home.

Can embarrassment be retrospective? In one photograph from the seventies, I'm caught seated, gesturing, in front of a news poster on display behind my chair at the editors' weekly conference. In big black type, the poster announces: UGANDA SENSATION. The poster, sent to my office for approval for distribution across the country, promoted a scoop we'd secured documenting the crimes of General Idi Amin, otherwise known as "the Butcher of Uganda," "Big Daddy," and "Emperor of All the Beasts and Fishes on Earth"—the bloodthirsty madman so vividly portrayed in 2007 by Forest Whitaker in the movie *The Last King of Scotland.*

We didn't allow visitors to our editorial meeting, but this week we had a guest by royal command: Prince Charles, the

Prince of Wales. He'd expressed an interest in how the paper was put together to Denis Hamilton and our managing director, whose wife was lady-in-waiting (personal assistant) to the Queen. I could hardly demur, but I wished a better day had been chosen. As head of the Commonwealth, Queen Elizabeth was about to receive a bevy of African leaders among the thirty-five prime ministers attending a Commonwealth conference during the Silver Jubilee of her accession to the throne. We intended to rebuke them for continually failing as a group to unite in condemnation of Amin. (A situation similar to the failure of African states to unite against the outrages of Robert Mugabe in Zimbabwe in 2008.) Prince Charles would now have to hear how we planned to attack guests of his mother.

Enough was known about Amin's reign of terror to feel repelled by the way racial fraternity had given him immunity from censure. It was bad enough that the Organization of African Unity, predecessor of the African Union, had not only looked the other way but in 1975 had unanimously elected him chairman. It would be contemptible, I thought, if the Commonwealth and the UN remained supine in light of the horrible story we were preparing for the coming Sunday.

The source of the sensation was a thirty-seven-year-old defector from Amin's government by the name of Henry Kyemba, who'd known Amin for twenty years and had been his minister of health for the past five. Kyemba had walked into my office a few days before in fear of his life. "I want to ensure," he told me, "that what I know does not die with me." That same morning I bundled Kyemba and his wife, Teresa, into an office car with a driver I knew I could trust and sent them to my weekend cottage in Alphamstone, Essex, with the writer Russell Miller. It was melodramatic but necessary. Amin had dispatched agents to kill Kyemba; one had already been detained at Heathrow Airport by an immigration officer alerted by the Home Office, which had granted asylum to the minister.

Kyemba's arrival in London had been daring. Sickened by what he'd seen and knowing that five of his cabinet colleagues had been murdered, he had made elaborate plans to defect while in Geneva heading Uganda's delegation to a World Health Organization conference. So as not to arouse suspicion, he'd left his two infant children in Kampala in the care of relatives. Only when he received word that they'd safely avoided Amin's goons and border guards by trekking through the bush to Kenya did he evade the other Ugandans and make his way from Geneva to my office.

It was a stroke of good fortune to have Miller ready to begin debriefing him immediately. Miller was well informed on Uganda because he'd prepared for an interview with Amin, fixed by a retired army officer who'd something to do with the "whiskey run," the twice-weekly flights of spirits, cigarettes, and luxury goods from Stansted Airport to Entebbe by which Amin secured the loyalty of his thugs. It was good fortune for Miller, too, since he'd been due the next day to catch a plane to Kampala. Had he been in Kampala representing the *Sunday Times* when we published Kyemba's story, he would not have survived. Amin had not hesitated to murder other journalists, including Nicholas Stroh, freelancing for the *Philadelphia Evening Bulletin*, and his associate Robert Siedle, who had been killed just for asking too many questions about a massacre at Mbarara barracks.

Kyemba was the first senior member of Amin's government able and willing to speak with unique authority on the reign of terror, because his position gave him access to all hospitals and mortuaries. By the next morning, when I rode my BMW motorbike to Alphamstone, Miller had already solved the mystery of the seventy-five-year-old British-Israeli grandmother Dora Bloch, who'd been among the 106 hostages held by Palestinian hijackers at Entebbe Airport courtesy of Amin. She was unlucky to miss the electrifying rescue of the hostages by Israeli commandos on the night of July 3, 1976. The night before the raid she'd choked on a piece of meat and been taken to Mulago Hospital. Kyemba visited her there and found her recovered. The morning after the Israeli raid she was nowhere to be found. In response to inquiries from the British High Commission, Amin said that she'd been returned safely to the airport an hour before the raid and had presumably been taken by the Israelis. Indeed, hospital records proved it. In truth, Amin had ordered Kyemba to falsify them.

In the peace of the Essex countryside it was chilling to listen to Kyemba's description of how Dora Bloch had become a victim of Amin's rage after the Israeli raid: "He went berserk. If he's provoked, he reacts like a wild animal and goes into a kind of fit. No one around him is safe." The morning after everyone else had been rescued, said Kyemba, four of Amin's "State Research" officers arrived at the hospital. Two of them carrying pistols and shouting for staff to stand aside grabbed Bloch from her bed and frog-marched her screaming down three flights of stairs and out the main hospital door, without shoes and dress and in full view of patients, staff, and visitors. They dumped her body by the road twenty miles from the city. A photographer who took a picture of her partially burned corpse was murdered.

Kyemba knew, too, what had happened to the Anglican archbishop of Uganda Janani Luwum and two cabinet ministers who'd all been reported killed in a car accident. He'd seen their bodies in the mortuary. "They were riddled with bullets, the archbishop shot in the mouth," Kyemba said. "The country is littered with bodies. They're fed to crocodiles in the river."

I left Miller at his typewriter and raced back to the office with a sketch of the hospital layout Kyemba had drawn; we had very little time before deadline.

Our Kyemba story had an instant effect. The prime ministers at the Queen's conference condemned Amin for "massive violations" of human rights. For the first time, African leaders allowed open discussion of the internal affairs of another African country. Britain broke off diplomatic relations with Uganda. America's ambassador to the UN, Andrew Young, denounced Amin in vivid language. Amin was ousted in 1979. He should have been tried as a war criminal for hundreds of thousands of murders, but Saudi Arabia gave him sanctuary as a convert to Islam. He lived there with his four wives, fancy cars, and chef until his death in 2003.

Only later did I realize that the UGANDA SENSATION might have been troubling to our guest that day, Prince Charles. Sitting to the right of him in our editorial meeting was Ron Hall. He'd given a party at his house in Hampstead and, lacking a downstairs cloakroom, had asked guests to leave their overcoats and umbrellas on the upstairs bed. When the first departing guests went to the room to collect their coats, they interrupted the writer wife of a political correspondent thrashing about under the coats with an African diplomat. "Don't mind us," she said blithely, "we're discussing Uganda." *Private Eye* at once seized on this unlikely response as a neat way of conveying gossip about the sexual mores of public figures, saying someone was "an expert on Uganda" or a couple met often "to discuss Uganda."

At this time Prince Charles, unknown to his public, was deep in an affair with Camilla Parker Bowles, which was to continue through his marriage to Princess Diana. The palace might not have been pleased to see the future King of England in front of that poster blaring UGANDA SENSATION.

*   *   *

It was not by chance that Kyemba came to our office to start the chain of events that led the African nations to disown Amin. He might have chosen any one of four or five newspapers with bigger circulations, but he regarded his appearance in the *Sunday Times* as a mark of authenticity.

The difficult part for me whenever there was a knock on the door from the bearer of apparently big news was making the judgment call: can we believe a word this person tells us? (And nowadays with pictures one must wonder if the photograph has been manipulated.) What if Kyemba was a fabricator? What if he wasn't who he said he was? What if half of what he said was true and half wasn't? That would have been gravely damaging to our reputation. We couldn't very well put in a call to Idi Amin, but we could check Kyemba's identity and assess his character and the consistency of his story with known facts. Almost always in these circumstances, we had to take some things on faith.

Given that, the excitement of a scoop can overwhelm elementary prudence: you want to believe. Redoubtable journalists fall for confidence tricks and hoaxes. Before I became editor of the *Sunday Times,* Denis Hamilton and the Thomson Organization had bought eighteen volumes of Mussolini's handwritten wartime diaries for book publication by a Thomson company and newspaper serialization. I knew nothing of the transaction, which had been conducted during his editorship by Hamilton and a skilled investigator, the former Insight supremo Clive Irving, who'd left the paper in 1965. Everyone had been sworn to secrecy. Three years later, in February 1968, the Italian newspaper *Corriere della Sera* reported that it had discovered a mother and daughter from Vercelli forging Mussolini papers. Only then did Hamilton rather shamefacedly let me in on his acquisition.

He called me to his office to say he'd kept quiet about it on my assuming the editorship because secrecy had been a condition of the sale (i.e., con) and in due course he'd hoped to make either me or the *Times* the present of a world scoop. Hamilton and the Thomson group had already parted with a down payment of £150,000 in advance of the diaries being translated and edited. I was led to understand that the Thomson group would rather the deal was forgotten, but to me it was clearly a story we had to do—and it was irresistible to send an Insight reporter to grill Clive Irving, his former boss.

Famous publications have been burned time and again. A *Washington Post* reporter named Janet Cooke fooled her editors and the judges of the Pulitzer Prize with her invention of an eight-year-old heroin addict; Jayson Blair long deceived the editors of the *New York Times*, plagiarizing other publications and pretending to go places and conduct interviews he never had; Stephen Glass fabricated more than twenty stories for the *New Republic* and other publications for several years before being caught out in 1988 when a drama of a teenage hacker and a computer company proved to be figments of his vivid imagination; and in 1983, a year after I'd left the company, the forgers of Hitler's diaries took in Times Newspapers in London and *Newsweek* magazine in New York. I felt for my former *Sunday Times* colleagues. Caught up in the excitement of a shattering scoop, their own doubts suppressed, they'd been let down by the vetting historian, Lord Dacre (previously Hugh Trevor-Roper), and my gullible successor as editor of the *Times*, Charles Douglas-Home, who initially had charge of the project. They'd been rushed and pushed into the folly by the commercial imperatives of Rupert Murdoch and his macho management, who would rather be caught dead than having second thoughts.

It could be said I was lucky in my editing years never to

be swept up in one of these disasters, and I suppose I was. Not a little of that, however, was because my door was always open. This was not a custom applauded by apostles of good line management, but anyone on the staff could barge in, waving a galley proof, and ask, "Harry, why are you publishing this crap?" Transactions presented "for your eyes only" flatter the ego, at the risk of having egg on one's face later. Had the paper's foreign staff been in on the Mussolini deal, it's very likely someone would have had a vague memory of the trial and conviction some years back of two women in Vercelli forging Mussolini papers, or at least thought to make a few discreet inquiries in Italy. Had Trevor-Roper as a Hitler scholar not contentedly accepted the idea that he was so experienced he could make the judgment all by himself, the falsification of the Hitler diaries would very likely have been detected by a reputable German historian.

Retailers of trash invariably impose haste — "We'll have to go to the *Observer* if you can't decide here and now" — and invariably insist on secrecy. When dealing with strangers, I came to regard both these conditions as red flags.

Who was Anthony Mascarenhas? The well-dressed man in his early forties who came into my office on May 18, 1971, had the bearing of a military man, square set and mustached, with appealing, almost soulful eyes and an air of profound melancholy. I'd never met Mr. Mascarenhas before, nor had the foreign editor, Frank Giles. We'd encouraged him to file freelance for us from Pakistan on the strength of his reports in the *Karachi Morning News*, where he was assistant editor. He had lived most of his life in Pakistan and held a Pakistani passport, but he was by descent a Christian from Goa, in India.

Two months before, in March, the Bengalis of East Pakistan,

fired by Bengali nationalism, had rebelled against what they saw as their ill treatment by the non-Bengali military rulers of the geographically divided nation. (President Yahya Khan and his administration were in Islamabad, in West Pakistan.) In an untimely and ill-starred bid to hasten independence, 175,000 troops in East Pakistan had joined thousands of Bengalis in a pogrom against non-Bengalis. Thousands of men, women, and children had been butchered. I'd kept a close eye on it because my youngest brother, John, was working for the Foreign Office in Islamabad. "Our man in Dacca," he wrote to me, "says the East Paks have been meat-hooking people, hanging them up and then slitting their throats like pigs." Reports of these atrocities had been filed by Mascarenhas and our own Nick Tomalin in Jessore.

At the end of March the government in Islamabad had sent in two army divisions to restore order. It also had expelled all international reporters and imposed a news blackout. Thereafter the news from East Pakistan was that the army had made the province peaceful again. Such was the story in Pakistan's press and television. Pictures were broadcast of villages and towns coming out in parades with Pakistani flags to celebrate the return of peace. A British parliamentary delegation went to West and East Pakistan and satisfied itself that all was well.

Mascarenhas, talking quietly for a long time with shafts of afternoon sunlight coming into my office, told a very different and very harrowing story. In late April he'd been one of eight senior pressmen taken to East Pakistan by the Ministry of Information. The government wished to discountenance sporadic reports of army killings in East Pakistan, retailed mainly by a fast-growing stream of Bengali refugees. "The way Islamabad put it," said Mascarenhas, "was [for us] to show in a patriotic way the great job the army was doing....But what I saw was genocide."

He'd been shocked by the Bengali outrages in March, but he maintained that what the army was doing was altogether worse and on a grander scale. It had not been content to do the necessary job of restoring order, nor was it confining its violence to rebels. Instead, Mascarenhas said, it had gone on a huge killing spree across the entire country. Soldiers were systematically moving from village to village, town to town, killing every Hindu (about 10 percent of the country's 75 million people), every one of the 75,000 non-Bengali Muslim mutineers they could catch, and many thousands of educated non-Bengali Muslims presumed to have been supporters of the rebellion: teachers, journalists, lawyers, students, left-wing political cadres. One of the victims, his body thrown in a brick-field, was my Dacca journalist friend Serajuddin Hussein, who had uncovered the child-kidnapping gang.

"The top officers," said Mascarenhas, "told me they were seeking a 'final solution.' I wrote down quotes all saying the same thing: 'We're determined to cleanse East Pakistan once and for all of the threat of secession even if it means killing two million and ruling the colony as a province for thirty years.'"

Was this man to be believed? Seven of the eight pressmen invited on the trip had written what they'd seen, and it was nothing like the story Mascarenhas was telling me. I asked him why he had not filed a contrary story for his own newspaper: "They wouldn't publish it, and they're under military censorship anyway." He said he'd had a crisis of conscience. "Either I had to write the full story of what I'd seen, or I would have to stop writing. I would never be able to write again with any integrity." But writing the full story, he said, was impossible anywhere in Pakistan; he'd been allowed to send us only a description of the Bengali atrocities. Even references to the danger of famine had been deleted by the censor. "That's why

I've come to London. I want the truth to come out, but I cannot tell it and stay in Pakistan."

Instinctively, I believed Mascarenhas. He did not ask for money and seemed propelled only by a decent Christian passion and immanent shame. Frank Giles, my deputy and the foreign editor, made the same judgment, while passing on the foreign department's caution that we had known Mascarenhas for only a short time. I was impressed and moved that the suffering he'd seen made him ready to sacrifice his life in Pakistan—to abandon all his possessions and his career and to uproot his wife and five children. His main anxiety was that he would first have to get his family out of Pakistan; nothing could be published before he did, nor could we make other inquiries that would point to him as the source.

I took the risk. I told him that subject to vetting and his own determination to see it through, we were ready to pay for the evacuation of his family, but I could not give him a job. He'd not felt it safe to write his story in Pakistan, so he'd memorized notes, then discarded them. His five-thousand-word report of ten days in hell was a detailed eyewitness account of unique precision and authority. It supplied the missing piece of the East Pakistani tragedy: why people were fleeing by the millions. He named names: Here was a pitifully skinny tailor, Abdul Bari, scared by the arrival of the army in his village, running away and brought back for execution. Mascarenhas, forsaking his neutrality, exclaimed to Major Rathore, "For God's sake don't shoot [him]." Bari was found to bear the marks of circumcision obligatory for a Muslim; he was not a Hindu to be shot out of hand and got away with a clubbing. But in army headquarters at Camilla, Mascarenhas saw truckloads of Hindus being brought into the compound and heard the screams as they were bludgeoned to death.

Everything Mascarenhas described from his travels throughout the province fitted the picture emerging like the big missing piece in the jigsaw of fragmented, unconfirmed accounts from refugees and missionaries. He'd arranged with his wife, Yvonne, that if I accepted his report, he would send a telegram to her saying "Ann's operation successful." That would be the signal for her to fly out to relatives in Rome, leaving everything behind. She received the telegram and escaped with the children, but on returning to Karachi, Mascarenhas himself was forbidden to leave; only one foreign trip a year was allowed. To escape, he took a flight to Peshawar, walked across the border to Afghanistan, and then sent our agreed-on message to a staffer's private address: "Export formalities completed. Shipment begins Monday."

I took the exceptional step of clearing the entire center spread of the June 13 edition. One page contained the single-word heading GENOCIDE in big black letters and an editorial titled "Stop the Killing."

Our breach in the curtain of silence was an international sensation. President Richard Nixon, wishing to retain Pakistan as an ally against the Soviets, ignored the genocide. "To all hands," he wrote in a memo, "don't squeeze Yayha [sic] at this time." But by the end of July more than five million refugees were in camps in India, and still more came. Years later, in Delhi, India's prime minister Indira Gandhi told me that the Mascarenhas report had shocked her deeply, setting her on a campaign of personal diplomacy in the European capitals and Moscow to prepare the ground for India's armed intervention.

The India-Pakistan War of 1971 ended with the creation of the state of Bangladesh. Mascarenhas had no political agenda; he was just a very good reporter doing an honest job. For that he earned the enmity of the Pakistani military and a telegram from the Black September group (which the following year murdered Israeli athletes at the Olympic Games): "You bastard, we'll get you, you went against your country." I put Mascarenhas on a retainer. He amply justified that and seven years later became a permanent member of the foreign staff with consequences I will relate in chapter 19.

The *Sunday Times* I inherited could fairly be described as a Conservative newspaper. Its editorials no longer slavishly echoed the party line as they had done in Lord Kemsley's time, but my conviction was that it should not have any party line at all.

I was well aware that even an independent, unpredictable editorial might have fewer readers than the TV guide, but the editorial page was where we could speak to the opinion formers and firmly establish the tone of the paper. The aspiration I brought to the page was that we should try to judge every issue on its merits, questioning the use of power by government, the courts, and corporations, but fairly, and always balancing respect for individual human dignity and freedom with the imperatives of order. That was easier said than done.

Editorials under Denis Hamilton had been written by William Rees-Mogg and Hugo Young, with some contributions by me. I straightaway replaced this troika with an editorial board of eight that I chaired for up to two hours every Friday morning. It included the foreign editor, the business editor, the religious affairs editor (who was also an expert on Northern Ireland), the labor editor, the political editor, a political columnist, and a former editor of the paper who had retired to academic life.

The group brought special knowledge to the arguments, which at times were strenuous. The most contentious issues, apart from the selectors' choice of fast bowlers for the cricket tests, were Britain's role in the European Union (go in and stay in); Pershing missiles from President Ronald Reagan (yes, please); what to do about overweening trade unions; the propriety of our disclosing cabinet discussions in extracts from the diaries of the late Richard Crossman; Enoch Powell's "rivers of blood" speech on immigration; internment and ill treatment of IRA suspects in Northern Ireland; and skirmishes between the editorial board's interventionists and the laissez-faire insurgents, all trying to find the way to the British economic miracle in the dark mazes of economic policy.

The inner strength of the editorials was that they were not spun off the top of the head. They drew on solid reporting, investigations we commissioned, seminars we organized on the economy and Northern Ireland, and reconstructions of major political events. Instead of the staple editorial bemoaning Britain's low levels of productivity, for instance, we asked the feature writer Stephen Fay to go into the factories and solve a mystery: why does a British welder in Ford's Dagenham plant produce 110 Cortina doors an hour when a worker in Germany, Belgium, or Spain, using the same machinery to the same management plan, produces 240 an hour? (Answer: labor-management trench wars.)

The tricky part of not having a party line came during general elections, when all newspapers conventionally endorse a party and the "red top" tabloids ramp up the propaganda war. Denis Hamilton had told me on appointment as editor, "You'll have total freedom from Roy [Thomson]—so long as you don't attack the Queen." That idea had never impinged on the fringe of my consciousness, but I tested the freedom of opinion in the October 1974 election.

Tory prime minister Edward Heath had called and narrowly lost an election in March based on the theme "Who governs Britain?" The coal miners, going slow in a wage dispute, had forced him into allowing commercial enterprises to use electricity only three days a week. We were certainly on his side in principle but were persuaded that Labour's "social contract" might end the warfare (it did only for a time) and that the Labour ministers—Roy Jenkins, James Callaghan, Anthony Crosland, Denis Healey, and Harold Lever—were a more impressive bunch.

Hamilton, reading my mind, had gently suggested that Lord Thomson would be displeased if the *Sunday Times* endorsed Labour. Thomson usually called me on a Saturday night to ask whether we'd yet overtaken the combined circulations of both opposition qualities (we were close). This Saturday I took the chance to mention that I was inclined to endorse Harold Wilson and Labour against Edward Heath and the Tories. Thomson made some shrewd comments on the two leaders and concluded, "Well, it's up to you, Harold. How's the run going?"

By 1979 the Labour Party was a shadow of its purposive self in the great days of Clement Attlee. It was frustrated by its ties to the trade unions and the public-sector unions in particular, which demanded more and more for less and less—their attitude toward the nobler ideals of socialism climaxing in the 1979 "winter of discontent" strikes, when they stopped cancer patients from going into hospitals for treatment.

Michael Jones, who'd become political editor, realized sooner than most that the Conservative leader Margaret Thatcher, waiting in the wings, could not be dismissed as a right-wing harridan whose middle-class accent and suburban outlook would doom the Tories to the wilderness. I agreed. When she was a backbencher, I happened to be at some stuffy City of London dinner, seated at the same table with a group of financiers. These were regarded as pillars of the Tory Party. She was not in the least in awe of their millions. I relished the way she assailed them for being more greedily interested in money manipulations than in investing in the business of manufacturing and managing the unions more effectively.

The decay of the Labour Party in the late 1970s was painful to report. It was infiltrated by Trotskyites creating cells in around one hundred moribund constituency parties, working by stealth to undermine any Labour man lacking a taste for a Soviet state. Jones tape-recorded one of the Trots in full flow promising "a civil war and the terrible death and destruction and bloodshed that would mean." It didn't seem much of a vote catcher to me. More serious were the strenuous efforts by left-wingers in the National Union of Journalists to impose a closed shop, meaning nobody could write for the paper unless he had a union card. Since a closed shop would hamper us in so many ways, I resisted the move, with support from Margaret Thatcher, while the Labour ministers I most respected sat on their hands. But as editors rallied, some moderates in the Labour Party dared put their heads over the parapet, and the legislation died.

All of us on the editorial board remained dismayed by two aspects of British life in the 1970s: the grip some recalcitrant unions had on the Labour Party and the stultifying secrecy in government. The great showdown was the diaries of Richard Crossman, a former Oxford don who was a member of the Labour cabinet from 1964 to 1970. The rule was that ministers had to wait thirty years to publish a documented account of their experiences, and if they or anyone else wanted to publish sooner, they had to accept official censorship on pain of a criminal prosecution under the Official Secrets Act.

Crossman's ambition was to illuminate how Britain was governed: he wanted to show that civil servants called the shots more often than the public realized, that cabinet meetings were not the decisive forum of popular imagination and MPs had little real power. He'd learned in September 1973, when I first invited him to lunch at the paper, that he had only six months to live. The priorities in his mind were such that his first action, even before he finalized his will, was to finish his two years of editing and give clear instructions to his executors completely to reject any censorship. He predicted there'd be pressure for suppression and truncation of his work, from both Whitehall (the civil service) and Westminster (the politicians), and he was right. After his death, his executors promised they'd not publish without official approval, and the government asked us to give the same promise.

Denis Hamilton was in favor of giving in, but when I assured him that we'd studied the law and prepared our case, he went along with the stratagem I devised. With only two or three on the staff in the know, I prepared an uncensored first serial and sent it to press on the night of Saturday, January 25, 1975. Roy Thomson and his son Kenneth happened to be paying a rare visit to my office that night. I told them that as soon as the prime minister's office got its hands on a copy, we expected a court order to stop the presses. Kenneth was worried; his father simply said, "You happy in your own mind, Harold?" I told him I was. There was no breach of national security. People should know how they were governed. "A good read, eh?" said the owner as he went happily off with his paper.

No court order reached us that night, but the noises from Whitehall were menacing. Every day we expected an injunction and had a bevy of lawyers on standby; I was advised we'd surely lose. Then Cabinet Secretary Sir John Hunt proposed to discuss what we might and might not publish in future extracts. I declined to meet with him. I sent two deputies because I couldn't trust myself to behave with the appropriate courtesy.

I wasn't aware of it at the time, but in 2005 Bernard Donoughue, who assisted the prime minister, published his *Downing*

Street Diary: With Harold Wilson in No. 10, which includes this entry on January 14, 1974, concerning a conversation he had with Attorney General Sam Silkin: "[Sam] had met Harold Evans for the first time the other evening at the American Ambassador's residence and thought he was a 'fanatic' for open government....Sam said, 'He's very tough. He said to me "It's granite against granite." He may be granite. I certainly am not.'" It didn't sound like me, but if I didn't recognize myself in this scene, I also didn't recognize the sheep the attorney general affected to be.

For nine weeks I played cat and mouse with the Cabinet Office, accepting some requests for deletions, but in the end we published 100,000 words and broke every restriction. The attorney general then shed his wool and bared his teeth. He sought a court order to force the publisher of Crossman's book to accept the censorship we'd defeated. I couldn't tolerate seeing the executors and publisher singled out in this way. Within days of the writ being served on them, we ran unpublished Crossman material and were duly joined in the legal action.

We lost in the High Court but won in the Court of Appeal. Soon afterward a committee of inquiry, to which I gave evidence, recommended that ministerial memoirs no longer be regulated by statute. The logjam had been broken, but an even fiercer contest with government was pending.

17

Death in Cairo

The only qualities essential for real success in journalism are ratlike cunning, a plausible manner, and a little literary ability.

I am quoting my colleague and friend Nick Tomalin, who protected himself—and entertained us—with irony and epigram. He concealed his real passion for a trade he described in a rare moment of self-revelation as "a noble, dignified and useful calling." In June 1973, before he took leave to write a history of the National Theatre, he cared enough to send me a critical appraisal of how far the *Sunday Times* and Britain's "so called quality press" were meeting the highest aspirations. Four months later, at the age of forty-one, he was dead on a battlefield.

Nick was immersed in reading the notations of Mozart and Beethoven, playing the oboe in one of the regular musical gatherings at his home, when we interrupted him on the early evening of Saturday, October 6, 1973. The Arab nations had chosen the holiest day in the Jewish calendar, Yom Kippur, to launch a war against Israel from Egypt and Syria.

Tomalin was a star writer, dazzling in his versatility but most renowned for his classic "The General Goes Zapping Charlie Cong," describing an afternoon in the gunship of a

Texas general who was proud to have killed more Vietcong than any of the troops he was commanding. We hesitated to break Nick's book sabbatical, but his closest friend and editor, Ron Hall, thought he would like a change. Typical of Tomalin—and indeed every reporter I ever asked to go into harm's way—he said yes right away. "Don't worry, it's safe enough," he told his wife, the literary biographer Claire Tomalin. "The Israelis take good care of the press."

In the first week he filed a briefing for a long Insight narrative on the war, without expecting a byline. On the Sunday he finagled his way into a closely guarded Tel Aviv hospital to bring a gift to his taxi driver, who'd broken a leg taking him to the Syrian front. He was visibly affected by the long lines of stretchers waiting for the wounded. The following week he headed back to the Golan Heights as the Israeli Army fought to retake sections they'd lost in last-ditch stands against massed Syrian armor. "I am only beta plus when it comes to courage," he remarked at a dinner on Tuesday, October 16, a self-deprecating acknowledgment of the apprehensions correspondents felt about the shifting, ill-defined front lines on the Golan.

Early Wednesday morning found him sharing a car with photographer Fred Ihrt of the German magazine *Stern* and their escort, Major Hannan Levy, necessary to get them through roadblocks and not accidentally run into fighting. They passed an Israeli artillery battery, whose soldiers gave Tomalin mail to post, then descended into a bleak, treeless valley to take pictures of clusters of wrecked tanks near a crossroads. Two hundred yards farther on they could see what looked like an abandoned bunker, and Tomalin drove them there. It was very quiet, no sign of life anywhere. In fact, without Major Levy realizing it, they'd come right up to the Israeli front line. Concealed from view inside the battered bunker were Israeli soldiers who'd endured accurate Syrian artillery fire for several days; by some fluke they failed to see the correspondents' car arriving and departing again.

Major Levy judged the risk of running over a land mine too great for Tomalin to drive them back the way they'd come by making a three-point turn against the bunker, so the major and Ihrt got out to direct Tomalin while he carefully reversed to the crossroads. He was turning there, with Ihrt and Levy some yards behind his car, when they heard a swooshing sound. Tomalin would have been unable to hear it above the car's engine. The noise was from an antitank missile being guided onto the target by a Syrian hidden in the hills. The missile flashed past Ihrt and Levy and blew up Tomalin's car with a direct hit, killing him instantly.

Moments later Syrian artillery shells were exploding around the crossroads. Ihrt and Levy were hiding in a rocky trench. A transporter arriving at the crossroads was hit by shellfire. Five survivors scrambled out, and Israeli commandos in the bunker were yelling for everyone to crawl back to shelter with them.

And then there was other movement, a man running down the hill into the valley floor and toward the killing ground at the crossroads. It was our Don McCullin, who'd arrived above the valley with photographer Frank Herrmann. At the top of a slope they'd been stopped from going further into danger by an Israeli tank commander. McCullin, one of the most celebrated war photographers—surviving under fire in Vietnam, Cambodia, Cyprus, Biafra, and Beirut—was impelled by a surge of emotion to argue the warning and hazard his life yet again, not for a picture but for a friend. He took off down the hill, running half a mile to the smoldering car in the valley, identified Nick, retrieved his broken glasses, saw there was nothing more he could do, and ran the half mile back, choked up, unable to speak.

The death of one journalist is only another digit in the

statistics of war, but I often wonder how much readers and viewers understand that the world-weary cynicism or vainglorious postures affected by the men and women who place themselves at risk conceal a deeply felt compulsion to "bear witness when others can't or won't." The phrase comes from the third of our reporters who lost his life, our adventurous and droll David Blundy, killed by a sniper's bullet in El Salvador in 1989 while attempting to file a last paragraph for the *Correspondent*.

The second at the *Sunday Times* did not die in war but in attempting to report peace. This was David Holden. We were plunged into many mysteries during my fourteen years as editor of the *Sunday Times*, but the most profound was right there in our own office. It turned on how we could answer two related questions: who assassinated Holden, our chief foreign correspondent, in Cairo in December 1977 and why? I've brooded over these questions for many years but have not written about the incident before. I'm writing about it now because what happened has only slowly and painfully become discernible through the shadows.

In 1977 Egyptian president Anwar Sadat made the momentous announcement that he would make an unprecedented trip to Jerusalem on November 19 to present an olive branch to Israel's parliament, the Knesset. He had ambitions to make peace with Israel on behalf of all the Arab nations he'd led to war in 1973 on Yom Kippur and also to finally resettle the Palestinians who'd lost their land. He was denounced as a traitor by the "rejectionist" states of Syria, Libya, Iraq, and South Yemen, as well as by all factions of the Palestine Liberation Organization (PLO). They arranged to meet for a "sorehead summit" in Tripoli in December as Israeli negotiators, and the world's press, arrived in Cairo.

David Holden, the foreign department's star on the Middle East, did not jump at our invitation to go to Cairo. He was writing a book on Saudi Arabia during the six-month leave of absence he took each year. We still hoped he might do it, but in the meantime Cal McCrystal, the foreign features editor, flew out on Friday, November 18.

At age fifty-three, Holden was a vastly experienced correspondent and broadcaster, one of the chroniclers of the end of Arabia as romance—"the immortal image of mystery," as he once put it. His career had spanned the end of an empire and the entrenchment of secular nationalism not yet threatened by Islamic fundamentalism. He shared the sense of style of his friend and *Times* colleague James (later Jan) Morris, who was to receive a last enigmatic message from him. Holden was a small, neat man—not a hair out of place—who somehow, with his bush jacket and debonair manner, still managed to bring a touch of Beau Geste to our newsroom hubbub. He evoked the dashing, young foreign correspondent of the *Times* of twenty years before, flourishing his British passport at the Yemeni border guard with a great curved dagger, seeking out the wicked old Imam Ahmed in his rocky fort, standing on a hilltop in Qartaba to observe rebel tribesmen around him opening furious fire on British soldiers across the valley. Nobody on either side hit anything, he reported back, except a goat.

Holden became intellectually absorbed by the politics of the transition as the former colonial states, through sacrifice and treachery, struggled to find their identity amid the eddies of big-power politics and the ascendancy of Israel. He moved easily through the Arab capitals; too easily, the Israelis thought. They regarded him as unduly sympathetic to the Arab cause. In 1967 he reported how the Israelis punished Palestinians for occasional sniping by demolishing Arab houses on the West Bank. He disliked what he saw, but he reported accurately and without histrionics. He did not hate Israel; the emotion was alien to his character. He wrote, also with amused tolerance, of "Arab venality, prejudice, opportunism and incompetence." If he hated anything, it was the categorization of countries as good or bad and the manipulation of people's minds.

He was a cultured man but unaffected, widely read in literature and history. He thought it impossible to write about the present without studying the past. Analysis rather than adventure became his strength. More information, he suggested, did not mean better information. The result of too much reporting was "to turn up the decibels on the Tower of Babel." He would not shun the ramparts, but he sought his realism elsewhere, in the nuances of his quiet meetings with diplomats and intelligence officers, academics and Arab editors.

Holden was not all that popular among a few of our harder reporters who'd covered the Six-Day War and the Yom Kippur War. On his infrequent stays in the office, they thought him rather detached, even condescending, remote from the graft of reporting. This was unfair. He was generous in providing contacts and very well aware of the dangers of practicing journalism in tense, exotic places. He'd been interned by the Egyptians during the Suez crisis. Reviewing a book by fellow foreign correspondent Noel Barber of the *Daily Mail*, he wrote, only a few months before his death, "Thank God I have never suffered either bullets or the steel tearing into my flesh, but I have felt the boots going in and I have heard the prison door close behind me, and I know how sickening the fear of such moments can be."

Holden stayed at home in London the weekend of November 19 and 20, but the following week he told us he would go to Egypt after all. We learned later that Anthony Austin, the articles editor of the *New York Times Magazine*, had reached him on "about the eighteenth" with a request to write an essay from

Egypt. Holden was, Austin recalls, "very enthusiastic," rather different from our impression. The *New York Times* asked the Egyptian embassy in Washington to telex Cairo to arrange an interview with President Sadat. The upshot of all this was that Holden arranged to go to Cairo, but first he would swing through Syria, Lebanon, Jordan, and the Israeli-occupied West Bank for us to test the strength of rejectionist feelings. He landed in Damascus on Sunday, November 27.

The plans for his murder had already been made.

Holden's first optimistic article, which we headed "Peace May Break Out After All," was filed from Amman on Saturday, December 3. The fire and fury of the rejectionist front had a "disintegrating quality," he said, adding laconically, "very Middle Eastern." His telex said that the following morning, Sunday, he would go to the simmering cauldron of the West Bank, where the Israelis were building settlements on conquered land. He wanted also to revisit Jerusalem, stay in the American Colony Hotel he loved in the Arab quarter, and then get back to Amman, crossing via the Allenby Bridge in good time to catch Royal Jordanian Airlines flight RJ 503 to Cairo on Tuesday evening, December 6.

Reviewing the news schedule on Wednesday, I asked what David proposed to write. Nobody had an answer. "We've not heard from him. Give him time to find his bearings." The foreign desk put in calls to Cairo's Meridien and Hilton hotels, where he had been tentatively booked. He'd not checked in, nor had he been in touch with the Reuters bureau, where he would normally establish communications. Nobody was alarmed. Communications in the Middle East were notoriously difficult; it was commonplace to have to wait up to eight hours to send a telex or get through on the telephone. "He'll pop up like a jack in a box, you just see."

By Thursday confidence had evaporated. We set off a full-scale search operation, calling British diplomats and fellow journalists he'd traveled with. Progressively through Friday we confirmed his departure from Jerusalem, his crossing of the Allenby Bridge, and his boarding of the plane to Cairo as planned. The foreign desk suggested an explanation for his silence. The Middle East was racked with cholera, his inoculations were out of date, and Egypt might have unceremoniously quarantined him for three or four hours in the isolation hut at the far end of the airport.

I saw the paper to press on Saturday, December 10, then around 10:00 p.m. went to spend the night at an office short-stay apartment near our building in Grays Inn Road. I was in the newsroom in five minutes when the dreaded call came. The British embassy, chasing the police, had heard that on Wednesday, December 7, the body of "an unknown European male" had been deposited in Cairo's Kasr el Ainy mortuary, the Dantean repository of all the city's accident victims. Bob Jobbins, the Cairo correspondent of the BBC, and Fuad al Gawhary, of Reuters, went to the mortuary and at once identified Holden. Jobbins was struck by the lack of any obvious injury, save a small exit wound in his chest. "An apparent execution," he presciently observed.

Holden's body had been found at 8:00 a.m. on Wednesday, nine hours after his 11:00 o'clock arrival in Cairo on Tuesday night. He lay on a sandy patch littered with old newspapers by the highway that ran beside the walls of Al-Azhar University. The area was unfrequented at night, but he was certain to be found as soon as day broke either by students, a passing motorist, or soldiers from a camp on the other side of the highway. He was on his back, his feet neatly together and parallel to the road, his arms folded across his chest in a mocking parody of repose. His expression was calm, his hair as sleek as ever, the only discordant note being the way the dark-rimmed spectacles he wore for driving were lodged crookedly over his eyebrows.

His shoes were clean, without a trace of the fine white dune dust to be expected if he'd walked or been walked to this spot.

There was nothing on his person or at the scene to indicate who he was. All marks that might suggest his identity or nationality had been removed, down to the maker's label inside his green-and-brown-check sports jacket. Someone had emptied the pockets. Only a few Jordanian coins remained untouched in one trouser pocket.

The manner of death was equally methodical. He had been shot once from behind by a short-cartridge nine-millimeter automatic, the classic shoulder-holster weapon. The range was so close, as little perhaps as two inches, that his jacket was scorched just below the left shoulder blade where the bullet had entered. The killer had aimed his gun downward as he fired so that the bullet would pierce David's heart. It left his chest with such little force that it was found in the folds of the polo-neck sweater he wore underneath his jacket.

The time of death was established at no earlier than 3:00 a.m., no later than 5:00 a.m. This meant that Holden had been alive for at least three hours after leaving the airport, possibly a captive all that time.

The shock at the *Sunday Times* was profound. David had not been as closely knitted into the competitive jousting and gossip of our office life as the convivially mischievous Nick Tomalin. But unlike Nick, who had bravely but knowingly exposed himself to risk in a battle zone, David had been reporting peace, and there seemed to be no explanation for his death. We all felt a passionate urgency to do everything we could to find one.

I called the Home Office and the commissioner of police at Scotland Yard. The commissioner assigned two of the most experienced homicide detectives, Chief Superintendent Ray

Small and Detective Inspector Tony Comben, to the case, but they had first to get permission to work on Egyptian soil, as well as in Syria and Israel. We wanted to move quickly while the trail was still warm. Within a few hours a team of six reporters was on the way to the Middle East: Insight editor John Barry and Cal McCrystal in Cairo, Paul Eddy and Peter Gillman in Amman, Tony Terry (a former British intelligence agent) in Jerusalem, and Helena Cobban in Beirut. Denis Hamilton discouraged this initiative; he was as distressed as any of us but believed we should leave inquiries to the police. I was well aware that our reporters could only ask questions. Despite a common exaggeration of the "powers of the press," we didn't have any of the means of coercion available to the Egyptian security services, nor did we have knowledge of Cairo's criminal networks. But we had our own contacts, we knew the way David worked, and our team was especially resourceful.

Barry and McCrystal visited the morgue, but their mission, apart from answering any questions the Egyptian police might have about Holden, was to track his movements in the last week of his life. They were to look for clues to some of the questions the murder posed: Who knew Holden was arriving on flight RJ 503? Who else was on the plane with him? Could he have spotted a terrorist on board? Was he seen leaving the airport with anyone and by anyone he knew? Was the motive for his killing something to do with his private life playing out as public drama? Or was the trigger his work? Nothing of his we had published could be regarded as offensive, although some Israeli commentators had condemned him for a *Sunday Times* Insight report on the ill treatment of Palestinian prisoners. The report, which had angered the Israeli government, was later confirmed by the U.S. State Department, but Holden had had nothing to do with the report, as we made clear, and those who compiled it were never molested in any way.

Was there something to suggest that Holden had been chosen as a high-profile target by Palestinian rejectionists or terrorists? Did they think that the death of a famous British correspondent on Egyptian soil would embarrass Sadat and demonstrate to the VIPs attending the peace talks that peacemakers were vulnerable? Was Egyptian security all that tight?

Who had Holden seen in his swing through the Middle East? Could one of the people he'd met there have learned the time of his flight to Cairo? Had he alarmed somebody, seeing them in a politically compromising situation? Or had he perhaps been asked to carry to Cairo a message or document too sensitive to relay over telex or telephone?

Most of Holden's last week alive, we found, was spent interviewing Arab leaders, including those of the PLO; the West Bank mayors of Bethlehem, Nablus, Hebron, and Ramallah; Arab journalists and academics; Syrian and Jordanian officials; and American, British, and Australian diplomats. We pressed them for recollections of what had transpired; none of them had any awareness of his travel plans, but we learned that on the West Bank he'd been given a petition to take to Cairo appealing to Sadat not to negotiate with Israel.

Three other curiosities emerged. We were intrigued by Kenizé Mourad, a thirty-year-old French reporter for *Nouvel Observateur*. She'd invited Holden for a drink on meeting him at the U.S. embassy in Damascus on November 30. In Amman on December 2 they spent time together, ending with dinner in the hotel coffee shop. The next day they went to a restaurant; at 11:00 p.m. she'd gone to his room for drinks and stayed until 1:00 a.m. She told us she angled to join him on his West Bank trip and he declined. On December 5, she said she'd gone back to Damascus, a curious move, we thought, for a journalist, since the Syrian leadership had flown to Libya for the

sorehead summit. At first, we wondered if she might have followed David for some reason, but she herself sought out Peter
Gillman and was very open about David being "a wonderful
man." I came to the view she was an eager younger journalist
admiring of an old Middle East hand.

We also came across two unexplained gaps in Holden's
schedule and discrepancies in two testimonies. In Jerusalem
on the afternoon of December 5, Holden had told Edward
Mortimer of the *Times*, with whom he'd been working, that
he was going alone for a walk in the Old City. The taxi driver
described to us how he'd dropped Holden at its main entrance,
the Damascus Gate. Later that day Holden had described to
Mortimer his long walk in detail, remarking how much the city
had changed in the ten years since his previous visit shortly
after the Six-Day War. But had he spent two and a half hours in
the Old City as he'd suggested? That certainly did not square
with the testimony of an academic at Birzeit University, who
told us the two of them had spent the afternoon in a village
twenty miles away where the Israelis had harassed the population. And what was the meaning of the postcard Holden had
sent from Jerusalem to his friend Jan Morris? He'd written only
nine words: "In the Old City, citadels still have their uses."

The next day, his last, produced a conflict about his time
in Amman. The manager of the Bisharat Travel Agency in the
lobby of the InterContinental Hotel said that he'd noticed Holden
around lunchtime, about the time he'd have arrived in Amman.
He saw him go into the hotel's coffee bar with two Americans,
writers and archaeologists John and Isobel Fistere.

Holden and the Fisteres had all been in Beirut for the first
two and a half years that Kim Philby had been there. (The gossip then was that the Fisteres were keeping an eye on Philby for
the CIA.) Ruth Holden told us of a dinner she and David had
given with Philby as a guest. In the files of the *Times* we found

that on January 8, 1957, Holden had recommended Philby, "the *Observer* man," to the paper's foreign desk as someone who could replace a departing *Times* stringer. The mere fact of knowing Philby at this time in Beirut was hardly significant, but what had surprised me, and others on the original Philby investigation in 1967, was that Holden had not come forward either during our inquiries or after publication.

The Fisteres gave a very different account of their meeting with David. They said they had seen him in the evening, not at lunchtime, and then for only about five minutes, when they'd exchanged a few words by the hotel press center. According to them, he had been "trying desperately to telex to the Cairo Hilton to confirm his reservation there." He'd looked "tired and dirty and worn-out from his travels, in a desperate hurry to catch his flight." The travel agent's account checked out better. No one in the press center or wire room could recall Holden trying to send any last-minute telexes, and if he had, he would have been given a telex from the Hilton that had been waiting for him since December 4. He'd caught his plane with time to spare.

I felt justified in sending the team to investigate when John Barry reported from Cairo that he was disturbed by the Egyptians' initial response to the murder. The death by shooting of an unknown European was a rare event. In thirty years only two foreigners had been murdered in Cairo, both victims of domestic disputes, and December 1977 was a period when Egypt was on the alert for the arrival of a thousand reporters from around the world, as well as the Israeli negotiators. Yet Barry said that the Egyptians had made zero effort to identify the body and had performed no proper autopsy. Had Holden not been identified when he was, he would have been buried in a common grave. The initial line of the Egyptians was that the murder was the work of foreign agents (Israelis heavily hinted), though the Egyptians were worried enough about the rejectionists to deport two hundred Palestinian militants.

The Scotland Yard detectives were still stuck in London, awaiting travel documents from the Egyptians, but the questions the *Sunday Times* team started asking galvanized the authorities. We were assured that President Sadat himself had ordered a massive investigation. Hundreds of police had been deployed. They had grilled the airport staff, and they said every one of the 128 passengers on the flight had been traced and questioned. None was suspected of terrorist links. They were mostly American tourists. Mrs. Willivene Bonnette from Clyde, Ohio, told us that Holden had had the aisle seat and would not get up to let her in, so she'd had to squeeze past. He'd been "sarcastic and kind of surly," telling her it was "absurd" she did not know what she was going to do and see in Cairo. He'd rebuffed conversation, saying only that he had been in Jerusalem "on business." His mood might be explained by a personal anxiety: the grumpy, experienced traveler wasn't sure he had a bed for the night. He had once held a booking at both the Hilton and the Meridien, but he had changed his itinerary so often that he had lost the Hilton booking and did not know that we had a room waiting for him at the Meridien. To arrive in Cairo late at night with no hotel booking was not an amusing prospect.

We tracked how he had on landing joined others in the wearisome scramble Egypt inflicted on its visitors. He'd changed traveler's checks for $200 at the National Bank of Europe, completed a form to obtain an entry visa, gone through passport control, and picked up his red Samsonite suitcase; he was alone at the time. That was the last fact about his life of which we could be certain. Presumably he'd walked through the "nothing to declare" channel in customs and through a pair of swinging doors into the open. A double line of crash barriers formed a channel into the foyer of the arrivals building. A police guard of a couple of armed men stood at the end to control the throngs. From that point to the curbside where the taxis waited was at most forty paces. In that distance Holden had disappeared.

There was one curious feature of his arrival, probably innocuous but possibly sinister. Everywhere on his journey he had entered his occupation as "journalist"; here he had written "writer." This meant he would avoid being drawn into the bureaucratic net the Egyptians had set up for the media arriving for the negotiations. "Journalists" and "press" were ushered into a pressroom next to the visa office and escorted directly to their hotels. It may have been a whim on his part, or someone might have advised him to do that so he would remain a free agent.

It was routine for the police at Cairo's airport to log every taxi picking up a fare. Hundreds of drivers were interviewed. The police concluded that Holden had not been picked up by one of the authorized, registered taxis. If there had been a line of people waiting, he might have veered right at the exit and gone to the parking lot to pick up one of the "pirate" taxis, but there had been plenty of regular taxis at the curb, and the cheaper gypsy cabs were uninvitingly small and uncomfortable. So perhaps someone had picked him up.

Near midnight on Thursday, December 15, four days after the identification of the body, John Barry was summoned to the police station at Dukki, a pleasant quarter of central Cairo on the west bank of the Nile. General Nabawi Ismail, soon to be minister of the interior, was there with a dozen beaming generals from security and criminal investigation, along with a battered white Fiat 128 without license plates that a Dukki resident had found abandoned. It had a tangle of wires below the dashboard, indicating that it had been started without an ignition key.

In the trunk they'd found Holden's red suitcase. In it were

427

two Christmas gifts for his wife and jumbled clothes. His Olivetti portable typewriter was in the car, too, along with unexposed rolls of film, a blue folder stuffed with a letter and notes for his book on Saudi Arabia, and the scattered pages of his loose-leaf contacts book built over three decades; the Egyptian section alone ran to eleven pages. Missing were his passport, traveler's checks, Olympus camera and lenses, exposed rolls of film, and any material he'd accumulated on his trip.

General Ismail and his team doubted the motive was robbery. Holden had been alive for at least three hours, possibly five, after leaving the airport; robbers would surely have taken what they could and fled. Nobody had attempted to cash the traveler's checks (and never did). Detectives had combed through the known outlets for stolen goods and found nothing of Holden's. Surveying the found and the lost, the general remarked, "It looks as if the killers knew what they were looking for."

Our immediate thought was that they had been looking for material for Holden's book on Saudi Arabia. We could not tell whether the pages of notes that remained were the total of his work. Kenize Mourad said he'd told her he'd uncovered corruption in high places, but he did not intend to include that in his book. There was a sufficient reason for this: the book was being written in cooperation with the Saudis, its viability resting in part on the hope that the government would buy ten thousand copies. And we found that the part of the manuscript that had been completed was a thorough historical survey—nothing more.

The police at first assumed that the Fiat was a gypsy cab that Holden had voluntarily taken from the airport. The team told me they were not convinced. It struck us all as highly unlikely that as experienced a traveler as Holden, tired from a day on the West Bank and Jordan, would consider the saving of a few

Egyptian pounds worth the discomfort and risk of a ride in a gypsy cab, especially if the driver had used the tangle of exposed wires to start the car.

Could he have been forced into the cab as in one of those scenes in the movies where the victim is told to keep quiet and keep moving with the prod of the abductor's concealed pistol in his back? It seemed implausible. The airport was teeming with people and security men. None of the travelers or officials noticed the slightest thing untoward in the exit area, nor inside the terminal before customs. To penetrate inside the terminal to identify Holden during the time he was exchanging money, collecting his visa, and picking up his suitcase would have required a pass to get through security. Conceivably he could have been met by an Egyptian security person, or someone posing as one, and invited to a waiting car, but by far the most likely scenario was that he was met outside the street barrier by one or more people who knew him and whom he knew he could trust.

If he'd been abducted in the white Fiat, it was not the car he died in. Just a little later, the police found another Fiat, abandoned at Tanta in the heart of the rich delta farmlands eighty miles north of Cairo. In the rear passenger compartment there was a cartridge case matching the fatal nine-millimeter bullet, and bloodstains were found between the front seats. The headrests on the passenger seat had been removed, making it easier for the gunman leaning forward from the rear seat to put a bullet through the heart. The headrest subsequently turned up in the first car used to capture Holden, the white Fiat dumped with the luggage at Dukki.

There were more provocative facts when we had the body flown home to London and a thorough autopsy indicated he had put up a fight, possibly that his wrists had been tied. The examination at London Hospital by Professor David (Taffy) Cameron noted: "Bruise on the principal knuckle of the left middle finger, to a lesser extent on the left little and ring fingers, and a bruise noted to front of the left wrist, approximately three inches above the wrist. There was also fingertip type bruising to the outside of the left arm above the elbow; and bruising was noted on the main knuckle of the right thumb." If Holden had indeed been in a struggle, we reasoned it was unlikely to have been at the airport, since this would have caused a commotion that someone would have been sure to notice. Our best guess was that he'd struggled on being transferred to the murder car. There, thinking they might have finished with him, he might have taken his front seat quietly enough.

Nearly a month later a third Fiat was found with documents from the murder car. All three had been entered in identical fashion by breaking open the quarter light, all driven by hot-wiring the ignition, two resprayed, one green, one red. The security police thought the logistics of the break-in, respraying, murder, transfer of the luggage, dumping of the body, and getaway would have required a team of eight people. Robbery having already been discounted, the police moved vaguely back to foreign agents, rejectionists now in the starring role. The theory gained momentum when they established that the owner of the first car found at Dukki was an activist, a twenty-two-year-old engineering student with a Jordanian passport (whose father had fled Jordan on terrorist charges). He was brought in for questioning as were the owners of the other two cars. All were cleared, we were told, but they did yield tantalizing information. The owner of the first car said he'd reported it stolen in the third week of November — around the time in New York and London Holden's trip to Cairo had been decided. The other two cars were stolen when Holden was set to move from Jerusalem to Cairo on December 6.

*   *   *

But who carried out what was clearly a well-planned abduction? Over the Christmas holiday, I had a conversation about the murder with a highly placed Egyptian visiting London. He told me the operation was carried out by Fatah hard-core rejectionists who would stop at nothing to sabotage Sadat's initiative. More he would not say. We followed up. Helena Cobban, our correspondent in Beirut, had a good working relationship with Fatah's chairman, Yasir Arafat. He promised he would investigate.

Barry and Peter Gillman were summoned to Beirut to hear the findings. "Finally, after much fussing about changing cars," said Barry, they were ushered into a heavily curtained room in a derelict building wrecked in the Lebanese civil war. In the gloom, a middle-aged man sat at a Victorian desk; they were given to understand he was head of Fatah intelligence. Nobody was identified, but Gillman had a tremor of recognition that one of the three men was Ali Hassan Salameh, believed by Israel to have organized the Munich Olympic kidnappings in 1972 (and subsequently blown up by the Israelis). Barry reported: "He said on the chairman's orders he'd made inquiries and could assure us that 'no arm of the resistance' had a hand in the murder. I asked if he could be so certain of "organs of resistance" other than Fatah, and he said no Palestinians would have wanted Holden dead. They had a policy, he said, of not killing journalists, and the *Sunday Times* had been regarded as "a friend to our cause" because it had published that report on the ill treatment of Palestinian prisoners.

I could not regard the interview as conclusive, but a strange development made Fatah's involvement seem less probable.

Even more alarming than the news from Cairo and the pathologist's report in London was the information Paul Eddy brought into my office in the second week of January 1978. He'd asked for a closed-door meeting, and in his cool, cryptic style he proceeded to astonish me. "The killers knew exactly when Holden would arrive in Cairo because they got the information from the horse's mouth—us." Eddy had discovered that copies of telexes between Holden and the foreign desk were missing. Hundreds of telexes were filed in an unmarked cupboard on the fifth floor, not far from my office. Nothing had been taken or disturbed except eight telexes relating solely to Holden's changing travel plans from the day he decided to go. With the messages stolen from the cupboard, the plotters would have been able to track him as he traveled from Damascus to Amman to Jerusalem, back to Amman, and finally to Cairo.

The foreign department was very well run. Could it not be, I suggested, that this was just a mix-up, an unusual act of carelessness? Eddy had another shock for me. The thefts were continuing in January. He had discovered the December thefts only in the course of looking for more recent messages and was stunned to find that some of these, too, had disappeared. Among them were travel plans and reports on the progress of the investigation from Barry and Gillman, who had returned to the Middle East in early January. One dispatch reported speculation that there might be a connection with the terrorist Abu Nidal's campaign to kill moderate Palestinians who favored a deal with Israel. (The key moderate PLO leader, Said Hammami, had been shot dead in London in January.)

Someone had gained access to the editorial floor, which was not too difficult in those days. There were at least six entrances to the deep, rambling building on Grays Inn Road. A thief could easily mingle with the hundreds of casual workers who were employed on Saturdays in the basement presses and in the huge distribution warehouse where copies came up from the basement for bundling and loading onto trucks. Those floors were removed from editorial on the fourth and fifth floors at the front of the building, but we were used to seeing new faces, assuming they belonged to casual messengers ferrying copy and coffee. Still, an interloper must have had intimate knowledge of the layout and procedures to find the foreign department cupboards when nobody was in the room. "Horrible thought," said Eddy. "We may have a spy on the staff."

On January 24 Eddy removed all material related to Holden from the foreign department and locked it in the Insight office, with only a single key to the filing cabinet. We did this very quietly, not wanting to alert a predator. The stealth was prudent, but it meant the wire room that transmitted and received messages did not know of the thefts from the foreign department— and we were not aware the wire room operators had developed a practice of keeping a second copy of messages sent to the foreign department. They impaled them on a spike in a corner of their office hidden away in a back corner of the building. It took the thief thirty-six hours to realize that fact and gain access to the wire room when it was unattended during the night of January 26–27. Every message was gone, including twenty-five related to the investigation. More surprisingly still, sometime between 8:00 a.m. and midday on January 27 Eddy asked the wire room for its copy of a telex from Gillman to Eddy announcing travel plans to the Middle East. It had vanished.

Again we sounded no alarm, but I spoke with Scotland Yard and the Foreign Office. Very soon after my call, our windows began to receive a thorough cleaning inside and out. The cleaners were from the Yard's C-10, known as "the watchers." Without detection they hid infrared cameras that would capture any intruder on tape. Eddy and the managing editor were the only staff people who knew.

We then baited the trap. Discussing the schedule in conference, the foreign editor said that Gillman and Eddy were reporting a breakthrough and that Eddy would travel to Cairo. "Tell them no heroics in any circumstances," I told the foreign editor. I wasn't really worried. Eddy, making sure he wasn't followed, did not go to the airport but instead headed for North Wales (only later did he tell me, by the oddest of coincidences, that he went to my very own Rhyl). The Eddy-Gillman plan was that from there he would contrive to send messages purportedly from Cairo, Beirut, and Jerusalem, while the Yard's concealed cameras kept watch on the foreign department and wire room.

Over ten days no interloper appeared on the recordings. Either the thefts were by someone on the staff pretending to go about their normal work, the trap had been rumbled, or the thief had concluded that we were not on a dangerously hot trail. I had got so jumpy, especially after the Philby cover-up, that I even began to think I'd made a mistake letting the Foreign Office know that we'd detected the thefts.

What if our own Secret Intelligence Service (MI6) had played some role in the abduction of Holden? What if we were caught in a convoluted winding down of the Philby betrayal? Hadn't I learned from Dorothy Sayers or Agatha Christie that it was a mistake to overlook the least probable suspect?

From these mad thoughts, I found comfort in the scientific principle of Occam's Razor, that the simplest explanation for which there is visible evidence should always be preferred. Certainly, the authorities in the shape of Scotland Yard could not have been more unstinting in their cooperation—while the Egyptians were not. Chief Superintendent Small and Detective Inspector Comben were still in London. Assurances that they would be welcomed were endlessly forthcoming. What was not were the necessary papers. In the end Comben and Small were never allowed to go to Cairo. This was baffling and infuriating because they were appalled by the Egyptian police work. An inquiry about whether fingerprints on the cars had led anywhere produced a negative—too many policemen had handled the vehicles. Instead of admitting the two Scotland Yard men, the

Egyptians sent a senior officer to London. He was as baffled as we were by the purpose of his visit. He thought he might perhaps go to Paris to interrogate Kenize Mourad. Unable to locate her, he settled for long shopping expeditions to Marks & Spencer.

It was all very frustrating, but the timing of the thefts of the cars and the raids on our office did put a different perspective on an early theory, first advanced in a Lebanese newspaper. Holden, it reported, had been mistaken for David Hirst, a *Guardian* correspondent. In Arabic the surnames Holden and Hirst have some differences, but they could have been mistaken for each other. Our access to the flight manifest found that European names were hopelessly garbled. A motive was apparent, too: revenge. Hirst had angered President Sadat and infuriated Mrs. Sadat by writing about corruption and high living. "True enough," Hirst affirmed. "Nine months before, four security men came to the Cosmopolitan Hotel. I was escorted out with a gun pointed literally at my head. On top of that I came back to Cairo deliberately when David Owen [foreign secretary] was visiting for two days, and Sadat was incensed that I'd been able to get a visa in Rome. They tried to stop me leaving on Owen's plane, but Robert Fisk [veteran Middle East correspondent] said he wouldn't leave without me."

It turned out that another journalist had been mistaken for Holden. In August and September of 1974 David *Halden,* on the staff of the Canadian Broadcasting Corporation (CBC), had flown into Cairo from London. He told us that on the first occasion, to his surprise, he'd been met in the arrivals hall. It was late at night, and he'd not told the Egyptians he was coming. Nonetheless, after he passed through visa and passport controls, he was approached by two men in somewhat scruffy clothes who said they were from the Cairo Press Center or the Ministry of Information (it wasn't clear) and had come to take him to his hotel. He presumed when they said "Mr. Holden" they were simply mispronouncing his name. They led him to the car park to the right of the exit area, where an old sedan was waiting, a driver already inside. Halden got in with the two officials. During the trip to central Cairo, they told Halden they'd managed to set up some of the interviews he'd asked for. Halden hadn't sought any (nor had "David Holden," so far as we could discover). He asked if they were sure they had the right man. The reply was "You are David Holden of the *Sunday Times*, are you not?"

They took him to his hotel.

Mistaken identity seemed the most plausible explanation to us for a time. Sadat was certainly very angry about David Hirst. One well-placed but very frightened informant confided that he knew Sadat had sent an assassination team to the airport and swore us to secrecy. The crucial difficulty was that David Holden was clearly the intended target. The thefts of the cars, and the thefts of telexes relating to Holden, could not be just a coincidence. And whoever held Holden for three hours would have known pretty soon that he was not David Hirst. Nor had Hirst signaled any intention to revisit Egypt.

We were forced back to the conclusion that the chesslike precision of the abduction, and the capacity to operate in both Cairo and London, must have been the work of an international organization with considerable facilities. The Egyptian police pressed this explanation on us, but we did not find it convincing for a number of reasons. To accept it one has to believe that an unknown group, undetected in Egypt's clampdown, arrests, and deportations, using methods without the slightest resemblance to other terrorist killings in the world, went to all this trouble to murder at random one of a thousand correspondents for indiscernible motives, remove his clothing labels for no apparent reason, and then disappear without a trace, leaving their achievement unclaimed.

There were other suspects who had the means to carry out assassinations and had been known to do so. Not excluding the

Egyptians themselves, there were the foreign intelligence agencies of Israel, the United States, Russia, and possibly even Britain; and the Saudis, we were told, handled this kind of work by contract with professionals. But what on earth could have been the motive? Was there an important clue in the killers so carefully leaving Holden where he would be found—a warning perhaps?

While the rest of the team resumed normal duties, I authorized Eddy and Gillman to continue the inquiry, as they much wished to do. To consider motives it was agreed we had to ask not just who killed David Holden but also who *was* David Holden? It's not an easily answered question about any of us; all identities are evanescent. His career was well documented— the son of an editor of the *Sunderland Echo,* educated at Quaker schools and Emmanuel College, Cambridge, a teacher of geography for three years (a job he said he "loathed"), a postgraduate student at Northwestern University in Illinois, a foreign correspondent for the *Times* and *Guardian.*

To go beyond these facts into the nuances and ambiguities of a personal life was a sensitive decision. I was troubled by the way newspapers and television in pursuit of the mass audience were intruding into private lives when there was not the slightest justification. People are entitled to personal privacy; it's integral to our sense of worth. Certainly there are gray areas where the private elides with the public; but photographers and reporters, and their editors, who regard private lives as fair game are for the most part taking the easy option. It is harder to expose the complications in a real public wrong than to make someone's life a misery (on the grounds of exposing hypocrisy, which is itself hypocrisy on stilts). Indeed, gratuitous breaches of privacy invite restrictive laws that protect the unscrupulous, who are all too ready to invoke the sanctity of private life while plundering the public purse. So I hesitated about authorizing our own inquiries into Holden's personal life; he was not around to defend himself.

Yet the thought persisted that the motivation for his murder might lie in some conjunction of the personal and public. I felt we owed it to him at least to explore the possibility of finding something relevant, without necessarily committing to publication what we found. This was how we ran into contention with the CIA and FBI.

The most important relationship Holden formed before his marriage was a passionate ten-year friendship with an older man he looked up to. He was a chameleon named Leo Silberman who'd been an ardent Communist, first anti-America then pro, a supporter of Israel on its founding and then vehemently anti-Zionist. The CIA came to suspect he was a British intelligence agent in Africa. Silberman had been born into a Jewish family in Germany in 1915. As Hitler rose to power, the family escaped to Britain, where Leo joined the Communist Party and, according to his brother Freddy, lost jobs because of his radical activities. He married a Communist Party secretary in Vienna in the 1930s—as Philby had done—and thus came to the attention of the FBI when he later applied for a visa to visit the United States and denied any Communist connections.

During the war Silberman studied and taught sociology at South African universities—brilliantly, according to his professors, although he gave himself the title "Doctor," to which he was not entitled. The British Colonial Office was impressed enough to provide him with a letter saying that he was working on their behalf in East Africa "in connection with social problems."

Silberman was loud and flamboyant, the opposite of Holden, but they were lovers, according to Silberman's brother Freddy. Holden and Silberman stayed close until Silberman's death in 1960, whereupon Holden married photojournalist Ruth Lynam, who worked for *Life* magazine.

We were surprised that Holden was bisexual. In letters to his brother Geoffrey and former teachers and in conversation,

Holden made constant references to girlfriends and sex. He wrote to Geoffrey about the lack of sexual opportunity in Arab countries, saying, "What is a fellow to do except turn queer?"

Holden's closeness to Silberman led us to ask the FBI first and then the CIA what they knew about him and Holden. An FBI official told us he had Holden's file in front of him. "It looks to me as if some of this stuff is classified," he said, adding that he'd have to ask if it could be released.

The agency dragged its feet so much that on August 15, 1978, I wrote to the FBI and the CIA asking them to meet their obligations under the Freedom of Information Act and retained the Washington law firm of Williams & Connolly to act for us. In the meantime we checked through unofficial sources and learned that within weeks of Holden being posted to Washington by the daily *Times* in 1954, he'd been observed meeting "a known Soviet bloc agent." None of us regarded this as conclusive, the FBI having an ability to put two and two together to make five. Many were the cases in the paranoid 1950s where individuals were put under surveillance for a chance meeting or an expression of social concern. A journalist might meet a Soviet agent, knowingly or not, in the course of his work. Indeed, I suppose I must have been observed meeting a number of Soviet bloc agents at diplomatic parties in London, and I'd stayed in Moscow (I'd been shown around by an Intourist guide so well indoctrinated that I quickly realized the truth was the exact opposite of what she told me).

The FBI declined to release any further details on the grounds of national security. The CIA was also less than forthcoming. Sixteen months after our requests under the Freedom of Information Act for documents concerning Holden and Silberman had produced no response, we filed a court action. John Barry met two CIA officials in Washington's Mayflower Hotel. They said the agency had nothing in its files about Holden and no knowledge of his murder. "I just don't believe you," said Barry. "You must have at least taken an interest in the murder of a British newsman at that critical time." They acknowledged the point, but all they had collected, they said, were rumors, no more, that he had been killed by European terrorists looking to use his press credentials somehow. They invited Barry to withdraw our suit; he didn't have to read my mind to decline their invitation.

In fact the CIA did have a file on Holden. The court action led to the agency providing us with an index, but not the contents, of thirty-three documents it had assembled, four of them about Holden and the rest about Silberman. We learned much later that this file on Silberman had been started when a CIA agent in East Africa had met him at a dinner party where Silberman, on the basis of the Colonial Office letter, had given the impression he was a British agent working under the cover of an American foundation grant. This annoyed the CIA man on two grounds: British intelligence had an "undeclared" operative in his area, and the agent was using an American foundation as cover, something American operatives were forbidden to do.

In addition to the thirty-three documents from its own files, the CIA said that it had turned over nineteen documents — one to the FBI, thirteen to the Department of State, four to the National Security Agency (NSA), and one to the International Communication Agency — to decide whether these could be disclosed to us. All of the agencies said no. The FBI affadavit of January 24, 1982, referred to "a very sensitive espionage investigation which still very much impacts national security."

We appealed these decisions; all our appeals were denied. Williams & Connolly advised that rather than go to trial, a slow and expensive business, we should propose that the documents be shown in camera to a judge who would rule whether the CIA was justified in maintaining secrecy. A judge supported the proposal; the CIA rejected it. Only when an appeals court ordered the agency to comply did it allow U.S.

District Court judge Maurice E. Lasker to see its "top secret" file in confidence.

He was swift. In a judgment on Februay 15, 1983, he ruled that disclosure would constitute a national security risk. The documents should not and would not be released.

What were we to make of this? A source told us that the CIA file simply recorded that Holden was "an informal contact," meaning that he would have met "second trade secretaries at U.S. embassies" on a fairly regular basis, presumably to exchange information. Holden was not, we were assured by this source, in the pay of or under the control of the CIA, but it would have been possible for "adverse parties" to mistakenly come to a more sinister conclusion.

But none of that could have persuaded a judge to seal the documents, certainly not the judge who'd forced the CIA to make them available for judicial inspection in the first place and was regarded as open-minded. We were compelled regretfully to consider whether David had in some way been involved in espionage for somebody and been killed for that reason, perhaps because he had been thought to be serving two masters. That would at least do something to explain why his body had been left as an obvious example of an intelligence killing. It was a warning: this is the price of betrayal.

But to go further into these shadows meant trying to identify which intelligence agency might have employed him in the first place as a straight agent, rather than a double agent, then which agency might have regarded this as treachery. Three agencies had surface plausibility: the CIA, Mossad (Israel's intelligence agency), and the KGB.

The CIA was the obvious first candidate, given its resistance to revealing its documents. There were incidents in David's life that lent some credence to the idea of a double identity on behalf of the CIA. Nobody could explain why he'd been arrested twice in Cuba and then deported. His flat repudiation of any CIA involvement in the bloody coup that had deposed Chile's President Allende in 1973 was also an uncharacteristic misjudgment and in uncharacteristically vehement language. And then there was the afternoon in Jerusalem when he had been in two places at once and sent that cryptic postcard to Jan Morris: "In the Old City, citadels still have their uses." The notion did occur to us that the uses of the "citadel" might have been sexual, not political. When I spoke to Morris, she discounted this and said that she had never had such a strange postcard from Holden on all his travels. Then we learned that the U.S. consulate in East Jerusalem maintained a clandestine meeting place in a small rented room in the Old City walls. We'd previously been assured that by agreement with Israel, there was no CIA post in Jerusalem, only in Tel Aviv. Moreover, we discovered that the academic at Birzeit University who'd said he'd been with Holden that afternoon was a paid agent of the CIA.

The theoretical case for Holden being a KGB agent was based on the one FBI sighting of him with a KGB operative and his association with Kim Philby. Holden might have been useful to the Soviets in gathering information and assessing trends: Moscow had been taken quite by surprise by Sadat's expulsion of the Soviet military in 1971.

And then there was Mossad, every paranoid's favorite mastermind. Rather than Holden being an agent for Mossad, however, the first hint the Egyptian police gave was that he'd been a Mossad victim. They said the bullet had been manufactured in Israel. Then they thought better of it and emphasized terrorists. But would Mossad have left such an obvious clue to a clandestine killing? Furthermore, unless one was totally cynical about the Sadat-Begin peace moves, would the Israelis have risked killing a reputable journalist who was writing favorably about the initiative they valued? I thought not. It was put to us more than once, however, that if Holden was an intelligence agent, Israel was the country he could best serve. It was the one nation denied access and travel throughout the Middle East. His journeys, though infrequent, gave him valuable insights into the options and intentions of Israel's immediate neighbors, including their military preparedness. Perhaps there was a wider audience for his observations than the regular readers of the *Sunday Times.*

Eddy and Gillman were still sporadically on the trail when I left the *Sunday Times* to edit the *Times* in 1981. They left, too, a few years later, but they kept in touch with people they were sure knew more than they'd admitted.

In 1988, after we had lost the Freedom of Information case, Gillman confided what we'd found to a senior U.S. contact in the Middle East, even allowing perusal of the Eddy-Gillman unpublished Insight notes. The contact, having digested all the information, said we had to consider the assassination in the context of the history of the CIA involvement in the Middle East.

In 1973, at the outbreak of the Yom Kippur War, American intelligence capability in Egypt had reached zero with the expulsion of the last active CIA agent, a woman who for cover worked for the splendidly named Société d'Alexandrie pour les Boissons Distillées et Vignobles de Gianaclis. After Egypt's defeat, the agency worked hard to reestablish itself in Egypt and to establish links with Egyptian intelligence. It was central to persuading Sadat to make his historic gesture. The peace negotiations, leading to the 1978 Camp David Accords, had gathered great impetus, with Egypt and Israel offered comparable aid packages from the Americans. Nothing was to be allowed to jeopardize the rapprochement.

The contact did not admit any direct knowledge of the murder but suggested that Holden would have been vulnerable if he had been suspected of playing a double game in any way that clouded the prospect of a peace agreement. The contact in

effect suggested we should not rule out a joint operation, instigated and encouraged by the CIA but carried out by the Egyptians. Why Holden should have been thought to be a hazard
could have been because he was believed to be a hostile intelligence agent or carrying messages from the rejectionist front.
I've mentioned he did have a petition for Sadat, given him on
the West Bank. The team had not regarded this as really significant because it was in mimeographed form (that is, typed on
a stencil and run off on a Cyclostyle machine) and by the time
Holden reached Cairo it had already been published by Edward
Mortimer in the *Times*. But the stakes were high in 1977.

It proved impossible to verify or even follow up this lead.
Eddy and Gillman had gone back to the source, but he'd left his
position, and over many months all efforts to find him in the
Middle East and the United States failed. Personally, I come reluc-
tantly to the view that there is force in the scenario, given the
unhelpfulness of both the Egyptians and the CIA. The nature of
the operation in Cairo certainly points to Egyptian involvement.
In the mists of circumstance and conjecture, we are left only
with the certainty that Holden was foully murdered and with
the aching suspicion that he died not for journalism but for some
secret cause he'd betrayed. Perhaps we should give him the benefit of the doubt, but no journalist should ever agree to act for an
intelligence agency, whatever the invocation or however strong
the desire to be patriotic. And we should relentlessly expose the
agencies and journalists who ever make that kind of arrangement. Vivid in my mind still is not only Philby passing himself
off as a correspondent in Beirut but our own Jon Swain, held captive by rebels in Eritrea and in mortal danger because of false
suspicions he might be a British spy. The credibility of journalism and the lives of individual correspondents are too valuable
ever to compromise.

18

Divided Loyalties

A newspaper is an argument on the way to a deadline. If there isn't any argument, there's not much of a newspaper. And the editor's decision is final. That sounds pretty straightforward, doesn't it?

The questions, in fact, are endless. Is this report credible and clear? Is it a rehash of the familiar, or does it advance public understanding? Does it justify its space and position in the paper? Is its readability derived from malice? Is it legally risky? Does it betray a source? Is it faithful to the paper's espoused values of seeking the truth fairly and without fear or favor?

When I was the editor of the *Sunday Times,* nothing impeded my ability to make those final decisions except my own ignorance or cowardice. But I did have to decide under the pressure of time, and paleontology kept me on the alert against procrastination—at least the paleontology from a fragment of verse by Bert Leston Taylor, a *Chicago Tribune* columnist, which I stuck in my science scrapbook at St. Mary's Road Central School:

> *Behold the mighty dinosaur*
> *Famous in prehistoric lore, . . .*
> *You will observe by these remains*

The creature had two sets of brains —
One in his head (the usual place),
The other in his spinal base.
Thus he could reason "A priori"
As well as "A posteriori."
If something slipped his forward mind
'Twas rescued by the one behind....
Thus he could think without congestion
Upon both sides of every question.
Oh, gaze upon this model beast;
Defunct ten million years at least.

In my own pondering I was not beholden to any party line. I did not have to duck a decision or temporize for fear of offending friends of the ownership or its commercial interests. When the Thomson Organization was bidding for licenses for North Sea oil exploration, I ran reports damaging to all the bidders, accompanied by an editorial saying the government's terms were too generous. To Thomson's abiding credit, I did not hear a word of complaint.

I published an Insight exposé of CIA involvement in elections in Guyana the day before a Thomson team met the government to sell a television station. The team was asked to leave the country forthwith. Something similar happened with a Thomson venture in South Africa. This sounds as if I was seeking confrontation with my own company. I wasn't. I knew about the oil licenses, but I didn't know about the activities in Guyana and South Africa. Even if I had, I'd not have felt obliged to delay or suppress the reports: independence from the commercial life of a very large conglomerate had been a condition of my appointment. It was honored both ways. Denis Hamilton, as editor in chief of Times Newspapers, did once have occasion to tell me he thought a business news report I'd published on the rigs of oil companies in the North Sea had been malicious and unfair, but that wasn't censorship; it was a professional judgment by a distinguished colleague—and he was, I fear, right. It was a reminder of the vigilance to be exercised in maintaining the paper's standards. The press is not noticeably different from other institutions in an aptitude for closing ranks under attack; it was important for me not to let our powerful esprit de corps protect errors.

Fact checking was the least of it. All the facts might check out, but that did not mean we should publish something as it stood. Have we put it in context? What are the foreseeable consequences of publication and nonpublication? With contentious material I made a point of testing it on various people, sometimes in groups but aware of the group dynamics. Is the one who has not joined in silent because he is scared to disagree with a peer group? I tried to cultivate suspicion of myself.

My emotional mind-set was publish-and-be-damned, so how could I offset that with reason? I was acutely aware that I was making decisions in a social context where my colleagues subconsciously shared my assumption that publication was good, suppression bad. There were issues where the weight of opinion in the office was so evenly balanced in logic and emotional force that I felt I had become the editor of a paper called the *Daily Dilemma*. The rise of full-scale terrorism in Northern Ireland from 1971 to 1997, for example, called for excruciatingly difficult judgments:

Should we talk with terrorists?

Should we seek and accept interviews if a condition is not to disclose the identity or whereabouts of someone wanted by the authorities?

If someone has information that could save lives, what measures are justified to get it out of him? Ill treatment, threats, cruelty, torture? If we know about these practices, should we keep quiet?

Should we suppress everything that might conceivably make things worse? (In the violently paranoid state of Northern Ireland, there was always the risk of endangering someone's life.)

Which comes first, truth or patriotism? As citizens protected by the rule of law in a civilized society, are editors obliged to be loyal first to the guardian state? (President John Kennedy, after the Bay of Pigs fiasco in 1961, put it this way: "Every newspaper now asks itself with respect to every story: 'Is it news?' All I suggest is that you add the question 'Is it in the interest of national security?' ")

The editor's decision was final at the *Sunday Times* in the sense that the story went to press as approved. But that was all that was final. A decision was never without repercussions. As I will relate, what I decided about Bloody Sunday in 1972, the British Army's shooting of thirteen unarmed civilians in Derry, was still being challenged thirty-five years later, not by the government but by one of our star reporters.

In the newsroom one summer Friday in 1975, the news editor, Magnus Linklater, seeking a decision, thrust folios of copy into my hand. "You'd better read this from Chris Ryder. I've questioned him. Pretty amazing." Ryder was our plump young staffer, a native of Belfast who still lived there. He was distinguished by his rolling Belfast accent and cheerful determination to ignore warnings from the extremists of both sides in the conflict. In the early days of the Troubles, the IRA, dedicated to achieving a socialist, united Ireland, were welcomed as defenders in the Catholic areas under siege by mobs. Since then, Ryder had reported, the Catholic community had become progressively more disillusioned by random violence and intimidation from the "Provos"—gunmen of the Provisional IRA, which had split from the "official" IRA.

Ryder had broken the news that three Provo women dressed as nuns had been foiled in attempting to rob a big Irish bank, but after the manager was contacted by the Provos at his home, the bank was so scared it paid up anyway. Ryder's latest report in my hand was that a number of Provos were operating "a new element in urban terrorism." It was said that behind the front of the Andersonstown Co-operative Society and Sinn Fein, the IRA's political organization, the Provos were using force and fraud to create monopolies for themselves in construction work and taxi services. It was also said that they had set up a chain of highly lucrative drinking clubs.

James Evans, our lawyer, came over to read the piece. It was, he said, actionable, but since the Provos were an illegal terrorist organization, it was highly unlikely the two men named would sue. One of them, however, was a spokesman for Sinn Fein, and if they did sue, we'd have to be sure we could prove that the link with the IRA/Sinn Fein was inextricable. The courts in Belfast, he said, were as exacting in their standards as mainland courts. "It's up to you, Harry."

That was the first decision: play it safe and not publish, or risk it? I risked it and published two reports by Ryder, in August 1975 and August 1976. A full six months passed after the second report before a libel claim was served on me on behalf of the two men we'd named, Seamus Loughran, the Sinn Fein spokesman, and Gerald Maguire, who'd been interned. They alleged that they'd been maliciously and falsely defamed.

At that time local and national news organizations were regularly settling libel claims by people who'd been interned and who'd argued that any mention of them in this context was defamation, since detention without trial was not a judicial process and no criminal conviction had resulted. So I had a second decision to make: should we do as everyone else did?

Making our defense more challenging was the fact that jurors and witnesses were regularly terrorized by the IRA. One witness to a terrorist attack had been killed. All criminal and terrorist cases had to be tried by a single judge and no jurors, so taking our case to a civil trial before a jury, where jurors and witnesses might be intimidated, was a big risk. Was it worth it? After all, the costs of paying compensation were likely to be much less than the monetary costs of fighting.

But that was only one consideration. It had been my decision to publish. Either I'd had confidence in the reporting then, or I hadn't. If I hadn't, I'd been reckless. If I had been satisfied with the reporting, I surely had a duty to stand by the reporter who'd exposed himself to harm. Retreat would be a rebuke to one reporter, but it would stain the integrity of all our reporting. Furthermore, it would be a betrayal of those who were willing to testify or sit as jurors. A newspaper operated under the assumption that the rule of law prevailed, how could we undermine it? "Accept service," I told our lawyers.

Two years later, in October 1979, I was summoned to appear in Belfast in the Queen's Bench Division of the High Court of Northern Ireland. I'd got used to testifying in the Law Courts in the Strand in years of suits brought against the *Sunday Times*. This experience was very different. It was nightmare time in the province. More than two hundred IRA prisoners were on "dirty protest," smearing excrement in their cells in a campaign to regain political status, culminating in hunger strikes. Killings had been trending down for years, but in March an IRA splinter group had blown up Airey Neave, the Conservative MP, as he drove out of the House of Commons parking yard. On the morning of August 27, the IRA had murdered Lord Mountbatten on a little fishing expedition in Sligo, and with him his fourteen-year-old grandson, a fifteen-year-old local boy, and eighty-four-year-old Lady Brabourne, the mother-in-law of his elder daughter. On the afternoon of the same day, two concealed bombs in the Northern Ireland town of Warrenpoint had killed eighteen men of the British Parachute Regiment, the Paras' biggest loss since their sacrifices holding the bridge at Arnhem in World War II and the single most disastrous day in Ireland for the security forces.

It was a bleak, wet morning with poor visibility when I was met at the airport by two detectives armed with pistols and small machine guns to ensure my safe passage to the fortified courthouse. By then nearly two thousand people had died in the Irish conflict; proportionate to population, it was as if a small English town the size of Darlington had been wiped off the map. The streets of terraced houses were like those I'd grown up among in Manchester—seeing a solitary man running along with a greyhound, I had a flash memory of my dad's betting days—but "desolation" was the adjective that came to mind. Even in the Blitz, our Newton Heath streets did not have the foreboding that hung like a fog over Belfast. Where there was color—murals and graffiti painted on a gable end—the message was death to the other side. Every pub in the city had armed guards, gunmen of both sides having found it tempting to burst open the doors and spray with automatic fire whoever was having a drink. There were distant sirens in the city, but the noises in my imagination were the wailing laments and rifle shots of the frequent funerals and the sobs of the widows.

No imagination was required to bend double in the car when one of my escorts shouted urgently, "Get down! Get down!" and the driver did a quick U-turn. They'd taken a wrong street. In parts of the city the security forces were afraid to run into a trap—a roadblock in front and sinister cars moving in behind. When we got safely to the fortified courthouse and awaited admission, my bodyguard was kind enough to point out two heavyset men on the other side of the anteroom. "They're the ones," he said, "we've got to watch for you."

It was good to find two experienced staffers, David Blundy and Phil Jacobson, waiting in the courthouse. They'd had armed escorts; so had the other witnesses. Ryder, who'd been assigned two bodyguards for the duration of the case, arrived in an armored Land Rover that varied its route every day. As the trial went on, this protection business became curiouser and curiouser. At one point a lookout for one of the more violent Loyalist groups was identified in the public gallery, so the police ended up having also to protect the IRA people who showed up in court.

I took the witness stand, facing a jury of three men and four women and Mr. Justice Murray. I had a hard time from Mr. Michael Lavery, QC, the lawyer for the men we'd written about. We were conducting a vendetta, weren't we? Didn't we realize these men were providing the community with jobs? Hadn't we invented the story about his clients because I was in business to sell newspapers and make money for myself or my employees? The *Belfast Telegraph* recorded:

> MR. LAVERY: Are you making the case that the plaintiffs
>   and the Andersonstown Co-operative were
>   committed or part of robbery, fraud and protection
>   rackets?
> MR. EVANS: Yes. I would stand by every word in the
>   two articles.

Ryder testified for three days, threatened with imprisonment for contempt of court if he refused to reveal all his sources. The lanky and deceptively casual young Blundy, who made us all laugh with his gift for puncturing egos (including mine), said under cross-examination that he had spoken with one of the defendants when writing earlier reports about the IRA, identifying him then only as "an IRA source." Lavery pounced. "So you're willing now to betray a source in the witness box?" Blundy replied that of course he'd protect the anonymity of a source, but if the source brought a lawsuit and threatened to kill one of his colleagues (Ryder), might not that immunity be regarded as questionable?

The lowering atmosphere of Belfast clearly affected me. That night, back in London, as I walked from the office toward an apartment, a man shuffled toward me and asked if I'd show him the way to Tottenham Court Road. His theatrical Irish accent made me jump out of my skin. In my nervy state I promptly told Scotland Yard. By morning I'd calmed down, but they insisted I go along to examine mug shots.

At the end of October the jury considered the evidence for a full day. When they returned in the afternoon, they accepted the thrust of our case, dismissing the libel claim by the two men. The Andersonstown Co-op was awarded a token £200 in damages. Loughran, who'd played a prominent part in the proceedings, was eventually relieved of his public duties as Sinn Fein spokesman on "health grounds." One of Ryder's sources clarified this: "It is more to do with his future health than his present health."

The whole experience reinforced my admiration for our reporters and my sadness at the miserable existence of the people of Northern Ireland. Life there was indeed brutish and nasty. The paramilitaries, but especially the IRA, didn't much care who died. The IRA incinerated men and women at a happy get-together of the Irish Collie Club at La Mon House hotel in Castlereagh. The Protestant "Shankill Butchers" gang abducted and slaughtered thirty Catholics picked at random. Loyalist members of the outlawed Ulster Volunteer

Force ambushed and machine-gunned the popular Showband Miami, a mix of Catholics and Protestants, returning to Belfast from a Catholic dance hall gig. In the Poppy Day massacre in the county town of Enniskillen, an IRA splinter group detonated a bomb to kill people gathered at the cenotaph to remember the victims of all conflicts. And then the bombings came to London by the score, and the terrorists almost succeeded in murdering Mrs. Thatcher.

Was it an inevitable tragedy? I've endlessly run over in my mind how journalism might have made a difference after I took over the paper in 1967.

Ever since the British government had partitioned Ireland in 1921, separating an independent republic of twenty-six counties in the south from a province of six British counties in the north, the people had been divided by faith and by flag as much as Shiites and Sunnis are divided by religion in Iraq. In the northern six counties, loosely called Ulster, Protestants formed more than half the 1.5 million population; the south was primarily Catholic. The Protestant Unionists ("Orangemen," after their protector King William, the Prince of Orange, who won the Battle of the Boyne in 1690) passionately saw themselves as British, loyal to the Crown and the Union Jack. They had their own Parliament in Stormont, just outside Belfast, with a large degree of self-rule, and they used it to suppress the Catholic minority, keeping them out of the best jobs and housing.

The Protestants were fearful of losing their cultural and political identity as their majority shrank against the faster-growing Catholic population. They were always on the alert for subversion by IRA revolutionaries, who regarded themselves as the true repository of the Irish identity and sought to force the six counties into the republic to the south (though that, too, they regarded as an illegitimate state). The Republican dream of "one Ireland" under the tricolor flag was anathema to the Loyalists. They saw no poetry in the terrible beauty attending the violent birth of the republic. The modern reality of "one Ireland" for them was a poor, priest-ridden state where Gaelic was the national language, where they would lose the benefits of the British welfare state, and where their personal liberties would be compromised by the ordinances of the Catholic Church. The "special position" of the church was then enshrined in the constitution, and it aggressively used its muscle. Divorce and the sale of contraceptives were banned; it had a plan for maternity care thrown out in 1951; and it controlled the schools, though the Irish constitution did not recognize an endowed religion. So the Protestant ("Proud to be Prod") Unionists rigged elections, controlled the Royal Ulster Constabulary (RUC), and could call up B Special police reservists; they maintained an omnipresent threat of violence.

The Catholics developed a burning sense of resentment and frustration, but in turn they fueled Protestant anxieties by insisting on their separate church schools and by continuing to talk of a united Ireland. "They are no more willing to renounce it," wrote our political insider John Whale, "than they are to renounce transubstantiation." The constitution of the Republic of Ireland, moreover, still laid claim to the whole of the island.

But the Irish calamity is not unique. The seeds of disaster there were comparable to those sown in Iraq, comparable to the earlier desegregation traumas in the American Deep South, comparable to the illusions of the Vietnam War. I have insufficient reserves of humility to suppress the conviction I developed from observing all of these episodes: you can't beat honest firsthand newspaper reporting—when you can get it. Governments may know a lot more about our lives than we care to contemplate, but frequently they know less about the world than we presume. They are captive to preconceptions, electoral concerns, political affiliations, special interests, and bureaucratic hierarchies that filter "truth." Government just cannot govern well without reliable independent reporting and criticism. No intelligence system, no bureaucracy, can offer the information provided by free competitive reporting; the cleverest agents of the secret police state are inferior to the plodding reporter of the democracy.

Yet to Fleet Street, for many years, and its readers, Ulster was about as riveting as Ecuador. I'd taken no interest in the province myself when I edited the *Northern Echo;* in fact I knew next to nothing about it. But the *Sunday Times* was very early in its reporting. In July 1966, when I'd just become managing editor, I read an item on the news schedule: Queen's visit to Belfast. The reporter assigned the story was Belfast-born Cal McCrystal, who'd been beaten up covering the riots of October 1964, when a Belfast Republican club provocatively displayed the Irish tricolor. His feature before the Queen's visit was so much more than the usual backgrounder. It was an authoritative depiction of the Protestant majority's crude apparatus of political and religious oppression, concluding that the real dilemma for the new Labour prime minister, Harold Wilson, was whether to allow the province to work out its own bizarre destiny or to "use reserve power to bring elementary social justice to Ulster." McCrystal's report appeared as the paper's main feature that week, and we headlined it "John Bull's Political Slum." In his study *How the Troubles Came to Northern Ireland,* the academic Peter Rose describes it as "one of the very few [articles] in the British press during those years which made a genuine attempt to warn mainland Britain of the consequences of the failure to tackle Catholic grievance."

I expected the feature would produce the same reaction in the Labour government as it had in me: a sense that political reforms were urgently necessary. That didn't happen. The report was immediately denounced by Stormont as biased. This made more impression on the British government than our firsthand report because the government took its advice from the Home Office in London—which in turn took its cue from Stormont.

The pity was that this would have been a perfect time for the British government to change direction. The hard men of the IRA trying to blast the two Irelands into one had faded; their successors, a left-wing leadership based in Dublin, opted for Marxist pamphlets and polemics rather than bombs; their agitation for a socialist workers' state implicitly recognized partition. (Happily, this lost them the Irish American funding that had always fomented violence.) The old IRA hands in the north grumbled at this pacifism, but leadership had moved principally to a new generation of educated middle-class Catholics who wanted to "take the gun out of Irish politics." They were building a civil rights movement that did not insist on Irish unification and was open to Protestants as well as Catholics. Even those of them who still yearned for a united Ireland, the constitutional nationalists, nonetheless set out to win social justice within by peaceful persuasion modeled on Martin Luther King Jr.'s movement rather than by the violent overthrow of the state. The Marxist-Leninist Roy Johnston, a computer specialist, described it as trying "to salvage the basic Enlightenment republican democratic tradition from various overlays of Catholic nationalism, Fenian conspiracies and quasi-Stalinist centralism which have infested it."

This new peaceful coalition was the window of opportunity. In Britain the Conservative—and Unionist—government had given way to Labour; there was a reformist prime minister in Belfast, Terence O'Neill; and the Catholic leaders best represented by Derry's visionary John Hume had entirely reasonable demands ("one man, one vote, removal of gerrymandered boundaries, allocation of public housing on a points system based on need"). Editorially we supported O'Neill in his struggle with the Loyalist hard-liners, and Hume in his antipathy to the bigotry of Catholic Ireland, but I wonder how much difference we could have made with an even more insistent advocacy coupled with extended reporting of the kind I'd urged on the American press over treatment of blacks in the South.

As excuse I can offer only that Northern Ireland was just one developing story. We had to rush teams to cover Israel's Six-Day War; we had reporters in the midst of America's never-ending war in Vietnam, in the civil war in Nigeria, and in the anarchy of the Congo. The Soviet Union and China were on the brink of a border war, and the world's first democracy (Greece) was taken over by a bunch of fascist colonels. But these excuses are not good enough; news is always at an editor's throat.

At the end of 1968, after violent clashes between the RUC and civil rights marchers, I committed the paper to continuously serious coverage and comment. To monitor what was happening on the streets, I set up a rolling team from the newsroom (two weeks in Northern Ireland, one week off), including Chris Ryder. The reporter I recruited from the *Sunday Telegraph* was its chief investigator, Tony Geraghty, who'd also made a name for himself on the *Guardian*. He could not be typecast by either side. He was a British subject and an Irish citizen—and a veteran of the British Paras (later to serve as a military liaison officer with U.S. forces in the Gulf War).

Geraghty's reporting convinced him that the "pusillanimous" Labour government was making a tragic error acquiescing in Stormont's approval of provocative Loyalist marches in the summer of 1969. He was right. The more radical elements of the civil rights movement, students in the People's

Democracy organization, staged a countermarch in Derry; police brutally attacked it in the "battle of the Bogside"; that was followed by wolf packs of Catholic youths in the Falls Road area of Belfast hurling rocks and petrol bombs at police stations. The RUC drove armored cars into the rioters, and Protestant mobs firebombed Catholic homes. Ten civilians and four members of the RUC were killed by gunfire on the night of August 14–15. The uneasy but viable mixture of peace and gradual reform was broken—for good as it turned out. When the Labour government in August 1969 sent in the British Army, it would have been wiser at the same time to impose direct rule from Westminster instead of assigning the soldiers to work as common-law constables with the distrusted RUC. The ancient fault lines remained.

Still, there was no excuse for the gross misrepresentation in the American media of the peacekeepers as an invading "army of occupation." Caught up in retailing Irish tribal folklore, local TV stations and the more thoughtless popular press in the United States quite ignored that Ulster was constitutionally as much a part of Britain as Massachusetts was of the United States; that without the army, there'd be civil war in which the Catholics would suffer most; and that the democratic Republic of Ireland also regarded the IRA as a menace to its own democracy.

We were supportive of the soldiers caught between the warring parties, but our reporting soon ran into difficulties with the army. Geraghty happened to be on the spot when a brigadier jumped out of a staff car and strode alone and unescorted into the "no-go," dangerously tense Falls Road, where Catholics, surrounded by sixty thousand Loyalists, had barricaded themselves against the mobs. "I'm going to see Father Murphy and these Citizens Defense chappies," said the brigadier. He had no objection to Geraghty tagging along to the door of the vestry of St. Peter's Pro-Cathedral.

He would say nothing when he came out. But among the emerging Central Citizens' Defense Committee (CCDC) delegates, Geraghty recognized a thirty-seven-year-old leader of the IRA. "We've got this back-of-the-envelope treaty with the British military," he told Geraghty, showing him the understanding that the CCDC would open the no-go areas within three days in return for the army and local vigilantes looking after security, to the exclusion of the distrusted RUC.

It was news, but it was news that could have consequences. It showed that the army was not one-sided and was engaged in some creative diplomacy. But the Loyalists might hate the army talking to anyone with an IRA connection. They did, and they rioted in protest. The day after Geraghty's report, our sister paper, the *Times*, briefed by Whitehall, knocked the report: "Diligent investigations by journalists have failed to reveal that the IRA is now nothing much more than a slogan out of the past." An army brigadier, who was director of public relations, came to my office to protest Geraghty's "inventive" reporting. This puzzled Geraghty. He wrote to me, "How could what every dog in the street in Belfast knows is true be denied in London 90 minutes' air time away?"

The answer was that Belfast was then three hundred years away from the Ministry of Defense and the army. They were just not as well informed as the reporter. General Ian Freeland, who'd been in charge for only two months and was incensed by our report, told me later, "The army did not know at that stage who were current members of the IRA." They should have if police and army intelligence had done their homework. The Northern Ireland Civil Rights Association opened its doors to anyone. Five days after I had received the indignant brigadier, the Scottish judge Lord Cameron issued his report on the disturbances of the previous autumn. It confirmed Geraghty's assertion that the IRA had become involved in the uneasy coalition forming the civil rights movement, though not yet as gunmen. They had virtually no firearms then to defend the Catholic areas, and some graffiti around the Lower Falls (Belfast) read, IRA = I RAN AWAY. What had been political heresy on Sunday morning was by Friday a judicially tested fact. Cameron's report, reinforcing Geraghty's observations, should have led to the army and police recognizing the weakness of their intelligence and alerted everyone to the terrible risk that defense of the Catholic ghettos against mobs might fall to a resurgent IRA. The old equation loomed: fear – trust = IRA.

The dragon's teeth had been sown. Irish American dollars, denied to the constitutional nationalists, started to flow again to bombers and shooters. As an admirer of American journalism, I was appalled by reports of what was being broadcast on local television in Boston, New York, Chicago, and Philadelphia. They gave time to IRA front men who, without challenge, retailed propaganda and incitement: "Violence is the only thing left"; "The only language the British ever understand is violence"; "The only real criminals in this matter are the English." In the bars along Second Avenue in New York, near the *Sunday Times* office at Forty-second Street, I was often approached to give dollars to Noraid, a charity supposedly raising money for the families of slain or imprisoned IRA men. The *Chicago Tribune* nailed the lie: "The money bankrolls the sort of sub-humans who can pack six-inch nails around a bomb and put it in a place where women and children and tourists will gather."

American audiences generally were given no idea of the truth that the killing was mainly the work of paramilitaries, not the security forces. Those who died as a result of army and police intervention in the end numbered fewer than half those killed by nationalist and Loyalist paramilitaries. And of the paramilitaries, the well-armed IRA killed at twice the rate of the Loyalists.

Seeing how distorted reporting could become stiffened my resolve to keep ours as straight as possible. In view of the risks our reporters were accepting, I became resentful of the reactions of Westminster and Whitehall, which became more dismissive when Edward Heath and the Conservatives assumed power in June 1970. Basically, they consistently ignored our warnings of increased disenchantment within the Catholic community, creating a sea in which guerrillas could swim. Junior army officers in Belfast did soon realize that military actions had to accompany notable visible improvements for the community, but their superiors saw it as their mission to submit upbeat reports to London. It was what London preferred to hear. (It was exactly the same scenario in the United States in the Iraq War starting in 2003. Not wanting to be accused of defeatism, the senior commanders shrank from conveying bad news to Washington as the insurgency gained strength, and Vice President Dick Cheney accused reporters who conveyed the unpalatable truth of being lazy, foolish, cowardly, and unpatriotic.)

All the reporting we were doing was fair and firsthand, and television's brave cameramen were routinely bringing the horrors into people's living rooms. But it was not possible to understand Northern Ireland by focusing on the latest outrage. Violence is always sure of space on television and in the press. Political change, being more subtle and dull, is frequently neglected until it explodes into "inexplicable" violence.

So we devoted hours to discussing what constructive suggestions we might offer on the editorial page, based on the reporting. I was responsible for both factual reporting and the opinion pages—the common British practice—and I think that helped to ground our comment in the day-to-day reality.

I can see the virtues of the American practice of separating opinion (church) from news (state), but that can dilute the concentrated focus necessary to make people sit up. I felt keenly when I was traveling in the Deep South in the 1950s that the separation of church and state preserved editorial chastity at the cost of delaying reform. That was similarly true of the Iraq misadventure in 2003. The U.S. momentum to invade was very strong. There was no shortage of critical comment. What was lacking, to induce second thoughts, was investigative reporting independent of government sourcing, coupled with argument based on it.

There were degrees of emphasis among the group in the weekly editorial conference deciding the paper's policy, but we agreed on pressing reforms harder while recognizing that the Provos were using the civil rights movement as a cover for armed insurrection, just as the Loyalists had long feared. We assailed Democratic congressmen in the States for appearing to condone violence. We were unsparing in our criticism of a major speech by Senator Edward Kennedy drawing a parallel between Ulster and Vietnam: "It is in most respects of a piece with the rest of his ill-researched, ill-considered and destructive speech."

The most important consequence of tying the reporting to comment was our conviction that London would make a catastrophic mistake if it started interning people without trial but simply on suspicion. In March 1971 we wrote of internment: "If it were done on a large enough scale, it would arouse more Catholic viciousness than it allayed." And again in August 1971: "Internment would worsen the army's chief problem which is mass Catholic hostility. More important it would carry the security forces beyond the frontier of what is ordinarily considered tolerable in a civilized society."

Again the government listened to Stormont, cheered on

by sections of the press in Britain which had frankly done far less on-the-ground reporting than we had. We were the only newspaper to come out against internment when 342 Catholic men were "lifted" in very rough raids on houses on August 9, 1971. In various political encounters I was made to feel as if I was letting "our" side down, but internment was a disaster. Intelligence had been too weak to capture the most dangerous men. By November, 908 were imprisoned, many guilty of nothing more than where they lived; by December, 1,576 had been arrested and 934 released. Not a single Protestant gunman was arrested. The key Provos escaped. The advocates of internment defended it as an emergency measure following the deaths of twenty-seven people in the first eight months of 1971. It had the opposite effect. In the remaining four months, there were forty-one deaths in the defense forces and seventy-three among civilians.

It was no pleasure at all to be vindicated. It was infuriating. The British public was bewildered. It was like coming into a movie halfway through. How had we got in this mess in the first place? Nothing made sense. How could Catholic women who'd come out to give cups of tea to soldiers in 1969 now be on the streets shouting to the tune of "Auld Lang Syne": "Go home, you bums, go home." How did the army's velvet glove develop, in August 1971, into the iron fist of internment?

Bruce Page made the inspired suggestion that Insight should be given the time and resources to answer such questions in a major historical reconstruction that he'd supervise. The editor of Insight was now John Barry, the disconcertingly omniscient baby-faced reporter who'd done well on Philby. He took himself off to the province with four reporters, and for three months they engaged in questioning hundreds: Catholics and Protestants, householders and activists, generals and IRA leaders, politicians and civil servants, newspaper observers in Belfast and Dublin, lawyers and academics. "It's proving absurdly easy to get everyone to talk," Barry wrote to me. "I think it's because nobody has ever asked them to look back."

Insight's report tracked the origins of the crisis from partition to the first stirrings of the civil rights protests and the rebirth of the IRA. I thought I was up to speed on Northern Ireland, but I read the report in November 1971 with a mounting sense of despair. It was like rewinding the tape on a terrible crime. It had been an unjust society, but here, step by step, one could see how it had begun to descend into murderous chaos and why — and why the reel was still unwinding. It was heartbreaking to read of the misperceptions, peaceful protest failing and degenerating, old prejudices hardening, and decent people feeling betrayed, so that the men with guns came to prevail. And, perhaps most astonishing, despite the conflict having already lasted so many years, until now nobody had bothered to look so closely.

The real base of terrorism was profound Catholic distress and disillusion in the north and tenacious Catholic sympathy in the south. "Too long a sacrifice," wrote W. B. Yeats, "can make a stone of the heart." The people who had refused to face Catholic disillusionment had only prolonged the agony. The Insight portrait of a disintegrating society, on the contrary, demonstrated that the province faced a crisis of governance, for which no solution could emerge from military action, despite all the innumerable acts of forbearance and individual courage by the soldiers assigned to policing.

Initially I'd cleared two full pages for the report. I was on the stone as trays of type arrived a couple of hours before press time. It was clear there was too much metal, not enough space — and still more copy was landing on the printers' desks. It was all too good to cut, so I cleared still more space. And still the copy arrived. I gambled on writing an announcement that this was a two-part series. It transpired that we had more than enough to justify that impromptu decision. The team's fifty thousand words, carefully edited by Ron Hall and Bruce Page, ended up taking eight pages in the end, the longest home news report the paper had ever published. I ran "Perspective on Ulster" over two weeks in November 1971. It wasn't just long, however, one of those lengthy newspaper series we mentally categorize as too important to read. Thanks to the skill of the writers and editors, it was a gripping fast-paced narrative, taking the reader into the minds of the competing characters, all acting for what they thought was best and together producing the worst. There was an enormous and typically extreme reaction to the series. The newspaper was lauded by some for "saving Ireland from insanity," when in reality we could only hope to accelerate a political debate. Alternatively, the reporters were accused of "doing the dirty work of the IRA."

There was an important news fallout from our commitment to writing an accelerated history of the Troubles. Insight's researcher in Belfast, Parin Janmohamed, made the rounds of Catholic lawyers who were trying to represent some of the men seized in the internment swoops by the police and the army. The lawyers were too frightened to say much, but in one of the offices she induced a lawyer to give her half a dozen handwritten statements smuggled out of prison. They laid out what internees alleged had happened to them—and what they'd heard had happened to a few others who'd undergone interrogation. They told of men being hooded, made to stand spread-eagled for hours, and deprived of sleep, but those allegations were secondhand. Parin went back to Insight's hotel headquarters and said, "You won't believe what I've just been told."

In one of the statements, a Michael Farrell said that he'd been forced to run barefoot over a path of broken bricks at Girdwood Barracks. John Barry hired a small plane to fly over Girdwood to see if the basic layout corresponded with the statements. It did, but the brick path story didn't sound credible. Insight asked the army. A path of broken bricks? Nonsense, Irish fantasies. Barry talked his way into a Catholic convent that had grounds adjoining the barracks. He climbed a tree to see over the wall, and there, facing him, was a long path of broken bricks, the foundations for a concrete path still to be laid. He remembers clambering down, thinking, *Oh, my God, what's been going on here?*

The brick path meant Farrell's allegation might be true, but it was not solid evidence. Insight was also told of Alsatians snapping at the internees as they ran over the bricks. Farrell's statement said one of the dogs had taken a bite out of the sleeve of his jacket. Barry persuaded Farrell's wife to get the jacket from prison. One sleeve was ripped. He took it to a forensic chemist. Yes, he reported, there were saliva stains around the tear, though he could not be absolutely sure they were canine.

Barry was convinced that Farrell was telling the truth, but he was baffled by talk of hooding, wall-standing, and deprivation of sleep at somewhere other than Girdwood. All the internees had been roughly treated, but if the statements were to be believed, a few had been subjected to five techniques that became known collectively as highly coercive interrogation (HCI): covering the prisoner's head with an opaque cloth with no ventilation (hooding); standing a prisoner against a wall with hands raised and fingertips to the wall for as long as twenty hours; subjecting him to high-pitched white noise; depriving him of all but bread and water; and denying him sleep. These practices fell under the Geneva convention barring cruel and degrading treatment. But how to check the facts? Nobody on the team had ever heard of anything like this before. In December 1971 the IRA had staged a great jamboree of a press conference in Dublin, putting on show three IRA men who'd escaped from jail in Ulster and claimed they'd been tortured with lighted cigarettes and needles in their bones. Photographs of a defaced leg and thigh flashed across the nation's television screens. The *Guardian* put the story on the front page: "IRA Men Show Wounds."

These horrific details of burning and bone scraping were, as it happens, without foundation. On December 19, 1971, Lewis Chester, a former Insight editor, documented the falsity of it all in a way that was far more effective than official denials. He was able to do it because for some time he'd been investigating on the ground and by hard work had uncovered some apparently genuine allegations of ill treatment under interrogation. Comparing these earlier statements and doctors' reports on the IRA men, Chester demonstrated that they were fiction.

How did the media correct their earlier acceptance of the false story? They didn't. Of the papers that had splashed the original story (the *Times* had played it much more cautiously), only the *Guardian* bothered to print a follow-up, but it was brief and relegated to the back page. And on television, there was silence.

We'd learned to be very wary of IRA propaganda, but Barry thought of someone who could help us on the nature of the techniques allegedly being used. A Special Air Service (SAS) man we'll call "Mike" had spent hours telling Insight of his adventures in Yemen in 1965 running a joint British-Israeli-Saudi covert campaign against Egyptian troops intervening in a civil war there. Suddenly one day Mike got scared that he might be identified and asked Insight to drop the story. We did. Back in London the reporters took him to their favorite watering hole. He felt he owed them one, so in the tiny glassed-in private cubicle that was Insight's home away from home, he said, "Sure, those are the interrogation techniques taught at Ashford." He was referring to the army intelligence headquarters. Mike opened up a bit more to say that the five techniques were designed to induce sensory deprivation and disorientation and that Ulster had been the first time they had been tried for real.

No one with a grievance understates it, but it seemed inconceivable that the wretched internees could have known enough to concoct all this. The question then was whether the interrogations had taken place somewhere Insight could check. The victims had been taken in helicopters to, they were told, the mainland. We wasted a week checking bases in Britain before one of the reporters thought to make friends with an air traffic controller who said yes, the helicopters had indeed flown eastward but had then turned round and landed back in Northern Ireland at Palace Barracks, Holywood. But how could we substantiate this? Another reporter pointed out that "Mike" had said that doctors had to be present at these interrogations. Those doctors must have been housed somewhere, so Insight combed the hotels around the base. Bingo—they found a chatty receptionist who told them about all those nice young British military medical men who'd stayed there for two weeks at just the right time. The reporter checked their names and dates against the register. They tallied.

At about the same time, and quite independently, John Whale came back to the office from Stormont to write a report incorporating a remark by a Northern Ireland cabinet minister: "Those fellows are singing like birds." We now had a multiplicity of statements of ill treatment tending to corroborate one another in substance and yet made by men who could not have coordinated their stories. I was satisfied that it all added up to a prima facie case.

The next question was whether there was a public interest argument against publication. I knew it would embroil the paper in still more controversy between those who would declare it unthinkable that Britain would do such a thing and those who felt that nothing was too harsh for the internees. I shared the repugnance for the unspeakable cruelties of the IRA. It was an evil enemy, its methods indiscriminately vicious; there could be nothing but admiration for the skill and bravery of the soldiers who disarmed its murderous explosive devices.

But further questions were raised. The first was that there was far from any certainty that the men in prison were members of the IRA or guilty of any crime. The second was that our report might incite retaliation. But one of the philosophies I'd absorbed at Durham was Immanuel Kant's maxim that one should act as if the principle one follows will become a universal law, and it seemed to me that condoning cruelty by keeping silent, for whatever reason, was immoral. So I ran the Insight-Whale report on the front page, albeit with a modest single-column headline: "How Ulster Internees Are Made to Talk."

The paper was roundly condemned. A group of Tory MPs came promptly and angrily to my office to say that what I'd done was close to treason. The establishment mouthpiece, the *Sunday Telegraph,* which had done very little frontline reporting, fueled the fire. *Crossbow,* the influential magazine of the Bow Group of younger Conservatives, caricatured me sinisterly reading a copy of the *Sunday Times* with the headline "Army Atrocity." When I entered a reception one evening, the dilatory home secretary, Reginald Maudling, called out, "Here comes the editor of the IRA Gazette."

This was rich. We'd been unequivocal in expressing our detestation; we'd exposed the IRA torture story the rest of the press had retailed and never corrected; we'd prominently featured the sufferings of the victims of bomb outrages; we'd depicted the lonely ordeals of army patrols; and later at Scotland Yard's request we would faithfully refrain from reporting that police had quietly flooded an area of London in the hope of trapping a murderous IRA gang (which they did in the Balcombe Street siege of December 1975, despite the stupidity of the *London Evening News* in revealing the tactic).

To his credit, Prime Minister Edward Heath appointed Sir Edmund Compton to head a three-man inquiry into our report. We were vindicated. Subsequently, on a complaint by the Irish republic, the European Court of Human Rights found that the five techniques used were "cruel, inhuman and degrading." It stopped short of calling them torture, but the British government gave a "solemn undertaking" that they would never be used again.

In five years of reporting on Ulster, everyone involved had been acutely sensitive that we'd gone out on a limb with every story that did not regurgitate the conventional wisdom. What happened on Bloody Sunday, January 30, 1972, tested our rigor.

In the space of twenty minutes in Derry, a company of British paratroopers fired 107 high-velocity bullets that killed thirteen unarmed Catholics and wounded fourteen. The event was immediately overlaid by propaganda from both sides and as I write this thirty-seven years later still has not been resolved. The Catholic Bogsiders were outraged. They believed a massacre had been planned. The British government immediately insisted that the paratroopers, sent into the confines of the Bogside to arrest violent rioters, had been fired on by IRA gunmen—and fired on first.

What I did about Bloody Sunday provoked controversy. Put baldly, why did the editor of the *Sunday Times* fail to publish an immediate article on the shootings? Was it because the writers "diverged from the official line," as the *London Review of Books* phrased it in 2002? Did I "help to bury the evidence" that the British Army planned the shootings in advance, as alleged in 1998 by James Ledbetter, the media editor of New York's *Village Voice*?

It is true I did not publish an article by two *Sunday Times* reporters. But the reasons were different from the ones implied. Immediately when I heard of the shootings that Sunday evening, I reached out for John Barry, the chief author of our reconstruction "Perspective on Ulster." He was on a bizarre vacation, riding a camel deep in the Sahara with a Tunisian antidrug patrol. I got hold of Murray Sayle and asked him to leave at once for Derry. He'd covered Northern Ireland extensively beginning in 1965, and in particular the riots that had followed the internments in August 1971. The newsroom assigned two reporters, Derek Humphry and Peter Pringle, who had contacts in Derry.

Sayle is a legend in journalism, a buccaneering figure with a large broken nose acquired in graduating from the University of Sydney and a spellbinding retailer of stories. His hilarious novel *A Crooked Sixpence* recounts his time as a vice reporter on the newspaper *People* exposing prostitution rings. (Editor Sam Campbell's instructions to him were to get offered sex for money, watch the lady disrobe, and then "make an excuse and leave.") Murray had climbed Everest, sailed the Atlantic, and reported on the battlegrounds of Vietnam, Israel, Czechoslovakia, Jordan (Black September), and Bangladesh, as well as anywhere else a foreign editor needed a reporter who could talk his way through a brick wall.

Sayle was the principal author of the report that reached our office on Thursday afternoon. Before I had a chance to read it, both Page and Hall, the responsible editors, came in to see me, very concerned. "You can't publish Murray's piece." Page was especially vehement. He said the report implied that an unprovoked army had plotted the killings, a serious charge that should be published only if it could be substantiated. Murray's piece did not do that: the sources had not been subjected to enough scrutiny, the findings were inconsistent, and there were too many "internal contradictions." It just did not meet the *Sunday Times* standards. It would damage the credibility we'd established by years of work on Ulster.

I said I'd read the piece and consider all their objections. It is generally a good rule not to let head office second-guess the reporter in the field, and Sayle was revered. But Page and Hall had investigated and edited many contentious stories. They were zealous guardians of the paper's unimpeachable investigative record, neither beholden to the other. The idea that either of them would toe an official line was ludicrous; even the idea of an official line would have roused their hostility.

Reading the piece, I noted that it said right at the start that not a single shot had been fired at the soldiers, then quoted one "official" IRA man as saying that he did fire a shot from a .38 pistol and later quoted Gilles Peress, the French photographer who brought back devastating pictures, as saying that he'd heard two pistol shots near Free Derry Corner when there were no paratroopers there. That inconsistency wasn't confronted. I could see that Sayle and the other reporters had worked hard. The background to the tragedy was lucid. The tumultuous scene in Derry was vividly depicted, assisted by a graphic street map of the action. But the piece bothered me. As research, it was probably as good a job as anyone could have done in four days, but it went beyond quoting witnesses. It tried to reconstruct a chaotic, fast-moving scene, reconcile conflicting stories, and reach conclusions. That is an objective I would normally applaud, but there just wasn't enough evidence in the copy I had. My immediate thought then was whether we could preserve the bones of the reporting while editing for internal consistency and dismantling the shaky hypothesis.

At this point James Evans made an appearance. He'd come in to support Hall and Page. The evidence wasn't good enough.

Before I had time to invite Page and Hall to discuss what we might do, the news desk rang to say the government had appointed Lord Widgery to conduct a judicial inquiry into the shootings. This complicated matters. The whole question of whether or not to publish would be moot if the Lord Chief Justice decided that the rule of contempt of court applied. I telephoned the Lord Chief Justice. I thought he might not take the call—judges in Britain don't jump to the telephone for pressmen—but I got through. I said we had done a great deal of interviewing and proposed to publish this Sunday. We also had compelling photographs. I told him I presumed contempt would not apply since nobody had yet been accused.

It would be an exaggeration to say he was aghast, but he made it very clear that it would be "unhelpful" to publish anything and yes, he would apply the rules of contempt. I told him that we would continue our own vigorous inquiries. I withheld the article, but that week I took the chance of publishing the shocking photographs by Gilles Peress of unarmed men being shot.

At the same time, I gave the Sayle article back to Hall and Page, asked them to make use of the reporting, and told them to get John Barry off his camel and without delay set in train our own parallel inquiry.

"It was the most intense period of our lives," remembers Barry. Insight interviewed 250 witnesses, including members of the IRA. It was essential to hear what they had to say. (Those who assert you can never "talk to the enemy" are more interested in party-line propaganda than the difficult business of weighing evidence.)

Eleven weeks after the shootings, Lord Chief Justice Widgery issued his report. He judged that some of the paratroopers' firing had "bordered on the reckless," but he basically exonerated the army of any premeditated plot to kill. But the report was not the whitewash the members of the Catholic community immediately said it was. Widgery confirmed that one of the thirteen people killed was an unarmed man shot from behind while crawling; that four other men had been killed by shots fired without justification; that an excessive number of rounds had been fired; that grounds for identifying targets had been nebulous; and that all this had happened in a battalion operation not clearly authorized at the brigade level, discountenanced by the police, and launched at a time when other methods of keeping order were succeeding.

Insight was ready. The team amassed five hundred photographs from all the sources that day, laboriously sorted these into sequence, and from them identified the witnesses who had been present at critical moments. Then they tracked those people down and questioned them. They tried, above all, not to create a seamless narrative where there wasn't one. Nobody in the army or media and no one among the rioters and politicians could offer a single perspective on a kaleidoscope of events in which a second of life was an eternity. We laid out what we knew and made clear what we didn't know.

Insight's four-page report was critical of Widgery. It differed from him on his certainty that the army fired only in response to IRA fire. Nor did it endorse the Sayle report's conclusion that the IRA did not fire a single shot: "The Provisionals admit to a burst of machine gun fire from the area of the Bogside Inn which is recorded by the army after 4:40 p.m. It is certain that they fired other shots. Eyewitness accounts vary from none to 50, but witnesses agree all shots were fired after 4:30 p.m. [when the army ceased fire]." The vicious assaults of the more reckless rioters were acknowledged, but the government was faulted for authorizing an attempt to scoop them up using heavily armed paratroopers. Militarily it went wrong in plan and operation; soldiers did shoot at obviously unarmed civilians. We added the rider that although the paratroopers' response was out of proportion, the vast majority of the 100-odd soldiers involved, under great stress, did not fire, let alone kill anyone.

Through the intervening years, Bloody Sunday has remained an open wound. Murray Sayle, the author of the first report I did not publish, recognized the legal constraints: "I don't blame Harold Evans for not publishing the story," he said in 1992 and reiterated in a series of e-mail exchanges with Peter Baker, editor of *Fingerpost*, a small magazine covering the Catholic community in Derry. But then he added: "Publication might have saved much subsequent bloodshed."

Here I part company with him. The original article, with its errors and shaky imputations, would likely have inflamed feelings even more rather than do justice to all those involved. The complexity of Bloody Sunday is exemplified by the fact that the tribunal of inquiry set up by Prime Minister Tony Blair in 1998 had by 2007 taken evidence under oath from nine hundred people, including the prime minister at the time, Edward Heath, and by 2009 it still had not reported its conclusions.

Among the Insight group, John Barry, Phil Jacobson, and Peter Pringle were summoned to testify, as were Sayle, Geraghty, and I. The entire Insight archive on Bloody Sunday, including the reporters' notebooks, Murray Sayle's rejected article, and my memos, was surrendered by the *Sunday Times* management after I left the paper, surprisingly without consulting any of us as to the sensitivity of our sources. Pringle and Jacobson have written a well-researched book on the event called *Those Are Real Bullets: Bloody Sunday, Derry, 1972.*

I remain proud of our Northern Ireland reporting. We revised the reconstruction we'd published as "Perspective on Ulster," corrected the inevitable errors, and extended the reports to create a paperback book called simply *Ulster.* It was a best seller, which paid for the costs of the reporting. The main characters were portrayed as more than cardboard cut-outs, but succinctly, and each step on the road to Armageddon was made maddeningly explicable from that point of view. It was one of the most important initiatives I ever undertook and made me more ambitious for that kind of contextual journalism. It was possible only because of the skill and integrity of reporters willing to suborn their individual egos in a collective effort to present as truthful an accounting as they could, informed by narrative energy but untainted by preconception.

After Bloody Sunday the British government, the British Army, the Provisional IRA, and certain Protestant activists continued to take positions they considered points of principle. Through the Anglo-Irish Agreement of 1985 and the Good Friday Agreement of 1998, the rate of wanton death declined, albeit with appalling slowness. Only the IRA was not willing to stop the killing. Yet gradually after the event, intelligence successes on the IRA side could be seen to fall farther and farther behind those on the British side. John Hume worked hard to convince Gerry Adams, leader of Sinn Fein, that there was yet another historic opportunity for peace. In 2001, on a side wind after the destruction of the World Trade Center, American money for IRA causes ceased to flow. Another change in 2007 at last brought Adams and Protestant firebrand Ian Paisley into a kind of fellowship. Sadly, such understanding as the two aging enemies have pieced together could have been enjoyed at any time in the previous thirty-five years following the 1973 power-sharing agreement between the British and Irish governments and Northern Ireland's leaders.

Millions of words have been written about the Troubles. But just four lines of verse by the poet Desmond Egan linger in my mind as an expression of the tragic futility of all the hate:

Two wee girls
Were playing tig near a car
How many counties would you say
Are worth their scattered fingers?

19

Showdowns

I opened the description of my *Sunday Times* years with a photograph on my wall of an editorial conference. I close with another photograph that is seared in my consciousness: a tall, lightly bearded man in a Russian fur hat, deeply tanned in midwinter and wearing dark sunglasses. He is exultantly linking arms with a group of others outside our offices in Grays Inn Road in 1980; in the foreground is a coffin labeled "Sunday Times."

The man is Reg Brady, a Communist "father of a chapel" in the pressroom. In more prosaic terminology, that's a trade union shop steward, in his case representing the unskilled casual workers who helped man the basement presses. His key achievement was to shut down the *Sunday Times* for a year and pave the way for its acquisition by Rupert Murdoch. It was not a solo effort. Brady's fellow unionist, a clerk who was father of the clerical chapel, Barry Fitzpatrick, had a hand in it. So did the members of another union chapel, the one hundred or so machine minders in the pressroom, led by a squat, tight-lipped man called Vic Dunn. They were perpetually fighting with Brady's members about pay differentials and who did what, arguments that held up the production of the newspaper. These issues were of graver concern than the multitude of demarcation sensitivities I found on first arriving in Fleet Street: every item of work was the jealous preserve of one union or another. If I hung up a picture myself or unplugged a reading light or changed a lightbulb at my desk, I was told the heavens would fall. "Good job nobody saw you do that," said the administrative editor. "We might have had a work stoppage."

Was he serious? I'd laughed like everyone else at the farcical antics of Peter Sellers playing Fred Kite the shop steward in the vintage 1959 film comedy *I'm All Right Jack,* but I'd thought of it as confined to the Midlands car industry. Our relatively small workplace at the *Northern Echo* in Darlington had been nothing like that, apart from the traditional prohibition against a journalist touching metal type in the composing room. At the *Sunday Times* I was pleased to see one secretary reading a novel every day; I simply preferred that she did it on her own time rather than at the office. But every effort to move this studiously redundant young woman to work at a typewriter or telephone or at some other similar hard labor was thwarted by Barry Fitzpatrick.

It would be fair to say that we in management did not excel in combating guerrilla warfare at the *Sunday Times.* It escalated in the economic squalls of the 1970s, and we became increasingly exasperated. The ink had not dried on an agreement before one or another of the chapels broke it. Fitzpatrick, a fluent, nattily dressed clerk in his thirties, had a genius for ceaseless negotiation stimulated by management's expectation that his members would do the work (mainly processing advertising) they were paid for. Brady had a different wheeze. He and his union had insisted that 540 casual workers were needed to get the paper out. Only half of the 540 actually bothered to show up on Saturdays, but 540 pay packets were collected and signed for every week. Managements throughout

Fleet Street closed a blind eye to this "old Spanish custom," but our labor editor, Eric Jacobs, was willing to venture into the basement with a flashlight. He discovered the Spanish custom was so ingrained that, apparently, we had working in the *Sunday Times* pressroom none other than M. Mouse of Sunset Boulevard, Hollywood, and one week, big joke, another payment receipt bore the name of Marmaduke Hussey, the managing director of Times Newspapers. We were tensed for a work stoppage when I published this story, but Brady and his merry men took it in their stride, sure that nobody would dare to do anything about it. They reckoned without the tax authorities, who were gratifyingly curious and eventually reported that in Fleet Street more than 50 percent of the pay packets in newspaper pressrooms were drawn under fraudulently false names.

Corruption was only one goblin in the serial nightmare. Wildcat stoppages and downright sabotage were others. If management demurred over some new demand, the pressroom chapels damaged production. A favorite dodge was to accidentally leave chewing gum on a reel of newsprint in the presses, producing a paper break and time-consuming rethreading. Thousands of copies failed to reach readers. In 1978 the *Sunday Times* was unable to fulfill all the orders on nine occasions; we became known as the "Sunday Sometimes." The importance of the news itself made no difference. In July 1977 the European Court of Human Rights report included as an appendix our long-suppressed draft article on the thalidomide children. The news came from Strasbourg at noon on a Friday. The machine minders chose this occasion of editorial triumph to ramp up a running battle with management on the number of minders required to print the seventy-two-page paper. The run began with only eight of the nine presses we needed. We fell badly behind.

It was line management's job to sort this out. I was on the

phone every hour. They answered my entreaties by trying again to reason with the minders. I didn't want to complicate the lives of these duty managers—the stress of dealing with the crews undoubtedly led to the heart attack that felled the director in charge—but at midnight, as anger overtook despair, I invited Vic Dunn and his chapel committee to my office to tell them of the significance of the thalidomide article. I beseeched them to work normally and argue later. I thought I'd persuaded them that extortion on this issue would be immoral. Their response was to persist with their inaction, losing us 540,000 copies, one-third of the print order.

Much more comprehensible to me than such bloody-mindedness in pressroom and clerical was a collision of tradition and technology. I was an early addict of the computer. In 1954, as a science reporter, I was introduced at Britain's National Physical Laboratory to code breaker Alan Turing's Automatic Computing Engine (ACE), which, wondrously then, informed the waiting world what day my birthday would fall on twenty-five years hence. I must have been one of the first British newsmen to use a touch screen and video stylus, in 1973, on a visit to innovators along Boston's Route 128. I came back from a tour of American newspapers to enthuse about the computer for typesetting and research.

Management didn't need any urging to adopt computer-assisted typesetting. A number of my editorial colleagues did. They were troubled that acceptance of the computer would take jobs away from the Linotype operators who set the type for stories and classified advertising and the "comps" who assembled the type into pages. We had long bonded with these men. Some of them joined editorial for a friendly postproduction beer at the Blue Lion. The comps were cheerful allies in the weekly battle to meet press times, loyal to the paper, and disgusted by the anarchy in the pressroom. Having helped to set my RAF newspaper by hand and written about typography, I was still in love with the whole romance of hot metal and appreciated the pleasure they took in their jealous craftsmanship. I spoke their language. I thought we could work out a civilized transition that, by attrition and retraining, would keep the comps at work in the company.

It would be more costly, but such an arrangement would be equitable—and it was essential for the future of the *Sunday Times*. Because it was a text-heavy newspaper, access to the computer would save millions of pounds and hours of work. When every minute counted, it was ridiculous for journalists to type on a clunky typewriter, manually returning the carriage, and then have the same keystrokes duplicated by a typesetter—a typesetter who had no use for the facility the computer offered for an accurate word count or the ability to transpose paragraphs without starting to type all over again. Moreover, because the *Sunday Times* was an investigative newspaper, I was eager for us to embrace computers for basic research (though even my untutored enthusiasm underestimated quite how valuable it would be).

In a negotiation with the printers' union, we proposed a phased introduction over several years, with the men most affected guaranteed employment for life. The adroitly charming anarchist of the far left of the Labour government, Tony Benn, referred to this as an attempt to impose our wishes by force. Our own workers might well have been amenable, but the national union leaders rejected every inducement out of hand, fearful that what we did would set a precedent for the whole industry. We got nowhere in endless negotiations, so for three years the computers we'd optimistically purchased lay unused under dust sheets, ominously referred to as "The New Technology." By 1979 nobody in Fleet Street had been able to introduce computers and display screens (then unappealingly called "VD" units, for visual display), although they were in all the American newsrooms I visited.

These are only glimpses of the obduracy that undermined the success of the *Sunday Times*. I was depressed and, frankly, bewildered by it all. Why couldn't the wreckers, as I saw them, realize that they were hazarding the whole ship? I had the conceit that I could make contact with workingmen of my dad's generation. In my no doubt sentimental reflections, they seemed to me to exemplify the cliché of "solid working-class values," preserving their natural dignity as they struggled through the bad times to keep their families together, proud of being able to do "an honest day's work," noticeably distancing themselves from the "slackers" and "scroungers" among them.

Perhaps I was so disappointed because I was nostalgic for the mythic north of my childhood, which began to vanish when close-knit "Coronation Street" neighborhoods with terraced homes and corner shops and pubs were replaced by drably anonymous housing estates, where the "telly" glowed every evening, inciting acquisitive envies. In the "bad old days" people were poorer, and they were more or less stuck in the place where they were born and grew up, but there was comfort in being rooted in a community and recognized within it as a good neighbor. The wartime spirit of solidarity had been very real, but it had evaporated along with the British Empire and the pride and affection for its glory that everybody felt but was not willing to admit. U.S. secretary of state Dean Acheson kept saying in the 1950s that Britain had lost an empire and had yet to find a role, and as a people we seemed to have lost one identity and were struggling to find another. The class divisions had faded, we assured ourselves, and we'd had reformist Labour governments, but the positions of power and privilege were still predominantly occupied by Oxbridge graduates as they had been for a hundred years. What would George Orwell make of it all?

*　　*　　*

Whatever historians have to say about our disintegrating society, cut adrift from its traditional moorings, I cannot blame
anyone else for the personal stresses I felt in these years. In the
crises of the 1970s I created a crisis of my own. After twenty
years of a serene marriage to Enid, moving from Durham to
Manchester to Darlington and finally to London and raising
three children together, I fell in love with a woman half my
age. Torn by the pull of a magnetic north and a magnetic south,
I inflicted great pain on others, my own pain the least of it.

Tina Brown came into my life through her writing. Literary agent Pat Kavanagh (who was later married to the novelist
Julian Barnes) sent me some clippings from the *New Statesman*
magazine. She urged me to think about commissioning features from the writer, who was about to graduate in English
studies at Oxford: "She's very young, won a place at Oxford
when she was 16, but has a wicked eye." I put the articles in my
briefcase; they got buried under other submissions and manuscripts from agents pitching book serials for the Review Front. I
didn't get round to the necessary archaeology until two weeks
later. One of the Tina Brown clippings was a description of the
stab-in-the-back gossip fest at a *Private Eye* lunch in Soho to
which she'd been invited by the literary critic Auberon Waugh,
who'd admired her contributions to the Oxford university
magazine. Cabinet minister Richard Crossman was the guest
of honor—that is, he was in the hot seat, where victims were
goaded to sing for their supper with confidences that the *Eye*
would wittily betray in the next issue. Brown's column about
the lunch was hilarious. I'd normally have passed it on to Ian
Jack, the editor of our Look feature page in what used to be the
women's section, but feeling guilty at my neglect in reading
the submission, I got on the phone at once to tell Miss Brown

how much I'd enjoyed her writing and would like her to come in to meet Mr. Jack.

"So pleased you liked my columns," she said. "But sorry, not today—my husband has friends coming round for dinner."

Wait a minute! Married before she'd even left Oxford? Wasn't that carrying precocity too far?

She went on to ask how I'd come across her writing in a Spanish magazine. It transpired that the Tina Brown I was talking to was known to her husband as Tina, but she was Bettina Brown, indeed a sharp writer but Tina Brown's mother. The husband whose dinner party took priority over the needs of the *Sunday Times* was the celebrated Pinewood film producer George Brown.

Duly fricasseed by Ian Jack for her lack of provincial training, the correct Tina Brown was nonetheless given a few trial freelance assignments by the paper and the color magazine. Her entry was apparently eased by the fact, which I hadn't realized, that she was known to the critics at the *Sunday Times*. They'd named her as the winner of the paper's annual student drama contest for her play *Under the Bamboo Tree*, a comic ménage à trois. A year or so into her freelance work, I heard she was going to America to write a new play. She asked if anyone could give her introductions, and I said I'd drop a note to induce S. J. Perelman to see her. I'd published a few pieces by Perelman, the resident wit at the *New Yorker* who had authored a couple of scripts for the Marx Brothers and the screenplay for *Around the World in Eighty Days*. The result two months later was a cross letter from Perelman: "I don't know why I am being cordial to a man who wrote me way back on November 1st that a beautiful blonde playwright (who had won your drama award) was coming here and would phone me. The only blonde I have seen around here is a Polish maid with fat thighs and no chest who persistently spills ammonia on my suede shoes. This can't be the woman you meant, Harry, or else you have a low opinion of me as a judge of feminine sexuality. Was Tina real or merely the product of an erotic opium dream?" He forgave me when they did meet, and they became soul mates.

Late in 1974, when I was in New York myself, I agreed to listen to some feature ideas Tina had. I ran late returning to the Regency Hotel, where I had arranged a dinner meeting of Insight reporters and the New York office manager. We were in the middle of our investigation of a scandal—the deaths of 346 people when a DC-10 airliner crashed near Paris after it shed a cargo door known to be defective. I'd been summoned to a court in California to press our claim for access to secret documents, and preoccupied by our discussions, I forgot that Tina was waiting to see me. When I realized I wouldn't be able to meet with her, I suggested that she write me a memo, which I promised to read when I got back to London. We corresponded about her work, and then about newspapers and literature and life, and so our relationship began. I fell in love by post.

It was absurd. She was twenty-five years younger and courted by the likes of the enfant terrible Martin Amis and our own dashing star reporter David Blundy. When it became apparent that I was attracted to her, she gave up freelancing for the *Sunday Times* so that there would be no question that any success she gained might be attributed to having caught the boss's eye. She began writing features for the rival *Sunday Telegraph* and won the Catherine Pakenham Award as young female journalist of the year.

My infatuation, I told myself, was a typical midlife crisis and I should get over it. But I couldn't. Sporadic panicky "goodbye and good luck" separations, initiated by both of us with resolve and good intentions, failed to last. One crazy night, when she was in Spain with her parents, I got on my BMW bike and raced to the airport for the last plane to Málaga, realizing upon landing after midnight that I hadn't bothered to find out precisely where in someplace called San Pedro de Alcántara Mr. and Mrs. Brown lived. Nor did my Spanish phrase book help me with "Do you know where I can find the Englishman who came to Spain before the civil war, made films out of Pinewood, speaks Catalan, and has a young blond daughter about five feet six?"

I was ashamed that I had begun a secret life separate from Enid. I took a company flat next door to the *Sunday Times* office, ostensibly to be close to work. The habit of quick decision making didn't travel a couple of doors from the office to the company flat. I could disentangle the complications in deciding whether and how to take on the government over publication of the Crossman diaries, but I couldn't sort out my own life. For two horribly fraught years, I preferred to park my conscience while I wrestled with nerve-racking events at the paper.

Tina was deeply conflicted, too, about her association with a married man, simultaneously rejoicing and regretting. She kept trying to withdraw, but the bond we had, professional and personal, was too deep to break. I was the older, supposedly more responsible one, but the thought of living without her completely paralyzed me. I was enraptured by her and her innocent integrity and wit. I moved from the large, bleak company apartment to the tiny walk-up she rented in Bloomsbury. If she was in town and not on assignment for the *Sunday Telegraph*, we'd walk over to nearby Charlotte Street in Soho to our favorite Greek restaurant, oblivious of everything about us.

When we escaped London together, we retreated to the safe haven of both our childhood summers—the English seaside. By the mid-1970s people who wanted to bake in the sun had fled by the millions on package tours to the Costa del Sol. There was an almost ethereal, seductively solitary air around the uncrowded British resorts, with their half-empty, wind-swept Victorian piers, timeless boardinghouses advertising VACANCY in the front window, and once intimidating grand hotels now too imposing for their own good.

On Sundays I'd collect Tina on the pillion of my bike, and we'd scout the coast for romantic hideaways. We'd hole up in some boardinghouse with a pile of books and magazines, eat at the baked-beans-on-toast cafés, scramble among the rocks for shells, and walk the downs atop the cliffs at Beachy Head. In Hastings one morning a downpour forced us to retreat to a smoke-filled pub, where we sat with the locals watching the Queen's Silver Jubilee celebration on television as the rain fell. On an excursion to the Irish coast at Connemara, we impracti-cally considered buying a boathouse where we could disap-pear from the world. One magical Sunday exploring the coast of West Sussex, we found a little house with a For Sale sign at Angmering-on-Sea, where the ocean lapped right up to the back garden. We dreamt of buying it one day when we could afford it.

Meanwhile, at the *Sunday Times* we were not alone in our industrial misery. Waves of strikes crashed into and over the remaining seawalls, culminating in the 1979 chaos of the "winter of discontent." In two months thirty million working days were lost. I saw pickets blocking cancer victims arriv-ing for treatment at St. Thomas' Hospital across the river from where I lived. Going to a restaurant through the entertainment center of Leicester Square, I walked past high piles of uncol-lected rotting garbage that earned it the name "Fester Square." The National Union of Journalists, pursuing a wage claim, made a mockery of years of press protests against secretive local authorities by actually asking council officers to deprive people of news about gas leaks, fires, building plans, rents, and rates. It was like asking Sweeney Todd for a close shave.

The Thomson Organization sanctioned a dramatic bid to start anew. It offered to invest millions of pounds to buy out obstructive practices and overmanning, but the chapels and their unions didn't want a brave new world. Every proposal was rejected. As a result the paper was shut down in November 1978—a temporary break, we all thought, until negotiations resumed.

I drank the cup of bitterness many times over as I walked through the silence of the dead composing room, with its shrouded Linotypes and darkened offices. Gathering dust in my "pending" tray was a scoop of world importance. Anthony Mascarenhas, the man who'd exposed the genocide in East Pakistan, detected that Pakistan was well on the road to possessing a nuclear bomb. He pointed the finger at the then unknown Dr. Abdul Qadeer Khan, whose thefts of blueprints from a European facility would enable Pakistan to become the first nuclear power in the Muslim world. Khan, wrote Mascarenhas, hadn't stopped there. He'd supplied both Iran and Libya with centrifuge components and information. As the weeks of suspension turned into months, I gave approval for Mascarenhas to send his report to the Australian magazine *Eight Days*, started in Sydney by former *Sunday Times* executive Colin Chapman. Trading a world scoop of historical importance killed any lingering feelings I had of conciliating the unions.

We were suspended for a full year, but even when an agreement was reached to restart, the recidivists in the pressroom worked their mischief again, and the comps' national leaders reneged on the computer deal we'd worked out together.

I've never forgiven the print unions for what they did. Kenneth Thomson, Roy's son and then head of the company, was deeply wounded. Ken was a kindly, somewhat absentminded man with a gentle sense of humor who thought the best of everyone he met. In Canada, where he lived, he was not "Lord Thomson"—"call me Ken"—and he never took his father's seat in the House of Lords. He delegated the management of Times Newspapers to a London board, but he took pride in the papers, as his father had. Even though the *Times* journalists had been paid normal salaries for a year of not working, soon after returning to work they called a strike for more money. That was the last straw, a betrayal of the Thomson family, which had spent millions to save the *Times*. Thomson sadly concluded that he could do no more. "I promised Dad I'd keep the *Times* going, Harold, but this is too much," he said. He put both papers up for sale. I led a management buyout bid for the *Sunday Times*, but Thomson's London management, and Denis Hamilton, thought that Rupert Murdoch and his News Corporation had a better chance of dealing with the unions.

I'd encountered Murdoch often enough to appreciate the delusiveness of his charm. He was a chameleon who could switch from good humor to menace. I'd heard every jolly swagman's yarn that placed him somewhere between Ned Kelly and Citizen Kane. I'd been at seminars on newspaper ethics where he'd acted like a caged lion, glowering his contempt for the do-gooders and sappy academics. I often agreed with him. Once, expressing admiration of the *Sunday Times'* investigations, he'd joked that I should take over the *Village Voice* and teach the journalists there the meaning of responsibility. My friend Australian editor Graham Perkins had declined to work for Murdoch but thought that within the hard exterior of the riverboat gambler, there might still be found the lost idealist of the "Red Rupert" of his Oxford days. I didn't think that, but after the years of hand-wringing at our board meetings, I did find his buccaneering can-do style refreshing. "Sure," he said with a laugh, "we'll sort out the unions. We're going to print the *Sunday Times* in two sections, Friday and Saturday, and go up in size." Music to my ears.

The journalists felt badly let down by the Thomson management; they didn't trust Murdoch. The Australians associated with the paper were especially vehement, saying that he had fired every editor who'd stood up to him and that he would have no respect for the paper's cherished independence or any promises he made. But when the *Sunday Times* journalists' chapel came to a vote at the end of a passionate debate (which as management I could not attend), it voted against a court action to force a reference back to the Monopolies Commission. Many of them feared that a breakdown would mean the end of our sister paper, the *Times*. Fourteen of them favoring legal action, members of the so-called Gravediggers Club, printed T-shirts bearing the cry DON'T BLAME US. WE VOTED AGAINST.

The Thomson Organization and Parliament had asked Murdoch for guarantees that the tradition of editorial independence of both papers would continue to be protected in two ways: by the appointment of independent national directors to the board and by five guarantees of editorial freedom. Murdoch readily promised that editors would control the political policies of their papers; they would have freedom within agreed annual budgets; they would not be subject to instruction from either the proprietor or management on the selection and balance of news and opinion; instructions to journalists would be given only by their editors; and any future sale of the titles would require the agreement of a majority of the independent national directors.

It was on the basis of these guarantees, and only because of them, that in February 1981 I accepted Murdoch's invitation to edit the *Times*, giving up the job that had given me such fulfillment and pride at the *Sunday Times* and my power base as a defender of press freedom. My ambition got the better of my judgment. I guess the bitter experience with the unions had made me eager for a new start. I hadn't been enchanted either by the furtiveness of Thomson's London management during the sale. Still, it was wrenching to leave my friends at the *Sunday Times*. It had been a partnership sustained by a conviction everyone shared: we were doing something worthwhile in bringing the public early intelligence they'd not get anywhere else and associating it with the highest levels of cultural commentary we could achieve. It was a community of shared values—not political values, but the values of purposeful, honest journalism. Selecting and promoting people of excellence who had the same ideals, and whom I could trust to live by them in a collaborative enterprise, had been one of my principal tasks as editor.

Despite the difficulties we'd had with the national leaders of the print unions, I also retained an affection for the printers who worked with us. On my last Saturday evening putting the front page to bed, I was touched that the comps' farewell was an honor rarely accorded to anyone outside their union: they "banged me out," which meant that everyone on the floor seized whatever piece of metal was to hand and hammered away, creating a tremendous noise as I waved goodbye holding my last page proof. The photographers later ended a more sedate dinner given by the company by hoisting me on their shoulders. A week later at the *Times,* on my first night as editor, the comps accorded me the privilege of pushing the front page into the foundry, a pleasant welcome that was not a harbinger of things to come elsewhere in the building.

In my first six months at the *Times,* Murdoch was an electric presence, vivid and amusing, direct and fast in his decisions, and a good ally against the old guard, as I worked to sharpen the paper's news values while retaining every element of its traditional coverage of Parliament, the law, obituaries, and the arts. I had his enthusiasm for a thorough overhaul—"Go to it, Harry"—making headlines more readable and letting photographs breathe. He overruled the squeaks from his advertising director when I swept classified advertising off the back page for an irreverent parliamentary sketch and an information service. I brought in new political writers and started a new tabloid-size arts section.

Twenty-one days into my editorship I was at dinner with Tina at Langan's Brasserie just off Piccadilly on the night President Ronald Reagan was shot. I left the dinner table in a tearing hurry to oversee our coverage, calling for the most detailed narrative, a separate report on the gunman, another on the violent history attendant upon American presidents, and a third on the character of the next in line, Vice President George Herbert Walker Bush. There was argument around the picture desk about which of three near-simultaneous photographs we should use—one of the president looking toward the shooter, one of him being hit, or one of him being bundled into a car. This was an unusual true sequence, and to choose just one or to use three small images would be to miss an opportunity. I schemed all three running six columns wide down the page. Finally I ruled that the whole front page would be given to all the Reagan elements, and I created a second "front page" in the normal *Times* style for other news. We developed the same approach for other late-breaking news: the *Challenger* shuttle explosion; Israel's bombing raid on Iraq's Osirak nuclear reactor; the assassination of Anwar Sadat; riots in London and Liverpool.

The Reagan front page was a departure from the traditional *Times* style, as dramatic as the event, and I'm still proud of it today. There were mutterings, of course, from some of the old guard I'd dislodged from positions they had come to see as tenured. But readers responded in the thousands. Circulation stopped falling. News Corporation's 1981 annual report said that the "exciting" editorial changes had the "extremely grati-fying" result of increasing the paper's circulation from 276,000 to more than 300,000.

My difficulties with Rupert really began in the autumn of 1981, as the economy showed little sign of recovery from a reces-sion. Mrs. Thatcher's government was facing a catastrophic fall in popularity. We supported her editorially on any number of issues, including her determination to curb excessive pay demands by the civil service, but we were critical of her reli-ance on monetary policy in a recession and disappointed that she seemed unwilling to tackle the abuses of the trade unions as she'd promised. (She made up for that later.) At the same time, we were unsparing in documenting the disintegration and spiritual collapse of the opposing Labour Party. We identi-fied the virtually unknown left-wing activists who were con-spiring to win control of the party leadership by changes in the party's constitution and with that gave fair weather to the rise of the Social Democratic Party. However, it soon became obvi-ous that nothing less than unquestioning backing of Thatcher on every issue would satisfy Rupert.

His mouthpiece, Gerald Long, wrote me a stream of memos asking me to downplay or suppress news that was bad for the government. In the spring of 1981 the chancellor of the exche-quer had said the recession was over and recovery would begin in the early summer. It didn't. Six months later the Cen-tral Statistical Office released figures showing that output had fallen for the sixth successive quarter. Long stood amazed at our temerity in printing a summary of this official report. Did I not understand that if the government said the recession was over, it was over? As far as I was concerned, his rebuke was red rag to a bull. I was not going to let anyone in management tell me to fix the news. (Output fell by 2.3 percent in 1981.)

The warfare with Long escalated through the winter of

1981–1982, with Murdoch himself giving instructions to editorial writers and continually ducking the pledge to give me a budget. (Of course this came in handy later for the bogus charge that I had exceeded nonexistent limits.) In fact, by this time he'd blithely broken all his editorial pledges. Stories mysteriously appeared that I was thinking of resigning or being asked to resign. Murdoch denied them all. On February 10, 1982, hours after I'd been named Editor of the Year in the Granada press awards, he issued a statement saying there were absolutely no plans to replace Harold Evans, whose outstanding qualities etc. The reality was that two weeks later, he went to the national directors to ask them to dismiss me and install a new editor. They refused twice. They told him that if he himself dismissed me, I had a right of appeal to them and no pressure should be brought on me.

It was a dark time, and then came the news that I'd long dreaded. Since receiving his gold watch (and his miserable pension) for fifty years on the railway, Dad had lived very happily with Mum in a bungalow by the sea in Prestatyn, North Wales. Into his eighties, he rode his bike to the post office and bowling green and played football with his visiting grandchildren, cajoling my first son, Mike, to shoot with both feet and eat his crusts. In the summer he put on his glossy peaked cap for a return to railway work, giving rides to children on a miniature steam train on the promenade at Rhyl; he took it as seriously as he had driving mainline expresses. Mum and Dad lived close to an unpretentious golf club, and Dad liked to walk to it through the sand hills for a game of darts and for the oxygen of his days—conversation about the world.

He'd been a staunch trade unionist all his life and on the Labour left, but he had a dim view of the irresponsibility that had come to pass for trade unionism. I have his diaries—an entry of his activities every day, written in a hand far more legible than mine—and notebooks of the family budget ("Good news railway pension increased by 40 pence a month from 7.23 to 7.63"). Every Sunday, I am touched to see, he had recorded the length of the suspension at the *Sunday Times*. The big highlight of their retirement was to cross the Atlantic twice to stay with my brother Peter and his wife, Dorothy, in Ontario. They took the dome-car train—naturally—to make the 2,400-mile journey to the Rockies and beyond to Vancouver, giving Dad a good excuse to wear a cowboy hat and ride in the canyons of his imagination.

Then the inescapable day arrived. Dad had recovered from the heart attack he'd had while visiting us in Kent and resumed his normal life in Prestatyn. Now, a year later, as I was sending the *Times* to press, word came that he had suffered a stroke and was in a coma in the hospital in Prestatyn. He was in his eighty-second year.

All the sons had kept in close touch with Mum and Dad, Fred especially since John was in distant parts on Foreign Office work and Peter had emigrated to work for an insurance company in Canada. We were all told that Dad would be in a coma indefinitely, and we were discouraged from visiting: he would not be able to see or hear anyone or speak to us. In about the third week, though, Enid went to the hospital to visit; my parents were fond of her and she of them. She was surprised to find him sitting upright in a chair by the bed. She asked him to nod if he could hear her; she thought he did. All four sons hastened to Prestatyn—Peter from Canada, John from Hong Kong, Fred from Gloucester, and me from London. Mum was too ill to be with us. We stood by his bed and one by one spoke to him, telling him that we were all together again for the first time in many years. We thought we detected a responsive flutter of an eyelid.

Dad died forty-eight hours later. His friends said, "He was waiting for his four sons," and I think he was. We buried him on the hill in Bluebell Wood cemetery at Coed Bell, overlooking the sea. Two months later Mum, brokenhearted, joined him there. For many years I couldn't bear to open the diaries of their good last years together.

On Tuesday, March 9, 1982, upon my return from my father's funeral, while I was supervising the newspaper's budget edition (a special edition presenting the chancellor's annual budget) Murdoch summoned me to his office. He leaned forward in his chair, took off his glasses, and stared at me. "I want your resignation today," he said. I was astonished at how calm I was: it was rather like the out-of-body sensation I'd had the time I was mugged in New York and seemed to be watching myself from above. I noticed how red the rim of his left eye was, the thickness of the black hair on the back of his hands. "You cannot have my resignation," I heard myself saying. "I refuse." I asked what criticisms he had of the paper. "Oh, you've done a good job with the paper, sure. We haven't signed your contract, you know [I didn't], but we'll honor it." And then he veered. "You've said I put pressure on you. I haven't put any pressure on you. I've always made it clear political policy is yours to decide." In the midst of these exchanges, his voice wavered. He began to say how much harder it was for him than for me. No need for me to worry. I'd get lots of jobs. He'd wondered whether I'd take a job with his News International but guessed I would refuse. He'd guessed right.

After some twenty minutes I said I had to get back to the budget edition. As I left, saying he did not have my resignation, I asked whom he had in mind for my exit. It was then I learned that he'd suborned my deputy, Charles Douglas-Home. "Can't bring in another outsider at this stage," Murdoch said. "He'll be all right for the time being."

Back in my office, I confronted Douglas-Home. Eton and the Royal Scots Greys, the second son of the second son of the thirteenth Earl of Home, "Charlie" was a member of the *Times* old guard par excellence. I'd only appointed him as a gesture to that faction. He'd been most ardent in expressing his determination to stand with me in preserving the paper from managerial interference, so I asked him how he could have conspired for my job. He replied, "I would do anything to edit the *Times*. Wouldn't you?" Saying "No, I wouldn't do anything to edit the *Times*" seemed wan in the glare of his ambition. Accustomed to having a loyal and supportive deputy at the *Sunday Times*, I'd underestimated how much Douglas-Home longed for the validation of being anointed leader of the "top people's paper."

I was glad that I had kept in touch with the four key original national directors out of the six (the two others were Murdoch appointees). They assured me of their votes if I wanted to stay on, but I now had to envisage what that would mean. Nothing in my experience compared to the atmosphere of intrigue, fear, and spite inflicted on the paper by Murdoch's lieutenants. I was confident I could stand up to the bullyboys, but why should I give any more of my time and energies to an enterprise where every man feared another's hand? I was certainly not going to dilute, still forsake, a lifetime commitment to journalism free of political manipulation. I got madder and madder. I spent a morning discussing tactics in a meeting with my chief ally among the national directors, the burly Lord (Alf) Robens, another Manchester man (and formerly in charge of Britain's nationalized coal mines). He expressed contempt for Murdoch and his "methods," a reference to a ploy by which Murdoch had attempted to move ownership of the papers' titles out of Times Newspapers and into News International without consulting the national directors as required. Robens affirmed my feeling: "You'll be in a lunatic asylum at the end of six months the way they go on in that place." On his advice I went back to the paper and continued editing and writing.

Murdoch had gone to New York, but his henchmen told the press I'd resigned, when I had not. They proffered statements praising my record. I was not about to comply with this pretense, so I took my time and continued with my news and opinion conferences with senior staff. After a week, besieged outside my house by TV cameramen and reporters, and only when my lawyers were satisfied with the terms, I resigned on ITN's *News at Ten,* citing "the differences between me and Mr. Murdoch."

It was March 15. Only later did I recognize the significance of the date. One of the Shakespeare passages my father knew well and liked to declaim was "Beware the ides of March."

Two decades later, when Murdoch's appetite for newspapers led him to acquire the *Wall Street Journal,* I could not restrain a mirthless laugh on reading that the controversial sale in 2007 was hedged about with guarantees enforceable by a well-remunerated troika of the good and wise. This illustrious tribunal very shortly afterward had the pleasure of reading that the editor had resigned without their knowing, not to mention their approving. Still, I have to say that Murdoch's spirited capacity for risk and innovation is proving better for this fine newspaper than the lackluster Dow Jones management and those Bancroft family members who sold it to him.

Frankly, I agree with Murdoch now that editorial guarantees are not worth the paper they are written on. At Times Newspapers, their invention enabled an air of respectability to be given to an unnecessary and hazardous extension of monopoly power, and they suggested that the *Times* tradition had been maintained when behind the fake ivy it could so easily be plundered. Much as I appreciated the stalwart support of the independent national directors, in reality outsiders are incapable of monitoring the daily turmoil of a newspaper. This has nothing to do with their theoretical powers, and increasing or entrenching them would make no difference. Arbitration is impossible on the innumerable issues that may arise at warp speed every day between editor and management. Moreover, any intervention on editorial matters inevitably hazards the future relationship between complaining editor and resentful proprietor.

That relationship has to be based on trust and mutual respect. I recognize that the proprietor who imposes a political policy and fires a recalcitrant editor can invoke his right to do what he will with his property. He is the one risking his capital. In the case of Times Newspapers, however, the situation was different—Murdoch unequivocally forswore that right when he signed the guarantees to Parliament.

Today I have no residual emotional hostility toward him. On the contrary, I have found many things to admire: his managerial effectiveness, his long love affair with newspapers, his courage in challenging the big three television networks in the United States with a fourth, and altogether in his pitting his nerve and vision against timid conventional wisdom. And there was even one issue where he proved positively heroic.

In my efforts at a staff buyout of the *Sunday Times* in 1981, the print unions at Times Newspapers had let it be known that they preferred Rupert Murdoch to the other bidders for the titles. "We can work with Rupert," a general secretary had told me. ("You mean *not* work," I'd rejoined.) The unions took Murdoch's shilling—and five years later he put them to the sword. It was an equitable sequel. Under the guise of starting a new evening paper at Wapping, he set up a new plant capable of producing all his papers and secretly gave bargaining rights to the sensible electricians union, which in turn reached an agreement for journalists and clerks to access computerized typesetting. He installed color presses capable of printing both the *Sunday Times* and the *Times*, as well as his other major titles, the *News of the World* and the *Sun*. Then on January 24, 1986, in an astonishing commando operation no less remarkable because it was planned in total secrecy, he overnight switched production of Times Newspapers from the battlefield of Grays Inn Road to a new plant at Wapping wrapped in looped barbed wire.

Six thousand members of all the unions went on strike and plunged the journalists on the papers into a crisis of conscience. A few refused to cross the picket lines. Two foreign correspondents who did, David Blundy and Jon Swain, said it was like being back in Beirut or Belfast, escorted by an armored car on the day they went through the barricades. People in all departments who wished to go on working assembled at secret pickup points that changed daily; they were collected in coaches with metal grids on the windows. On Saturdays they were greeted by thousands of "flying pickets," demonstrators bused in from far and wide. The pickets rocked the coaches going in, the politer ones shouting "Judas" or "Effing scab," and tried to stop the trucks going out with the papers. Only the presence of mounted police prevented the violence from getting out of hand. As it was, hundreds were injured and a thousand people were arrested.

At the height of the siege of Wapping, as it came to be known, a British television company called me in Washington, where I was now working, to ask if I'd appear on a program about it. On the morning of the show, the producers explained the lineup: "We have so-and-so defending Murdoch, and you and someone else attacking him."

"Wait a minute," I said. "You've got this all wrong. Murdoch is right. What he's doing is long overdue."

There was a pause. "We'll get back to you." An hour later they did. "Sorry, we have to drop you. Hope you understand. You don't fit the scenario."

But Murdoch did. The old script of endless warfare on Fleet Street that had always ended with a management whimper was being rewritten. The siege of Wapping lasted a full year, but not an issue of any of the papers printed there failed to come out. I didn't have any doubt where I stood. Murdoch and his managers had struck a redemptive blow for the freedom of the press. We in the old management that cared so much for responsible journalism had failed, and he'd succeeded. Wapping was brave in concept and brilliant in execution. What was achieved there made it possible for other newspapers to follow. Not only that, but it opened the way for new publications to begin. The *Independent* newspaper was nourished at birth by this victory (staffed in part by a diaspora from the *Sunday Times*). For that every British newspaperman is in his debt. The carnivore, as Murdoch aptly put it, liberated the herbivores.

20

My Newfoundland

American lives, said F. Scott Fitzgerald, have no second acts. I beg to differ. At least this Englishman had a second act in America — and for that I have to thank America and Rupert Murdoch, too. If he hadn't given me a shove, I wouldn't have enjoyed twenty-five exuberant years exploring new frontiers. And America produced a marvelous convergence in my life with Tina.

In 1968, when Ben Bradlee took over the editorship of the *Washington Post*, I'd been editing the *Sunday Times* for a year, so we got together to compare notes and we became friends. Later on, the timing in our personal lives was the same. He fell in love and made a second marriage with his paper's intrepid and glamorous young Style writer, Sally Quinn. I'd been amicably divorced for some time from Enid (and preserved a friendship that has endured to this day). Bradlee thought I was being much too slow about popping the question to Tina, which I was, largely because I feared she wouldn't say yes. "What are you waiting for, Evans? She'll get away!"

I seized a moment on a short vacation we took to Cape Cod in August 1981. She was under the weather, so I said it would be prudent to have a blood test, without mentioning that a blood test was required for marriage. Sweetly, she fell for it. Then I popped the question. With our legendary impatience, we decided to do it immediately. I called my coconspirator Bradlee, and he suggested a perfect site for the Brown-Evans civil wedding at the end of that week. The Bradlees had just finished restoring the near-derelict Grey Gardens, the shingled beauty of a house near Georgica Pond in East Hampton on Long Island which had been the fabled retreat of Phelan and Edith Bouvier Beale, uncle and aunt of Jacqueline Kennedy Onassis. At a day's notice, a number of close friends managed to make it to Grey Gardens: Tony Holden, the former *Sunday Times* Atticus, who'd become the *Times* features editor; Mortimer Zuckerman, the real estate tycoon with whom I'd first become friends when he'd come to London two years back to ask me to edit his first media acquisition, the *Atlantic;* journalist Marie Brenner; critic John Heilpern; essayist Nora Ephron; and *Sunday Times* New York correspondent David Blundy, with his daughter Anna, who was maid of honor.

Bradlee was best man. He hid a tape recorder in the bushes so that Handel could join us as Tony Holden walked the bride through the bougainvillea and the presiding judge pronounced us man and wife. After champagne and cake, we drove into Manhattan for a honeymoon—all of one night at the Algonquin. In a simultaneous moment of panic at what we'd done, we exchanged written promises that we could part at any time simply by returning the signed piece of paper. The next day Tina had to go back to London to her job editing *Tatler* magazine. Before going home, I had to meet Henry Kissinger at the Rockefeller family estate in Pocantico Hills, New York, where I was editing a second volume of his White House years.

Two years later we were back in America for good.

I still don't know quite how it happened. Not long after I left the *Times,* I was invited to be a visiting professor for a term at Duke University in North Carolina. It was all I needed to gamble on the promise of a new life — Mr. Micawber's instinct that something would turn up under the big blue skies. At least, I thought, I'd escape having to answer people asking whether I was "all right," as if I'd just been let out of Broadmoor, and seeing the mix of disappointment and incredulity on their faces as I explained that no, I wasn't bitter about the *Times*. The new Mrs. Harold Evans (not that she ever called herself that) was ready to cut loose, too, having resigned from *Tatler* a year after its acquisition by Condé Nast. Over the years I'd made a number of friends in New York, Washington, Rochester, and St. Petersburg, who might, at the end of the Duke term, point us in the direction of gainful employment.

The immediate plan was for Tina to enroll in a course in American literature at Duke while I took an alarmingly bright group of law and politics students into the thickets of the First Amendment and the vicissitudes of English law. On the way to the United States we paused in Barbados for a Christmas break. A phone call from New York to the beach cottage disrupted our vacation. The legendary editorial director of American Condé Nast magazines, the gray fox Alexander Liberman ("Tsar of All the Russias"), was on the line asking if Tina would come right away to meet him and his chairman, S. I. (Si) Newhouse Jr. They'd relaunched the great Frank Crowninshield magazine of the twenties, *Vanity Fair*, and after ten issues and two editors it was sinking fast amid media ridicule and advertising collapse. Tina flew to New York for lunch and returned to Barbados two days later in a state of anxious excitement. She'd been invited to move to New York immediately to take over as editor in chief of *Vanity Fair*. It would mean a commuter marriage since I was committed to Duke for six months.

Of course I urged her to do it. She could take a rain check

on Melville, Hawthorne, and James; they'd still be there, but *Vanity Fair* might not. New York, though, did take a bit of getting used to as a resident rather than a visitor. Our first apartment was a beginners' blunder, a sublet in a glass tower on Third Avenue, Midtown. We found the agent through the Yellow Pages, paid the five thousand bucks cash deposit into his homburg hat, and faithfully followed his instruction to use assumed names for entry. We never saw him again. The apartment itself had so much furniture that if you tried to walk across the living room quickly, you risked being precipitated against the glass walls, and no doubt through them if you had attained sufficient velocity. I opened a closet, and out fell half a ton of pornography.

Tina speedily found another apartment, on Central Park South, while I was teaching at Duke. It was a romantic, touristy address, its ritziness an attraction for a better class of cockroach. It was another disaster. For a start, on my first visit the doorman wouldn't let me in. "But Tina Brown," I told him, "is my wife, and that's my apartment."

"Sir, Mr. Brown is already up there."

So he was: Tina's father. Not long afterward we fled to a two-bedroom rental at 300 East Fifty-sixth Street in time for the birth of our son, George.

We soon realized that New Yorkers don't muck up their kitchens by doing breakfast. We got into the habit of walking down Second Avenue and trying every restaurant, bar, and diner, moving from Irish to Italian, from the tolerable to the smart to the intolerable in the space of six blocks. Within a very short time the New York vortex kicked in. When you are at the outer edges, you can swim quite happily in cool waters, but as you get closer, you get sucked into a level of activity that is calculated to drive you crazy. There was a *New Yorker* cartoon that caught it perfectly: man on the phone saying, "How's

Wednesday? No? A week the following Thursday? Or the Wednesday after that? No? How's *Never* for you?"

It was exciting and very eighties. The city was a temple of conspicuous consumption—people liked arriving at the Plaza in stretch limos—but it was disconcerting to see white-collar drug transactions in Midtown and around the magnificent New York Public Library on Fifth Avenue. The intellectual excitement of competing in the media capital was high, though, and America seemed on top of the world. It was like going to dinner with some wonderful person and looking underneath the table and finding mouse droppings. Years later, when New York had become the safest city in the country, we were to find our way to a ground-floor co-op apartment at Sutton Place with a small ivied garden, and from that seclusion we gradually learned how to adapt to Manhattan's throbbing and very proximate cultural life.

Twelve months later the young woman whose prose style I'd admired became the toast of New York for saving and re-creating *Vanity Fair.* David English, the editor of the *Daily Mail,* wrote a droll article about how the James Bond of British journalism, as he was pleased to call me, had become a wistful shadow of a successful wife. The gossip columnist Liz Smith referred to me as Mr. Harold Brown. But I was thrilled for Tina; I admired her bravery and rejoiced in her success. She'd supported me in the traumas at the *Times,* and I'd supported her as she'd tried to find her way in her first editorship at *Tatler.* And within no time at all after Duke I was running hard myself, in charge of a distinguished publishing house, Atlantic Monthly Press, with offices in Boston and New York, and at the same time editorial director of *U.S. News & World Report* in Washington, back at the throbbing heart of news.

I rented a tiny house on N Street in Georgetown, former slave quarters for the big houses, a few doors down the street from Ben and Sally. They lived in a glorious mansion with gardens and a tennis court, where occasionally I was Ben's doubles partner trying to put a couple of senators in their place. On the weekend I scurried back to New York to be with Tina.

Even now, I marvel at the thrilling speed of the changes in our lives, all for the better. I'd been back to America many times since my first taste of the country in 1956, traveling through forty states in the golden Eisenhower years. I remained fascinated by its opportunities and contradictions, attracted by its openness and freedoms, appalled by racial discrimination, excited by the ideal of the American dream of individual fulfillment through equal opportunity, and intrigued by how a society so thrusting and ambitious could protect the values of a civilized society. No doubt I romanticized my first experience in the fifties, maybe actuated a little then by the knowledge that while in 1949 I was trying to find a crack in the Norman walls preserving higher education for the elite in Britain, millions of American ex-servicemen were going straight to college on the GI Bill. I thought America had a franchise on the future, and I wanted to be part of it.

I could not get over how fast Tina and I were welcomed and absorbed into American life in 1983. We were received warmly even by colleagues in journalism who saw plum jobs go to a couple of foreigners. We told ourselves that the reception was no better than Ben Bradlee and Sally Quinn would have received had they arrived in London in similar circumstances, but who were we kidding? I doubt that Fleet Street in the eighties would ever have accepted interlopers the same way America embraced us two expats.

*   *   *

For me to be entrusted with the editorial content of both a book company and a newsmagazine so soon after arriving in America was a curiosity. It happened because of Mort Zuckerman's appetite for public affairs. He had barely appointed me editor in chief of Atlantic Monthly Press, at the end of my Duke stint, than he bought *U.S. News & World Report* and urgently wanted its potential developed as the most serious of the three competing newsmagazines, its rivals being *Time* and *Newsweek.* The magazine had a circulation of more than two million and was plugged into Washington politics. This time, after Murdoch, I was more cautious: Zuckerman had a reputation for being mercurial.

Zuckerman's commitment to the magazine's integrity was tested early on. I wrote an editorial identifying the blatantly false statistics used in advertisements by the powerful National Rifle Association (NRA) to justify a bill that would make it easier for criminals, drug dealers, and lunatics to get guns. The new chief executive of the magazine dropped by my office. This was Fred Drasner, Zuckerman's business partner, a lawyer new to publishing. He was known as "Firestorm Fred" for his passion to incinerate anyone and anything that stood in his way. "Whaddya writing this week, Harry?" I told him. The embers glowed: "Hey, you can't do that. I just sold the NRA thirty thousand dollars of ads."

I'd no time to debate. I had to catch a train to New York for a meeting at Atlantic Monthly Press, where my associate publisher, Walter Weintz, was in the throes of publishing an art scoop, the sketchbooks of Pablo Picasso. That afternoon I got a message from the equable David Gergen, whom we'd recently appointed as the editor of *U.S. News.* Would I mind writing another editorial in a hurry? I imagined David's hair was still smoldering. I told him I would mind, and no, I wouldn't write another editorial. On the Monday when I picked up the magazine, my NRA editorial was there as I had written it. Zuckerman had overruled Drasner (who lost his deal). Rather impertinently, I told Zuckerman that he'd completed his apprenticeship as an owner in record time; indeed, throughout he remained steadfast on all the issues of principle that counted. He proved immensely well informed, with a phenomenal memory. In 1984 he was the first mainstream journalist to dare to comment on the growth of the new black underclass. Later he was at one with Nobel laureate Paul Krugman in warning very early that the 2005 housing bubble would burst, with attendant financial dangers.

I had things to learn myself. I put a lot of effort into writing editorials for the magazine, acutely aware that I was a foreigner, but I was often surprised, even after so many years of being immersed in American culture, by the subtle differences between British and American English. I was deflated early on to be told by a colleague that the editorial I'd written on terrorism was "quite good." Pray, I asked, in what way was it deficient? "Oh, none at all. It really was *quite* good." It dawned on me that in British usage "quite" means "not very," but in American usage it means the opposite.

Reentering big-time journalism—interviewing President Reagan, getting hold of the smuggled letters of Soviet dissident Andrei Sakharov—was exhilarating. I could hardly believe my luck as I walked on crisp fall mornings from N Street across the bridge and into the *U.S. News* office. I did the round of diplomatic lunches and receptions, taking time out to swim at the Watergate complex and run a few miles along the Georgetown canal, but I spent most of my time in the office, engaged in an extensive study of the magazine's strengths and weaknesses. In the early months I worked on a redesign undertaken by Edwin Taylor, who'd transformed the *Sunday*

Times and the *Times*. While our former colleagues in London were still chained to typewriters, the considerable British talent for innovative design stupidly wasted, we worked at *U.S. News* on the cutting edge of modern technology. I had unfettered access to the computer for writing and editing and for seeing the pages we laid out. I got sad and angry when I heard from my friends in Britain how they were impeded in their daily lives by demarcation rules and by the kind of resistance I'd come across to changes in the *Times*. In an atmosphere like that, it's often not worth the aggravation to risk making changes, and so a company, and eventually a nation, becomes stultified.

I'd expected the attitude toward change to be different in an American organization, perhaps not always for the better. What I found altogether liberating was to be anonymous in the United States, by which I mean accepted for who I was without being immediately typecast by my accent or where I was educated or what class I was from. I discovered that anyone can reinvent himself in America, probably more easily than anywhere else in the world, because of the scale of the country and Americans' attitudes. You are allowed to fail without being cast into outer darkness. I cheered the American business leader Mark Gumz, the president of Olympus, who said, "Success comes from failure and acting upon this knowledge."

For all the satisfaction of working at Atlantic Monthly Press and *U.S. News*, after two years of daily absence from Tina and the constant travel, I was ready to move. Then I got a call from Si Newhouse, who opened by saying he'd gone crazy. He'd persuaded himself that he should start a travel magazine; was I interested? Some of my friends thought it was me who'd gone crazy: "Why on earth would you leave the sharp end of journalism for a travel magazine?" But I did, and I'd say to anyone who loses a job in midlife not to get stuck in who you were.

Reinvention as the editor of a monthly glossy was enormous fun. I was given a quiet room next door to the main Condé Nast building to ensure that the new boy wouldn't be distracted by the high-stepping models strutting into the offices of *Vogue, Glamour,* and *Vanity Fair.* All I had to begin with was a no-nonsense, silver-haired secretary and a few blank sheets of paper on which I could scribble headlines and layouts for miracle marriages of subjects, writers, and photographers for hypothetical stories I'd like to read. But travel journalism was ripe for a revolution.

There was no shortage of information in bulk. Travel was a marketplace with a million hawkers. It was bewildering enough to choose among the honest vendors, but there were also travel journals tied to the travel business, travel writers who took free trips and portrayed the never-never land where all headwaiters bowed. There were guidebooks that did not reveal that they had taken baksheesh. Still in my mind was an incident at the *Sunday Times.* One of the reporters had got sick on a cruise, a misery he'd shared with several hundred others, but he hesitated to write the story because he'd been on a freebie. Thereafter in my budget at the paper, I always provided for us to pay our own way, and Si Newhouse agreed that *Condé Nast Traveler,* too, should invest in honesty. I compressed our philosophy in the slogan "Truth in Travel."

I recruited a young staff eager to make waves but spiced with a few seasoned executives who could coax fine, cultivated writers and adventurous photographers. I wanted to combine enjoyable writing and photography with a passion for the environment (not yet a fashionable subject) and harder-edged journalism. Early on I enlisted the innovative Clive (Idea-a-Minute) Irving, the former *Sunday Times* managing editor who'd come to the States to make films and forgotten to go home. I persuaded the graphic artist John Grimwade of the *Sunday Times* to risk an adventure in New York. We carried out prodigious research to identify the safest and worst airlines. Oh, you'll never get away with that, I was told by the cognoscenti in the trade. Such no-holds-barred reporting would cost us any hope of attracting advertising. The prophecies were soon borne out. One month, in a small news item, we advised people with breathing problems of the risks of air pollution in Mexico City. An advertising agency angrily canceled all its business because we'd printed an item "unsuitable for a travel magazine." I published the protest and defended our policy—with a reaction better than we could have dreamt. The agency itself was then denounced by the travel industry and by Madison Avenue, sensitive about its image. They all signed on for truth in travel.

Condé Nast Traveler took off, an instant success that thrives today in America and Britain.

In my fifth year at *Traveler*, Alberto Vitale, the hard-charging chief executive of the Newhouse book companies, barreled into the *Traveler* office "to look around a magazine operation," then surprised me by saying that the visit was only a cover for his real purpose. Once inside my office, he shut the door and asked, "Would you like to run a publishing house?" He'd only just taken over Random House, the largest trade publisher in the United States, comprising three major houses: Random House ("little Random"), Knopf, and Crown. With Newhouse's approval, he was inviting me to be president and publisher of Random House trade; I'd also have the Times Books and Villard imprints in my portfolio, with the enterprising editors Peter Osnos and David Rosenthal, respectively. It was an interesting challenge, one I hadn't expected at the age of sixty-one. My passion for books had been unbounded since filing book jackets for Mum's little lending library and haunting Failsworth Public Library, but it was also an opportunity to return to journalism on the scale of the *Sunday Times*.

I knew a lot about the writing and editing of books, and by now I knew most of the formidable publishers in New York. As a visitor from London looking for good books we might acquire for serialization in the *Sunday Times*, I'd been impressed by the authority of Sam Vaughan at Doubleday, whom the great and the good invariably chose as their publisher; by Phyllis Grann's dominance of fiction blockbusters; by the determination of Dick Snyder at Simon and Schuster, who'd more recently beaten me off when, as the apprentice editor in chief of Atlantic Monthly Press, I'd flung everything we had into trying to secure the memoirs of Reagan's indiscreet budget director, David Stockman ("None of us really understands what's going on with all these numbers"). Snyder could also call on the editorial flair of Michael Korda, who strolled into meetings wearing jodhpurs and riding boots and found time to write best sellers of his own.

Militating against any anxiety I might have was the artillery of Random House, its editors at "little Random." In publishing the editors are key. They acquire (with the publisher's approval); they nurture the author from conception to line editing, caring for every word. My job as publisher was to judge the merit and value of manuscripts editors wished to acquire, to do some acquiring and editing of my own, and to ensure the viability of the house. I had no doubt I could work happily with the editors. They treasured literature; they saw themselves, with justification, as defenders of American cultural values and feared the corporatism to which the industry was apt to succumb. I heard of a bureaucrat put in charge of a new imprint who in his first cost-cutting exercise complained, "What's that fellow doing in the company? Whenever I pass his office, he's always just reading."

Three of the editors I'd be working with were renowned. Jason Epstein, Joe Fox, and Bob Loomis had a hundred years' experience between them. Epstein was perhaps the most creative force in the history of modern publishing, always seeking new frontiers. At twenty-two, fresh from Columbia, he'd invented the groundbreaking trade paperback as a format for quality books—distinct from the pocket-size softcover mass-market books, a profitable format that everyone imitated. He'd been a cofounder of the *New York Review of Books* and a participant in the founding in 1979 of the Library of America series of classics seeded by state dollars. He had an omnivorous appetite intellectually and in the kitchen. You never knew whether his next disquisition would be on the virtues of Saint Thomas Aquinas or a properly prepared artichoke. He was also, it has to be said, captain of the praetorian guard of pessimists, so I discounted his warning, when I called him, that the job of publisher had become "impossible." More challenging was that at Random House I'd be responsible for a $100 million business habituated to its own way of doing things.

Vitale was pleased, inordinately pleased, when I said I'd like him to take me through their system for managing the nuts and bolts of profit-and-loss predictions, printing, binding, warehousing, and selling into stores. I'd stumbled onto someone as didactic as I was. He was an immigrant himself, a former Olivetti executive impervious to doubt, his preference for order and certainty expressed in his smart buttoned-up, double-breasted suits and his handwritten notes ALWAYS IN BIG CAPITAL LETTERS. But he appreciated books, and he kept his promise that I'd have pretty much a free hand as the custodian of a pantheon of the greatest American writers. I took over as president and publisher of Random House at the start of November 1990.

Every author, said one of the founders of the house, is a son of a bitch. It was not a considered judgment. Horace Liveright had just had a cup of hot coffee flung in his face by Theodore Dreiser. But as the author of seven books myself, I was instinctively on the author's side. I knew the angst provoked by contemplation of the first resoundingly empty page, the tension waiting to hear from the publisher, the feeling that once the manuscript is delivered, you might as well have died and have done with it. Writing a book, as our prized novelist E. L. Doctorow put it, is "a lot like driving a car at night. You never see further than your headlights but you can make the whole trip that way." To which I'd add that the editor marks the route with signposts and is always at hand with a jack and spare tire. I took an oath of office that we'd be swift in our responses to authors and agents and that we'd repay the mental exertions of the writer by putting real promotional muscle into letting everyone know there was something very much worth reading here.

The galaxy of writers in the history of Random House was stunning: William Faulkner, Eugene O'Neill, Theodore Dreiser, John O'Hara, Ayn Rand, Upton Sinclair, James Joyce, Robert Penn Warren, W. H. Auden, Truman Capote, Jane Jacobs, Daniel J. Boorstin, and Theodore Seuss Geisel (Dr. Seuss) of *Cat in the Hat* fame. Some of the greats were still with us: William Styron, Shelby Foote, Pete Dexter, Robert Ludlum, Mario Puzo, Dave Barry, Norman Mailer, James Michener, Gore Vidal, Maya Angelou, David Halberstam, John Richardson, Hunter S. Thompson, Edmund Morris, and Doctorow.

Styron hadn't written much lately. On one occasion Tina asked me to accompany her to join a psychiatrist friend's table at a dinner benefit for medical research. Styron was there, persuaded to speak for the first time about the reasons he'd not been able to write. He talked about his struggles to overcome a long depression (in the years before it was understood what medication might do). It was moving to hear him. Tina right away went over to his table to persuade him that if he wrote an article for *Vanity Fair* describing his experience, he would help so many others who felt isolated and ashamed. He did. Inspired by Milton's *Paradise Lost*, Tina wrote the headline "Darkness Visible." Styron then felt encouraged to write a book under that title, and we published it at Random House, where it rode the best seller list for many weeks.

Clearly we had to find new authors of similar eminence, marrying their literary excellence with a number of commercial blockbusters, without managing to shed the authors we had. I was sorry to lose one writer within a few weeks of taking over. Rupert Murdoch withdrew his memoirs. Pity. I'd have done a good job for him.

Gore Vidal was unhappy about Jason Epstein's initial read of a new "novel-concoction," as Jason called it. I flew to Miami to see Vidal and express our undying loyalty (soon justified by a magnificent collection of his essays, *United States*, which won the National Book Award). In my eagerness to expound on how great it was to have both Vidal and Norman Mailer in the same house, I had to reverse course in mid-flow when I remembered that the two never missed a chance to beat up on each other.

Front-list fortunes are notoriously unpredictable. I had to grow a reliable backlist of steady sellers we could count on for income when new acquisitions didn't realize our hopes. It makes sense to read the DNA of an institution; Tina had done it on taking over *Vanity Fair* (and would do so again at the *New Yorker* in 1992). The original animating spirit of Random House was Bennett Cerf. He'd died in 1971, but I listened to him. His ebullience came through loud and clear on a tape his son Christopher Cerf dug up from the archives, in which Bennett had recorded how he'd been assisted by the womanizing habits of the owner of the Modern Library (inexpensive classics), Horace Liveright, in 1925. Liveright, having agreed to sell to Cerf, was hesitating to sign, when a cuckolded husband arrived in the office with murder in his heart. Liveright escaped the wages of sin this time, but intimations of his own mortality induced him to sign the sales agreement. Cerf built on the Modern Library to publish regular books "at random."

I was delighted at the end of my first week as president when Vitale called to say he'd like to amble down and talk about the Modern Library. He appeared in my office with Sonny Mehta, the subtle, reflective, and quietly competitive publishing legend at Knopf. The proposal was that they'd help me out by relieving me of the Modern Library and combine it with Everyman's Library, which Knopf had just acquired.

Thanks but no thanks, Alberto and Sonny. The Modern Library was dear to my heart. I remembered my astonishment when, as a Harkness Fellow skimping to get by, I found that I could buy its volumes of Edward Gibbon's *Decline and Fall of the Roman Empire* for less than the cost of breakfast.

Jason had misgivings about my enthusiasm, but I'd already begun an evaluation of the list, looking for other great works we might acquire, and I'd scouted new members for a Modern Library board. Most of all, I was impatient to begin a phenomenal project originally inspired at the *Sunday Times* by Godfrey Smith. He'd suggested that the *Sunday Times* identify the best hundred novels published in the English language in the twentieth century and feature them, with biographies and photographs, in the color magazine he edited. I'd planned to accompany the launch of the series with an inexpensive reissue of every title by arrangement with all the original publishers. We were halfway there when I left to edit the *Times*. At a handover meeting with the new management team Murdoch had installed at the *Sunday Times*, I proudly presented the great books package. Rarely have I been more swiftly deflated. No, thanks, Harry, they said, one of them adding genially, "Fuck literature!"

So I brought the orphaned project to Random House. Closeted with a committee that included Edmund Morris, Daniel Boorstin, Shelby Foote, John Richardson, A. S. Byatt, Arthur Schlesinger Jr., and Gore Vidal, I found discussing which novelist should make the cut and which should not at once an education and an entertainment. I could claim to have read most of the preliminary list; they seemed to have read everything twice, and the divisions of opinion were arresting: "Edith Wharton? Never!" "*Ulysses*? Unreadable!" The project was simpler than it had been in London. Random House already owned a good proportion of the copyrights of the fancied titles; for the rest the publishers who held the copyrights joined in the fun. We told them we had no intention of ranking the list other than alphabetically. The renovated Modern Library again became the backbone of a profitable backlist, and I'm pleased still to be on its board.

I'd worried that working with editors preoccupied with their manuscripts might give me a sense of desolation compared with the hurly-burly of the newsroom and the incessant changes on a monthly glossy. I'd been in the job just over two months when it became clear that the coalition armies President George Herbert Walker Bush had assembled would use force to eject Saddam Hussein from Kuwait. I fretted that any one of the three newsmagazines would be gearing up to produce special issues or books if and when war came. What was to stop me from producing an instant illustrated history? Well, I didn't have an art department that could interrupt its normal work, I didn't have the staff to acquire hundreds of photographs or the space to display them, and I didn't have the writers and editors on tap as a newspaper does. In short, nothing compared to flinging an army into the desert against a dug-in enemy armed to the teeth.

Vitale, exemplifying the American can-do spirit, swiftly organized printing and distribution and pledged 50 percent of the net proceeds from the book's sales to the Gulf Crisis Fund of the American Red Cross. I induced Ray Cave, the former editor of *Time* magazine, and his wife, Pat Ryan, a former editor of *Life,* to acquire and lay out photographs in a war room I secured at Condé Nast. I commissioned the foreign editor of the *Economist* in London, Peter David, to write thirty-five thousand words; deployed *Traveler*'s John Grimwade on a war-front graphic; and went to the Pentagon to describe our package to the chief of the armed services, General Colin Powell, in the hope that he'd write a prologue. (He was tickled that I could, on command, recite my number in the Royal Air Force.)

The ground war began on February 24, 1991. It was over in one hundred hours. I'd thought the coalition armies would give us more time. Still, the picture pages were pretty well laid out, Powell's prologue was in, the dust jacket was at the printer, and Grimwade was finishing his 3-D graphic of the battlefront. All we lacked was the text. That was in London. It was a magical experience in those days to put the phone down on David writing away at the *Economist* in St. James's Street, walk from the Random House offices on Third Avenue to our Condé Nast war room on Madison Avenue, and find that the thirty-five thousand words had got there before me, transmitted from David's computer to ours. Not only that, it was already in the pages with Ray Cave's headlines.

Triumph in the Desert, published on Memorial Day, was a nice success as the first illustrated history of the Gulf War in color. I was well placed to secure Powell's life story two years later on his retirement as chairman of the Joint Chiefs of

Staff. The bidding war for the American hero was hot. It was my first experience of an auction where you started with six zeros and the only question was the number you put in front of them. Vitale calculated that a $5 million bid would be viable and would probably succeed. I recalled Duff Cooper's observation that the United States is more subject than any other country to inundation by great waves of conviction: "What elsewhere might be called a craze becomes there a creed." The creed in 1995 was that Powell would run for president in 1996 and win. From my conversations with him and his wife, Alma, I guessed that all the speculation was froth. My fascination was less with his political future than with his past: how did this Harlem-born soldier who came home as a wounded Vietnam vet in the sixties and was refused service at a hamburger joint in Alabama get to be chairman of the Joint Chiefs of Staff?

Si was always ready to back his publishers, so we all took a deep breath and bid again when our original $5 million was topped by Phyllis Grann at Putnam. Not yet scarred by bidding wars that got out of hand and ended in disaster, I was keen to go higher. (The scar in the cultural memory of Random House was John Grisham, lost to another house for the sake of saving a final $25,000.) But here we were talking hundreds of thousands of dollars, maybe a million or more. We ended up bidding another $1.5 million. We were into David Stockman territory—"all these numbers"—our bid an act of faith by Si, Vitale, and me. It was our final throw. We were outbid again, but Powell ended the bidding, and we were told he would come to us. We hired the author Joe Persico to help Powell, and I edited it with a promising junior called Jon Karp, but it was very much Powell's book: he is a natural storyteller. The only difficulty we had was settling on a title. After yet another session with the marketing department, I recoiled from the favored "My American Dream" and typed up a note to Powell I still have:

I have come up with a title that everyone here likes a lot. Let it brew with you and Joe and we'll pick up when I get back:

Colin Powell
My American Journey
An autobiography

I think it is better than My American Dream because it avoids the MLK connections. It is more active, more of an adventure and less of an introspection. And it has been quite an adventurous journey—the boy from the south Bronx who made something of his life and something that is redolent of America and opportunity. And again it is a journey that is not complete. It is a cool title, not thrusting but with a quiet emphasis.

It was one of the more remarkable experiences of my life to travel with Powell on part of his thunderously popular multicity book tour. President Bill Clinton was worried that Powell might threaten his chances of winning a second term; nobody knew what party affiliation Powell might have. Thousands lined up around three or four blocks in every city, buying the book and urging him to go for the White House. He'd sign three or four thousand books, wisecracking with the customers in line, and then cheerfully set off for the next city and more of the same. When we were well and truly launched, I was touched to receive from Powell a framed copy of the memo I'd sent him. Typically gracious, he'd written across the bottom in red ink, "Harry, You were right, as usual. God Bless."

Happily, in good time the red ink vanished from our accounts. *My American Journey* was a fabulous No. 1 best seller. It kept selling in paperback, and in a few years our faith was amply rewarded.

There is no way of removing the risk from publishing. It is easy to forget, in the excitement of an auction, that you and your rivals might be wrong. Maybe the big name is just a big name. And how do you calculate the price you will pay for an author with no track record at all—or no name at all? I had no idea who the author was who'd sent a bunch of type-written pages to the agent Kathy Robbins. She gave them to me in a brown paper shopping bag over breakfast at the Waldorf in 1992 with the warning that if I liked what I read, I was not to try to discern or guess the identity of the author, nor ever suggest that the characters were based on real people. I could have the pages exclusively for the weekend provided I coughed up $250,000. The manuscript, titled "Primary Colors," was a compelling piece of fiction about the turmoil and intrigue of a governor seeking the presidential nomination. Wild horses couldn't drag from me the admission that I thought it bore a marked resemblance to the 1992 Democratic primaries, which had ended in the nomination of Governor Bill Clinton.

On the Monday, when I said snap to "Primary Colors," Kathy and the unknown writer insisted that they wanted it published under a pseudonym. I wasn't keen on promoting a bogus name, then I remembered what a fuss there had been in Britain in the sixties during Harold Macmillan's premiership when the *Times* had published a series of caustic political articles by Anonymous. So Anonymous became the author of the shopping bag pages that became *Primary Colors* that became a runaway best seller and a Mike Nichols movie starring John Travolta.

The speculation about who might be the author of a No. 1 best seller "who dares not speak his (or her) name" became a media craze. Nobody believed me when I said I didn't know. It was true. I was guessing like everyone else. We might never have known but for an unusual lapse among the sales force. Rather than let them have galley proofs, we distributed a few numbered copies of the edited manuscript. They were instructed to return them, but after publication one landed in an antiquarian bookstore, and David Streitfeld of the *Washington Post* bought it, did some detective work on the handwriting, and announced that Anonymous was Joe Klein, a *Newsweek* political writer. The death of Anonymous was regretted by all concerned.

I considered the manuscript of *Primary Colors* well worth the investment, but l never dared to hope it would bring in millions of dollars as it did. Why didn't we publish only profitable titles like that? It's a nonsense question, but that doesn't stop it from being asked (with movies, too). The truth is, nobody can predict with certainty whether a book will take off or bomb. Fortunately, a publisher's fortunes rest not on one or two books, but on the whole list, year in and year out, along with the backlist—with the important proviso that it is the publisher's sacred duty to find the right market for each author.

We didn't have to do much to let people know that General Powell had written his life story, but by some means or other we had a duty to find the right audience for nonfiction books that would never make a headline, books by new authors that might not command review space, books of all kinds whose budgets did not justify advertising monies, and books by foreign authors who would not be available for television. And we had to be quick about it, bearing in mind the dictum of publisher Howard Kaminsky that "new books last in the stores about as long as milk takes to turn into yogurt."

I'd inherited excellent people in publicity and marketing (overseen by the imperturbable Walter Weintz, who seemed not to have had enough punishment at Atlantic Monthly Press), but typically they were overstretched. I augmented their efforts with a literary magazine called *At Random*, collating interviews, photographs, and articles about our authors. It was edited by Helen Morris, whose interview with Martin Scorsese led to marriage and a Scorsese-Morris daughter. I created a special events department of four people headed by Jonathan Marder, an inventive marketer I poached from BBC America. I was apprehensive about his idea that Random House should, every month, invite the public to a literary breakfast panel at Barneys on Madison Avenue, open to authors from all publishing houses. I would moderate the discussion from a platform surrounded by people munching bagels, and we'd record the proceedings for national radio distribution. I didn't expect many busy New Yorkers to turn up at an ungodly hour to listen to authors debate the legitimacy of Truman Capote's technique in his book *In Cold Blood* or the reality behind science fiction, but the city has a concentration of book lovers, and they packed the place every month. You could pretty well guarantee that if we were discussing the life and novels of a late-lamented author, there'd be someone in the audience with intimate knowledge of his working methods and moods. One morning Brendan Gill of the *New Yorker* intervened to explain how John O'Hara became the "master of the fancied slight," furiously ending his association with the magazine.

And if the topic was movies based on a book, there'd be someone at a breakfast table who had directed, starred, cast, wrote the script, composed the music, or sued the studio. Director Michael Winner's adaptation of Raymond Chandler's *The Big Sleep* got even more arresting when we learned from Sarah Miles of the mayhem on the set.

Marder was the magic man who pulled rabbits out of the hat. On the collapse of the Soviet Union, I commissioned a researcher to go to Moscow to collect photographs the Soviets had suppressed over the years and create a book called *The Russian Century*. But I also needed a venue for an exhibition of the photos. Marder came into my office: "Do you want the good or the bad news first?" The bad news was that the Russians had run out of money for redecorating their beautiful beaux arts consulate building in New York where he'd hoped we could stage the exhibition. The good news was that Marder had raced around the city and persuaded designers and stores to finish the redecoration for free—a generous gesture that produced an appreciative front-page arts feature in the *New York Times*, a crowded exhibition, a good sale of *The Russian Century*, and an overclose embrace for me from the redoubtable wife of the consul general.

Gerald Posner had been working for years with his editor, Bob Loomis, on a book called *Case Closed* about the assassination of President Kennedy. There had been some creditable attempts to penetrate the mysteries, but they'd been overlain in the public imagination by thirty years of conspiracy stories. Posner's manuscript proved that these were paranoid garbage. I was impressed by his assembly of incontrovertible medical, ballistics, and scientific evidence proving that there had been no gunman on the grassy knoll; Lee Harvey Oswald had been the lone rifleman firing three shots over eight seconds. Everywhere around town when I mentioned that we had a sensation, I got the same response: "Not another Kennedy book! Give us a break!" Bookstore buyers reacted the same way. How could we make people pay attention when the sensation was that there was no sensation? Clearly we had a big marketing problem.

This was a profoundly important book. The ever prudent Loomis had let a few academics and journalists of invincible integrity have sight of the manuscript. Tom Wicker, the veteran political reporter and columnist of the *New York Times*, was seized by the significance. Posner's work, he said, could do much to restore faith in government and democracy because it demolished the insidious insinuations that the highest officials of the U.S. government had been involved in their president's murder.

I became so exasperated, I quite lost my temper over lunch with a publisher from London when I was told yet again that the public had passed the point of satiation on the death of Kennedy. "We're naming the guilty men!" I cried out. The publisher sat up. "You mean the men behind the killing? Wow, that *is* something!" No, I said, the guilty men are all those who ignored the evidence and misled the world. I was grateful to the publisher. He'd provoked me into a spur-of-the-moment response that might solve the marketing problem. On the napkin I roughed out the outline of an advertising campaign, leading off with a big GUILTY splashed across photographs of the principal propagators of conspiracy. We made that the overture to the campaign, backed up by a special *U.S. News & World Report* prepublication issue. The result was spectacular. It was not only a huge best seller but a blast of cold air on the fetid distortions; it was a contribution to a nation's sanity and faith in its institutions. The conspiracy industry, of course, saw our book and ad campaign as another conspiracy. I was warned we'd be sued, and we were. But we won every court case.

There were times when my enthusiasm betrayed me. I was convinced that we had a literary and commercial masterpiece in Jonathan Harr's book *A Civil Action*, telling of the fight by a small law firm to recover damages from a polluter suspected of afflicting children with leukemia. It was so riveting I'd stayed reading on the plane to a sales conference and barely escaped being carried to the next destination. My absorption in the book induced me to sign off on a weak jacket (which the author liked), and we made little of an endorsement by John Grisham. The book was a flop. I was so convinced that people would be sorry to miss it, and feeling we bore the blame, that I did something many thought a waste of money. I relaunched the book in hardback with a new jacket and invested still more on publicity. It worked, as it would have the first time if I had not made an assumption treacherous in publishing: it was so good that it would sell itself.

Given the inescapable uncertainties, we needed more surefire authors who would regularly sell into the top of the best seller list—easier to achieve in fiction, where an author might produce every second year, whereas serious nonfiction authors such as Robert Caro on Lyndon Johnson or Robert K. Massie on World War I might need five years or more. Even a list of hugely popular novelists provides no assurance of profitability; blockbuster authors just secure larger advances. The one-off celebrity book is clearly desirable if it is of high quality and you judge it will repay its advance and cover your unpredictable losses on other books. So I pursued and promoted celebrity books that I judged might be worth the risk. I was moved going to the hospital where the unbelievably brave Christopher Reeve (Superman) lay paralyzed from a fall while show jumping and hearing him, between breaths from a tube, say that he'd like to tell his story. It was a success. Kate Medina listened to the way NBC anchor Tom Brokaw talked, decided he was a natural author, and signed up *The Greatest Generation*, a runaway best seller.

But you could never tell. My attempt to secure the memoir of Marlon Brando and the sequel was more bizarre. I'd heard he made a habit of humiliating publishers who flocked to his Beverly Hills hilltop retreat with open checkbooks. He satisfied himself that they were all East Coast phonies by inviting them to express their enthusiasm by going down on their knees in front of him. I was ready for that. When the call came for me to make the trip to Hollywood, I planned to tell him that declining to kneel was not a mark of disrespect but a recognition of physics: a skiing injury, I'd say, meant that I'd never be able to get up again and he'd have a problem disposing of the body.

For me he had a different test. After a restaurant dinner during which he accused me of being a CIA agent and asked what music I planned to die to, we went back to his house for several hours of erratic conversation. He flitted from topic to topic — the American Indian, the genius of Dr. Salk, diet, Israel, blood pressure, the proximity of American history, the horror of living in New York... When we finally got round to the book, he said, "I know how to write an interesting story, get the people in. I know this is necessary." Then he gave me a hard stare. "What you hear about me is nonsense. I don't want to hurt anyone when I write. There are things I will not put in. I will not write about the night at the White House with John Kennedy when I could have fucked the First Lady in the darkened kitchen, something I thought about when she became the widow in weeds." (Could this shocker be true? I did check and found that he had indeed had dinner with the Kennedys at the White House a few months before the assassination.) At midnight, when I tried to get away, standing by a limo in the moonlight, he demanded that I there and then give him a sample of my handwriting to deduce whether I was lying about the CIA.

On the next visit, when he met me in a kimono draped over his three-hundred-pound body, we played chess all afternoon as he beautifully intoned his favorite passages of Shakespeare. Eventually we sealed our understanding sitting in his fiendishly hot sauna into the early hours. Perhaps he calculated that I was about to expire in the heat, but he finally relaxed enough to talk about his son's killing of his daughter's boyfriend in the house we were in. The book he wrote with Robert Lindley, *Songs My Mother Taught Me*, was highly readable, but getting him to promote it was a nightmare and a farce. (He suggested that we make a film in which he would dress as a woman and I would interview him.) I winced as I watched the interview he finally organized himself with Larry King on CNN. King allowed him to go off on various wild riffs, ending with Brando kissing King on the lips. It was the kiss of death for my hopes, stopping the book dead in its tracks in its rise on the best seller list.

Brando's brooding menace was theatrical. The sense of physical menace I experienced when I got smuggled into a Miami jailhouse was palpable. I was in a cell with General Manuel Noriega, the deposed dictator of Panama and alleged torturer, who'd intimated to a go-between that he was ready to spill on the involvement of U.S. agencies in drug smuggling. The next day back in New York, entirely on impulse, I called an author who'd written on Panama. "I knew you were going to call," he said. "How come?" I asked. "A friend in the CIA told me." Since I'd decided to go to Miami only at the last minute and told nobody, and since I'd called the author without warning, this was spooky. I suppose the prison cell was bugged, so I was glad I'd told Noriega he was hated in America and peppered my questions with assertions that Uncle Sam would never lie.

When we published Noriega's book, a number of worrywarts asked how we could do such a thing when he'd been convicted. This provoked me into my earnest worst. Didn't they know the meaning of "publish"? It means "to make known."

Were we publishers intent on "making known" whether we liked the subject or not, or were we in the business of not making known? In short, were we censors? Bennett Cerf found Ayn Rand and Whittaker Chambers politically repugnant, but he published them.

The thought police were active again in 1993 when Richard Nixon asked me to edit a book he was writing as a foreign policy manifesto for America. I didn't hesitate for a second. Even his critics—count me among them—conceded that he had an original approach. His manuscript tackled the key questions of the day: Should we punish China for its abuses of human rights? Was it wise for America to stay aloof from the genocide in Bosnia? Was it cowardice or prudence for the United States, confronted by a handful of thugs, to back away from its mission to restore democracy in Haiti?

I'd go to Nixon's house in New Jersey with my editorial observations, and he'd invite me to stay for lunch with him and his astute assistant, Monica Crowley (later author of *Nixon Off the Record*). In our meetings he was not the Nixon of the White House tapes—no growls at criticism, all expletives deleted. He was never less than intriguing, his forefinger stabbing, the melancholy folds in his face uncreasing, his slow voice deepening as he expounded on the spiritual crisis—the spiritual deficit—he saw facing America, manifesting itself in crime, race relations, and what he called "the corrosive culture of entitlement, one of the greatest threats to our fiscal health."

What he loved talking about most of all was American history. It was uncanny how he could segue from some foreign confrontation in the day's headlines into an analysis of Woodrow Wilson, when he couldn't have known (could he?) that this was the point I'd reached in writing my political history of the second hundred years of the Republic, *The American Century*. On another visit I asked if he thought General Eisenhower had made a mistake in not taking Prague in May 1945, thereby letting the Soviets occupy the city. He made it very clear that he did: "It sealed Czechoslovakia's fate." All these lunch meetings ended with the same ritual. He'd sign the label on the fine bottle of wine we'd consumed and give it to me. (I should have asked for a full bottle.)

Nixon completed *Beyond Peace* in February 1994, but he asked me to hold it up until he'd returned from a March visit to Moscow and briefed President Clinton. In April we agreed on the jacket and final text—he was receptive to all my pencil marks—but shortly thereafter he suffered a stroke. At Random House we were already on a crash publishing schedule; we then went into a crash-crash schedule to get the book to him in the hospital as his family wished. He was too impatient to reorder the next world. He died on April 22, four days after his stroke.

His daughter Julie Nixon Eisenhower asked me to join the two thousand friends and former opponents at his funeral in the sunshine at Yorba Linda, his boyhood home, where the house his father built still stood. Officially it was a state funeral. The representatives of eighty states sat in chairs in the garden. A military band played "Hail to the Chief" as the flag-draped coffin was carried to a plinth in front of us; four jets flew overhead, and a twenty-one-gun salute followed. For all that, the occasion had the feel and quiet dignity of a family gathering, its mood caught in the deep bass voice of Henry Kissinger. The presence of the five living presidents—Carter, Reagan, Ford, Bush, and Clinton—symbolized, Kissinger suggested, that Nixon's long and sometimes bitter journey had ended in reconciliation. "He achieved greatly, and he suffered deeply."

For most businesses there is only one balance sheet. For publishing houses there are two, the numerical and the cultural.

Over a number of books and over a period of time, the numerical balance sheet, which is a complex of factors, has to be positive unless one has a patron—a Medici or an Emperor Francis I.

But I became convinced that the purpose of a publishing house, or an imprint, cannot merely be defined in terms of numbers, no more than the purpose of architecture can be defined by the arithmetic of quantity surveying. The house has first to be defined by its cultural balance sheet, by the creativity of its writers and its editors striving to enlighten and entertain. The identity of the house may not matter to the casual book buyer, but it does to authors, their agents, and the buyers of subsidiary rights, such as Hollywood. My experience in newspapers and magazines had persuaded me that provided we were not reckless, quality would produce a viable numerical balance sheet, whereas the simple notion of following the numbers wherever they might lead—the tyranny of numbers!—would diffuse rather than enhance the purpose of the enterprise. It was gratifying to see the policy vindicated year after year in the best seller lists: between them our titles appeared on the *New York Times* weekly list 173 times in 1992, 117 in 1993, 156 in 1994, and 205 in 1995. There were commercial as well as cultural benefits to establishing our watermark. When we sought to sign Jimmy Buffett, the music star who was also a best-selling commercial fiction writer, his agent directed him to Putnam. He came to us, despite a bid several hundred thousand dollars more than ours, because he wanted to be in the same house as William Styron, Norman Mailer, and Gore Vidal.

Throughout Random House and our imprints (Times Books and Villard), we sought to establish our identity by publishing books of intellectual merit, literary merit, and journalistic authority. To this end we signed the novelists and storytellers John Irving, John Berendt, Robert Harris, Anna Quindlen,

Alan Furst, Stephen Fry, Christopher Buckley, Barbara Taylor Bradford, Marc Salzman, Ethan Canin, and Caleb Carr. In public affairs and biography we signed Henry Louis Gates, Carl Sagan, Jeffrey Toobin, Clive James, Lewis Lapham, Sy Hersh, David Remnick, Sylvia Morris, Robert K. Massie, Gail Sheehy, Ron Chernow, and Paul Kennedy. And in the arts we signed Richard Avedon, Adam Gopnik, Alexander Liberman, and John Richardson.

But the perils of the publishing business are illustrated by the year 1993, when we had no fewer than eight of the twelve books on the American Library Association's list of the year's best books. Wanting to demonstrate that quality pays, I asked my finance director to tell me how much those books had made for the company. He came in with a long face. "Sorry, Harry, you lost $370,000 on those eight."

I asked him to check the results for the twenty-one titles of ours chosen by the *New York Times* as the year's most notable books. He looked even more miserable. "No good. You lost $698,000 on those." Then he gave me the big smile he'd been holding back: "But they are all still selling, and on two other titles alone you made a profit approaching two million dollars."

If you fancy yourself as a publisher, try guessing which four of the eight books on the American Library Association's list were viable in the year of publication: *Preparing for the Twenty-first Century* (Paul Kennedy); *A Tidewater Morning* (William Styron); *United States* (Gore Vidal); *Fraud* (Anita Brookner); *Dead Man Walking* (Sister Helen Prejean); *FDR: Into the Storm* (Kenneth Davis); *Lenin's Tomb* (David Remnick), *Selected Stories* (Mavis Gallant). Out of respect for the authors, I'll not give the details, but it should never be forgotten that good books have a long life. Jason Epstein always said when beating down opposition in-house to one of his many brilliant titles, "This book will be read long after we're all gone."

In 1994 we had a submission by a young first-time writer, not long out of university, whose contract with another house had been withdrawn for failure to deliver on time. Thanks to the alertness and judgment of a young Random House editor, Henry Ferris, at Peter Osnos's imprint at Times Books and the superb quality of the writing when I took a look, we judged the book worth an advance of $40,000. It was called *Dreams from My Father,* by a community organizer named Barack Obama. When Tina met him on the eve of his presidential inauguration, she remarked, "My husband signed the contract for your book."

He gave that wide radiant smile. "Worth a lot more now!"

A young boy walks on a beach with his father. This time it is not Rhyl in 1940; it is Quogue in 1998, and I am the father. The boy is my son George; he's twelve, as I was on Rhyl beach, and his mother is Tina. His younger sister, Isabel, was born just as I took over Random House. Tina, meanwhile, had reached the pinnacle of her profession, accepting Si Newhouse's invitation to move from the now profitable *Vanity Fair* to edit the *New Yorker.*

She worked very hard at the *New Yorker,* and then six years later on her *Talk* magazine start-up, killed by the advertising collapse after 9/11, while still being devoted to George, who'd been born prematurely, and Isabel. In work Tina and I remained the mutual support team we'd always been in editing and writing at all levels. I'd taught her layouts at *Tatler* and advised on the *New Yorker* design; she'd taught me about glossy magazines and covers when I started *Condé Nast Traveler.* We enjoyed life in New York, finally settling into our apartment at Sutton Place. Fifty years after playing in the English Open championships, I came across the American who'd won, Marty Reisman (aka "the Needle"), so I installed a table tennis table in the basement, and a group of us find it therapeutic to whack the celluloid ball. Reisman is still unbeatable.

As George and Isabel grew up, Tina and I split the evening engagements in New York so that one of us was always home. Our solo appearances at social functions caused New York tongues to wag, but that didn't affect us. We were living an American idyll—work in Manhattan, and on weekends we'd at last found our seaside dream, an old house on a beach on Long Island, twenty miles from where we were married in 1981.

The American predilection for the car is such that we had been regarded by some of our friends as English eccentrics when we took our first summer foray by train from the city, looking for a place to rent away from the heat. We rode the Long Island Railroad out, relaxing for two hours in the parlor car while a man in a straw boater served cold beer and the engineer sounded the whistle through the dreary suburban crossings and then joyously into the rolling pine barrens. At the end of a disappointing day of squally rain spent inspecting exorbitant glitzed-up beach huts in Westhampton, the letting agent drove us to nearby Quogue, a secluded seaside village of quiet lawns and white picket fences—a community of Waspy literary folk rather than the high rollers of East Hampton and Southampton. The seashore road was flooded by a tidal surge in the inland waterway, and the agent turned us round to go back. "You wouldn't want to see that house anyway," she said. "It's very old-fashioned." Our hearts leapt: "Yes, yes, show us right away."

The house on Dune Road, set down amid beach plums and dune grass, turned out to be a gray clapboard beach cottage with dormer windows. Built in 1928 and shielded from the ocean by a great double dune, it had survived the great hurricane of 1938. Every stick of furniture and ornament was from the same period in the 1930s. Little card tables were set for a game of bridge, like a scene from an Agatha Christie detective novel. Framed on one wall was the original owner's share certificate for the Siscoe gold mine, dated 1937.

We took it, of course. This was the dream seeded in those secluded spots at Angmering-on-Sea and Connemara when we first fell in love. In our house on the dunes, we lived the sepia print of an American summer, cocooned in a time warp while Tina edited her *New Yorker* articles and I immersed myself in American history and wrote and illustrated the story of the nation's ascent from 1889 to 1989: *The American Century.* It became a best seller, and I followed it with *They Made America,* a history of innovation over two centuries, made into a four-part PBS series. The old iron stove broiled local flounder pretty well, the ancient radio wafted in a narrative of baseball from somewhere, and every day for our morning dip the sun showed up promptly.

Twenty summers later, having saved up to buy the old house, we're still there with George, now twenty-three, and Isabel, nineteen, neither impressed that we can't tell them about the mysterious Siscoe mine. We retain our friendships and links with Britain. Enid came to Quogue for the wedding of our second daughter, Kate, who's settled in America. Our son Mike has worked in Los Angeles as a photographer and then in New York and later London as a specialist in computer printing. Ruth has managed London bookstores. I am proud of them all.

Tina and I now have dual citizenship; I became an American citizen in 1993 and Tina seven years later. When we can, we cross the Atlantic to Britain by sailing on Cunard's *Queen*

Mary 2, a nostalgic journey for me, since I returned to Britain in 1957 on the original *Queen Mary.* Around the time of 9/11 Isabel, then eleven, was asked at school whether she was British or American. She said she was "Amerikish." Some months after 9/11 her homework for a class in Greek mythology was to make a Pandora's box. We asked her what she'd put in it. She showed us an empty plate for hunger, a Tylenol bottle for disease, a cracked mirror for vanity, and a chocolate for greed. There was also a tiny colored drawing she had made of the Stars and Stripes.

"And that?" we asked.

"Hope," she said.

I often think of that today. I flew into America on the wings of hope, and it has not let me down. When I walk on the beach worrying what to put in this memoir and what to leave out, I hear the distant long, soft whistle of the locomotive rattling through the Hamptons, I see my father on his footplate, and I think of my own journey from the steam age of newspapers to digital delivery and all the people I have been privileged to work with in journalism and publishing. At the beginning I never conceived this memoir as a valedictory to a vanishing world. Now I hear so much about the imminent end of newspapers, it's a relief on a morning in New York to find that I can still walk to the corner newsstand for a bunch of them—meaningful stories on paper produced by what the Web world calls "human agents" rather than a bunch of bloodless algorithms. In fact I'm not alone. In the United States there are another 49,999,999 people similarly engaged. Fifty million people read a daily newspaper here, ten million in Britain.

Yet even as I have been writing this memoir, several major American newspapers have closed, and other famous titles have gone into bankruptcy. I am pained for the men and women who dedicated themselves to work they saw, rightly, as essential to a functioning democracy. My hopeful nature makes me believe that we are in a period of transition, at the end of which we will see a perfect marriage of the Web and the traditional newspaper, with its dedication to discovery, careful calibration of news values, and eclectic cultural mix. Technology will deliver a digital newspaper to our homes over the Internet, and we'll be able to choose to read it online or print it out in tabloid format to read over breakfast. (Disclosure: in 2008 Tina founded and now edits a comprehensive and exciting Web site, the Daily Beast, which I call up every morning.)

In fact the necessary worrying about what is happening with newspapers and their staffs tends to obscure the fantastic utilities of the Web. Internet journalism sites have immense potential, not just for their speed but also for increasing our comprehension and enjoyment. Hyperlinks open a panorama of global sources. We, the skeptical or curious readers, can explore primary documents quoted. We can replay a political rally caught on video by a spectator and posted to YouTube. We can keep track of a hurricane from a weather center or watch the performance of a new theatrical star the critics are acclaiming. And we can be sure that misstatement and tendentious entries will be stung to death by a thousand blogging bees.

The question is not whether Internet journalism will be dominant, but whether it will maintain the quality of the best print journalism. In the end it is not the delivery system that counts. It is what it delivers. There has never been such access to knowledge in all its forms. What we have to find is a way to sustain truth seeking. If we evolve the right financial model, we will enter a golden age of journalism.

I was exceptionally lucky to practice my craft for so long in the creatively free atmosphere cultivated by the Thomson and Newhouse families, Westminster Press, the *Guardian* and *Evening News*, and for that matter William Hobson Andrew— Mr. Will—with his milk can and impossible questions in Ashton-under-Lyne.

How many words, Evans, in a memoir?

Enough!

Acknowledgments

What are your sources? Are they sound? Why don't you name them? The questions I've answered as a reporter and asked as an editor now demand answers from an author.

Well, I'm glad you asked. It's an opportunity to acknowledge my considerable debts. When I set out to follow my paper trail through the labyrinths of memory, I had the sometimes enigmatic diaries I'd kept over the years in Pitman shorthand I could still read; I had school reports, wartime ration books, letters, photographs, articles, and transcripts of radio and television programs I'd been involved in; I had years of my newspaper files I cherished; and I had innumerable notes. I learned early, when challenged on a story, that if you wanted to survive as a journalist, you never threw away anything (and it works if you have a researcher as good as Jolene Lescio). Still, knowing that memory plays tricks, especially on sequence, I became an intruder on other people's tranquility, ransacking their recollections to affirm or amend my own.

My premier debt is to my younger brother Fred, curator of our family folklore, who wrestled me to the ground on various things I'd got wrong in our family history (just a bit!), as he used to wrestle me in boyhood. Fred was my guide when I revisited our haunts in Manchester and North Wales; I thank his widow, Christine, for her forbearance when I took away Fred from home. My brothers Peter and John also helped re-create those vanished times as did John's widow, Margaret. Alf Morris—sorry, Lord Morris of Wythenshawe—was of course the source of the story that as a schoolboy I was known in the neighborhood as "Posh" Evans, an attempt by Alf to under-mine my working-class credentials. His own are sensitively portrayed in Derek Kinrade's biography of Alf's ascent from Newton Heath to Labour minister in the House of Lords. It is a fine social history of northern working-class life.

My knowledge of my father's working life was much enriched by the recollections of Ken Law, his fireman mate on many an adventure on the footplate of steam locomotives. To check my memories of my start in newspapers, I revis-ited the town of Ashton-under-Lyne and the library at Sta-lybridge, and I thank the librarians there. It was an exercise powerfully assisted by Derek Rigby, who graduated from carrying Mr. W. H. Andrew's milk can to making headlines as an enterprising reporter. My two closest *Ashton-under-Lyne Reporter* pals, Eric Marsden and Frank Keeble (all in our early teens when we met), reassured me that various eccentricities I remembered really were true; our Weegee, Charlie Sutcliffe, scoured his photo library to my benefit. As for my years in the Royal Air Force, yanked out of Ashton, it's all in that Lubyanka Ministry of Aviation Records Office at Innsworth if anyone cares to check, and they'll have a record, too, of another air-man, Peter Spaull of South Wirral. He heard me on the BBC's *Desert Island Discs* and touched down out of the blue to testify to the fun of producing the *Empire Flying School Review.* He vol-unteered the information that my tapping him to write film reviews and gossip items eventually led to him covering music and the arts for BBC radio and to writing a column in the *Liv-erpool Daily Post. Per ardua ad astra.*

My diaries at Durham University reflect my joy in meeting Enid Parker, and I am grateful for the assiduity she brought to checking the details of those days and our years of married life. It was delightful re-creating the glow of those years with her and with Derek and Daphne Holbrook, Roy Arnold, Brian and Shirley Scrivener, John (Lofty) Morland, and Keith Nodding. Durham meant a lot to all of us and to the others reminiscing at Castle reunions: John Perkins, John Hollier, Bill Burdus, John Bridges, Lou Hamer, Edgar Jones, Geoff Pulling, Ridley Coats, Roy McKenzie, Eric Thompson, and Chuck Metcalfe. The Master of University College, Maurie Tucker, went out of his way to be helpful.

I was lucky that amid the paper storms at the *Manchester Evening News,* when my diaries went blank for days, I had a colleague from those times possessed of total recall, the writer Duncan Measor. I thank Duncan and his wife, Marjorie. I did find it stimulating to retrace steps when I could, and a visit to the *Manchester Evening News* offices was most rewarding. I thank the *Evening News* editor Paul Horrocks and his resolute assistant, Lisa Brealey; chief executive Mark Dodson; deputy editor Maria McGeoghan; Tom Waghorn; and the reporters, subs, and photographers I interrupted on their way to a deadline. Bob Corfield's film on the paper's centenary caught the atmosphere well. Andy Harvie, the news editor in my time, was helpful, as was Jane Futrell, the daughter of Denys Futrell and Tony Watson, head of the Press Association. On this visit to Manchester I had the big benefit of the hospitality and knowledge of my school chum Peter Charlton, the official historian of Newton Heath, and his wife, Lillian. My friend Barrie Heads, one of the redoubtable producers of Granada Television in its early glory days in Manchester, was kind enough to let me read his hilarious television memoir before its publication. I am sorry I failed his high standards of pronunciation.

Absolutely indispensable from the *Northern Echo* on was

Joan Thomas, my first-ever secretary, who later joined me in London. I'd not have been able to reach so many who shared the excitements without Joan's indefatigable resource in tracking people I'd lost touch with. Michael Morrissey, the paper's first news editor, and David Spark, the assistant editor, were extraordinarily generous with their time. Ken Hooper was helpful in retracing our cervical cancer investigation. I also thank Peter Ridley, Ray Robertson, Bill Treslove, and that kid photographer of the rock stars Ian Wright, who grew up to be a celebrity in his world. Don Berry, like Joan Thomas, came from Darlington to the *Sunday Times,* in his case via the *Rochester (NY) Times-Union,* and brought his superpowered sub's black pencil with him. I thank him for his wry observations.

I could fill a telephone directory with all the people who made the *Sunday Times* what it was in my fourteen years of editing (not forgetting the late Mike Randall, Peter Sullivan, Jack Lambert, Peter Harland, Steve Brodie, Malcolm Crawford, Peter Roberts, and Tony Bambridge). We were a community, sharing our passion for journalism, and I am forever indebted to them all for their skill, courage, and companionship. It's wonderful that the head printer, George Darker, is nearing one hundred years of age, despite the stresses to which we subjected him.

I can only make particular mention here of those *Sunday Times* individuals who failed to evade my long arm when I sought to test my recollections and records on theirs, chief among them John Barry, Godfrey Smith, Bruce Page, Godfrey Hodgson, Phillip Knightley, Edwin Taylor, Paul Eddy, Peter Gillman, Elaine Potter, Cal McCrystal, Tony Holden, Keith Richardson, Tony Rennell, Magnus Linklater, Peter Pringle, Philip Jacobson, Tony Dawe, Colin Chapman, Michael Ward, Parin Janmohamed, Charles Raw, Lewis Chester, Frank Giles, George Darby, Don McCullin, James Evans, and Anthony Whitaker, along with the recently much-mourned Hugo Young, John Whale, and Peter Wilsher.

Yvonne Mascarenhas, the widow of the brave Anthony, told me the story of her escape from Pakistan, which Anthony had kept to himself. Clive Irving, creator of the early Insight pages, filled in the gaps in my knowledge and understanding of those days before I joined the paper. For images, but also recollections, I drew freely on the skills and energies of photographers Bryan Wharton, Sally Soames, Peter Dunne, Mark Ellidge, and Ian Berry. Lord Snowdon graciously agreed I might use on the book jacket a portrait he took of me at a typewriter during my editorship.

My review of our Northern Ireland work owes much to John Barry, the former Insight editor (now with *Newsweek*), who challenged and enriched my account (though he's responsible for nothing that invites criticism) and with him the intrepid Chris Ryder. Chapter 17, "Death in Cairo," owes a great deal to Eddy and Gillman, who never gave up on the story. I very much appreciate how Scotland Yard was ready, as the saying goes, to assist us in our inquiries. I am indebted to the cooperation of Sir Ian Blair, then Metropolitan Commissioner of Police at Scotland Yard; Commander Simon Foy, head of homicide; Inspector Graham Jenkins; and former detectives Ray Small and Tony Comben. For their readiness to help, I must also acknowledge Jan Morris, David Holden's friend; Sy Hersh at the *New Yorker*; Steve Emerson at the Investigative Project on Terrorism in Washington, D.C.; Roger Louis, director of British studies at the University of Texas; and Professor Alan Weinstein, the ninth Archivist of the United States.

I had interesting discussions about the future of newspapers and the Web—a scene changing too rapidly to do full justice to their observations—with Paul Steiger of ProPublica; Clark Hoyt, the public editor at the *New York Times*; and ex-editors Gene Roberts and Clive Irving.

My Paper Chase—which is what it truly was—might never have been finished on time (well, only a year off) without the needling of my agent and friend Ed Victor. Cindy Quillinan, my assistant, had survived the vicissitudes of my book and television series on innovation and crested the waves of organizing manuscript "Mark XI" with uncanny calm.

Geoff Shandler, editor in chief at Little, Brown, whose original idea it was to divert me from recording other people's history to my own, proved to have reservoirs of patience as deep as his editorial judgment. At that crucial moment in the life of a book when an author is wondering whether to turn tail and run, I was vastly encouraged by Michael Korda, who has vibrant memories of his own of those years in Britain and life in the RAF, and I thank the historian Edmund Morris for some suggestions. I am grateful that Little, Brown's copy editor Barbara Jatkola proved to have 20/20 vision for all sorts of mistakes. An early manuscript was also read by Don Ross of the Newseum in Washington, D.C. He and I were partners in an exhibition the museum staged on war correspondents. As a Marine, he was wary of a mere airman, but it was a successful collaboration, and I thank him for volunteering to see that in this memoir I did not appear on early parade with Briticisms untranslated, infinitives split, tenses mixed, and the placing in sentences of prepositions up with which he would not put. I apologize for any faults of this kind that sneaked in, for assuredly they were the fault of RAF Corporal Evans and not U.S. Marine Corporal Ross.

I was most fortunate that John Heilpern, who grew up in Manchester and was a star on the *Sunday Times'* rival, the *Observer,* took an early interest in what I might do to retrieve those vanished times—his phrase. A brilliant biographer and theater critic himself, he urged me not to skimp on my early life and family, and in many a conversation he enabled me to retrieve the half-remembered and cherish it anew. His critical overview of the manuscript was invaluable, and I will always be grateful to him.

Throughout, from that daunting first blank page, during periods of uncertainty and distractions, I was sustained by the discerning eye, professional skill, and loving support of my gifted wife, Tina. My driving fear was of disappointing her, and my driving hope is that our children, George and Isabel, will regard the memoir as some compensation for those days in the present when I was lost in the past.

The author is grateful for permission to use the following: "For the Fallen" by Laurence Binyon. The Society of Authors as the Literary Representative of the Estate of Laurence Binyon; excerpt from "Annus Mirabilis" by Philip Larkin from Collected Poems *by Philip Larkin. Copyright © 1988, 2003 by the Estate of Philip Larkin. Reprinted by permission of Farrar, Straus and Giroux, LLC; "The Northern Ireland Question" by Desmond Egan from* Elegies, Selected Poems, *The Goldsmith Press Ltd., Ireland.*

Principal *Sunday Times* Books

The Zinoviev Letter, by Lewis Chester, Stephen Fay, and Hugo Young (Heinemann, 1967). How the famous "Red letter," which helped to defeat Ramsay Macdonald's Labour government in 1967, was forged by White Russians and circulated by the Conservative Party's Central Office with secret service help.

Philby: The Spy Who Betrayed a Generation, by Bruce Page, David Leitch, and Phillip Knightley, with an introduction by John Le Carré (Deutsch, 1968).

An American Melodrama, by Lewis Chester, Godfrey Hodgson, and Bruce Page (Deutsch, 1969). History of the U.S. presidential election of 1968, during which Richard Nixon was elected and Robert Kennedy was murdered.

Journey to Tranquility, by Hugo Young, Bryan Silcock, and Peter Dunn (Jonathan Cape, 1969). History of man's assault on the moon.

The Secret Lives of Lawrence of Arabia, by Colin Simpson and Phillip Knightley (Nelson, 1969). Documentation of Lawrence's sadomasochism and unsuspected role in Middle East politics.

The Pound in Your Pocket, by Peter Wilsher (Cassell, 1970). Century of Sterling, 1870–1970.

The Strange Voyage of Donald Crowhurst, by Nicholas Tomalin and Ron Hall (Hodder, 1970). The mystery of Donald Crowhurst, who vanished from his trimaran during the *Sunday Times'* single-handed nonstop race around the world.

Do You Sincerely Want to Be Rich? by Charles Raw, Bruce Page, and Godfrey Hodgson (Deutsch, 1971). Subtitled *Bernard Cornfeld and*

IOS: An International Swindle. Investigation of Investors Overseas Services (IOS) and its creator, Bernie Cornfeld: how it operated as an "offshore" company responsible to the law of no single nation and what it did with the billion dollars entrusted to it by a million savers.

Hoax, by Lewis Chester, Stephen Fay, and Magnus Linklater (Deutsch, 1972). The forgery and retailing of Howard Hughes's autobiography by Clifford Irving.

Ulster, by the Insight Team (Deutsch, 1972). Results of four months of inquiry into the origins of the Troubles.

The Thalidomide Children and the Law, by the *Sunday Times* (Deutsch, 1973). Documents and texts.

Watergate, by Lewis Chester, Stephen Aris, Cal McCrystal, and William Shawcross (Deutsch, 1973).

Death of Venice, by Stephen Fay and Phillip Knightley (Deutsch, 1975). Investigation of the threat to the survival of Venice.

The Exploding Cities, by Peter Wilsher and Rosemary Righter, with a foreword by Barbara Ward (Deutsch, 1975). Stimulated by a *Sunday Times* conference with the United Nations Fund for Population Activities at Oxford University.

Insight on Portugal (Deutsch, 1975). Portugal's return to democracy.

Nicholas Tomalin Reporting (Deutsch, 1975). Ron Hall introduces reporting by his colleague and friend, killed on duty for the *Sunday Times* in October 1973.

The Yom Kippur War, by the Insight Team (Deutsch, 1975). Sequel to the *Sunday Times'* 1974 book *Insight on the Middle East War.*

The First Casualty, by Phillip Knightley (Deutsch, 1975). War correspondent as hero, propagandist, and mythmaker from Crimea to Vietnam.

The Crossman Affair, by Hugo Young (Jonathan Cape, 1976).

Destination Disaster, by Paul Eddy, Elaine Potter, and Bruce Page (Hart-Davis, MacGibbon, 1976). Investigation of the DC-10 crash in Paris.

On Giant's Shoulders, by Marjorie Wallace and Michael Robson (Times Books, 1976). The story of thalidomide victim Terry Wiles.

Slater Walker, by Charles Raw (Deutsch, 1977). Jim Slater tried to prevent the publication of Charles Raw's four-year investigation, which concluded that in all its various forms, the investment company Slater Walker was really about one thing—the manipulation of share prices.

The Abuse of Power, by James Margach (W. H. Allen, 1978). The war between Downing Street and the media, from David Lloyd George to James Callaghan.

The Fall of the House of Beaverbrook, by Lewis Chester and Jonathan Fenby (Deutsch, 1979). How Trafalgar House acquired the *Daily Express, Evening Standard,* and *Sunday Express.*

Jeremy Thorpe: A Secret Life, by Lewis Chester, Magnus Linklater, and David May (Deutsch, 1979).

Suffer the Children, by the Insight Team (Deutsch, 1979). The thalidomide story.

Siege! by the Insight Team (Hamlyn, 1980). How the Special Air Service rescued hostages at the Iranian embassy in London in 1980.

Stop Press: The Inside Story of the Times Dispute, by Eric Jacobs (Deutsch, 1980). The year of the suspension of Times Newspapers (1978–1979).

Lawsuit, by Stuart M. Speiser (Horizon Press, 1980). Lawyer in the DC-10 case opens his files on other celebrated cases.

The Vestey Affair, by Phillip Knightley (Macdonald, 1981).

Bibliography

Alterman, Eric. "Out of Print: The Death and Life of the American Newspaper." *New Yorker,* March 31, 2008.

Bacon, Robert William. *Britain's Economic Problem: Too Few Producers.* London: Macmillan, 1978.

Barnett, Steven. "Future of the Printed Word: The Press; Reasons to Be Cheerful." *British Journalism Review* 17, no. 1 (March 2006): 7–14.

Bayley, Edwin R. *Joe McCarthy and the Press.* Madison: University of Wisconsin Press, 1981.

Behr, Edward. *Anyone Here Been Raped and Speaks English?* London: New English Library, 1982.

Bell, J. Bowyer. *The Irish Troubles: A Generation of Violence, 1967–1992.* New York: St. Martin's Press, 1993.

Benn, Tony, and Ruth Winstone. *Conflicts of Interest: Diaries, 1977–1980.* London: Hutchinson, 1990.

Blundy, David, and Anthony Holden. *The Last Paragraph: The Journalism of David Blundy.* London: Heinemann, 1990.

Boyd, Ruth. *Stanley Devon: News Photographer.* England: D. Harrison, 1995.

Braddon, Russell. *Thomson of Fleet.* London: Collins, 1965.

Brandon, Piers. *The Life and Death of the Press Barons.* London: Secker, 1982.

Briggs, Susan. *The Home Front: War Years in Britain, 1939–1945.* New York: American Heritage, 1975.

Brown, Anthony Cave. *Treason in the Blood: H. St. John Philby, Kim Philby, and the Spy Case of the Century.* Boston: Houghton Mifflin, 1994.

Brown, Derek. "Future of the Printed Word: Cyberspace; Joe Blog's Turn." *British Journalism Review* 17, no. 1 (March 2006): 15–19.

Butler, David, and Anne Sloman. *British Political Facts, 1900–1975*. London: Macmillan, 1975.

"The Changing Newsroom." Pew Research Center's Project for Excellence in Journalism, July 21, 2008, http://journalism.org/node/11961.

Coleridge, Nicholas. *Paper Tigers: The Latest, Greatest Newspaper Tycoons and How They Won the World*. London: Heinemann, 1993.

Compton, Edmund. *Report of the Enquiry into Allegations Against the Security Forces of Physical Brutality in Northern Ireland Arising Out of Events on the 9th August, 1971*. London: HMSO, 1971.

Coogan, Tim Pat. *Michael Collins: A Biography*. London: Hutchinson, 1990.

———. *The Troubles: Ireland's Ordeal and the Search for Peace*. New York: Palgrave, 2002.

Cottle, Simon. "Reporting the Troubles in Northern Ireland: Paradigms and Media Propaganda." *Critical Studies in Mass Communication* 14, no. 3 (1997): 283–96.

Crossman, R. H. S. *The Diaries of a Cabinet Minister*. Vol. 3, *Secretary of State for Social Services*. London: Hamish Hamilton, 1975.

Cudlipp, Hugh. *The Prerogative of the Harlot: Press Barons and Power*. London: Bodley Head, 1980.

Cuozzo, Steven. *It's Alive: How America's Oldest Newspaper Cheated Death and Why It Matters*. New York: Times Books, 1996.

Davies, Nick. *Flat Earth News: An Award-Winning Reporter Exposes Falsehood, Distortion, and Propaganda in the Global Media*. London: Chatto & Windus, 2008.

Deakin, James. *Straight Stuff: The Reporters, the White House and the Truth*. New York: William Morrow, 1984.

Dean, Joseph. *Hatred, Ridicule, or Contempt: A Book of Libel Cases*. London: Constable, 1953.

Donoughue, Bernard. *Downing Street Diary: With Harold Wilson in No. 10*. London: Jonathan Cape, 2005.

———. *The Heat of the Kitchen*. London: Politico's, 2003.

East, P. D. *The Magnolia Jungle: The Life, Times and Education of a Southern Editor*. New York: Simon and Schuster, 1960.

Eckley, Grace. *Maiden Tribute: A Life of W. T. Stead*. Philadelphia: Xlibris, 2007.

Edwards, Robert. *Goodbye Fleet Street*. Sevenoaks, Eng.: Coronet, 1989.

Edwards, Ruth Dudley. *Newspapermen: Hugh Cudlipp, Cecil Harmsworth King and the Glory Days of Fleet Street*. London: Pimlico, 2004.

Egerton, John. *Speak Now Against the Day: The Generation Before the Civil Rights Movement in the South*. New York: Knopf, 1994.

Elliott, Geoffrey. *I Spy: The Secret Life of a British Agent*. London: St. Ermin's Press, 1999.

Evans, Harold. Foreword. In *Killing the Messenger: Report of the Global Inquiry by the International News Safety Institute into the Protection of Journalists*, 2–5. Brussels: International News Safety Institute, 2007.

———. Introduction. In *Don McCullin*, by Don McCullin, 12–14. London: Jonathan Cape, 2001.

———. "The Suez Crisis: A Study in Press Performance." Master's thesis, University of Durham, 1965.

Friendly, Fred W. *The Good Guys, the Bad Guys and the First Amendment: Free Speech vs. Fairness in Broadcasting*. New York: Random House, 1976.

———. *Minnesota Rag: The Dramatic Story of the Landmark Supreme Court Case That Gave New Meaning to the Freedom of the Press*. New York: Random House, 1981.

Geraghty, Tony. *The Irish War: The Military History of a Domestic Conflict*. London: HarperCollins, 2000.

Giles, Frank. *Sundry Times*. London: John Murray, 1986.

Giussani, Vanessa. "The UK Clean Air Act, 1956: An Empirical Investigation." Center for Social and Economic Research on the Global Environment, 1994.

Glover, Stephen. *Paper Dreams*. London: Jonathan Cape, 1993.

Goff, Peter, and Barbara Trionfi, eds. *The Kosovo News and Propaganda War*. Vienna: International Press Institute, 1999.

Greenhill, Denis. *More by Accident*. York, Eng.: Wilton 65, 1992.

Greenslade, Roy. *Press Gang: How Newspapers Make Profits from Propaganda*. London: Pan Books, 2004.

Grundy, Bill. *The Press Inside Out*. London: W. H. Allen, 1976.

Haines, Joe. *The Politics of Power*. Sevenoaks, Eng.: Coronet, 1977.

Hamilton, Denis. *Editor-in-Chief: The Fleet Street Memoirs of Sir Denis Hamilton*. London: Hamish Hamilton, 1989.

———. "The Sunday Times." *Punch Magazine,* December 23, 1964, 944–47.

Hampton, Henry, Steve Fayer, and Sarah Flynn. *Voices of Freedom: An Oral History of the Civil Rights Movement from the 1950s through the 1980s.* New York: Bantam Books, 1990.

Harris, Geoffrey, and David Spark. *Practical Newspaper Reporting.* London: William Heinemann, 1966.

Hattersley, Roy. *Fifty Years On: A Prejudiced History of Britain Since the War.* London: Little, Brown, 1997.

Heads, Barrie. "Medium Close-up." Unpublished manuscript.

Hennessy, Peter. *Having It So Good: Britain in the Fifties.* London: Allen Lane, 2006.

Herd, Harold. *The March of Journalism: The Story of the British Press from 1622 to the Present Day.* London: George Allen and Unwin, 1952.

Hetherington, Alastair. *Guardian Years.* London: Chatto & Windus, 1981.

Hilty, James W. *Robert Kennedy: Brother Protector.* Philadelphia: Temple University Press, 1997.

Hobsbawm, Julia, ed. *Where the Truth Lies: Trust and Morality in PR and Journalism.* London: Atlantic Books, 2006.

Hobson, Harold, Phillip Knightley, and Leonard Russell. *Pearl of Days.* London: Hamish Hamilton, 1972.

Hodgson, Godfrey. *America in Our Time.* Garden City, NY: Doubleday, 1976.

Hoggart, Richard. *The Uses of Literacy: Aspects of Working-Class Life with Special Reference to Publications and Entertainments.* Harmondsworth: Penguin Books, 1958.

Holden, Anthony. *Of Presidents, Prime Ministers, and Princes: A Decade in Fleet Street.* London: Weidenfeld and Nicolson, 1984.

Hooper, David. *Official Secrets: The Use and Abuse of the Act.* London: Secker & Warburg, 1987.

Howard, Anthony. *Crossman: The Pursuit of Power.* London: Pimlico, 1991.

Isaacs, Jeremy. *Storm over 4: A Personal Account.* London: Weidenfeld and Nicolson, 1989.

Jack, Ian. *Before the Oil Ran Out: Britain, 1977–1986.* London: Secker & Warburg, 1987.

Jackson, Brian. *Working Class Community: Some General Notions Raised by a Series of Studies in Northern England.* London: Routledge & Kegan Paul, 1968.

Jenkins, Roy. *A Life at the Centre.* London: Macmillan, 1991.

Jenkins, Simon. *Newspapers.* London: Faber and Faber, 1979.

———. *Thatcher and Sons: A Revolution in Three Acts.* London: Penguin, 2007.

Keen, Andrew. *The Cult of the Amateur: How Today's Internet Is Killing Our Culture.* London: Nicholas Brealey, 2007.

Kennedy, Ludovic. *10 Rillington Place.* London: Panther Books, 1972.

Kennedy, Robert F. *The Enemy Within.* New York: Harper & Row, 1960.

Kingston, Shane. "Terrorism, the Media and the Northern Ireland Conflict." *Studies in Conflict and Terrorism* 18, no. 3 (July/September 1995): 203–31.

Knightley, Phillip. *A Hack's Progress.* London: Jonathan Cape, 1997.

Kovach, Bill, and Tom Rosenstiel. *The Elements of Journalism: What Newspeople Should Know and the Public Should Expect.* New York: Three Rivers Press, 2007.

———. *Warp Speed: America in the Age of Mixed Media; A Century Foundation Report.* New York: Century Foundation Press, 1999.

Kurtz, Howard. *Media Circus: The Trouble with America's Newspapers.* New York: Random House, 1993.

Lapping, Brian, ed. *The Bounds of Freedom.* London: Constable, in collaboration with Granada Television, 1980.

Leapman, Michael. *Barefaced Cheek.* London: Hodder and Stoughton, 1983.

Leigh, David. *The Frontiers of Secrecy: Closed Government in Britain.* London: Junction Books, 1980.

Lennon, Peter. *Foreign Correspondent: Paris in the Sixties.* London: Picador, 1994.

Lloyd, Chris. *Attacking the Devil: 130 Years of the* Northern Echo. Darlington, Eng.: Northern Echo, 1999.

Lords, Walter. *A Night to Remember: The Classic Account of the Final Hours of the* Titanic. New York: Henry Holt, 2005.

Madigan, Charles M, ed. *-30-: The Collapse of the Great American Newspaper.* Chicago: Ivan R. Dee, 2007.

Mansfield, F. J., and Denis Weaver. *Mansfield's Complete Journalist: A Study of the Principles and Practice of Newspaper-making.* London: Pitman, 1962.

Marr, Andrew. "Future of the Printed Word: A Changing Culture; Brave New World." *British Journalism Review* 17, no. 1 (March 2006): 29–34.

McLuhan, Marshall. *Understanding Media: The Extensions of Man.* London: Abacus, 1973.

Meyer, Philip. *The Vanishing Newspaper: Saving Journalism in the Information Age.* Columbia: University of Missouri Press, 2004.

Morton, J. B. *Beachcomber: The Works of J. B. Morton.* London: A. Wheaton, 1974.

Nasaw, David. *The Chief: The Life of William Randolph Hearst.* Boston: Houghton Mifflin, 2000.

Neil, Andrew. *Full Disclosure.* London: Macmillan, 1996.

Orwell, George. *The Road to Wigan Pier.* London: Victor Gollancz, 1937.

Orwell, Sonia, and Ian Angus, eds. *The Collected Essays, Journalism and Letters of George Orwell.* Vol. 2, *My Country Right or Left, 1940–1943.* Boston: David R. Godine, 2000.

Page, Bruce. "Future of the Printed Word: The Dangers; It's the Media That Needs Protecting." *British Journalism Review* 17, no. 1 (March 2006): 20–28.

Page, Bruce, David Leitch, and Phillip Knightley. *The Philby Conspiracy.* Toronto: Fontana Books, 1968.

Philby, Rufina. *The Private Life of Kim Philby: The Moscow Years.* New York: St. Ermins Press, 1999.

Pimlott, Ben. *Harold Wilson.* London: HarperCollins, 1992.

Polsgrove, Carol. *Divided Minds: Intellectuals and the Civil Rights Movement.* New York: W. W. Norton, 2001.

Powledge, Fred. *Free at Last? The Civil Rights Movement and the People Who Made It.* New York: Harper Perennial, 1992.

Prevett, J. H. "Actuarial Assessment of Damages: The Thalidomide Case I." *Modern Law Review* 35, no. 2 (March 1972): 140–55.

———. "Actuarial Assessment of Damages: The Thalidomide Case II." *Modern Law Review* 35, no. 3 (May 1972): 256–67.

Prichard, Peter. *The Making of McPaper: The Inside Story of USA Today.* Kansas City, MO: Andrews, McMeel & Parker, 1987.

Pringle, Peter, and Philip Jacobson. *Those Are Real Bullets: Bloody Sunday, Derry, 1972.* London: Fourth Estate, 2000.

Righter, Rosemary. *Whose News? Politics, the Press and the Third World.* London: Burnett Books, 1978.

Roberts, Gene, and Hank Klibanoff. *The Race Beat: The Press, the Civil Rights Struggle, and the Awakening of a Nation.* New York: Vintage Books, 2007.

Rose, Peter. *How the Troubles Came to Northern Ireland.* New York: St. Martin's Press, 2000.

Rose, Richard. "On the Priorities of Citizenship in the Deep South and Northern Ireland." *Journal of Politics* 38, no. 2 (May 1976): 247–91.

"Rover Boys Rewarded." *Time,* April 8, 1957.

Sampson, Anthony. *The Changing Anatomy of Britain.* London: Hodder and Stoughton, 1981.

"Scandal in Portland." *Time,* June 4, 1956.

Schama, Simon. *A History of Britain.* Vol. 3, *The Fate of Empire, 1776–2000.* London: BBC Worldwide, 2004.

Sebag-Montefiore, Hugh. *Dunkirk: Fight to the Last Man.* Cambridge: Harvard University Press, 2006.

Shepard, Richard F. *The Paper's Papers: A Reporter's Journey Through the Archives of the* New York Times. New York: Times Books, 1996.

Smartt, Ursula. *Media Law for Journalists.* London: Sage Publications, 2006.

Smith, Richard Norton. *The Colonel: The Life and Legend of Robert R. McCormick, 1880–1955.* Boston: Houghton Mifflin, 1997.

Smith, Zay N., and Pamela Zekman. *The Mirage.* New York: Random House, 1979.

Spark, David. *Investigative Reporting: A Study in Technique.* Oxford: Focal, 1999.

"The State of the News Media 2008." Project for Excellence in Journalism, March 17, 2008, http://www.stateofthenewsmedia.com/2008/.

Steiger, Paul E. "Read All About It: How Newspapers Got into Such a Fix, and Where They Go from Here." *Wall Street Journal,* December 29, 2007.

Swanberg, W. A. *Citizen Hearst: A Biography of William Randolph Hearst.* New York: Scribner, 1961.

———. *Pulitzer.* New York: Scribner, 1967.

Thomson, Roy Herbert. *After I Was Sixty: A Chapter of Autobiography.* London: Hamish Hamilton, 1975.

Trevor-Roper, H. R. *The Philby Affair: Espionage, Treason, and Secret Services.* London: Kimber, 1968.

Walker, Martin. *Powers of the Press.* London: Quartet, 1982.

Waterhouse, Robert. *The Other Fleet Street: How Manchester Made Newspapers National.* Altrincham, Eng.: First Edition Limited, 2004.

Waugh, Evelyn. *Scoop: A Novel About Journalists.* Harmondsworth: Penguin Books, 1976.

Weatherby, W. J. *Breaking the Silence: The Negro Struggle in the U.S.A.* New York: Penguin, 1965.

Wendt, Lloyd. Chicago Tribune: *The Rise of a Great American Newspaper.* Chicago: Rand McNally, 1979.

Whale, John. *The Half-Shut Eye: Television and Politics in Britain and America.* London: Macmillan, 1969.

Wilkinson, Brenda. *The Civil Rights Movement: An Illustrated History.* New York: Crescent Books, 1997.

Williams, Francis. *The Right to Know: The Rise of the World Press.* Harlow, Eng.: Longmans, 1969.

Winchester, Simon. "13 Killed as Paratroops Break Riot." *Guardian,* January 31, 1972. http://www.guardian.co.uk/uk/1972/jan/31/bloodysunday.northernireland.

Winocour, Jack, ed. *The Story of the* Titanic: *As Told by Its Survivors.* New York: Dover Publications, 1960.

Young, Hugo. *The Hugo Young Papers: Thirty Years of British Politics—off the Record.* Edited by Ion Trewin, with forewords by Harold Evans and Alan Rusbridger. London: Allen Lane, 2008.

———. *One of Us: A Biography of Margaret Thatcher.* London: Macmillan, 1989.

———. "Rupert Murdoch and the *Sunday Times:* A Lamp Goes Out." *Political Quarterly* 55, no. 4 (October 1984): 382–90.

Index

Abbott, Joe, 53
Ace in the Hole (movie), 60
Acheson, Dean, 484
Ackerman, Bob, 149
Ackner, Desmond (later Lord), 363–64, 365
Adams, Gerry, 477
Adams, William Henry, 98
African Union, 396
Agate, James, 90
Agricultural Research Council, 284
airline scandal, 326, 487
Albania, 345–46
Alcock, J. W., 173
Alder, Ralph "Raphie," 80
Alger, Horatio, 312
Allcock, Ron, 71
Allen, Edgar, 127
Allende, Salvador, 442
America. *See* United States
American Air Force, 97
American Beauty (movie), 231
American Cancer Society, 277
American Century, The (Evans), 532, 538
American Chamber of Commerce, 227
American Dilemma, An (Myrdal), 194
American Indians. *See* Native Americans
American Journal of Obstetrics and
    Gynecology, 363
American Library Association, 535
American Red Cross, 521
Amin, General Idi, 376, 390, 395–400
Amis, Martin, 487
Anatomy of Oxford (anthology), 241
Andersonstown Co-operative Society, 449,
    452, 453
Andrew, William Hobson ("Mr. Will"),
    83–85, 95–96, 541
Andrews, Sir Linton, 246
Angelou, Maya, 517

Anglo-German Friendship Society, 334
Anglo-Irish Agreement (1985), 477
Angus, W. W., 117
antibiotics, 12
antiques swindle, 326
Apache Indians, 218
appeasement (Munich pact). *See* Chamberlain,
    Neville
Arab-Israeli wars. *See* Israel
Arafat, Yasir, 431
Aris, Stephen, 376
Aristotle, 162
Arkansas Gazette, 225
Ashley, Jack and Pauline, 372–76,
    379–81, 383
Ashmore, Harry, 225
Ashton-under-Lyne Reporter, HME at, 74–99,
    110, 151, 162, 179, 187
Aspinall, Neil, 281
Associated Press (U.S.), 139
Associated Society of Locomotive Engineers
    and Firemen, 27
Astaire, Fred, 193
Astbury, Frederick, 357
Astor, David, 214, 304
Astor, Lord, 318–19, 321
Aswan Dam, 205
Atlanta Constitution, 225, 228
Atlantic magazine, 505
Atlantic Monthly Press, 508, 510, 512, 515, 526
Atlas, Charles, 55
Atomic Energy Commission (AEC), 346–47
At Random (literary magazine), 526
Attenborough, Richard, 291
Attlee, Clement, 168, 310, 409
Auden, W. H., 517
Austin, Anthony, 418–19
Avedon, Richard, 535
Ayerst, David, 161

Index

Bacon & Woodrow (law firm), 368
Bagehot, Walter, 162
Bailey, David, 392
Baker, Peter, 292, 476
Baldwin, Stanley, 22
Bangladesh, creation of state of, 406
Barber, Anthony, 278
Barber, Noel, 418
Bari, Abdul, 405
Barnes, Julian, 485
Barnes, Thomas, 177
Barrett, Donald, 371
Barrett, Vivien, 383
Barrington-Ward, Mark, 242, 244–45, 248, 258
Barrington-Ward, Robert M., 248
Barry, Dave, 517
Barry, John, 329, 331, 391, 422; on Holden
    case, 425, 427, 431–32, 439–40; on Ireland,
    464–65, 467–68, 472, 474, 476
Batchelor, Mr. (subeditor), 152
Bateman, John, 53, 64
Bay of Pigs disaster, 251, 346, 448
BBC (British Broadcasting Corporation),
    59, 141, 171, 321, 367, 372, 420; BBC
    America, 526; "BBC voice," 41, 64, 75,
    310, (Queen's English) 283; radio, 297,
    373, (Goon Show) 60, 310, (HME hosts
    discussion program) 317, (Radio 4
    program The World at One) 341; suppresses
    news, 22, 43; television monopoly, 188,
    (broken) 162, 188–89; television programs,
    282, 367, 377, (about Northern Echo) 263
Deale, Phelan and Edith Bouvier, 505
Beano (comic book), 45
Beatles, the, 280–82, 392
Beau Geste (movie), 60
Beavan, John (later Lord Ardwick), 96, 112–13,
    120, 146
Beaverbrook, Lord (William M. Aitken), 148,
    305–6
Bede, Saint, 116
Beedham, Brian, 198
Beethoven: His Spiritual Development
    (Sullivan), 92
Begin, Menachem, 442
Belfast Telegraph, 452
Bell, Alexander Graham, 193
Bengalis in Pakistan, 402–4
Benn, Tony, 483
Bentham, Jeremy, 136
Bentley, Derek, 163–64, 167
Berendt, John, 534
Berlin, Irving, 193
Berlin Philharmonic orchestra, 171
Berlin wall, 133, 251; airlift, 109, 115
Berlioz, Hector, 316
Bernstein, Cecil, 189
Bernstein, Sidney, 189
Berra, Yogi, 193

Betjeman, John, 130
Betzinez, Mr. and Mrs. Jason, 218, 233
Bevan, Aneurin, 168, 185
Bevin, Ernest, 310, 319
Beyond the Fringe (comedy revue), 310
Beyond Peace (Nixon), 533
Bible, the, 38, 223; Welsh translation of, 14
Bickers, David, 357
Big Sleep, The (Chandler), 526
Billings, Josh, 9
Bill of Rights, American, 204
Bingham, Barry, 223, 261
Bingham, Lord Chief Justice Thomas, 164
Binyon, Laurence, 53
Birkenhead, Lord, 22
Birmingham Gazette, 241
Black, Cilla, 281
Black Hawk (Indian leader), 232
blacks: in England, 65, 253, 254, (vilified) 356;
    in southern U.S., 203–4, 222–31, 253, 455,
    457, (migrate to Chicago) 205, 219
Black September group, 406–7
Blackshirts, the, 165
Blair, Jayson, 401
Blair, Tony, 186, 476
Blake, Peter, 392
Bloch, Dora, 398
Bloody Sunday. See Ireland
Blundy, Anna, 505
Blundy, David, 416, 452, 487, 502, 505
Blunt, Anthony, 340–42, 352
Boer War statue (Manchester), 178
"bogus Burgundy" story, 326
Bolam, Silvester, 130
Bonnette, Willivene, 426
Boorstin, Daniel J., 517, 520
Bordrez, Maurice, 128
Bourne-Arton, Anthony, 273
Bowles, Camilla Parker, 399
Boxer, Mark, 315, 317, 319–20
Boyle, Andrew, 341
Boy Scouts, 31, 38, 308, 322
Brabin, Justice, 297–98
Brabourne, Lady, 451
Bradford, Barbara Taylor, 535
Bradlee, Ben, 504–5, 509
Bradley, Mamie, 203–4
Brady, Ian, 84
Brady, Reg, 479–80, 481
Brando, Marlon, 202, 530–31
Brave New World (Huxley), 358
Bray, Jeremy, 278
Brenner, Marie, 505
Breslin, Harold, 216
Bright, John, 175
Briscoe, Peter, 365
Britain, 437; declares war on Germany, 7–8,
    40, (wartime rationing) 63–64, 65–66,
    200–201; exaggerated ideas of prowess

564

of, 68; immigrants to, as "threat," 356, 408; interest on U.S. loan to, 207–8; in Ireland, (Irish Protestant loyalty to) 454, (and torture of internees) 466–71 (*see also* Ireland); as portrayed to/seen by U.S., 196, 210, 214; postwar, Empire diminishes, 168, 484; in Suez crisis, *see* Suez canal; thalidomide in, *see* thalidomide affair
British Agent (Whitwell), 342
British Army of the Rhine (postwar), report on equipment of, 183–84
British European Airways, 169
British Expeditionary Force (BEF). *See* Dunkirk
British Gazette, 22
British Information Service, 167, 211
British Parachute Regiment (Paras), 458; fatalities among, 451
British Railways, 20, 121, 156
Broad, Sarah and Roger, 380
Broadbent, Geoffrey, 273
Brokaw, Tom, 529
Bromhead, Dr. Peter, 127
Brooke, Gerald, 349
Brookes, Rupert, 45
Brooklyn Dodgers, 202
Brookner, Anita, 535
Brown, A. W., 173
Brown, Bettina, 486
Brown, George (Foreign Secretary), 330, 350–51
Brown, George (film producer), 486
Brown, Gordon, 23, 382
Brown, Tina, 485–89, 494, 504–5, 512; editorships of, 506–9, 517–18, 536–38, 540
Brown v. Board of Education, 223, 225–26, 228
Buber, Martin, 153
Buckley, Christopher, 535
Buffett, Jimmy, 534
Bulgaria, holocaust in, 235
Burdon, Eric, and the Animals, 282
Burgess, Guy, 330–34, 338, 344, 345, 352
Burke, Edmund, 110, 125, 126, 328
Burnet, Alistair, 198
Bush, George Herbert Walker, 494, 520, 533
Bush, George W., 10, 193
Butler, Rab, 292
Butler Education Act, 115, 310
Byatt, A. S., 520

Callaghan, James, 409
Cameron, David (Taffy), 429
Cameron, Lord, 460–61
Campbell, Sam, 472
Camp David Accords (1978), 443
Canadian Broadcasting Corporation (CBC), 435
Canberra jet bomber, 169–70
cancer research/treatment, 275–78, 325, 355, 376, 489
Canin, Ethan, 535

Canterbury, archbishop of, 22
Capa, Robert, 390
capital punishment. *See* death penalty
Capone, Al, 196, 197
Capote, Truman, 517, 526
Capra, Frank, 193
Cardus, Neville, 151
Carlile, Richard, 176–77
Caro, Robert, 529
Carr, Caleb, 535
Carr, George, 280
Carter, Hodding II, 225, 229
Carter, Jimmy, 533
Casablanca (movie), 60
Casanova Brown (movie), 87
Case Closed (Posner), 527–28
Cash, Wilbur, 230
Castle, The (Kafka), 82
Cathcart, John, 282
Catherine Pakenham Award, 487
Catholic Church, 9, 219, 334; Catholic activists in Germany, 340; in Ireland, 448, 454–59, 461–66, 475–76, (Protestant slaughter of Catholics) 453–54, 471, ("special position" of) 455
Catholic Herald, 297
Cat in the Hat (Geisel, "Dr. Seuss"), 517
Cave, Ray, 521
censorship, 447, 532; of Crossman's memoirs, 411–12; military, in Pakistan, 404; theater, abolition of, 392; World War II, 4
Cerf, Bennett, 518–19, 532
Cerf, Christopher, 518
Ceylon Observer, 238
Chalfont, Lord (Alun Gwynne Jones), 336, 338
Challenger shuttle explosion, 494
Chamberlain, Neville, 7, 40–42, 44, 53, 64; and appeasement, 23, 304, (opposed) 247, 271
Chambers, Whittaker, 134, 532
Chandler, Raymond, 194, 526
chaos theory, 329–30
Chaplin, Sid, 247, 261, 287
Chapman, Colin, 490
Charles I, king of England, 53, 288
Charles, prince of Wales, 395–96, 399
Charlton, Peter, 62
Chatham House reports, 167
Chemie Grüenthal, 358, 361, 362–65, 378, 383
Cheney, Dick, 462
Chernow, Ron, 535
Cherokee Indians, 219
chess, 88, 92–93, 199, 530
Chester, Lewis, 316, 329, 468
Cheyenne Indians, 219
Chiang Kai-shek, 134
Chicago, 203; black migrants in, 205, 219; HME's stay in, 196–97, 203–14
Chicago American, 211
Chicago Tribune, 196, 208–11, 214, 445, 461

Chichester, Francis, 318
China vs. Soviet Union, 458
Chowdhury, Amitabha, 240
Christiansen, Arthur, 284
Christie, John Reginald Halliday, 164, 289–94
Christie, Julie, 392
Chronicle (San Francisco), 216
Churchill, Randolph, 312, 320
Churchill, Sir Winston, 21, 186, 214, 271; early
    memoirs reprinted, 279; as prime minister,
    wartime and postwar, 22, 44, 59, 64, 168,
    193, 236, 272, (successor to) 205; quoted,
    (on Dunkirk) 7, (on naval tradition) 125,
    (on truth) 8–9; skepticism about, 22–23, 68
Church of England, 170
Chuter Ede, Lord, 294–95, 297
CIA (Central Intelligence Agency), 344–46, 355,
    424, 530, 531; HME's exposé of, 446; and
    Holden case, 438, 439–44
Citizen Kane (movie), 60, 61
Civic Trust, 178–79; for the North East, 273
Civil Action, A (Harr), 528–29
civil rights movement. *See* Ireland
class, hierarchies of, 21, 24, 309–11, 352, 392,
    484; and accent, 41, 93, 310; lack of, among
    bomber crews, 103–4; and MI6, 350
Clayton Players, 90
Clean Air Act (1956), 176
Cleese, John, 60
Climate of Treason, The (Boyle), 341
Clinton, Bill, 523, 524, 533
Clinton (Tennessee) *Courier*, 223
Coal Board, 273
Cobban, Helena, 422, 431
Cobden, Richard, 175, 178
cold war, 10, 23, 115, 201, 217, 346–47. *See also*
    Philby, Harold Adrian Russell "Kim"
Coleridge, Samuel Taylor, 328
Collett Dickenson Pearce (CDP), 393
Collier, Richard, 6
Collins, J. D., 266
Collins family, 14, 15
Comben, Detective Inspector Tony, 422, 434
Commonwealth Fund, 193–95, 203
Communism, international, 133, 438; anti-
    Communist hysteria, 134, 195, 201; in East
    Berlin, 184; in Indonesia, 317; and Philby
    case, 330, 333–34, 340, 346; and sabotage of
    production, 387, 479
Complete Journalist, (Mansfield), 142
Compston, Ken, 317–18
Compton, Sir Edmund, 471
computers: proto-computer, 173, 177; use of, vs.
    Linotype, 482–83, 512
Conan Doyle, Sir Arthur, 54, 296
Condé Nast magazines, 506, 521
Condé Nast Traveler magazine, 513–14, 521, 536
Congo, the, 458
Coningsby (Disraeli), 173

"conkers," 49
Connolly, Cyril, 304
Conran, Terence, 324
Conservative Party (Tories), 21, 41, 135,
    176, 214, 292; attacks on, 246–47; and
    commercial television, 162, 188; interviews
    with members, 167; and Ireland, 9, 327, 457,
    462, 470; Labour vs., 168, 185, 271–72, 311,
    352, 457; newspapers and, 85, 246, 273, 304,
    (advertising refused) 285, (news coverage)
    317; Profumo scandal and, 310; Thatcher
    and, 394, 409
Constitution, U.S., 223; First Amendment to,
    216, 506
Cook, Peter, 392
Cooke, Alistair, 198
Cooke, Janet, 401
Cooper, Duff, 522
Co-operative Society chain, 36–37; Co-op café,
    88, 92–93
Copenhagen (drama), 339
Cornforth Men's Choir, 288
Cornish, Norman, 247
Corn Laws, repeal of, 175
Coronation Street (TV program), 189, 283
Correspondent, the (the newspaper), 416
Corriere della Sera (newspaper), 400
cotton export investigation and Cotton Board,
    180–83, 184
Count of Monte Cristo, The (Dumas), 48
Court, Hazel, 108
Court of Appeal, 296, 367, 412
Coward, Noel, 100
Craig, Christopher, 163–64
Craven, Charlie, 226
Crewe (steel) Works, 16
Cromwell, Oliver, 53
Crooked Sixpence, A (Sayle), 472
Crosby, Bing, 60
Crosland, Anthony, 409
Crossbow (Conservative magazine), 470
Crossley Brothers diesel works, 63
Crossman, Richard, 408, 410–12, 485
Crowley, Monica, 532
Crowninshield, Frank, 506
Crown Publishers, 514
Crowther, Geoffrey, 197
Cudlipp, Michael, 315, 320
Cursley, Sidney, 167, 169
Czechoslovakia, 53, 533

Dacca (East Pakistan), missing children in,
    240–41
Daily Beast (web site), 540
Daily Dispatch, 66, 148
Daily Express, 58, 66, 148, 150, 198;
    "Beachcomber" column in, 59–60;
    optimism of, 7–8, 43, 284–85
Daily Herald, 148

Daily Mail, 43, 82, 297, 367, 373, 418, 508
Daily Mirror, 5, 8, 144, 148, 271, 285, 292, 351; staff at, 85, 130, 328
Daily News (Chicago), 211, 212–13
Daily News (New York), 209
Daily Sketch, 285
Daily Telegraph, 94, 148, 196, 283, 309, 315, 333
Dalton, John, 173
Dandy (comic book), 45
Daniels, Jonathan, 226
Darlington and Stockton Times, 250, 256
Dave Clark Five, the, 281
David, Peter, 521
Davidson, Bruce, 392
Davidson, L. C., 22
Davies, Howard, 56–57, 58
Davies, Hunter, 309, 314
Davis, Chester, 394
Davis, Miss Kennard, 338
Davis, Kenneth, 535
Dawson, Geoffrey, 209
Day-Lewis, Cecil, 241
Day of the Sardine, The (Chaplin), 261
D-Day landings, 72. *See also* World War II
Dead Man Walking (Prejean), 535
death penalty, 163–64, 167, 289–97, 312, 392; abolished, 298
Declaration of Independence, American, 126
Decline and Fall of the Roman Empire, The (Gibbon), 519
Delta Democrat Times, 225
democracy, 113, 459; world's first (Greece) taken over by fascism, 458
Democracy (drama), 339
Des Moines Register and Tribune, 216
Despatch (Darlington), 249–50, 256, 259–60, 275
Dexter, Pete, 517
Diageo company, 383
Diana, princess of Wales, 399
Dickens, Charles, 51, 126, 174
Disraeli, Benjamin, 135, 173, 246
Distillers Biochemicals, 357–71, 378–83
D Notice Committee, 339, 348
Dobb, Maurice, 330, 333
Dobrik, Nick, 382
Doctorow, E. L., 517
Doctor's Orders (two-act farce), 90
Donoughue, Bernard, 411
Donovan, Terry, 392
Dors, Diana, 108–9
Doubleday Publishers, 515
Douglas, Kirk, 60–61
Douglas-Home, Sir Alec, 311
Douglas-Home, Charles, 401, 498–99
Downing Street Diary: With Harold Wilson in No. 10 (Donoughue), 411–12
Drasner, "Firestorm Fred," 510–11
Dreams from My Father (Obama), 536
Dreiser, Theodore, 517

Driberg, Tom, 345
drive-in restaurants and movie theaters (U.S.), 202
Drogheda, Lord, 285
Dudgeon, Professor L. S., 276
Duff, Sir James Fitzgerald, 134, 195, 197
Duffy, Brian, 392
Duke University, HME teaches at, 506–7
Dulles, John Foster, 205–6
Dunkirk, BEF survivors of, 3–4, 5–7, 58, 301; histories of, 6, 7
Dunn, Vic, 479, 482
Durham Advertiser, 250
Durham Cathedral, *son et lumière* concert in, 287

East, P. D., 228–30, 233
East African Standard (Nairobi), 94
Easthope, Reginald, 130
Eccles Journal, 13
Eckersley, Peter, 283
Eclipse of God (Buber), 153
Economist, the, 167, 192, 194, 197, 198, 521; Philby as correspondent for, 333, 340, 350; and pollution issue, 175–76; and thalidomide, 359, 366
Edalji, George, 296
Eddowes, Michael, 292
Eddy, Nelson, 30
Eddy, Paul, 329, 388, 422, 431–34, 437, 443–44
Eden, Sir Anthony, 44, 186, 205, 207, 211, 214
Edinburgh, Philip, duke of, 169
education, 14, 16, 21, 91, 112–13, 115, 310; adult, 164–65; educational elite, 352; "eleven-plus" examinations, 50–51, 54, 87; grammar-school, 10, 53, 57; and language, *see* BBC; literacy, 236. *See also* Evans, Harold Matthew (PERSONAL LIFE)
Egan, Desmond, 478
Egypt, 468; and Holden case, 422–23, 425–36; 1950s events in, 205–7 (*see also* Suez canal). *See also* Sadat, Anwar
Eight Days (Australian magazine), 490
Einstein, Albert, 193
Eisenhower, General Dwight D. "Ike," 201, 205–6, 210, 218, 252, 509, 532–33; in 1956 election, 212, 217
Eisenhower, Julie Nixon, 533
Electricity Board, 187
Eliot, T. S., 130
Elizabeth, queen mother, 282, 341
Elizabeth II, queen of England, 163, 298, 339, 341, 408; coronation of, 161–62, 169; Silver Jubilee, 396, 489; visits Belfast, 456
Ellis Island (New York), 193
Empire Flying School (EFS), 102, 110
Empire Flying School Review, 108–9, 129, 243
English, David, 367, 373, 508
"English Revolution," 316

Index

Enlightenment, the, 126, 457
Entwhistle, Jimmy, 164
Ephron, Nora, 505
Epstein, Brian, 281
Epstein, Jason, 516, 518, 519, 535
Erthein, Herb, 200–203
European Court of Human Rights, 382, 471, 481
European Union, 376, 407–8
Evans, Albert, Dick, and Len (uncles), 15
Evans, Beattie (aunt), 15, 49
Evans, Don (no relation), 261, 270
Evans, Fred (brother), 497; early life, 4, 12–13, 18, 28–29, 31, 35–36, 59–60, 305, (education) 46–47, 51, 55, (World War II), 40, 43, 62–63
Evans, Frederick (father), 29–37, 42, 65, 114, 127, 136, 163, 199, 305; education, 14, 16–17, (mathematical skill) 19–21; illness and death, 496–98; marriage, 18–19; as train driver, 4, 12, 24–28, 44, 51, 55, 61, 74, 153, (promoted) 38–39, 180, (smog and) 174; wartime life, 3–7, 43–47, 50, 56, 58, 61–64, 71, (skepticism) 68
Evans, Mrs. Frederick (Mary Hannah "Polly," mother), 12–21, 29–33, 50, 114, 120–21, 136–37, 149, 163, 199, 496–97; illness and death, 497–98; wartime life, 4, 43–45, 55–56, 61–63, (runs shop) 33–38, 44, 65–66, 71, 74, 110
Evans, George (son), 507, 536–38
Evans, Harold Matthew (HME)
  PERSONAL LIFE
  childhood and early years, 3–5, 12–15, 18 21, 25, 28 38, 305, (and newspapers) 7, 10, 50–61, (war) 7, 40–47, 50, 61–69, 66–67, dual citizenship, 538; education, 10, 41, 44–58, 69–71, 372, (postwar) 109–11, 112–21, (at University College) 122–37, 142; love of music, 91–92, 307, (pop stars) 280–82; marriages, 132, 161, 485, 504–5 (see also Brown, Tina; Parker, Enid); motorbike, 127, 131–32, 386, 397, 487, 489; with RAF, 100–111, 118–20, 169, 184, 185, 195, 307, 521, (starts station newspaper) 106–9, 129, 483; visits United States, 199–216, (camping trip) 217–22, (in Chicago) 196–97, 203–14, (in Deep South, arrested) 222–31, (in New York City) 202–3, 296, 487, 507–8, (in Paris, Illinois) 231–33
  PROFESSIONAL LIFE
  at Ashton-under-Lyne (first newspaper job), 72–94, 151, 162, 179, 187, 259, (conditions during war) 95–99, (returns after war) 110; books by, 532, 538; as editor, 8, 14, 94, 225, (of college paper) 128, 195, 197, (named Editor of the Year) 496, (studies Suez crisis) 213–17, (thalidomide case) 9, 353, 355–84, (in the United States) 505–36; and politics, 135; teaches at Duke, 506–7.

See also Manchester Evening News; Northern Echo; Random House; Sunday Times; Times, the; U.S. News & World Report
Evans, Mrs. Harold Matthew. See Brown, Tina; Parker, Enid
Evans, Isabel (daughter), 536–38, 539
Evans, James (no relation), 364–66, 370–71, 374, 449, 474
Evans, John (grandfather), 13–14
Evans, Mrs. John (Sarah Jane Collins, grandmother, later Granny Jones), 14, 44–45, 47–49, 62
Evans, John (brother), 4, 36, 62, 63, 199, 403, 497
Evans, Kate (daughter), 265, 313, 538
Evans, Maggie (aunt), 15
Evans, Michael (son), 280, 305, 313, 496, 538
Evans, Peter (brother), 4, 36, 62, 63, 136, 497
Evans, Ruth (daughter), 243, 265, 313, 538
Evans, Timothy John (no relation), 164, 375, 376; tried and executed for murder, 289–98, 302
Evans, Wild Jack (uncle), 15, 20
Evening Standard, 320
Everest, British conquest of, 161–62
Examiner (San Francisco), 217

Fantasia (movie), 92
Farnol, Jeffrey, 54
Farrell, Michael, 467–68
fascism, 334, 458
Fatah (rejectionist group), 431
Faulkner, Alex H., 196
Faulkner, William, 191, 230, 517
Fawkes, Captain Guy, 29
Fawlty Towers (TV program), 310
Fay, Stephen, 408
FBI (Federal Bureau of Investigation), 228, 345, 347; and Holden case, 438–40, 442
FDR: Into the Storm (Davis), 535
Fenby, Charles, 241–44, 246, 249, 255, 274, 286–87
Fermi, Enrico, 193
Ferris, Henry, 536
Fielding, John, 361
Financial Times, 241, 285, 315
Fingerpost (Catholic magazine), 476
Finnegan, Mr. (subeditor), 152
First Amendment, 216, 506
First Casualty, The (Knightley), 7
Fisk, Robert, 435
Fistere, John and Isobel, 424–25
Fitzgerald, F. Scott, 504
Fitzpatrick, Barry, 479–80
Fleet Street. See newspapers
Fleming, Ian, 304, 309, 313–14, 344, 386
Food and Drug Administration (U.S.), 358
Football League, 28, 42; Cheshire League, 88
football pools, 42, 285
Foote, Shelby, 517, 520

Index

Ford, Gerald, 533
Ford Foundation, 196
Ford Motor Company, 393, 408
Foreign Correspondent, The (movie), 60
Foreign Office: in Holden case, 433, 434; in Philby case, 336–40, 343, 345, 350
Forrest, Lt.-General Nathan Bedford, 147
Forster, E. M., 341
Fort Sill, Oklahoma, 218
49th Parallel, The (movie), 60
Foster, Stephen, 30
Fox, Joe, 516
France: in Suez crisis, 206; in World War II, 6, (falls) 7, 58, (occupied) 338
Franco, General Francisco, 334
Franconia, RMS, 199
Franks, Oliver, 197
Fraud (Brookner), 535
Frayn, Michael, 149, 282, 339–40
Freedom of Information Act (U.S.), 439, 440, 443
freedom of the press, free speech, 107, 209, 216, 361, 382, 503
Freeland, General Ian, 460
Freeman, Eddie, 357
Freeman, Shirley, 279
Freson, Robert, 392
Friendly, Fred, 209
Front Page, The (movie), 60
Fry, Stephen, 535
Fuchs, Klaus, 346
Furst, Alan, 535
Futrell, Denys, 152, 160
Fyfe, Sir David Maxwell, 163, 291–92

Gaiety Theatre (Manchester), 177
Gaitskell, Hugh, 186
Gallant, Mavis, 535
Gallipoli, British assault on, 22, 23
Gandhi, Indira, 406
Gary, Indiana, 203, 207, 210
Gates, Henry Louis, 535
Gawhary, Fuad al, 420
Geddes, Sir Eric (Lord Inchcape), 21
Gedye, Eric, 333
Geiger, Hans, and Geiger counter, 173
Geisel, Theodore Seuss (Dr. Seuss), 517
General Strike (1926), 22, 24
Geneva convention, 467
Geraghty, Tony, 458, 459–61, 476
Gergen, David, 510–11
German internment camps, 3
Germany, 170; Britain declares war on, 7–8, 40, (German forces) 5–6, (Luftwaffe) 6, (Manchester area as Luftwaffe target) 62–63, 69, 87; East and West, 184, 185, (border closure and airlift) 109, 115, 133, 251; Nazi, (Belgian resistance to) 93, (Churchill sees as menace) 23, (Jews persecuted by) 289, (-Soviet

Nonaggression Pact), 349; Russia as foe of, 68; thalidomide in, 362–65, 383. *See also* Hitler, Adolf
Geronimo, 218
Gibbon, Edward, 519
Gibbons, Bob, 150
GI Bill (U.S.), 115, 509
Gibson, Pat, 242
Giles, Frank, 314, 319–20, 322, 340, 402, 405
Gill, Brendan, 526
Gillman, Peter, 422, 427, 431–34, 437, 443–44
Gladstone, William Ewart, 246
Glamour magazine, 513
Glasgow Herald, 98
Glass, Stephen, 401
global warming, 176
Goddard, Lord Chief Justice, 163–64
Goebbels, Joseph, 165, 377
Gold Rush, The (movie), 60
gold standard, 21–22
Gomulka, Wladyslaw, 207
Gone With the Wind (movie), 60
Good Friday Agreement (1998), 477
Goodman, Lord, 316, 382
Gopnik, Adam, 535
Gordon, General Charles George, 52
Gorton and Openshaw Reporter, 110, 112, 120
Gowing, Margaret, 347
Graham, Philip and Katharine, 302
Graham, Ruth, 276
Granada Television "Granadaland," 189–91, 280, 282–83, 286, 330; press award given to HME, 496
Grand Canyon, 220–22
Grann, Phyllis, 515, 522
Granta (Cambridge magazine), 315
Grapes of Wrath, The (Steinbeck), 194
Gray, Reginald, 245, 256, 258
Great Depression, 165, 193, 218
Greatest Generation, The (Brokaw), 529
Greece, 346, 458
Greeley, Horace, 296
Greene, Graham, 336, 339, 354
Greenhill, Angela, 337
Greenhill, Sir Denis, 337–38, 348
"green revolution," 179
Gregan, J. E., 177
Greis, Oberschütze Walter, 104, 109, 185
Grey, Zane, 194
Grieve, Lt. Colonel Angus Alexander MacFarlane (Master at Durham), 118, 122–23, 128, 136
Grimwade, John, 514, 521
Grisham, John, 522, 529
Groves, General Leslie, 347
Guinness group, 383
Gumm, Ed, and Gumm family, 232–33
Gunga Din (movie), 60
Guy Fawkes Night, 29–30, 32, 125

Gulf War, 458, 521

Gumz, Mark, 512

Guyana, 446

gypsy television program, 190–91, 282

Hackett, Bert, 178, 187, 273

Haggard, Henry Rider, 54

Hailsham, Viscount, and Hailsham Plan, 271–72

Halberstam, David, 517

Halden, David, 435–36

Hale, Nathan, 208

Haley, Sir William, 141, 146, 309, 319, 321

Halifax, Lord, 198

Hall, Joe, 70

Hall, J. R., 89

Hall, Ron, 315, 320, 327–29, 348, 371, 399, 414, 466, 472–74

Hallé orchestra (Manchester), 91, 92, 177

Hamilton, Charles Denis "C.D.," 304–5, 311, 313–22, 325, 396, 446–47; editorials under, 407; and Holden case, 422; interviews HME, 301–3, 306–9, 324; and "Mussolini papers," 400–401; and Philby case, 336–37, 348, 351–52; and politics, 408–9, 411; and thalidomide affair, 371; and unions, 491

Hammami, Said, 432

Hammon, Oklahoma, 219

Handel, George Frideric, 54

Hansard Parliamentary Debates, 167

Hardy, Thomas, 87

Harkness, Anna and Stephen, and Harkness Fellowships, 194–99, 204, 236, 331

Harkness, Edward, 194

Harling, Robert, 386

Harman, Nicholas, 366

Harr, Jonathan, 528

Harris, Robert, 534

Harrow-Wealdstone disaster (train crash), 153–58

Haselum, Lucy (grandmother), 15, 18

Heads, Barrie, 189–90, 280, 283

Head Wrightson firm, 273

Healey, Denis, 409

Hearst, William Randolph, 61

Heath, Edward, 333, 373, 376, 379–80, 408–9; and Ireland, 462, 471, 476

Heilpern, John, 505

Henderson, Scott, 291–92

Henry, T. E. "Big Tom," 138, 145, 162–63, 168, 172, 196, 220, 243, 252, 261; HME's assignments under, 165, 166–70, 174, 178, 180–87, 236–37, (television program) 190; and Manchester football club, 146, 195; praises, warns HME, 159, 242, 286; rewrites by, 152, 170; scoops world on end of war, 171

Her Majesty's Stationery Office, 272

Herrmann, Frank, 390–91, 415

Hersh, Sy, 535

Hetherington, Alastair, 207, 214, 236, 241

Hides, John David Michael (JDMH), 81–82, 110–11, 162

Hinchcliffe, Sir Raymond, 363–64, 366–69

Hindley, Myra, 84

Hindus in Pakistan, 404

Hirst, David, 364–65, 435, 436

Hiss, Alger, 134

History of the Peloponnesian War, The (Thucydides), 113

Hitler, Adolf, 58–59, 99, 104, 165, 209, 356, 438; appeasement of, 247, 304; "diaries" of, 401–2; officers' plot to kill, 340

Hobbes, Thomas, 110, 126, 132, 162

Hockney, David, 392

Hodgson, Godfrey, 329, 364

Hoffa, Jimmy, 216

Hogg, Quintin McGarel. *See* Hailsham, Viscount, and Hailsham Plan

Hoggart, Richard, 8, 16

Holden, Anthony "Tony," 388–89, 505

Holden, David, 416, 417–44

Holden, Geoffrey, 439

Holden, Ruth Lynam, 424, 438

Hollywood, 60–61, 190–91, 195, 534

Hood, Frances, 126–27

Hooper, Ken, 275–77

Hoover, J. Edgar, 347

Hope, Bob, 60, 193

Hopi Indians, 219

Hordon Colliery Band, 288

Hotspur (comic book), 45

Hotspur, RMS (destroyer), 150

House of Commons, 244, 295, 298, 351, 373, 379; Speaker of, 374–75

House of Lords, 244, 271, 491

House Un-American Activities Committee, 134

How the Troubles Came to Northern Ireland (Rose), 456

Hughes, Howard, 394

Hume, David, 328

Hume, John, 457–58, 477

Humphreys, Christmas, 292

Humphry, Derek, 472

Hungarian Revolution, 207

Hunt, Sir John, 411

Hurt, John, 291

Hussein, Saddam, 520

Hussein, Serajuddin, 240–41, 404

Hutchins, Robert, 197

Huxley, Aldous, 358

Idle, Eric, 60

Ihrt, Fred, 414–15

I'm All Right Jack (movie), 480

Imperial Chemical Industries (ICI), 267–70, 272, 360

In Cold Blood (Capote), 526

Independent (London), 282, 503
Independent (Nigerian weekly), 264
Independent Television News, 198
India: gains independence, 168, 236, 302; HME in, 236–39, 242; Pakistani refugees in, 406
India-Pakistan War (1971), 406
Indonesia, violence in, 317
infant mortality, pre-antibiotics, 12
Inglis, Brian, 283
Ingrams, Richard, 60
Inky Way (annual), 142
insurance fraud, 325
International Brotherhood of Teamsters, 215
International Communication Agency, 440
International House (Chicago), 204, 206–7, 214, 217
International Press Institute (IPI), 196, 237–38, 242, 302, 317
Internet, the, 139, 140, 147, 540
In Which We Serve (movie), 60
Iran, 490
Iraq, 416, 454, 455, 494
Iraq War, 10, 206, 462, 463
Ireland: British partitioning of (1921), 454, 465; Bloody Sunday in, 327, 376, 448, 471–77; Catholics in, *see* Catholic Church; Central Citizens' Defense Committee (CCDC), 460; civil rights movement in, 327, 376, 457–61, 463, 465; internment issue, 463–64; Loyalist forces in, 452–55, 458–61, 463; newspaper studies of, 456–57, 464–76; Northern, 9, 327, 407, 408, (High Court of) 450, (life in) 453, (terrorism in, internees tortured) 408, 447–54, 458–62, 465–71; peace efforts, 460, 478, (Anglo-Irish and Good Friday agreements) 477; Protestants in, 454–59, 464, 477, (Parliament [Stormont] of) 454, 457, 463, 468, ("Shankill Butchers") 453; Republic of, 455, 471, (IRA as seen by) 459; Sinn Fein, 449, 453, 477; the Troubles in, 448, 466, (1964 riots) 456, (number of violent deaths during) 451, 461
Irish Collie Club massacre, 453
Irish Republican Army (IRA), 448, 459–60, 473; IRA prisoners, (protection of) 452, (protest by), 450; Irish-American funding of, 457, 461, 477; new leadership, pacifism of, 457; Provisional "Provos," 449, 463–64, 475, 477; rebirth of, 465; and torture of internees, 408, 466–71, (false claims) 468, 470; violence and terrorism by, 356, 449–50, 453–54, (army response to) 466–76, (peace efforts ignored) 477
Irving, Clive, 400, 401, 513
Irving, John, 534
Isaacs, Sir Jeremy, 282–83, 330
Islam, 332; Amin converted to, 399; Muslims in Indonesia and Pakistan, 317, 404–5; and nuclear power, 490

Ismail, General Nabawi, 427–28
isolationism, 211
Israel, 170, 438, 468; -Arab wars, 206, 326, 390, 413–18, 443, 458, 494; athletes killed at Olympic Games, 375, 407, 431; in Holden case, 422, 432, 437, (Holden's reports on) 417–18, 422; Israelis taken as hostages at Entebbe, 398; Mossad of, 441, 442–43; Sadat seeks peace with, 416, 442, 443–44, (rejectionists against) 423, 430, 431, (rejectionists deported) 426; West Bank, 419, 423, 444
Italy, earthquake in, 391
ITN (Independent Television Network), 500
Ittefaq (Dacca daily), 240

Jack, Ian, 485–86
Jackson, Peter, 354
Jacobs, Eric, 481
Jacobs, Jane, 517
Jacobson, Phil, 452, 476–77
Jagger, Mick, 280
James, Clive, 535
Jameson (Ashton reporter), 95, 96
Janmohamed, Parin, 466
Jefferson, Thomas, 110
Jenkins, Roy, 298, 409
Jenkins, Simon, 329
Jerome, J. K., 60
Jesse, Tennyson, 292
Jevons, William, 173, 177
Jim Crow laws, 225
Jobbins, Bob, 420
John, Elton, 282
Johnson, Alan, 383
Johnson, Lyndon B., 251, 529
Johnson, Dr. Martin, 353
Johnston, Roy, 457
Joint Matriculation Board examinations, 50–51, 57; results, 69, 71
Jolson, Al, 30
Jones, David, 366, 368–69, 377
Jones, Edgar, 132
Jones, Sir Elwyn, 379
Jones, Granny. *See* Evans, Sarah Jane Collins (grandmother)
Jones, "Gravedigger Jack," 45, 47–48
Jones, Michael, 409–10
Jonson, Ben, 252
Jordan, 419, 430
Joseph, Sir Keith, 373
Joyce, James, 517
Jugantar (Bengali paper), 240
Junor, John, 285, 306

Kafka, Franz, 82
Kaminsky, Howard, 525
Kant, Immanuel, 126, 470
Karachi Morning News, 402

Karp, Jon, 522
Kavanagh, Pat, 485
Keeble, Frank, 82, 84–85, 88
Kelsey, Dr. Frances, 358
Kemsley, Lord "K," 304, 309, 407
Kennedy, Edward, 463
Kennedy, John F. "Jack," 216, 251, 301, 346, 448, 530; assassination of, 279, (book about) 527–28
Kennedy, Ludovic, 292, 296, 297
Kennedy, Paul, 535
Kennedy, Robert "Bobby," 215–16
Kentucky Fried Chicken restaurants, 202
Kenyatta, Jomo, 94
Kessel, Jacqueline Henriette Alphonsine Marie Dirix de "Jackie," 93–94
Keynes, John Maynard, 109, 162, 328
Khan, Abdul Qadeer, 490
Khan, Yahya, 403, 406
Khrushchev, Nikita, 201, 207, 251, 331
Kimber Bull (law firm), 361
King, Larry, 531
King, Martin Luther Jr., 224, 228, 457
Kipling, Rudyard, 141
Kirkpatrick, Lyman B., 344–45
Kissinger, Henry, 376, 505, 533
Kitson, Timothy, 379
Klein, Joe, 525
Knightley, Phillip, 7, 372; and Philby case, 330, 335, 340–45; and thalidomide case, 362, 368, 370, 378
Knopf publishers, 514, 519
Knox, Valerie, 274
Korda, Michael, 515
Korean War, 133, 168, 201
Kramer, Billy J., 281
Krugman, Paul, 511
Kyemba, Henry and Teresa, 396–400

Labour Party, 135, 328, 352, 372, 376, 496; collapse of, 495; Conservatives win over, 168, 185–86, 272; and death sentence, 163, 293–94; economic policy, 109, 246, (attacked) 394; interviews with members of, 167; and Ireland, 456–59; and nationalization, 127, 186; newspapers' disdain of, 85; and Philby, 332–33; prewar, 23–24; reformist, 484; and thalidomide issue, 373, 379, 383; and unions, 483, (union control of) 409–10; victory of, 309–11, 457
Lake, Veronica, 108
Lambert, Tom, 283
Lambert, William, 215
Lamour, Dorothy, 60
Lapham, Lewis, 535
Larkin, Philip, 280
Last King of Scotland, The (movie), 395
Lavery, Michael, 452–53
Law, Ken, 19, 31

Lawrence, D. H., 176
Law Society, 358
Law Society Gazette, 377
Leacock, Stephen, 60
Leader magazine, 241
League of Nations, 208
Lebanon, 419
Ledbetter, James, 472
Legal and General Assurance Society, 380
Leitch, David, 330–31, 333, 336, 345, 348
Lenin, V. I., 67, 330
Lenin's Tomb (Remnick), 535
Lennon, John, 281, 282
Lever, Harold, 409
Leviathan (Hobbes), 126
Levin, Bernard, 297
Levy, Major Hannan, 414–15
Lewenhak, H. K., 190–91, 282
Lewis, Mr. Justice, 290
Lewis, Sinclair, 231
Lewis, Wyndham, 310
Leyden, Dr. Wolfgang von, 127
Liberal Party, 21, 85, 135, 246, 292; interviews with members of, 167; in Timothy Evans case, 293, 295
Liberman, Alexander, 506, 535
Libya, 416, 424, 490
Lichfield, Patrick (Lord), 392
Lidell, Alvar, 64
Life magazine, 438, 521
Lindley, Robert, 531
Linklater, Magnus, 448
Linotype printing, 75, 85, 95, 143, 145, 252; computers vs., 482–83
Little, Tom, 272, 287
Liveright, Horace, 517, 519
Liverpool; bombing of, 61; riots in, 494
Livingstone, David, 52
Livingstone, R. W., 113
Lloyd, Bill, 152, 162
Locke, John, 110, 126
Locomotion (Stephenson), 261
Logic Piano (proto-computer), 173, 177
London: bombing of (World War II), 61; IRA bombings in, 454; riots in, 494
London, Midland and Scottish Railway (LMS), 18, 20, 28
London Evening News, 471
London Review of Books, 472
Long, Gerald, 495
Loomis, Bob, 516, 527–28
Loreburn Business College, 70, 120
Lorenz, Edward, 329
Loughran, Seamus, 449, 453
Louisville Courier-Journal, 223, 261
Low, David, 161
Low Countries, Hitler invades, 58
Lowe, Frank, 393
Lowry, L. S., 12, 190, 283

Lubbock, Eric, 295–97
Ludlum, Robert, 517
Lulu (rock group), 281
Luwum, Archbishop Janani, 398
Lynes, Tony, 378, 380

McBride, William, 365
McCarthy, Senator Joseph, 134, 170, 201, 215, 217, 333
McClellan, John L., and McClellan Committee, 215
McCormick, Colonel Robert "Bertie," 196, 208–10
McCrystal, Cal, 417, 422, 456
McCullin, Don, 390, 415
McDonald, Sir Alexander, 357, 378, 380
MacDonald, Jeanette, 30
McDonald's restaurants, 202
McGill, Ralph, 225–26, 228
McKenna, Frank, 24
McLachlan, Donald, 350
Maclean, Donald, 330–34, 344, 346–47, 352
McMahon Act (U.S.), 347
Macmillan, Harold "Supermac," 44, 266, 271, 283, 301, 310–11, 524; and the economy, 246–47; and Philby, 332, 350
McPhee, Jock, 107–8
McVeigh, Michael, 133
Mad Men (TV series), 393
Maginot Line, 5
Magnet (comic book), 45–46, 58
Maguire, Gerald, 449
Mahler, Gustav, 82
Mailer, Norman, 517, 518, 534
Main Street (Lewis), 231
Malaya, 168
Malayala Manorama (newspaper), 238
Manchester: bombing of, 61–64, 69, 87, 177; housing in, 172–73; industry in, 173–75; neglects heritage, 177; "Newspaper City," 148, 177; St. Ann's Square in, 177–79, 260; smog in, and fight against, 173–76
Manchester City Council, 174
Manchester Education Committee/Council, 45, 57, 67, 71
Manchester Evening Chronicle, 147, 148, 161
Manchester Evening News, 66–67, 96, 261, 286, 541; campaigns for urban renewal, 178; cotton export investigation by, 180–83; HME at, 137, 138–39, 141–65, 195, 248, 321, 324, 339, (promoted) 166–80, (sent abroad) 180–85, 192, 236–42, 302, (takes leave) 198–99, (television program) 190–91, (writes column as "Mark Antony") 187–88, (writes editorials) 205–6, 210; letters to, 172; rivalry with *Chronicle*, 147–48, 161; and television, 189–91
Manchester Guardian, 7, 113, 178, 214, 468; HME with, 207, 210–11, 236, 324, 339, 541; staff at, 81, 111, 171–72, 241, 283, 309, 435, 437, 458; and thalidomide, 359
Manchester Observer, 177, 214, 236, 304, 309, 330, 347, 349; Philby as correspondent for, 333, 340, 350, 425; scoops *Sunday Times*, 385
Manchester United football club, 28, 42, 146, 178, 195
Manchester University, 110, 173, 186
Mancroft, Lord, 285
Manhattan Project, 347
Mann, Manfred, 281
Mansfield, F. J., 142, 143
Mao Zedong, 133
Marder, Jonathan, 526–27
Margach, James, 320
Margaret, Princess, 302
Marines, U.S., 390
Marsden, Eric, 86–88, 90–94
Marshall, Alfred, 109
Marsland, W. L., 51, 52–53, 57–58; testimonial from, 73–74, (sought) 120
Marx, Karl, and Marxism, 24, 131, 185, 328, 333–34, 457
Mascarenhas, Anthony, 402–7, 490
Mason, David and Vicki, 367, 370, 371–72, 373, 380
Mason, Louise, 357, 367
Massie, Robert K., 529, 535
Mather, Bill, 178–79
Mather and Platt engineering firm, 63, 69, 127, 178
Mathew, K. M., 238
Matthews, Stanley, 17
Maudling, Reginald, 470
Maxton, Jimmy, 23
Mayor of Casterbridge (Hardy), 87
Mays, Benjamin, 224–25, 233
Meakin, Bert, 6
Measor, Duncan ("Mr. Bow Tie"), 138, 142, 147, 150, 159, 167, 172
Medina, Kate, 529
Mee, Billy, 80, 87, 93
Mehta, Sonny, 519
Meigs, Dr. Joe V., 276
Men in Shadow (play), 107
Menzies, Sir Stewart, 336, 338, 350
Mercer, Lorraine, 383
Metro-Vickers plant, 69
MI5 (counterespionage agency), 333, 335, 342, 348, 350
MI6. *See* Secret Intelligence Service
Miami Herald, 394–95
Michener, James, 517
Middlehurst, Dennis, 75, 80, 94
Middlehurst, Mr. (John W., "Jack"), 74–80, 82–90, 94–95, 99, 108, 142, 187
Middlesbrough riots, 254–55, 265
Miles, Sarah, 526
Miles, Police Constable, 163–64

Index

Mill, John Stuart, 126
Miller, Russell, 396–97, 399
Milligan, Spike, 60
Mind of the South, The (Cash), 230
Ministry of: Aviation Records, 101; Defense,
    460; Education, 115; Food, 66; Health, 277;
    Transport, 324
Mirror Group, 286
Mitchell, Alex, 345
Modern Law Review, 368–69
Mollenhoff, Clark, 216
Monopolies Commission, 319, 321
Monroe, Marilyn, 109, 202
Monsters of the Moors (Hindley and Brady), 84
Montgomery, Field Marshal Bernard, 301
Monty Python (TV program), 60, 310
Moore, Dudley, 392
Morehouse College, 224
Mormons, 394
Morning Telegraph (Sheffield), 81
Morris, Alf (later Lord Morris), 38, 44, 51,
    372–73, 376, 379, 381
Morris, Edmund, 520
Morris, Helen, 526
Morris, James (later Jan), 417, 424, 442
Morrison, Herbert, 310
Morrissey, Mike, 264–65, 266
Mortimer, Edward, 424, 444
Mortimer, Raymond, 304
Morton, John Cameron Andrieu Bingham
    Michael, 60
Mosley, Oswald, 165
Mossad (Israeli intelligence agency), 441, 442–43
Mountbatten, Lord, 356, 450
Mourad, Kenize, 423–24, 428, 435
Mugabe, Robert, 396
Muggeridge, Malcolm, 316, 343
Mullis, Miss Edith, 244
Murdoch, Rupert, 252, 286, 306, 401, 504, 518;
    and *Sunday Times,* 479, 491–92, 501–3, 519;
    and the *Times,* 492–96, 498–503
Murphy, Father, 459
Murphy, Pat, 303, 313, 320
Murray, Arnold and Gertie, 15, 31, 63
Murray, "Big Eva" and "Little Eva," 15, 65
Murray, Justice, 452
music (pop concerts), 280–82, 318
Muslims. *See* Islam
Mussolini, Benito, "papers" of, 400–401, 402
My American Journey (Powell), 523–24
My Early Life (Churchill), 279
Myrdal, Gunnar, 194

Nader, Ralph, 380
Nashville Tennessean, 216
Nasser, Colonel Gamal Abdel, 205–6, 301, 312
National Book Award, 518
National Council for the Training of
    Journalists, 303

National Enquirer, 282
National Guard, U.S., 223
National Health Service, 9, 168, 276, 355, 378
national interest, 9, 10
nationalization, 127, 168, 186, 187
National Liberal Club, 317
National Physical Laboratory, 184, 482
National Rifle Association (NRA), 510–11
National Security Agency (NSA), 440
National Theatre, history of, 413
National Union of Journalists (NUJ), 96, 112,
    410, 489
Native Americans, 218–20, 232
Navajo Indians, 219
Near v. Minnesota, 209
Neave, Airey, 450
Neguib, Colonel, 170
Nehru, Jawaharlal, 236, 237
Nelson, Horatio, Viscount, 68
Nettleton, John, 132
Newcastle Journal, 260, 261, 263
Newhouse, S. I. (Si) Jr., 506, 512–13, 522, 536
Newhouse companies, 514, 541
Newman, Arnold, 392
New Republic, 401
News and Observer (Raleigh, N.C.), 225
News at Ten (TV program), 500
News Corporation's annual report, 494–95
News International, 498, 499
News of the World, 8, 96, 502
Newspaper House (London), 242
newspapers: American, (closures of) 539–40,
    (events in Ireland misrepresented by) 459,
    461, (investigations by) 215–17; amnesia
    of, 225; British wartime, 140; confidence
    tricks and hoaxes played on, 400–402;
    and Conservative Party, 85, 246, 273, 304,
    317, (advertising refused) 285; as "Daily
    Surprise," 58–61; editorial decisions,
    445–54; Fleet Street, 306, 314, 389, 456,
    480–83, 503, 509; HME's applications to,
    72–74; Indian and Far Eastern, HME and,
    236–41, 250, 302; movies about, 60–61;
    public trust in, 7–8, (betrayed) 43–44
New Statesman magazine, 485
Newstead, Mrs. Matthew (Matt), 13
Newsweek magazine, 214, 224, 401, 510, 525
Newton, Isaac, 252
New York City, HME in, 202–3, 296, 487, 507–8
New Yorker magazine, 486, 507, 518, 526,
    536, 538
New York Herald Tribune, 283
New York Review of Books, 516
New York Times, 224, 302, 388, 401, 419, 527, 528;
    book lists, 534, 535
New York Times Magazine, 418
Nichols, Mike, 524
Nicholson, A. L. (Leslie), 342, 345
Nicholson, Douglas, 295

574

Nidal, Abu, 432
Nigeria, civil war in, 458
Night and Day (play), 389
Nixon, Richard M., 217, 375, 406, 532–33
Nixon Off the Record (Crowley), 532
Nocturne in Black and Gold (Whistler), 323
Noises Off (farce), 339
Noraid (supposed charity for IRA), 461
Noriega, General Manuel, 531
Norman, Philip, 282, 318
North Atlantic Treaty Organization (NATO), 168, 184
North Eastern Railway Company, 21
Northern Echo, 235, 242, 318; HME with, 243–62, 263, 287–98, 302–6, 308, 456, 480, (circulation increases) 279, (grassroots reporting) 270–73, (hires news editor) 263–65, (investigations by) 264–98, 325–26, 370, ("Man on Our Conscience" story) 295–97, 302, 376, (and photographs) 390, (and pop music) 280–82, (*Teenage Special*) 281, (Teesside Smell story) 265–69, 325, (on television panel) 282–87, (thalidomide affair) 353–55, 360; London editorials and features in, 245–46, (replaced by local) 253–55; ownership of, 285; readership of, 249; redesigned, 273
Northern Ireland. *See* Ireland
Northern Ireland Civil Rights Association, 460
Northern Sinfonia orchestra, 247
North of England Newspaper Company, 250, 303
North Sea oil exploration, 446, 447
North West Gas Board, 149
Norway falls to Hitler, 58
Norwich Union Insurance Society, 285
Notting Hill riot (1958), 254
Nouvelle Observateur, Le, 423
Nulsen, Dr. Ray O., 363
Nuremberg trials, 207, 208

Obama, Barack, 186, 222, 536
Offa's Dyke, 47
Official Secrets Act (OSA), 103, 325, 335, 337, 348, 410
Ogden, Betty, 54
O'Hara, John, 517, 526
Old Chicago (movie), 87
Oldfield, Will, 98
Oliver Twist (movie), 109
Olympic Games (1972), 375, 407, 431
Onassis, Jacqueline Kennedy, 505
O'Neill, Eugene, 517
O'Neill, Terence, 457–58
"Orangemen," 454. *See also* Ireland
Orbison, Roy, 281
Oregonian (Portland), 215
Orwell, George, 36–37, 309–10, 484
Osnos, Peter, 514, 536

Oswald, Lee Harvey, 527
Ottoman Empire, 235
Our Man in Havana (Greene), 336
Owen, David, 435
Oxford Mail, 241–42
Oxford Union, 314

Page, Bruce, 327–29, 464, 466, 472–74; on Philby case, 330, 333–36, 338, 340–42, 345, 347, 350; on thalidomide case, 368–72, 381
Paget, Dr. Edward, 360
Paine, Thomas, 110
Paisley, Ian, 477
Pakistan: East, genocide in 402–7, 490; as nuclear power, 490
Pakistani Army, 241
Palatinate (university biweekly), 128–35, 195, 197, 309
Palestine Liberation Organization (PLO), 416, 423, 432
Palestinians: vs. Israelis, 417; militants deported from Egypt, 426; terrorists, 423, (hold hostages at Entebbe) 398, (at Olympic Games) 375, 407, 431
Palin, Michael, 60
Pall Mall Gazette, 235, 244
Papanicolaou, Dr. George, and Pap smear, 276–77
Papworth, Squadron Leader, 103, 105
Paris: anti-Gaullist street battles in, 390–91; Comintern, 333
Paris, Illinois, 231–33
Parker, Alan, 393
Parker, Enid, 61, 206, 497, 538; courtship and married life, 131–32, 161, 180, 199, 243–44, 260, 274, 313, (on U.S. travels) 217–22, 230–31; marriage ends, 485, 488, 504
Parkinson, Michael "Parky," 318
Parkinson, Norman, 392
Patterson, Eugene, 228
Patterson, Robert, 230
Pawley, S. J., 54
Pearce, John, 392–403
Pearson Industries, 285
Peet, Ron, 380
People (British newspaper), 8, 148, 285, 472
People's Democracy group (Ireland), 458–59
Pepper, Bill, 169
Perelman, S. J., 60, 486–87
Peress, Gilles, 473–74
Pericles, 113
Perkins, Graham, 491
Persico, Joe, 522–23
Petal Paper (weekly newspaper), 228–30
"Peterloo Massacre," 177
Peters, Frank, 257–58, 296
Peterson, Sir Maurice, 344
Phantom Ranch, 220; Jay and Ray of, 222

Philadelphia Evening Bulletin, 397
Philby, Aileen, 348
Philby, Eleanor, 330, 333, 347, 349
Philby, Harold Adrian Russell "Kim," 330–52, 424–25, 434, 438, 442, 444, 464
Philby, John, 348–49
Philby, St. John, 332
Phillips, Dr. Montagu, 361–62, 370, 381–82
photojournalism, 81, 349, 391–94
Picasso, Pablo, 510
Pickles, Wilfred, 41
Picture Post magazine, 241
Pierrepoint, Albert, 290
Pitman shorthand, 70, 77, 249
Pitney, Gene, 281
Please Please Me (record album), 280
Polish workers in Gary, Indiana, 207
pollution, 284–85, 308; and fight against, 173–76, 269–70, 273
Ponchielli, Amilcare, 92
Popper, Sir Karl, 328
Poppy Day massacre (Ireland), 454
Popski's Private Army (World War II), 81
Portland spy ring, 341, 349
Posner, Gerald, 527–28
Potter, Elaine, 368, 375, 381
Powell, Albert, 6
Powell, General Colin, 521–23, 525
Powell, Dilys, 315
Powell, Enoch, 277–78, 355–57, 359–60, 373, 381, 383, 408
Prejean, Sister Helen, 535
Preparing for the Twenty-first Century (Kennedy), 533
Presley, Elvis, 202
Press Association (Britain), 139, 153, 157
Prevett, John, 368–69, 370, 371
Priestley, J. B., 41
Primary Colors (Klein), 524
Pringle, Peter, 472, 476–77
Private Eye (TV program), 60, 306, 392, 399, 485
Profumo call girl scandal, 310
Protestants in Ireland. *See* Ireland
Pulitzer Prize, 401
Putnam Publishing group, 522, 534
Putt, Gorley, 199
Puttnam, David, 393
Puzo, Mario, 517

Queen magazine, 315
Quindlen, Anna, 534
Quinn, Sally, 504, 509

"race riot," 254. *See also* blacks
Rachman, Peter, and Rachmanism, 285, 326
Radstrom, Par, 204–5
Rand, Ayn, 517, 532
Rand, Michael, 392

Random House: HME at, 514–18, 526–36; Modern Library, 519–20; Powell's autobiography, 521–24; *Primary Colors*, 524–25
Rathore, Major (Pakistan), 405
Rave On (Norman), 282
Reagan, Ronald, 408, 511, 515, 533; shot, 494
Red Army. *See* Soviet Union
Red Wharf Bay murder, 94
Reed, John, 343–44
Rees-Mogg, William, 100, 306–7, 314–15, 319–20, 356, 407
Reeve, Christopher, 529
Reisman, Marty "the Needle," 536–37
Remnick, David, 535
Reuters news bureau, 321, 419, 420
Rexinger case, 217
Reza Shah Pahlevi, shah of Iran, 301
Rhodes scholars, 194, 208–9
Ricardo, David, 136
Richardson, John, 517, 520, 535
Richardson-Merrell company (U.S.), 358, 363
Rigby, Derek, 84
Roads to Ruin: The Shocking History of Social Reform (Turner), 125
Road to Wigan Pier, The (Orwell), 36
Robbins, Kathy, 524
Robens, Lord (Alf), 499–500
Roberts, Mrs. Amy, 12–13
Robeson, Paul, 23–24, 30
Robinson, Anne, 388
Robinson, Police Constable, 29
Robson, Flora, 200
Rockefeller, John D., 194, 204
Rockefeller Foundation, 196, 237
Rockwell, Norman, 194, 231
Roe, Alliott Verdon, aircraft factory of (Avro), 62–63, 60, 173
Rolling Stones, the, 281, 392
Rollins, Babette, 205
Roosevelt, Eleanor, 209–10
Roosevelt, Franklin D., 59, 64, 68, 193, 208, 257
Roosevelt, Theodore, 213
Rose, Jim, 236–37, 238, 242
Rose, Pamela, 242
Rose, Peter, 456
Rosenthal, David, 514
Rousseau, Jean-Jacques, 110, 126
Rove, Karl, 231
Royal Air Force (RAF), 6, 62; Air Traffic Control, 106; All-Weather Squadron, 102; bombs Egyptian airfields, 206; Fleet Air Arm, 87, 91; Flying Training Command, 102; HME in, 100–111, 118–20, 129, 169, 184, 185, 195, 307, 483, 521
Royal Antediluvian Order of Buffaloes ("Buffs"), 32
Royal Army: Corps of Signals, 4, 6, 97; Engineers, 98; Pay Corps, 81

Royal Automobile Club (RAC), 386, 387
Royal Flying Corps, 17
Royal Naval Volunteer Reserve, 149
Royal Opera House, 282
Royal Ulster Constabulary (RUC), 455, 460;
    clashes with, 458, 459
Runyon, Damon, 194
Ruskin, John, 323
Russell, Leonard, 315, 317, 318
Russian Century, The (photographs), 527
Rutherford, Ernest, 173, 177
Ryan, Pat, 521
Ryder, Chris, 448–49, 452–53, 458

Saatchi, Charles and Maurice, 393–94
Sac Indians, 232
Sackur, John, 339–41
Sadat, Anwar, 442; assassinated, 494; and
    Holden case, 419, 423, 426, 435–36, 444;
    and peace with Israel, 416, 423, 431, 442,
    443–44
Sagan, Carl, 535
St. Aidan's Society, 131
St. Ann's Square and St. Ann's Church
    (Manchester), 177–79, 260
St. Cuthbert and St. Cuthbert's Society, 116, 119,
    133, 288; St. Cuthbert's hospital, 354
St. Mary's Road Central School, 50–58, 68– 70,
    120; school magazine for, 66–68
St. Peter's Fields, and "Peterloo Massacre,"
    176–77
Sakharov, Andrei, 511
Salameh, Ali Hassan, 431
Salote, queen of Tonga, 169
Salvation Army, 99
Salzman, Marc, 535
Sands, Bob, 85
Satherly, Richard, 366
Saturday Evening Post, 231
Saudi Arabia, 399, 437, 468; Holden's book on,
    417, 428
Saxon, Eric, 178
Sayle, Murray, 472–73, 475–76
Schlesinger, Arthur Jr., 520
Scoop (Waugh), 306
Scorsese, Martin, 526
Scotland Yard, 324, 453, 471; in Holden case,
    421, 426, 433–34
Scott, Charles, 149
Scott, C. P., 151
Scott, Laurence, 149, 178–79, 243
Scott, Ridley, 393
Scott, Robert Falcon, 52
Scott, Sir Walter, 54, 116
Scott Trust, 148
Scrantonian (Pennsylvania), 216
Seale, Patrick, 349
Searchers, the (rock group), 281
Secombe, Harry, 60

Secret Intelligence Service (SIS, MI6), 333,
    335–40, 342–45, 348, 434; -CIA joint
    operation, 346; class consciousness of, 350
Seigenthaler, John, 216
Selected Stories (Gallant), 535
Sellers, Peter, 60, 480
Senior, Stanley, 251–52, 257, 259, 266
September 11 attacks, 10, 536
Shanks, Edward, 141
Sheehy, Gail, 535
Shenstone, Mr. (of British Airways), 169
Sherwin's Political Register, 177
Shout! (Norman), 282
Showband Miami group machine-gunned, 454
Shrimpton, Jean, 316, 317
Siedle, Robert, 397
Silberman, Freddy, 438
Silberman, Leo, 438–39, 440
Silkin, Sam, 412
Silverman, Sydney, 163, 298
Simon and Schuster, 515
Simpson, Colin, 390
Simpson, Guy, 281, 282
Sinclair, David, 282
Sinclair, Upton, 517
Singing Fool, The (movie), 30
Sinn Fein. *See* Ireland
Sivori, Antonio and Fred, 33–34
Six-Day War, 390, 418, 424, 458
Sjostrom, Henning, 362
Skyner, Gary, 357
Slater, Oscar, 296
Small, Chief Superintendent Ray, 421–22, 434
"Smalltown USA." *See* Paris, Illinois
Smith, Godfrey, 304, 311, 314, 318, 320, 392, 519
Smith, Ian, 339
Smith, Liz, 508
Smith, General Walter Bedell, 345
smog. *See* pollution
Smuts, Jan, 301
Snowdon, Lord, 282, 302, 324, 392
Snyder, Dick, 515
soccer, 17, 28, 152
Social Democratic Party, 495
socialism, 23, 41, 312, 409, 448
Socialist Party, 135
Social Studies, 115–17, 119
Société d'Alexandrie pour les Boissons
    Distillées et Vignobles de Gianaclis, 443
Songs My Mother Taught Me (Brando and
    Lindley), 531
Soskice, Sir Frank, 293, 295, 297
Sousa, John Philip, 17
South Africa, 446
South Yemen, 416
Soviet Communism: A New Civilisation?
    (Webb and Webb), 24
Soviet Union, 134, 195, 201, 207, 410; and atomic
    bomb, 346–47, (fallout from tests) 284–85;

Index

Soviet Union *(cont.)*
British anti-Soviet operations, 342–43; and China, border war with, 458; collapse of, 527; and Czechoslovakia, 533; Egyptian arms deal with, 205; as foe of Germany, 68, 109; and Holden case, 437, 439, 441–42; -Nazi Nonaggression Pact, 349; Pakistan as U.S. ally against, 406; Philby as agent for, 331, 334–35, 342, 344, 349, 351; Red Army of, 184; romantic view of, 24; secret service (NKVD, later KGB), 343, 350, 441–42

Spanish Civil War, 332, 334

Spark, David, 254, 267, 270, 274, 287

Special Air Service (SAS), 468

Sporting Chronicle, 148

Springfield, Dusty, 281

squash games, 386–87

Stagecoach (movie), 60

Stalin, Joseph, 24, 109, 133, 193, 201, 338, 346–47, 349, 457

Stalybridge and Hyde Transport Board, 82

Stamford, Ossie, 267–68

Standard English, 41, 310

Standard Oil Company, 194

Staniforth, Frank, 250

Stanley, H. M., 52

State, U.S. Department of, 422, 440

Stay-at-Home Holiday campaign, 56

Stead, William Thomas, 235–36, 242, 243–44, 246, 260, 262, 325

Steinbeck, John, 194

Steiner, George, 304

Stephenson, George, 52, 261

Stern (German magazine), 414

Stevenson, Adlai E., 201, 205, 212, 217

Stewart, Michael, 295

Stockman, David, 515, 522

Stockton and Darlington Railway, 52

Stoker, R. R., 179

Stone, Jonathon, 382

Stones, The (Norman), 282

Stoppard, Tom, 389

Strauss, Admiral Lewis, 346

Streitfeld, David, 525

Stroh, Nicholas, 397

Student Representative Council (SRC), 129, 131, 132, 134

Stuttaford, Thomas, 373

Styron, William, 517–18, 534, 535

Suez Canal, 68; British intervention at (Suez crisis), 150, 186, 201, 205–8, 246, 304, 418, (HME's study of) 213–17, (press view of) 214

suffrage, unversal (for men), 176

Sukarno, 317

Sullivan, J. W. N., 92

Sulzberger family, 302

Sun, The, 286, 502

Sunday Empire News, 88

Sunday Express, 148, 285, 305, 349

Sunday Mirror, 271

Sunday Telegraph, 350, 359, 377, 385, 458, 470, 487–88

Sunday Times, 275, 282, 285, 301, 311, 486; buyout bid for, 491, 501; editorials of, 407–8; HME at, 303–7, 309, 313–22, 323–29, 504, 515, (airline scandal) 326, 487, (Holden case) 416, 417–32, 434–44, (Idi Amin case) 395–400, (Irish Troubles) 448–78, (Philby case, "Project X") 330–52, (thalidomide affair) 9, 326, 355–84, 481–82, (workday routine) 385–88; HME leaves, 443, 476, 492–93, 519; libel suits against, 325, 356, 449, 450, (dismissed) 453; Murdoch and, 479, 491–92, 501–3, 519; and politics, 407–12; redesigned, 511–12; staff of, 90, 94, 388–89, 499, 505, 513–14, (photographers and photojournalism) 389–94, (war and other casualties) 415–16, 420 (*see also* Holden, David); union problems at, 306, 479–84, 489–95

Sunderland Echo, 437

Supreme Court, U.S., 209; *Brown* ruling, 223, 225, 227, 228

Sutcliffe, Charlie, 80–81, 93–94

Swain, Jon, 389, 444, 502

Swan Hunter, 272

Sweeney Todd: The Demon Barber of Fleet Street (school performance of), 58

Syria, 416; and Holden case, 419, 422; in Yom Kippur War, 414–15

Systematic Theology (Tillich), 153

table tennis, 71, 103, 128, 132, 135, 187, 536–37

Tale of Two Cities, A (Dickens), 126

Talk magazine, 536

Tarelli, Dick, 249–50, 259–60

Tatler magazine, 505, 506, 508, 536

Taylor, A. J. P., 377

Taylor, Bert Leston, 445

Taylor, Edwin, 371, 511

Taylor, Laurence, 77, 78, 79, 88, 92

team journalism, 326–29, 391

Teesside Smell, 265–69, 325

television, commercial, 162, 188–91, 280, 281, 367, 500; Channel 4, 282; government ban on, 170; HME on panel, 282–87, 330, 362; U.S., 501, (vs. British) 202. *See also* BBC

Tennyson, Alfred Lord, 292

10 Rillington Place (movie), 291

Territorial Army (Terriers), British, 17, 308

terrorism: in Northern Ireland, reporting on, 447–54; Palestinian, 398, 423, (at Olympic Games) 375, 407, 431; Sept. 11 attacks, 10, 536; and truth vs. lies, 9

Terry, Tony, 422

Terry, Walter, 82

thalidomide affair, 9, 326, 353, 355–84, 481–82

Thames Television, 330

Thatcher, Margaret, 165, 341, 394, 409–10, 454, 495

That Was the Week That Was (TV program), 392
They Made America (Evans), 538
Thomas, Harford, 241
Thomas, Joan, 248–49, 251, 279, 289, 387
Thompson, Hunter S., 517
Thompson, William Hale "Big Bill," 196, 209–10
Thomson, Kenneth, 319, 321, 411, 490–91
Thomson, Roy (Lord Thomson of Fleet) and Thomson group, 301–4, 311–13, 351, 352, 386, 394–95, 446, 490–93, 540; and merger with *Times*, 318–21, 325; and politics, 408, 409, 411
Thomson, Tommie, 82
Thornton, Norman F. "Nifty," 142–47, 149–50, 152–54, 157, 160, 162, 174, 257
Those Are Real Bullets: Bloody Sunday, Derry, 1972 (Pringle and Jacobson), 477
Thucydides, 113–14, 118
Tidewater Morning, A (Styron), 535
Till, Emmett "Bobo," 203–4, 225
Tillich, Paul, 153
Time magazine, 214, 224, 510, 521
Times, the, 401, 500, 502, 524; HME joins, 14, 443, 492–94, 497, 519, (difficulties begin) 495–96, (leaves) 498–500, 505–6; Holden case, 437, 439, 444; and merger, 318–21; misinformation from, 43, 209; Murdoch and, 492–96, 498–503; Philby with, 332, 334, 424–25, (leaves) 335; redesigned, 512; staff at, 130, 282, 314, 505, (great editors) 100, 141, 177, 248, 307; and thalidomide, 356, 359; unions and, 491, 512. *See also Sunday Times*
Times Newspapers, 318–19, 321, 401, 446, 491, 499–502
Tinsley, John, 354–55
Tirpitz (German battleship), 63
Titanic, the, 235
Tito, Josip Broz, 346
Tocqueville, Alexis de, 227
Tomalin, Claire, 414
Tomalin, Nicholas, 315, 316, 320, 403, 413–16, 420
Toobin, Jeffrey, 535
Tories. *See* Conservative Party
Towards the End of the Morning (Frayn), 339
train crash, 153–58
train drivers, 24–28, 38–39
Travolta, John, 524
Treslove, Bill, 254, 273
Trevor-Roper, Hugh (later Lord Dacre), 343, 401–2
Tribune, the, 297
Trinder, Tommy, 65
Trinity Review, 341
Triumph in the Desert (David), 521
Trotskyites, 410
Truman, Harry, 226, 252
Truman Show, The (movie), 231
truth, 8–9; patriotism vs., 448

Turing, Alan, 482
Turner, E. S., 125
Turner, J. M. W., 116
Turner, Wallace, 215
Tuskegee University, 224
Tweedy, Guy, 382
Twenty Four Hours (TV program), 367
Tyas, John, 177
Tyne Tees Television, 281

Uganda, 376, 390, 395–99
Ulbricht, Walter, 251
Ulster Volunteer Force, 453–54
Uncle Mac's amateur shows, 56
Under the Bamboo Tree (play), 486
Union Society, 124, 128, 131, 133
unions, trade, 27, 496–97; Labour Party and, 483, (union control of) 409–10; and newspapers, 479–84, 489–95, 501–3, 512, (print unions) 306, 493
United Nations, 186, 208, 210; and Idi Amin, 396, 399; Security Council in Suez crisis, 206
United Press International (UPI), 212
United States, 437; accusations against, 355; Air Force, 109; and atomic weapons, 347; Britain as portrayed to/seen by, 196, 210, 214; church-state separation in, 463; deceptions by, 10; Declaration of Independence, 126; enters World War II, 64–65, 97, 193; GI Bill in, 115, 509; investigative newspapers in, 215–17; and Iraq, 206; and Ireland, funding for and press misrepresentation of events in, 457, 459, 461, 477; as menace to peace, Union Society debate on, 134; mid-1950s euphoria of, 201–2; southern, 463, (blacks in) 203–4, 222–31, 253, 455, 457; in Suez crisis, 205–6; thalidomide in, 358, 360; visits to as adventure (1956), 193, (HME visits, *see* Evans, Harold Matthew PERSONAL LIFE); waives interest on loan to Britain, 208; witch hunts in, *see* McCarthy, Senator Joseph
United States (Vidal), 518, 535
U.S. News & World Report, 214–15; HME at, 508, 510–12, 528
University College, Durham "Castle," 116–21; HME at, 122–37
University of Chicago, 203
"useless man," 114

Vanity Fair magazine, 506–7, 508, 513, 518, 536
Vaughan, Gerard, 373
Vaughan, Sam, 515
Vaux Breweries, 273, 295
Vice, Anthony, 314, 320
Vidal, Gore, 517, 518, 520, 534, 535
Vietnam War, 10, 376, 455, 458, 463; veterans of, 331, 390, 414, 415, 522
Village Voice (New York), 472, 491
Vincent, Claude McClean, 102–3

Vitale, Alberto, 514, 516, 519, 521–22
Vittachi, Varindra Tarzie, 238–39, 317
Vogue magazine, 320, 513
Volkov, Konstantin, 343–44, 348

Walker, Jim, 296
Wallace, Marjorie, 377–78
Wall Street Journal, 394–95, 500
Walters, "Stuffy," 211, 212–13
Walton, Dick, 70
Waples, Professor Douglas, 203, 207
Ward, Michael, 376
Wardle, Miss Polly, 54
Warren, Robert Penn, 517
Washington Post, 224, 302, 401, 504, 525
Watergate affair (U.S.), 376
Waterhouse, Keith, 312
Waterloo, Battle of, 122
Watts, David, 282
Waugh, Auberon, 485
Waugh, Evelyn, 60, 130, 306
Way, Mr. Stanley, 276–77, 278
Way Ahead, The (movie), 87
Weakest Link, The (quiz show), 388
Weatherby, Bill, 149
Webb, Sidney and Beatrice, 24
Webster, Bill, 279
Wedgewood, Maurice, 255–59, 279, 296
Weintz, Walter, 510, 526
Welch, Colin, 283
Welles, Sumner, 210
Wellington, Arthur Wellesley, duke of, 68, 122
Werth, Alexander, 7
West, Rebecca, 316
Westberg, Charles, 259, 267, 280–81
Westminster Press group, 241–42, 246, 250, 267, 285–87, 541
Whale, John, 455, 469–70
Wharton, Bryan, 389–91
What the Papers Say (TV program), 282, 285, 286–87, 330, 362
Whipp, Eddie, 53
Whistler, James McNeill, 323
Whitaker, Forest, 395
White Citizens Council, 227, 230
white slave traffic, 244
Wicker, Tom, 528
Widgery, Lord Chief Justice, 474–75
Wild, Very Reverend John, 287–88
Wilde, Jimmy, 17
Wilde, Oscar, 186
Wiles, Terry, 378
William III, king of England (Prince of Orange), 454
Williams & Connolly (Washington law firm), 439, 440
Wilmers, John, 357–58, 361, 369
Wilson, Harold, 310–11, 317, 320, 337, 351–52, 409, 456; and thalidomide case, 379, 381
Wilson, Woodrow, 208, 210, 532

Winner, Michael, 526
Wintour, Anna, 320
Wintour, Charles, 320
Witherow, John, 384
Wizard (comic book), 45
Wodehouse, P. G., 60, 200
Wolfe, Herbert, 289–90, 293–95, 297–98
Wolsey Hall, 109–10, 112
women in 1930s, 37
Women's Royal Naval Service (Wrens), 56
Woodard, Isaac Jr., 225
Word in Edgeways, A (radio program), 317
Workers' Educational Association (WEA), 164, 261
World Almanac and Book of Facts, 44
World Court, 208
World Cup, 318
World Health Organization, 397
World Trade Center destroyed, 477
World University Games (hockey), 134
World War I, 17, 22–23, 53, 58, 102, 184, 245, 291
World War II, 236, 338, 345; Britain declares war on Germany, 7–8; casualties, 86, 97, 184, 451; censorship, 4; children evacuated to countryside, 44, 46–49; cost of, to Britain, 168; D-day landings, 72; Dunkirk, British retreat from, 3–7, 58, 301; German occupation, 338, (resistance against) 93; home front preparations for, 43–44, 72; Philby and, 340; phony war ends, 58, (Manchester area bombed) 61–64, 69, 87, 177; rationing during, 63–64, 65–66, 81, 200–201; survivors of Japan and Europe, 149–50; U.S. enters, 64–65, 97, 193; war in Europe winds down, 95, 99. *See also* Royal Air Force (RAF)
Worsthorne, Peregrine, 377
Wren, Christopher, 177
Wren, P. C., 54
Wright, Ian, 280–81
Wright, Rowland, 268
Wroe, James, 177

Yank at Oxford, A (movie), 112, 118
Yeats, William Butler, 465
Yemen, civil war in, 468
Yeomans, Dick, 250–51, 253–54
Yom Kippur War, 326, 413–16, 418, 443
Yorkshire Post, 246, 260, 264
Young, Andrew, 399
Young, Graham, 389
Young, Hugo, 331, 346–47, 407
Young Journalists' Club, 96
Yugoslavia, 346

Zhukov, Marshal Georgi, 68
Zimbabwe, 339, 396
Zog, king of Albania, 346
Zuckerman, Mortimer, 505, 510–11

About the Author

HAROLD EVANS is the author of the *New York Times* best seller *The American Century* as well as *They Made America: Two Centuries of Innovators* and *Good Times, Bad Times*. He was the founding editor of *Condé Nast Traveler,* editorial director of *U.S. News & World Report,* and president and publisher of Random House, where he published a record number of nonfiction best sellers. Editor of the influential London *Times* between 1967 and 1981, Evans was voted by British journalists as the greatest all-time editor. He was awarded the European Gold Award for his investigations and campaigning, notably for winning justice for children affected by thalidomide, and in 2004 he was knighted for his service to journalism. Since 2002, he has been editor-at-large of *The Week* magazine. He lives in New York with his wife, Tina Brown, and their two children.